Mícheál Ó Súilleabháin

A Life in Music

Frontispiece: Mícheál Ó Súilleabháin, St Mary's Cathedral, Limerick, 2014.
PHOTOGRAPHER: MAURICE GUNNING

Mícheál Ó Súilleabháin

A Life in Music

Edited by Helen Phelan, Marie McCarthy
and Nicholas Carolan

CORK
cup
UNIVERSITY
PRESS

First published in 2024 by
Cork University Press
Boole Library
University College Cork
Cork T12 ND89
Ireland

Library of Congress Control Number: 2024945691

Distribution in the USA Longleaf Services, Chapel Hill, NC, USA.

British Library Cataloguing in Publication Data

A CIP catalogue record for this book is available from the British Library.

ISBN: 9781782050162

Printed by BZ Graf in Poland

Design and typesetting by Alison Burns at Studio 10 Design, Cork

www.corkuniversitypress.com

CONTENTS

PART II: EDUCATOR 101

Gaiseadh/Flowing

Oileán/Island

Works by Mícheál Ó Súilleabháin:
Discography, Writings and Select Scores

List of Figures

List of Abbreviations

BBC	British Broadcasting Corporation
BC	Boston College
CMC	Contemporary Music Centre
ICO	Irish Chamber Orchestra
ICTM	International Council for Traditional Music
ITMA	Irish Traditional Music Archive
ITMS	Irish Traditional Music Society
IWPAV	Irish World Performing Arts Village
NCH	National Concert Hall
QUB	Queen's University Belfast
RTÉ	Raidió Teilifís Éireann
RTÉ CO	Raidió Teilifís Éireann Concert Orchestra
RTÉ NSO	Raidió Teilifís Éireann National Symphony Orchestra
SEM	Society for Ethnomusicology
SMEI	Society for Music Education in Ireland
SMI	Society for Musicology in Ireland
UCC	University College Cork
UCD	University College Dublin
UCG	University College Galway
UCH	University Concert Hall
UL	University of Limerick

Acknowledgements

In preparing this volume, the editors are deeply indebted to the contributors, who have so generously shared their personal memories, collaborative experiences, and works inspired by Mícheál's legacy.

The project would not have been possible without the generous financial support provided through The Ireland Funds for which the editors are extremely grateful.

We wish to thank the staff at Cork University Press, in particular Mike Collins, Maria O'Donovan and Sinéad Neville, for their support and encouragement of the project. We are grateful to the reviewers of the manuscript for their valuable feedback.

We gratefully acknowledge Mícheál's personal archive and the Irish Traditional Music Archive, as well as the archives at University College Cork, University of Limerick and Boston College, for access to materials. We have endeavoured to credit all photographs correctly.

We are grateful to the following for their assistance in furthering the volume: Mary Louise O'Donnell for her excellent management of the project and careful editing and formatting of the essays, Maurice Gunning for support in sourcing and curating the photographic plates, Fióna Bolger, John McAuliffe and Vincent Woods for support in engaging the poetry community, as well as Tríona Ní Shíocháin, Lillis Ó Laoire and Áine Uí Cheallaigh for their generous assistance with Irish-language texts.

The editors wish to acknowledge all of Mícheál's colleagues from the Irish World Academy of Music and Dance, as well as all those musicians, academics, friends, colleagues, and family who gave so generously to the project.

The editors are grateful to Cló Iar-Chonnacht for permission to publish extracts from poems by Seán Ó Ríordáin, and to the Heaney family, Faber and Faber, and Farrar, Straus and Giroux for permission to include extracts from the poems and essays of Seamus Heaney. Lines from 'Leaves' by Derek Mahon from *The Poems: 1961–2020* (2021) have been reproduced by kind permission of the author's estate and The Gallery Press (www.gallerypress.com).

The editors also acknowledge Carcanet Press, Dedalus Press, Many Rivers Press and The Gallery Press for permission to republish the following complete poems:

> Paddy Bushe, 'Equinox Concert', *To Ring in Silence: New and selected poems* (Dedalus Press, 2007).

Moya Cannon, 'Between the Jigs and the Reels', *Carrying the Songs* (Manchester: Carcanet Press, 2007).

Michael Coady, 'Between the Beats at the Moorings Bar', *Going by Water* (The Gallery Press, 2009).

Tom French, 'Irish Destiny, *The Last Straw* (The Gallery Press, 2018).

Eiléan Ní Chuilleanáin, 'Air: The map of the world', *The Map of the World* (The Gallery Press, 2023).

Mícheál Ó Súilleabháin, 'Early Music', *Early Music* (Many Rivers Press, 2021).

David Whyte, 'The Music of the Morning Sun', from *Still Possible* © 2022 and *The Seven Streams: An Irish cycle* © 2024 (Reprinted with permission from Many Rivers Press, Langley, WA). www.davidwhyte.com

Enda Wyley, 'Eurydice Speaks', *The Painter on His Bike* (Dedalus Press, 2019).

Introduction

On 11 December 2011, the president of Ireland, Michael D. Higgins, visited the newly opened Irish World Academy of Music and Dance building on the University of Limerick campus. The president's address paid tribute to the students and faculty, as well as to Mícheál Ó Súilleabháin, whose creative vision was the driving force behind the flowering of the Academy, describing it as 'the best version of our future that we might possibly aspire to'. In his closing remarks he stated:

> This is the version of Irishness that is open and that is welcoming the world and that is full of joy and it is celebratory because it is of the heart and of the spirit. It is neither empty nor false, nor relying on rating agencies or anything else. The only rating agency that matters in the end is the profound sound that comes up from all the music of the world when it is able in its different homes to tolerate each other and also promise new sound and new shapes and new colours.[1]

No publication can hope to articulate or evaluate the sum of a life's journey. As Ó Súilleabháin's most quoted poet, Seamus Heaney, writes, '[U]seless to think you'll park and capture it'.[2] Nonetheless, something of the essence of Ó Súilleabháin's journey is captured in the lines by the president. Any engagement with the traces of Ó Súilleabháin's life – his compositions, recordings, publications, media outputs, cultural work, as well as his many students from decades of working in higher education – reveals a notable consistency of vision that cross-fertilised all this work. At its heart, this was the belief that our truest selves grow and emerge through engagement with others. These others may be from a different culture or tradition, or reside within ourselves. The engagement requires openness, courage, celebration, creativity and sometimes great struggle.

Mediating these different voices demands the balance of a tightrope walker or the precision of a gyroscope – a scientific instrument used for maintaining orientation, which Ó Súilleabháin always kept on his desk. Move too close, and there is the danger of losing yourself or your identity; stay too far away, and one risks cultural or personal isolation. For Ó Súilleabháin, the place of greatest equilibrium and creative tension was the space 'between worlds':

> By mediation, I mean that middle voice which opens up a channel of communication between separate energies. In the case of music, I am referring to musicians who, through a mix of artistic talent, temperamental disposition and what some would call historical accident, find themselves in a position where their natural accent speaks to opposite sides. Such figures are frequently involved in a musical fusion which can quickly become a musical confusion if things start to go wrong. The musical mediator can be viewed as a bridge which allows listeners access to parts of their society and their experience of which they were unaware or perhaps just suspicious. And like any bridge, people walk across it – often with little regard for that which conveys them to another place, another world.[3]

This theme of mediation reoccurs across five decades of writing, teaching, composing and performing. Very early in his career, he was marked by the legacy of Ó Riada and Fleischmann and his commitment to the dialogue between Ireland's dual inheritance of 'classical' and 'traditional' musics. The creative tension in this lifelong engagement was added to by Ó Súilleabháin's primary mode of musical expression: the piano. In a review of his first album, which featured no less than five keyboard instruments – the clavichord, harpsichord, piano, pedal organ and mini-moog synthesiser – Bill Meek wrote: 'Mick Sullivan is a keyboard man, possibly almost in spite of himself, because no one would better understand the problems of the KB [keyboard] family in its wooing of traditional music.'[4]

Both as a musician and an educator, Ó Súilleabháin became known for challenging the dominance of western classical music in formal institutions, whether these be concert halls or lecture theatres, drawing on cultural theorist Edward Said in interrogating the role of classical music as a mode of dominance in sustaining social structures.[5] Like Said, Ó Súilleabháin took up this challenge as someone deeply committed to the importance of western classical music, but insisting that it recognise other musical traditions on their own terms. Changing one aspect of a social system, he was convinced, had far-reaching, subversive effects across wider cultural and political frameworks. He described the decision to allow traditional musicians entrance to the music degree in University College Cork, for example, as one such subversion: 'Since 1982 when we changed our entrance exams to allow traditional students to study for a music degree, nothing has been the same since. It was like letting off a bomb …'[6]

Ó Súilleabháin's musical recordings, compositions and performances bear witness to what he called 'the redress of music'. From his earliest works, such as the *Concerto for Traditional Musician and String Orchestra* in 1979 (a piece which would be reworked and rebirthed as the title track of the album *Oileán/Island* in 1989), his approach strove to bring about an encounter between musical worlds which diminished neither in the meeting: 'Ó Súilleabháin is one of those rarities: a musician who grasps absolutely both the classical and traditional idioms and his take seems to be that, not only can they co-exist, they should burst forth together in something that goes beyond mere fusion.'[7] In attempting to describe this process, Ó Súilleabháin sometimes resorted to gesture. Noeleen Dowling wrote in 1989:

> To illustrate, he draws his hands wide and slowly moves them until they are about two inches apart. He nods to the space between them, 'That's like the effect you create with bringing the two types of music together – the excitement is in narrowing the space between them. But the space has to continue to exist'.[8]

While he is best known for this creative dance between Irish traditional and classical music, his introduction to the world of ethnomusicology as part of his doctoral studies in Queen's University Belfast (QUB) convinced him that the Irish story, like any cultural story, has global resonance. In attempting to describe this, his writings turned continuously to the language of poetry, art, architecture and gesture:

> Linking the local to the global is a catch phrase now but it is one which for me is full of meaning. My attention was drawn last year to a 'cultural village' architectural concept which the Italian architect Renzo Piano designed in New Caledonia off the coast of Australia. It is a strikingly beautiful series of buildings based on the local tribal huts of the Kanak people. Someone described this kind of architecture which was at once local and global as 'glocal'. As I thought about the word – especially its hardness and musical aggression – I was drawn towards a different amalgamation of the two words local/global into 'lobal'. Quite apart from its softness, 'lobal' carries resonances of the lobe of the ear, of a kind of listening. Because 'lability' listens to the process of becoming, because it is the dance of T.S. Eliot's 'still point of the turning world', it leads us towards a kind of 'real presence' where creativity resides.[9]

Ultimately, Ó Súilleabháin recognised that the encounter between the self and the other, whether this took place in the cultural, educational, spiritual or psychological sphere, was beyond words: '[T]he intimate connection between all of that and my music making – both as a performer and a composer – is too deep for me to articulate.'[10] Where words left off, the desire to continuously create 'a music that you never would have known to listen for'[11] appeared to be the North Star guiding and propelling his life's journey.

It is far too early for an in-depth analysis of the impact of Ó Súilleabháin's work, not least because his vast personal archive will take several years to categorise and digitise. In the final months of his life, however, he had an idea for a collection of writings by musical peers, educational colleagues, poets, dancers, visual artists, cultural historians, as well as his many students, which might bounce off, and interact with, his work. There was no doubt in his mind that the two people best positioned to help us with this project were Nicholas Carolan and Marie McCarthy, whose meticulous scholarship and cultural knowledge he had long admired. Mícheál had sustained personal and professional relationships with all three of the editors and felt confident in their musical and academic understanding of the nuances of his life's work, as well as their knowledge of potential contributors. While Mary Louise O'Donnell came on as project coordinator later in the process, she had also worked closely with Mícheál, first as a doctoral researcher and later as a fellow musician and academic. A few months after Mícheál's death, I came across the notes we had made around the idea for a book. I contacted Nicholas and Marie and have been immensely grateful for their immediate, generous and sustained response to the proposal, as well as Mary Louise's invaluable contribution to the project.

While this collection of essays, personal reflections and poetry takes as its point of departure some aspect of Ó Súilleabháin's work, each contribution develops its own thread and trajectory. Some segue into a resonant theme or topic from the author's own work. Others position his work within a wider social, cultural, educational or political context. Many are deeply personal, sharing stories and memories from the well of creative collaboration. The styles of presentation embrace a wide spectrum of scholarly, anecdotal and poetic approaches. As editors, we have not attempted to impose a common style across the contributions, but rather to allow the work to present itself in a manner as idiosyncratic, multi-faceted and immense as the musical life it engages.

The most challenging aspect of the work was to find a structure on which to hang such an array of writing. Recognising that no structure could contain the cross-fertilising nature of his work, we nonetheless created three sections to highlight the three parts of his professional identity: musician, educator and cultural mediator. Each part is further divided into three sub-sections, with titles from Ó Súilleabháin's recordings used as framing devices for each of these nine sub-divisions.

Part I looks at Ó Súilleabháin the musician, as a recording artist (Elver Gleams), a performer (Becoming) and composer (Between Worlds). Part II focuses on Ó Súilleabháin the educator, from his early years in Cork and Belfast (The Dolphin's Way), the development of the Irish World Academy of Music and Dance (Templum) and his educational impact internationally (Lumen). Part III explores Ó Súilleabháin's role as a cultural mediator including his engagement with the Irish language, particularly through song (Casadh/Turning), his love of poetry (Gaiseadh/Flowing) and his wider impact on Irish culture (Oileán/Island).

Ó Súilleabháin cultivated a lifelong engagement with the writings of Seamus Heaney. In Heaney, he found a resonant language of mediation: 'consciousness can be alive to two different – some might say opposite – dimensions of reality and still find a way of negotiating between them'.[12] In his keynote address to the International Council of Traditional Music in 2017, he reminded his audience that the ultimate mediation was between the ordinary and the extraordinary, or between the practical and the poetic. Heaney writes, 'We must keep our feet on the ground to signify that nothing is beneath us, but we should also lift up our eyes to say nothing is beyond us.'[13] Ó Súilleabháin believed that our best selves emerged through the crossing and re-crossing of this frontier:

> I want to affirm that within our individual selves we can reconcile two orders of knowledge, which we might call the practical and the poetic; to affirm also that each form of knowledge redresses the other and that the frontier between them is there for the crossing.[14]

Finding his creative home at the crossroads between these orders meant never arriving at a final destination. In a similar fashion, this book eschews any attempt at arrival, nor does it presume to capture the essence of a life. Rather, through its shared stories, poems, personal and critical reflections, it offers a kaleidoscopic glimpse into the flow of a life lived in music.

Helen Phelan

Editors

Helen Phelan is professor of arts practice, and director of the Irish World Academy of Music and Dance, University of Limerick. She is founder of the PhD Arts Practice programme at the Academy, and founding Chair of IMBAS, a national network for artistic research. She is an award-winning scholar for her work in music, ritual and migration.

Marie McCarthy is professor of music education at the University of Michigan. She has been a regular contributor to music education in Ireland for over three decades. Her awards include honorary life member of the Society for Music Education in Ireland and the International Society for Music Education.

Nicholas Carolan is director emeritus of the Irish Traditional Music Archive, of which he was founder-director 1987–2015 and general editor of its publications. A researcher, writer, producer and lecturer, he is best known for the archival television series *Come West along the Road* and *Siar an Bóthar* (1994–2014).

Mícheál Ó Súilleabháin: A biography

Helen Phelan

Early years

Michael O'Sullivan[1] was born on 10 December 1950. His mother, Ellen (Nellie), inherited a shop from her aunt, Bridget Barrett, at 39 Mitchell Street, Clonmel, County Tipperary, where the family also resided. His father, Ambrose, was a private in the army stationed at Kickham Barracks in Clonmel before his marriage. His mother and father ran the grocery shop together. They had two sons: John, born in 1949, and Michael, a year later.

While neither of Ó Súilleabháin's parents were known as musicians, he spoke about their latent musicality, particularly his father's, in several interviews. He described his father as 'always humming, tapping and lilting'.[2] Ó Súilleabháin recalled hearing the tune 'The Blackbird' for the first time when his father lilted it. He also played the mouth organ on occasion and sang a small number of Irish songs in English. His mother was drawn to music such as Thomas Moore's *Irish Melodies* and was the one who encouraged both sons to take music lessons. Ó Súilleabháin and his brother were members of the Clonmel Pipe Band, where Michael played pipes and John was a drummer. The band was run by a local priest, Fr William Meehan, and by a neighbour, Tony O'Keeffe, who was also Ó Súilleabháin's godfather. O'Keeffe would play an important role in Ó Súilleabháin's early musical formation.

Both Michael and John were sent for piano lessons to another neighbour and customer at the shop, Mamie Morris, or Mrs Morris as she was known to her students. Mrs Morris introduced Ó Súilleabháin to the piano via the classical music examination system but it soon became apparent that her own musicality also drew on the influence of traditional fiddling and céilí vamping. Ó Súilleabháin's recollections of his early musical years speak of the element of chance in his musical formation. As well as learning piano, his mother decided that he should also play a second instrument. Ó Súilleabháin recalls being fascinated by a harp in the window of a music shop in Clonmel. The harp was full of woodworm and they bought a violin instead:

> … anyway we didn't get it, but I came very near. It's really interesting, isn't it, in a way, you know, very near to actually learning the harp … there's that element of chance; it's fascinating, isn't it?[3]

Mrs Morris' husband was a traditional fiddler and she brought this knowledge to teaching Ó Súilleabháin the classical examination repertoire, but lessons were soon overtaken by sessions with Ó Súilleabháin sight-reading on violin from tune collections and Mrs Morris vamping on the piano.

The Clonmel traditional fiddler Tom Barrett was a friend of Mrs Morris and she invited him to attend a few lessons, giving Ó Súilleabháin his first exposure to traditional music off the page:

> I think he came twice and in a way I suppose it would have been sensible if perhaps she had released me to him, you know what I mean? And if I had been going up to him for my weekly lessons … which would have been interesting because I think if I had done that, and maybe been drawn down a stylistic road … because remember, there was no style passing.[4]

Ó Súilleabháin recalled being a very good sight-reader at a young age and picked up tonic-solfa quite easily when it was introduced through singing in primary school. He enjoyed the speed and mechanics of playing tunes from notation but identified the playing of Tom Barrett as his first realisation that music could be played differently to how it was written. The violin was to fall away as the piano took over, and new musical influences also came to the fore in early adolescence.

As for many young people in the 1960s, radio, television and recordings opened up the world of popular music. Strongly influenced by The Beatles, Ó Súilleabháin purchased an electric guitar and amplifier and started a local band with friends called The Sea Cliffs. At the same time, his godfather, Tony O'Keeffe, who played in a dance band, invited Ó Súilleabháin at the age of fourteen to perform at dancehall gigs for an older audience, who were listening and dancing to the music of the 1950s. Both these experiences provided early exposure to the business and touring side of the musician's life. Ó Súilleabháin noted that while the dance band played covers, The Sea Cliffs provided the first opportunity to write and perform his own music. The Sea Cliffs were later reformed as a band called C.Y.N. and, under the influence of the ballad boom, Ó Súilleabháin also formed a four-piece ballad group called The Puppets. This led to his first television appearance, where Ó Súilleabháin played the double bass with The Puppets on *Ballad Sheet*, a popular studio-based music programme on Ireland's RTÉ television network hosted by Shay Healy.[5]

Ó Súilleabháin's formal school education took place at both primary and secondary level through the Christian Brothers schools in Clonmel. Though individual teachers shared their enthusiasm for music, it was not taught as a subject in these schools. Ó Súilleabháin discovered by chance towards the end of his fifth year in secondary school that music was an examination subject in the Leaving Certificate. He eventually found a teacher in Sr Ita Moloney, a Presentation nun, who met with him every Sunday afternoon for four hours to teach the Leaving Certificate curriculum. She also loaned him a record player and a box of *Reader's Digest* records. Ó Súilleabháin noted this as the first time he heard Bach's *Brandenburg Concertos*:

> I remember it not making musical sense, and all of that polyphony, you know? Really complex counterpoint, and you know the way you say about Bach, he's a musician's musician, and it's all very intellectual kind of stuff, hitting that wall, and just not being able, and this is not – I was well up, I was sixteen years of age. This happened at sixteen, so I can remember the shock of non-recognition. And I remember Brian Boydell, being on *The Late Late Show*, with … an early music group kind of thing. I'm sure Barra his son must have been in it at that stage, and Jenny and Andrew Robinson and all those people. But he was interviewed by Gay Byrne, and he was enthusing about Bach's *Brandenburg Concertos*, and … I think he was saying, these are the most important pieces of music, I mean these are just blowing me away and everything else. This guy obviously knows an awful lot. But a professor of music in Trinity, he's also performing, doing that stuff that sounds kind of weird to me, and it's kind of nice. I had a little alternative feeling because it was early music perhaps, as well, you know? And you know, they weren't all in dicky bows. So I was kind of intrigued on a number of levels … Anyway, I sold my electric guitar and amplifier to buy a record player, and a two-album set of the Bach *Brandenburg Concertos*, which I still have. Yehudi Menuhin, the Bach Festival Orchestra. Exchanging one for the other, which is the real symbolic act in a way. Didn't want to sell the electric guitar, but there was [a] sense of changing cultural worlds I suppose as well.[6]

The educational reforms introduced by Minister for Education Donogh O'Malley in the late 1960s included the revision of the scholarship system for third-level education, introducing a means-tested grant system. Ó Súilleabháin repeated his Leaving Certificate to qualify for a grant and was awarded a place in music at University College Cork (UCC) in 1969.

UCC student years

While his music teachers were encouraging him towards the degree programme in Trinity College Dublin, Ó Súilleabháin notes Ó Riada as an important factor in his decision to go to Cork.

> I remember vividly a programme about new bank notes that he introduced … he was running some kind of a late-night magazine, artsy kind of a programme, which wasn't just music. Oh yeah, he was fronting it. And there were various things, and it was very kind of arty and cutting-edge stuff, and it was Ó Riada doing his thing. Loads of panache. Just waltzing around the studio, sort of loving every minute of it.[7]

Ó Súilleabháin spoke often in interviews and publications about the seminal influence of both Aloys Fleischmann (1910–92) and Seán Ó Riada (1931–71) during his student years. Although Ó Riada's early passing in 1971 meant that Ó Súilleabháin had less than two years of exposure to him as a teacher, the impact of that encounter and of Ó Riada's public persona would last a lifetime. As a university student, however, the primary influence on his education was Aloys Fleischmann:

> … his strengths were in systematic musicology, analysis and composition, anything like that, that had manipulation of the notes, which was something I would have liked, but a lot of our course was counterpoint and harmony exercises. And these I loved, so you went off and you did them two or three, four times a week. You spent hours in the library, just like doing crossword puzzles. Hours doing crossword puzzles, poring over these crossword puzzles, and seeing could you get them right, faster, and then when you got them faster, he'd give you more complex ones. It was all terribly graded. I loved it, I was good at it you see, the maths, I'm sure.[8]

The craft of western art composition that would ground much of Ó Súilleabháin's later output was developed during these years, culminating in a master's in Composition with Fleischmann between 1972 and 1973. Studying piano with Annette de Foubert in Cork, he was awarded a licentiate diploma in piano performance from Trinity College London (LTCL) in 1973.

Another key development during Ó Súilleabháin's student years was his engagement with the Irish language. While Ó Riada would have opened this door, Ó Súilleabháin credits fellow students such as the composer Máire

Ní Dhuibhir with bringing confidence and enthusiasm to his pursuit of the language. The introduction of oral courses for beginners at the university was also important:

> Even though you weren't doing Irish you could still attend them free of charge ... the basic ideology of his course was the music of the language. So you know that was the first time anybody had got you to pronounce a word, beautiful ... that would give you a whole confidence then, and your mouth and just, there was something, right. So important.[9]

In the first summer of his degree, Ó Súilleabháin went to the Corca Dhuibhne Gaeltacht in Kerry to the Dún Chíomháin centre owned by University College Cork. He described this visit as an epiphany experience, as well as his introduction to the Irish-language poetry of Seán Ó Ríordáin, to which he would return throughout his compositional career.

In remembering these formative university years, Ó Súilleabháin often recounted that the first person he met in the Music Department was his future wife and long-time musical collaborator, Nóirín Ní Riain. Ní Riain was also a student of music, and as a singer was equally caught up in the Irish-language renaissance and engagement with Irish music. She was a member of a popular traditional student music group called Pangur Bán, created by Ó Súilleabháin, which made a number of television appearances. Ó Súilleabháin and Ní Riain both completed their education in Cork in 1973 and entered teaching positions in Ó Súilleabháin's hometown of Clonmel.

Clonmel and the Ring Gaeltacht

Ó Súilleabháin's first position was in the Central Technical Institute, Clonmel. Part of the Vocational Education Committee (VEC) system, it included teaching responsibilities in mainstream school, evening adult education classes and community initiatives. During his year teaching in Clonmel, Ó Súilleabháin established a string orchestra called the Clonmel Chamber Orchestra and the Clonmel Chamber Choir. In a publication from 1985, he noted this early teaching experience as formative in his understanding of the limitations of the system of formal music education in Ireland:

> The first indication I got that the idea upon which school music is based was 'out of tune' came during the final class which I gave to first-year girls. It was the end of my first year as a music teacher and having

> spent the year introducing Mozart and Stravinsky along with the usual dose of music notation to my reluctant students, I had decided that this class should be turned back on itself in the form of invitations to entertain with song and story. Things were proceeding as expected until a set of twins in the first row were eagerly called upon to sing by their classmates. I might mention in passing that their surname was Fortune and that they were affectionately known to all as The Miss Fortunes: but their singing was neither misfortunate nor unfortunate. I immediately recognised the vocal timbre as that of a certain form of contemporary pop music: what in musicological terms I was later to discover was called 'Afro-American'. The clean-cut, impeccably performed ornamentation would, I knew, be beyond the capability of the average-schooled classical musician. There was a sensitivity to intonation which showed itself in the use of microtones and glissandi. My own feeling of being let down can only have been matched by the feeling of alienation which these students must have experienced in the face of my doctrinaire patronising approach.[10]

These pedagogical insights concerning the importance of recognising and teaching all musical genres with parity of esteem would inform the ethos upon which he would later build the Irish World Academy of Music and Dance. Ó Súilleabháin and Ní Riain married in the summer of 1974. Fearing that they were losing contact with the Irish-language epiphany they had shared in UCC, they decided to leave their positions in Clonmel and move to the Ring Gaeltacht in County Waterford where they both once again secured teaching positions. Ó Súilleabháin continued to work within the VEC system, this time teaching three days a week in Dungarvan and two in Kilmacthomas. The Ó Riada influence can been seen again in Ó Súilleabháin's creation of the vocal group Claisceadal na Rinne, modelled on Ó Riada's Cór Chúil Aodha, as well as a musical group based on the ensemble format of Ceoltóirí Chualann called Tiompán. Tiompán was inspired by the Déise piper Tommy Kearney and the album *Óró Damhnaigh*, which the group recorded and published in 1977, featured John Dwyer, Matt Fahy, Tommy Kearney, Nóirín Ní Riain, Tomás Ó Catháin and Mícheál Ó Súilleabháin. The album also featured a young Mel Mercier. Ó Súilleabháin's performance career would be marked by an enduring musical partnership with Mercier, particularly around their piano and traditional percussion collaborations.

With Ó Riada's passing, Tomás Ó Canainn initially stepped in to teach the Irish traditional music classes in UCC. In 1975, the position was advertised at a junior level and Ó Súilleabháin was appointed to the post, marking the start of a lifelong professional engagement with higher education in Ireland.

The Cork years

As well as teaching classes in general musicianship, Ó Súilleabháin's position included the design and delivery of modules on Irish traditional music. Using the precedent of employing non-academic native speakers of foreign languages as language tutors, he drew in an array of traditional musicians and dancers as performance tutors to back up the general academic lectures on the subject.

In 1976, he produced his first solo album. Published by Gael Linn Records, the album marked the public change to his Irish-language name, *Mícheál Ó Súilleabháin*, as the title of the album. Its experimentation with dance tunes, songs, harp compositions and airs on a variety of keyboard instruments contains several stylistic precursors of the signature piano style which would reach maturity in the later *Dolphin's Way* recording. The response to the liminal and experimental nature of the work was prophetic of the sometimes controversial reaction his work would evoke throughout his career. For example, the *Irish Times* music critic Charles Acton wrote somewhat enigmatically that 'the record is undoubtedly of interest and will give a lot of pleasure to many people but to me it is somewhat misconceived and while entertaining, dangerous'.[11]

Ó Súilleabháin's public and media profile began to grow during this period, particularly in Irish-language radio and television. Television appearances included *An Fear agus a Chuid Ceoil* with Riobard Mac Góráin, a pioneer in the development of Irish music, film and theatre and a founder of Gael Linn.[12] His third album, *Cry of the Mountain*, featured music recorded between 1974 and 1978 for radio and film including music from *The Green Linnet*, the award-winning radio series produced by Tony MacMahon, and *The Cry of the Mountain* by acclaimed Irish naturalist Éamon de Buitléar.

The late 1970s were a turning point musically and academically. Following mixed reviews of a major concert marking the centenary of the birth of Pádraig Pearse, Ó Súilleabháin felt at the end of a musical road, which had been strongly influenced by his musical mentors in Cork, and the need to find his own approach to mediating between musical traditions. He also sensed that he had brought Irish music as far as he could in the university context, which still created barriers of access to traditional musicians. His musical breakthrough came in the form of a commission by the Gorey Arts Festival, resulting in the *Concerto for Traditional Musician and String*

Orchestra. The piece marked Ó Súilleabháin's break away from the Ó Riada model of the traditional music ensemble, to a form of encounter between western art and Irish traditional music. The first traditional musician to perform the piece was flute player Matt Molloy:

> ... that really was the key piece. And really I suppose the most important piece. And I wouldn't let Matt play any classical music, and I wouldn't let the classical musicians play any of Matt's music. It had to be separate. But I used what I later – do you know in that article 'Creative Process', where I talk about set accented tones – I identify these set accented tones and I pick them out and use them as a sort of a tone row. So there's a hidden connection between what the string music is playing and the jig ... it's like a tonal version of serialism. Now, you're not supposed to hear it but just interestingly enough there is a kind of a, like, a little connection there.[13]

In 1980, Ó Súilleabháin took his first sabbatical from UCC. His first child, Eoin (Owen), was born the same year and the period marked a significant engagement with the Benedictine community of Glenstal Abbey, resulting in a trilogy of recordings produced and arranged by Ó Súilleabháin featuring Nóirín Ní Riain and the monks of Glenstal Abbey: *Caoineadh na Maighdine* (1980), *Good People All* (1982) and *Vox de Nube* (1989). At the same time, a growing interest in ethnomusicology led to the beginning of a relationship with John Blacking and John Bailey in the Department of Anthropology at Queen's University Belfast and Ó Súilleabháin's eventual registration as a doctoral researcher under the supervision of Blacking. A musical and educational exchange with India in the mid-1980s had increased Ó Súilleabháin's desire to situate Irish music in a more global context and ethnomusicology provided a theoretical framework for this. Compositional work during that period included incidental music for Brian Friel's adaptation of Chekov's *Three Sisters*. He also wrote *The Bodhrán*, a manual for beginners based on fieldwork he had conducted as an undergraduate student.[14]

Ó Súilleabháin's return to UCC coincided with a new phase of traditional music in the university. The changing of entrance requirements, allowing more traditional musicians to join the music programme at UCC, created a growing body of traditional expertise within the student body, as well as from the increasing numbers of internationally recognised Irish traditional music tutors interacting with the university. A regular series of lunchtime concerts brought additional traditional musicians onto campus. In 1983, Cork University Press published *Bunting's Ancient Music of Ireland*, an edition based on the original manuscripts by Donal O'Sullivan and completed by Ó Súilleabháin after O'Sullivan's death.[15] He completed his doctoral research on innovation and tradition in the music of Tommie Potts in 1987, a year which marked another important crossroads in his recording, performing and compositional life.

Ó Súilleabháin's own piano playing was reaching further into the structural elements of dance tunes and airs, while developing signature approaches to ornamentation and harmony. In 1987, this work found a new recording home:

> Early this year, he was phoned at his County Limerick home by Declan Colgan, an executive in Richard Branson's giant Virgin Records group. Colgan explained that he had been given the go ahead to start a new label, Venture, within the Virgin Empire. It was to be a vehicle for innovative music ... *The Dolphin's Way* is Ven001.[16]

The Dolphin's Way became the first comprehensive public record of Ó Súilleabháin's signature piano style. Featuring Colm Murphy on bodhrán and Mel Mercier on bones, it included piano presentations of pieces such as 'Oíche Nollag/Christmas Eve', 'Merrily Kiss the Quaker' and 'Fiach an Mhada Rua/The Fox Chase', among others. These were pieces to which he would return frequently and reimagine in other manifestations including string quartet, string orchestra and full orchestral versions. The recording was also the start of a professional relationship and friendship between Ó Súilleabháin and Colgan which would result in the release of several more albums with the Venture label. *Oileán/Island* (1989) featured a re-working of the *Concerto for Traditional Musician and String Orchestra* and also marked the beginning of a recording relationship with the Irish Chamber Orchestra. *Casadh/Turning* (1990) saw Ó Súilleabháin return to the harpsichord while *Gaiseadh/Flowing* (1992), featuring Neil Martin, Mel Mercier and the Irish Chamber Orchestra, included some of his most popular pieces including 'Woodbrook', and '(must be more) Crispy' co-written with Mel Mercier.

In 1990, Ó Súilleabháin and his family, including his second son, Mícheál, born in 1984, relocated to Boston where he was Visiting Professor at Boston College (BC). During this time he founded an archive for Irish traditional music in America, located in the Burns Library at BC. The archive was partially funded by a CD recording of a fiddle festival he coordinated entitled My Love is in America. The CD, which he produced, was released in 1991 and honoured by an award from the Library of Congress. On his return to UCC, he produced a series of five CD recordings of live traditional music events held in Cork from 1991 to '95 called Éigse na Laoi. The first four recordings were released by Nimbus Records and featured music from Donegal and the Shetland Islands (*Fiddlesticks: Irish traditional music from Donegal*, 1991); America (*Dear Old Erin's Isle: Irish traditional music from America*, 1992); Cape Breton, Canada (*Traditional Music from Cape Breton Island*, 1993) and England (*Across the Waters: Irish traditional music from England*, 1994). The fifth, *The Gathering: A world of Irish music*, was directed by Mel Mercier and Niall Vallely and released by the Real World Records label in 1997.

Ó Súilleabháin's continued interest in writing for theatre and film is also evident during this period. In 1989 he worked with community arts group Theatre Omnibus on a performance piece based on the songs of Johnny Patterson. In 1993 he wrote a newly commissioned score for *Irish Destiny*, the last silent film to be produced in Ireland. The screening of the film's re-release, with live music from Ó Súilleabháin and the RTÉ Concert Orchestra, was attended by Mary Robinson, president of Ireland. Music from the score would be recorded as part of the *Becoming* album in 1998 and a DVD version of the film with music was produced in 2004. In 1993 Ó Súilleabháin also formed the ensemble Hiberno Jazz, to explore the confluence of Irish, classical, jazz and world music influences.

1993 marked another major turning point in Ó Súilleabháin's life. Having spent eighteen years in higher education, he was offered the chair of music in both UCC and the University of Limerick (UL). His decision to move to Limerick was prompted by a growing desire to develop a new centre for music and dance education in Ireland, one that he could build from the ground up and that would incorporate his vision for a more inclusive approach to performing arts education. In correspondence with Anne Dhu Shapiro, a colleague from Boston College, he wrote in 1992, 'I am obsessed now with a vision of a world music centre which I feel should be located in Ireland … this has been with me on and off since 1989 and it now seems to be taking on a life of its own. I think something is either going to happen quickly now or else the idea will fall on its face.'[17] On 1 January 1994 Ó Súilleabháin commenced the development of the Irish World Music Centre at UL.

The Limerick years

The Irish World Music Centre, which would evolve into the Irish World Academy of Music and Dance, was initially dedicated to postgraduate research. Ó Súilleabháin was determined that the centre would complement rather than compete with the programme at UCC. His creation of the centre coincided with an impulse to professionalise and decentralise the Irish Chamber Orchestra, and a dialogue between the orchestra's chief executive John Kelly and Ó Súilleabháin resulted in a decision by the then minister for arts, culture and the Gaeltacht, Michael D. Higgins, on the recommendation of the Arts Council, to relocate the orchestra to the UL campus.

In 1995 the Irish World Music Centre and the Irish Chamber Orchestra commissioned a joint report on global models of best practice in performing arts education. Published in 1996, the recommendations of *The PIPA Report* provided a blueprint for a five-year plan of programme development (1996–2000).[18] The report's author, Helen Phelan, was appointed academic coordinator from 1996 to '99 with a mandate to facilitate the development of a suite of taught postgraduate programmes. A second report, *Artful Knowing*, by David Elliott,[19] articulated the core philosophy of the Academy. Elliott and Ó Súilleabháin met in the context of the Music Education National Debate (MEND), which had also commenced in Ireland in 1994, and Elliott's philosophy of praxial music education, articulated in his 1995 publication *Music Matters: A new philosophy of music education*, had a strong influence on the growing centre.[20] This period also saw the beginning of a relationship between Ó Súilleabháin and The Atlantic Philanthropies (TAP). Founded by entrepreneur and philanthropist Chuck Feeney in 1982, TAP invested over 1.3 billion dollars in the Republic of Ireland to advance higher education, human rights and services for the young and old. Significant funding from TAP facilitated a year-long residency by David Elliott at the evolving centre, as well as an ambitious series of sixteen international seminars from 1996 to '97. Coordinated by Helen Phelan with a core panel consisting of David Elliott, Kari Veblen and Mícheál Ó Súilleabháin, 'the PIPA seminars' brought international artists and academics to Limerick to assist in the creation of unique programmes of global standard, including programmes in music therapy, contemporary dance performance, Irish traditional dance performance, community music, festive arts, Irish traditional music performance, classical string performance, ethnomusicology, ethnochoreology, ritual chant and song, and music education.

The evolution of these educational programmes, in combination with an extensive programme of artists-in-residence, artistic commissions and community engagement, grounded the philosophical vision of the Academy in a synergistic network of interweaving scholarly and performative research, teaching and learning. Helen Phelan, Ó Súilleabháin's second wife, worked closely with him for over two decades on this development, first as academic coordinator and later as associate director of the Academy. Also central to the early evolution of the Academy were Paula Dundon, the first academic administrator of the Academy; Margaret O'Sullivan, who coordinated the Toyota Arts Initiative from 1995 to 2000 following a gift from Toyota Ireland leading to the creation of the Sionna festival, and numerous artistic commissions and residencies; Ellen Byrne, publicity and performance coordinator; as well as Sandra Joyce and Niall Keegan, who were central to the development of the Irish traditional music programmes and would become director and associate director when Ó Súilleabháin stepped down as director in 2012.

While the Academy was originally called the Irish World Music Centre, Ó Súilleabháin was determined to also include dance in its offerings. Influenced by his exposure to ethnochoreology during his doctoral research in Belfast, two of the first programmes developed at the new centre were in ethnomusicology and ethnochoreology. With founder-director of Daghdha Dance Company Mary Nunan, as well as ethnochoreologist and traditional dancer Catherine Foley, the centre developed ground-breaking postgraduate programmes in contemporary and Irish traditional dance performance.[21]

The creation of the Irish World Music Centre coincided with Ó Súilleabháin's growing media presence. In 1995 he devised, scripted and presented a joint RTÉ and BBC Northern Ireland TV series called *A River of Sound: The changing course of Irish traditional music*. The series sparked a heated debate in Ireland over the depiction of innovation and tradition in Irish music and was strongly featured as a topic at *Crosbhealach an Cheoil, The Crossroads Conference 1996: Tradition and change in Irish traditional music*. In 1995 Ó Súilleabháin was also invited to write the interval piece for the Eurovision Song Contest, which had included the enormously successful *Riverdance* interval act the previous year. *Lumen* featured vocalists Nóirín Ní Riain and Brian Kennedy, as well as *sean-nós* singers and the monks of Glenstal Abbey. The internationally acclaimed percussionist Evelyn Glennie also featured. Ó Súilleabháin had worked with Glennie the previous year on a new mass composition, *Missa Gadelica*, the influence of which can he heard in the compositional style of *Lumen*. *Lumen* was featured on the album *Between Worlds* released the same year.

Ó Súilleabháin also played an increasing role in educational and musical institutions across the state. He was the chairman of the Irish Traditional Music Archive for two terms (1993–99) as well as serving as a board member of the Irish Chamber Orchestra, Daghdha Dance Company, the University of Limerick Concert Hall, and the Contemporary Music Centre. In 1999 he called for public dialogue around the proposed new Irish Academy of Performing Arts, fearing that its design, influenced by the

European conservatoire model which often centralised its conservatoires in key urban centres, might not best serve Ireland as it moved towards the twenty-first century: 'I'm very concerned that an opportunity like this comes once in the lifetime of a nation ... Dublin should certainly not be the assumed location.[22] In 1994, Ó Súilleabháin worked with Clare activist Harry Bohan to create Maoin Cheoil an Chláir, a music school grounded in Bohan's vision of community-led values and Ó Súilleabháin's belief in the role of the arts in fostering inclusive educational and social models.[23]

1999 also saw the launch of *Sources of Irish Traditional Music c. 1600–1855.*[24] Started by Aloys Fleischmann in the 1950s and passed to Ó Súilleabháin after his death in 1992, the 1998 publication brought together some 7,000 tunes sources from all known manuscripts and collections up to *c.* 1855. With the additional editorial assistance of Paul McGettrick and consultancy from the 1980s from Nicholas Carolan completing the collection was a labour of love for Ó Súilleabháin, who had first started working on it with Fleischmann while a student. Recording and media work at this time also included the three-part television series *In Search of Ancient Ireland* directed by Leo Eaton with a musical score by Ó Súilleabháin. The programme was produced by WNET/RTÉ and broadcast in Ireland and the United States in 2002. A piece based on the programme's music was also incorporated into his album *Templum*. Featuring the Irish Chamber Orchestra and the National Chamber Choir of Ireland, it was released in 2001.[25]

Ó Súilleabháin's work as a musician, educator and public figure was increasingly recognised by a number of awards and appointments. In 2003 he was given the title of ard ollamh of the Fleadh Cheoil na hÉireann in Clonmel by Comhaltas Ceoltóirí Éireann, the first time in the history of the organisation that such an honour was given.[26] He was awarded an honorary DMus by the National University of Ireland/UCC and an honorary alumnus award from Boston College in 2005. In March 2005 the minister for arts, John O'Donoghue, announced the appointment of Ó Súilleabháin as the first chair of a new initiative called Culture Ireland with a brief to promote Irish culture abroad.[27]

Ó Súilleabháin's recognition internationally made him a strong choice for this position. He was well known as a musician and educator, particularly within the Irish diaspora in North America, indicated for example by his nomination as the *Irish Echo*'s Traditionalist of the Year in 2007. The *Irish Echo* has the largest circulation of an Irish-American weekly newspaper in the United States. Writing about this award, Earle Hitchner noted the uniqueness of Ó Súilleabháin's widespread musical appeal and impact of his educational work: 'Although the world of academia can be insular and frequently goes unnoticed by the majority of music followers, what Mícheál Ó Súilleabháin, a professor of music at the University of Limerick, has accomplished at the Irish World Academy of Music and Dance is unprecedented and unrivalled.'[28] While Ó Súilleabháin was best known within the Irish diaspora, his compositional reputation also led to international commissions such as *Madison's Descent*, a masque in ten movements for voice, choir and orchestra which was commissioned by Peak Performances and premiered in Montclair State University, New Jersey, in 2006.

On the tenth anniversary of the Irish World Music Centre in 2004, it was announced that the Centre would change its name to the Irish World Academy of Music and Dance in recognition of the central role of dance, and the expansion of vision from a research centre to a fully fledged academy with undergraduate and postgraduate students, artists-in-residence and a network of community-based partnerships. By 2007 a new, state-of-the-art building for the Academy was announced, to be located on the banks of the river Shannon.[29] The €20 million building, funded largely by TAP, was specifically designed to combine the elements of research, performance and teaching by leading French architect Daniel Cordier, who was appointed following an international design competition. Inspired by the architecture of the beehive huts on Skellig Michael, it accommodates two performance workshop theatres as well as dance performance studios, recording spaces, music performance practice rooms, seminar rooms, exhibition areas and an international research centre.[30] The building was officially opened by An Taoiseach Brian Cowen in September 2010. In the same year, Ó Súilleabháin released a compilation recording of new and selected works called *Elver Gleams*. In 2011 he received the TG4 Gradam Aitheantais/ Special Recognition Award.

With the building accomplished, he decided to take his first sabbatical since arriving in Limerick. In 2012 he relocated with Helen and son, Luke Phelan, to the University of Notre Dame as the Patrick B. O'Donnell Visiting Professor of Irish Studies. On his return to the Academy, he announced that he would be stepping down as director to facilitate the transition between then and his retirement in 2016. Sandra Joyce continued in the directorship of the Academy and in 2016, following an international search, Mel Mercier was announced as the new chair of performing arts to succeed Ó Súilleabháin.[31] In 2022, Helen Phelan was announced as the new director of the Irish World Academy.[32]

As he approached retirement, recognition of his work was marked both locally and internationally. In 2016 he was awarded the freedom of Clonmel and honoured with a mayoral reception from Limerick in 2017. In the same year, he received an honorary doctorate from the Royal Conservatoire of Scotland. 2017 also marked his first invitation to curate a performance with the National Symphony Orchestra (NSO). He was increasingly drawn to writing for a larger orchestral palette and relished the opportunity to compose new music for these forces. The sell-out concert in 2017, featuring two major works with Iarla Ó Lionáird and orchestra, was followed by a second invitation in 2018 in which he featured his newest work based on a series of poems by Seán Ó Ríordáin, performed with the NSO under conductor David Brophy and singers Lillis Ó Laoire, Síle Denvir and Iarla Ó Lionáird. His final performance was at the 2018 Fleadh Cheoil na hÉireann in Drogheda. On 2 November 2018 Mícheál was granted honorary life membership by the Society for Music Education in Ireland. He passed away following an extended illness on 7 November 2018. Tributes from around the world noted his central role in reimagining Irish music globally. Christopher Fox, professor of English and the director of the Keough-Naughton Institute for Irish Studies at the University of Notre Dame, noted:

> In the world of Irish music, there was no one more important and innovative than Mícheál Ó Súilleabháin … [H]is contribution to Irish music and culture was absolutely astonishing, and he leaves behind a lasting legacy in his stunning compositions and in the Irish World Academy of Music and Dance.[33]

President of Ireland Michael D. Higgins described his legacy as an indelible contribution to the Irish cultural landscape, both nationally and internationally:

> A representative of much of what is Irishness at its best, Mícheál Ó Súilleabháin has left us with an indelible legacy, both through his music and through the Academy, which he led for over two decades … His music and outstanding work will forever be enjoyed by countless people, celebrating his humour, his fearless sense of exploration, and his talent for harmony, joy and mobilising the peerless power of music.[34]

PART I
MUSICIAN

Foreword

Nicholas Carolan

Music was at the centre of Mícheál Ó Súilleabháin's being. From his precocious childhood involvement with music and its performance – all kinds of music, popular, traditional and classical, chiefly instrumental but also vocal – there developed in time his ambitious, brave and unique musical life. An omnivorous student, an arresting and instantly recognisable performer, a widely popular composer and arranger, an innovative and influential educator, and a national and international public cultural figure, he has left a rich musical legacy, one centred on Ireland but one with a far wider reach. Available now on commercial sound recordings, in compositions and published writings, in institutions and organisations he led, on archived radio and television programmes, and in his continuing effects on generations of students and musical colleagues who came into personal contact with him, this varied interconnected legacy will have a future influence also on those who will benefit from the changes he introduced into third-level music education in Ireland.

It seems appropriate therefore to begin this memorial volume with considerations of Mícheál as a musician, conveyed through the personal memories and reflections of friends and colleagues who played music with him or sang to his accompaniments and arrangements, or who brought his music to the world. They come from Dublin, Limerick, Mayo, Belfast, Galway, Clare, Cork and Kerry.

Fiddle player Paddy Glackin, deeply traditional but welcoming of experiment, was a well-met early collaborator in the exciting 1970s, when a whole generation of young virtuoso traditional musicians were coming to the fore in Ireland, and radio and commercial recording opportunities were opening up for them. Fiddle player Martin Hayes recalls the inspiration he received from Mícheál on the radio as a teenager in the same decade and later personally as an emigrant in Boston and at the Irish World Academy of Music and Dance in the University of Limerick on his return to Ireland. Cellist, uilleann piper and composer Neil Martin is likewise grateful for radio example and for the personal support given him in performance and composition over years in his marrying of traditional and classical streams. Saxophonist Kenneth Edge, who joined Mícheál in the group Hiberno Jazz and in other settings from their first meeting in the early 1990s, illustrates his essay with visual memorabilia and manuscript scores.

Singers have their perspectives. Nóirín Ní Riain remembers their days in the 1970s student group Pangur Bán but focuses on their decades-long exploration of religious *sean-nós* and plainchant song and her resultant recordings with the monks of Glenstal Abbey. Choral director John O'Keeffe shared in this experience of the blending of traditional and liturgical song in the 1980s and later in its academic study at the Irish World Academy. Brian Kennedy began his many collaborations at the deep end in 1995, performing on Mícheál's Eurovision extravaganza *Lumen*. Iarla Ó Lionáird, who explored the older Irish-language song culture accompanied by Mícheál on piano in later years, ponders the depth and mystery of their performances.

Bhí an ceoltóir Máire Nic Fhinn páirteach le Mícheál ina chéad-seoladh ar an domhan mór, an tráth i 1976 a thaifead sé a chéad cheirnín, do Ghael Linn, agus a nasc sé é féin le híomhá agus le hidéalachas na heagraíochta. Record producer and executive Declan Colgan follows Mícheál's record career on to the beginnings of international exposure as the first signing by Declan of the Virgin Venture label of London. Gerard Keenan, chief executive officer of the Irish Chamber Orchestra, looks back to adventures in studio and concert hall from the 1980s and the ensemble's crucial 1994 re-siting to the University of Limerick. Conductor David Brophy traces the fine detail of Mícheál's music and of their many key symphonic interactions on the concert hall platform. Sinead Hayes revisits concerts of Mícheál's music she conducted in Manchester and Dublin in partnership with him and the National Symphony Orchestra. Film archivist Sunniva O'Flynn relives the nail-biting 1993 premier of the War of Independence silent film *Irish Destiny* for which Mícheál composed the score and performed it live with the RTÉ Concert Orchestra, the first of many occasions. Playwright Mary Coll and actor Joan Sheehy discuss their memories of the 2010 Limerick play *Anything but Love* for which Mícheál also composed the score. As a capstone to the section, musician and *Journal of Music* editor Toner Quinn considers Mícheál Ó Súilleabháin's critical reception as a composer and explores his contributions to Irish composition.

1
The Making of Fresh Music
Paddy Glackin

Paddy Glackin is a fiddle player from Clontarf in Dublin. He performs as a soloist and with a variety of other traditional musicians. From the early 1970s he collaborated on a number of musical projects with Mícheál Ó Súilleabháin.

In 1973, for a young musician playing traditional music, everything seemed so definite and fixed, particularly when it came to playing the fiddle. Tunes were collected from many sources and modified to give them a new shape and expression. This process was conducted within very strict parameters which, although not written down, were clearly understood. Not adhering to these unwritten tenets left one in an isolated space and made playing an isolated activity. Individuality was encouraged on one level but was scorned if the musician stepped outside the normal structures. Exploration of tunes in a truly free sense was a lonely pursuit and was largely conducted within the confines of your own home. For a young fiddle player with a fair degree of energy and curiosity, it was difficult to navigate these forces which were pulling in different directions. A casual meeting with Mícheál Ó Súilleabháin and Nóirín Ní Riain was to change that sense of isolation and frustration and open up a new and exciting musical horizon.

The encounter took place at a *féile cheoil* in Lixnaw, County Kerry in 1973. I was playing at the closing concert with the late accordion player Paddy O'Brien of Nenagh. At the post-concert get-together I was approached by a young couple who were most complimentary about my playing. Their curiosity in relation to my approach to music and fiddle playing was striking. Their questions and incisive comments struck an immediate chord and gave me a confidence boost that was required at that time. Essentially, it was a welcome and an important validation of a young apprehensive fiddler in 1973.

The first concert I attended involving this duo was later in 1973 in Theatre L of University College Dublin, Belfield, where they were part of the group Pangur Bán. They performed a wide selection of tunes and songs from various regions and presented them in a very contemporary way. I could sense the influence of Seán Ó Riada in their approach, but I was also very taken with influences coming from other genres. Rhythmically and structurally, the tunes and songs went in a direction I hadn't encountered before and I was particularly interested in the accompaniment and approach of the keyboard which, to my ear, was borrowing from a jazz which sounded very much like the playing of Dave Brubeck. The entire evening was a revelation to me and I left Belfield that evening with a sense of excitement about the possibilities for new ways of expressing the music.

Around this time, another force was emerging on the traditional music scene in the form of a Raidio Teilifís Éireann radio programme called *The Long Note*. It was the creation of the Clare accordion player Tony MacMahon. The basic philosophy of the programme was to create a new conversation around traditional music and to challenge the clichés and unfounded claims that abounded at that time. Tony believed fervently in the integrity and artistic merit of Irish folk music and he set about redefining the priorities. His intention was to focus on the music of the individual and to give a platform to those who had been marginalised by the musical establishment of the time. The second element of the process was to encourage a younger generation of musicians to explore the possibilities of the music through experimentation and the creation of new approaches. The programme encouraged robust debate by its rigorous reviews and broadened the musical landscape to include the music of other Celtic countries, particularly the music of Scotland and Brittany.

Mícheál Ó Súilleabháin was ideally placed to be part of this new broadcasting experiment. He was invited by Tony to arrange a version of the programme theme tune and to create a series of 'stings' or audio separators. Mícheál invited me to play fiddle on these sessions with others, such as Matt Molloy on flute, Mel and Paul Mercier on bodhrán and Paddy Keenan on pipes. Our first get-together in Studio 1 in the RTÉ Radio Centre was a mind-expanding experience. The boldness of the arrangements, along with the energy emanating from Mícheál, was infectious, and after four to five hours of intense playing we left RTÉ tired but utterly exhilarated! The reaction to the recording was along predictable lines – positive and negative – but our youth and conviction insulated us from any negative response. This was only the start.

Our next project was another radio programme. Produced again by Tony MacMahon, it was RTÉ's entry to an international radio competition. The theme of the programme was Napoleon Bonaparte, once a hero of Irish folk culture. Mícheál, as musical director, assembled six musicians to play his arrangements of melodies popular in Ireland which celebrated Napoleon's place in history. Tunes such as 'Napoleon Crossing the Rhine', 'Napoleon's Grand March' and 'The Downfall of Paris' were given modern arrangements, with an emphasis on a pulsating rhythm that underpinned the tune structures. As usual, energy was at the core of this project and it was suitably augmented by the wonderful singing of Seosamh Ó hÉanaí of Galway and the text by the Dublin poet Pearse Hutchinson.

At this stage, I was invited by the Dublin Irish-language organisation Gael Linn to record a solo fiddle album. While the idea of a solo album was an honour and a challenge, I wanted it to reflect my recent musical experiences. I was energised greatly by the record's producer Tony MacMahon and of course by Mícheál, who was most generous with suggestions for tune treatments. We took the slow air 'Seán Ó Duibhir a' Ghleanna', played it in a straight manner and moved into an abridged setting of Clare fiddle player Bobby Casey's set-dance interpretation. It was notable for the explosive passages in the opening and closing sections of the set dance played by Mícheál on harpsichord. We also took a single-jig version of 'The Frieze Britches' on the final track and had the most wonderful fun playing it in different keys. It was described by Séamus Ennis as 'a humorously boastful gift-knot'.

That recording was to be the first expression of our mutual interest in the music of the contemporary Dublin fiddle player Tommie Potts. We took tunes like 'Top it Off' and married it with a reel version of the related tune that is known as 'The Sunny Banks'. We spent many hours discussing Tommie's music and were forever trying to figure out how on earth he came on the versions of tunes like 'My Love is in America'. Of course Mícheál was later to bring his understanding of Potts to a much higher level as he chose Tommie Potts and his music as the subject of his PhD thesis.

The phenomenon of tunes appearing in different time signatures and dance metres was an area that Mícheál was to explore as part of his thesis. It was an area of interest to me also, having been introduced to it by Paddy O'Brien. Over many meetings in that period, Mícheál and I explored this interesting aspect of the music and we uncovered many instances of tunes in different metres which we regularly used as a device in our performances at that time.

One of my most enjoyable experiences with Mícheál was our collaboration on an album called *Cry of the Mountain* which was a celebration of his work for radio and film between 1974 and 1978. Part of the album featured tunes from the RTÉ Napoleon programme. It also featured two interesting and imaginative compositions which showed how Mícheál was being influenced by other musical traditions. The title track 'Cry of the Mountain' and a track called 'The Kinkisha' illustrated his sense of curiosity and were described by Gerard Victory in his introductory notes as 'linking Irish music quite brilliantly with the exotic procedures of the Orient and South America'. He further observed that this revealed 'a growing inclination somehow, to develop a new musical language spanning East and West and rooted in great ancient cultures which, when examined, reveal fundamental bonds between their traditions'.

Cry of the Mountain included an expanded version of our original arrangement of 'Seán Ó Duibhir a' Ghleanna' which Mícheál described as a 'concertino for fiddle'. It also featured Dave Hennessy on accordion, Ursula Willis on cello, Mel and Paul Mercier on bones and bodhrán, and Seamus Tansey on flute. This version was significant in that it allowed the lead instruments to explore different approaches to the basic theme. One of my outstanding memories of this project was a rehearsal which took place upstairs in the Phoenix Bar in Cork. It was a joyous and exciting occasion, as it was here that Mícheál encouraged us to freely interpret the basic theme of the piece and to go in whatever direction felt comfortable. Seamus Tansey rose to the challenge with a wonderful reel that showed all his great musical qualities to fine effect.

Despite our close personal and musical relationship, public performances were rare and only occurred when Gael Linn were celebrating different milestones. One such occasion was a musical celebration in the Gaiety Theatre, Dublin in 1979 which was notable for the inclusion in our ensemble of two guest musicians playing Indian sitar and tabla. It was a very interesting experiment listening to tabla and bodhrán blending and it was also a new experience to play tunes like 'The Sunny Banks' with differing rhythmic patterns. This was an area which Mícheál and Mel would continue to develop over many years.

That was to be our last time to play together until 2013. This occasion was a celebration of the twenty-fifth anniversary of the Irish Traditional Music Archive at the Abbey Theatre in Dublin. It brought us together with Kildare uilleann piper Liam O'Flynn and Belfast cellist Neil Martin. The event was initially thought of as a one-off occasion, but the enjoyment we derived from playing as a quartet was so uplifting that we decided to play more concerts should there be a demand. Over the next two years we performed at different events in Ireland and Europe and each performance left us really looking forward to the next one. Unfortunately, it came to its end with the sad passing of Liam in March 2018 and of Mícheál in November of that same year.

I consider my association with Mícheál over forty-five years as a truly great gift bestowed upon me. Musicians need those in their lives who can inspire and encourage a sense of adventure. Mícheál did that in a spirit of huge generosity. Anytime I needed advice or suggestions, the response was immediate and given with the same enthusiasm I first encountered all those years ago. Our paths diverged but the spirit of humanity and friendship never diminished.

2
An Bóthar Ard ón gCrosbhóthar

Máire Nic Fhinn

Ag plé le hearnáil na siamsaíochta ó thús a saol oibre le Ceirníní Gael Linn. D'oibrigh le RTÉ mar láithreoir-iriseoir agus mar oifigeach cumarsáide agus na Gaeilge. D'fhoilsigh Coiscéim beathaisnéis a scríobh sí dar teideal Riobard Mac Góráin: Ceannródaí ildánach (Ceirníní Gael Linn idir na 50idí agus na 70idí) *i 2018.*

Chuir mé aithne ar Mhícheál Ó Súilleabháin trí Ghael Linn go luath ina shaol mar cheoltóir sna 1970idí. Is maith is cuimhneach liom an fear óg a tháinig isteach san oifig chugainn agus é fuinniúil, meanmnach. Anuas air sin, bhí bua na cainte aige a bhí tógálach. Cé nach raibh sé ach i lár na bhfichidí an tráth sin, bhí comharthaí ceannaireachta agus bealach ar leith a bhí le sonrú ina phearsantacht. Ba thréithe iad a tháinig in inmhe níos faide ar aghaidh ina shaol mar ghníomhaí réabhlóideach i réimsí an cheoil, an oideachais agus na fiontraíochta.

Bhí sé díreach ceaptha ina léachtóir cúnta le ceol i gColáiste na hOllscoile Corcaigh, áit a ndearna sé staidéar faoi stiúir Sheáin Uí Riada agus Aloys Fleischmann. Ní raibh aon aithne phoiblí air ach bhí sé aitheanta i measc a chomhpháirtithe ceoil mar scoláire, mar ghinias ar mhéarchlár agus mar oidhre an Riadaigh. Agus cé go raibh neart comparáidí a d'fhéadfaí a dhéanamh le Seán Ó Riada, tháinig Mícheál Ó Súilleabháin ar an bhfód mar ealaíontóir ard-bhuacach a raibh fís dá chuid féin aige.

Chuaigh a shuim sa cheol traidisiúnta siar go dtí a óige i gCluain Meala agus é ag éisteacht le clár raidió seachtainiúil Ghael Linn sa bhaile lena mhuintir. Deir sé go raibh tionchar ag an gclár air sa mhéid is gur mhúscail sé a shuim sa chultúr Gaelach. Dá bhrí shin, bhí bá nádúrtha aige leis an eagraíocht agus é ag smaoineamh ar a chéad cheirnín a thaifeadadh. Theastaigh uaidh a bheith páirteach san íomhá agus san idéalachas a bhí á gcothú aici.

Bhí modhanna nuálacha á dtriail aige féin lena shaothar ceoil a fhorbairt agus a chur i láthair. Ba mhór aige gur thug Riobard Mac Góráin, a bhí i gceannas ar lipéad Ceirníní Gael Linn, cuireadh dó teacht ar chlár teilifíse a bhí aige dar teideal *An Fear agus a Chuid Ceoil* (RTÉ, 1975). B'in thart ar an am céanna a raibh sé i mbun ábhar a réiteach dá chéad cheirnín. Dúirt sé go bhfuair sé 'éisteacht, saoirse agus spreagadh' ó Riobard agus a chuid smaointe á gcur ina láthair aige.

Tháinig an ceirnín sin dá cheol uirlise amach i 1976. Cuireadh ainm Mhichíl i láthair go feiceálach sa chéad áit ar an gclúdach tosaigh ar a raibh pictiúir de chuid Jack B. Yeats. Ba sheift mhargaíochta í a tharraing aird ar a ainm mar aon le raon a chuid tallainne. Bhí nuálaíocht ag baint leis an taifeadadh mar shaothar. Ba é a chúram teicníc méarchláir a leagan ar na foirmeacha agus ar na cineálacha éagsúla den cheol Éireannach. D'úsáid sé cúig ghléas méarchláir – clabhchorda, cruitchorda, pianó, orgán troitheán agus sintéiseoir. Léirigh Mícheál a chumas i réim agus fíneáltacht an cheoil ar uirlisí nach samhlófaí de ghnáth le ceol na hÉireann. Ba thaifead trialach a bhí ann ar mhórán bealaí mar nach raibh a leithéid déanta roimhe sin agus níorbh fhios cén chaoi a nglacfaí leis. Mheall an ceirnín lucht leanúna breise i dtreo an cheoil thraidisiúnta. Spreag sé ceoltóirí eile le bheith níos misniúla le cóiriúcháin nuálacha agus na cineálacha uirlisí a raibh ceol Gaelach á sheinm orthu.

An bhliain chéanna, eisíodh an ceirnín *Óró Damhnaigh*, ar a raibh dréachtaí aonair uaidh féin agus ó ghrúpa ceoltóirí aitheanta faoina stiúir, ina measc John Dwyer. Cloiseadh freisin, den chéad uair ar thaifeadadh, glór álainn an amhránaí Nóirín Ní Riain, a bhean chéile ag an am. Léirigh sé dhá cheirnín eile a rinne Nóirín le Gael Linn ina dhiaidh sin, *Seinn Aililiú* (1978) agus *Caoineadh na Maighdine*, cnuasach d'amhráin dhiaga thraidisiúnta (1980).

Ba é an ceirnín *Cry of the Mountain* (1982) ar a raibh ceolta a thaifead Mícheál don raidió agus do scannáin idir 1974 agus 1978, an ceann deiridh a rinne sé le Gael Linn. Bhí a aigne casta i dtreo na margaí tráchtála idirnáisiúnta faoin am seo agus mar a tharla le cuid mhaith oirfideach a thosaigh amach le Gael Linn, fuair sé tairiscint a chomhlíon a uaillmhianta sa treo sin. Chuaigh sé le comhlacht nua a bhí Virgin a bhunú in Éirinn agus tháinig *The Dolphin's Way* amach i 1987 le Venture Records. Rinne sé iliomad taifeadtaí leosan agus le comhlachtaí eile ó shin.

Lean Mícheál sruth na nuálaíochta ina chuid ceoil ó rinne sé a chéad fhadcheirnín le Gael Linn. Cosúil leis an Riadach roimhe, bhí an traidisiún mar fhuaimrian ina chumadóireacht agus ina chuid cóiriúchán. Agus cé go raibh sé dílis don traidisiún, tháinig sé faoi thionchar seánraí ón iasacht ar nós snagcheoil agus cheol an oirthir. Bhain sé leas as iliomad cineálacha méarchláir, uirlisí sreanga, cnaguirlisí agus gaothuirlisí ar nós an tsacsafóin, ina chuid cóiriúcháin do ghrúpaí ceoil thraidisiúnta.

Faraor, ní raibh glacadh lena chur chuige i ngach cearn. Chothaigh sé míshuaimhneas i measc chaomhnóirí an traidisiúin a mheas go raibh lagú ag teacht ar théagar an cheoil de bharr fhórsaí tréana na nuálaíochta. Sroicheadh crosaire sa díospóireacht sna 1990idí. Ghéaraigh ar phlé deighilteach faoi cad air a bhféadfaí ceol traidisiúnta a ghlaoch feasta i bhfianaise na gcineálacha áirithe stíle a bhí ag teacht chun cinn ó oirfidigh áirithe. Bhí Mícheál chun tosaigh sa dioscúrsa sin. Bhain sé le cohórt a chreid má bhí coimhlint ann nach raibh cúis ar bith ach go bhféadfadh an dá fhoirm maireachtáil comhthreomhar le chéile. Forbairt nádúrtha na linne seachas lagú an sainmhíniú a chuir sé chun cinn sa tsraith teilifíse a chuir sé i láthair dar teideal *A River of Sound: The changing course of Irish traditional music* (RTÉ–BBC 1995).

Is amhlaidh a ghríosaigh sé sin lucht a cháinte. Bhí Tony MacMahon ar dhuine díobh siúd a bhí glórach ag cosaint an traidisiúin. Bhí seisean imníoch go mbeadh máistrí aonair an cheoil lena gcuid stíleanna áitiúla agus réigiúnacha i mbaol ó thionchair ón iasacht. B'íorónta mar scéal é mar gurbh é Tony a léirigh an ceirnín ceannródaíoch méarchláir a rinne Mícheál do Ghael Linn fiche bliain roimhe sin.

Tharla buaicphointe poiblí na hargóna nuair a reáchtáladh comhdháil dar teideal *Crosbhealach an Cheoil* (1996) i mBaile Átha Cliath. Thug Mícheál agus Tony – beirt fhathach i saol an cheoil – aghaidh ar a chéile i gcomhrac a bhí fíochmhar ar uairibh. D'éirigh díospóireacht teasaí ina ndearna Tony scagadh agus cáineadh ar shaothar Mhichíl. Má chuir an cáineadh pearsanta aon mhairg ar Mhícheál, tháinig a chuid uaisleachta chun cinn sa gcomhrac. Níor chaill sé radharc ar an mbóthar ard. Is féidir a rá, díreach mar a shamhlaigh sé, go nglactar go forleathan leis an nuálaíocht anois mar fhorbairt leanúnach na linne seachas é bheith ina bhagairt don traidisiún.

Ba fórsa gníomhach ar son an athraithe é Mícheál i ngach gné dá shaol mar cheoltóirchumadóir, mar oideachasóir agus mar fhiontraí. Bhí sé flaithiúil lena chuid ama le cairde, ar choistí agus ag tacú le heagraíochtaí cultúrtha. Tá liodán a chuid éachtaí pearsanta agus poiblí rólíonmhar le meabhrú san amharc gearr seo ar a shaol. Mairfidh a oidhreacht i nDámh Chruinne Éireann Rince agus Ceoil i Luimneach, mar chloch le carn ar a chuid gníomhaíochtaí go síoraí.

Máire Nic Fhinn, who worked for the Irish-language cultural organisation Gael Linn in Dublin, remembers Mícheál Ó Súilleabháin's early musical impact. As a young academic, he made the first of several LPs for the company's label in 1976, encouraged by executive Riobard Mac Góráin. His well-received novel keyboard approach to Irish traditional music encouraged experimentation in younger players but also engendered resistance from others. Public tradition-vs-innovation controversies in which he was involved in the 1990s have died away and his approach is now regarded as having been a beneficial force for change.

3

'This is, in several ways, an experimental recording ...'

Declan Colgan

Declan Colgan has worked in the music industry for nearly fifty years and currently runs Panegyric Recordings & Books with his wife from their base in Buckinghamshire, England.

That was either a very brave or an immensely foolish thing to state on the front of a vinyl album sleeve in 1976. Even more unusually, almost uniquely in fact, it wasn't on what would in later years become known as a 'hype sticker', something along the lines of 'featuring all of Carolan's harp hits on a single disc'. But it was printed as the first line of a full descriptive paragraph on the sleeve front, a manifesto in miniature which could be read either as an enticement to investigate further or a warning to put it back in the rack and find something less daunting. The paragraph included a surprising list of keyboard instruments used on the recording.

The album sleeve was simultaneously intriguing and puzzling. The artist and album name *Mícheál Ó Súilleabháin* sat atop a Jack B. Yeats illustration, under which the paragraph appeared. I should have realised then that he was a teacher. Had I known, I would definitely have put it back in the rack. Instead, I looked to the back of the sleeve, where dual-language Irish/English notes identified a series of pieces and confirmed the instrument used for each: piano, harpsichord, clavichord, pedal organ, moog. And a mini-moog at that.

Sold.

In 1974 I had been fortunate in getting a part-time job, weekends and school holidays, in one of Dublin's best record shops. Having started with a level of knowledge of records that was probably fairly typical of a compulsive teenage record-buyer, music-press reader and haunter of record shops, my mind and ears were then treated over the course of the next few years working there to rock music in all its myriad forms. And while I was initially very dismissive of other forms of music, just as rock had extended its tentacles into jazz, country, folk and anything it could part-absorb, I extended my listening to match. Jazz-rock, country-rock, folk-rock inevitably led to the purer drops of those genres – music with the word 'rock' absent. This was the advantage of working with the only slightly older, but much more knowledgeable, full-time shop staff with their greater exposure to records, films and books, many of which I might not have discovered myself. Even Irish traditional music which, pre-work, I would have ignored was now part of that mix. It would have been impossible not to become familiar with it as almost all record shops in Ireland played Irish music in some form or other during the summer to attract tourist cash.

The more I heard, the more I wanted to hear. But I was always willing to give piano/keyboard players a first option when confronted with a pile of unheard albums. By 1976 that meant trying to trace the catalogues of the likes of Keith Jarrett, McCoy Tyner, Chick Corea, Herbie Hancock and Joe Zawinul, alumni, for the most part, of stints with Miles Davis and John Coltrane. The range was from solo piano concert recordings to those of small groups, and to larger, more 'out there' free-jazz improvisations.

It was in the midst of this awakening to music's possibilities that Mícheál's album arrived in the shop, largely unheralded and with little or no advance notice or accompanying information. This was the treatment commonplace with all but established major artists, who hardly needed the push, or with the select few chosen among the major labels' newer signings who were deemed bound for glory.

Traditional music (not just Irish) was also then looking to a larger international audience, cross-pollinating with other forms of music, its audience expanding. Planxty, possibly to their regret, were signed to Polydor, not the more obvious Gael Linn or Claddagh labels. Outside Ireland, The Chieftains were signed to Island Records, in company with Bob Marley, Traffic, Free and, at that point, King Crimson and Roxy Music. Likewise The Bothy Band appeared on Polydor in the UK and France. Even the descriptions were changing. If The Chieftains was an ensemble that performed concerts, The Bothy Band was a group that played gigs. Horslips, incorporating traditional elements into a rock band setting, brought large public-address systems to halls that had previously hosted showbands. They released and recorded via their own Irish label Oats, their albums appeared variously on Atco/Atlantic, RCA, Mercury and DJM in the UK, United States and other countries.

But Irish traditional music that was played, even in part, on a multi-tracked mini-moog was taking those possibilities further. While the more studio-based, less roadworthy analogue moogs had been used by The Monkees, Simon & Garfunkel and The Beatles, the sturdier, more familiar mini-moog is more readily identified with early 1970s progressive rock bands. Despite its appearance a year earlier on a single split between a proto-Bothy Band song and a Clannad tune (the mini-moog belonging to Dónal Lunny), it's not what anyone would have expected on an album of Irish tunes. And certainly not on Gael Linn, the label most associated with Seán Ó Riada and often seen somewhat unfairly as representing the status quo of the tradition.

Of course no music springs to life uninformed by that which precedes it. Ó Riada had himself played keyboards with the idea that the harpsichord could echo the Irish harp, and Mícheál had studied with Ó Riada. But the overall aim displayed on Mícheál's debut album – that of presenting traditional music on a variety of unaccompanied keyboards – was novel. If the clavichord and harpsichord could be seen to represent the harp, the pedal organ and the mini-moog represented the uilleann pipes, but only in a general sense. Nobody would have multi-tracked pipes in quite the same manner as the mini-moog was layered here.

The music was, as a result, never in any way directly imitative of its perceived instruments of origin. It was abundantly clear that this was an album by a keyboard player. The flourishes and embellishments may have echoed the tradition they represented, the feeling of chances being taken may have better reflected an informal session than a harpsichord recital, but the sense of if being grounded in pianistic interpretation was key to the recordings. Importantly, this wasn't what Wendy Carlos had done successfully with Bach or Isao Tomita with a variety of composers, using synthesisers to replicate the timbres of orchestral music. This was Irish traditional music played and interpreted by a piano and keyboard player steeped in the music.

Perhaps that also explains why the piano pieces seem to have had the most emotional impact, at least on this listener. The precedent for the use of harpsichord had already been set. The mini-moog had the shock of the new to it. But the piano pieces seemed to convey, most accurately, Mícheál's intent as an arranger and performer. These were the pieces which stayed in the mind long after the record ended, from the bare-bones simplicity of 'Oíche Nollag / Christmas Eve' – the tune with which he later became most associated in a very different arrangement – to the harmonic beauty he brought to 'Carúl Loch Garman/The Wexford Carol'. These were the pieces I extracted for a cassette compilation of piano recordings of favoured pianists that I played until it snapped. These were the pieces that came to mind again for a very different purpose over a decade later.

Towards the end of 1986, as the commercial impact of the compact disc was heralding a new era of discovery among buyers of recorded music, I was asked to set up/operate/curate an 'eclectic music' label for Virgin Records in London. This was to echo, to an extent, Virgin's own roots as a label of diverse music and specifically its Caroline Records label, which in the mid-1970s released records by Dudu Pukwana, Klaus Schulze, Glenn Phillips, Fred Frith and many more.

In trying to find the right artists to launch the label I went back to Mícheál's first Gael Linn album, referencing in particular the solo piano pieces and its self-description as 'an experimental recording'. Having tracked Mícheál down with help from Virgin's Dublin office to University College Cork, at the moment when he had just completed a doctorate in ethnomusicology in Queen's University Belfast, I discovered that his mind also had turned to thoughts of recording again. So the timing was mutually ideal. The notion of piano – as opposed to more general keyboard recordings – was one he found particularly appealing, and he suggested that he be accompanied by Colm Murphy on bodhrán and Mel Mercier on bones. Virgin approved and Mícheál became the label's first signing. The recordings were made at the smaller of the Dublin Windmill Lane studios near Stephen's Green over two days, and were issued in 1987 as the first album on Venture Records. The title *The Dolphin's Way* came from a line from a Seamus Heaney poem which we were kindly allowed to quote by the poet and his publisher.

Mícheál seemed able to distil the essence of all of the traditional music he had heard and played over the years into a series of performances which made the piano sound like a natural instrument of the tradition. Still an experimental recording (two separate pianos were used in the sessions, a Yamaha for the fast tunes and a Bösendorfer for the slow airs), it now had a confidence and maturity of style, a depth of interpretation and a fluidity of playing that was only hinted at on his debut Gael Linn record. But nothing of the sense of wonder of that recording was lacking.

As someone who was closely involved with signing the artist, organising the recording sessions and producing and overseeing the mastering of the recordings, it's not for me to judge its impact. But on more than one occasion over the years other musicians told Mícheál (and me) how important that record was to them. It seems to have a resonance with audiences, especially musicians, that went far beyond that which anyone involved in it would have imagined when it was being made. I felt then and continue to feel privileged to have had an involvement with it and with many of the recordings that followed it.

It sold in sufficient numbers, from a purely record-company perspective, to enable Venture to continue with Mícheál as he expanded his vision of composing, arranging and performing with the Irish Chamber Orchestra. He recorded several more albums with the label and was the sole artist to have been there from its inception, before that particular cycle of the industry ended in 2002 with the absorption of what remained of Virgin Records into EMI. The piano remained central to all of his recordings: half of the *Casadh/Turning* album returned to the solo piano or piano with percussion style, with Mel playing both bodhrán and bones on this occasion. On many occasions we discussed the idea of a full solo piano album; 'The Dolphin's Return' became the shorthand method of referring to the potential project. Indeed Mícheál even planned recording a sequence of Carolan tunes, many of which he premiered in concert settings, including at London's Wigmore Hall in 2016.

Sadly, the opportunity to suggest, even facetiously, the 'featuring all of Carolan's harp hits on a single disc' hype sticker to help sell such a record never presented itself. The best summation, one that could be applied equally to all of his recordings, was his own. It was there at the start, on the cover of that eponymous Gael Linn album: 'This is, in several ways, an experimental recording …'

4

It Began Literally as a Dream

Nóirín Ní Riain

Nóirín Ní Riain PhD is a spiritual singer, theologian, author, teacher and interfaith minister. She has performed, lectured and recorded worldwide and is the holder of the first doctorate in theology to be awarded by Mary Immaculate College, University of Limerick in 2003.

A dream come true, actually. Some months before we had ever met the monks, Mick and I were staying in my parents' home, Mount Marian, in Caherconlish, County Limerick. In the middle of the night, I sat bolt upright in the bed, still in sleep-time. 'Look at the monks, Mick,' I cried out excitedly. 'They're singing with us.'

So convinced was Mick of the vision that he asked, 'How many of them?'

'Twelve,' I replied. I can still recall the dream but one detail is amiss: the dream-time monks were processing in brown habits; Benedictines wear black.

From the outside it would seem that there was no real connection between the monastery and us. Glenstal was a bastion of Anglo-Irish sensibility with little sympathy for the traditions which we were embracing at the time. The lifeline was made through song. The monks were the guardians of an ancient tradition of music which they used on a daily basis for their worship. Monks had sung plainchant for centuries and this recently installed offshoot of a fifteen-hundred-year-old Benedictine tradition was something of a shopfront for the brand in Ireland. Glenstal Abbey and Gregorian chant had become synonymous.

In the summer of 1976, we, newly-weds, headed for the Benedictine Abbey of Solesmes, France, where we ventured on a very basic course on the mystery of Gregorian chant and semiology with the great, iconic Dom Eugène Cardine. One privileged moment was when he led us into the monastic archives to show us the original early manuscripts.

From that time on, Mícheál and I were always fascinated by theories and resonances around ornamentation within the Irish traditional *sean-nós* (old-style) singing tradition and the neumes in plainchant. A neume, coming from the Greek, could be derived either from pnεῦμα *pneuma* meaning 'breath' or νεῦμα *neuma* meaning 'sign'. Either way, it is the basic element of western and eastern systems of musical notation prior to the invention of five-line staff notation. The earliest neumes were inflective marks that indicated the general visual shape of a melody but not necessarily the exact notes or rhythms to be sung.

Our conversations and questions were many. Was plainchant simply unfurled ornaments? What were the essential melodies and the notes on the periphery? Why are some *sean-nós* singing techniques from different corners of Ireland so diverse and strange to each other? For instance, the Donegal style is so stark, un-ornamented and purely melodic as opposed to that of An Rinn, Baile Bhúirne or Corca Dhuibhne which are so richly iced with many cherries on top!

We would experiment, devising neumes to transcribe *sean-nós* ornaments. This slowly and eventually developed into a system which I devised for a publication – *Stór Amhrán: A wealth of songs from the Irish tradition* (1988, 2007) – of adapting the five lines and four spaces of western classical notation. Mícheál would play an instrumental version of scores on the piano and I would adapt and follow his advice on re-scoring the songs to transcribe them from the oral to the written in as precise a manner as possible. (This was a blueprint that we followed in the years to come as I transcribed *na hamhráin cráifeacha* – the traditional religious songs of Ireland – for the booklets of two Glenstal recordings.)

I am primarily a singer who learnt these religious songs by ear from Pilib Ó Laoghaire, and then wrote them down not only from the recordings of Ó Laoghaire himself, but often from my own memory. The hand becomes the scribe of a music heard and then sung by the voice, an incarnation of tradition through the body processing it through the brain. Almost as a fingerprint is inked onto a page, the preservation of the music in pictorial image on the sheet of manuscript is the final act of a process involving the whole body as instrument from the ear to the fingertip.

Mícheál was always concerned about musical repertoires which predated or had been marginalised by the colonial monopoly of classical literate musical notation. Here were two such outsiders. Could they be brought together and salvaged?

Caherline church: the first acquaintance

Our first music-making encounter with this monastic community of Glenstal was not within the monastery but for the opening of a local church in Caherline, County Limerick in 1977. My invitation to bless the opening in song came because I was the local singer. The curate invited the monastery to add what he whispered to us before they arrived as '*a bit of claawss*'! The organist at that time was Dom Paul McDonnell and over the tea later he spoke, to our great surprise, about his friendship with our former university lecturer and inspiration Seán Ó Riada, who passed over in 1971.

Dom Paul invited us to a liturgy in Glenstal Abbey on the following Sunday. Afterwards, reminiscent of our Solesmes manuscript epiphany, he brought us in to show us a scribbled hand-written transcription of the now very familiar setting of the 'Ár nAthair' (Our Father) from Seán. This was prompted when Dom Paul first sent him, Christmas 1968, a greeting card with a transcription of a plainchant gospel acclamation. Mick was very moved that Seán Ó, as he fondly called him, had been there before him.

The time was right

The 1970s was a time of transition for the Benedictine community at Glenstal Abbey. The monks had lost a dynamic young abbot, a past pupil of the school, Dom Joseph Dowdall, the first Benedictine abbot in Ireland since the Reformation. He was only twenty-nine when he was elected for life. He would still be abbot today at the age of ninety-two if he had lived, and who knows what Glenstal might have become under his enthusiastic guidance. The monks elected in his place Augustine O'Sullivan who had been a primary-school teacher before entering Glenstal: a solid, decent, upstanding and, above all, holy and humble man. He was a fluent Irish speaker, played the piano and had a deep devotion to Mary, the Mother of God. Our conversations were primarily in Irish and our repertoire of traditional religious songs, which is mainly centred on Mary, soon also became very dear to his heart.

The personal story

Prior to the musical collaborations, there was a very profound personal friendship between this young newly-wed couple and the community. A reciprocal curiosity was satiated: we were fascinated by their vocation, spiritual daily prayer stops and routine; on the other hand, they could glimpse as intimately as imaginable the experience of married life. Other bonds of belonging emerged, tennis for instance. For over twenty years Mick and I were average players, but partnered with two fine athletes, Brother Patrick and Brother Simon, we had the perfect combination for a good game. Secondly, we became pregnant with both of our sons during these years and that created a further connection between us. That association with Eoin and Mícheál continues to flourish since they spent their secondary school years as boarders in the Glenstal Abbey school. Thirdly, when Eoin was two years old, we went to live on the monastic grounds for nine months while

Mícheál was on sabbatical from University College Cork (UCC). Monks visited us frequently in Chapel Lake Cottage and we diligently staggered our daily attendance at the monastic liturgy of the hours.

We were, therefore, no strangers to this community when the time was ripe to bring our musical conversation to the public. Neither was this a financial enterprise. The very opposite. This was all about shared sonic prayer. The recordings meant the world to Mícheál and, as in everything that he embraced, this venture had to be full of integrity and of the highest musical perfection achievable. He had already established a strong liaison with Gael Linn through his own music, so that avenue opened wide to enable the production of these recordings.

Caoineadh na Maighdine (The Virgin's Lament), 1979

Abbot Augustine welcomed Mícheál's direction of our recordings. He invited us both on many occasions to join the choir and even hosted a monastic champagne launch to birth our first Gael Linn recording in 1979! With the accession of Augustine as abbot, members of the community hitherto unrecognised began to blossom and to breathe. In particular the scholar and lover of Irish language and folklore Seán Ó Duinn, who featured on the cover of the booklet accompanying that first CD, *Caoineadh na Maighdine*. Glenstal was ready for this injection of traditional Irish rhythm. Abbot Augustine was the ideal leader to champion the cause, and the sentinels standing on the parapets in the community were sufficient in number to open the doors to the guests bearing new gifts.

The young first chanter at that time was Brother Ciarán Forbes. He, along with a number of the community, was a fluent Irish speaker, and had a great love of music and a natural singing voice untouched by formal training. Mick heard the still small voice in this community. He also had the charm, the genius and the diplomatic skills to coax the timid, harness the egos and produce the goods.

Caoineadh na Maighdine still captures the sound of that year for me. We had great enjoyment and amusement during rehearsals and the recording was nothing less than miraculous. The 'twelve' gathered to record in the dead of night in the church – the quietest, most reliable time to avoid the noise of aeroplanes landing in Shannon Airport. With one candle lighting on the altar, every note was a prayer. We had an intuitive, unspoken accord that we would sing each song once, not involving ourselves with multiple takes, which might wound the original purity. Because I had completed a master's degree in UCC on these song-prayers, I was tuned into the objective musicology – the silent analysis of every song on paper; it was pure joy for us to find another, deeper expression of these songs through singing them with others. Dom Kevin Healy was the willing scribe who transformed all my basic notations into beautiful melodic scores.

Good People All (The Wexford Carols), 1982

The repertoire for the second monastic recording which Mícheál produced and directed, *Good People All*, was inspired by the traditional seventeenth-century Christmas carols still sung today in Kilmore, County Wexford. Yet again, the memory of Seán Ó Riada unconsciously returned and hovered. One morning in 1970, during one of our music lectures with Seán, he announced that, for this class, he was going to play a series of piano variations on 'The Wexford Carol'. He placed an open red book – *The Oxford Book of Carols* – on the piano stand and played this ancient tune over and over again. Then, with his usual impish manner he invited any one of us to approach the piano to play. Mick grasped the challenge and from that little hymnal, played the carol. Seán was fascinated and although not a person to be effusive, he described Mícheál sometime later as a genius and the most talented student he had ever encountered. That same Wexford carol – 'Good People All' – he would record and perform again and again and it was one of the first traditional songs which he taught to the monks at Glenstal Abbey eight years later.

However, that was simply the beginning of our relationship with the Christmas carol-singing tradition alive and well in Kilmore Quay; we were soon to be surprised, enchanted and obsessed by this still – even now – little-known unique song repertoire. During our university days, Mícheál, inspired by Seán Ó's Ceoltóirí Chualann, gathered together a bunch of students to form a traditional band called Pangur Bán. On the way out of the radio studios in Cork after doing some recordings one afternoon, the producer, Breandán Ó Cíobháin, brought out a reel-to-reel recording and played the singing of the six Kilmore Quay men, under Jack Devereux. We had never heard such singing, much more reminiscent of Scots-Gaelic psalm singing than *sean-nós*, and we were hooked!

One book, *A Smale Garland of Pious and Godly Songs*, by Bishop Luke Waddinge, printed in Ghent in 1684, and one manuscript, *A New Garland Containing Songs for Christmas*, assembled around 1728 by Fr William Devereux, are the sources for the texts of these carols. Tune titles appear underneath some of the sacred poems, presumably secular tunes of the time which have survived to this day. Although our interpretation of these melodies on the recording differs from that of the male Kilmore singers, particularly in tempo, we were always respectful of the source. Both Mícheál and I had a great desire to share this unique traditional treasure-trove with a wider audience.

The third Glenstal recording, *Vox de Nube* (Voice from the Cloud), which Mícheál produced in 1989, was a completely different venture; the circle expanded from the former stable diet of plainchant and traditional religious song in Irish to embrace chants of Hildegard von Bingen and the visionary songs of the Swiss Lutheran mystic Joa Bolendas. The liner notes here summarise the aspiration of the entire trilogy:

> Our vision of Western chant has come about through a subversion of a thousand-year-old manuscript tradition. The voice searches the depths of aural consciousness for something of the music's original breath. Masked – perhaps even protected – by an eclectic repertoire, flashes of emotive colour surge through the sound surprising us like the wild flower among rocks ... as the cactus flowers, we are challenged to break ground from beneath. This incisive voice is the perfect means of cutting a way through the over-growth, and the Word reverberates to this voice of praise, inviting us to link earth with Heaven. Under the light of the 'Voice from the Cloud' we are drawn into God's own time.

Reveries of public performances that ensued

Following the launch of the recordings and the unexpected media response, we were inundated with invitations to perform. Of course, Mícheál was the lynchpin here; without his direction and conductorship, none of this would have been possible. Here follows just a few of these diverse invitations:

The Late Late Show begged us to appear live in studio but Archbishop Ryan of Dublin intervened and advised the monastery against this;

We travelled to Quimper in Brittany in 1989 to give a concert in the Cathedrale St Corentin. It sold out immediately and we were invited to do another sell-out performance later that evening in that same Gothic Breton national monument;

The chapel in Trinity College Dublin was another packed venue in 1982 for what was more of a sacred ritual than a performance entitled *Coicead* (The Fifth Province);

The German composer James Last invited us to be his guests in St Patrick's Cathedral, Dublin in 1986. Mícheál chose our shared repertoire and scored the orchestral arrangements. Rehearsals were called for the day before in the cathedral. Mick stood beside James as he took to the podium to conduct. But as he had absolutely no sense of the music, style, and particularly the free tempo, he was soon at sea in it all. Eventually after some hours of confusion all around, Mick stepped up to Hansi, as he liked to be called, and suggested that they swap places! Instantly, Mick's leadership and conducting saved the day. The performance was pre-recorded and no-one knew the difference as James Last stood there waving his arms with great panache!;

At the International Cork Choral Festival, a yearly event in the City Hall, we received the award for the best sacred singing presentation throughout the festival;

When His Holiness the XIVth Dalai Lama paid a visit to the University of Limerick, Mícheál invited a monastic schola to be part of this musical welcome in April 2011;

Mícheál was commissioned to write a central showpiece for the Eurovision Song Contest in 1995. Here, in a composition called *Lumen* he created and witnessed his own cross-pollination of music genres: *sean-nós* singers on one side of the pews, as it were, singing antiphonally to a monastic schola on the other, held together and in harmony with a classical orchestra and an array of traditional Irish musicians. Almost twenty years later, in 2014, Mícheál gathered together the same forces for a concert of his music which was the culmination of Limerick city's Year of Culture in 2014.

Coda

What we realised during the Glenstal collaborations was the connection between *sean-nós* and plainchant. The work Mícheál sought to achieve during those ten years was to cross-fertilise and reveal the unique sound created by their practical interconnection.

This happened through the realisation of these recordings and the effect of an MA in Ritual Chant and Song at the Irish World Academy of Music and Dance on the daily use of this medium in the prayer life of the monks at Glenstal Abbey. Expert teachers from all over the world resurrected the dry bones of plainchant as it was preserved and annotated by monks before any standardised idiom of transmission had been devised. Three of the monastic chanters from Glenstal Abbey attended this course in succession and the outcome of this on each one personally acted as yeast in the dough of the whole community.

11 October 2017 was the final time Mícheál stepped onto the altar of Glenstal Abbey. The occasion was the funeral mass of An tAthair Seán Ó Duinn. The chanter, Fr Senan Furlong, invited us to provide the music for the Communion. I sang a musical setting of Mícheál's to one of Seán's most beloved traditional hymns to Mary, '*A Mhuire na nGrás*'. Mícheál then played a truly beautiful improvisatory lament on a low G whistle which mesmerised the entire congregation well beyond the duration of the distribution of communion. Time stood still and we were aware of the power of his music to allow the soul to leave the body and enter the realm of never-ending joy.

Go bhfanfaidh a n-anamnacha i suaimhneas síoraí – May their souls rest in everlasting peace.

5

'Let's start with an improvisation': Playing the saxophone for Mícheál Ó Súilleabháin

Kenneth Edge

Saxophonist-composer Kenneth Edge began his musical career by winning the 'RTÉ Young Musician of the Future' competition in 1983. He was the original saxophonist for Riverdance *and has inspired many Irish composers to create new works for him. Kenneth teaches saxophone at the Royal Irish Academy of Music.*

Introduction

In the liner notes of the 1995 CD A *River of Sound* Mícheál Ó Súilleabháin writes:

> Our music is a water of life, whiskey of passion. It uplifts us, marks our joy and sadness. It is a music to live and die for… As Irish music flows into that great singing ocean of music which is surfacing in our own time around the globe, it is timely to chart its course so that the flow may be more abundant.

The depth of Mícheál Ó Súilleabháin's engagement with Irish traditional music is evident in the above quotation, as is his inimitable eloquence, his poetic way with language. In a 2006 essay, 'Wisdom of the River', Mícheál writes of the river Shannon as it 'opens out into the Shannon estuary like a singing mouth'.[1]

His love of the mythology of the river was central to his creative imagination. When, in 1993, he was appointed first chair of music at the University of Limerick (UL), on the banks of the Shannon, the breadth of his vision alongside his energy, dynamism and a seemingly bottomless well of ideas led to the creation of one of the world's most important centres of musical learning, the Irish World Academy of Music and Dance. Mícheál's achievements at UL are well documented and widely fêted and to some extent they fall outside the scope of this essay. He wore many hats and fulfilled many roles, yet everything was connected. I can't speak of Mícheál as a pianist, for instance, without reference to him as a composer, I can't speak of him as a colleague without thinking of him as a friend, and I can't write purely objectively about performing with him without struggling to find a way of describing my embodied subjective awareness of making music with him. On a deeply intuitive level it's clear to me that Mícheál's performative artistry, his 'river of sound', had as its source the two indivisible wellsprings of his musical creativity – playing the piano and composing – and in this essay I offer my thoughts and insights into Mícheál the performer. I also present a brief first history of Mícheál's compositions for solo saxophone, all of which I premiered.

Meetings

The first time Mícheál and I met was at the Gaiety Theatre, Dublin in early 1993. We were both performing at a gala event and were introduced to each other in the green-room bar afterwards. I recall being flattered by Mícheál's comments about my playing, he was particularly taken by the stylistic gear-shifting I employed in switching between classical and jazz styles. During this period I was starting to explore the saxophone, particularly the soprano saxophone, as a chameleonic voice, sonically apt across a broad spectrum of musical styles, so this fortuitous first encounter with Mícheál Ó Súilleabháin could not have been more timely. A few weeks after our initial meeting, Mícheál invited me to participate in a recording session at Tadhg Kelleher's Sulán Studios, situated in the exquisitely picturesque surroundings of Ballyvourney, County Cork. The performers for the recording would be Mícheál, myself, percussionist Mel Mercier, double-bassist Andy Baker and the singer Nóirín Ní Riain. The recording sessions were to be filmed by the television network Teilifís na Gaeilge (now TG4).

I said that of course I'd be delighted to be involved, so a second meeting was duly scheduled, this time at the Davenport Hotel, Dublin, to discuss possible repertoire for the recording. Mícheál arrived with his briefcase stuffed with handwritten orchestral scores and CDs for me, all of which I still have. The CDs Mícheál gave me to study were *The Dolphin's Way*, *Oileán*, *Casadh*, and the recently completed *Gaiseadh*. His recommendation to me was: 'Have a listen and see what you think might work on the sax.' The sheet music he gave me to study included *So Merrily Dance* (Figure 5.1).

He also gave me a handwritten full score of the wonderful rhythmic composition *(must be more) Crispy*, which he composed in collaboration with Mel Mercier (Figure 5.2).

An intriguing and elegiac score that Mícheál asked me to consider was *Ah! Sweet Dancer*, which he had originally composed for solo 'free reed' (Figure 5.3).

Figure 5.1: Bars 1–3 of Mícheál Ó Súilleabháin's *So Merrily Dance*, score handwritten in pencil.

Figure 5.2: Bars 1–6 of Ó Súilleabháin/Mercier, *(must be more) Crispy*, score handwritten in black ink.

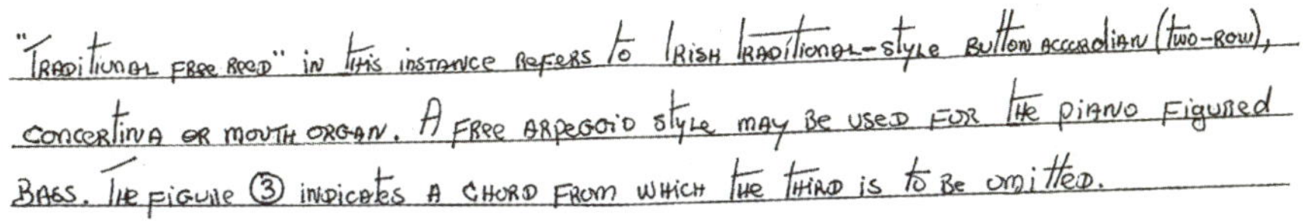
"TRADITIONAL FREE REED" IN THIS INSTANCE REFERS TO IRISH TRADITIONAL-STYLE BUTTON ACCORDIAN (TWO-ROW), CONCERTINA OR MOUTH ORGAN. A FREE ARPEGGIO'D STYLE MAY BE USED FOR THE PIANO FIGURED BASS. THE FIGURE ③ INDICATES A CHORD FROM WHICH THE THIRD IS TO BE OMITTED.

Figure 5.3: Mícheál Ó Súilleabháin's performance instructions on the back page of the score of *Ah! Sweet Dancer*, handwritten in blue ink.

Mícheál felt that *Ah! Sweet Dancer* would work on a fixed-reed instrument such as the soprano sax, as the solo melody line is ideally suited to the saxophone (Figure 5.4). Mícheál also gave me some hand-notated melodies (Figure 5.5).

For certain other compositions, such as 'By Golly' and 'Oíche Nollag', Mícheál asked me to learn them by ear from the CDs and to think of them as works to freely improvise over.

Figure 5.4: Mícheál Ó Súilleabháin, *Ah! Sweet Dancer*, bars 1–5, score handwritten in black ink.

Figure 5.5: Mícheál Ó Súilleabháin, 'The Gentle Maiden – *An Mhaighdean Cheansa*', handwritten on manuscript paper in black ink.

Hiberno Jazz

I recall these recording sessions with Mícheál at Sulán Studios as one of the most enjoyable experiences I have had as a musician, and I'm delighted to say that in preparation for this essay I came across a cassette tape of the Sulán recordings which I presumed had been lost during the intervening twenty-seven years. Re-listening to this recording has proved both nostalgic and exhilarating. The excitement level of the performance is thrilling – having learned *Crispy* through score study and listening to Mícheál and Mel's recording on *Gaiseadh*, for instance, I was prepared for a tempo of crotchet = 120bpm, but on listening back now to the Sulán recording I note that we launched into this piece at the much faster tempo of crotchet = 132bpm. Our recording of 'By Golly' was a riot of free improvisation and 'Oíche Nollag' an intoxicating mix of traditional, classical and jazz styles. From these first musical experiments the group Hiberno Jazz was born and would continue to grow with the later inclusion of the extraordinary flute player Niall Keegan and the singer and bodhrán player Sandra Joyce (Figure 5.6).

Figure 5.6: Promotional video cassette for Hiberno Jazz, produced by Mícheál Ó Súilleabháin in 1993.

Ag *déanamh ceoil* – making music

Something that struck me from the outset about Mícheál was that he seldom used standard rehearsal talk to communicate his musical intentions. He made these intentions clear through his embodied gestures, either through his piano playing or his conducting. Words seemed unnecessarily superfluous. The most technically detailed instruction he would give me would be something along the lines of 'Would you improvise a descant line above the string chords?' Mícheál's utter avoidance of musical dogmatism spoke to the trust and respect he felt for the musicians he chose to collaborate with. It also spoke of Mícheál's awareness of the ineffable qualities of music and his conviction that music exists solely through performance. In a 1982 essay, Mícheál writes that: 'The [Irish] phrase *ag déanamh ceoil* (making/doing music), for example, refers to the act of performance, not to any process of musical predetermination.'[2] In the same essay he writes of 'the traditional musician's perception of what music is: a floating body of melodic patterns which become set when subjected to the discipline of performance'.[3]

Although Mícheál is writing specifically of the Irish traditional musician, the point he makes has great relevance for performers within the western art music tradition, where it can be argued that no matter what the degree of forensic detail employed by a composer in their score notation, the music itself has no existence on the page except as an abstraction, coming to life only when someone performs it into being. This involvement with and animation of music has been referred to as 'musicking', a term coined by the New Zealand musicologist Christopher Small (1927–2011).[4] Small offers this definition:

> To music is to take part, in any capacity, in a musical performance, whether by performing, by listening, by rehearsing or practicing, by providing material for performance (what is called composing), or by dancing.[5]

The phrase *ag déanamh ceoil*, as used by Mícheál above, is indistinguishable from Small's concept of 'musicking' and this parallel outlook is worthy of further study.

'Let's start with an improvisation': Mícheál Ó Súilleabháin's compositions for solo saxophone

I am blessed to have been in regular contact with Mícheál since 1993, both as a musical collaborator and friend, and I'm honoured to have performed the premieres of all his compositions for solo saxophone. Space doesn't allow for a detailed performer's analysis of all of Mícheál's saxophone works, but I'd like to discuss three of his works that have a special resonance within me: *Templum*, *Lumen* and *The Brook of Donode*.[6]

Templum (1994)

The first work Mícheál composed for me was *Templum*, originally written as the 'opening meditation music' of his large-scale composition *Missa Gadelica*.[7] Since its premiere, *Templum* has received many performances as a stand-alone piece for soprano saxophone and chamber orchestra, as well as being recorded in a version for soprano saxophone, chamber orchestra and chamber choir.[8] When I performed *Templum* with an orchestra Mícheál would act as conductor, a role at which he excelled, as he was the very embodiment of his music, full of expressive nuance and gestural clarity. His ability as a conductor is seldom mentioned; he himself would play down this facet of his craft and would often reference the opening lines of Seamus

Figure 5.7: Mícheál Ó Súilleabháin, *Templum*, bars 1–25 of solo saxophone part.

Heaney's poem 'In Memoriam Seán Ó Riada':

> Ó Riada's white head was Easter snow,
> the silver knob on a swordstick.
> He conducted the Ulster Orchestra
> like a drover with an ashplant
> herding them south.[9]

Mícheál told me that his method of composing the solo line of *Templum* was to record a series of improvisations on tin whistle, from which he constructed the soloist's melody. This solo part when notated at concert pitch is written in D Major, and it is clear from looking at the melody line just how suitable it is for performance on a D whistle (Figure 5.7).

Lumen (1995)

After *Missa Gadelica*, the next major musical involvement I had with Mícheál was *Lumen*, which he composed as the interval act of the 1995 Eurovision Song Contest, held at The Point Theatre, Dublin. *Lumen* was scored for large forces[10] and opened with an improvised ascending saxophone line. Mícheál didn't write a specific sax part for *Lumen*; instead he requested that I improvise around the vocal soloists and join in on the main melody at various points. The one thing he did stipulate was that the opening saxophone flourish should resemble a 'skyrocket' and that the end of *Lumen* should have a more slowly ascending 'skyrocket'. While researching this essay, I found myself very moved when I came across my original performance part of *Lumen*. Although not conventionally notated, it's what I had on my music stand on the night of the Eurovision performance, and it acted as a guide and stimulus to performance, rather than a conventionally scored roadmap (Figure 5.8).

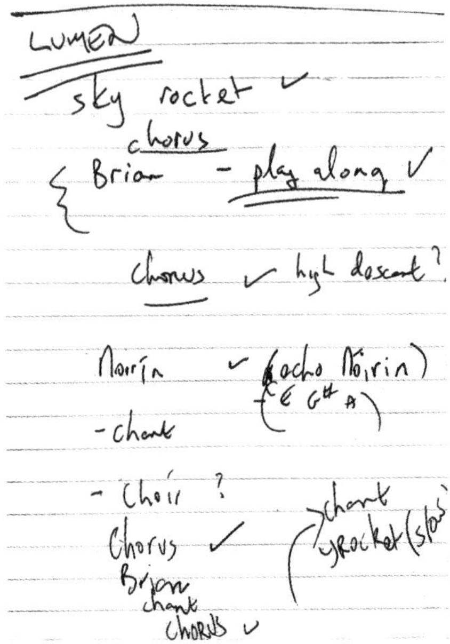

Figure 5.8: Kenneth Edge's handwritten saxophone guide for the premiere performance of Mícheál Ó Súilleabháin's *Lumen*.

The Brook of Donode (2014)

The final work that Mícheál wrote for solo saxophone was the exquisite, meditative work *The Brook of Donode*, composed to a commission from Mairéad Mason as a birthday gift to her husband Maurice Mason. *The Brook of Donode* is scored for soprano saxophone and concert harp and received its world premiere performance at a private event at the Masons' home in Ballymore-Eustace, Kildare on 17 January 2014. The performers were myself on soprano saxophone and Geraldine O'Doherty on concert harp. The musical score of *The Brook of Donode* has Seamus Heaney's poem 'St Kevin and the Blackbird' prefacing it, and the performance at the Masons' home was preceded by a recitation of Heaney's poem by Mícheál Ó Súilleabháin. As I've already said, Mícheál seldom used words to describe music but in the case of *The Brook of Donode* he used Heaney's poetry to open a window onto his musical intentions. A few days before the performance he wrote to me:

> Regarding mood, that should be easily evident from the poem attached to the score. St Kevin has 'forgotten the river's name', and this music thus exists in his head – as the poem asks: 'Is there distance in his head?'

> In a way the music title gives us the name of the river – Donode – which runs alongside the house of the person for whom the music has been commissioned, Maurice Mason. He likes to walk the brook and we might imagine him listening to this on his iPod as he does so. The recurring harp motif is surely the water's onward tranquil movement. The sax is commenting on the surround of nature: the underwater life, the wood, trees, clouds, wildflowers, perhaps the occasional wildlife (no ducks or seagulls, Ken! Maybe an occasional waterhen).[11]

Mícheál's allusion to seagulls takes me back to the very first live gig that Hiberno Jazz did, which was in the Falls Hotel, Ennistymon, County Clare in 1993, shortly after the original Sulán recording sessions. Mícheál asked me to create a sound similar to the mewing of a seagull over the top of the piano introduction to his composition *Casadh na Gráige*. I'd forgotten the *craic* we had with that sonic caterwauling until the above communication of twenty-one years later!

Although many of Mícheál's scores are meticulously notated, areas of nuance are left to the discretion of the performer. For instance, in bar 9 of *The Brook of Donode*, the saxophone part contains the following instruction: 'Sax may ornament throughout *ad lib* including timbral variation'. This seems like a vague performance instruction, but as discussed above, Mícheál displayed absolute trust in the performers he chose to work with, and would often comment playfully, 'Let's not over-rehearse.'

'Let's end with an improvisation'

Although this essay is of a mostly scholarly nature, with its lists, illustrations and endnotes, I'd like to set scholarship aside and speak of the pure subjective joy of making music with Michael Ó Súilleabháin. We performed many times together and our working relationship spanned a quarter of a century, taking us to China, Italy, Chicago's Symphony Centre, London's Royal Albert Hall, so many wonderful experiences and memories, but I will never forget how that first gig in Ennistymon felt. The sheer joy of the performance and the feeling that I was discovering an entirely new way of thinking of the saxophone as a vehicle for self-expression.

My final concert with Mícheál took place at the National Concert Hall, Dublin on 8 September 2017. The concert was titled *Elver Gleams* and was a celebration of Mícheál's music, featuring various soloists with the RTÉ National Symphony Orchestra, conducted by Sinead Hayes (Figure 5.9).

Elver Gleams

A CELEBRATION OF THE MUSIC OF

Mícheál Ó Súilleabháin

RTÉ National Symphony Orchestra

Mícheál Ó Suilleabháin piano
Iarla Ó Lionáird vocalist / **Brendan Power** harmonica
Kenneth Edge saxophone / **Mel Mercier** bodhrán
Pádraic Keane uilleann pipes
Sinéad Hayes conductor

Presented by **Mícheál Ó Súilleabháin** and **Paul Herriott** RTÉ lyric fm

PROGRAMME

Templum (soprano sax and orchestra)
Flowan (piano and orchestra)
Termōn (pipes and orchestra)
So Merrily Dance (piano and orchestra)
Port na bPúcaí (voice and orchestra)
(must be more) Crispy (piano, sax, harmonica, bodhrán/bones, orchestra)

INTERVAL

Bean Dubh an Ghleanna (soprano sax and orchestra)
Oileán/Island: Three movements (harmonica and orchestra)
An Buachaill Caol Dubh (voice and orchestra)
GELLAN

All music composed/arranged/orchestrated by Mícheál Ó Súilleabháin except: *(must be more) Crispy*: composed by Mel Mercier and Mícheál Ó Súilleabháin and orchestrated by Mícheál Ó Súilleabháin.

The following compositions are based on Irish traditional airs: *An Buachaill Caol Dubh*: commissioned by Iarla Ó Lionáird and the RTÉ Concert Orchestra, *So Merrily Dance*: based on a West Cork slide, *Port na bPúcaí*.

FRIDAY 8 SEPTEMBER 2017 National Concert Hall

1

Figure 5.9: Programme for *Elver Gleams* concert at NCH Dublin, 8 September 2017

Sadly, the *Elver Gleams* concert was the last time I had the pleasure of performing with Mícheál and it was also the last time we would meet.

For his funeral in Kilrush, County Clare, where the river Shannon opens into the Shannon estuary, Mícheál was as thoughtful and meticulous in his planning as ever, writing a running order detailing his express wishes for every aspect of his funeral service. He requested that I play *Templum* with the Irish Chamber Orchestra as an opening meditation as he arrived at the church. He also requested that I perform a solo improvisation inspired by *Templum* at the small private service at Shannon crematorium.

Templum was the first piece that Mícheál Ó Súilleabháin wrote for me and the last piece I played for him. I think of Mícheál's final request of me as the greatest musical gift and personal honour that I have ever received.

6
The First Time I Met Mícheál O'Smoothie-Phone
Brian Kennedy

Brian Kennedy is an Irish singer-songwriter from Belfast. He was invited by Van Morrison to tour the world for six years and sing on six of his albums. To date Brian has released seventeen solo albums and published two successful novels.

I was singing with Van Morrison in Galway in the early 1990s at the Arts Festival, and the show that night was very special for all kinds of reasons. Van was on particularly brilliant form and had also generously given me loads of space to sing and duet and improvise with him that night. At the end of the concert a tall, enthusiastic fella approached the stage and was instantly so complimentary about my voice and what I had just done in the context of Van's blues and soul revue set. It was Mícheál Ó Súilleabháin himself and I was thrilled to meet him because I adored his album *The Dolphin's Way* but only knew him by reputation. His first wife Nóirín was just as excited. We swapped numbers.

Over the coming weeks Mícheál told me he had a secret project in mind for me that, between the jigs and the reels of emails and phone calls, turned out to be a piece of music called *Lumen* which was to be performed during the now-famous interval spot in the Eurovision Song Contest. Ireland had won the year before in 1994 with Paul Harrington and Charlie McGettigan singing 'Rock 'n' Roll Kids', written by Brendan Graham. The interval that year introduced the world to the phenomenon that would become *Riverdance*. So, the new coveted interval spot fell to Mícheál in 1995 and he dreamed up a spectacular majestical ensemble of musicians and singers, including the Brennan sisters from Clannad, the monks from Glenstal Abbey, Kenneth Edge on soaring saxophone, and Nóirín and myself sharing lead vocals. It was the way in which Mícheál had constructed the piece that was so unusual and memorable. It was as if we were instruments in his extraordinary orchestra that also included the deaf percussionist Evelyn Glennie.

The performance was a great success and became a platinum seller in Ireland. It marked the beginning of an incredible personal and professional friendship between us. I had grown up on the Falls Road in west Belfast and never had any kind of vocal training, so Mícheál instinctively came up with a way to teach me the melodies he had written. We worked on some incredible projects and live shows over the years; he would often look over the top of his sheet music and wonder how on earth I was able to remember everything that he was teaching me. I loved it that he had no snobbery about music at all, and in fact delighted in pairing the most unlikely people and instruments.

I was bemoaning the fact that I wanted to move back to Ireland but I wasn't sure where. That was when he told me about Killaloe with the now late John Kelly and the Irish Chamber Orchestra and how it was so easy to commute via Shannon Airport as opposed to Dublin. It also turned out that an old friend, Ken Rice, that I knew from early London days was also living in the area. I flew over from London for the weekend just for a look around and by that Monday I had found a wee house in the hills of Ballina, County Tipperary, overlooking Lough Derg, that I ended up buying and living in for years. Ironically, long afterwards when Mícheál separated from Nóirín and I was offered a chance to be the lead singer in a specially adapted version of *Riverdance* on Broadway in New York, I decided to rent my house out. I couldn't believe it when the auctioneer told me that it was Mícheál himself who rented it for around three years in the end.

We worked on another project called *Madison's Descent* that has yet to see the light of day on a sound recording, but here's hoping those beautiful songs that he wrote for it will one day be issued. I never met anyone like him. He had an incredible natural, elegant energy about him, not only in the way that he spoke but particularly when his fingers touched the keys of any piano. His style is recognisable instantly and the way he married traditional Irish music with the temperature of classical music remains ground-breaking even today. I feel so lucky to have known him although I hate having to use the past tense. When I myself was first diagnosed with cancer, it was so unexpected and wonderful when little cards would periodically turn up in the post from him in that unmistakable wild flourish of handwriting asking how I was doing and telling me not to hesitate if I needed anything. Given that he was in poor health himself, it is all the more moving to me that he would take the time to do that.

The last time I saw him was in Dublin at a restaurant, purely by chance, and it was obvious that he wasn't long for the world. I know it's such a cliché, but I take great comfort in the knowledge that he has left behind an unparalleled body of work that I'm privileged to be a small part of. Anytime I hear his music now I feel such a profound sense of pride that I knew him, that I sang with him, that he encouraged me when I was just getting started really. I can still hear him calling me playfully 'BK' with his big arms outstretched to greet me at his home or at the incredible University of Limerick. I called him 'Smoothie-Phone' as opposed to Ó Súilleabháin and it always made him laugh.

7
Mícheál and the ICO: A musical journey
Gerard Keenan

Gerard Keenan has worked all his life in music as both a performer and a manager and has enjoyed a long career managing different ensembles. Appointed orchestra manager of the Irish Chamber Orchestra in 2006, he became its chief executive officer in 2012.

I first met Mícheál in 1988 in the very top floor of the small Irish Chamber Orchestra (ICO) office in Kildare Street, Dublin. He literally walked in off the street, introduced himself and asked if I'd be interested in some of his music with a view to a recording. I recognised Mícheál and had an awareness of his music as his first CD *The Dolphin's Way* had received a lot of radio airplay. I should say at this point that I always had a wide-ranging interest in all sorts of music despite spending my life principally in classical music. I had only taken the job as manager of the ICO the year before and loved the idea of doing something different. Mícheál was, I think, surprised and pleased. That brief encounter in Kildare Street led us to many years of happy collaboration in both the studio and the concert hall.

Our first recording was an album entitled *Oileán* which we recorded in Lombard Street Studios. It nearly started disastrously as we were supposed to be back in Dublin from a tour of Italy the day before the recording. We were due to fly out of Pisa but were fogbound! Eventually the pilot decided to go for it, and to be honest it was one of the most terrifying take-offs I have ever experienced. On arrival in Heathrow we had to run to try and make our connection to Dublin. Whilst running between terminals we saw our double bass being dropped twelve feet from the hold of our plane; it miraculously survived! A good omen, although the bass player Andy Baker didn't think so.

The recording was a happy and productive event as we were working for the first time with some legends of Irish music: Matt Molloy, Tony MacMahon, and the then rising star Mel Mercier. Matt was the soloist in the title work and was an outstanding player. He wasn't however a great counter of bar rests so I asked the cellist John O'Kane to give him a kick just before he was to come in; John dutifully obliged! The album was for the Virgin label and the producer was Declan Colgan. He was a huge fan of Mícheál's music and went on to produce all Mícheál's albums for Virgin. My abiding memory of the recording was the wonderful mutual respect for both traditions shown by all the musicians, which had not always been the case previously when traditional musicians met classical musicians. Mícheál and I collaborated on two further albums: *Casadh* in 1990 and *Gaiseadh* in 1992. The latter two were recorded in a magical setting in Sulán Studios in Baile Bhúirne, west Cork, engineered by Tadhg Kelleher. There were some epic nights in the local hostelry of An Mhuileann (the Mills Inn) which remain in the memory to this day.

The success of the Virgin albums led to many concert bookings for festivals and concert series: we appeared at Mayfest in Glasgow, at the Manchester Irish festival and in London. I will concentrate on one concert, in particular, which took place in August 1991. We were invited to perform at Féile an Phobail in west Belfast and were the first orchestra to perform there (it should be noted that the conflict was ongoing at this time). The festival itself began in 1988 and was created to portray a more positive view of the community and to provide entertainment for people at prices they could afford. It has gone on to be one of the most successful community festivals in Europe. Our concert was in the Andersonstown Leisure Centre and we arrived onstage to a packed hall of over 600 people. It was clear that this was to be a special event. The concert was in full swing when for no reason the fire curtain started to slowly descend! There were frantic efforts to halt it by those of us side-stage (which included local MP Gerry Adams), but to no avail. We carried on the concert with Mícheál in front of the curtain and the ICO behind. The following day's *Andersonstown News* had the epic headline 'ICO Plays behind the Iron Curtain'. After the concert we were presented with a handmade Eamon Maguire bodhrán, beautifully inscribed as being from the people of west Belfast. We still have it in pride of place in the ICO studio.

Eventually I moved on from the ICO for a while and didn't see much of Mícheál, but our paths crossed again for another recording in 2001. This time it was *Templum*, on which the National Chamber Choir (with which I was then working) featured.

It is important to note the following: just before I moved on in 1993 from the ICO there was talk of the orchestra moving to Limerick, a move they completed in 1994, due in no small measure to the persuasive powers of Mícheál! This move proved to be the making of the ICO and led to its continued growth over the years. I once again joined the ICO as orchestra manager in 2006 and Mícheál and I re-established our connection.

We worked together successfully for years and one of the last acts of his leadership of the Irish World Academy was to ask me to relaunch the MA Classical String Performance for the Academy, something I was happy to do. He took a huge interest in the project even after his retirement and I believe the advancement of the course made him very happy. During those years with the ICO I was involved again both in commissioning Mícheál and performing his works. Sadly, the last time I organised for him was to provide the musicians for his requiem mass, which was a total honour. His wife Helen presented us all with a beautiful Kevin O'Dwyer commission of a silver wild hazel nut; I treasure it and wear it with pride for many of our concerts. It was an emotional moment when I handed all Mícheál's scores to Helen in July 2020. On gathering the scores, it was so moving to see my handwriting on so many of them from over thirty years ago! I dearly hope that our MA programme will be a continuing and fitting tribute to Mícheál. I know for sure that his music will continue to provide inspiration and entertainment for generations to come.

Mícheál Ó Súilleabháin made a massive impression on music in Ireland and indeed on myself; I am so lucky to have shared so many positive experiences with him. *Ar dheis Dé go raibh a anam dílis*.

8
A Bridge between Worlds
Sinead Hayes

Irish conductor Sinead Hayes is a graduate of the Royal Northern College of Music master's conducting programme. She is emerging as a leading interpreter of contemporary music and opera in Ireland. As a traditional fiddle player, she has performed with members of the Berlin Philharmonic in the orchestra's family concert series.

To say that Mícheál Ó Súilleabháin was a major influence on my career as a conductor and fiddle player is an understatement!

I remember hearing a radio interview with Mícheál about his work to develop the BMus course in University College Cork (UCC) in the 1970s and '80s. He described lecturing in the 'Ó Riada Room' in the Music Department, sharing his knowledge with the young classical music students, while seeing the traditional musicians outside, passing the window. The traditional players were studying physics and engineering – not music. He set out to change that, and as a result, Irish traditional musicians were given the chance to study music in UCC alongside their classical colleagues.

In the 1990s I was one of those musicians, studying civil engineering, not music, at University College Galway (UCG). It was almost impossible to imagine a future life in music, let alone a career that could somehow combine my interest in both classical and traditional. But a couple of years before I started at UCG, Mícheál's ground-breaking television series *A River of Sound* had made quite an impression on me. The confluence of Irish traditional, classical, contemporary and so many other styles suggested a tradition that was open and outward-looking. The seeds of possibility were sown!

Moving to London in 2000 to pursue a master's degree in engineering gave me a chance to see the tradition, and my place in it, with a new perspective. The divisions between classical and traditional seemed somehow blurred with distance, and London provided the ideal environment for the germination of seeds planted by *A River of Sound*. My career as a structural engineer was relatively short-lived, and when I discovered a whole world of orchestral music that I simply had no access to in the west of Ireland, the conducting bug bit! Funded by my now part-time engineering job, I undertook a music degree in City University London. Here the perspective shifted yet again, as I reluctantly learned to view Irish traditional music through the lens of ethnomusicology. My resistance to 'theorising' the music stemmed from a sense of ownership, and the somewhat inflated sense of authority that this sense of ownership endowed. Thankfully, these insular ideas were soon dissipated, affording Irish traditional music a seat as musical equal around the artistic table – in my world at any rate!

My master's in conducting brought me to Manchester where in 2012, tired of the 'plastic shamrock' image of traditional music in the UK, I decided it was time to try to bring my two worlds of Irish traditional music and conducting together. I emailed Mícheál.

The plan, half formed, vague and ambitious, was to produce and conduct a concert of contemporary Irish music for the St Patrick's Festival in Manchester, with Mícheál's traditional flute concerto *Oileán* as the centre piece and the Manchester traditional flute player Michael McGoldrick as soloist. The answer came within hours: a supportive 'Do it!', practical help with getting music, and even a promise to try to make it across the Irish Sea for the concert. Over the course of the next few weeks Mícheál's support for the project was unflagging. The concert was to be funded by projected ticket sales and a small tax refund I had received from Her Majesty's Revenue Commissioners. I can still hear Mícheál's mischievous chuckle at the idea of the UK government part-financing a concert featuring his music! When concert day arrived, so did Mícheál and his partner Helen. No fanfare, no fuss, just a whirlwind of reassuring energy when it was needed by a nervous conductor-concert promoter. The concert, in a sold-out Manchester Cathedral, was unforgettable, with the audience rising as one in ovation at the end of Michael McGoldrick's brilliant playing of *Oileán*.

Fast-forward five years, to an unexpected email from the National Symphony Orchestra with an invitation to conduct a concert of Mícheál's music, with the legend himself at the piano. Mícheál had recommended me as the conductor. Unbelievably, it was his debut concert with the National Symphony Orchestra. My answer was immediate: 'Yes, it would be an honour.' In the weeks before the concert, music scores seemed to come from all corners of the land, arriving by courier to Galway. The concert programme featured some of Mícheál's best-known works including *Oileán*, *Bean Dubh an Ghleanna*, *Tearmon*, and one of my all-time favourite pieces *(must be more) Crispy*. I remember as a teenager sitting at the piano with a cassette tape of Mícheál's album *Gaiseadh/Flowing* (1992) trying to work out the rhythms in the piano part of 'Crispy' – the track eventually wore out from all the rewinds! To get a chance to conduct the piece with Mícheál, Mel Mercier and the NSO was very special indeed.

The rehearsals for the concert in September 2017 were a whirlwind. We had a world-class set of soloists: Kenneth Edge (saxophone), Pádraic Keane (uilleann pipes), Iarla Ó Lionáird (voice), Mel Mercier (percussion), and Brendan Power who played harmonica in *Oileán*. Each brought their unique artistry to their part of the programme, creating new worlds with every piece, all with the musical support of Mícheál. The fantastic players of the National Symphony Orchestra were warm and enthusiastic throughout, sensing that this was going to be a concert like no other. The concert itself, *Elver Gleams*, was unforgettable, and remains one of the highlights of my musical life. Not only did he play brilliantly, but Mícheál also presented the concert, introducing each piece with characteristic grace and eloquence. And for the encore, he had one more trick up his sleeve, persuading me to take out the fiddle to join in with his famous version of the reel 'Christmas Eve'.

It was a privilege to work on Mícheál's music from inside the notes, teasing out the various strands to bring the essence of the pieces into the spotlight in Manchester and Dublin. His music engages players and audiences not just with its subtle craftsmanship, but with a flair for dramatic narrative and pacing that is an extension of Mícheál himself. He had an uncanny ability to effortlessly bring people into his world. In those Manchester and Dublin concerts, I could feel the entire audience being brought on a journey, as we weaved the melodies of *Oileán* and the other works into the charged ether.

In many ways that special Dublin concert was Mícheál in musical microcosm, building bridges between the worlds of traditional and classical music with energy, grace and humour, and with a few surprises thrown in for good measure! His legacy will live on, not only in his music and the visionary infrastructure he created for Irish music at the Irish World Academy in the University of Limerick, but through his students, his family, and the countless number of musicians he inspired to dream beyond the boundaries of genre and tradition. Mícheál Ó Súilleabháin made this world a richer place, and we are the poorer for having lost him too soon.

9

Inspirational Torch Bearer

Martin Hayes

Martin Hayes is a fiddle player deeply grounded in the music of east Clare who also is open to new musical possibilities through collaboration with musicians from different musical backgrounds. He has been instrumental in creating ensembles such as The Common Ground Ensemble, The Martin Hayes Quartet and The Gloaming.

During my father's earlier years, Irish traditional music was mostly in decline, especially during the 1940s and '50s when young people were turning their backs on it. Its future seemed very uncertain at that point. The music was not embraced by the wider society, which was a major factor in this decline. Traditional music didn't really begin to be more fully accepted in the broader Irish society until the 1990s. Along this road to greater acceptance there were a number of important voices who championed the music at different stages. Some of those who come to my mind are Seán Ó Riada, Séamus Ennis, Ciarán Mac Mathúna and Tony MacMahon, all of whom advocated for and spoke eloquently on behalf of the deepest and most authentic elements of the music. To me, Mícheál Ó Súilleabháin was one of those essential voices. As a musician he successfully championed our music, broke new ground artistically and inspired his fellow musicians. He also achieved great success as a scholar, composer and educator.

Mícheál and his music impacted on me at many different points in my career. When I was a teenager his music inspired me from afar. I grew up inside a rich musical world of old musicians, old styles and old ideas. In that musical world of east Clare, the sounds from his eponymous first commercial recording still managed to break through. During my teenage years I religiously listened to *The Long Note* programme on RTÉ radio every Monday evening. This celebrated the old tradition while also heralding new emerging ideas within the music. Mícheál's playing was regularly featured on this programme, where on occasion I might hear him performing some innovative take on an old tune, followed perhaps by a version of an air played by Séamus Ennis or a simple tune played by Micho Russell. In the seventies Mícheál's music was part of that tapestry of new and emerging sounds that offered my generation new vistas and new possibilities for Irish music. I remember his version of the tune 'The Long Note' itself being featured. It was very edgy and progressive, even by today's standards, and yet for me it sat perfectly within the tradition. His music seemed to be grounded in a philosophical view that embraced both old and new ideas, ideas around pushing boundaries while simultaneously embracing the deepest elements of the tradition.

I first saw Mícheál perform and heard him speak while attending the Scoil Éigse in Ennis in 1977 when I was just fifteen. I was already familiar with his music and was very taken with how he actually played tunes on the piano. I had grown up listening to piano accompaniment, which I liked very much. The conventional wisdom at the time was that the piano had limited possibilities in terms of playing the melodies of Irish dance music. But his playing of the tune 'Oíche Nollag' broke through this dance-tune melody-playing barrier on the piano. He developed a dry staccato style that allowed for the delivery of traditional tunes with a clarity and percussive punch that had not been previously heard on the piano.

I didn't meet Mícheál again until I was a young man in my twenties living in America. In 1990 he invited me to participate in the Boston College Fiddle Festival which he was curating. At that point I had drifted far away from the core of the traditional music community and this was for me an important and welcome invitation back to those very roots and into the fold of the tradition. Later in my career I regularly taught fiddle at the Blas Summer School and in the MA Irish Traditional Music Performance programme at the Irish World Academy of Music and Dance at the University of Limerick (UL), both of which he personally established. During my time as artist in residence at UL, I enjoyed many conversations with Mícheál about music and our shared love of the music of the great fiddler Tommie Potts.

Potts and his innovative musical approach was a perfect subject for Mícheál, who saw no conflict between tradition and innovation and who seemed to view traditional music within a broader philosophical, historical and cultural context than was common within the tradition at that time. My musical vision was formed largely from digging deeply into the ideas and understandings that underpinned the music of the older players of the county. Though my musical journey at the time seemed pointed in a different direction to his, I still found it very encouraging that Mícheál Ó Súilleabháin was simultaneously pushing musical boundaries and could speak out on behalf of the music in a competent and articulate manner. It felt important for me, coming from the humble roots of the music, to be associated by genre with someone linked to a wider artistic world, a wider intellectual world that implicitly respected my sources and where I was coming from musically. When I was a teenager traditional music was still marginal within society, so belonging inside a bigger musical tent was very important for me and was a significant moral support in terms of pursuing my musical goals with confidence and enthusiasm. His intellectual and musical heft provided a framework of thought and musical vision that served as a kind of bulwark against the widespread ignorance of the music that only began to properly dissipate towards the middle of the 1990s.

We now live, thankfully, in a very different musical landscape where traditional music is widely accepted and cherished. Mícheál had a lot to do with making all of that possible. A visionary musician who innovated, he has left a huge impact that will live on through his music and through his Irish World Academy of Music and Dance in Limerick.

10

Moments

Iarla Ó Lionáird

Iarla Ó Lionáird, singer and songwriter from the Gaeltacht of Cúil Aodha, County Cork, comes from a line of traditional singers. Beginning with Seán Ó Riada's local choir, he has performed throughout the world and in many musical contexts, recording solo and with the Afro Celt Sound System and The Gloaming.

> Somewhere in the heaven
> of lost futures
> the lives we might have led
> have found their own fulfilment.
>
> 'Leaves', Derek Mahon

Mícheál once told me that the thing which puzzled and enchanted him most about our performances together was those moments where I stood in front of the microphone and hesitated just after his introduction on the piano and just before beginning to sing. Something about that space in time especially captured his attention; his focus drawn intensely upon those moments, mere seconds that seemed freighted with mysterious properties within which lay an otherness, generative of a strangely sacramental nothingness, a special silence – that wellspring of song.

I did not inquire further as to what he meant by this observation. But looking back now at our many occasions of very special music-making together it begins to suggest to me some kind of manual, an instruction set or perhaps even a map of sorts of what our work together meant to him, what he saw in it, wished for it and drew from it. And what it meant to me.

Mícheál doubtless had a very significant interest in our older song culture. It was genuine, deeply felt and almost reverential in character. It is likely that he first perceived its centrality in terms of an understanding and appreciation of our general folk-music culture as an undergraduate in University College Cork. This would have come about through his interactions with Seán Ó Riada, although not exclusively so. As with many others of that generation, Ó Riada's influence might be regarded as epiphanic. But he too belonged to a stream of parallel influences that included, within that orbit of the city and university at the time, presences such as Seán Ó Tuama, Daniel Corkery and Seán Ó Riordáin. Together they might be appreciated as powerful mentors and guides who harnessed a new optimism that foregrounded our language, culturally and economically, our music culture and our Gaelic literary heritage as touchstones of identity that were ripe for assertion and contemporary exploration through art and intellectual inquiry.

My overriding impression of their likely influence upon Mícheál and indeed the influence of that milieu in general upon his development is that he took much from their thinking and that those impressions signalled and resonated within him to his final days. And they would serve, I would suggest, as coordinates on a musical map which he in turn fleshed out and upon which I and many others too were invited to roam.

But Mícheál, being of a different generation, would not be fettered by any provincialisms or easy dogmas that might derive from some narratives characteristic of that era. He was simply too gifted and informed a scholar to allow for simplification as such, and would instead see our culture as having a manifold genealogy – a rich and at times perhaps difficult-to-acknowledge history, being mottled and storied, bestowed with multiple narratives and imbued with paradox and surprise, rupture as well as continuity. Nevertheless Mícheál undoubtedly extended the range and depth of his appreciation for our native music and language through his experience as a young scholar at that time. His work and scholarship on the various collections of our music subsequently attest to the foundational basis of his remarkable knowledge and surefooted and subtly perceptive navigation of our music and song in his work both as performer and composer. Arguably this wider and keenly informed perspective on our music frequently placed him on the front foot, in danger of encroaching on others of narrower persuasions. I look back now and see more clearly that Mícheál waited patiently for many of us to catch up and move to where he already was – beyond the binary and static models that dogged discourse on identity, and in particular our traditional music, into new dynamic territories of open possibility and potential.

Mícheál was something of a globalist when it came to believing in the potential of our culture as a whole, and he revelled in imagining and witnessing its ability to navigate well beyond our shores. I recall with particular fondness his presence at a concert performance by The Gloaming in Brussels, and his evident delight and curiosity at yet another manifestation of our tradition in music and song. It was humbling to see the pride with which he regarded our work. What *he* may not have perceived on that occasion was that we saw him as a *ceannródaí*: a pioneer trailblazing entirely new methodologies and approaches for our music and particularly on the piano, an instrument central to our own success as a group. Our American pianist Thomas Bartlett claimed on that occasion that Mícheál's explorations on the keyboard were a major influence on his own trajectory as an artist.

These competing energies of the local and the global as they might be perceived were, I feel, the source of Mícheál's particular strength – being possessed of a radical belief in the value of our native culture and having equally a confidence in its ability to transfigure and translate beyond its purported origins. This belief informed indelibly his approach to education, where he sought to bring our practices and particular knowledge as makers of a folk music within the embrace of all other epistemologies – there to be held in equal esteem and with parity of voice, while simultaneously acknowledging and challenging the ineffability and mysteries of performance through scholarly endeavour. It was a call, an invitation to achieve new fulfilments and enriched connectivities in lives lived equally well in music and in thought.

In all of my years performing with Mícheál, usually just the two of us, what I am left with is a deep sense of kinship. A mutual love for word and song, their inseparability, and yes, the intangible mystery of music itself, of its happening at all. An Indian raga as a magic carpet of interwoven modes and notes for a performance of 'An Buachaill Caol Dubh', the richly pan-psychistic and lofted settings for renderings of 'Sliabh na mBan', 'Aisling Gheal' – an encoded message to Ó Riada that we were still here, still attending to the work, to the dream – and 'Port na bPúcaí', Ó Riordáin's words spoken while fingers plotted out the coordinates of the phantom tune. Each one a layered cartography in service of an attentiveness to the unknown.

Téir faobhar na faille siar tráthnóna gréine go Corca Dhuibhne,
Is chífir thiar ag bun na spéire ag ráthaíocht ann
An Uimhir Dhé, is an Modh Foshuiteach,
Is an tuiseal gairmeach ar bhéalaibh daoine:
Sin é do dhoras,
Dún Chaoin fé sholas an tráthnóna,
Buail is osclófar D'intinn féin is do chló ceart …

On a sunlit evening take the cliff road out to Corca Dhuibhne,
and out on the horizon you will see shoaling there
the Dual Number, and the Subjunctive Mood,
and the vocative case on people's mouths:
that is your door,

> Dun Chaoin in the evening light,
> knock and there will be opened your own mind and your right shape.
>
> 'Fill Arís', Seán Ó Riordáin (trans. Barry McCrae)

Soon we will find ourselves on stage again to celebrate his music, this time and for the first time in his absence. And we will recall how one felt the presence of Mícheál's hand within reach of the tiller as our culture continued to swirl and swell, careen and flow towards evermore unfolding destinies. A shielding, steadying hand, defiantly Irish but with an explorer's ear to the world. And it is this hand and its reassuring friendship and presence that we will miss …

11

Distant Beating Hearts

David Brophy

Freelance conductor David Brophy, a music graduate of Trinity College Dublin with a career extending to radio, record, television and film and embracing a wide variety of music, is a former principal conductor of the RTÉ Concert Orchestra. He has conducted extensively in Europe, Africa, the United States, Canada and China.

Má castar libh fear léinn sa tslí,
bhur rún ná ligidh leis, bhur sians.
Ní dá leithéid a cumadh sibh:
tá baint agaibh le bualadh croí
ar chuma an éinín bheannaithe.

– '*Seo Libh, a Dhánta, tríd an Tír*',
Seán Ó Ríordáin

Now if an expert crosses your path,
don't betray your song or secret.
Not designed for the likes of him,
you're on the side of the beating heart,
the same wing as the holy spirit.

– 'Onward, Poems, through the Land',
Seán Ó Ríordáin (trans. Frank Sewell)

I first read these lines in June 2018. Mícheál and I were knee-deep in rehearsals with the RTÉ National Symphony Orchestra for what was to be our last concert together. He had just given me Seán Ó Ríordáin's *Selected Poems* (ed. Frank Sewell) as a thank-you gift, an appreciation for whatever meagre offerings I managed to bring to rehearsals. I use the word 'meagre' here deliberately, as this is how my contributions genuinely felt as we prepared for concerts together. In physical, intellectual and linguistic terms, Mícheál was a giant of a man.

Our concerts saw Mícheál seated at either the piano or, less frequently, a harpsichord. I will never forget our first rehearsal together. He was at the piano, I was conducting the RTÉ Concert Orchestra, and we were rehearsing his ever-popular *Woodbrook*. All musicians bring a certain ebb-and-flow to their playing, something that naturally reveals itself in all styles of music. In so-called 'classical' music, this is referred to by the Italian term *rubato*, simply meaning stolen. The speed within a phrase is stolen from one part and given back to another part through subtle acceleration and deceleration of the overall tempo. This flexibility of tempo is central to the style of many composers, Puccini being the composer who most readily comes to mind. Mícheál's *rubato* was like no other and I quickly realised how much I had to learn from this utterly unique musician. He took so much time from one part of the phrase, quickly giving it all back in glorious extremes of fluctuating pulses, that I regularly put the stick – and therefore the beat – in entirely the wrong place. Unlike many musicians, Mícheál's wide-enveloped *rubato* never came across as an affectation. His sense of the tides within a tempo were totally of himself, drawn from a heart that always pumped the lifeblood with purpose, no matter the context. To make music with Mícheál was to acquaint oneself with the inner workings of the man himself, as much as the composer. Faced with such openness and honesty of expression, there was little option but to give of yourself, wholly, to his way, and I was more than willing to sacrifice everything and anything I held dear as I pursued an understanding of his musical vernacular. Mícheál cajoled me to ask questions of myself, simply by playing the piano. He managed to know so much, yet play with the disarming innocence of a child. In so doing, he asked questions of all who made music with him, slowly prising our minds apart, opening our hearts to him and his world. What a gift he was!

Mícheál the composer was equally beguiling. The self-acknowledged influences of Aloys Fleischmann and Seán Ó Riada were always clear, but only up to a point. Like his teachers, Mícheál drew on technical aspects beloved of the modernist European avant-garde. However, Ó Súilleabháin employed these techniques not necessarily as means to an end, but as merely one of a number of ways to propel his musical narrative. In doing so, he skilfully masked his music's ever-shifting technical scaffolding, allowing intrinsic thematic momentum itself to drive both form and structure. Despite initial appearances, his willingness to deploy established tropes from a variety of seemingly disparate musical byways was both brave and deft. The ease with which he fused Irish traditional dance, walking-bass jazz piano and the faintly televisual sound-world of a 1970s or 1980s Ronnie Hazlehurst in 'Oíche Nollag' strikes me now as one of his most audacious musical achievements. In *(must be more) Crispy*, Mícheál invokes an antidote to Bernstein's *Mambo!* calling for the less bawdy two-syllable word of the work's title to be whispered by the orchestra as an interjection within ever-shifting metres, recalling the restless rhythmic vitality and additive motivic development found in much of Stravinsky's music. In fusing the traditional and the baroque, *Francesco Walks* presents musical style itself as a kind-of aural mirage, the antiphonal interplay between two seemingly opposing disciplines forcing the listeners to question their own ears amid ever-blurring familiarity.

Through the aforementioned works and many more, Mícheál had, over more than three decades, firmly established his truly original voice. However, like all great artists, the desire to delve deeper into oneself, to re-examine approaches and styles, took hold of his ever-restless creative muse. The final years of his life witnessed a desire to dig deeper into the soil that gave life and form to his voice, simultaneously demanding more of himself and of us performers too. I will never forget the September afternoon in 2013 when myself and Iarla Ó Lionáird stood in front of the RTÉ Concert Orchestra to give Mícheál's setting of the traditional Irish air 'An Buachaill Caol Dubh' its first read-through. I had appreciated its shape, its arc and its trajectory in pre-rehearsal studies, but there was something utterly breathtaking in actually hearing it released into the air for the first time. His monolithic harp ostinato, standing firm amid barely audible strings, their smoking timbres gently percolating, still excites my ear today as I recall the opening bars. For centuries the fine art of coordinating singer and orchestra has been central to the craft of all composers and performers. Here, Mícheál purposely layered the pulsating harp – its ticking rhythmic drive recalling the central motif of Beethoven's Fifth Symphony – under the free-flowing vocal air, drawing attention to their polar-opposite functions – utterly uncoordinated – while eschewing the need to fit, unite, or in any way align themselves. The music, through harp, voice and strings, reveals its transcendental self as solid, liquid and gas, all at once. Over the course of more than twelve minutes, Mícheál punctuates the vocal stanzas with quietly dignified cascading horn-calls, echoing fragments from the vocal line, as the texture slowly prises itself apart, heaving and groaning until it eventually explodes. Not unlike the opening of Richard Strauss' *Also Sprach Zarathustra*, the final bars witness the timpani take a stentorian stranglehold of the harp's opening motif, finally heralding the very first entry of wind and heavy brass with only seconds remaining. Its impact on me was profound. It was breathtaking, audacious, defiant and utterly triumphant. I shall never forget it.

I remember looking at Iarla after the final chord, acknowledging, in silence, what we both knew. We had witnessed something very special. Mícheál had found something new. I am convinced that he himself knew that this was somehow different. He had found a new way to sculpt disparate forces, languages and expressions. He had managed to marry the timeless and the ephemeral. He had found the heavenly sweet spot between the real and the unreal, the us and the them, the earthly and the extra-terrestrial. As the title of our final concert together in 2018 suggested, less than five months before his untimely passing, Mícheál had manged to navigate his voice into the space 'Between Worlds'. As I continue to mourn the loss of him, I can only begin to imagine what riches the ever-expanding horizons of his voice might have revealed in time.

I regularly pick up Ó Ríordáin's *Selected Poems* to this day, recalling the way Mícheál, at the time, enthused about the importance of their relatively recent translation into English. He rightly saw Ó Ríordáin as a wholly original voice and thinker, one of global importance. His father a native Irish-speaker, his mother an English-speaker, Ó Ríordáin committed his life to exploring ways in which language itself had the ability to mould our thinking, our speaking and our being. In gifting Ó Ríordáin's poetry to me, Mícheál – ever the pedagogue – opened my mind to viewing his own life's work in a wider cultural context. Like Ó Ríordáin, he viewed tradition and modernity as interdependent, their continued relevance relying on a certain acknowledgement of each other's ways and means. Both men sought ways of communicating through a universally authentic tongue, one that found its roots within Ó Ríordáin's *bualadh croí*. For Mícheál, however, music – the ultimate global language – could only find its path through not one, but many beating hearts. In his hands, the palpitations of 'classical', 'jazz' and 'traditional' could – and did – synchronise their pulses, allowing the contrast and juxtaposition of syntax to serve a more global purpose. In this way, it could be said that Mícheál's expression transcended mere music itself. It gave voice to elusive truths, from distant beating hearts.

12
Mícheál Ó Súilleabháin: A force for good

Neil Martin

Belfast-born composer and musician Neil Martin enjoys a most varied and rewarding career encompassing dance, opera, theatre, film, television, radio, concert hall and studio. Recent compositions include an opera, Nobody/Somebody, *a violin concerto,* dall'ombra, *and* Sweeney, *an orchestral song-cycle. His work with the West Ocean String Quartet has been widely lauded.*

Mícheál was a man of so many diverse parts that writing about any one aspect of his being is not really possible – pianist, composer, arranger, visionary, teacher, academic, professor, fierce 'dacent' man, friend – the full gamut. His various tributaries naturally flowed off and effortlessly rejoined the main source, and for me that main source was sharing and communication at many levels. I was immensely fortunate to have been in his orbit for more than four decades and we collaborated in different ways at different times.

He was first and foremost an undeniable and significant influence on my life. I remember yet with a crystal clarity listening to *The Long Note* programme on RTÉ Radio as a young teenager in the mid-1970s and hearing the *auteur* sounds of jigs and reels being played with ornamentation on the piano, cuts and crans and rolls that felt like an aural illusion. To hear those energies jumping out from the radio caught my breath – it was a new colour and it broke the mould. It also chimed deeply with me because by then I was dipping into the two camps of classical and traditional music. Playing cello, piano and uilleann pipes, I found Mícheál's world immediately beguiling. And then his version of 'Seán Ó Duibhir a' Ghleanna' with its descending bassline absolutely affirmed to me that cross-collaboration was a world of endless possibilities.

Whereas I had always found classical and traditional music wholly compatible myself, in my youth it was made known to me that there were some who opposed this notion. I was told by some traditional players that because I read music and played cello that I could never be a proper traditional musician. Certain classical musicians looked down on traditional music, seeing it as a lesser artform. Insignificant and vapid matters now of course, and no more than speedbumps to a teenager back then. At Scoil Éigse in Ennis in 1977 I attended an afternoon lecture of Mícheál's on the correlation of Carolan and certain elements of contemporaneous baroque music and I remember Vivaldi's *L'Estro Armonico* being used by Mícheál to illustrate connections. The lightbulb was again sparked. Afterwards I boldly introduced myself to Mícheál and he encouraged me to pursue both music forms fearlessly and to pay no heed to any negative whisperings. I listened to him.

We next met in the early 1980s when I was an undergraduate student at Queen's University in Belfast and the Music Society (of which I was treasurer) invited Mícheál up to give one of our weekly Thursday lunchtime recitals in the Harty Room. More bravura piano playing and reaffirmation of the potential of it all and an overriding sense of *positivity* – he brought so much of that to everything he touched. Zeal for music and people and poetry and arts and life. It was palpable from him, contagious.

We'd occasionally bump into each other in various situations over the next few years, and then in 1990 Mícheál asked me to premiere and record *flowansionnamare*, a new piece he was writing for uilleann pipes and chamber orchestra. Punchy, edgy, adventurous music, in which the demands on pipes bring them outside of the standard traditional framework, melodically and rhythmically. After a rehearsal in his then home of Murroe we went to a local pub for a quiet pint before dinner and I told Mick about another passion in which I was engaged: collaborating with Belfast filmmaker David Hammond in making documentary films for Flying Fox Films, David's independent company. 'When all your various strands meet up, it'll be fascinating,' he said. This was to happen a few years later and Mícheál was involved. The *flowansionnamare* concert and recording went swimmingly.

During the first half of the 1990s, as well as his busy composing and performing schedule that he somehow managed to run alongside his academic obligations at University College Cork, Mícheál was a presenter of television programmes. One substantial undertaking was *A River of Sound*, a weighty and courageous series on traditional music and its associations, produced by Philip King and Nuala O'Connor for BBC and RTÉ. During the shoot for this series I got a letter from him, written during a recording break and whilst he was in the bath of some hotel, trying to compose a movement for a new mass: 'Water, water everywhere, trying to compose a Sanctus in the bath,' he wrote in his distinctive hand. Extraordinary and boundless levels of energy coupled with an unfailing capacity to handle many detailed and complex things simultaneously and all the while making time to drop a friendly and humorous line. *Quel homme*! When I once enquired as to how he found time to juggle all these differing strands of his life, he told me that he'd sit down of a Sunday afternoon and plot the week ahead to the very minute, from meetings and lectures and rehearsals right down to the duration of phone calls. He wasted no time, Mick Sul.

Mícheál had a profound love of all arts, was well-read, open-minded, and I know that poetry was a source of great joy to him. Shortly after Seamus Heaney became a Nobel Laureate in 1995, Mícheál, now recently established at the University of Limerick (UL) as the inaugural director of the Irish World Academy of Music and Dance, phoned to ask if I'd play uilleann pipes at the conferral of an honorary doctorate by the university on Seamus. I know that Mícheál took great pride and delight in delivering his beautifully crafted words of praise to Seamus that day – it meant the world to him. And in the fifteen minutes between rehearsal and the ceremony itself, he outlined for me on a flipchart his twenty-year aspiration for music at UL.

David Hammond was a fine singer as well as a fine filmmaker, and around 2002 Flying Fox Films made a series of television programmes about him for the BBC: *David Hammond's Ireland*. Davey was keen for Mícheál to be part of this and a date was set, a location booked and a Steinway concert grand brought in for Mícheál to play. He took the train from Limerick to Belfast for the shoot, and from a taxi between trains he phoned to ask me to sing the melody of the song Davey would be singing that afternoon. 'And roughly what key might he sing that in?' Regardless, it became immediately obvious that not much rehearsal was needed. Both men were very comfortable and delighted to be in each other's company. I was directing that day and after a few short rehearsal verses I called 'cut' and we re-set for the one, magical take. Mícheál's words from 1990, 'When all your various strands meet up, it'll be fascinating', seemed to come full circle that day.

Over the next decade or so we'd see each other occasionally, perhaps collaborate now and again, but we met socially as well and had some terrifically warm and hospitable evenings in his home in Newport. It was in 2013 that the Irish Traditional Music Archive (ITMA) was having an evening concert in the Abbey Theatre in Dublin to mark its twenty-fifth anniversary and Nicholas Carolan, the director of ITMA, asked Kildare uilleann piper Liam O'Flynn to put together a quartet for the evening's concert. That quartet was Liam, Mícheál on piano and harpsicord, Paddy Glackin on fiddle and myself on cello. We rehearsed, we enjoyed, we'd a blast of a gig, and over the following three years we went on to perform together from time to time, enjoying it all the more with each gig. There was such pleasure playing in that ensemble, employing an extensive palette of musical possibility which spanned many decades of making music in all sorts of situations, one that we collectively delighted in sharing. We were planning on doing more, on upping the output, when early in 2017 both Mícheál and Liam became ill. The loss of both those towering figures in 2018 took a great toll on music in Ireland and I wished we had all been able to have had longer in each other's company, both on and off stage. Cherished times they were.

I garnered much from Mícheál's words of encouragement at various points in my own compositional career, and one early example of this was my composing and arranging for the West Ocean String Quartet from the late 1990s. The quartet occupies a space somewhere in-between the worlds of classical and traditional music, a world not dissimilar to Mícheál's. He shared thoughts on some of the early drafts and recordings and offered a few gentle suggestions, delivered as always with grace and care. I am convinced that the seeds to mine this world *between musics* were sown at least in part by his positivity towards that teenager in Ennis all those years before.

It was those seemingly small but indelible gestures – a word here, a text there, an email, a letter, a phone call – that left a lasting impact. Mícheál phoned me during the interval of a concert the Irish Chamber Orchestra (ICO) was giving in Limerick and at which Brian Kennedy was singing songs arranged by both Mícheál and myself. Knowing that I'd be sitting at home in Belfast wondering about it all, he phoned at the interval just to say how well my arrangements were working. Now, *there* was a great generosity of spirit. Heartsome, selfless and kind. He was a most approachable man, generous with his time, and no matter how busy he was, which of course was always, he'd find time to check in with you.

His love of poetry, literature and other world musics and their easy cohabitation within his own musical palette was another important avenue of inspiration to me. The title of the final track on *Gaiseadh*, his album on which *flowansionnamare* features, was taken from T.S. Eliot's 'Burnt Norton', the first poem of his *Four Quartets*. *At the Still Point of the Turning World* is Mícheál's arrangement of 'An Buachaill Caol Dubh' framed within a north Indian alap/raga-like figure that gradually sets out the mood and colour of the piece – in his hands their union sounded completely natural. It was, and still is, mesmerising and inexplicably moving. I was fortunate to have been in the studio as he recorded it and when I listen to it now more than thirty years on, I get goosebumps yet.

I believe that I work hard, composing and performing to my best. I'm always busy. But when I mull on Mícheál's lifetime's output – his recordings, his decades of collaborations with the ICO, his scores for theatre and film, his boundless energies presenting and collaborating on television, his orchestral compositions including *Oileán* and *flowansionnamare*, his immeasurable academic career and his zealous enabling of thousands of musicians to up their game, his orchestrations for Liam O'Flynn and Iarla Ó Lionáird *inter alia*, his choral and devotional compositions, the countless electrifying performances around the globe of his own music – it's enough for several lifetimes. The breadth and extent of his compositional opus alone is significant, and that so much of it was ground-breaking further allows us to appreciate the scale of his imagination. His compositions and arrangements all have his mark, their own unmistakable stamp, and that is quite something to achieve and sustain over a lifetime. He ploughed his own furrow relentlessly and dedicated himself to it unfailingly. Those lucky enough to be around him were swept along in his contagious and enthusiastic wave of squeezing as much out of life as possible. You couldn't ignore the force of energy that was Mícheál Ó Súilleabháin.

Mícheál was for me a reliable and constant feature throughout more than forty years, an enabler, a constructive force and an affirmative voice, a friend and a colleague. His influence is ingrained in me and I'm in his eternal debt. Down through the years I always eagerly awaited his own new musical offerings, knowing full well that with every new work, he'd open some new door for us all, offer another view. His eternal composition 'Ah! Sweet Dancer' and his sublime arrangements of 'Port na bPúcaí' and 'Bean Dubh an Ghleanna' will forever hold wonder, awe and love for me.

The scale of Mícheál's legacy may not be entirely appreciated for some time to come. But let us be assured that he enriched this place and our music and our lives. He gave with great grace of his very best. Good man, Mick Sullivan – *go gcluinfear do cheol binn go deo*.

13

A Conversation on Music and Memory

Mary Coll and Joan Sheehy

Mary Coll is a Limerick poet, playwright and broadcaster. Her publications include All Things Considered *(Salmon, 2002) and* Silver *(Arlen House, 2018). She has made numerous contributions to arts and culture programmes on radio and television and has worked as a critic for national newspapers.*

Joan Sheehy is an actor and director from Granagh, County Limerick. She has performed with all the leading Irish theatre companies and toured nationally and internationally. More recently, she has directed many acclaimed productions and can be seen as Úna in the award-winning film An Cailín Ciúin.

In 2010, to celebrate the re-opening of the Belltable Arts Centre, Limerick, Mary Coll was commissioned to write a new play, *Anything But Love*, directed by Joan Sheehy, with an original score written and performed by Mícheál Ó Súilleabháin. The play was based on *The Ante-Room*, a novel published in 1934 by the Limerick writer Kate O'Brien. It is the story of three siblings gathered in their family home during the final days of their mother's life and has all the accompanying drama one would expect in these circumstances. Modernised to a contemporary Limerick setting, the original music composed by Mícheál was far more than a soundtrack, it became a significant additional character in itself, bridging past and present and moving effortlessly through each scene in the play. Following the production in the Belltable Arts Centre, *Anything But Love* was then recorded for broadcast by RTÉ Radio as part of their 'Drama on One' series; this took place before a live audience in the Mill Theatre, Dundrum, County Dublin, with Mícheál performing his score in person on the night.

M. I remember from the outset, Joan, that we both only ever thought about Mícheál in terms of the soundscape for *Anything But Love*. Were you ever worried he mightn't go for it? What was his first reaction?

J. The moment Mícheál's name was mentioned I couldn't imagine the play without his contribution and I was so excited at the prospect of our collaboration that I didn't even entertain the thought of him not agreeing. It was just as well that his first reaction was a hearty, passionate 'Yes, when do we start and how do we do this?'

M. He was always such a great supporter of theatre, very clear in conversation with me after any performance in the Belltable about what he felt had worked and what didn't on the stage.

J. Yes, he had immediate and often very uncompromising reactions! I discovered that these came from a profound understanding of the nuance of performance and the structure of a piece of drama.

M. Kate O'Brien's novel *The Ante Room*, the inspiration for *Anything But Love*, is set in the 1880s but there is nothing dated about the themes it addresses: love, infidelity, loss and loyalty. I often wondered what Mícheál made of it all on his first reading.

J. I think that his emotional understanding of the material and his instant yet sophisticated response was the most memorable element of our first discussion. I thought I would be teasing out the narrative for him while he spoke about music but he was right there with me and very quickly we agreed that the music would be integral to the drama and not just a punctuation. We both imagined the spirit of the dying woman, the mother of the household, as the musical centre of the collaboration. He was completely immersed in the story and had a great sense of Kate O'Brien's place in literature and her importance to Limerick.

M. I know that as a writer I heard in my head what I thought was the sound of the play, the music that I felt would surround the family in their home. What shocked me was how Mícheál could create that exact music without any need to talk to me about it. Was there a lot of conversation between you both beforehand to achieve that perfect fit?

J. He had an immense practicality about him, there was no pretence of mystery around the process of creating work. We would break down the script and identify the areas where music would be integrated. He loved working out where the action peaked or ebbed, where the music led or underscored or completed the narrative.

M. Writing a character who was a concert pianist was more than a bit of a stretch for me but Mícheál's music made the character of Richie real in a way that writing alone might not have achieved. He really understood him, didn't he?

J. Mícheál loved the colourful rogue that was Richie, the fact that he was a concert pianist was meat and drink to him and allowed another rich layer of music into the play. In his very careful choice of music for Richie and his own playing of that, he brought so many elements of the man to life. It was a fantastic opportunity to integrate music organically into the dramatic action.

M. Kate O'Brien had a great love for classical music and opera and it comes through in all her novels. In *The Ante Room* she references a variety of composers but Mícheál went straight for Chopin, the great romantic, without hesitation or apology, which of course fit perfectly in terms of the love stories of the play.

J. Oh yes, Chopin was his man. He looked for the romance, the sadness and the playfulness in the pieces he chose to include.

M. You and I had some great 'discussions' around the script, about what would work and what wouldn't, and we both know how resistant writers are to direction. I'm wondering was it very different working with a composer?

J. Mícheál actually loved collaboration and was open to the most naive of suggestions but was also very strong on why something would not work. I never had the feeling of a musical maestro talking down to me – he was heart and soul in the process of making a play great and he relished the collaborative cut and thrust.

M. So there was none of the drama you usually get from temperamental writers?

J. There was robust discussion as there was with you, but I have to admit there were no strops or tantrums from either of you. I guess I wore you both down! It is sometimes said that the greater the artist, the easier it is to work with them, and this was especially true in Mícheál's case. He didn't need to prove anything, he was interested in creating great work and was fascinated by the journey.

M. When we eventually got to the nuts and bolts part of the production I was amazed how willing Mícheál was to get stuck in at the coalface of bringing it all together. He didn't just mail in the score and be done with it.

J. He particularly loved the often painful process of technical rehearsal in a freezing Belltable. He loved seeing the set, lighting and costume adding to the weave. We were a team pulling this production together and his insights, his black humour and his spirit of comradery kept us all going!

M. He was protecting his work too though, wasn't he, there were going to be no shortcuts when it came to how it would be presented.

J. Indeed, it was at this stage I saw the absolute steel in him as he dealt with the sound system, the operators, the fluctuating levels and all the other technical elements that impacted on the music. The only occasion when he 'lost it' was during a preview where the prologue music couldn't be heard properly, and let's just say that he made it abundantly clear that if he had invested so much in creating this music it needed to be heard!

M. I can remember his response to anything that fell short of excellence, there was never any doubt as to his priorities.

J. That was the joy of working with Mícheál, and indeed the challenge – excellence was a given for him. His clarity at all times during the creation of the work was breathtaking and he demanded clarity in response. I learned a great deal through the process of working with him.

M. His music really added a unique extra dimension to the play, one that was quite moving and almost surreal. I had written five characters but his music became a sixth presence throughout.

J. It truly did. The play deals with so many hidden passions and losses and Mícheál's music managed to embody all that inner, unspoken turmoil.

M. And it had a very real emotional impact, didn't it? It was never simply a soundtrack.

J. No, the script, music and acting all developed and fused together into a unique performance. Of all the great experiences with Mícheál, the live recording of the play for RTÉ Radio Drama was the highlight. It was in the Mill Theatre, Dundrum, as part of the Dublin Theatre Festival. On stage, Mícheál played live while the actors performed at microphones and it was an extraordinary experience, starkly dramatic and deeply moving.

M. I know. I wrote a play, but whenever I think back about it now what I hear is Mícheál's music, it was transcendent and unforgettable.

14

Irish Destiny: The movie, the music, the maestro

Sunniva O'Flynn

Sunniva O'Flynn is head of Irish film programming at the Irish Film Institute where she is responsible for curation of Irish film and bringing new and archival cinema to national and international audiences. An extensive knowledge of Irish film history, stemming from many years with the IFI Irish Film Archive, informs her programming practice.

Few Irish silent feature films were ever made and, due to the instability of the nitrocellulose-based stock on which they were processed, fewer survived. So, when in 1991 a print of the silent Irish War of Independence feature film *Irish Destiny* was unearthed in the Library of Congress in Washington, it was a cause for great celebration. The film would be restored and repatriated and a score commissioned which would complement and complete the film and render it digestible for contemporary audiences.

The 35mm print, which had been in distribution in the United States in the 1920s, carried some musical cues for accompanists in its opening frames. *Musical Themes* - - 'Mother Machree' and 'Danny Boy' it instructed. Needless to say, we in the Irish Film Institute (IFI) were looking for something a little less clichéd and a little more sophisticated. We needed a composer who would be unintimidated by the anachronistic challenge of writing a full seventy-eight-minute score for a silent film; who would understand how a silent film score must enhance, not overwhelm, the picture; who would be sensitive to the political underpinnings of the film and who would, ideally, interweave traditional and classical traditions to properly amplify the national and universal themes within. With advice from folks with better musical nous than we had (such as Dermot McLaughlin, then traditional music officer in the Arts Council) we learnt that Mícheál Ó Súilleabháin was the only man for the job. Upon approach, Mícheál jumped immediately on board with curiosity and boundless enthusiasm for a project which would see the creation of a full orchestral score for a silent Irish feature film, a first in the history of Irish cinema.

And so Mícheál set to work to score a film that, unlike other Irish features made to date, was *not* based on a pre-existing literary work but was instead written for the screen (by its producer, Dublin pharmacist Dr Isaac Eppel) and was all the better for that. Innately cinematic, the film was bursting with romance, drama and acts of derring-do played out against sweeping rural landscapes and bustling city streets. Of particular distinction was its bold representation of the War of Independence (told through drama and newsreel footage) which had taken place a scant five or six years before. Mícheál dove in, working gamely away with a time-coded VHS tape, set at 20fps, the speed at which, silent-film historian Kevin Brownlow advised, would create the most natural and fluid movement in both the acted and newsreel sequences.

The day finally arrived in December 1993 when the score was complete, the meticulously restored print had been repatriated, and the only job left was the transformation of the National Concert Hall into a cinema for the film's premiere. The RTÉ Concert Orchestra, conductor Proinnsías Ó Duinn and composer-performer Mícheál Ó Súilleabháin were standing by. A 35mm mobile projector had been booked from the UK and was en route in a truck on the B+I car ferry. But a storm was brewing and the ferry was forced to anchor in the middle of the Irish Sea. We had no option but to hire a private helicopter to fly over, winch the truck off the boat and head for Dublin. But first there was a pit-stop at an RAF airbase in Valley in Wales where the irony of the RAF facilitating the screening of a Black-and-Tan/Irish republican drama was not lost on Mícheál, who told the story (with some forgivable embellishments) with great relish for years after. In Dublin, a high-speed dash from the airport through the city with garda out-riders was followed by a super-quick set-up with mere moments to spare before the rehearsal-free curtain-up. The orchestra took up their positions. Mícheál seated himself at the grand piano, centre stage. Conductor Proinnsías Ó Duinn took to his podium, raised his baton, and, as the projector whirred to life and the title sequence unspooled, the opening notes of Mícheál's magnificent score filled the hall. But suddenly – the baton dropped. The music stopped. Proinnsías walkie-talkied, 'Stop the film! – There is an overture to be played!' Much laughter from the audience – with, according to the *Evening Press*, 'President Robinson, a patron of the IFI, particularly amused'.

A frantic rewinding of the 35mm reels. Baton up. Mícheál and the orchestra played the full three-minute overture and then, upon Proinnsías' very dramatic signal, the projector kicked back into life and *Irish Destiny* burst forth again to delight a new generation.

Mícheál's score does its job at its most basic level. It facilitates effortless viewing of a film from a distant era by engaging the emotions and drawing the viewer into the world of the film. Mícheál disregarded the rather trite musical suggestion of the United States distributors, and while he did not adhere slavishly to musical styles contemporaneous with the film's release, he did allude to musical precedent in his reference to 'Amhrán Dóchais' and Seán Ó Riada's score for *Mise Éire* (George Morrisson's 1916 newsreel montage film made in 1959). The score deftly underpins the story, matching dramatic sequences with music that is romantic, exciting, menacing and poignant as befits the action. Mícheál's glorious piano sequences are particularly agile in their illumination of character and parsing of plot. But the music does far more than simply follow the action, it adds a significant further narrative dimension to the work. In adopting a clear point of view, it carries us along as it articulates a political response to the horrors of war and expresses hope and pride in the newly formed state. As Mícheál himself said, 'My hopes for the music are that it is questioning without being apologetic, that it is proud without being arrogant, that above all else it praises the human spirit of freedom in whatever tradition it is found.'

In the years following the exciting premiere, the film screened again, live with RTÉ and other concert orchestras – in Dublin, Paris and Brussels – and occasionally with a nimble hybrid of Mícheál playing live alongside the pre-recorded orchestral score. One of Mícheál's favourite, most triumphant performances was in 2007 when the film, once banned in Britain because of its subversive political content, screened with full orchestra in the Barbican Centre in the presence of the lord mayor of London. The audience, which included the descendants of director Dr Isaac Eppel, cheered the good guys and hissed and booed the bad guys in true silent film fashion.

I believe Mícheál was very proud of *Irish Destiny*, enjoyed every performance and was delighted to see it made more widely available when it was broadcast and released on DVD in 2006. It was our great good fortune to be part of this project, to work with Mícheál Ó Súilleabháin over many years and to be nurtured by his enthusiasm, his genius and his great *joie de vivre*.

15
Along the Enchanted Way: Recollections of a church musician

John O'Keeffe

John O'Keeffe is director of sacred music at St Patrick's College, Maynooth, and director of choral groups at Maynooth University. In 2021 he was awarded the Knighthood of St Gregory for his services to Irish church music.

Within the continuum of my own musical development, I can recall a number of occasions when I came into contact with Mícheál Ó Súilleabháin's work in the general domain of church music. The first was a concert given in Trinity College Chapel in 1982 with Nóirín Ní Riain and the monks of Glenstal Abbey as part of the Dublin International Organ Festival, with Mícheál at the organ. It was a memorable event, framed in the context of a native Celtic spirituality, long before such things became fashionable. Looking back, the recorded collaborations of that exciting period have stood well the test of time. The exchange of music between the traditional female soloist and the monastic choir was daring yet convincing, and for a young student of liturgical music provided a very attractive window into the music of both traditions.

As the 1980s progressed, the question of the integration of Irish language and music into the then recently vernacularised liturgy tended to be eclipsed by developments on the English-language front and the proliferation of church music from American publishing houses. By way of response, a Tionól Cheol Eaglasta was convened in Maynooth in 1987, organised not by any official body but by two students of the college, Tomás Ó Caoimh and Frank Lawrence. At the symposium Nóirín Ní Riain presented the fruits of her studies in Irish traditional religious song and Mícheál himself was also a contributor, being joined in the discussions by his friend and colleague Tomás Ó Canainn. All three had studied with or worked alongside Seán Ó Riada at University College Cork. The discussion was lively and good-humoured and in those days it seemed the most natural thing in the world that musicians of that calibre should be deeply concerned with and exercised by questions surrounding the music employed in Irish liturgical worship.

The 1990s witnessed the birth and development of the Irish World Music Centre/Irish World Academy of Music and Dance and Mícheál's emergence as a broadcaster, most notably in the 1995 BBC series *A River of Sound*. The central *sean-nós* episode of that series features a performance by Iarla Ó Lionáird of 'Caoineadh na dTrí Muire', a representative example from the native religious song tradition whose textual content, form and musical expression brings the listener particularly close to the world of liturgical chant.

Mícheál's longstanding fascination with chant took on academic flesh in the ensuing years as he set about establishing a master's in chant performance degree at Limerick. In typical fashion, he cast his net wide and landed an exciting catch in the form of Katarina Livljanić, by then a well-established chant performer and academic who had studied in Zagreb, Graz and Paris. Well-drilled in traditional scholarship and performance as she was, her musical instincts took her down the road of medieval chant as a discipline primarily grounded in orality. One can imagine Mícheál's eyes dancing at the interview as she presented her vision of chant performance as a vital, living, personalised process set within the broader framework of a richly oral liturgical tradition.

I was fortunate enough to be amongst her first batch of Irish students in 1998. My contact with her proved transformative, and profoundly shaped my views on the question of chant, not just in the context of the existing Latin tradition but perhaps more importantly in the evolving arena of vernacular liturgical music. At our introductory session, by way of audition, she surprised us all by asking us to deliver, not a piece of chant, but any song that we liked to sing, from any musical genre that we felt comfortable in. Using this approach, she cut quickly to the essence of each musician before her, and gave a clear signal that, whatever its purpose, religious or secular, singing is first and foremost a deeply human activity. Mícheál himself was not at that inaugural class of the plainchant programme (no doubt tending one of the many other academic fires he was lighting in that same year) but he may as well have been, for it epitomised what seems to me to have been his own instinctively healthy approach towards music of all genres.

Many of the threads mentioned above would later come together in my own academic work, and my final contact with this uniquely influential musician came late in 2017 in the form of an email from him, *as Gaeilge*, marking the launch of my book *The Masses of Seán and Peadar Ó Riada: Explorations in vernacular chant* (2017). The study builds on a number of themes that were close to his own heart, endeavouring as it does to establish more concrete and demonstrable connections between *sean-nós* and the orally derived monophonic repertoires of plainchant and medieval secular song, and signalling the exciting possibilities inherent in the fusion of a rich repository of structurally varied ritual texts with the musical language of a living cultural tradition. Mícheál's message was enthusiastic and gracious, as was typical of the man, but, more importantly for me, it underlined his keen appreciation of the compositional significance of the combined Ó Riada liturgical corpus. Of the many messages received at the time, it is one I shall particularly treasure.

16

The Mediator and the 'Disappointment': Understanding Mícheál Ó Súilleabháin's contribution to Irish composition

Toner Quinn

Toner Quinn is a musician, writer about music, founder and editor of the online publication The Journal of Music, *and a lecturer in publishing at Ollscoil na Gaillimhe – University of Galway.*

One of the curious twists of fate in my life is that, at the age of seventeen, I made a mistake on the Central Applications Office form for university entrance that meant that, although I had been accepted into University College Cork (UCC) after an interview and audition with Mícheál Ó Súilleabháin, to my shock I did not get to go there and study with him.

After Ó Súilleabháin died, I thought about that moment. It was clear from the decades that followed that our interests overlapped, to the extent that he referred to my views on Irish music in a newspaper article in 2013.[1] Had I studied with him, might my musical journey have been different? As it was, my knowledge of the composer and musician was learnt from a distance: discovering the albums *The Dolphin's Way* and *Oileán/Island*, viewing his television series *A River of Sound* and his Eurovision interval work *Lumen*, reading his essays in books and journals, and attending his keynote speech at the Crossroads Conference in 1996.

In subsequent years, as I worked in the domain of publishing, our worlds connected occasionally: publishing the book *Anáil Dé, the Breath of God: Music, ritual and spirituality* in 2001,[2] to which he contributed, and his review of a book on Aloys Fleischmann in the *Journal of Music in Ireland* in 2007.[3] But in 2016, after his retirement from the University of Limerick had been announced, I decided that I needed to have a much more in-depth conversation with Ó Súilleabháin about his work. I arranged to interview him at his house in Newport, County Tipperary, and we spoke for over two hours, but only reached the 1990s as we worked through the chronology of his career. I followed our conversation up with some emails, but then struggled to find the time to work on the piece, so large had it grown. It was never published. When he passed away, I drew on the interview to write a tribute for the *Journal of Music*.

That tribute, 'Mícheál Ó Súilleabháin's Example will Continue to Inspire',[4] tried to capture his achievements in education, performance and composition, but although he was a celebrated figure in Irish music, we should not pretend that Ó Súilleabháin's compositional work was universally appreciated. Indeed, any discussion of his composed music should involve an exploration of the musical disagreements that his work tended to draw out, because they tell us something about the period of Irish musical life he lived through. In this essay I look at the critical reception, often negative, that his music received, suggest why this might have been, and make the case for what I think was his key contribution to Irish composition.

Musical mediators

Composing in Ireland has often been a subject of disagreement because there are contrasting traditions and influences tugging on it, namely western classical music and Irish traditional music. Ó Súilleabháin's music drew on both, and thus his music was sometimes a flashpoint for debate. He was not unaware of this situation. He once grouped the eighteenth-century harper Turlough Carolan, the composer Seán Ó Riada and the fiddle player Tommie Potts together as 'musical mediator[s]'[5] in Irish music. Mediators, Ó Súilleabháin said, acted as bridges between different musics; they could have different audiences. And they could also divide opinion because they sat in neither group comfortably. Ó Súilleabháin did not describe himself as a mediator, but it was clear he was one.

And as with the artists above, Ó Súilleabháin's work was, for periods, questioned or rejected by different sides of Irish musical life. In the case of Irish contemporary music, his work, as we shall see, never received full acceptance during his lifetime. Critics did not regard his style of music as what Irish composers should be writing in the late twentieth and early twenty-first centuries. One voice said Ó Súilleabháin's work made the very concept of original composition in Ireland 'a meaningless term';[6] another, in a complete survey of twentieth-century Irish composition, made no mention of him at all.[7]

Ó Súilleabháin realised that his engagement as a composer with traditional music was considered a 'disappointment' (Ó Súilleabháin's word, from our interview).[8] Unfortunately, those negative views of his work tended to become so widespread that critical opinion did not interrogate them fully by exploring the full range of his work. This had real consequences for his music. Two years before he died, the Composing the Island festival – a three-week, twenty-eight concert celebration of one hundred years of Irish composed music – took place at the National Concert Hall to mark the centenary of the Easter Rising. Ó Súilleabháin's forty years of work was excluded. When I asked him about this, he explained it away calmly, saying that he had other opportunities to have his work performed and indeed the RTÉ Concert Orchestra had given over entire concerts to his work in the preceding years.[9] This was true, but it wasn't the point; Composing the Island was about asserting that the country had a substantial tradition of composed music. To exclude Ó Súilleabháin was shocking.

At the same time, a major book on Irish music published to accompany the festival only included a brief reference to a couple of tracks from his 2001 *Templum* album.[10] Even Ó Súilleabháin's page-long entry in the 2013 *Encyclopaedia of Music in Ireland* fails to discuss a single work he wrote.[11]

There are actually over seventy works by Ó Súilleabháin listed with the Contemporary Music Centre, including several substantial orchestral and choral works. If we are considering Irish musical culture as a whole, and the environment in which he worked, this critical reception for Ó Súilleabháin's work is significant.

Musical politics

In an obituary for the composer in *The Irish Times*, published a few days after he died, the writer describes Ó Súilleabháin's compositional output as follows:

> Like Ó Riada, [Ó Súilleabháin's] interests straddled the worlds of classical music and Irish traditional music. Unlike Ó Riada, *he never essayed large-scale work in a purely classical style* [italics mine]. But his career path followed that of Ó Riada, as the pull towards the traditional proved much stronger than the magnetism of any other style or form.[12]

In those two sentences, there are a number of issues that remind us of the thinking that Ó Súilleabháin grappled with throughout his career.

For it is not simply a description of a composer that is presented here, but an entire view of music. The obituary carefully uses the phrase 'purely classical style', but what does that mean in this context? We could think of the orchestral works of Haydn, Mozart and Schubert, but the twentieth and twenty-first centuries have expanded the lexicon of western 'classical' music exponentially, and the various types of oeuvre that composers produce, from electronic to the freely improvised, are all accepted as being part of this diverse tradition, so why does the idea of a 'purely classical style' suddenly come into play in an obituary of an Irish composer in the twenty-first century? It only makes sense if its purpose is to exclude.

The reference to Ó Riada also needs to be interrogated. Ó Riada had often been rejected by composers and critics as a model for contemporary Irish composers, because of the small number of works he wrote. In 2003, composer Benjamin Dwyer wrote: 'How often, one might ask, has Ó Riada's music actually been performed? Are his scores studied avidly as examples of excellence by younger generations of Irish composers?'[13] Later, in his book *Different Voices: Irish music and music in Ireland* (2014), Dwyer added: 'Alas, if it registered at all, Ó Riada's impact on art music in Ireland was minimal, mainly because the few works he wrote in the European style were of very mixed quality.'[14]

This view is not unrepresentative of opinions in contemporary Irish music, and yet, in the Ó Súilleabháin obituary, Ó Riada was presented as the standard to be met. Ó Súilleabháin was of course influenced by Ó Riada, his lecturer at UCC, but the younger composer was also part of a post-1960s musical world in which contemporary composition had diversified radically (Ó Súilleabháin's eponymous debut album in 1976 reflected this, containing traditional music played on synthesiser) and by the 1980s he had moved on from some of Ó Riada's thinking, and indeed challenged it.[15] He also had other important influences, so the blanket statement that 'his career path followed that of Ó Riada' is only true in the broadest sense. As we shall see, Ó Súilleabháin's compositional approach was a significant advance on what Ó Riada did.

Perhaps the most surprising aspect of the *Irish Times* obituary, however, is that it is factually wrong. There are, in fact, several large-scale works that Ó Súilleabháin wrote that *are* in a 'purely classical style' (taking that to mean a multi-movement orchestral work), such as the three-movement work *Oileán/Island* for flute and orchestra (1988, rev. 2016); the three-movement orchestral work *Session #1* (1991); *flowansionnamare*, a concerto for three instruments and string orchestra recorded on *Gaiseadh/Flowing* (1992); and *Madison's Descent*, a cantata in ten movements for voice, choir and orchestra (2006).

But still, putting all of these political matters aside, it is important to explore what Ó Súilleabháin's contribution to Irish composition ultimately is, and its significance for the development of our musical culture over the past five decades, and for future composers.

Stepping away from Ó Riada

When Ó Súilleabháin graduated from UCC in the 1970s, his concern as a composer was initially the same as that of Ó Riada, the 'creation of a native Irish art music by bypassing the western orchestra'.[16] His *Concertino for Fiddle* in the same decade was certainly that, a multi-movement work for traditional musicians. But in the 1980s Ó Súilleabháin stepped away from Ó Riada's vision, moved back to the western orchestra and produced what is one of his most significant works, *Oileán/Island*, a concerto for traditional musician and string orchestra. He also produced his ground-breaking solo piano album *The Dolphin's Way*.

It is important to recognise that, at the same time as he was producing these works in the mid- to late 1980s, he was engaged in a detailed PhD study of the work of the Dublin fiddle player Tommie Potts (1912–88), a musician who had developed a unique way of playing traditional music. As Ó Súilleabháin made clear in a 1999 essay, he was deeply interested in Potts' musical innovations and honed in on a number of them.[17]

Firstly, Ó Súilleabháin noted the way that Potts deconstructed tunes by breaking the 'round', that is, the standard repeat of tunes that is essential for performance with dancing and that reflects the social origins of the music. Challenging that basic community essence of the music's structure was a radical step by Potts. Secondly, Potts also altered the basic structure of a melody, swinging away from it and back to it with a particular type of improvisation that diverged significantly from traditional practice, flying 'out and upwards with wonderful control', as Ó Súilleabháin described it.[18] Thirdly, Potts would take short phrases from other pieces of music, particularly classical, popular and jazz, and insert them into his performances of tunes.

Together, these innovations gave Potts an approach that allowed him to hold a line between traditional practice and something new. Ó Súilleábháin was excited by these aspects of Potts' music and adamant that this 'separate yet inextricably linked musical expression' could 'honour rather than negate' the original music from which it came.[19] Understanding the influence of Potts is key to appreciating the composer's work. Ó Súilleabháin's approach to composition was often about expressing, through classical forces, innovation and creativity in traditional melody – just as Potts had. Unless you understand traditional music expression, therefore, it is difficult to see the innovation in Ó Súilleabháin's work, which is probably why his music has been dismissed by successive classical music scholars.

Interrogating traditional melody

Ó Súilleabháin's *The Dolphin's Way* (1987) was a pioneering album in the performance of traditional music on the piano. Like Potts, he was both developing and experimenting with traditional music. And as with the fiddle player, Ó Súilleabháin breaks the 'round' (repeat) of tunes, significantly alters the melody with improvisations, and, both on this album and on *Casadh* three years later, inserts sections inspired by jazz, classical and popular music. There are a number of significant examples: 'Merrily Kiss the Quaker', 'The Old Grey Goose' and 'Brian Boru', but perhaps the most startling is 'Christmas Eve'.

Ó Súilleábháin originally recorded 'Merrily Kiss the Quaker' on his debut album in 1976 as an entirely straight, ninety-second rendition of the tune, very much in a traditional style. Eleven years later, under the influence of Potts, and perhaps even feeling that Potts' innovations gave him permission to diverge from standard traditional practice, he reimagines the tune as a combination of classical, jazz and traditional styles – disassembling the tune into phrases and improvising around them, breaking the round by pausing after certain motifs, and also improvising entirely away from it. The opening sequence, which contains a series of rising phrases, and the later improvisations have clear resonances with Potts. Although Ó Súilleabháin's 'Christmas Eve' may still be regarded, even more than thirty years later, as outside traditional music practice, it is possible that he perceived it as having a clear link to the tradition via Potts.

This intense engagement by a composer with the melodic structures of Irish traditional music in this and dozens of other short piano works, following an equally intense study of one of the genre's most individual players, expanded the sonic world around the genre and presented a number of new ways into this music. Ó Súilleábháin is often presented simplistically as a direct descendant, musically, of Ó Riada, but his work with traditional dance melodies as a composer is much more complex. This is also evident in the orchestral work *Oileán/Island* (1988), which features the traditional flute player Matt Molloy on the original recording (1989). Ó Súilleábháin created the work around Molloy's classic renditions of traditional tunes, notably the 'Hare in the Heather' reel.

In the first part of *Oileán*, after a first full round of a jig by Molloy, Ó Súilleábháin again breaks the round and provides a passage that seems to point to corners of another jig without playing a full phrase from it. This process is then repeated, before returning to the first jig. The second slow movement again involves flute and orchestra circling each other, pointing to tunes and phrases but never fully embracing them. The third and final movement allows Molloy to perform a full two rounds of a reel without interruption, before Ó Súilleábháin – Potts-like – moves to tangential phrases and motifs, inspired by the melodic and rhythmic 'model' of the tune, trying to engage with it without actually doing so in an obvious way.

For the remainder of the movement, as Molloy again performs two complete rounds of the reel, Ó Súilleábháin is constantly trying to move away from it, the orchestral accompaniment initially sympathetic but gradually deconstructing the structure around the tune until finally the flute stops and the orchestra proceeds on its own path. A slow truce between flute and orchestra appears at the end before the orchestra picks up pace again and moves on.

The important point about these musical approaches is that this engagement with traditional melody appears to have been born out of a deep engagement with Potts and with traditional music more generally. It does not simply follow on from what Ó Riada did in the 1950s and '60s, which was to employ elements of traditional music but, as Ó Súilleabháin has written, from outside the music rather than within it.[20] This melodic intensity within traditional repertoire is a characteristic of much of Ó Súilleabháin's work from the later 1980s onwards, and it has provided Irish composers and musicians with a form of compositional expression that was previously not available to them.

The critical reception given to Ó Súilleabháin's work during his lifetime, however, was not informed by an understanding of the depth of his engagement with traditional music, and how that opened up new compositional avenues. As I write in 2022, Irish musical life is a diverse tableau of cultural strands and sounds. Ó Súilleabháin's compositional work is undeniably an influence on many levels, but perhaps not an obvious or widely acknowledged one. Yet more Irish composers and adventurous musicians are engaging with Irish traditional music in a new, sophisticated way.[21] Ó Súilleabháin's work was an essential bridge to this new era, not only as an educator who helped to build the culture that allowed a richer overall engagement with traditional music, but as a composer who interrogated the melodic tradition in such an intricate manner in his piano and orchestral works that he demonstrated rich new channels into the genre. Today, Irish traditional music, western classical music, modern popular music, improvisation and experimental practices are the underlying strata of an Irish musical language that is developing among the new generation of Irish composers – and that is something I am sure Ó Súilleabháin, the mediator, would celebrate.

PART 2
EDUCATOR

Foreword

Marie McCarthy

Mícheál Ó Súilleabháin's legacy as artist-teacher and educational leader is central to his life in music. His vision as educator was grounded in his practice as performer and creative musician. It was underpinned by a culturally diverse view of music that was informed by multiple disciplines and enacted in curriculum, degree programmes, and collaborations he created and enabled at University College Cork and the University of Limerick. Part II, focused on Mícheál the educator, is organised in three sections: The Dolphin's Way, Templum and Lumen.

In section one, The Dolphin's Way, former students describe Mícheál's immense influence on the course of their musical lives and document the innovative curriculum and partnerships he created during his tenure at University College Cork (UCC). Mel Mercier weaves a poetic narrative around his musical collaborations with Mícheál beginning in the mid-1970s and his studies with him at UCC. Drawing on her own story and those of several classmates who studied with Mícheál, Sandra Joyce creates a portrait of his qualities as teacher, set in the context of a dynamic and flourishing Music Department in the 1980s. Liz Doherty offers humorous vignettes to illustrate his way of connecting with people through music, as she pays tribute to the 'huge magnetic force' of his presence as teacher and mentor. Niall Vallely captures the vitality of Mícheál's approach to innovating the tradition and his capacity to inspire students to find their voice within it. Based on an intimate knowledge of the Music Department as undergraduate student, research student and now lecturer, Mary Mitchell-Ingoldsby documents his multi-faceted pioneering work at UCC – curricular innovations, and the creation of an archive, lecture series, society and festivals. Alongside his monumental efforts to transform music in the academic setting at UCC, he completed a PhD at Queen's University Belfast. Ethnomusicologist John Baily, lecturer at Queen's at the time, identifies persons and events that influenced Mícheál and validated his worldview of music.

The essays in section two, Templum, are organised around the early formation of the Academy at UL, followed by essays documenting the evolution of its degree programmes between 1996 and 2017. Past-president of UL, Edward Walsh, recalls how he recruited Mícheál to fill the inaugural chair of music at UL and supported his plans to build a progressive centre for music in higher education. Fundraising was a priority to set the project in motion. Margaret O'Sullivan describes how funding from the Toyota Performing Arts Initiative helped bridge the worlds of traditional music in the community and in the Academy. Folklorist Ríonach uí Ógáin reflects on Mícheál's deep interest in Irish language, myth and folklore, and how they informed and inspired his vision for the design of the Academy building. Architect Daniel Cordier, whose design concept for the Academy was selected during an international contest, recounts vividly his conversations with Mícheál as the design evolved and was realised. Music education philosopher David Elliott guided the direction of programmatic development in the early years and here he reflects on twenty years of 'music makings, takings, and sharings' at the Academy.

Essays recounting the evolution of the Academy are followed by a series describing the development of each programme. Authors represent current and former faculty directors, programme advisors and graduates. While the essays are too numerous to list, the degree programmes and the authors who document their development are highlighted. The earliest post-graduate programmes established in 1995–6 were in Ethnomusicology (John Morgan O'Connell; Susan H. Motherway), Ethnochoreology (Catherine Foley, Orfhlaith Ní Bhriain and Mats Melin), and Music Education (Jean Downey and Ernestine Healy). A suite of six programmes was launched in 1998–9: Classical Strings Performance (Diane Daly and Ferenc Szűcs), Ritual Chant and Song (Edward Foley and Sr Sidonia Freedman), Music Therapy (Tríona McCaffrey and Jane Edwards), Dance Performance (Mary Nunan), Irish Traditional Music Performance (Niall Keegan) and Community Music (Kari Veblen and Kathleen Turner). Two baccalaureate degrees were added – Irish Music and Dance in 2002 and Voice and Dance in 2008 (Jennifer de Brún, Hannah Fahey and Óscar Mascareñas), and a PhD in Arts Practice in 2009. Additional MA programmes were added in Festive Arts in 2013 and Songwriting in 2017 (Carl Corcoran). The section closes with insightful narratives from graduates of the PhD programme who acknowledge Mícheál's impact on their academic formation and the space he created at the crossroads of 'artistic practice and academic rigour' (Mary Louise O'Donnell and Matthew James Noone). The authors represent complementary doctoral programmes grounded in traditional research and arts practice, respectively.

In section three, Lumen, international scholars familiar with the Academy bring to light Mícheál's pedagogical gifts and the broad sweep of his influence on music education locally and globally. Patricia Shehan Campbell considers his qualities as a teacher and how his role as public educator impacted audiences beyond the Academy through his broadcasts on TV and radio. In a similar vein, Anya Peterson Royce speaks to the generosity of his teaching and the centrality of conversation in the educational process he nurtured at the Academy, 'a place of light and of welcome'. The deep impressions that he left with these scholars are reflected again in Tran Quang Hai's vignettes of three meetings with him between 1985 and 2017. The evocative recollections of Christopher Frayling speak to the 'kindred spirit' he found in Mícheál as peer leader of the arts in higher education, captured in the metaphor of Mícheál as 'the candle and the light'. Regina Murphy offers a perspective on multiple aspects of his educational leadership in Ireland – from institutions, to initiatives such as the Music Education National Debate, to professional organisations such as the Society for Music Education in Ireland (SMEI). His influence in communities beyond the island is portrayed by ethnomusicologist Svanibor Pettan who describes contributions to the International Council for Traditional Music. Boston College librarians Elizabeth Sweeney and Christian Dupont describe Mícheál's visits to the college beginning in 1979. The authors provide evidence of how he influenced the development of academic music and archives in the college and, more generally, how he advocated for the inclusion of traditional music and dance in the discipline of Irish studies. I close the section by placing Mícheál's educational vision in the context of international trends and reforms in music education in the late twentieth and early twenty-first century.

17

Reflections from the Well

Mel Mercier

An award-winning composer and performer, Mel Mercier is Professor Emeritus and former Chair of Performing Arts at the Irish World Academy of Music and Dance. Mel collaborated as a percussionist with Mícheál Ó Súilleabháin for forty years. He is director of the Irish Gamelan Orchestra, MÓNCKK, and PULSUS, the first Irish traditional percussion ensemble.

> So, when I'm playing with bodhrán, it reinforces something in me, and I try to have it reinforce something.[1]

Introduction

I met and played music with Mícheál Ó Súilleabháin for the first time in the mid-1970s, in Studio 1 at the RTÉ Radio Centre in Dublin, where he was recording music for the traditional music programme *The Long Note*. Tony MacMahon, the well-known accordion player and producer of the show, had invited me and my brother Paul to add the pulse of the bodhrán and the rattle of the bones to Mícheál's inventive musical arrangements of short musical links for the programme. I was fifteen years of age and Mícheál was about twenty-four, and that first encounter marks the beginning of a defining relationship in my life.

The fifteen years that followed saw the maturing of Mícheál's hybrid piano style and, alongside it, the emergence of our piano and percussion duet. Over the course of the following forty years, Mícheál played a central role in Irish musical culture, and I was blessed often by his invitations to travel with him on his visionary journeys in music and education. On innumerable concert stages, from Boston to Bandon, and Calcutta to Cork, I sat with my bodhrán and bones in the well of the piano, swept up and transported by the force of Mícheál's ebullient sonic energy, searching out the deepest grooves in his unique synthesis of traditional, classical and jazz musics.

In this essay, I return to the well of the piano and the studio, take my place again in the classroom and the pub session, and dip into conversations and memories to offer a loosely woven tapestry of reflections and recollections, brief scenes from the story of a lifelong friendship and musical and professional relationship.

Prelude

In 2016, in an interview I conducted with Mícheál for a documentary I was making about my father, Peadar Mercier,[2] he proposed that, when they perform, musicians release the immanent, culturally encoded sounds of the musical instruments they play. He spoke of the 'encodement of the culture, or the sonic culture' in the musical instrument itself, and explained it as, 'some fusion between the morphology, or the actual structure, shape, texture of the materials of the instrument itself and the non-material aspects of the sound world out of which it has come'.[3]

Mícheál suggested that the musician unlocks these culturally encoded sounds in the interaction – the play – between his or her body and the musical instrument. He illustrated the point by referring to what he imagined might occur when a European child holds the African instrument known as *mbira* for the first time:

> Now, if you give an *mbira* to, let's say, a European child, not even an African child, or a child who has never heard African music at all, and you get out of the way and the element of *homo ludens*, or the playing person, or that element of play comes in and the child starts to fiddle with the *mbira*, African sounds begin to come out.[4]

In our conversation, Mícheál went on to draw a parallel between this idea of the musician reaching in, unlocking and releasing something that is indwelling in the instrument, and his conception of the pedagogical relationship between teacher and student. When you have 'a really good teacher and a really good student', he said, 'the teacher does not impress knowledge upon the student, but the teacher operates all kinds of magical techniques to release the fertility of knowledge in the student, which he or she already has in a very deep, fertile, creative manner'.[5]

In the scenes that follow, Mícheál Ó Súilleabháin, *homo ludens* and *homo docens* – the playing man and the teaching man – is centre-stage. I am also present, in his company, as I often was, in the wings waiting to enter, or on the stage. In this meandering dramaturgy, this disembodied duet, I continue our conversation, muse with him on his embodied relationship with just some of the instruments that he played, not least the bodhrán itself, and bear witness to the alchemical – the magical – in his teaching.[6]

Thumb piano

In 1976, just a year or two after we first met him in the RTÉ studios at *The Long Note* recording session, Mícheál invited my brother Paul and me to perform on his soundtrack for John and Tommy McArdle's film *The Kinkisha*. Mícheál had played piano and harpsichord in his musical arrangements for *The Long Note* and, while the harpsichord also featured prominently in his score for *The Kinkisha*, he also played two non-western instruments, an African *mbira* and an Indian sitar.

Mícheál had recently received the *mbira*, an Igbo version of the African 'thumb piano' called *ubo aka*, as a gift from the Nigerian musician and scholar Meki Nzewi.[7] A member of the plucked idiophone family, the *ubo aka* is one of the Igbo 'talking instruments'. Traditionally used for communication, its eight tuned metal 'tongues', mounted on a bowl-shaped gourd resonator, are linguistically tuned, meaning that the melodic contours sounded by the instruments may correlate with the tonal dimension of Igbo speech.[8] Jostling for contact with the delicate, tightly packed metal musical tongues of the instrument, Mícheál's chunky thumbs and first fingers produced a mesmerising flow of bubbling melorhythms,[9] issuing an irresistible call to my brother and me to lift and strike our own idiophones and join him in the discovery of our first Hiberno-African groove.

In the same recording session, Mícheál's early cross-cultural embrace of musical instruments and sounds was evidenced further in his playing of the Indian sitar to accompany the singing of Nóirín Ní Riain, whose improvisation on the Waterford Déise version of 'A Rí an Domhnaigh'[10] was included as part of his soundtrack for the film. The provenance of the sitar instrument played by Mícheál in this 1976 recording is not clear. Its appearance predates the arrival, in 1982, of a collection of Indian musical instruments that were gifted to Mícheál and the Department of Music at University College Cork (UCC) by the Indian Council for Cultural Relations (ICCR). In addition to the sitar, the collection included the drone instruments called *tanpura* and *shruti* box, a portable harmonium, a bowed sarangi, and tabla drums.

The gift came on the back of Mícheál and Nóirín's first trip to India in 1982, where they performed concerts at the invitation of the ICCR.[11] Following the arrival of the instruments, Nóirín began to experiment with the harmonium and *shruti* box to accompany various genres of spiritual song, which she sourced from the *sean-nós* and Gregorian chant repertoires, and, later, the music of Hildegard von Bingen.[12]

Drone

On 16 September 1979, three years after the recording of the soundtrack for *The Kinkisha*, I sat on the stage of Dublin's Gaiety Theatre with Mícheál, Paddy Glackin, Matt Molly, Nóirín Ní Riain and Keshav Sathe, a Bombay-born, indo-jazz fusion tabla player. The event was the Pádraig Pearse Centenary Concert, with President Patrick Hillery in attendance. The programme consisted of Mícheál's arrangements of traditional music and song, and his newly composed *Fill Arís – In Ómós do Phádraig Mac Piarais*, which was based on the poem 'Fill Arís' by Seán Ó Ríordáin. For the performance of *Fill Arís* Mícheál moved from the piano stool to take his place on the floor of the stage, where, sitting cross-legged alongside Nóirín, Keshav, myself and the other Irish traditional musicians, he strummed the *tanpura*, an Indian long-necked, four-stringed drone instrument.

Charles Acton, the music critic at *The Irish Times*, was in the audience. In a colourful review of the concert, he wrote the following of Mícheál's new composition:

> Mícheál Ó Súilleabháin's much heralded work 'Fill Arís – In Ómós do Phádraig MacPiarais', to a poem by Seán Ó Riordáin, did not add much to the poem or be of particular importance. By introducing the Indian tabla (expertly played by Keshav Sathe) and the plucked string drone tanpura (played by himself) he produced irrelevant elements, which were neither assimilated nor contrasted together – apart from imposing the inconvenient posture of squatting on cushions upon his Irish musicians.[13]

Mícheál continued to include Indian instruments in his music through the 1980s and into the 1990s, and throughout his life he returned often to the sonic and functional dimensions of the Indian drone in his compositions.

Bodhrán

Mícheál first heard the sound of the bodhrán in the mid-1960s, in his teenage years, when he attended a performance of John B. Keane's play *Sive* in his hometown of Clonmel.[14] In the play, Keane exploits the shamanic resonances of the instrument, placing it in the hands of his character, Carthalawn, the travelling tinker-seer who beats the drumskin to underscore his portentous verse. Mícheál had no interest in Irish traditional music in his teenage years; throughout the sixties he was inattentive to the new sounds being created by Ceoltóirí Chualann, The Chieftains and others. It wasn't until he became a student of music at UCC and fell under the influence of Seán Ó Riada, one of his lecturers, that he developed an interest in traditional music and began to take notice of the bodhrán. He recalls seeing the instrument on the television in the hands of Ó Riada and my father, Peadar Mercier. He also saw my father play it at Ceoltóirí Chualann's final concert, which took place in Cork City Hall in 1970 and which he attended as a student usher: 'So, I was collecting tickets at the door. So, I actually saw them on stage that night. I stood at the back and I witnessed the whole sound.'[15]

Mícheál's interest in the bodhrán endured and, in 1972, in the final year of his BMus degree, he carried out some fieldwork with traditional bodhrán makers and players and wrote a dissertation on the instrument: 'I wrote a small dissertation on the bodhrán itself, and I got some help from John B. Keane indeed in that, and talked to bodhrán makers and bodhrán players in north Kerry, in south Tipperary, in Clare and in west Limerick.'[16]

What he discovered in his fieldwork was that there were three ways of playing the bodhrán: a single-ended stick style, a double-ended stick style, and a style that used the hand only. Mícheál believed that the defining ergonomic element in all three styles was the way the playing hand was turned. 'If you imagine,' he explained, 'having a pen in your hand and turning your wrist around, so that a swivelling motion – a bit like opening a door – that swivelling motion of the hand is, in a sense, the Irishness of the bodhrán.'[17] In 1974, Mícheál wrote two papers based on his fieldwork, which both appeared in *Treoir*.[18] In the first paper he discusses the history and construction of the bodhrán,[19] and in the second he explores traditional bodhrán performance techniques.[20] The focus of these short articles reveals Mícheál's early fascination with both the morphology of musical instruments and the relationship between the performer's body and the musical instrument being played.

Reflecting on the knowledge he gained about traditional bodhrán-playing practices through his fieldwork, and the progressive developments in the role of the bodhrán he witnessed in the music of Ceoltóirí Chualann and The Chieftains in the early 1970s, in my interview with him Mícheál identified this period as one of transition for the instrument. In this period, he suggested, the bodhrán was leaving behind a fading folklife world, 'which is in rural Ireland, where the instrument exists in the hands of one of the wren boys on the 26th of December every year, St Stephen's Day', and moving into the new world, 'onto the stage, in [Ó Riada's] professionalisation and formalisation and institutionalisation of traditional music'.[21] Ó Riada elevated the status of the bodhrán as a musical instrument by bringing it onto the concert stage, in his own hands, to lead his pioneering Irish traditional music ensemble, Ceoltóirí Chualann. When, later, he moved to the harpsichord to lead the ensemble he passed the instrument into my father's hands. In Mícheál's words, in that moment 'Peadar became the conduit or the mediator between the old world and the new world of the bodhrán'.[22]

In 1975, Mícheál was appointed, at a junior level, to the lectureship formerly held by Seán Ó Riada at UCC,[23] and in the following years he laid the foundations of his enlightened approach to music education. He also sustained his research interest in the bodhrán and continued to track innovations in bodhrán performance technique. In the late seventies he invited Johnny 'Ringo' McDonagh and Tommy Hayes, two of the leading exponents of an emerging 'modern' style of bodhrán playing, to UCC, where he filmed interviews with them and arranged for them to perform for his students and an audience drawn from the wider campus community. Subsequently, he wrote a short piece about contemporary developments in bodhrán playing, which was published in 1981.[24] In 1984, his book *The Bodhrán: A practical introduction*, which synthesises his bodhrán research to that point, was published by Waltons.[25]

Duets

A performance with Tommy Hayes in a concert at St Canice's Cathedral, Kilkenny on 26 August 1983, as part of the Tenth Kilkenny Arts Week, marks a significant moment in the evolution of Mícheál's relationship with the bodhrán.[26] The main item on the programme that evening was an orchestral performance of Shaun Davey's *The Brendan Voyage: Suite for uilleann pipes and orchestra*, conducted by Noel Kelehan, with soloist Liam O'Flynn playing the uilleann pipes. Mícheál was invited to perform the opening set and he, in turn, invited Tommy Hayes to join him, for the first time, to play several pieces, including 'Oíche Nollag/Christmas Eve'. The concert programme note reads:

> The concert will be opened by Mícheál Ó Súilleabháin of Cork with traditional music played on the piano in a style first demonstrated by Seán Ó Riada. Complementing rather than accompanying on the bodhrán will be Tommy Hayes.[27]

This, to my knowledge, was the first sounding of an Irish piano and bodhrán duet. Previous to that, in all of my musical encounters with Mícheál, the bodhrán and the bones were played as part of larger ensembles, which Mícheál led, almost always, from the harpsichord or the piano. Reflecting on his experience of sitting at the piano performing this duet with Tommy, Mícheál described being 'very taken with the fact that the fit was there. It hadn't happened before'.[28] There was, at the same time, he noted, something incongruous and beguiling about the sight of it:

> It looked kind of strange, still looks sort of strange, especially if you have a fine big grand piano that somebody has hired in, that's worth about one hundred and thirty thousand euro, or something [*laughs*]. And then, you know, even a classy set of drums beside that doesn't seem to argue with it visually, but to put the goatskin drum up against it, in a way is also fascinating.[29]

Cork

From 1979 to 1986, my study and work commitments kept me in Dublin, and with Mícheál immersed in his work in Cork there was less contact between us.[30] In that period I encountered John Cage and the avant-garde through my participation in Cage's *Roaratorio: An Irish circus on Finnegans Wake*, which I performed with my father, Joe Heaney, Paddy Glackin, Liam O'Flynn, Seamus Tansey and John Cage himself.[31] My experience of Cage's juxtaposition of Irish traditional music, traditional musicians, contemporary dance and his music of chance in this beautiful avant-garde cacophony was boundary-shattering. It left an indelible mark on me. It changed my perspective on what music could be and expanded my perception of what being a musician might mean for me.

One evening in 1985 I was standing at the bar in a pub in Dublin when I saw Mícheál and the Cork bodhrán player Colm Murphy on the television playing on *The Late Late Show*. I can't remember if I heard Mícheál speak with Gay Byrne about his work at UCC on that occasion, but I already had a sense from the occasional messages I had picked up on the airwaves that his integration of Irish traditional music into the university curriculum had reached a tipping point and, critically, that the invitation to traditional musicians to come and study music at UCC was open and real. Watching Mícheál and Colm that evening, I felt an irresistible pull to Cork and to music. Just a few months later I attended the UCC Department of Music open day to find out more about the course and, encouraged by Mícheál and what I witnessed there, I followed up with an application for entry to the undergraduate programme as a mature student.[32] In spring 1986, as part of the formal entrance examination, I played my bodhrán and bones with Cork fiddle player Matt Cranitch. That part of the process went well, but I failed the music theory test. Fortunately, I passed the repeat test a few months later and was accepted as a student on the three-year BMus degree programme commencing in September 1986.

By the time I began my studies at UCC as a bodhrán- and bones-playing traditional musician, Mícheál had established music-making and musicians at the core of his approach to music education. With the support of several of his academic colleagues, he had also made significant progress in the achievement of an equality in status between Irish traditional music and 'classical music', and he had led the integration of Irish traditional music studies into the university curriculum, creating an unprecedented point of access to a progressive university education in music for young Irish singers and instrumentalists.[33]

Classes in traditional music and dance were delivered by Mícheál and a team of music and dance tutors. The tutors provided practical tuition that complemented Mícheál's lectures on aspects of style, repertoire and history in Irish traditional music and dance. In 1975, in his first year as a lecturer in the Department of Music, Mícheál invited the well-known Cork uilleann piper Mícheál Ó Riabhaigh to teach the pipes to his students.[34] Ó Riabhaigh was the first of many traditional musicians, singers and dancers that Mícheál would welcome into the university, with an invitation to share their artistic and cultural knowledge. Some of the tutors he appointed in his first ten years at UCC, and who were teaching there when I arrived in 1986, still teach there at the time of writing, among them the box player Bobby Gardiner and the fiddle player Connie O'Connell.

No talk

In 1983, when Mícheál invited him to teach at UCC, Connie O'Connell was regarded as one of the finest exponents of the Sliabh Luachra style of Irish traditional music.[35] Connie accepted Mícheál's invitation and began teaching for a couple of hours every week in the Department of Music building. Because teaching space was limited in the building, Mícheál had to vacate his office while Connie and his students occupied it.

In the early days, Mícheál would occasionally stand outside the door, listening, excited and curious about what was happening in the lessons. There was, he told me, 'No talk. Just music'.[36] Connie taught his students as he, himself, had learned, through oral transmission. Mícheál described how he heard 'an initial phrase fragment played by Connie followed by six or so fiddle students attempting to repeat what they heard by ear, and then 'that same fragment repeated and the class response. Then, yet again, and again, and again'.[37] As the lesson progressed and the students began to master the basic phrases, Connie added in ornaments or a small variation, again with no comment or verbal explanation. In Mícheál's words, Connie 'delivered no heady analysis ... no fuss. No baggage. No heady conceptual frameworks. Just music as an intelligence of its own, as a knowledge that undercut language and went beyond it somehow'.[38]

Talk

The 'Ó Riada Room', one of the department's two multi-purpose teaching rooms, was located just a few steps from Mícheál's office.[39] As I remember it, this *was* a space of 'heady analysis' and 'conceptual frameworks'.[40] Here, in the presence of Seán Ó Riada's death mask,[41] my lecturers, among them Nick Sandon, Paul Everett, Jeremy Dibble, Geoffrey Spratt and Mícheál, performed their research-led teaching. The airwaves crackled with narratives of historical and contemporary performance practices, cultural and social contexts, and the recorded sounds and analyses of Machaut motets, Vivaldi concertos, Schubert symphonies, Beethoven string quartets, Stravinsky ballet scores and west Munster *sean-nós* singing.

In the autumn of 1986, sitting in the 'Ó Riada Room' as a first-year BMus student, I witnessed, first-hand, the crafting and delivery of Mícheál's rich, compelling and affirming narratives of creativity, orality and transmission in Irish traditional music. Like many of my fellow students – traditional and classical musicians alike – I was inspired by Mícheál's eloquent and erudite mapping of the coordinates of traditional music, song and dance. He rendered a multi-dimensional landscape of Irish traditional music and dance and located it within a global cartography. He validated our unique, emergent musical identities and he signposted multiple possible directions of travel: to the centre, to the margins, and off the map. When he was in full flow he illuminated the performative detail of creative process and expression, and he conjured imaginative spaces of lineage and affinity, community and individuality, belonging and difference. He lifted us up, and then he got out of the way.

The Rock

During my years as a music student, the Rockview Bar on Gilabbey Street in Cork was the venue for the weekly student traditional music session. These gatherings were at the heart of my undergraduate, extra-curricular musical experience. Curated by the student-run Irish Traditional Music

Society, the sessions were actively supported by Mícheál; he was a constant, centring presence, even if he wasn't always there. When he was at the session, Mícheál sat cheek by jowl with his exuberant students, hemmed in by them, playing into a heaving soundscape, at the centre of his own emergent vision. It was in this milieu that I saw the Nigerian *ubo aka* for the first time since the *Kinkisha* sessions, ten years previously. In the years since my first sighting of the instrument, Mícheál had concentrated his performance energies on the forging of his unique, hybrid piano-playing style, which found its full expression on his signature album *The Dolphin's Way* in 1987.

The *mbira*, which had sat, relatively silent, for more than a decade, spoke again at the Rockview sessions. I sat beside him on many of those memorable nights, stitching thumb-piano ostinatos and bodhrán and bones rhythms into rich tapestries woven of Niall Vallely's searching concertina, Méabh Ní Fhuartháin's vivacious flute, Angela McLaughlin and Brendan McDonagh's effervescent tin whistles, Maria O'Connell and Liz Doherty's swooping fiddles, Gerry Diver's burbling banjo, Mary Mitchell-Ingoldsby[42] and Max Busch's noble pipes, and Frank Torpey and Jim Higgins' propulsive bodhrán grooves.

'Crispy'

During my years as an undergraduate student, Mícheál and I played together often, deepening our musical rapport and consolidating our piano and percussion duet. In 1989 I graduated from UCC and spent the following two years studying for an MFA in World Percussion at the California Institute of the Arts (CalArts) in Los Angeles. When I returned to Cork in 1992 I began teaching classes in Indian, Javanese and west African musics at UCC on a part-time basis, and Mícheál and I took to playing together again regularly.[43] At this time, Mícheál suggested that we co-compose a piece of music to perform at our concerts. I never asked him what moved him to propose the co-creation of a new piece. Perhaps it was his way of acknowledging a shift in our relationship, a marking of my transition from student to junior colleague, and a desire to find another point of connection in our musical relationship to celebrate that. Whatever his motivation, I was excited by the invitation to meet him, for the first time, in the space of composition, and it led to the making of *(must be more) Crispy*, one of only two pieces of music that we co-composed.[44]

At CalArts I had taken lessons on the tabla and had become familiar with north Indian drum language, a system of spoken mnemonic syllables (or *bols*) that can be used to 'speak' and memorise complex rhythm patterns.

Michael (Mícheál) (r) with mother Nellie and brother John, 1950s.

Mícheál, Clonmel Pipe Band, 1960s.

Mícheál (r) with The Sea Cliffs, 1960s.

The Castle Stars showband with Mícheál's godfather Tony O'Keeffe (l) next to Mícheál, 1960s.

Mícheál as a student in UCC (back row, r), 1970s.

With Nóirín Ní Riain and Pangur Bán, 1970s.

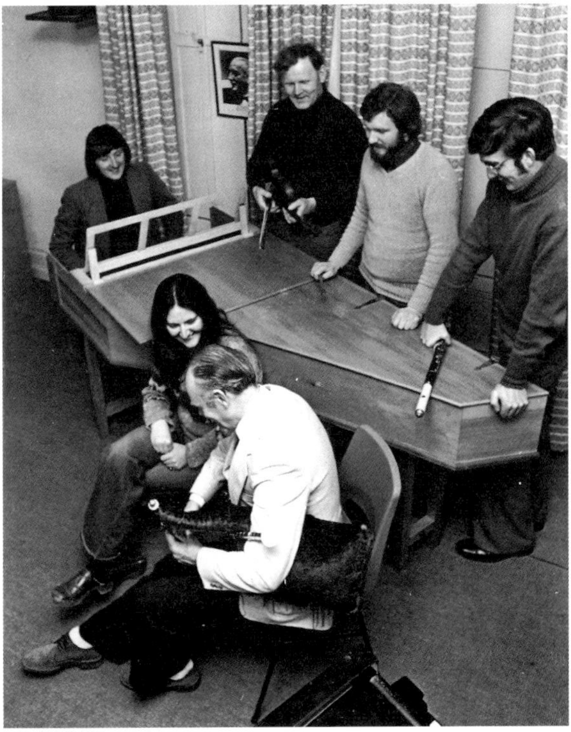

With Nóirín Ní Riain and Tiompán, 1970s.

Mícheál (r) with mother Nellie and brother John.

With father Ambrose.

Aloys Fleischmann (front row, centre) with Mícheál and Nóirín (back row, r) and class at graduation, UCC, 1972.

Mícheál in office in UCC, 1970s.

'Across the Waters', Éigse na Laoi, Triskel Arts Centre, Cork, with musicians Billy and Julia Clifford, 1994. PHOTOGRAPHER: TONY KEARNS

With The Chieftains, UCC.
PHOTOGRAPHER: TONY PERROTT

Mícheál, Nóirín, Eoin (on bike) and Mícheál 'Moley'.

With Mel Mercier and Colm Murphy, publicity photo, *The Dolphin's Way*, 1987.

Teachers' Club, Dublin. PHOTOGRAPHER: COLM HENRY

While I had three wonderful tabla teachers at CalArts – the master tabla players Pandit Taranath Rao and Pandit Swapan Chaudhuri, and my drumming mentor John Bergamo – I was a novice player. I was a more competent and experienced exponent of bodhrán playing, more entrained and tuned in to the pulse and rolling dance rhythms of Irish traditional music. My encounters at CalArts with north Indian rhythms, and other sophisticated percussion traditions from south India, Ghana and Java, had, however, brought me into an embodied engagement with an extensive body of complex drumming practices and their associated repertoires of rhythm patterns and compositions. Sitting cross-legged on the floor, with my hands on the tabla drums, I was plugged into a multi-dimensional matrix of rhythmic structures and compositions, and I chose to draw on this new knowledge to create the rhythmic structure and phrases of 'Crispy'.

Over a period of weeks I applied the common Indian rhythm compositional methods of reduction, expansion and repetition to some basic combinations of tabla strokes to form longer patterns or phrases. In this way, the four-beat rhythmic cell '*Tiri Kita Dha* __' expanded to become the fourteen-beat phrase 'Tiri *Kita Dha* __, *Dha Tiri Kita Dha* __, *Dha Dha Tiri Kita Dha*'. This pattern emerged as the signature phrase of 'Crispy'. It also turned out to contain the rhythmic DNA of the composition, with almost all of the materials generated from combinations and permutations of its cells.

The rhythm composition I eventually brought back to Mícheál was in the form of a chorus and variations. I suggested that we call it *(must be more) Crispy*, a catchphrase made popular by my friend Dan Morris, a CalArts student, who quoted it, somewhat mischievously, from his south Indian percussion teacher Poovalur Sriji, whose feedback to him on his efforts to master the small lizard-skin frame drum, known as *kanjira*, often included the phrase 'very good, Dan, but must be more crispy'. Mícheál chose to learn the rhythms by playing them on the *mbira*, and from there he transposed them onto the piano, where they took on a melodic and harmonic guise. Meanwhile, I set about transposing the tabla rhythms onto the bodhrán, a process that required some innovation in my approach to the instrument, specifically the development of new bodhrán sticking patterns to articulate the asymmetrical rhythms that had quite naturally fallen under my fingers on the tabla.

We played 'Crispy' often over the next twenty years and more. We always enjoyed telling the audience how we made it together and we loved to invite them to join us in whispering the word 'crispy' in the middle of the chorus:

Mícheál: 'It goes something like this …'
Mel: 'Tiri Kita Dha __, Dha Tiri Kita Dha __, Dha Dha Tiri Kita Dha,
Tiri Kita Dha __, Dha Tiri Kita Dha __, Dha Dha Tiri Kita Dha,
Tiri Kita Dhin …'
Mícheál and Mel: 'Crispy.'

And then we hurtled through it, riding the exhilarating rollercoaster twist and turn, climb and drop of its hybrid asymmetrical rhythms, revelling in the shared, sublime thrill of it. I am not sure that we ever quite mastered the performance of it, but perhaps that's the point. Encoded with our shared pulse, and our friendship, it holds a special place in our playhouse, the memory palace of our lifelong duet.

18

The Scholar's Harvest Home: Mícheál Ó Súilleabháin and the student experience of traditional music at third level

Sandra Joyce

Sandra Joyce, singer and bodhrán player, is executive dean, Faculty of Arts, Humanities and Social Sciences, University of Limerick. She was director of the Irish World Academy of Music and Dance, 2013–22. With Mícheál Ó Súilleabháin and Niall Keegan, she has been central to the development of traditional music degrees at UL.

Introduction

Mícheál Ó Súilleabháin was a seminal figure in many aspects of Irish culture, not least as a composer, academic, performer and writer. However, he was also an inspirational teacher, someone who impacted the learning experience of students in profound ways. This paper explores his role as educator in a third-level context, and specifically his influence on the student body while he was a lecturer at University College Cork (UCC) from 1975 to '93. Ó Súilleabháin's transformational pedagogical contributions have been discussed in different contexts, including recently in Jack Talty's work.[1] This paper builds on past literature, and provides perspectives through an ethnographic and auto-ethnographic approach, featuring my own recollections as well as interviews with fellow students from their time as students of music at UCC in the mid- to late 1980s. The unique environment that Ó Súilleabháin created and nurtured, and which developed as a result of his influence, included instrumental, dance and song classes; weekly pub sessions; weekly live performances on campus; festivals; lectures from visiting lecturers, broadcasters and performers.

In short, Mícheál had a profound impact on the way traditional music was located at the university, working as a two-way conduit between the traditional music community and the institution. The results of this were manifold, and included the opening up of access for traditional musicians to study music at third level, as well as the drawing of musicians of other genres to traditional music. Focusing on the student experience, the paper assesses the impact on the lives and career choices of those who studied with Mícheál at this time. It asserts his position as one of the most important educators in the history of Irish traditional music, as well as any context in which musics meet in an institutional setting.

The title of this paper references 'The Scholar' and 'Harvest Home', two well-known tunes in the Irish tradition. The term 'Harvest Home' can mean a gathering or a festival held when the harvest has been completed, and I will return to this idea towards the end of the paper. 'The Scholars' was also the name of a bar close to the Music Department in UCC where there were vibrant and exciting music sessions during the time when I studied and Mícheál worked there. The combination of the names of the tunes in this context therefore brings together many themes explored in this paper, including the ways Mícheál inspired students as an educator, the environment he created for traditional music in UCC at that time, and the legacy he has left.

When asked to consider contributing to this volume, I was inspired to reach out to fellow students from my time at UCC to investigate their experiences and to explore how they would articulate Mícheál's influence.[2] As someone who worked with him for a considerable time at UL, it was important to me to reach out to those who had taken different paths, both within and outside of music. I contacted thirteen people who I knew personally from my own time at the Department of Music at UCC to progress this paper. I deliberately chose not to speak to people who had worked with Mícheál at UL, as I was anxious to gain the perspectives of those graduates who have gone on to work in different contexts, to gain an insight into the impact, if any, that studying with Mícheál had on their subsequent musical careers both in and outside of academia, as well as in their formal music teaching and performance.

I asked four main questions of the informants:

1) What is your memory of being a student in the Music Department, UCC? What genre(s) of music did you particularly engage with prior to coming to UCC?
2) What is your memory of Mícheál Ó Súilleabháin as an educator and/or performer from that time?
3) What do you believe Mícheál's impact was on the Music Department at that time?

4) What, if any, impact has studying with Ó Súilleabháin had on your subsequent musical career?

I randomly assigned each respondent with a number from one to thirteen, which is given beside the quotes included. This paper will undoubtedly be critiqued because of its overly positive viewpoint, but it is reflective of the responses I received from former students who came from a variety of music, social and geographical backgrounds. The fact that these responses were overwhelmingly favourable could, of course, be partly due to feelings of nostalgia for an important formative time in the participants' lives, as most were in their late teens/early twenties at that time. It may also reflect the fact that the informants were aware that I had worked with Mícheál for many years and may have felt that negative responses would not have been welcome. However, it is significant that they spoke of Mícheál's influence in such positive terms in this context.

The Scholar(s)

When I reflect on my time as a student of music in UCC, I certainly have mixed feelings. Like many people in their late teens/early twenties, I had many insecurities and painfully remember my immaturity at that time, alongside the many great times I and my fellow students had in terms of musical development, friendship and opportunity. As Heewon Chang states: 'Confessional/self-critical/self-evaluative writing tends to expose self – inequities, problems or troubles – providing a vehicle through which self-narrators work to come to resolution or self-learning.'[3] Chang also says that 'autoethnography is an excellent vehicle through which researchers come to understand themselves and others'.[4] In hindsight, and as has been expressed in the interviews I did for this paper, many of us believe that there was something exceptional happening in terms of traditional music at UCC in the mid- to late 1980s. Traditional music was becoming important, possibly the most important and vibrant of the musics studied and reflected in the curriculum. This was due to a variety of factors, including an influx of traditional musicians into the student community, a vibrant and active Irish Traditional Music Society and, of course, the prominence and influence of Mícheál Ó Súilleabháin. As two of my informants stated:

> Of course, at the time I didn't realise the ground-breaking transformations that were happening in terms of traditional music within higher education and in terms of the new synergies happening within Cork city as what was happening on Western Road began to seep out into

> the town.[5] I was – with my fellow students – caught up in being part of something that was bigger than any of us really knew or imagined! (Informant No. 4)

> A lot happened in that period [in UCC Music Department] that changed things forever. (Informant No. 3)

Many of the people studying music at that time in UCC have subsequently greatly contributed to diverse aspects of music, such as education (teaching in second- or third-level contexts); as influential professional musicians; or by holding positions in important national music organisations.

It is important to note that UCC Music Department had a long and distinguished association with the teaching of traditional music that stretched back to the early twentieth century.[6] As Talty notes:

> The music department at UCC is intrinsically linked to the story of the development of Irish traditional music pedagogy in Irish higher education. … Although the institution has been closely associated with Irish traditional music studies and seminal figures such as Seán Ó Riada, traditional musicians were once ineligible to audition for the BMus programme unless they performed Western classical music on an appropriate instrument associated with the Western classical tradition. It was not until Mícheál Ó Súilleabháin's tenure at UCC that traditional music, song, and dance became accepted as performance options, firstly for students who had gained access to music at UCC through classical music performance, and subsequently, for students whose primary or only performance medium was Irish traditional music, song, or dance.[7]

This is supported by a number of my informants, who also noted the importance of the legacy of Seán Ó Riada in terms of Mícheál's developments at UCC. For example:

> I think for those who were interested in traditional music before they got there he validated their decision to come to UCC; he certainly did that for me. For those who weren't particularly interested in traditional music before they got there (or perhaps had simply not been in a context where it was part of their musical experience), he opened a door to a whole other world. Notwithstanding Ó Riada and Fleischmann's interests during their time in UCC, Mícheál, in my view, was the key figure in creating parity of esteem for traditional music and traditional musicians

> not just in UCC but at other institutions as they were compelled to respond to what was happening in UCC and his influence there. Through strategic curriculum development and embedding traditional music in the UCC Music Department he transformed third-level music education in Ireland. (Informant No. 1)

Two of my informants were directly inspired to study music at UCC as traditional musicians because of the environment Mícheál had created. One puts it succinctly: 'I chose UCC purely because of the traditional music element of the course' (Informant No. 9). This environment included an exciting series of weekly lunchtime concerts featuring many nationally and locally renowned musicians, as well as the opportunity to engage with weekly tutorials in traditional music, song and/or dance. These tutorials are described by the same informant as having 'opened up Irish music to everyone'. Another graduate, who came primarily from a classical music background prior to studying in UCC, states that she joined set dancing lessons by the dancing teacher Joe O'Donovan, which 'integrated [her] into the trad world and was a social outlet as well as being a chosen activity' (Informant No. 6).

Despite the fact that they came from diverse musical backgrounds, all informants referred to traditional music in the context of Mícheál's influence on them in their time at UCC Music Department, as well as subsequently. Of the thirteen informants, five described themselves as primarily classical musicians before coming to study at UCC, with a further four describing themselves as coming from mixed musical backgrounds which didn't really include traditional music (for example, one of these informants described Irish ballads as being one of three genres he engaged with). The impact of this cannot be overstated. I was one of those who arrived at UCC with what I believed was a scanty knowledge of traditional music, even though reflection has revealed to me that it was a great part of my soundscape when growing up in Tuam, County Galway. For example, I studied harp for many years at the Presentation Convent, as well as limited exposure to the tin whistle and Irish dancing. But it was Mícheál who opened up the world of traditional music for me, who validated it as an area not just worthy of study but also amplified its importance and gave it an equal status to other forms of music. This is something which influenced all my subsequent life choices, and enhanced my life in so many ways, as I went on to work in traditional music at university level – and I was not alone in this. As my informants noted:

> He lived and breathed the tradition so much so that it was impossible not to be drawn in. I had never given trad much thought before but he elevated this music for us and made us proud of our heritage. (Informant No. 5)

Mícheál created an amazing 'clique'/merry band of trad players – I always felt like they were a special crew when I was there – and I think that it was all Mícheál-generated. There was a real buzz about the trad heads there. It was a really special time for trad music – there were so many future influential musicians in UCC in my day that I felt like I was there for a really special time in the history of the Music Department, even though I wasn't part of the trad set myself. (Informant No. 7)

Another writes:

> I remember Mícheál's energy as an educator. He loved what he did and wanted you to love it too. He loved to play piano and punctuated his lessons with dashes of music to prove a point, to strengthen a point made, just to play. I was amazed to hear Irish traditional pieces being played on the piano. He encouraged a love of Irish traditional music, a genre I had little knowledge of. I was also introduced to other world music through his classes. He swept you along with his enthusiasm and his love of music. (Informant No. 12)

Mícheál's ability to draw people towards traditional music, particularly through performance, came through strongly from the responses, as can be seen in the quotes above.

However, a number of informants also credit Mícheál with expanding and developing the curriculum, and broadening it in terms of the introduction of ethnomusicology. Again, this is something which greatly affected me on a personal and professional level, and which broadened and diversified perspectives for those studying many musics at that time, including traditional music:

> Suddenly I found that ethnomusicology was a large area of my studies. I had never heard of it, nor did I know anything about it prior to showing up in Cork and getting my class schedule! I did not appreciate at the time what a rare and special opportunity it was, or that I had accidentally fallen into one of the very few places in Europe, let alone the world, that one could study in that area at an academic level. (Informant No. 10)

> Mícheál's ethnomusicological approach contextualised the discussion in a world-music space and opened up our frame of reference. (Informant No. 9)

Performance was an important part of Mícheál's efficacy as an educator. He understood and valued the integration of performance into the curriculum, as already discussed. But his personal prowess as a performer and his growing profile were an inspiration.

> *The Dolphin's Way* came out in our earlier days in UCC and we were gobsmacked: his rhythm, his harmonic palette, his ability to improvise on a melody, his ease in different genres and his ability to weave them into Irish music whilst retaining its essence. (Informant No. 9)

As well as performing in more formal contexts – such as in what one person describes as a 'spellbinding performance' in the Aula Maxima in UCC with 'new student' and longtime collaborator Mel Mercier (as referred to by Informant No. 2), Mícheál also frequented traditional music sessions in venues such as the Rockview Bar, College Road. I regularly attended these sessions and they were high-energy, exciting and infectious events, driven by the rhythm and flow of the music as well as the dynamism of the atmosphere. I remember that Mícheál mainly played the ukulele in these sessions – another respondent talks of him also playing the 'African *mbira* thumb piano and his Irish flute' (Informant No. 2). This connected him to the student body on an important social and participatory level, and undoubtedly influenced his popularity and efficacy as a lecturer who in a very real way embodied the music practice he was speaking about in class. His method of teaching has also been described by one graduate as a performance: 'The lectures were kind of a performance … I came out of [a lecture by Mícheál] the way you might come out after a gig … you'd have had some moment of revelation or something, and the putting across of things was a sort of a performance in itself' (Informant No. 3).

Harry White writes of 'the reanimation of Ó Riada's productive cult of musical personality so effectively espoused by Mícheál Ó Súilleabháin'.[8] Although I would have some reservations about this reference, given the potential negative political connotations around the term 'cult of personality',[9] his point is relevant to the way Mícheál's influence is articulated in the responses to my interview questions from this diverse group of people. There is no doubting the respect and gratitude for Mícheál which came through in all the responses – his generous and open personality is something that many informants referred to directly. As one states:

> Mícheál took a huge personal interest in his students. I loved his classes, I was particularly impressed by his open mind and his open heart to those who did not come from a pure Irish music background; he saw interest, he saw an appetite, he saw he could bridge the gap between my world (classical) and the world I wanted to be part of [traditional music]. (Informant No. 6)

Another writes:

> I remember him to be very dynamic, positive, encouraging and enthusiastic. He related very well to the students, looking out for them, guiding them and going out of his way at times to help them … Mícheál was extremely generous, dedicated, inspirational and creative as an educator. He brought the subject to life. He was very good-humoured and his passion for the subject was infectious. For someone who was so talented and gifted he was very down to earth and approachable. (Informant No. 8)

In their 2018 article on collegiate band, choir and orchestra members' preferred teacher interpersonal behaviours, Royston and Fischer state: 'When asked to describe effective music teachers, the students' responses included descriptors such as warm, caring, friendly, personable, encouraging, and inspirational.'[10] Many of these words came through in the responses to the questions I posed for this paper. One contributor's articulate contribution particularly resonated with me:

> Mícheál … was not an educator who saw his role as simply transferring his knowledge onto his students; he was all about creating the moments to allow each of us to dig deep, rise to the challenge, and certainly in my own case, surprise myself! He could always see more potential in me (and all of his students) way beyond what I could see, at that moment, in myself. And he always found the right task or opportunity or invitation to allow each one of us to discover and realise that potential within ourselves. He certainly never saw his role as spoonfeeding his learners full of facts. Instead, he was curious about each individual's potential and saw his role as being about encouraging that, of drawing it out, of setting the conditions to allow us to find ourselves. (Informant No. 4)

I personally benefited from Mícheál's ability to inspire confidence in his students as well as those who worked with him to organise festivals and other events that now seem extraordinary, and this was something he carried into his work well beyond his time in UCC. Many respondents articulated similar sentiments:

> What I can say with confidence is that Mícheál was consistently encouraging and challenging in equal parts. For me, he created opportunities that I simply would not have had as an undergraduate otherwise in terms of developing intellectually, musically and indeed gaining professional skills (though I didn't recognise them as such at the time). (Informant No. 1)

Yet another gave a perspective that I like to think Mícheál would have been particularly proud of, especially in terms of his philosophy in establishing the Irish World Academy of Music and Dance at UL:

> Mícheál brought a very uniquely Irish perspective to the programme at UCC by (a) his presence and personality and (b) his advocacy for including young traditional musicians alongside classical musicians at the academic level. I recall a gradual breaking down of some of the prejudices between the two as we [were] all learning to respect and appreciate the value of each over time. There was an eventual sense of 'we're all in this together' that I experienced. (Informant No. 10)

The equal honouring of diverse musical and dance practices and the bringing together of these energies in the innovative programmes at the Irish World Academy was something that he achieved to great success when he moved from UCC to UL in 1994. It is very important to note that Mícheál's focus on traditional music was never at the expense of other musics. Marie McCarthy speaks of the late twentieth century when '[p]luralism and heterogeneity began to take precedence over the narrow, essentialist view of Irishness as the basis for a cultural ideology'.[11] Mícheál brought native Irish culture into the institution on an equal footing with other musics while maintaining the plurality and global engagement of that tradition. 'I believe that Mícheál was all about "fusion". His fusion of Irish traditional and classical music, developed more by his unique style of piano playing, was such an important part of my studies. He showed me that all genres of music are equal' (Informant No. 13).

Another striking aspect of this research was the fact that all respondents spoke positively of the impact that Mícheál's role as educator had on them in their subsequent career and life choices. One person, who has forged a career outside of music but who has continued to engage with choral singing, states: 'Mícheál's influence has most certainly stayed with me during my musical life. It was a privilege to have had the opportunity to study under him during his time at UCC' (Informant No. 11).

Others referred directly to the way he integrated performance into his classes: 'I am a music teacher in a secondary school. I would hope that I have reached the students I have taught, helped them, supported them, passed on the interest in the way I was taught by Mícheál' (Informant No. 8). But perhaps the greatest legacy for this group is, again, the way he endowed his students who had little or no experience of traditional music with the knowledge and confidence to engage with this tradition. One respondent, who works as a church musician outside of Ireland, states:

> My experience at UCC with Mícheál and the broad nature of the curriculum there that was influenced by him equipped me to work with all these different levels and abilities of musician, volunteer and professional, with a confidence and understanding, and a lack of prejudice for one approach or another, that I do not think I would otherwise have. ... Mícheál taught me that while knowledge and understanding are invaluable, the only real way to enter the soul of any type of music is to at least attempt to play it. This has been a fundamental aspect of my work with musicians (especially the young) during my career in church music. (Informant No. 10)

Another writes: 'Studying with Ó Súilleabháin opened up to me the world of Irish traditional music' (Informant No. 8). Others contributed the following:

> Even now as a teacher of twenty-nine years I still tell my students about him and what a thrill it was to be witness to his genius in the classroom. I really never liked trad before I met Mícheál and so he brought me into the world of traditional music and made me love it. (Informant No. 7)

> It gave me a greater respect for our Irish traditional music genre. I got my introduction to Irish traditional music at UCC, a greater love of Irish culture which strengthened when I left Ireland to live abroad. I had a bit more understanding and a lot more respect for Irish music and culture. I still loved telling people he had been one of my lecturers. (Informant No. 12)

Conclusion: Harvest Home

This paper touches on the influence and impact of Mícheál Ó Súilleabháin on some of those studying music at UCC in the 1980s. It is hard for me to describe the effects that his energy, his insights into traditional music and his musical prowess had on me as a young person navigating their way in the strange and intimidating environment of third-level music education at that time. As has strongly come through in the responses, Mícheál greatly influenced the student experience by creating a dynamic and exciting environment, full of opportunity and possibility. Some of the informants' statements reflect more of a professional outlook while others are more personal. But all those interviewed stated that studying with Mícheál shaped them in many different ways, and most still draw on his recordings and/or his teaching ethos in their current careers.

One of his great successes was creating the space for and attracting established traditional musicians to UCC, but also, and perhaps more importantly, creating an environment inclusive of those for whom traditional music was a relatively new experience. By igniting interest in traditional music, he gave it a respect and status that we, as students, benefited from and participated in on many levels. His personal engagement and dynamic personality was a potent part of the success of his student engagement. He didn't just impact music in UCC; he impacted the landscape and development of music and dance education across third level in Ireland, and internationally. His passion for the parity of esteem of different arts practices is something which I know has inspired colleagues working in diverse institutions across the world.

Returning to the title of this paper, which has been inspired by the tunes 'The Scholar' and 'Harvest Home', seems fitting at this stage. My primary memory of Mícheál Ó Súilleabháin will always be his gathering and drawing people of varied social and cultural backgrounds to him – his mere presence was a celebration for most people. His legacy is indeed an abundant harvest, which continues to yield many riches. I will leave the final words on this to my informants:

> Mícheál is the primary reason for my subsequent music career … [he] instilled a belief in the possible. … What he taught me musically could not be put into words. … I am forever indebted. (Informant No. 9)

> Not only do I feel privileged to have studied with him but indebted to him for helping me pursue the career path I have taken. In the course of any lifetime, many people will cross your path but it is not every day you

meet someone who is as inspirational, as generous and as encouraging as he was. I feel very lucky to have met him and this view I know is shared by many. (Informant No. 8)

Studying music with Mícheál has had a huge impact on my career. I'm still doing now at fifty years of age what I learnt to do under his tutelage and that is testament to the man. (Informant No. 2)

So much of what's happened in the academic research side of Irish traditional music goes back to that time. … The presence of traditional music possibly in all the universities in Ireland now is another thing that's essentially entirely down to him, and the students that came out of there … (Informant No. 3)

Since 1987, his guiding hand, listening ear and gentle nudging has absolutely shaped everything I have done – whether consciously or subconsciously on my part. To be honest, even though he is not with us now, I kind of feel that he still is – and I find myself often taking a moment to consider what Mícheál would advise me about this or that. I am so grateful for every minute that I got to have with him as my teacher and mentor. And I think that he will continue to shape my musical path for a long time still to come. (Informant No. 4)

19
Francesco Walks: A personal reflection
Liz Doherty

Fiddle player Liz Doherty is founder and director of I Teach Trad: Professional development for Irish traditional music teachers. *A national teaching fellow, she lectured at UCC (1994–2000) and Ulster University (2007–20). She published* The Cape Breton Fiddle Companion *in 2015 having completed her PhD on the topic at UL.*

Dear Francie,

How I laughed out loud when you started signing emails and cards as Mícheál a.k.a. Francie. This was your nod to Francie Jimmy Annie, the wandering violinist (modelled on the baroque composer Francesco Geminiani) whom you imagined leaving Dublin and travelling to Donegal, encountering traditional fiddlers along the way and engaging in colourful musical duels. 'Francesco Walks' – the piece that you composed to celebrate Francie's journey – was commissioned for the Ar Ais Arís festival in Buncrana in 2007. What a performance that was! A rabble of local musicians processing through a slightly bewildered audience, the string ensemble on stage, yourself positioned in the centre with harpsichord and piano – between the two worlds; the baroque strings presenting, the trad tunes being stated, and then the rising energy as the musical conversation between the two began in earnest. Remember that hair-rising-on-the-back-of-the-neck moment when Grace Toland put her full vocal power behind the words 'my Buncrana'? You looked over at me – that knowing look that seemed to say, 'That's it, right there, that's what we were looking for!'

You were *so* fond of Francie Jimmy Annie. You imagined that piece in so many ways. A scaled-back version for performances with the RTÉ Concert Orchestra, included as part of the *Lumen i Luimneach* concert, and later with the RTÉ National Symphony Orchestra on a memorable June night in the National Concert Hall in 2018. There were plans for a tour with the Irish Baroque Orchestra. And the dream – the whole theatrical stage version. 'Francesco is going to walk again and again,' you said.

It's interesting now, looking back, that as well as the absolute musical thrill of being part of a live performance with you, 'Francesco' re-ignited the mentoring relationship that I was so privileged to have experienced with you for over thirty years. While this had been a constant since 1987, the more frequent conversations we were having around 'Francesco' meant that you were tuned in to some current decisions that I was grappling with around my academic career. You encouraged me and challenged me. You helped me to dig deep, to believe in myself and to take big action. And those conversations still ring in my ears: 'Never think small, imagine the possibilities, start big … and close the loop. Do the work. Create the magic. Change is OK. Close the loop. Move on to the next possibility. Seek out the next opportunity. Close the loop.'

You were this huge magnetic force that first of all drew me from Donegal to UCC where, during that period of the late 1980s–early 1990s, there was a new energy being created between traditional music and academic life. You generated spark after spark, left each one out there burning, and anyone who wished to do so was invited to pick them up and see where they would lead them. Cape Breton was one such spark that I couldn't wait to run with. I remember the afternoon when you called me into your office to discuss my two-week absence from class. I had been off on a tour of Scotland with a group of Donegal fiddlers – so was justifying myself by waxing lyrical about a Scottish fiddler I had met called Alasdair Fraser, who was fascinated by these amazing tunes from a place called Cape Breton. You (time-efficient as always) were opening a pile of mail as you were listening to me, and literally, out of one of the envelopes fell a cassette tape of a young Cape Breton fiddler, Natalie MacMaster. You handed it over to me, invited me to go off, listen to it and report back at a later stage with more insights into this fiddle tradition. A couple of years later, on the eve of me embarking on a HDip, you clearly sensed my lack of enthusiasm for the prospect and asked me, 'If you could do anything at all for the next year, what would you do?' And once I replied that I would go to Cape Breton, that was it. I was going to Cape Breton. You were on the phone then and there, reaching out, opening the door … and believing (far more than I was) that I would walk through it.

You used to laugh and call Cape Breton my Tír na nÓg. And, you know something? That is exactly what it is to me to this day. Remember the Cape Breton Éigse na Laoi? Of course, the whole five of those festivals were special. And what a model! Again, you had that vision … make magic happen … and close the loop. The five-year programme was scoped out. And no matter how brilliantly it was going, five years was all it was going to be. You never wavered on that. Even when everybody else would have loved it to have run for another five years! The first Éigse, in 1991, was Fiddlesticks, a celebration of Donegal and Shetland fiddle music. That was the first time I was ever part of a recording. What an opportunity. And then, in 1993, we got to bring Cape Breton to Cork. Talk about epic! I'll never forget going to the airport, supposedly to pick up the sixteen invited musicians and dancers. I swear, I thought that plane would never empty! They kept emerging … Cape Bretoners and Cape Bretoners living in Boston. The excitement and the energy was palpable. Something magic was happening. And the memories! Jerry Holland and Hilda Chiasson playing the most driving set in the Aula Max, the bemused Irish audience reactions to the spontaneous applause mid-tune as a step dancer showed a particularly nimble step – before joining in whole-heartedly, Dwayne Coté and Seán Maguire having a musical duel backstage in City Hall, and the marathon Ireland–Cape Breton dance off down in the Mardyke. We were all caught up in the magic and the energy of the moment. And how lucky were we that you had the vision to have this all captured for a recording. That Nimbus CD tells such an amazing story – indeed it reminds everyone of their own stories, their own memories, of that special time. For me, it was another moment where you invited me to move out of my comfort zone, to step up, programme the event, secure the funding, make it happen. You opened the door, and I walked through.

For all the doors that you opened for me. For believing that I could – and would – walk through them. And for being there to counsel, encourage and challenge. Thank you. I am forever grateful.

Liz D.

20
A Creative Process: Mícheál Ó Súilleabháin at UCC

Niall Vallely

Born in Armagh in 1970, Niall Vallely has established himself as one of Ireland's most significant musicians and composers. Niall has toured throughout the world, recorded on over fifty albums, and his compositions have been recorded on more than 100 albums. He earned a BMus and PhD in music from University College Cork.

Embarking on a music degree in University College Cork (UCC) in 1988 I really had no idea of the impact Mícheál Ó Súilleabháin would have on my life as a musician. However, I did start to realise quickly that I had arrived in a time and place where something significant was happening. Although the study of Irish traditional music had been pursued at the Department of Music at UCC since the early twentieth century, this was a point in time where it had reached a critical mass and, in many ways, took centre-stage.

In his lectures Mícheál introduced a way of talking about traditional music that took it seriously and put it in a historical and global context that respected its deep intrinsic worth as music. He had no fear of intellectualising traditional music because he knew it was important. At the same time he ensured that the study of the music was rooted in practical music-making. For those of us who had grown up with traditional music we learned a way of articulating what we already knew as well as a way of interrogating the received wisdom about the music. But everything always came back to playing and performing and listening – the traditional ways of passing on traditional music. The students who were new to traditional music learned to play, sing and dance as well as learning the history, structure and theory of the music. Mícheál assembled a team of tutors that ensured that students were continually connected to the core of the music, and then he brought in the cream of traditional performers to inspire us in weekly performances. He fostered an atmosphere of creativity around traditional music. He didn't portray the music in a purely academic way that might have focused on preserving the past glories of the tradition; rather he saw what we were all doing as part of a vital and living music culture.

Mícheál's creativity extended beyond his own performance and composition. He simply had a creative way of being. He created an atmosphere in the Music Department where traditional music was not only acceptable, it was valued. He created a scene which enabled the students' own creativity and musical curiosity to flourish. He created festivals, concerts, sessions, recordings. He created an interest in the music among students who had never been exposed to it before and he created a self-confidence among the traditional musicians that maybe hadn't been encouraged before. Mícheál empowered the students in both creative and practical ways. He was constantly coming up with schemes and ideas which, once he had set the ball rolling, the students would become deeply involved in putting into action. Events such as the weekly Seomra Caidrimh recitals and the Éigse na Laoi festivals were initiated by Mícheál and then developed into student-led events. Students like myself were not alone exposed to the best of traditional music performances at these events but we got a first taste of event management: booking performers; looking for sponsorship; liaising with venues, with the college authorities, the Arts Council, the city council etc; booking sound engineers; designing posters and programmes and dozens of other jobs. We were often thrown into the deep end but gained an introduction to a whole other side of the music industry that has stood many of us in good stead. Mícheál approached the organisation of events in a creative way also. Éigse na Laoi, in particular, the five-festival series that ran from 1991 to 1995, couldn't be just another music festival. He always had a vision for something that would be of greater significance than what might be apparent on the surface. These festivals stood apart in their effort to reimagine how a traditional music festival might work. They helped to cement a long-lasting connection between the university and the wider traditional music community as well as connecting with the people of Cork city in a way that college events seldom did. Mícheál also ensured that the festivals were documented with a series of high-quality recordings that not only continue to make a deep artistic impression but also helped fund a series of initiatives such as the Irish Traditional Music Archive and archival projects in England and Cape Breton.

Mícheál seemed to be able to effortlessly switch between lecturing, performing, composing, playing the ukulele and *mbira* in a session, making TV programmes, dealing with the college authorities, recording albums. His enthusiasm for music was a constant. He created a whirlwind of musical activity and he brought us all along in his wake. He was constantly coming up with new schemes and ideas. The range of music-making we were involved in as students was extraordinary: from the avant-garde recording and performance of *Eklego* through performances of Mícheál's own music from his albums *Oileán* and *Casadh* to the anarchic 'Johnny Patterson's Travelling Circus'.

Mícheál cared about Irish traditional music and its value in the world of music. He espoused a broad and universal outlook on music that valued the creators and performers of the music past and present. He had a vision of a situation where Irish traditional music would stand on an equal footing with all the other musics in the academic setting. Previously, traditional music, if it wasn't ignored entirely, was at best an optional extra within Irish university music departments. 'Music' actually meant 'western art music', and other types of music needed a qualifying adjective. Nowadays all the Irish universities have some element of traditional music in their music degrees and UCC has actually realised that vision of valuing all musics equally.

Mícheál was a huge inspiration to me personally as a musician, performer, composer, academic and educator. He was also an inspirational figure to many other students in Cork at that time and the impact of his influence can still be felt through their work as performers and composers, teachers, academics and administrators. He was always incredibly supportive of his former students and, I think, proud of their achievements. Right from the beginning of my career as a performer with the band Nomos, his encouragement and backing were incredibly important not least through playing on our first album. In 1999 he launched my first solo album and later wrote an introduction for my book of tunes, *Malfunction Junction*. I particularly felt this support when I started to compose music and he conducted the premiere performance of my first major composition *Flight/ Imeacht*. He was always interested, and in our final conversation he was much more keen to talk about my upcoming *Concertina Concerto* than about himself. Mícheál changed the course of my musical life and created ripple effects in Irish music that will be felt for generations to come.

21
'The Dolphin's Way': Mícheál Ó Súilleabháin's pioneering work at the Department of Music, University College Cork (1975–93)

Mary Mitchell-Ingoldsby

Mary Mitchell-Ingoldsby is a lecturer in Irish traditional music at the Department of Music, University College Cork where she also manages the department's Traditional Music Archive and is organiser/co-editor of the Ó Riada Memorial Lecture Series. An uilleann piper, music collector and a performer, she has published and performed extensively.

In 1975, Mícheál Ó Súilleabháin was appointed full-time lecturer in music, with responsibility for Irish traditional music, at the Department of Music, University College Cork (UCC). This was a position he held for the following eighteen years and during his tenure he was appointed senior lecturer and head of department. He was an innovative and inspirational teacher and leader who displayed enormous creativity, vision and energy in all that he did, most particularly in the area of Irish traditional music. He created his own distinctive voice within that tradition and he revolutionised the teaching of Irish traditional music in the department and ultimately at third-level institutions. While his teaching was innovative, he also kept a keen eye on the past and on the great tradition-bearers of Irish traditional music.

The Department of Music, UCC has a rich history in the area of Irish traditional music stretching back 100 years to 1922, when it became the first university in Ireland and arguably in Europe to include the traditional music of its own country as part of its music degree curriculum. It has remained an integral part of the music degree at UCC ever since. Earlier appointees in this area were Carl Hardebeck (1922–3), Dr Annie Patterson (1923–34), Seán Neeson (1934–62)[1] and Seán Ó Riada (1963–71).[2] Tomás Ó Canainn (1971–5) was appointed on a part-time basis as he was already lecturing at UCC's Department of Engineering. Mícheál Ó Súilleabháin arrived in the middle of that 100-year history, initially as a student and later as a member of staff shortly after graduating. He subsequently contributed enormously to the development of the Irish traditional music curriculum and to the BA and BMus degrees in general, together with postgraduate studies at UCC. This paper will explore many of these exciting developments.

Performance courses in Irish traditional music

As a member of staff Mícheál quickly achieved an impressive number of firsts for the department and the university. One of his early innovations was the introduction of Irish traditional music performance courses. As most music students at UCC up to the mid-1980s came from a western art music background, Seán Ó Riada in the 1960s decided that all students should play traditional music on a traditional instrument (usually a slow air and a dance tune) as part of the Irish traditional music component of the BA and BMus degree courses, and this was in itself a revolutionary idea.[3] In the first year of his appointment Mícheál took this idea further and invited the highly respected Cork uilleann piper, teacher and chairman of the Cork Pipers' Club, Mícheál Ó Riabhaigh, to teach whistle to the undergraduate music students, thereby becoming the department's first tutor of Irish traditional music performance. These courses were a first for any university in Ireland. Shortly afterwards fiddle classes were organised and music graduate and engineer Matt Cranitch was appointed as tutor. This part of the course proved very successful and popular and, although it was only initially offered to first-year students, by the mid-1980s this was extended to include second-, third- and later fourth-year students. In 1983, when Matt Cranitch moved to another position, Mícheál engaged the highly respected Sliabh Luachra fiddle player Connie O'Connell to replace him. In that same year he also recruited the renowned button accordion player Bobby Gardiner, and both continue to teach at the department to this day. The study of uilleann pipes, flute and set dancing all followed quickly in the late 1970s and early 1980s. However, in March 2015, in a speech he delivered at UCC at the launch of Connie O'Connell's book of tune compositions, *Bóithrín na Smaointe*, which is also housed on the main UCC website, Mícheál recalled:

> … at the start there was opposition to the idea of employing traditional musicians as tutors, even on a part-time basis. After all, it was argued, they did not have qualifications such as diplomas or degrees and this made nonsense of the university idea. I counteracted the argument at the time by pointing to native language teachers in French and Spanish, not to mention Irish and other languages, on the basis that they were naturally

> fluent in their native tongue in terms of oral speech performance. Some of these did not have university or higher education diplomas or degrees either. The argument won the day and the way was cleared for future development, expansion and consolidation.[4]

Since that time, experts in the field of Irish traditional music performance have been teaching in the department, whether they have formal qualifications or not, and all are highly respected musicians and teachers.

Mícheál had a great interest in dance. He appreciated the importance it has within the tradition so he incorporated Irish traditional dance into the music degree curriculum in the early 1980s. This was once again a first for any music department in a university in Ireland. Traditional singing classes and *sean-nós* singing classes followed. By the late 1980s virtually a full suite of Irish traditional music performance courses was on offer and today these courses not only attract undergraduate students but also overseas and postgraduate students.

In 1975 the performance element of the Irish traditional music course constituted just 10 per cent of the overall Irish traditional music component of the degree course and, even if students did play Irish traditional music, they did not include it as part of their main degree performances. However, this began to change in 1976 when Matt Cranitch played fiddle in the second half of his major study recital in his final year.[5] Nollaig Casey did the same thing the following year. In 1977 I became the first person to take an Irish traditional instrument, the uilleann pipes, as a primary instrument throughout a music degree in Ireland. Mícheál was delighted with these new developments. From the mid-1980s the number of Irish traditional musicians studying music at UCC increased steadily year on year, with the result that some of the most outstanding young Irish traditional musicians still constitute a substantial cohort of the overall student body.

Curricular developments and reform

Apart from his extensive teaching commitments, an important part of Mícheál's work in the department included curricular development and reform. In the early 1980s the curriculum began to change slightly but the real change began to happen *c.* 1986. The BMus degree was extended to four years and former colleague Paul Everett explained that this meant there was a greater degree of flexibility for staff to teach courses in their own particular areas of interest and 'it was the beginning of what we would later call research-led teaching at undergraduate level'. He also explained that, rather than asking students to study every area of music after first year, they were allowed to choose courses within specific categories, like a menu system, so that their choices formed a flexible core that still maintained its integrity, encompassing some western art music, some Irish traditional music, some ethnomusicology and some performance, but which also encouraged students to specialise and develop their skills.[6]

That significant curriculum revision also resulted in the creation of the first schemes of distinct performance options, both in Irish traditional music, song and dance, and also in other musical genres. The credit weighting for these courses, previously delivered as part of the core courses, increased significantly. Together with his colleagues, in particular Professor Nick Sandon and Paul Everett, Mícheál worked hard on this new curriculum and on the idea of parity of esteem between all musical genres,[7] which had been an aspiration of Mícheál's for many years.[8]

During the mid-1980s Mícheál redesigned the entrance test in collaboration with his colleagues so that the assessment of potential would be given at least as much weight when assessing incoming students. The written part of the test was also tailored to suit students from different musical backgrounds.

A separate course for ethnomusicology was also developed at this time. Mícheál had a particular interest in the music of India, as Seán Ó Riada had before him, and Mícheál brought back various instruments from his travels to India. During a visit to the department the Indian ambassador donated a number of Indian instruments, books and records.[9] Mícheál appointed a teacher of sitar during the 1983–4 academic year,[10] an instrument which is still studied in the department to this day. Students have also studied and explored the music of many other countries as part of this course.

Mícheál's interests were not limited to Irish traditional music and ethnomusicology. He was largely responsible for the introduction of jazz to the music degree curriculum, which was another first for UCC.[11] A designated lecturer in jazz, Paul O'Donnell, was appointed in the early 1990s and, to this day, it is an important and very popular part of the curriculum. Early in his tenure Mícheál approached Comhaltas Ceoltóirí Éireann suggesting they fund a scholarship for two music students,[12] and two first-year traditional music students are awarded a small scholarship annually.

Fieldwork and archives

Mícheál had a great interest in and respect for the practice of fieldwork, specifically collecting and documenting the music of some of our finest tradition-bearers. He recorded many of these musicians himself, including Ben Lennon, Seán de hÓra, Micho Russell and Tommie Potts. Apart from their music, Mícheál was also interested in documenting what he referred to as 'biographical notes; conversation on philosophy of music; concepts, change, tradition, musical understanding, attitudes'.[13] During his time at UCC Mícheál was either directly or indirectly involved in setting up numerous traditional music archives both in Ireland and overseas. In 1989–90 he was invited by the Irish studies programme at Boston College (BC) to become a visiting professor[14] and, while on sabbatical there, he set up the Archive of Irish Traditional Music in America which is still housed within the prestigious Burns Library in Boston College.[15] The Irish Traditional Music Archive (ITMA) in Dublin was launched in 1991 by President Mary Robinson and in 1993 Mícheál became chairman of the board of directors for two terms of three years from 1993–9.[16] He also played a key role in establishing the Muckross House Music Collection which began in 1980. The then manager of Muckross House, Ned Myres, who was the driving force behind the music collection, contacted and met with Mícheál, who helped in numerous ways, initially by providing collectors from the graduate community of UCC. He arranged that Tony Perrott and the staff of the university's Audio Visual Services would support the collectors as regards recording devices, also providing them with the necessary high-quality 5" reel-to-reel BASF tapes. Mícheál designed index sheets to document the recordings and he attended numerous meetings in relation to the collection. Tom Munnelly of the Folklore Department of University College Dublin also helped train the collectors.

Irish Traditional Music Archive, Department of Music

Mícheál was instrumental in founding the Irish Traditional Music Archive at the Department of Music, UCC. For most music students, fieldwork was either a major or a minor part of their music course and Mícheál stressed the importance of using good-quality recording equipment. From 1975 to the early 1990s an Uher reel-to-reel tape recorder was used by students which was in line with that being used by RTÉ at that time. Mícheál was very aware of the importance of documenting the collections properly and he impressed this on his students. He designed fieldwork sheets where students documented their collections; each collection was accompanied by either an essay or a dissertation. Students very often collected music from musicians living in their own locality, so not only was the fieldwork course a useful teaching tool but also a means of collecting and documenting music from all over Ireland, thereby rapidly adding to the archive collection in the department.

Under Mícheál both undergraduate and postgraduate students were engaged in important research work resulting in many excellent projects, dissertations and theses in Irish traditional music, song and dance. All of these are now housed in either the Irish Traditional Music Archive of the department or in the Special Collections section of the Boole Library at UCC, while all the recordings are housed in the department's Irish Traditional Music Archive.

In 1980 Mícheál arranged to send the Henebry-O'Neill collection of wax cylinders, which were made in the early twentieth century or late nineteenth century by Captain Francis O'Neill and the Rev. Richard Henebry, to the British Sound Archive for the purpose of transferring them to reel-to-reel format, this being the most advanced technology at the time, and I have since digitised this reel-to-reel collection.

My own involvement with the archive goes back to 1983 when Mícheál asked me to collect music in north Kerry for Muckross House Museum, later Muckross House Research Library (MHRL). I continued to do so for the following eight or nine summers and in 1991 he suggested that I complete a research master's based on the north Kerry music collection made by both Geraldine Cotter and myself, which numbered 2,000 pieces of original fieldwork. The master's was supervised by both Mícheál and Nicholas Carolan, the director of the newly launched ITMA.

I was to create two databases in line with ITMA's database system designed by Nicholas Carolan but it was to be tailored by me to suit the fieldwork collection of MHRL. The trustees of Muckross House kindly agreed to fund the work and once completed they received both a hard and soft copy of the two databases, that is the sound recordings database and the biography database. They also received all the inputted information in the database plus the second section of the thesis which included a discussion on the life and music of six musicians from five different corners of north Kerry.

Following the completion of this work, Mícheál asked me to design a database for the department's archival material and to catalogue the department's collection of recordings and associated documents. This database was again designed in line with what was being used by ITMA. The projects and theses have been numbered and catalogued, making it a valuable collection stretching back almost fifty years with more than 3,000 pieces of original field recordings and associated documentation plus recorded concerts and other events organised by the staff of the Department of Music. The archive also houses many valuable documents relating to the development of Irish traditional music at UCC over the past fifty years as well as old photographs, ephemera and instruments. We have digitised the entire collection of recordings and this work was grant-aided by the Ireland Funds, and by royalties from the *Dear Old Erin's Isle* commercial recording.

The archive is continually growing and being added to by our students and staff and by outside donations. Fieldwork continues to be part of the undergraduate degree within relevant courses, including 'Collectors, Collections and Fieldwork in Irish Traditional Music', and it can often be part of postgraduate degrees.

Many researchers and doctoral students have used the archive, including Professor Tríona Ní Shíocháin who resurrected and subsequently published songs from the Muskerry Gaeltacht which had gone out of circulation. Colin Dunne researched the recordings of Tommie Potts as collected by Mícheál and based a TG4 (*Gradam Ceoil*) award-winning performance on this collection. Conal Creedon researched the Henebry collection for a television documentary on the life of the celebrated Fr O'Flynn. For his doctoral studies Dr Ciarán Ó Gealbháin listened to the recordings of Nioclás Tóibín and to the Henebry collection in search of recordings of Nioclás' mother Cití Shíle Ní Mhuirgheasa Bean Tóibín. Some archival pieces have also been of value to our MA in Composition students, who have utilised very old recordings from the Henebry collection to form new compositions. Numerous undergraduate and postgraduate students have availed of the archive whether they come from UCC, the University of Limerick or other institutions or indeed are independent researchers. Therefore, on a national level, it is an invaluable resource for all those working with Irish traditional music.

The Traditional Music Society

Mícheál was aware of the advantage of setting up communities of musicians within the university. He encouraged students to form an Irish Traditional Music Society, which was established during the academic year 1980–1. This was again a first for any university in Ireland. Committee members included Gearóid Ó hAllmhuráin, Sorcha Ní Riada and myself, and through the years it has been hugely successful, winning numerous awards, especially under auditors Mel Mercier, Aoife Granville and Jack Talty. The society had the three goals of being educational (classes), social (sessions, concerts) and academic (lectures). Therefore, it took over the organisation of weekly concerts in the Seomra Caidrimh on the main campus of UCC which Mícheál had originally organised and which were again a first for any university in Ireland. The society also organised weekly sessions and an annual festival, all of which still take place today. Mícheál continually met, supported and encouraged the students in their work. The sessions were extremely popular, with many wonderful evenings of music taking place in various locations around Cork city where students and staff would play on a specific evening. It was a wonderful meeting place for all students, including visiting students who also became part of the Irish traditional music community, and all were welcome whether musicians or listeners. Mícheál was at the heart of these sessions and he played with just as much enthusiasm as the students, usually on the ukulele. It was amazing the energy he could bring to these gatherings on such a simple instrument. Sometimes he would play the piano or an African instrument called the *mbira*.

Ó Riada Memorial Lecture Series and further publications

In 1985 Mícheál, together with the Irish Traditional Music Society, initiated the Ó Riada Memorial Lecture series at UCC whereby an invited speaker would deliver a lecture on a specific topic in Irish traditional music (see Figure 21.1).[17] The lecture would then be published and launched at

Figure 21.1: Mícheál Ó Súilleabháin launches 'A Key to Sources of Irish Traditional Music', *Ó Riada Memorial Lecture 6*. PHOTOGRAPH BY COLM HENRY

Figure 21.2: Mícheál Ó Súilleabháin (r) with Professor Aloys Fleischmann (centre) and Donal Counihan (l), Cork University Press, at the launch of *Bunting's Ancient Music of Ireland*, January 1984. PHOTOGRAPH COURTESY OF *THE CORK EXAMINER* (NOW *IRISH EXAMINER*)

the following year's lecture. The first speaker was Breandán Breathnach and, thirty-nine years later, this lecture is still an annual event. This series now constitutes a valuable collection of lectures delivered by some of the most eminent speakers, researchers and performers in the world of Irish traditional music.

Mícheál encouraged and supported the development of the Harp Society, another first for UCC. He had a great interest in the harp and one of his earliest major publications was *Bunting's Ancient Music of Ireland*, co-edited with Donal O'Sullivan and published by Cork University Press in 1983 (see Figure 21.2).[18]

Festivals

During the 1989–90 academic year, another of Mícheál's activities while on sabbatical at BC was to organise the highly successful My Love is in America festival which featured sixteen of arguably the finest fiddle players in America, both Irish and American-born musicians. The final concert was held on Sunday, 25 March 1990 and all sixteen fiddle players, accompanied by Mel Mercier on bodhrán, were recorded live at BC. Mícheál produced a commercial recording from this festival and he decided that the royalties would go towards providing seed-money for the newly established Traditional Music Archive at BC. The recording was a great success and it received an award from the American Library of Congress.[19]

On his return from BC in 1990 Mícheál organised a series of annual festivals that were larger even than the society's annual Éigse na Laoi festival. These festivals took place over a five-year period and he was greatly helped by both students and staff of the department, most notably by Niall Vallely with all five festivals, Mel Mercier with the second to the fifth festival, and Liz Doherty with the third festival together with the Traditional Music Society.[20] Each year the festival had a different theme, for example Fiddlesticks featured music from Donegal and the Shetland Islands while Dear Old Erin's Isle featured music from America (see Figure 21.3). From 1991 to 1995 these festivals brought top-class traditional musicians and dancers from all over the world including Scotland, the US, Britain

Figure 21.3: Mícheál Ó Súilleabháin performing at the Johnny Patterson Concert in the Everyman Theatre as part of the Dear Old Erin's Isle festival, Cork, 1992. PHOTOGRAPH BY TOMÁS TYNER, AUDIO VISUAL MEDIA SERVICES, UCC

and Cape Breton Island to UCC and Cork. The final festival was called The Gathering and featured musicians from all the above-mentioned places and further afield. However, by the time this final festival took place, Mícheál had departed to the University of Limerick.

A commercial recording was usually produced from recordings made at these festivals and the royalties went to various traditional music archives.[21] These helped to raise the profile of each archive and of Irish traditional music in Ireland and overseas. Mícheál mentions in a correspondence that while the amount of money was quite small, the main advantage, as he saw it, was to provide seed-money and to highlight the existence of a specific archive in a way that could attract sponsorship.[22] The first festival's recording benefited the ITMA; the second benefited the Traditional Music Archive, Music Department, UCC; the third featuring music from Cape Breton benefited 'The Cape Breton/Ireland Musical Bridge'.[23] The commercial recording produced from the second festival, *Dear Old Erin's Isle: Irish traditional music from America*, also received an award from the American Library of Congress.[24]

Teaching skills

Mícheál was an imaginative teacher and, for those students who were new to Irish traditional music and often more than a little indifferent towards it, Mícheál helped them listen to the music with fresh ears and to open their minds to the beauty and complexities of the music and song traditions. Many of my fellow classmates remarked at the time that he changed their minds, and one said that she never even liked Irish traditional music until she heard Mícheál talk about it and play it. He spoke about the music with great enthusiasm, depth and energy and students were often amazed by the way his fingers seemed to dance along the blackboard as he followed the notes of a particular tune or song as he lilted. His piano-playing in class was exciting, original and inspirational. He also guided students in the right direction when it came to specialisation or postgraduate studies. Many of the composers who graduated from the department were influenced by his arrangements and compositions. One such accomplished composer, Marian Ingoldsby, who was a student between 1982 and 1985, said that it was the atmosphere and the people teaching in the department that inspired her to become a composer. She was greatly influenced by Mícheál's arrangements and harmonies. He gave her a lifelong love of figured bass and in his analysis classes he often took an innovative approach and would incorporate Irish traditional music for analysis purposes.[25]

Figure 21.4: Mícheál Ó Súilleabháin with Max, Maeve, Neil and Anne Fleischmann at the launch of *Sources of Irish Traditional Music*, Aula Maxima, UCC, 8 January 1999.
PHOTOGRAPH BY VALERIE O'SULLIVAN, COURTESY OF *THE IRISH TIMES*.

Sources of Irish Traditional Music

In 1980, after Professor Fleischmann's retirement, Mícheál became increasingly involved with Fleischmann's magnum opus, *Sources of Irish Traditional Music* (see Figure 21.4). Numerous graduates and helpers had already worked on this project[26] and Mícheál and Professor Fleischmann would meet regularly to discuss and categorise tunes for this huge work. Nicholas Carolan, at the request of Professor Fleischmann, agreed to act as consultant to the project in 1988.[27] Following Professor Fleischmann's death in 1992 it was left to Mícheál to bring the work to the next level. He was ably assisted by some of his very talented postgraduate students, most notably Paul McGettrick, who acted as associate editor. This monumental work of well over 6,000 tunes including a complete catalogue of the collection, was published by Garland Publishers of New York in 1998 in two large volumes. It was launched by President Mary McAleese on 8 January 1999 in the Aula Maxima, UCC.[28]

By the late 1980s and early 1990s, as well as a large and growing number of undergraduate students, a substantial number of postgraduate students were coming to UCC to study specifically with Mícheál. These students not only came from different parts of Ireland but also from overseas, and many of these students have now become a part of the academic, performance, educational and artistic structure of Ireland.

Mícheál Ó Súilleabháin did it his way! It has been a privilege and a pleasure to document just a little of his pioneering work, or his 'dolphin's way', in the place where it all began in the Department of Music at UCC.

22
Mícheál Ó Súilleabháin, Ethnomusicology and Queen's University Belfast

John Baily

John Baily (DPhil, PhD) is a British ethnomusicologist whose research is focused on the music of Afghanistan, from two years' fieldwork in the 1970s and continuing intermittently with the Afghan diaspora in Pakistan, Iran, the United States, Europe and Australia. His monograph is War, Exile and the Music of Afghanistan *(2015).*

Mícheál Ó Súilleabháin and Nóirín Ní Riain entered my life in the early 1980s. Mícheál was contemplating embarking on a PhD programme of research on the innovative and much-admired compositional work and Irish fiddle style of Tommie Potts and was drawn to Queen's University Belfast (QUB/Queen's) by the allure of anthropologist and musicologist Professor John Blacking, who had taken up the newly created chair in the Department of Social Anthropology in 1972.

Blacking was brought up in the highly musical environment of Salisbury Cathedral Close, where his father was the architect looking after the fabric of the cathedral and other local churches.[1] John was an accomplished classical pianist and in his youth contemplated becoming a professional musician. He read social anthropology at Cambridge University and, after two years' national service, mostly in Malaysia, worked for fourteen years in South Africa, becoming in due course professor of anthropology at Witwatersrand University. His research on the music of the Venda people of South Africa had received international acclaim, especially in the US, and with his appointment, QUB showed strong support for his plans to develop a special interest in ethnomusicology within their newly established Department of Social Anthropology. Meanwhile, having recently been awarded a DPhil in experimental psychology for work on human movement and spatial coordination, I was looking for a university department where I could develop my interest in ethnomusicology. I visited Blacking in Belfast on 21 July 1972 (commonly referred to as 'Bloody Friday') and we discussed at length my proposals to investigate relationships between music structure and human movement, an issue already of great interest to Blacking. In due course this resulted in my becoming a research fellow for five years at Queen's, funded by the Social Science Research Council, which included three periods of fieldwork in the city of Herat, in western Afghanistan. Back in Belfast, between periods of fieldwork, I could see for myself the progress Blacking was making in his plans for establishing QUB as an alternative to UCLA and other American universities for graduate studies in ethnomusicology. By then he had already attracted several PhD students from Africa, others from the US, Brazil, Argentina, Canada, Germany and the UK.

In 1978 I was appointed lecturer in ethnomusicology in Blacking's department and became fully involved in teaching the MA in Social Anthropology (Ethnomusicology) programme for the next five years. The syllabus had been created in outline by Blacking and included course units on Theory and Method in Ethnomusicology, Anthropology of Music, Ethnography of World Music and Dance, and the music and/or dance of a special area. It was my responsibility to teach the 'Blacking approach' in ethnomusicology; Blacking's role was to supervise MA and PhD dissertations.

During the five years I taught at Queen's there was usually an intake of three to five MA students per year. They came from a variety of backgrounds, including several from Northern Ireland. The dissertations were substantial in length and in content, and usually researched, written and submitted in a second year of registration. I have only two dissertations in my possession: 'The Lambeg Drum in Ulster' (1982) by Fionnuala Scullion, then working at the Ulster Folk Museum; and 'Taxonomy of Musical Instruments of Mbaise, Nigeria' (1981) by Chinyere Nwachukwu from Nigeria. In addition to the MA lectures there were weekly ethnomusicology seminars, given by visiting speakers or by our own MA and PhD students presenting aspects of their research, and there were occasional classes in African drumming, dance, and Afghan long-necked lute playing.

Blacking managed to persuade The British Council to fund occasional visits by distinguished colleagues from abroad, such as Mantle Hood and William Malm from the US, Gerhard Kubik from Austria, and Hormoz Farhat from Iran. In 1983 we hosted a week of ethnomusicologists and ethnochoreologists from Poland, Bulgaria, East Germany and Hungary, that in turn led to the creation of the European Seminar in Ethnomusicology. In 1975 the department hosted the annual conference of the Association of Social Anthropologists on the theme of the Anthropology of the Body. John Blacking gave the keynote address, justifying this new approach in anthropology. A further aspect of ethnomusicology at Queen's was the university's Folk Music Society, which held weekly sessions in the department. Some of Northern Ireland's leading singers and instrumentalists performed at these sessions.

It was into this hive of ethnomusicological and ethnochoreological activity that Mícheál Ó Súilleabháin and Nóirín Ní Riain entered in the early 1980s. I have no doubt that Blacking's seminal book *How Musical is Man?*, published in 1973, stimulated Mícheál's visit to Belfast and, having already completed an MA at University College Cork, he was in due course enrolled as a part-time doctoral student at QUB. Mícheál and Nóirín contributed greatly to our class discussions and seminars and to the life of an international scholarly community devoted to research in ethnomusicology and ethnochoreology. I believe that it was the example of this rich and dynamic international milieu that later inspired Mícheál to create, with more than a little help from Irish-American multi-billionaire Chuck Feeney, the inspirational Irish World Academy of Music and Dance with one of the most talented academics, keyboard players and composers of his era at the helm. Once the Academy was up and running I had the pleasure of making a number of visits, usually to attend selection panels for the appointment of new members of staff. I am honoured to have had a role in helping to bring Mícheál's vision to fruition.

23
Mícheál Ó Súilleabháin
Edward Walsh

Edward Walsh is the founding president of the University of Limerick. He has been elected member, New York Academy of Sciences; member, Irish Academy of Engineering; member, Royal Irish Academy; fellow, Royal Society of the Arts; and honorary member of the Royal Hibernian Academy of Arts.

A university president's prime task is the recruitment and development of talent. I am happy to believe that, during the twenty-eight years of involvement in establishing the University of Limerick, recruiting Mícheál Ó Súilleabháin and supporting his vision was one of my more successful initiatives.

The Republic's first new university was established in Limerick with World Bank and European Investment Bank finance. Its mission at the outset was to prepare new generations for the challenges and opportunities arising from Ireland's membership of the European Economic Community and to act as a catalyst in attracting high-tech inward investment. From the beginning, there was a commitment in Limerick to blend the arts and the sciences: engineering and science degrees in electronics and advanced materials were launched alongside Ireland's first degree in European Studies. However, it was not until the arrival of the remarkable philanthropist Chuck Feeney that the new university was in a position to consider the introduction of music to the curriculum.

In 1990 Feeney secretly agreed to finance half the cost of building Ireland's first purpose-designed concert hall on the Limerick campus on the understanding that I would secure matching funding from the state. I had a good relationship with the minister for education, Mary O'Rourke, who managed to get the necessary commitment more readily than I expected; I suspect because the Department of Finance assumed it was most unlikely Limerick would ever succeed in raising the necessary £6 million in private funding. However, with Feeney's commitment on the table we were able to claim the state funds immediately. United States and Irish architects were commissioned to draw up the plans, and construction of the 1,000-seat University Concert Hall commenced in 1991.

I was aware of the remarkable work Mícheál Ó Súilleabháin had been doing at UCC and invited himself and his most talented wife Nóirín Ní Riain to lunch. I briefed them on plans for the new concert hall and my hope that it would act as a catalyst for a rich programme of music at the university. I was surprised that Mícheál had not yet been appointed as professor of music; University College Cork (UCC) appeared to be taking his extraordinary talents for granted. Before lunch concluded I told Mícheál that, provided he agreed to be a candidate, Limerick would advertise a professorship of music. Discussions followed. I got his agreement and the professorship was advertised. Days later UCC advertised a similar professorship and moved swiftly to interview. So swiftly indeed that Mícheál was interviewed in Cork on a Friday and offered the chair before we were due to interview him on the following Monday. That evening Mícheál had two professorships on offer: one from Cork and one from Limerick.

UCC had been less than helpful, over the years, as efforts were made to establish a university in Limerick. So, in addition to head-hunting Mícheál Ó Súilleabháin, I considered it would be just retribution were UCC to lose such a superb talent to Limerick. However, I knew that it was a big ask to expect Mícheál to uproot himself from UCC and abandon the rich musical environment, created over decades by Aloys Fleischmann and Seán Ó Riada, for a new university that had none. So it was clear I had to make some special commitments when I phoned him that Monday evening. In addition to offering him the challenge of creating a completely new faculty of music, I committed myself to actively fundraising on his behalf to secure the finance that would give him the freedom and resources necessary to transform his vision into reality. To my great satisfaction Mícheál accepted the offer to come to Limerick and shortly afterwards he and Nóirín purchased Dromore House, not far from our own home in Newport.

We lost no time in attempting to fundraise, and on a bleak November evening Mícheál and I were heading through Dublin traffic for a meeting with Tim Mahony, the founding chairman of Toyota Ireland. As we drove I cogitated that a musician and an academic had not much prospect of convincing Tim and his car-salesmen colleagues that giving away money was a good idea. However, to my great surprise I had to do no more than introduce Mícheál and he took over. I could see that his latent charisma and people skills quickly captured the imagination of these hard-nosed businessmen. Tim agreed to make a gift of £500,000 that provided Mícheál with the resources and freedom to start building his vision for the Irish

World Academy of Music and Dance. He lost no time either in convincing John Kelly, the chief executive of the Irish Chamber Orchestra, that it would benefit from a move from Dublin to Limerick. This it did in 1992 and took up residence in the University Concert Hall when it opened in 1993. The hall also incorporated some additional booty from Cork: the great Savoy cinema organ which was purchased and rebuilt in a dedicated complex within the concert hall. Its inauguration was marked by a special concert given by Mícheál Ó Súilleabháin.

Once Chuck Feeney met Mícheál he too was captivated, and soon plans and funding emerged to house the Academy. The splendid €8 million building, opened in 2010 with its forty music rooms, two theatres and vibrant art was fondly christened by the students: Taj Mícheál. Mícheál's performances in the Concert Hall over the years are memorable, but the most brilliant, I believe, was his first impromptu concert when he, Nóirín Ní Riain and his first students took to the stage and in a far-from-structured performance left us in no doubt that Mícheál was about to make something extraordinary happen – and this most wonderfully he did.

The last concert Mícheál created was performed at his own funeral in St Senan's church in Kilrush on 12 November 2018. Over 500 mourners, including the president of Ireland, were present. They listened to a wealth of music offered in Mícheál's memory by those he had inspired, and by those who had especially inspired him – Helen Phelan and Nóirín Ní Riain. We all knew that we had lost not only an exceptional talent but an incomparable member of humanity.

24
Always Unfolding Knowing: Toyota Performing Arts Initiative as curriculum of event, cultural object and lived experience

Margaret O'Sullivan

Margaret O'Sullivan holds a doctorate in curriculum studies at the University of British Columbia. As head of quality, support and development with Music Generation Ireland, her research focuses on quality of music-making and learning experience for children and young people.

In 1990 or 1991, during my undergraduate music degree, I remember attending one of Mícheál Ó Súilleabháin's lectures. The image in my mind's eye is from my customary position with my back to the bay window of the old Rectory building. The death mask of Seán Ó Riada surveyed the room. Two chairs faced an 'audience' of maybe thirty or forty students. Mícheál's distinctive voice could be heard guiding a tall elderly gentleman into the room. He was strong and broad, with a flat cap shoved high at a jaunty angle on his large forehead. Micho (Mike-O) Russell was visiting University College Cork (UCC) to play a lunchtime concert, and to give another concert in the Lobby Bar that night. I hadn't heard him playing live despite having grown up in County Clare. His legendary status was well established by this time, and he had been touring overseas to places like the United States and Germany, far away from the small farm on the north coast of Clare where he lived with his two musician brothers from birth.[1]

Mícheál formally welcomed and introduced Micho. For a short time he played and sang and answered questions, interspersing his performance with stories and remembrances that illuminated his stark, playful style on the tin whistle and in song. His speech was evocative of my grandparents, a husky, almost conspiratorial, tone. Micho started each spoken or sung phrase softly, building to a deeper final elongated syllable, drawn out for dramatic effect. The apparent simplicity of his music was almost shocking to some students, schooled in the notion that to be a musician of great renown was to labour in the pursuit of excellence, a disembodied concept entangled with a kind of athleticism that had little in common with the steady flow of pulse, breath and ornament that characterised Micho's style. I remember Mícheál facilitating lightly, leaving space for Micho's way of being in music, and in the world, to reveal itself.

With the passage of time, memories emerge and are shaped and re-shaped with each telling and each re-telling to the self and to others while retaining the essence of the event's meaning for the narrator.[2] Through the reconstruction of my memories of this and other events I seek to understand the impressionistic nature of the lived experience of curriculum. The purpose of my story is to illustrate how the event of curriculum continues to unfold in the consciousness of one who experiences it. In this essay I relate my memory of Micho Russell's visit as a starting point for a consideration of the role and presence of Mícheál Ó Súilleabháin as a profoundly influential educator who integrated artists and events in a deliberately holistic approach to curriculum. Drawing on the curriculum theory of Madeleine Grumet,[3] I reflect on how curriculum curation and design lead strongly from the politics and presence of the educator. I share further experience and story from my time as performing arts coordinator at the fledgling Irish World Music Centre with a view to thinking about the event *of* curriculum and curriculum *as* event, as cultural object, and as lived experience, that continues to resound and reverberate beyond the moment in ways that are impossible to know.

A rich seam of curriculum

Of course, I could not have articulated it in this way at the time, but the impression of this event has remained deeply embedded, regularly surfacing for repeated consideration. The presence of such a musician in an Irish university lecture theatre was rare at that time, but for students of music in UCC it was part of a rich seam of curriculum. For at least some of us it soothed an ache that we did not know we had or perhaps couldn't name, as Irish students navigating a deeply colonial music curriculum towards finding our own ways of being in music. I understood that this event ran counter to the established values of the wider academy. Although I grew up in County Clare, my prior music education was largely in the classical tradition. I deeply loved classical piano, but my vague sense of desire to learn about 'other' musics, and particularly to learn Irish traditional music, had drawn me to UCC. As a mandatory curricular element, the incorporation of practical instrumental and vocal learning had opened the door to the employment of traditional musicians as teachers. Both the phenomenon of a regular faculty of Irish traditional musicians and a programme of complementary events generated the possibility of encounters with the counter-cultural (in the academic sense) presence of musicians like Micho within the music department of a national university.

In a body and way of being that did not typically 'belong', the essence of Micho's music and presence interrupted the normative narrative of classical music as the essential underpinning of a university music curriculum. While the 'inclusion' of marginalised musics, such as Irish traditional music, took place without disrupting established world views within the academy, the curriculum events I experienced at UCC from 1987 to '92 went beyond mere structural accommodations within normative knowledge systems. They can be seen as a move towards acknowledging space for protocols and understandings for gathering around the music, or at least for an awareness of traditions within their own terms of reference and operation, and of appropriate sites of performance and music-making.

It is unlikely that Mícheál could have anticipated all of the ways in which an encounter with a musician like Micho might continue to act upon those who experienced it. The impossibility of knowing what is really taken up in the *event* of curriculum points to the reality that a curriculum with prescribed outcomes is largely reflective of the desire of the curriculum designer and the demands of the institution/society, and cannot but fail to anticipate the full potentiality of the educative encounter. The outcome of a curriculum event is prescribable only in terms of what can be known and made legible within the disembodied terms of reference of the institution, that fail to comprehend the multiple subjectivities present in those experiencing the encounter – students and educators alike.

Educator as coder and code breaker

Setting up the case for a politics of the presence of the educator, for being present, known, and named in curriculum choices, curriculum scholar Madeleine Grumet argues that politics is always present in curriculum and its contestation, and that 'it should always be contested as citizens struggle over what matters, what is worthy of their children's attention and effort'.[4] Knowledge of who decides, the what and the how of design and curation of curriculum, requires presence and embodiment in and of the educator. Elsewhere, Grumet adds that 'curriculum codes what matters to us in representation systems – academic disciplines, in texts and tests'.[5] Meanings and ideologies become obscured within received codes embedded in curriculum choices. When an educator breaks the established code, challenging curriculum conventions by introducing knowledges contained in bodies that do not traditionally belong, as in the form of the event described, an opening arises out of the tensions that reverberate beyond the code-breaking event itself. The embodied choices of the educator make visible the politics and presence of the educator within curriculum. Signalling a politics and presence of Mícheál as educator, through an event of curriculum such as the visit of Micho to UCC, an opening is unveiled that points to multitudes of possibilities for what a music curriculum in an Irish institution can be, a curriculum that makes space for recognition of special knowledges and of knowledge keepers providing context for non-institutionalised ways of knowing.

Grumet, Anderson and Osmond propose three forms for curriculum inquiry: first, through the curriculum phenomenon as a *cultural object*; second, the study of the curriculum object as *event*; and third, through the study of curriculum from the *perspective* of the researcher/learner.[6] To understand a curriculum event as *cultural object*, the curriculum's social, cultural and ideological underpinnings are emphasised. In the *event* of curriculum, whether in the everyday happenings in schools or within different contexts of study, the *lived experience* of actors – participants of and witnesses to the event – are considered as primary source material. The researcher/learner's *perspective* is found not only in lived experience but in the individual's consciousness of their particular histories and experiences (beyond identity) to understand the immersive influence of curriculum in shaping their perspective. Remembering the lived experience brings the individual's subjectivity into the encounter, as in the student in a lecture hall experiencing a code-breaking event of curriculum, that also signifies as cultural object and calls researcher perspective into view.

Toyota Performing Arts Initiative (1995–2000)

About seven years after Micho Russell's visit, I found myself in a glass elevator with *sean-nós* singer Dara Bán Mac Donnachadha and his brother-in-law Seán. They had just arrived from Carna in Connemara that morning and I was showing them around the University of Limerick (UL) Foundation building, meeting staff and students. I first met Dara Bán the previous summer at his home in Carna, where he had lived his whole life farming the small stony fields of his homeplace by the sea. Lillis Ó Laoire and I went along with filmmaker Michael Ruane to spend time with Dara Bán in the making of a short film we commissioned as part of the Toyota Performing Arts Initiative. Our essential idea was to film and record Dara Bán in a way that conveyed and celebrated his way of being in song and in the world, as a project within a whole series of events centred around Dara Bán as *sean-nós* singer-in-residence.[7] Lillis skilfully and gently mediated these processes to facilitate Dara Bán's interactions in song and story fully through Irish. In the glass elevator I vividly remember Dara Bán singing and joking shyly, intrigued by the dramatic architecture, amused by the flying man sculpture, peering out through his thick glasses at the flamboyant mosaic in the atrium below.[8] 'A Mheaig', he called me, his very own singular diminutive of Mags, as we floated upwards in the glass box, Dara Bán singing under his breath.

The invitation to Dara Bán Mac Donnachadha to become the first *sean-nós* singer-in-residence at UL was part of a colossal project called the Toyota Performing Arts Initiative of which I was coordinator. Having discovered a love of arts organising while volunteering with UCC's Éigse na Laoi festivals (1990–5), I had pursued a career in arts management after my degree. At the end of 1995 I moved to UL to work with Mícheál and the growing team at the Academy. In support of Mícheál's vision as chair of music, Tim Mahony of Toyota Ireland donated half a million pounds that facilitated the imagining of a curriculum of events and happenings to orient and complement a suite of postgraduate programmes of music and dance studies. The unfolding curriculum positioned Irish traditional and contemporary music and dance at its heart, around which were stacked seminars, concerts, commissions, festivals and events that brought diverse artists into contact with each other, with audiences and with students. In small and large teams, over lengthy brainstorming and research sessions, we generated grand-scale events including the annual Toyota concerts, diverse artist residencies, Sionna festivals, Comhaimseartha/Of Our Times series of lunchtime concerts and seminars, annual specialist events such as Lá na nAmhrán and Tráth na gCos, as well as diverse once-off celebrations of niche traditions and practices. Archiving and documentation processes were initiated, and the many ups and downs of implementation of a rapidly growing, wildly ambitious programme by a tiny team of coordinators rolled out over five years.[9]

Many of the original events continue to live on in the current Irish World Academy of Music and Dance. Repudiating the modernist post-colonial framing of academic music curriculum with classical music at the centre, this was a programme that aimed to position practice, tradition and innovation at its heart through the event of curriculum. There are too many highlights to accurately document here, but the programme took the form of ambitious and eclectic nights of music and dance as part of the first Sionna festival at Limerick's Potato Market (1996), Evelyn Glennie's first solo performances in Ireland at University Concert Hall, and the commissioning of a new set dance, *The Limerick Tumbler*, that has since entered the mainstream dance repertoire. Niche events such as Mind your Ps and Qs, a festival celebrating Celtic music and dance from regions across the UK and Europe, always featured a twist by including artists beyond those identities. Uniquely beautiful imagery was generated for all events by UL's graphic designer and celebrated print artist David Lilburn.[10] Commissions were premiered annually by the Irish Chamber Orchestra and Daghdha Dance Company, featuring diverse composers, creators, musicians and dancers.

Into the midst of this carnival of ideas and events came the shy, partially sighted, fair-haired, bird-like body of Dara Bán Mac Donnachadha, with his voice of light and shade and honey and limestone, first-language Irish speaker, specialist knowledge keeper and storehouse of non-institutionalised ways of knowing and being in song and in the world, a counter-cultural presence amidst the modernist and enthusiastically neo-liberal structures of UL. As *sean-nós* singer-in-residence, Dara Bán was facilitated by Lillis in giving song workshops and performances, and generously giving of his art to create a significant body of archive recordings. Grumet's idea that 'curriculum codes what matters to us'[11] can be understood in the significance of Dara Bán's way of being in song and in the world encoded in the curriculum of events that gave form to his artist residency, and in the wider curriculum centred around his treasure of songs. What mattered to the emerging curriculum was his deep immersion in tradition and repertoire, and the connections his presence signified stretching back over one hundred years of unbroken family song tradition. Within Dara Bán's way of being in song was his aunt's way of singing to him nightly, and his father's way of teaching him to sing and passing on of songs he had learned from generations before, to Dara Bán and other local singers including Joe Heaney. Understanding curriculum as event is an attempt to describe the situation itself and to demonstrate it from the perspectives and understandings of the actors within it, and in this case from my lived experience of the event. I experienced Dara Bán's presence as centred in an event of curriculum within the potentiality of the emerging Academy, in a way that had been signalled in the more 'inclusionary' events of my undergraduate years, inclusionary in the sense that events like Micho Russell's visit occurred without fundamentally unsettling the world view that instituted long-established music curriculum conventions.[12] With the freedom afforded him in creating the Academy, Mícheál was empowered to structure curriculum around a figure like Dara Bán, positioning *sean-nós* song at its centre, creating space for gathering around the music and the artist in ways that could but try to emulate and represent protocols and understandings ever changing within the tradition.

Why does this particular lived experience of encounter with Dara Bán continue to unfold in my memory, out of hundreds of extraordinary events with music and dance artists of those five years? Apart from my awareness of the privilege of close proximity to an artist of Dara Bán Mac Donnachadha's irreplaceability, is the importance of the event as cultural object for those who were fortunate to experience it. Acknowledging that the terms of reference and operation of the *sean-nós* tradition could not be replicated within the Academy, Dara Bán's residency worked to make space for the art form in new sites of performance and music-making that celebrated the presence and embodiment of Dara Bán as knowledge keeper, allowing access to a way of being in song that is always already under threat of erosion, a fact of which Dara Bán was deeply aware. When I use the term 'way of being' I am not romanticising a fixed singing style, repertoire or way of life, but striving to convey the complex and transitional mix of elements involved in the artistry of Dara Bán (and Micho Russell and all those who have gone before), including embodied familial histories, inheritances and responsibilities, the embeddedness of storytelling, Irish as first language, the immersive quality of his relationship with place, language, story and song. It is of course possible for a singer to learn a song disentangled from all of these dimensions. The singer's way of being in song will be singular to the set of conditions experienced by the singer, and will be newly negotiated as it moves from song to singer and from singing to performance. Similarly, in instrumental music, performance becomes the predominant value that renders the action of music-making legible within the academy. In other words, if the dominating framework for the experience of music is in performance and in the composed work, as in the classical music tradition, that emphasis on performance continues to be reproduced within the instituted structures and understandings of the academy. Within a predominantly performance-oriented framework, it is unlikely that the artistry of either Dara Bán or Micho Russell could be fully experienced and understood. To understand the event of curriculum as cultural object, a break with conventional curriculum ideology as centred around a modernist framework of performance allows for attention to the many dimensions of being in music and in the world that are part of an artistic encounter in the present moment.

These events of curriculum that I experienced continue to unfold in me, as the multiple subjectivities of those who experience an event of curriculum are unknowable in their potentiality. The presence and embodiment of the artist within the curriculum event as cultural object reverberates in the lived experience of actors within the event beyond the event itself. The political leanings of the educator, in this case Mícheál and subsequently in tandem with Lillis, myself and many others involved in developing the emerging curriculum of the time, are embodied in their curriculum choices and actions. With increasing emphasis on practice and performance, particularly under the influence of performative values, how can we continue to make space for these events of curriculum that will continue to reverberate in the multiple subjectivities of those who experience them? Events of curriculum that centre the artist in their way of being in song and in music make possible and celebrate the impossibility of knowing what is really taken up.

25

An Dúghabháil: Reifying the source

Ríonach uí Ógáin

Ríonach uí Ógáin is former director of the National Folklore Collection UCD. She has published widely on aspects of traditional music and song. She is former editor of Béaloideas: The Journal of the Folklore of Ireland Society. *Her most recent publication is* Colm Ó Caodháin: An Irish singer and his world *(2021).*

Among his many great achievements we must not lose sight of Mícheál Ó Súilleabháin's contribution to engaging with vernacular Irish culture and the Irish language in a way that made them relevant to current scholarship. His discussions in this realm underlined and demonstrated the regard he had for Irish and its capacity and possibilities in his world.

My personal reflection portrays aspects of Mícheál's engagement with vernacular Irish culture and language and discussions that took place surrounding them. His love of Irish frequently finds expression in album and tune titles and all our conversations moved easily through Irish and English. Much of our conversation focused on delving deeper into earlier tradition and Irish terminology and how they might be reimagined in facets of his work. *Dúghabháil* as expressed in the title of my reflection means the 'intense capturing of' or 'intense engagement with' the source as words and phrases were reified and as concepts were revealed. We attempted to find a way of unravelling terms and finding English equivalents before agreeing that they were the appropriate Irish term. Our aim was to encompass the nuances of Irish and identify a deeper metaphorical expression.

One of his earliest discussions with me concerned the river Shannon which flowed so closely to the Irish World Academy of Music and Dance when it was established in 1994. His research query entailed a great deal more than the meaning of An tSionainn, which comes from the Old Irish *Sinann* and was probably a woman's name, most likely a goddess associated with wisdom. He wanted to know all that was to be learned about popular belief regarding the river's source which was said to be in the Otherworld. He was fascinated with the river's association with wisdom, knowledge and learning. He was taken with the concepts of *tairseach* (threshold), *teora* (boundary) and the marginality of rivers. Rivers were seen as sources of inspiration, as reflected in Irish poems that appeared sometime between the tenth and the twelfth centuries. These poems tell us that nine hazel trees grew at a well on the Shannon and as the hazel nuts ripened and fell they were eaten by the salmon. The juice of these nuts produced bubbles that contained wisdom. Sinann, a beautiful girl from the Dé Danann, possessed every gift except that of wisdom and although women were not supposed to approach the spot, she went in search of the bubbles of wisdom and drowned. The river is said to be named after her. Mícheál was intrigued with the personification of rivers and with the fact that Irish and international mythology affirm their female deification and personification. He had a particular affinity with the word 'liminality' and expressed some of this in 'Idir Eatarthu/Between Worlds' on the recording *Oileán* (1989). In 2004, a project was in train to create a three-dimensional animation of the story of *Sinann*, who Mícheál imagined might have a very tribal, almost African look. The project was part of a proposal to rename the Irish World Music Centre.

He drew on the symbolism and folklore attached to key aspects of his vision and as ideas came about, we frequently conversed about these. His queries inevitably led me to seek out source material and to find examples of motifs, phrases and narratives. This occurred before online resources such as DIL.ie, duchas.ie and logainm.ie became available so there was much poring over dictionaries to find instances. One of his most recent research questions related to the phrase *cothrom Féinne* (fair play) which stems from the folk belief and perception of the mythical Fionn Mac Cumhaill and his band of warriors, Na Fianna, as representing justice and truth. Although we discovered that the earliest known use of the phrase was as late as the early nineteenth century, we were in agreement that *cothrom Féinne* is most likely an expression of folk etymology where the trigger for the phrase came about because of the popularly held belief in truth and justice as deeply rooted aspirations in Irish society.

The meaning of some words is best conveyed by reference to belief and symbol, and the sense of a word or phrase is at times best communicated through examples of usage. The words *éigse* and *imbas* overflow with meaning and Mícheál asked about these words as consideration was being given to renaming the Zen garden at the Academy. The fact that Zen gardens are described as 'frozen movement or music' made him mindful of the liminal space between stillness and movement, and of the twelve bells of midnight when time is suspended and the hero just has time to chase into the fairy fort to rescue the stolen child. Returning to the folktale of the river Shannon, he thought that the garden might be imagined as a hazelnut holding the secret of wisdom. Both *éigse* and *imbas* underline wisdom and great knowledge. The strongest distinction between *éigse* and *imbas* is that *imbas* includes some kind of ritual performance in order to gain foreknowledge.

On another occasion he sought some verses to include in a musical dedication to *imbolc* or St Brigid's Day. He was keen to include something from Irish tradition. We exchanged opinions on relevant verse and narrative and one suggestion he liked was to include the words spoken by a member of the household during the re-enactment of Brigid calling to houses on the eve of St Brigid's Day:

> *Gabhaigí ar bhur nglúine,*
> *Fosclaígí bhur súile*
> *Agus ligí isteach Bríd bheannaithe.*
> [Go down on your knees, open your eyes and admit blessed Brigid.]

The broad canvas of material in the National Folklore Collection appealed to Mícheál. It was the ideal source from which he could choose what was needed. His enthusiasm and desire to share and spread knowledge came to light in numerous ways but essential aspects were his commitment, energy, curiosity and desire to educate. These factors ensured that he arrived at accurate definitions, translations and interpretations. He was open to suggestion, and was very much drawn to reapplying words that are associated with an earlier world to find new, relevant life in contemporary society and academic discourse. We reached new understandings of the subtleties of words and their aptness to particular contexts. He was pleased with his words on the cover of the brochure for his Academy: *Of Our Times/ Comhaimseartha*. My act of reflection contributes a further comprehension of him and of how keen and determined he was to excavate and explore core meanings and contexts in Irish as they related to his own innovative musical, cultural and academic pursuits.

26
The CÉILÍ and the HOUSE OF LIGHT

Daniel Cordier

Daniel Cordier is from Orléans, France. He moved to England in 1972 and received a degree and diploma in architecture from Oxford Polytechnic in 1980. Belief in multidisciplinary practice led to major design projects in the UK, Europe and Ireland. He founded his own practice in 2003.

The journey leading to my meeting with Mícheál began in London in the 1990s with the design of the Materials and Surface Science Institute (MSSI) at the University of Limerick (UL). On completion of this project, my activities moved to the university's masterplan in readiness for its major expansion north of the river Shannon into the comparative rurality of County Clare, but late in 2003 I left London to start my own practice. News of the launch of a two-stage international design contest soon followed and early in 2004 the design contest brief for the Irish World Performing Arts Village (IWPAV) was published by UL. On the basis of my recent knowledge of the campus I decided to apply.

Stage 1 called for a design concept (see Figure 26.1) conveyed on a single A1 board with a succinct written statement, from which five anonymous entries would be selected for the second stage.

Invitation to Stage 2, delivered line by line by the fax machine, called for a more detailed definition of the proposals. The selection of my Stage 2 submission by UL led to my first encounter with Mícheál at 9.15 a.m. on 18 October 2004 in Plassey House. The meeting's purpose was to put faces to names, for me to explain the design concept in more detail and for all of us to team-up and engage creatively to develop the brief to detailed design stage to deliver a working building. It was the first of many meetings with Mícheál to shape the future of the IWPAV.

Whilst we were new to each other and from different disciplines, both of us shared the same unifying goals for the project and I felt we got along very well from day one. Mícheál's personality was central to this success – his quick grasp of ideas, his collaborative nature in developing concepts and addressing issues, and his remarkable natural ability to express himself spontaneously. He embraced with empathy what appealed, and rejected what did not without delay or offence, and this too impressed me as much as

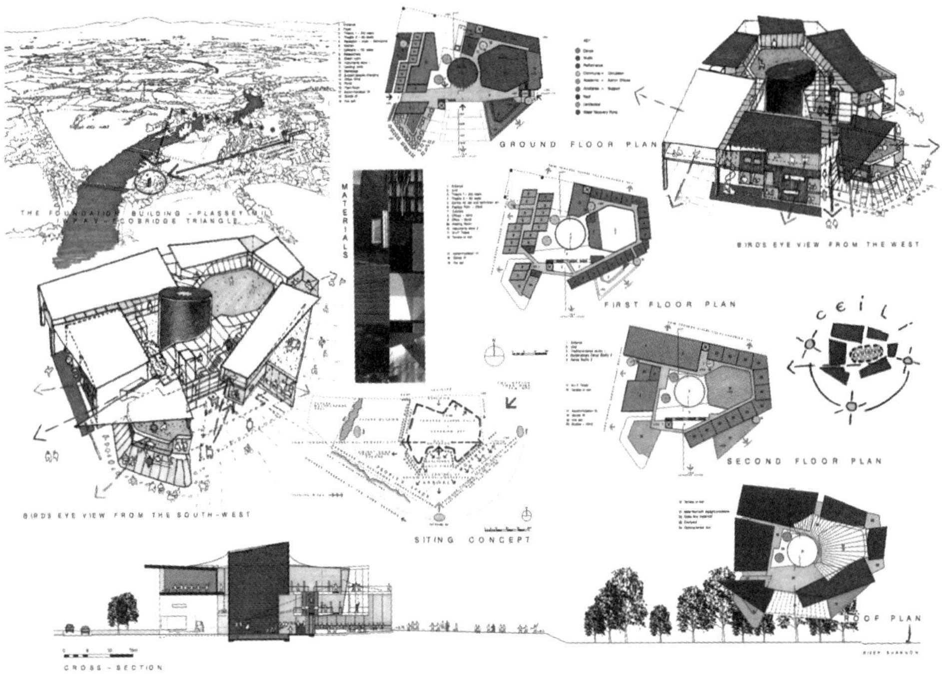

Figure 26.1: Stage 1 – Design concept submission.

his contagious highly spirited enthusiasm. He always found the right word or formula to capture and develop the kernel of an idea into the next level, infusing its spirit around him and often taking on the lead role to promote it. To this day I envy his confident ability for improvisation.

Mícheál's influence in the cultural dimension of the contest brief became clearer as I got to know him – the response to the Shannon's monastic communities, the presence and energy of a living Shannon and the goddess Sinann's legendary tale inspired Mícheál's many faceted aspirations for the IWPAV.[1] These references were another strong link which resonated with me as I had studied Cistercian monastic and religious architecture. The word 'village' in the design brief title also caught my imagination, implying a mixed community characterised by innate Irish sociability, an identity which goes beyond music and dance. I could not have had a better client than Mícheál. He was a natural, clear-headed, charismatic chieftain with outstanding communication skills and a clear vision for the IWPAV; he was always part of the team rather than above it, with an introspective ability to creatively question a process in motion.

The name 'Irish World Performing Arts Village' would become the first victim of his questioning approach and after prolonged reflection it became the Irish World Academy of Music and Dance (IWAMD) which, although lengthy, reflected Mícheál's logic, a cultural ambition for the global outreach of his native art forms. Academia was his milieu and music his chosen mode of expression, with dance the natural extension of performance delivery.

An inflight magazine article had caught my attention with a *circa* 1960 picture of Old Bunratty Road, a single parked car and about fifty people in small groups, on and off the pavement in conversation. This village sociability and sense of place through public interaction matched my view of buildings as fractals of urbanism and it became an obsession. The Academy required a heart – the DRUM THEATRE, and an informal street of spacious but humane dimensions naturally engaging with the movements of people between their social spaces – the FOYER. Inspirational as it was for the design concept, the loss of the word 'village' was a shock but the associated values and imagery were strong enough for it to remain unaffected. The layout of the main theatre space became the second and last victim of Mícheál's questioning approach. It was the right decision and it took with it the terrace above it which converted to a large indoor dance studio, but none of these impacted the overall concept. Yet, in spite of these valuable sources of inspiration, my first two weeks on the project proved to be a near soul-destroying impasse arising from the masterplan geometry and the varied types of accommodation in the brief which did not readily stack-up in an orderly manner. Whilst it did not need to, the campus buildings generally adhered to simple rectilinear volumes and this somewhat unruly departure from this norm required a strong rationale.

Architecture is like a good book. It requires a strong story line expressed with discernible clarity. I eventually got to a possible solution and showed my 'work in progress' – a wordless concept diagram – to my daughter Emily who, unprompted, said 'It's a *céilí*' (see Figure 26.2). Realising Emily had seen the clarity of what I had done, it was a eureka moment and her shorthand expression of the concept provided me with the confidence to proceed.

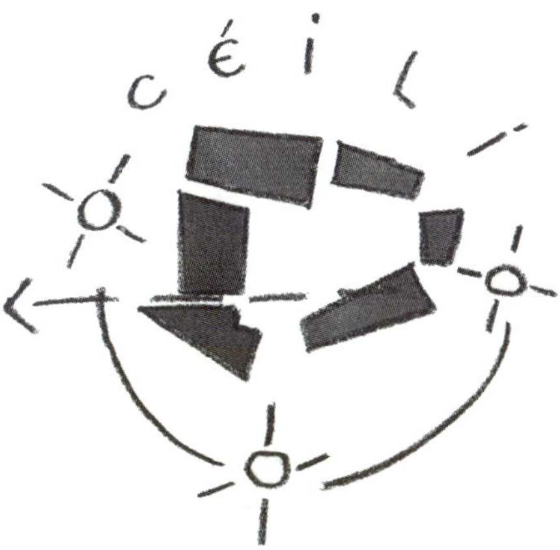

Figure 26.2: Concept diagram – The CÉILÍ.

I recall the positive atmosphere and the freedom of expression Mícheál created around him that enabled individuals to be and to work together. It all felt constructive and creative, the nononsense can-do attitude, the absence of pretence but directness with a sense of common purpose, all facilitating communication and teamwork. From operating out of existing accommodation disseminated around the university, Mícheál's personal vision and his knowledge-based experience as client input essential values and strengths to the successful development of the brief into a fully functioning building and department.

For a long time, Mícheál worked towards the building being sited alongside the flowing Shannon, thus echoing a global principle of monastic tradition as well as celebrating an upstream settlement. His success placed the Academy at the living heart of campus, making it the vista on the tree-lined journey across the Living Bridge to the foothold piazza in County Clare. The warmth and transparency of the FOYER's southern aspect, with its entrance, associated café, terrace and street, celebrate a sense of welcome whilst maintaining the secretive shared visual connection to Plassey tower and the Foundation building that provides visual unity and anchors the FOYER's east–west axis. The FOYER STREET hosts Desmond Kinney's mosaic and Robert Ketchell's Zen garden, both of which celebrate goddess Sinann's enhancing connections to the river and key community spaces, and it captures the spirit of what Mícheál and I liked to call the HOUSE OF LIGHT, reflecting his personal values and warmth of spirit. The ritual pit and stone laid in front of the DRUM THEATRE further enhanced the sense of home and foundation.

One powerful event resulting from my collaboration with Mícheál stands out in my memory. On one of my inspection visits, two young ladies, arm in arm, came up to me smiling and enquired if I was the architect. On hearing my reply the young lady on the right said how much she'd enjoyed the building; she was impressed by its sound and the upbeat mood and liveliness of the atmosphere. She said it had a noticeably different sound and feel from other buildings and she had derived much pleasure from her visit and, being blind, this mattered to her.

27
Of Our Times
David J. Elliott

David J. Elliott is Professor Emeritus of Music and Music Education at New York University. He is co-author of Music Matters: A new philosophy of music education, *2nd edn (2015), and* Musical Bodies, Musical Minds: Enactive cognitive science and the meaning of human musicality *(2022). He has also published fifty-two journal articles and forty-seven book chapters.*

I am very fortunate to have had a strong relationship with many of the people who compose and embody the mission, ethos, creativity and deep humanity of the Irish World Academy of Music and Dance.[1]

My relationship with the Academy began in 1995 when I was invited to be one of several keynote speakers – including Mícheál Ó Súilleabháin, Richard Colwell, Marie McCarthy, Patricia Campbell and Kari Veblen – at the first Irish Music Education National Debate. After the conference, Mícheál invited me to speak at a subsequent conference of his own at the University of Limerick (UL), which was followed by a reception where he talked to me about his vision for the Irish World Academy of Music and Dance. I was captivated – heart, mind and soul.

As I learned, the president of UL facilitated a clear road for Mícheál, as the inaugural chair of music, to create and develop innovative graduate music programmes that would offer courses unavailable elsewhere in the Republic and, in some cases, the rest of the world – including Irish Traditional Music and Dance Performance, Ritual Chant and Song, Classical String Performance (in association with the Irish Chamber Orchestra, which had relocated from Dublin to the new Academy on the UL campus), Contemporary Dance Performance, Music Education, Ethnomusicology, Ethnochoreology, and Community Music. An important part of the plan was to foster students' creativity and self-development by encouraging them to move across degree programmes.

I was extraordinarily honoured that Mícheál and his colleagues, many of whom had started to gather around him as his doctoral students, planned to put into practice several important concepts and practical strategies I proposed in *Music Matters: A new philosophy of music education* (1995), including the book's emphasis on praxis – the basic idea being that musical concepts of all kinds must be continually integrated with all forms of musical actions (performing, improvising, etc.) and applied in real-world contexts.[2] For example, the study and performance of Irish traditional music and dance in the Academy would be taught and learned in the ways it is authentically taught, learned and performed by masters of the tradition and put into action in real-world situations. The establishment of a vibrant cross-genre artist-in-residence initiative (entitled *Cónaí*, the Irish word for home) in 1995 has already seen twenty years of residencies covering some thirty artists and arts institutions (including the Irish Chamber Orchestra, Daghdha Dance Company, Rex Levitates/Liz Roche Dance Company, The Chieftains, and Fidget Feet Aerial Dance Company, the latter of which has now moved its base full-time to the environs of the Limerick campus as a direct response to the residency). Furthermore, a cultural community pathways structure (entitled *Bealach*, the Irish word for path) was established at the same time, linking the tapestry of Academy curricular offerings to a variety of social energies (including NOMAD – linking to the Irish Traveller community, and SANCTUARY – linking to the New Irish).

In the twenty years since its founding, the Academy has gone from an absolutely zero base to offering nineteen degree programmes with graduates from more than fifty countries worldwide, and it has attracted a blend of public finance and private philanthropic funding in excess of €50 million.

In 1996 Mícheál invited me to spend one year living on the campus of UL, participating with his colleagues in the creation of the curricula for the Academy's programmes. It was to prove to be one of the most joyful and meaningful periods of my life. At the time, we only had three small offices in the Foundation building. As I recall, we hurtled through the back roads of Ireland with Niall Keegan at the wheel on a national tour to raise public awareness of the new Academy. Now, twenty years later, the original dream has come true: the Academy is one of the most innovative and rigorous international schools of music and dance in the world. And it has taken up its home, finally, in an extraordinarily beautiful, innovative and creative building that embodies its mission on the banks of the river Shannon as the river flows majestically through the middle of one of the world's most elegant, spacious and ecological campuses.

During my 1996/7 residence at UL and every time I've visited the Academy during the last twenty years, I'm transported back to my earliest childhood memories of my grandfather and father playing Irish traditional music in our home in Toronto. Permit me to reminisce a bit about my family and link it to the kinds of doings, makings and sharings that occur every day at the Academy. I trace my heritage to the south-west of Ireland. My great-grandfather was a farmer in County Clare. My grandfather (Harry) was the youngest of thirteen children and learned to play the Irish button accordion as a child on my great-grandfather's farm. Harry was well known in the area for playing at Irish dances as a teenager. Like others in Ireland at the time, my grandfather wanted to leave for a new life in the United States or Canada. He was booked on the *Titanic* but missed the boat when it stopped at Cobh. He eventually made it (via New York) to Toronto, where some of his brothers had settled before him and where my father was born. Harry continued to play the box throughout his life, and he 'taught' my father and me. As a labourer working at all sorts of back-breaking jobs, Harry was still able to buy my dad a piano, but he had no money for lessons.

My father taught himself to play the piano extremely well. He instantly learned (by ear) hundreds of popular songs, big-band tunes, jazz, and so on. My musical inheritance is rooted in – and was gifted to me by – the Irish world of music-making, informal musical gifting-and-sharing, and the stories and poetry of my Irish past. In addition to the welcoming warmth, hospitality and humanity of my colleagues at the Academy, I'm 'back home in Ireland' each and every time I visit.

For what is music, and what is it for, if it's not about networks of relationships? Relationships between self and another and multiple others; relationships between the past, present and future; and relationships between my worlds and your worlds in our moments of shared musical oneness. Let me examine for a moment a key idea in *Music Matters* that Mícheál and his colleagues have actualised.

Music is not simply one or more pieces of music. *Musics* – all the different kinds of music in the world – are actually, at their centres, networks of people. That is, each individual kind of music is actually a 'musical practice' – meaning people (music makers and listeners) who form specific musical communities (e.g. Irish fiddlers and listeners; Indian tabla drummers; jazz bebop players; baroque performers) and who share certain musical abilities, understandings, histories and values in common and who therefore make and value 'their musics' for themselves and others.

In other words, a musical practice is a set of human–musical relationships. A musical practice is something that a particular group of people organises towards some kind of practical end. In praxial terms, music is vital to all societies and cultures because its doings-and-makings help to define, embody and reflect a society's values by fulfilling a wide range of divergent and evolving needs. Thus, the diverse human practice of 'musics' includes thousands of specific socio-musical practices and communities that thrive at local and regional levels, across national borders, and overlap for a variety of reasons and purposes. Again, in praxial terms, specific kinds of sounds are valued as 'music' according to the personal, social and cultural functions they serve. In short, 'musics' are made by people for people. Thus, musical values and meanings are not intrinsic, they are not 'fixed-in' sonic forms or captured in notated scores; musical values are socially assigned to sounds according to how sounds are used, experienced and understood as being 'good for' various purposes in people's personal and social lives.

As Tia DeNora says, 'Music is not about life but is, rather, implicated in the formulation of life; it is something that gets into action, something that is a formative, albeit often unrecognized resource of social agency.'[3] To quote from William Butler Yeats' 'Among School Children': 'O body swayed to music, O brightening glance, / How can we know the dancer from the dance?' We *are* because of the music we make and celebrate.

These ideas take me back to the beginning. 'You're very welcome' were the first words Mícheál spoke at the 1996 UL conference. I'd never heard these words of welcome and hospitality in that way before. A common turn-of-phrase in Ireland (as I later learned), they were extremely meaningful on a personal level, but also musically significant to me. As I understood and felt them then and now: 'Let me welcome you into my world, and, also, welcome to our worlds of music at the Academy on the river Shannon.'

The music makings, takings and sharings at the Academy have been part of my body, mind and spirit for twenty years. They've enabled me to be the thinker in/for musics that I am. They've helped me deepen and extend my understandings and experiences of the many actual and potential values and 'goods' that lie in and surround musical relationships.

The Academy has gifted me the deepest possible relationships. Because of the Academy's continual welcomes – your human welcomes – I have been reminded of my past, present and living heritages. The people and the music-making at the Academy are central parts of my life's narrative, and the relationship of music and dance has once again lifted us all into a new station where a shared humanity can be sung, danced and celebrated.

28
Towards a National Ethnomusicology

John Morgan O'Connell

John Morgan O'Connell is an Irish ethnomusicologist with a specialist interest in cultural history. Currently professor of ethnomusicology at Cardiff University, he designed and taught the MA in Ethnomusicology at the University of Limerick. A specialist in musical traditions of the Middle East, he recently published research on staged folklore in Ireland with Susan Motherway.

'Towards a National Ethnomusicology'[1] was the subject of the first symposium organised by the International Council for Traditional Music (ICTM) Ireland.[2] Convened to celebrate the newly recognised status of the ICTM Ireland as a national committee for ethnomusicology,[3] the meeting attracted ethnomusicologists (amongst others) from the leading educational and archival institutions on the island of Ireland. At the conference, the discussions ranged from deliberations upon language and music, folklore and anthropology. They embraced considerations of the national and the transnational, the individual and the institutional. Of course, Mícheál Ó Súilleabháin played a prominent role in the plenary session at the event. With specific reference to his mentor, Seán Ó Riada, Mícheál showed how ethnomusicology occupied a central position in the formation of a national consciousness. For Mícheál, Ó Riada was unique at the time for his simultaneous articulation of a local and a global identity, a veritable ethnomusicologist who had an individual perspective.

Indeed, Mícheál would frequently represent ethnomusicology as 'the international study of traditional musics'. In part, this definition presented Mícheál with a plausible gloss for the field, especially to those who were less familiar with the academic subtleties of disciplinary classification. In part, this strategy allowed Mícheál to view traditional music in general and Irish (traditional) music in particular as expressive media worthy of serious consideration. This explains his reference to Ó Riada in ethnomusicological terms. As part of the same mindset, Mícheál sought in Ireland the same level of validation for traditional music as 'classical' music both in terms of its status and sponsorship.[4] Ó Riada also shared this concern, as is evident in his compositional output and ensemble participation. By defining ethnomusicology as an international study, Mícheál could also offset the critical scrutiny of his educational ambitions either by conservative members of the traditional music community or the disparaging condescension of the national arts establishment.

It is noteworthy that ethnomusicology was at the heart of Mícheál's vision for a college of performing arts.[5] Along with ethnochoreology, ethnomusicology was one of the first permanent appointments to be made at the Academy. Placing music and dance at the core of his institutional philosophy, Mícheál clearly indicated his interest in developing an academic study of performance practice, a focus that had long been central to the fields of ethnomusicology and ethnochoreology. I was appointed as the ethnmusicologist and Catherine Foley was appointed as the ethnochoreologist. Although Catherine had an established research profile in the areas of Irish music and dance, my areas of expertise lay elsewhere. With a specialist interest in the musical traditions of west Asia, my appointment took many by surprise.

At the interview for the position (23 May 1996), Mícheál asked me about my interest in the Middle East. Aware that he was fascinated by an 'eastern' reading of the Irish tradition,[6] I responded by highlighting the long engagement by Irish historians with west Asiatic and north African sources especially in the religious and artistic domains. Even Ó Riada was not impartial to this distinctive interpretation of the Irish past. While such a comparative perspective might seem odious in certain intellectual circles, it does position Irish music as an occidental pole in the orientalist discourse of colonial difference.[7] In this way, Irish music could be viewed as an epicentre in the world of music. As Ó Riada might have argued, Irish music was simultaneously local and global. In the heady aftermath of *Riverdance* (1994), Irish music had indeed become a world music. And the Academy was a cogent reminder of this progression.

I came to the interview prepared to talk about my own 'World of Music', a seminar syllabus that was specifically designed to place Irish music in a global arena. Organised around relevant ethnomusicological issues (such as diffusion and diaspora) and musical concepts (such as composition and improvisation), I aimed to demonstrate how a theoretical idea could be realised in musical practice. The module was tailored specifically to meet the didactic needs of students already immersed in different aspects of the Irish tradition. Through careful juxtaposition of world musics, thorny questions in Irish music surrounding subjects like tune families[8] and vocal styles[9] could be analysed and scrutinised. Knowing that Irish (traditional) music would be taught separately, I gave pride of place in the curriculum to the music of the Celtic world, showing how the notion of 'celtitude' was articulated differently in the musical traditions of the Celtic fringe.[10]

I came to the interview also prepared to present my signature seminar, The Anthropology of Irish Music. Avoiding the word 'traditional', I aimed to find an inclusive definition of Irish music, one that embraced the popular and the 'classical', the national and the transnational from an anthropological perspective. Distinguishing between the *what* (the materials of music) and the *who* (the actors in music), I considered the *where* (the contexts of music) before reflecting upon the *why* (the economic, social, political and aesthetic dimensions) of Irish music as an important articulation of Irish identity. Here, I organised the module into distinctive theoretical approaches by covering the symbolic (such as interpretative anthropology) and the structuralist (such as practice anthropology), by considering the social (such as social anthropology) and the musical (such as cultural anthropology). In this way, I aimed to transcend the disciplinary distinctions in my anthropology of music which historically fell into a European strand and an American branch.

Had I had time, I should have added that hermeneutic theory informed my approach to curriculum design. Invoking an anthropological precedent,[11] I structured each lecture around three moments in the hermeneutic cycle, namely experience, reflection and interpretation. Experience is the domain of ethnography, an ethnographic description of a musical moment. The experience could involve listening or viewing, learning or performing. Reflection is the domain of analysis, a critical evaluation of a musical moment. The reflection might involve musical or linguistic analysis, audible or visual evaluation. Interpretation is the domain of understanding, an individual reading of a musical moment where anthropological theory is used to fashion a 'partial truth' or a provisional understanding. Of course, understanding as an ontological moment in the hermeneutic cycle embraces the verbal as well as the non-verbal. Here, music or dance, performance or composition represent distinctive ways of what Heidegger called 'being' (gr. *Dasein*).[12]

It is noteworthy that Mícheál described my Anthropology of Irish Music as ground-breaking. Why? To answer, it is important to look at ethnomusicology in Ireland at the time. In principle, ethnomusicology was taught at two institutions, one in Belfast at Queen's University and the other at University College Cork (UCC). In the former, the approach was, broadly speaking, anthropological and in the latter the approach was, generally speaking, musicological. Of course, there were ethnomusicologists at other institutions (such as at University College Dublin and Trinity College Dublin). However, there did not seem to be a unified approach to Irish music or a unifying aspiration towards a national ethnomusicology.

Indeed, research into Irish music in Belfast was for the most part sidelined. Although there were exceptions (with Mícheál being notable in this regard), the failure to engage with an anthropology of Irish music was due in part to political considerations and in part to academic distinctions.

At the time of my interview, Ireland was still experiencing the scourge of internecine strife. In this context, Irish (traditional) music had become a significant site of contestation. Although the performance of Irish (traditional) music had in the past transcended religious boundaries,[13] it had by then become the cultural capital of a nationalist community. To study it had political implications, especially at an institution known for its unionist credentials. The professor of anthropology at Queen's University, John Blacking, understood this. As a former pupil, Andrée Grau,[14] informed me, John Blacking believed that the study of non-western music provided a neutral space for interrogating social inequalities and political divisions not only abroad but also at home. For him, Irish [traditional] music was not sufficiently 'non-western' to be the subject of anthropological inquiry. It was a folk music more suited to the national study of folklore than the international scrutiny of anthropology.

Of course, anthropologists have studied in western contexts and folklorists have conducted research in non-western regions.[15] And many have worked in both contexts. Significantly for me, the folklorist Henry Glassie is a good example of this, Glassie having worked both in Ireland and Turkey.[16] Indeed some scholars have noted the recent convergence of the two ethnologies on the island of Ireland, namely anthropology and folklore. However, as Ó Giolláin argues, anthropological publications about the Irish tradition have tended to be completed by non-Irish scholars (mostly British and American), while folkloric studies of the same tradition have, generally speaking, been conducted by Irish academics.[17] In this sense, Blacking could claim that anthropology in Ireland was indeed an international endeavour while folklore was a national pursuit.

Earlier, Ó Giolláin posited a more critical assessment of this difference.[18] With respect to Ireland, he believed that anthropology had a practical application in the imperial past while folklore had an ideological application in the national present. For him, anthropology was international by virtue of its 'outward ethnographic gaze' but folklore was national by implication because of its inward ethnographic focus. Ó Crualaoich provides a perceptive reading of this situation with respect to Belfast.[19] Considering the history of inter-institutional relations there, he notes that anthropology had flourished in Queen's University 'without, it would appear, overmuch concern for or contact with the ethnological activities being pursued at

Cultra'; that is, with folklore at the Ulster Folk Museum. This perhaps explains Blacking's ambivalent attitude towards an anthropology of Irish music. However, it also points to a wider consideration of traditional music as music folklore rather than as music anthropology.

Ó Giolláin makes this point with respect to UCC.[20] When speaking about the institutionalisation of ethnomusicology in Ireland, he noted that Ó Riada 'brought Irish folk music into the ambit of a university musicology department'. In this context, he highlighted the relationship between Ó Riada and Mícheál, detailing Mícheál's seminal role in the foundation of the Irish World Music Centre and emphasising the central position of ethnomusicology and ethnochoreology in its formation. Ó Giolláin says nothing about how Irish 'folk music' is studied or researched there. He merely concludes that 'folk music continues to have an important presence in Irish life'.[21] Here, it is somewhat confusing that Ó Giolláin refers to Irish (traditional) music as (Irish) folk music. After all, the International Council for Traditional Music changed its name from the International Folk Music Council after much public debate more than thirty years before.[22]

Perhaps Ó Giolláin was thinking back to the long history of music folklore in Europe. In this chronology, Béla Bartók played a pivotal role by developing a comparative approach to music folklore as a means of ascertaining the national in music.[23] Of importance, this method of comparison was musicological rather than anthropological in character. It was a system that was widely emulated throughout Europe, especially in those nation states that emerged after the First World War. As one of these states, Ireland adopted the analytical methods of music folklore to establish a national patrimony. In this, Ó Riada (as a composer) and Aloys Fleischmann (as a musicologist) at UCC performed a crucial role in the musical classification of relevant genres. Indeed, Mícheál was instrumental in publishing an annotated catalogue of sources that concern Irish (traditional) music, prints and manuscripts which had originally been collated and edited by Fleischmann.[24] The two volumes still represent an important reference for the scholarly study of Irish music.

But what of the traditional in Irish music? Ó Giolláin includes a chapter on music in his edited consideration of Irish ethnologies. Written by Anthony McCann (an ethnomusicology graduate of the Academy), the chapter examines the ambivalent definition of tradition employed by leading scholars and performers in Ireland.[25] By juxtaposing 'two rivers' (namely, the show *Riverdance* with the documentary *A River of Sound*), McCann interrogates the strategic use of natural metaphors (such as rivers) to represent the polemical debates that erupted in musical discourse during the 1990s. Principal among these was the volatile axis, tradition vs innovation. McCann places Mícheál squarely in the innovative branch of this axis, since Mícheál advocated for an avant-garde stream in traditional music (by way of innovators such as Tommie Potts who experimented from within) and for a third stream in world music (by way of innovators such as Dónal Lunny who experimented from without).

In these debates, Mícheál grounded his arguments musically both as a performer and as a scholar. As McCann points out, Mícheál emphasised the sonic attributes of traditional music. In developing a traditional style of piano performance, Mícheál memorably stated: 'I began to realise for the first time that between the written note and the sound was where the tradition flowed.'[26] Recalling the Ireland–India connection proposed by Cowdery,[27] this statement was indeed an Irish take on an Indian phenomenon. Elsewhere, Mícheál would demonstrate musically with reference to his own compositions the sonic gradation between the traditional and the innovative by showing exactly where the musical break with tradition had occurred. Most interestingly, he talked about the sound world of traditional musicians, especially the harmonic consciousness of those musicians whom he recorded as a field researcher. Noteworthy for Mícheál were the distinctive notions of musical intonation and metric organisation to be found in traditional practice.

At the time of my interview, I was well versed in what McCann calls the 'uncivil wars for the soul of Irish Music'.[28] Unlike McCann, I was convinced by Mícheál's musical explication of the traditional and the innovative. Like McCann, however, I was less convinced by Mícheál's theoretical explanation of this distinction. As McCann reminds us, the concept of tradition in Irish music has become rhetorical. Repeated enough times, the traditional becomes the truthful.[29] If, as Ó Giolláin remarks provocatively, '[f]olklore is predicated on the death of tradition',[30] what then of music folklore and the death of a musical tradition? Do the musicological methods of music folklore serve merely to ossify and stultify? Do they ultimately result in the death of a musical tradition? As some critical commentators might contend, even the monumental Fleischmann collection represents a suitable tome to grace such a tomb.

For me, a national ethnomusicology should honour a national tradition of music folklore while drawing simultaneously upon an international tradition of music anthropology. The solution lies in the systematic acknowledgement of two ethnologies within the interpretative framework, with the world of music presenting a fertile space for musical comparison and the anthropology of (Irish) music providing a critical platform for anthropological conceptualisation. Interestingly, folklore and anthropology come together in the domain of field research, in this way providing both fields with a unified method for ethnographic description. To complete the hermeneutic circle, three levels can now be identified: experience (as ethnographic description), reflection (as musical analysis) and interpretation (as anthropological theorisation). In this way, a tripartite programme in ethnomusicology that includes ethnographic methods, musical analysis and anthropological interpretation might present a durable template for realising a national ethnomusicology, one that is both local and global, and both individual and inclusive.

It is satisfying to know that these three streams of ethnomusicology still flow in the great river that has become the Academy. Indeed, Mícheál and I agreed that Irish music should be allowed to seep into the murky waters of world music. However, this should not be its only destination. As mentioned above, Mícheál used ethnomusicology and ethnochoreology to validate his dream of founding a performance academy. And this he achieved. However, we disagreed about the nature of performance in such an academy. Should it be a performance academy (using lower case) where music and dance were studied academically by following the anthropological principle of ethnographic inquiry? Or should it be a Performance Academy (using upper case) where music and dance were studied practically following the musical principles of 'classical' excellence. I fear that the latter has taken precedence over the former, the spectacular now being preferred to the special, with significant consequences for the development of a national ethnomusicology in Ireland.

29
Engaging Traditional Ears in the Irish World Academy's Ethnomusicology Programme

Susan H. Motherway

Susan Motherway completed postgraduate degrees in ethnomusicology at the Irish World Academy of Music and Dance. Her doctoral thesis 'The Globalisation of Irish Traditional Song Performance' *was published by Ashgate in 2013. She lectures at the Munster Technological University and has co-edited a collection of papers on staged folklore in Ireland with John O'Connell.*

1994 was a landmark year for Irish traditional music and dance performance as a result of a global fascination with *Riverdance*.[1] It also proved a landmark year for traditional music education, when Mícheál Ó Súilleabháin established the Irish World Music Centre at the University of Limerick (UL). As a fresher that year at University College Cork (UCC) it was hard not to feel the sense of loss which imbued the music department he had just departed. Indeed, Ó Súilleabháin's charismatic personality, creative drive and desire to explore all music traditions and their junctures had left an indelible mark there. Following in the footsteps of pioneering academics such as Seán Ó Riada (1931–71) and Tomás Ó Canainn (1930–2013), he had established a comprehensive Irish traditional music programme within the BA and BMus degrees, which signalled to prospective students the department's openness to traditional musicians (who were not accepted in other colleges).[2]

His international reputation as a composer, arranger and performer drew budding musicians to study with him, happy in the knowledge they would evolve not only as music historians but also as innovative thinking performers. Irish traditional musicians were not only visible in the Department of Music at UCC, they also established a vibrant Irish Traditional Music Society on the college campus. In 1995, while still a fresher, the society in conjunction with the Department of Music delivered The Gathering. This was the fifth in a series of traditional music festivals Ó Súilleabháin had established in UCC to celebrate the music of the Shetland Isles, Cape Breton, England and the Irish diaspora.[3] Students

Figure 29.1: Siamsa Tíre Dancers perform to Mícheál Ó Súilleabháín's 'Oileán' on RTÉ's *Music of the Night* (1992). PHOTOGRAPH COURTESY OF RTÉ ARCHIVES

recognised that while Ó Riada had enabled Ireland to establish a national consciousness through its music, Ó Súilleabháin was striving to articulate a global identity for Irish traditional music. An identity he later honed at the Irish World Academy of Music and Dance.

While I missed out on Ó Súilleabháin's instruction at UCC, I was fortunate, through my involvement with Siamsa Tíre, the National Folk Theatre of Ireland, to have performed with him in 1991. His suite *Idir Eatarthu/Between Worlds* inspired Siamsa Tíre to collaborate with the choreographer Anne Courtenay in devising a work that juxtaposed traditional and contemporary dance. A subsequent performance of the work at the National Concert Hall for Raidió Teilifís Éireann, alongside Bill Whelan's *Seville Suite*,[4] brought me into the hub of traditional music experimentation and debates around innovation and tradition. Ó Súilleabháin's *A River of Sound* (1995), a joint RTÉ and BBC Northern Ireland production, flamed this debate further by reaffirming that the tradition could be reinvigorated by experimenting with musical sounds and concepts underpinning other music traditions to produce forms of musical hybridity, fusion, deconstruction and bricolage. This ignited discussions in the Irish traditional music community in relation to musical change, acceptable limits of innovation and the impact of commercialisation and the music industry on traditional music. The culminating *Crosbhealach an Cheoil, The Crossroads Conference 1996* that took place in Dublin drew over forty academics to grapple with ideas around revival, decline, intellectualisation and transmission in Irish traditional music.

The Irish traditional music community's engagement with the themes of the conferencesignalled a growing desire to discuss and debate issues effecting the ebb and flow of the tradition. The graduate ethnomusicology programme developed by Ó Súilleabháin at the Academy in 1994 provided an appropriate environment for this to continue, by enabling students to document the tradition at different stages of its development and stimulate discussion within the academic community in relation to musical change as a result of external influences, be they economic, social, cultural or technological. Ó Súilleabháin's motivation for this programme came from his experience of the ethnomusicology programme at Queen's University Belfast (QUB), led by his mentor and PhD supervisor Professor John Blacking. While Blacking's programme was forged within an anthropology department, Ó Súilleabháin established his within an academy of music and dance, a programme that valued the oral and literate tradition equally. In so doing, he broke away from the hegemonic art music model found in music departments around the world, striving instead to create a broader community of sound. This development not alone vindicated Irish traditional music but enabled graduates like myself to engage with global scholarship and continue our journey in academia. Students no longer had to travel abroad for training in ethnomusicological methods, and staff for Irish music and world music programmes in Ireland could be recruited locally. Most importantly, it enabled emic perspectives of Irish musical life in all its richness and diversity to emerge.

UL's central role in establishing a national committee for the International Council for Traditional Music (ICTM) in Ireland (2005) further cemented the significance of the field to Irish music and established a network amongst academic institutions and societies of related disciplines[5] on the island of Ireland. In time, the Irish committee for ICTM strove to broaden the ethnocentric focus of ethnomusicological study in the country so as to include other cultures on the island of Ireland and abroad. It also problematised the concept of a national ethnomusicology by exploring trans-national, post-national and regional dimensions.

The demands of PhD supervision and academic leadership meant that Ó Súilleabháin was unable to deliver the new MA programme. However, his contribution to the innovation and tradition debate within the media, his work under John Blacking in QUB,[6] his later publications on the creative process in Irish traditional music[7] and his compositional activity had initiated the translation of ethnomusicological concepts to an Irish context. Grounded in musical analysis, his publications explain the building blocks of the tradition and how performers improvise their own individual style using processes of alteration, variation, and concordance to melody, phrasing, rhythm and structure. Benefiting from Blacking's anthropological background, Ó Súilleabháin also developed a taxonomy for analysing Irish traditional music which included folk terms and metaphors alongside more analytical and descriptive terms.[8] He also studied musical behaviour, recognising the impact of the performance situation on a musician's performance and in particular the interaction between the musician and the dancer. He was deeply interested in musical intelligence and explored the relationship between creativity and musical dexterity.[9] In his life's work on Tommie Potts we also see him explore the psychological and emotional world of the performer in order to find the essence of his style and artistic expression. Ó Súilleabháin looked towards international academics such as J.H. Kwabena Nketia (1921–2019) and Nazir Jairazbhoy (1927–2009) to uncover models of experimentation in other oral music traditions and determine what might be considered prophetic or peripheral. Indeed, his set accented tone theory[10] presented a model of audibility which determined the limit of deviation from the standard tune which was acceptable to Irish traditional ears.

In 1997 John Morgan O'Connell became the course director for the MA Ethnomusicology programme, bringing with him his experience of ethnomusicology at UCLA. The curriculum design provided a very strong theoretical grounding in ethnomusicology. The History of Ethnomusicology and Anthropology of Music modules explicitly trained students in the history of the field and its theories, while the World Music Survey module provided an intense overview of musical systems. Musical enquiry was further supported by modules in Ethnomusicology and Fieldwork Methods. For their final project, students were encouraged to reflect on their musical encounters and present written, composition or performance projects that would articulate some element of their experience. This prompt led me to revisit my experience with Siamsa Tíre and explore the authenticity of re-presenting the past on stage. The course catered for students from a variety of academic backgrounds, which in my year were predominantly music and cultural studies. It also catered for a variety of music interests, which in my case (academic year 1998–9) included British, Chinese, Irish and popular music interests. The course constantly required students to reflect on their own musical experience, and guest lectures and seminars in Irish music provided additional critical engagement with current topics in the field for Irish scholars. However, having progressed from world music lectures in African drumming, Indonesian gamelan and Indian classical music at UCC, where the practical engagement was prioritised in the experience of the student, the programme suffered from a lack of active engagement with and experience of world music.

Soon after graduating I took a post at the Munster Technological University Kerry (MTU Kerry), where they were delivering a programme in folk theatre. In this context traditional song performance was used as a tool for setting the historical context, providing emotional expression as well as enabling storytelling and character development. Debates on traditional and innovative performance practices were prevalent, as were discussions on sources, language, arrangement and regional styles. My desire to gain a greater understanding of what constituted traditional song performance in a modern context and how performers mediated the divide between local and global audiences led me to undertake a PhD at the Academy. While I benefited considerably from the knowledge gained during this degree, it was the experiences that made it valuable. My supervisor John Morgan O'Connell prompted me to engage with academic groups and forums internationally. I became a student representative on the US-based Society for Ethnomusicology Council, secretary for ICTM Ireland, visiting research associate at QUB, and Ireland Canada University Foundation scholar at the Memorial University of Newfoundland. In 2013 Ashgate published my PhD thesis and Ó Súilleabháin travelled to Tralee to launch *The Globalisation of Irish Traditional Song Performance*[11] for me, a proud day.

My training on the MA and PhD programmes has stood to me as my career evolves and I adopt my teaching approach to fit other areas such as music technology, creative media and music education. This influence moves beyond the use of drumming to develop improvisational skills, or the use of ethnographic methods to investigate the role of the producer in the studio, but focuses more holistically on my approach to music education. Indeed, I apply an ethnomusicological perspective to the study of all music. I have also adopted the UCC approach to world music education established by Ó Súilleabháin by combining music analysis and contextual studies with

Figure 29.2: Mícheál Ó Súilleabháín attending the Staged Folklore Colloquium in Siamsa Tíre, Tralee in 2018 with Susan Motherway, Pat Ahern and Dermod McCarthy.
PHOTOGRAPH BY JOHN WALSH

creative performance elements of the music modules offered in MTU Kerry. What differs is that my instruments are predominantly computers. In 2018 I once again revisited the area of folk theatre to document fifty years of performances by Siamsa Tíre in Tralee. Here again, my faithful colleagues O'Connell and Ó Súilleabháin came to my support, offering their unique insights to the development of a colloquium and edited collection of papers on the theme of Staged Folklore in Ireland.[12] When Ó Súilleabháin passed I felt the loss of a mentor and friend, and wondered who else could provide such a leading voice in Irish traditional music studies. I feel so fortunate to have met him and thankful that he started me on my academic journey.

30
Ethnochoreology and Traditional Dance in the Irish World Academy

Catherine E. Foley, Orfhlaith Ní Bhriain, and Mats Melin

Catherine Foley is emeritus senior lecturer in ethnochoreology, University of Limerick; founding director of the National Dance Archive of Ireland; and chair emeritus of Dance Research Forum Ireland. She has published extensively including two monographs, Irish Traditional Step Dancing in North Kerry *(2012) and* Step Dancing in Ireland: Culture and history *(2013).*

Orfhlaith Ní Bhriain is senior lecturer in dance at the University of Limerick. She directs the MA Ethnochoreology, MA Irish Dance Studies and MA Irish Dance Performance programmes. An accomplished performer and teacher of Irish music, song and dance, she has published extensively in the field of arts and health.

Mats Melin is a Swedish-born traditional dancer, choreographer and researcher. Mats has worked professionally with dance in Scotland since 1995 and in Ireland since 2005. He has been engaged in freelance work nationally and internationally. Mats is a lecturer emeritus in dance at the University of Limerick.

This essay presents the voices of three ethnochoreologists who engaged in the study and teaching of ethnochoreology and traditional dance practices at the Irish World Academy of Music and Dance (hereafter, the Academy). These ethnochoreologists are Catherine Foley, Orfhlaith Ní Bhriain, and Mats Melin. As founding director of the Academy, Mícheál Ó Súilleabháin was instrumental in finding a place for these fields within his vision for the Academy. The essay examines this trajectory focusing on how each of the three ethnochoreologists encountered Mícheál and how they contributed to the vision and to the development of the fields of ethnochoreology and traditional dance practices within the university education system in Ireland and, in particular, the Academy.

Catherine E. Foley
Encountering Mícheál Ó Súilleabháin

I first formally met Mícheál in 1975 as a second-year undergraduate student on the BMus degree programme at University College Cork (UCC). Mícheál had taken over as lecturer in Irish traditional music from Tomás Ó Canainn, who in turn had taken over from Seán Ó Riada. I had known Mícheál from an earlier encounter. My sister Pat worked for the Cork International Choral Festival during the early seventies and she had heard Mícheál play Irish traditional music on the piano at the festival. She informed me about Mícheál's playing, and on learning that he would be playing with the UCC Irish traditional music group Pangur Bán the following weekend, I went to Blarney to hear them. Having grown up immersed in Irish traditional music, song and dance at home in Cork city, my interest had been sparked. Side by side with this traditional music immersion was my formal training in Irish dance with Peggy McTeggart, Cork, and classical music training on piano with Angel Climent at the Cork School of Music, and later Geraldine Neeson in Cork. It was, however, a later informal dance performance by me at the Cork International Choral Festival in 1976, during my third year of the BMus degree, that Mícheál, Professor Aloys Fleischmann – our professor of music at UCC– and my fellow classmates discovered that I was an Irish dancer. This performance motivated Professor Fleischmann to invite me and another BMus student, Aidan O'Carroll, to perform at the following year's choral festival. The acknowledgement of me as a dancer, as well as a musician, would be significant for my later academic trajectory into dance and ethnochoreology and Mícheál would play an important supportive role in this.

Muckross House and collecting Irish traditional music, song and dance

While employed as a secondary school teacher of music in Baile Mhúirne in the west Cork Gaeltacht, I received a letter enquiring if I would be interested in being interviewed for a part-time position as a collector of Irish traditional music, song and dance for Muckross House in Killarney. I was interested, and I was subsequently interviewed by Mícheál and Tom Munnelly. I was successful, and in the summer of 1980 my work as a collector commenced and this continued each summer from 1980 to 1985.[1] This work included identifying traditional musicians, singers and dancers in the region and collecting, recording and transcribing their materials. Aware at the time that I did not have an equivalent documentation system for dance as I had for music, I went to the LABAN Centre for Movement and Dance at the Goldsmiths' College, University of London in 1984 to learn Labanotation and to undertake a PhD, based on the traditional dance component of my collection. Mícheál was very supportive of this undertaking. In 1988 I successfully completed the PhD, which was the first ethnographic examination of Irish traditional step dancing undertaken anywhere in the world.[2] Going to London to undertake the PhD was necessary at the time as no university in the Republic of Ireland had doctoral research opportunities in dance. Undertaking a PhD with John Blacking at Queen's University Belfast was an alternative but I had been advised that LABAN in London would be a better choice due to its training in Labanotation – the system for documenting movement. Once I completed my PhD, Mícheál invited me to cover for him in the Department of Music at UCC while he went on sabbatical to the US. I lectured on Irish traditional music, song and dance, provided music and dance workshops, and designed and delivered a module on Ethnochoreology/Irish Dance Studies. This was the first time that such a module had been delivered at undergraduate level within the university system in the Republic of Ireland. During this time, Mícheál applied for funding to the American Ireland Fund for the establishment of a Centre for Irish Dance Studies at UCC; the application had the support of the president of UCC, Dr Tadhg Ó Ciardha. The application, unfortunately, was not successful at this time. In 1989 Mícheál returned from the United States and we made a joint presentation to international business entrepreneurs at Muckross House, Killarney for financial support for the establishment of the Centre for Irish Dance Studies at UCC. We would have to wait longer, however, until 1996, before this initiative, as part of a broader vision for the indigenous performing arts at the University of Limerick (UL), would become a reality.

Pioneering the fields of ethnochoreology and Irish traditional dance performance into the university system

In September 1996 I took up an appointment as lecturer in ethnochoreology with a specialisation in Irish traditional dance at the Academy.[3] John Morgan O'Connell took up another appointment in ethnomusicology and both of us were to lead in the design of MA programmes in ethnochoreology and ethnomusicology. I was aware that the establishment of an MA in Ethnochoreology programme was new within the university system in Ireland and, indeed, within the university system in Europe. Mícheál, then chair of music and founding director of the Academy, was instrumental in facilitating this inclusion as part of a broader vision for the performing arts and their study within university education in Ireland.

Joining the academic team at UL in 1996 as an ethnochoreologist with a specialisation in Irish dance placed both ethnochoreology and Irish dance within the university structure. With my joint passions for ethnochoreology and Irish dance performance, the MA Ethnochoreology programme was designed not only to provide advanced training in theoretical, conceptual and methodological issues pertaining to the field of ethnochoreology, but to facilitate the pedagogical journeys of the student scholars/dancers/artists on the programme. To this end, practical dance workshops were integral to the programme and students had the choice to undertake final presentations either as a full thesis or a combined thesis and performance/choreography. The programme had its first intake of five students in September 1997 with ethnochoreological training that included modules in the History and Theory of Ethnochoreology; Methods in Ethnochoreology; Dance Documentation Skills – Labanotation; World Dance Survey; The History of Irish Dance; and elective modules where students could select either an academic-based or practice-based module of study and practice.

The student profile for the MA Ethnochoreology over the years consisted of Irish and international students, all coming with their movement research interests. For example, students specialised in contemporary dance or Irish dance practices such as step dancing, competitive Irish dance, *sean-nós* dancing, or set dancing; others examined yoga, martial arts, or specific dance practices such as flamenco, Oriental dance, salsa, casino, Scottish step dancing, and hip-hop. Theoretical foci included identity, diaspora, gender issues, embodiment, transmission, cosmopolitanism, politics, ethnicity, ageism, and more. I was course director of the MA Ethnochoreology programme for twenty-three years until my retirement in 2019 from UL. During this time, several of the MA Ethnochoreology students continued with doctoral studies. Some students pursued research doctorates while others pursued arts practice doctorates, where they integrated their performance practices into their research. A number of these doctoral students progressed on to higher-education posts in the field. Orfhlaith Ní Bhriain and Mats Melin were two of these students (see below).

As well as my work in developing ethnochoreology at the Academy, Mícheál also asked me in 1999 to lead a team in the design of an MA Irish Traditional Dance Performance programme; this would be the first master's programme in Irish dance performance at any university in the world. This was an exciting initiative and the university subsequently approved the programme design. In September 1999 the programme commenced with three students. For the first year of this new and internationally unique master's undertaking, Stirling Productions in Northern Ireland produced a thirty-minute documentary on the MA programme entitled *The Dancing Masters* (2000). It was one of a six-part television series on Irish dance named *Rising Steps*, and it was broadcast on RTÉ in 2000 and numerous times later in Ireland and elsewhere.

The MA Irish Traditional Dance Performance programme focused on developing and enhancing students' dance skills and their cultural, analytical, interpretive and choreographic skills for performance. With a specialisation in Irish dance, the programme also exposed students to contemporary dance principles, dance documentation skills, world dance practices and academic reflection. Students devised and performed their own original solo choreographies and worked with other students and mentors in developing and performing new ensemble dance works. Students also shared some classes with ethnochoreology students where they learned fieldwork techniques, world dance practices and the importance of contextualising and historicising dance practices.[4]

The student profile for the MA Irish Traditional Dance Performance programme was again Irish and international. I was course director for the programme for fifteen years, until 2013, when the position was taken up by Orfhlaith Ní Bhriain.

In 2016, there were further programme developments. Mats Melin, Orfhlaith Ní Bhriain and myself designed an MA in Irish Dance Studies; Mats Melin was appointed course director of the programme. Similar to the MA Ethnochoreology and MA Irish Traditional Dance Performance programmes, the student profile was both Irish and international.

Other initiatives

While directing the MA Ethnochoreology and MA Irish Traditional Dance Performance programmes, I established and directed a three-day dance festival called Tráth na gCos in 1997. As always, Mícheál was supportive of the festival, which became an annual event in the Academy's calendar until 2005. The festival generally consisted of dance workshops, concerts and seminars;[5] these were recorded for archival, research and pedagogical purposes. An outreach aspect was integral to the festival, where some events were open to the general public.

Also, as part of the inclusion of indigenous arts within the Academy, Blas: The International Summer School of Irish Traditional Music and Dance was established by Mícheál and P.A. Moore in 1997 at the university; I was a founding director of the summer school with Niall Keegan and Sandra Joyce. Lectures, concerts, workshops and a fieldtrip were included in the summer school, illustrating the integration of practice and academic reflection. This summer school successfully continues at the Academy to this day (see below).

In addition, with the objective of raising the profile of dance research in Ireland within a global context, I established Dance Research Forum

Ireland (DRFI) in 2003 during the hosting of the Society of Dance History Scholars 26th International Conference at UL. A board of directors was appointed and I was elected chair.[6] DRFI was established as an international, inclusive and multidisciplinary organisation for the promotion, sharing and development of dance research – both academic and practice-based research.[7] Again, this initiative had the support of Mícheál and the 1st International Conference of DRFI took place at UL in 2005. Proceedings of DRFI conferences were produced and published to contribute to dance research and knowledge in Ireland and further afield.

Also, with the support of Mícheál and Gobnait O'Riordan, director of the Glucksman Library at UL, DRFI was successful in acquiring funding from the Arts Council of Ireland for a feasibility report to be undertaken for the establishment of a National Dance Archive;[8] a dance archive had been a primary objective of DRFI since its inception in 2003. Following the feasibility report, written by Dr Victoria O'Brien, seed funding was awarded by the Arts Council of Ireland to UL for the National Dance Archive of Ireland (NDAI) to be established at the Glucksman Library in 2009; I was appointed the founding director of the archive, again with Mícheál's support.

With my involvement with the International Council for Traditional Music (ICTM) since 1996, and particularly the ICTM's Study Group on Ethnochoreology, Mícheál supported the hosting of the ICTM's 27th Symposium of the Study Group on Ethnochoreology at the Irish World Academy in 2012; I fulfilled the role of chair of the local organising committee for the symposium with assistance from colleagues at the Academy including Orfhlaith Ní Bhriain, Mats Melin and Colin Quigley. In addition, we successfully hosted the ICTM's 44th World Conference at UL in 2017; I was co-chair with Colin Quigley of the local organising committee. Mícheál was invited to present the keynote address at the conference. The address, 'The Redress of Music: Music, mediation and parity of esteem', was later published in the ICTM *Yearbook*.[9] At one of the three concerts that took place during the conference, Sionna – A World of Music and Dance, Mícheál performed, as well as other members of faculty, and past and current students of the Academy.

Throughout my career at the Academy, I have often performed there and elsewhere with Mícheál, Niall Keegan and others. In 2005 Mícheál commissioned me to choreograph a new set dance as part of the Sionna festival; this became the *Sionna Set Dance* and with an award from the Arts Council of Ireland it was published in 2007 as a multimedia educational package, with graphic design by Michael McCabe and Mediatician Multimedia Design.[10]

Figure 30.1: The *Sionna Set Dance*. Dancers: Catherine Foley, Brian Morrissey, Orfhlaith Ní Bhriain, Michael McCabe, Maria O'Connor, Mats Melin, Maldon Meehan and Robert Kelly. Choreographer: Catherine Foley, 2005. PHOTOGRAPH BY MAURICE GUNNING

Mícheál supported and facilitated my academic journey and the various dance initiatives and projects I aspired to create, host or develop. He was a champion for the parity of esteem in music and dance and without his encouragement, support and generosity of spirit, the vision that is the Academy would not have come into existence.

Orfhlaith Ní Bhriain

1994 was a very special year in the evolution of Irish dance. It was the year when *Riverdance* was performed as an interlude piece for the Eurovision Song Contest. It was also the year when Professor Mícheál Ó Súilleabháin relocated from Cork to Limerick and established the Academy.

I had first encountered Mícheál in the early 1980s during a live recital that he gavein Halla Íde, a venue in Limerick city centre run under the auspices of Conradh na Gaeilge. He spoke about music and how just about any melody could be played in any tempo. He then went on and played well-known songs and anthems in a variety of time signatures with a range of different time grooves and this made me reflect on my understanding of Irish dance music.

Years later I took a career break from my teaching job and made an appointment to see Mícheál in UL; he advised me to meet with the faculty members who were leading the ethnochoreology and ethnomusicology programmes, namely Dr Catherine Foley and Dr John Morgan O'Connell. I enrolled on the ethnochoreology programme in 1997 under the directorship of Dr Foley and that changed the course of my life. I had been immersed in all aspects of Irish culture since childhood and had never entertained the possibility of studying it in an academic context. The year spent at the Academy changed my world view and changed my career path from primary education to postgraduate studies and dance pedagogy.

Mícheál was an ardent supporter of and advocate for dance, specifically Irish dance and contemporary dance which he promoted and facilitated constantly. Having completed the MA programme, my first tutor's hours were teaching Irish dance to study abroad students at UL. I was also brought on board for Irish-language interviews and programmes at the Academy. Mícheál had a wonderful way of drawing you in to a project. He was a visionary and a compelling leader. He was fearless, and demanded the highest levels of commitment from himself and from those around him.

I received a part-time contract to lead the Irish dance component of the BA Irish Music and Dance in 2003. This enabled me to commence my doctoral studies at the Academy on 'Documenting the Creative Processes in Competitive Irish Step Dance'. At the time, in the early 2000s, we didn't have a dedicated building and we utilised every building on campus that had a wooden floor for our Irish dance classes. I also had the opportunity to act as course director of the BA Irish Music and Dance.

I was invited by Mícheál, Niall Keegan and Sandra Joyce to co-direct Blas International Summer School in 2003 alongside my friend and colleague Michael McCabe. Mícheál wanted people to experience music and dance at the Irish World Music Centre and he even took to the floor to dance a polka set at the summer school céilí. Mícheál did not see obstacles but rather viewed challenges as opportunities or *féidireachtaí*. As the dance programme expanded, space was always an issue and Mícheál, Paula Dundon and I even sought alternative spaces off campus in Kilmurry church, local hotels and buildings in the city centre.

When construction in Ireland came to a standstill during the recession, Mícheál persisted with his vision and facilitated the building of the Academy, which commenced in 2008. He ensured that world-class dance studios were provided for in the design and I have a fond memory of a hard-hat tour of the building when it was just a shell with brickwork and cranes. Mícheál however could hear the music and see the dancers.

Mícheál and I shared a connection to garrison towns, coming from Clonmel and Limerick respectively, and possibly as a result of this we had a shared passion for the Irish language which opened up further opportunities for me in documentaries on radio and television. During a programme on the life of Kitty Linnane, which I presented for TG4 in 2013, I had an opportunity to play a piano duet with Mícheál. As a person, scholar and academic, his presence filled the room, yet he was willing to share the stage. He also supported my academic endeavours for the *Terminology of Irish Dance* text published in 2008 and *Jigs to Jacobites* in 2018.

On reflection, I was lucky to encounter the Irish World Music Centre, and I appreciate the personal opportunities and also the legacy for Irish dance through Mícheál's work with Catherine Foley and later myself and Mats Melin, both alumni of the MA Ethnochoreology programme.

Mats Melin

I first met Mícheál in 2000 when I visited the Academy during the Tráth na gCos festival with fellow Scottish dancers and Gaelic singers. I remember him as a vibrant and energising person with a great presence in the room and one who made you feel present and valued too. After I had finished my MA studies in ethnochoreology under Dr Catherine Foley in 2004–5, I was asked by Mícheál to join the Academy faculty team. I primarily and initially worked on the undergraduate level, to help expand the curriculum in my areas of expertise in aspects of ethnochoreology and research methods, Scottish and Cape Breton dance traditions, and to further encourage connections with the Scandinavian traditions and third-level institutions there. I was delighted to do these tasks, as it gave me an opportunity to further extend my own research into these areas. In particular, I was able to pursue my doctoral research into the Cape Breton step dance tradition, an area that both Mícheál and Catherine encouraged me to study deeper. Through my research I have been able to expand the Academy portfolio of knowledge to students on all study levels and I personally developed new ways of teaching and feeling movement. Perhaps the greatest highlight of my interaction with Mícheál over the years was the 2015 launch of my book *One With the Music*, a result of my PhD research into Cape Breton step dance transmission and tradition.[11] A full circle was completed when visiting Cape Breton musicians and dancers, together with our own Academy students, celebrated this tradition through music and dance in the Academy building, and Mícheál did the formal book launch.

I feel privileged to have studied, researched, created choreographies and worked as part of Mícheál's team at the Academy. He made me feel that my research interests were valid and continually asked about my progress and suggested new ideas to pursue. Encouraged by his creative energies, I continue to write about and teach my research in percussive and related dance forms of Scotland and Cape Breton.

Conclusion

With his vision, Mícheál influenced the integration of ethnochoreology and traditional dance into the university system in Ireland. He was a huge supporter of the notion of the parity of esteem in the arts and, as such, indigenous practices sat side by side with western classical arts. As ethnochoreologists and music/dance practitioners, we benefited from Mícheál's vision as he made way for all three of us to be part of this vision at the Academy.

31

Music Education at the Irish World Academy

Jean Downey and Ernestine Healy

Jean Downey is course director for the Professional Master of Education (Music) at the Irish World Academy of Music and Dance, UL. She is chief advising examiner for Leaving Certificate Performing, Composing and Listening. She is an active member of the Post-Primary Music Teachers' Association where she established the New Music Teachers' Forum.

Ernestine Healy is a traditional musician and secondary school music teacher. She was course director and lecturer at the Irish World Academy of Music and Dance, UL and tutor in the School of Music, UCC. She is currently a full-time advisor to the junior cycle music team, Department of Education and Skills.

Jean Downey

In this essay the reader is provided with insight into Mícheál Ó Súilleabháin's contribution to music education. The journey begins with Mícheál as lecturer in University College Cork (UCC) and it continues with his role in the establishment of Maoin Cheoil an Chláir, acknowledged as a significant milestone for music education in the west of Ireland. His contribution to music teachers, and in particular to post-primary music teachers, is then outlined. Finally, the development of music education postgraduate programmes at the Academy is presented, followed by part two of this essay contributed by music education graduate Ernestine Healy.

First encounter with Mícheál Ó Súilleabháin

The years in which I studied for the BMus degree with Professor Aloys Fleischmann in UCC were very special. The Music Department was housed in the old rectory on Western Road. Professor Fleischmann, the chair of music, was a wonderful teacher. He recognised the potential in all his students and his manner was always formal. He appreciated Irish music and it was core throughout the course of our study. Just five years before I began my BMus studies, Mícheál Ó Súilleabháin was a student in the same degree programme.

In our first year of study, modules on Irish music were taught by traditional musician and singer Tomás Ó Canainn who had undertaken this role as lecturer in Irish music following the untimely passing of Seán Ó Riada in 1971. When we were starting our second year of study in 1975 a young Mícheál Ó Súilleabháin was appointed as lecturer in Irish music. Mícheál taught us Irish music for the remaining years of our BMus programme. Among my peers in our BMus class were some outstanding traditional Irish musicians and dancers, including Catherine Foley whom I would join as a colleague at the Academy in the late 1990s.

Mícheál was a gifted teacher. I was trained as a classical musician with little background in traditional music. Under Mícheál's direction I learned to play tunes on the tin whistle with some success and on the fiddle with less success, but always with great encouragement from Mícheál. As a lecturer Mícheál's manner of addressing us was less formal than that of Professor Fleischmann. It was clear that a very special bond existed between them and they both had a great love and huge respect for the Irish music tradition. Mícheál's lectures were delivered with great passion, ensuring that we all developed an understanding of traditional Irish music and of its performance styles. Engagement with the music was key and we learned to connect with the music aurally and in performance. He introduced us to the music of outstanding local and national performers such as Seán Ó Sé, Tomás Ó Canainn, Tommy Hayes, Na Filí and The Chieftains, to mention but a few. A highlight throughout the years while he taught in UCC was when he brought these musicians into the Music Department.

In our final year of study we all had to undertake an Irish music fieldwork project. This was a double challenge. Fieldwork research was new to most of us and, secondly, many of us were not traditional musicians. Mícheál provided us with the skills we needed to undertake our research, lifelong skills which would be used in our future careers and musical journeys. He also directed us towards the traditional community so that we could undertake our research. Singer and tin whistle player Finbarr O'Mullane was a member of our local church choir. It transpired that Mícheál knew Finbarr's teacher and, to my surprise, I was able to undertake my research in my own urban locality. Our studies with Mícheál in our final year brought us beyond the realm of Irish traditional music. He introduced us to the traditional music, language and culture of Scotland; it was clear that he had a great interest in these traditions and this enriched our learning. Many years later I was to recall this interest when travelling with him to and from Maoin Cheoil an Chláir. Mícheál would recount his conversations with his scholar friends in Scotland, they speaking in Scottish Gaelic and Mícheál speaking in Irish.

Maoin Cheoil an Chláir

The enabling of music education for everyone was very important to Mícheál. He often spoke about the 'bridge' between traditional music and classical, which reflected his own upbringing:

> Mícheál was more exposed as a child and young teenager to pop music, classical music, light opera and choral singing than he was to traditional music. There was no Comhaltas branch in Clonmel and traditional music was, at this stage (in the 1950s), more associated with the rural hinterlands than the towns like Clonmel.[1]

It is no surprise then that a particularly significant achievement was the founding of Maoin Cheoil an Chláir by Fr Harry Bohan and Mícheál Ó Súilleabháin. In 1992 Fr Bohan contacted Mícheál to discuss his plan for an inclusive music school. The two found that their ideas converged, and they agreed that such cultural development was at the root of all other developments, economic and social. Mícheál chaired the enterprise, wrote a description and assembled committees to develop the plan and to appoint a director. Andrew Robinson was appointed director in 1993[2] and the school was opened by President Mary Robinson in October of that year. Based in Erasmus Smith House in Ennis, the school was unique in its time and offered music tuition to traditional and classical music students. In an interview with Denise Meaghar, Mícheál spoke about the grounding of his vision for the school:

> The more you dug into traditional music, certainly in my time, the more you dug into the local soil, the more you came up in some other part of the world. In other words, studying traditional music in any one area – let's say it is west Clare fiddling or something – suddenly and, particularly through academic disciplines like ethnomusicology and the study of traditional music in different cultures, suddenly you are going, 'Oh hang on a minute, that is the way they do it in Africa or certain people in Asia do it'. So there is a process here. You were actually releasing yourself into a global form of music-making, in other words, what we would call playing by ear, which is the global norm of the classical tradition of playing by ear and by eye – [it] is exceptional and is only a tiny minority of what World music does.

It is that connection of the feet and the head, of being grounded and at the same time having a vision; all of that of course, through the energy of the human body, resurrected or standing on the earth itself, suddenly becomes more and more relevant, more and more powerful, not just a symbol but an actual manifestation of whatever actually is emerging in our own times.[3]

At Maoin Cheoil music education and culture were nourished and cherished, at one point having over 500 students enrolled. Throughout the lifetime of the school it was led by a number of creative and inspiring directors, among them Colette Moloney and Hans Boller. The school was set up with a grant from the European LEADER scheme, 'which combats rural decline, as a model for a new style of music school suitable for areas where there is a local musical culture to be cherished'.[4] This inclusive music school was led by community education values and many years later Mícheál recognised it as a model and forerunner of the new Music Generation programmes which have been established in many locations in Ireland. Mícheál was an extraordinary and gifted chair of the school's board of directors and remained an active and loyal member until his untimely passing, when Seán Conlon became chair of the board. Many students were provided with both a traditional and a classical music education in this unique music school, taught by excellent teachers and encouraged by Mícheál. In Maoin Cheoil an Chláir traditional and classical lessons take place side by side, with specialist teachers for each discipline, and 'while no diluting of one form or another is entertained, many students find no trouble in crossing over between the styles'.[5]

The school music-teaching community

At the time Mícheál moved to the University of Limerick (UL) in 1994, I was a music teacher in Presentation Secondary School in Ballyphehane in Cork. From 1996 to '98 I was seconded by the In-career Development Unit of the Department of Education as a member of the Curriculum Support Team for Music to support teachers in the rollout of the new Leaving Certificate music programme. One of our tasks was to create resources for teachers and students. To that end recordings of some of the prescribed works were undertaken, one such recording being that of Irish composer Gerald Barry's *Piano Quartet No. 1*. Martin Barrett, a member of the Curriculum Support Team and a former student of Mícheál's at UCC, liaised with Mícheál in this regard. Mícheál invited the composer, the musicians and the team to the Academy to make the recording. The work and information provided by Gerald Barry were recorded in the Performing Arts Centre, a lovely intimate space of the Academy in the Foundation building at UL. A copy of the recording was subsequently presented to every secondary school music teacher in the country and to libraries and education centres. It was a great joy to meet with Mícheál once again and to make my first visit to the dynamic space he created at the Academy. Mícheál's welcome was, as always, warm and generous. He was very anxious to support the music education community.

The Post Primary Music Teachers Association is a national association which aims to assist teachers in the development of music education in post-primary schools. Local branches of the association are active throughout the academic year and a conference takes place annually. Mícheál's contribution to the association is widely acknowledged. The inspirational keynote address which he presented at the national conference on 30 September 2000 in the Rivercourt Hotel in Kilkenny is warmly remembered. Mícheál's final musical performance at a more recent national conference on 14 October 2016 in the Heritage Hotel in Portlaoise is another treasured memory. His love of poetry was well known, and he would enthral and inspire by quoting time and again from the works of great poets, especially Seamus Heaney. He is deeply missed by the music-teaching community, while he continues to live on through his music in schools and classrooms throughout the country.

Students in Irish post-primary schools have the option to take music as a subject right up to Leaving Certificate. The Leaving Certificate syllabus of the Department of Education states that students are required to be familiar with 'the range and variety of Irish music heard today, Irish musical idioms and influences, and to have an understanding of traditional and modern day performing styles'.[6] Reference to the music of Mícheál Ó Súilleabháin is made in many school music text books. It is clear, based on conversations with teachers across the country over the last five decades, among them Noreen O'Sullivan, a music teacher in Bishopstown Community School in Cork city and a former student of Mícheál's, that music students have experienced Mícheál's music and have an understanding of his contribution to the tradition and to Irish music of today. Some of the music teachers themselves were students of Mícheál's in UCC and were well placed to inform their students of his life and works.

Programme development

In 1996 Mícheál Ó Súilleabháin set up an international design team to establish a one-year postgraduate music education programme at the Irish World Music Centre. The programme was a Graduate Diploma in Education

(GDE) (Music) and it was to be jointly taught by the School of Education and the Academy. Those on the design team included Mícheál Ó Súilleabháin, David Elliott, Marie McCarthy, Helen Phelan and Kari Veblen from the music subject discipline, alongside Tom Kelly who was the course director of the sister programme, GDE (Business). The newly designed GDE (Music) programme was then, and continues to be today, unique in the Republic of Ireland. The teaching and the pedagogy is subject-specific. Students are prepared to be post-primary school teachers and their professional qualification enables them to be registered as teachers by the Teaching Council. During their course of study students are encouraged to take elective modules in musical performing, thereby enabling them to further their own musical practice as they begin their professional journey as music teachers. Under the expert direction of Helen Phelan, the founder and first director of the programme, the first class of student music teachers began their course of study in 1997. School placement is an important element in the programme and in its first year this was carefully monitored by Helen, Martin Barrett, and Marie McCarthy who was completing her book *Passing It On* while resident at the Academy. McCarthy references 'an innovative programme to prepare second-level music teachers which was developed by Mícheál Ó Súilleabháin during the 1980s where prospective teachers were trained in traditional as well as classical music'.[7]

In 1998 I arrived and took over the course directorship of the programme for one year, and I am still in that position. The music education programme from its foundation to the time of writing has been run under the careful guidance and direction of its external examiners, Barry Burgess (University of Ulster Coleraine), Gary Spruce (Open University), Graham Welch (University College London), Marie McCarthy (University of Michigan) and Patricia Shehan Campbell (University of Washington). My time as course director has been the most inspirational time of my professional career. It is impossible not to be inspired in such a creative space with wonderful students and for much of that time under the artistic leadership and vision of Mícheál Ó Súilleabháin.

In the past twenty-four years, graduates of the music education programme have returned to the Academy to undertake master's degree programmes in disciplines such as chant and ritual song, community music, ethnomusicology, Irish music performance and music therapy.

In 2003 Mícheál met with Elizabeth Shannon, and the William V. Shannon Fellowship link was established with the Academy.[8] The fellowship facilitated links between the music education programmes at Boston University and at the Academy by funding two students of the GDE

(Music) programme to complete their teaching practice in the prestigious Boston Latin School and Lexington High School. Tim Treacy, graduate of the GDE (Music) and of the MA Community Music programme, was awarded the fellowship to undertake his PhD studies at Boston University.

In 2004 it became apparent that some of the graduates who had qualified with the GDE (Music) were keen to progress to master's-degree level, specifically in music education. An internal design team was set up and external guidance was provided by Graham Welch. The MA Education (Music) degree was established and the first cohort of students began their studies in 2006. To support the new programme, Mícheál was offered an annual bursary by the Knights of the Round Table in Limerick which provided the funding for each of the MEd (Music) students to travel to London for a short visit where they were able to progress their research with Graham Welch and his colleagues at the Institute of Education, University of London.

In 2005 Mícheál met with Janie Orr, MBE, chief executive of EMI Music Sound Foundation, and an annual bursary was established. EMI Music Sound Foundation, now Universal Music UK Sound Foundation, has provided strong and consistent support for students at the Academy. Initially awarded to students of MA Community Music, the bursary in recent years has supported community music, Irish music performance and music education students. The trustees of the Universal Music UK Sound Foundation[9] have given very welcome support and guidance to Academy students through this bursary by providing a generous contribution towards the fees of the recipient and by keeping in contact with them throughout their studies.

In 2012, two years after the beautiful state-of-the-art Academy building was opened and became our home, the GDE (Music) was replaced by the Professional Diploma in Education (Music) as required by the HEA and the Teaching Council. The course structure remained unchanged. Prior to the intake of students in 2014, the minister for education and the Teaching Council directed a change in all teacher-training programmes. As a result, 2014 saw the first intake of students on a newly designed two-year Professional Master of Education (Music) programme. While the programme continued to be taught by the Academy and the School of Education, the course structure changed to meet the requirements of a master's degree. Included in the changes were the requirements for each of the students to undertake two full-semester school placements and to write a master's dissertation, alongside an increase in the number of modules taken, including music modules. Each year since the music education programmes were first introduced, students who graduated from the programme were hired as music teachers in secondary schools in Ireland and beyond. In time, the students of these teachers arrived to take various undergraduate music programmes at the Academy, thereby completing the circle.

In 2013 Mícheál enabled a series of school and community lunchtime concerts at the Academy. On every Wednesday of the semester a school or community group is welcomed to the Tower Theatre to perform their lunchtime concert.

> Wednesdays at the Irish World Academy are alive to the sound of visiting school and community groups. The experience begins when the visiting performers arrive into the beautiful Theatre 2 at midday to rehearse for their lunchtime concert. For many, it is their first time to perform in a university environment. The excitement is palpable. The concert takes place at 1.15 p.m. The campus community, families and friends are invited to attend. This is a very special time at the Irish World Academy when we experience the beautiful music making, song and dance presented by our visiting school and community groups.[10]

The warm Academy welcome characteristic of Mícheál continues to be extended to all the talented performers who come to entertain us each week.

Graduates of the music education programmes

Graduates from the music education programmes at the Academy are to be found teaching in school music departments in the Republic of Ireland, Northern Ireland and farther afield in England, Scotland, Spain, UAE, Australia, New Zealand and the United States. The network has spread far and wide and technology has enabled all to stay in regular contact and to share professional resources as well as continuing friendships. Some of the graduates have opted not to teach in school music departments but to teach in schools of music or set up their own schools of music, with great success. Many of the graduates are examiners with the State Examinations Commission for the junior cycle and Leaving Certificate examinations. Some graduates continue to serve on the national executive of the Post Primary Music Teachers Association, while others run local branches and take on other tasks such as webmaster and forum moderators. Other graduates are now in management roles in their schools, principals and deputy principals, ensuring advocacy for music. The Junior Cycle Support Team and the Professional Development Service for Teachers are both initiatives of the Department of Education and are populated by a number of music education graduates.

Other graduates are associates in the Professional Development Service for Teachers, providing in-service training and continuing professional development for their peers. The musical energy of the graduates knows no bounds. A very active body of graduates at the time of writing are those who are seconded from their schools as full-time advisors to the junior cycle music support team. Ernestine Healy, a music education graduate, who is co-author of this chapter, will take up the conversation here. A former student at the Academy, Ernestine has also been a member of faculty as lecturer and tutor and is a former director of the Blas Summer School.

Ernestine Healy

As I sit here and listen to 'Oileán' by Mícheál Ó Súilleabháin, my mind wanders back to my teenage years and how I was in such awe of this inspirational man, whom I had yet to meet. Growing up in Mayo in a house engulfed in music and sport, I learnt music from the age of six attending lessons with music teacher Bernie Geraghty. I was always intrigued with melodies, composing my own all of the time, but it was in harmonies, arrangements and orchestration where it all came alive for me. So much so, I always seemed to land myself in performances that involved being in the middle of the music and having the space to come up with some harmonies.

In 1992, *The Late Late Show*[12] had a full programme dedicated to Irish traditional musician Sharon Shannon. This is where my musical mind started to change. From there, still very young, I knew that all I wanted to do was study music in college. But the turning point for me was in 1995 when *A River of Sound*[245] was launched. Mícheál Ó Súilleabháin, the mastermind behind the series, appeared on an episode of *The Late Late Show* dedicated to the series in February of that year and his words struck a chord with me. I was inspired by his vision and wanted to attend the academic institution that he was leading.

As the courses at the Academy at the time were for master's students, in order for me to attend UL I first had to complete an undergraduate degree in another academic institution. I decided to attend UCC, where Mícheál had worked for numerous years and where all of the musicians who played on *The Late Late Show* programme had studied. I still remember my audition and interview with Mel Mercier, who had played with Mícheál on the piece *(must be more) Crispy*. I was a little awe-struck but we did engage in some great conversations about *A River of Sound*. I had taken up piano two years previously with my school music teacher Mary Benson, and I found Mícheál's ideas about posture and gesture of how musicians play the piano in different styles really interesting.

After spending four years in the Music Department in UCC, I moved to Limerick to complete the GDE (Music). On the first day of the course, all of the students gathered in the Performing Arts Centre or 'the PAC', where we were introduced to the faculty, many of whom I recognised as leading academics and musicians. When Mícheál spoke, you were immediately taken through a journey of creativity, inspiration and innovation. He spoke to us about what we would experience as students at the Academy and also of his hopes and dreams for the future of the Academy. You were brought straight into his vision.

My experience in the GDE programme was a significant and valuable one. Jean Downey was not only our course director, but a mother and friend to us all. It was difficult at times as we were engaging in placement as student teachers in schools along with engaging with lectures and assignments, but the most beneficial part was the space and time given to each of us to explore our own paths as both educationalists and musicians. Having time and opportunity to further your own musical practice as musician, composer and academic was something I know Mícheál insisted on, and that, I feel, was a very important aspect of the course. You were not only in the programme as a future music teacher and educator for the next generations coming through, you were also there as a developing musician. Embedded in the course was the belief that as a teacher and educator you never stop learning and you continue your practice as a performing musician.

While other students in the GDE (Music) course engaged with elective modules in performance, my classmate Catherine Clohessy and I decided to record a CD. After speaking to Jean, we were sent to meet with Niall Keegan to discuss the project. When we started to look at the idea of having some of our own compositions on the CD, Niall didn't hesitate to take up the phone to Mícheál to say he would be sending some students his way to chat to him. I remember thinking about how welcome Mícheál made me feel. Here I was sitting with someone who to me was an inspiration as a composer, academic, musician and visionary, but he had the ability to make you feel you belonged in that conversation with him, just having a chat about music.

On finishing the GDE in 2001, I moved back to Cork to take up a position as a music teacher in a secondary school in Fermoy. After a number of years I decided it was time to take a career break and return to the Academy as a student on the MA Irish Music Performance. I began the programme in 2007 and consider that year a turning point for me in so many different ways – as an educator, performer, composer and director.

I owe a lot of what I engaged with that year to Mícheál's vision for the Academy, that space which has an important balance of academic and performance reflection. Niall Keegan and Sandra Joyce played an immense part, their support and guidance allowing me to direct my own path for the year. An important aspect of the experience is the opportunity to engage with leading artists and academics. They are available on a regular basis and every effort is made to match the student's interests with both faculty and external artists' expertise. In following my own path, I was allowed to engage with composition projects, work with a number of orchestrators and write an undergraduate music business module. For composition I was again very fortunate to have an opportunity to meet with Mícheál on a number of occasions to chat with him and look at the direction I was taking with my pieces. It was inspiring to receive guidance and insight on how he perceived music. He always brought out the best in the ensembles he wrote and orchestrated for, and that was evident in our interactions too. You always left his office wanting to take another angle with something that you were working on.

In June 2008 before I finished my master's programme, I received a call to attend a meeting where I was asked to consider joining the faculty as acting course director for the GDE for 2008/9, as Jean Downey was going on secondment. During my time as acting course director, I was also invited to sit on the board of Maoin Cheoil an Chláir for a year. As mentioned by Jean earlier, Mícheál's talent as chair of the board was evident and the school reflected what he felt education, and especially music education, should be – inclusive by all and for all, encompassing important community education values. I continued to be part of the Academy staff for a number of years. In 2009 I lectured on the BA Irish Music and Dance programme, but returned to my secondary school teaching position in autumn 2010. In spring 2010 I became director of the Blas International Summer School of Irish Traditional Music and Dance and continued in that role until autumn 2016.

When I reflect on my career as a secondary school music teacher so far, the one name that has and will always inform conversations with my music students is Mícheál Ó Súilleabháin. We always engage with his pieces of music, look at his career and the legacy he has left with us. Every year I have a number of students who want to further their own journey in music education, and each year I spend time with them considering where that path should lead. In those conversations I say to students to always look further and set and engage new pathways in everything they do, to have a vision and strive for it. This was something that I embodied and adopted from my experiences both as a student and a faculty member in the Academy.

For me, music education is something that is important for all students. Music is a potential in every individual as it has the ability to contribute to many aspects of a student's development. As I currently engage with the new junior cycle music curriculum, I often think of Mícheál and how he would support it. So much of what the curriculum aims to do reflects his vision for music education: 'This music specification aims to contribute to the development of artistic awareness and understanding, self-expression, self-esteem, imagination and multicultural sensitivity, and therefore to the development of the whole person.'[13] That space for students (12–15 years of age) to be creative and innovative in their engagement with a composition portfolio and to reflect on that process; their ability to research and internalise the pieces for their practical examination through the programme note; and the space to engage with music as a curriculum where it allows them as students to develop skills to be the future of music education in our country. In all of these qualities I see so much of Mícheál and what he inspired us as students to do, through his vision for music education and the Academy. As music educators we engage and enable music-making among so many students in our schools. It is here that we can open minds and set up a generation who can see music through reflection and practice.

On bestowing an honorary life membership of the Society for Music Education in Ireland on Mícheál on 3 November 2018, Regina Murphy captured the legacy that he has left behind in his work, energy and vision for music education in Ireland: 'It is this ability to see what might be, what we might become, individually and collectively, that is Mícheál's gift to us – a love of music and all our ways of envisioning and embodying it.'[14]

Conclusion

By creating a music education programme in a university music department for those who wished to become post-primary school music teachers, Mícheál ensured that students would learn to become teachers while continuing to engage in their own musical performance practice. The music education programme at the Academy has provided music teachers across the island of Ireland and further afield, with graduates teaching music in an international context. At the time of writing 450 students have graduated from the Academy as music teachers and there are currently thirty-two student teachers in the programme across the two years.

The late Bridget Doolan, then director of the Cork School of Music, spoke in 1980 of the influence of Professor Aloys Fleischmann: '[I]t is really due to this one man that music education, certainly in Munster and in very many schools throughout the country, is in a very healthy state.'[15] Decades later we look at the inspired vision of Mícheál Ó Súilleabháin. Mícheál had an extraordinary vision for music education at the Academy and each year this is being further realised. Each year he reminded the graduates that as post-primary teachers they would enable music-making among many young students throughout their careers. In enabling music education at the Academy, Mícheál Ó Súilleabháin championed the cause of music education, of school music and of teachers in Ireland and internationally. For this legacy we are truly grateful.

32

Lighting the Fire: Perspectives on the development of the Classical String Performance programme at the Irish World Academy

Diane Daly and Ferenc Szűcs

Diane Daly is a violinist, educator, community musician and academic researcher. She is a member of the Irish Chamber Orchestra and is course director of the MA Classical String Performance at the University of Limerick, where she also teaches Dalcroze eurhythmics, Kodály, improvisation and creative embodied string performance.

Ferenc Szűcs is senior lecturer emeritus at the Irish World Academy of Music and Dance and had a key role in establishing and directing the master's programme in Classical String Performance. As a professional cellist he performed in over fifty countries and has associations with numerous orchestras, ensembles and institutes worldwide.

This chapter explores the development of the MA Classical String Performance at the Irish World Academy of Music and Dance, drawing its connections to the Irish Chamber Orchestra. The chapter is structured in three parts. In Part One, Diane Daly, violinist with the Irish Chamber Orchestra, graduate of the MA Classical String Performance in 1999 and course director of the programme since 2018, provides a historic overview. In Part Two, Ferenc Szűcs offers a personal reflection from his time as the founding course director, and in Part Three, Diane illustrates how Mícheál's vision has been realised through the growth of the MA programme.

Diane Daly

Part One: Irish Chamber Orchestra – connecting performance and teaching

I am a violinist and member of the Irish Chamber Orchestra, and like many musicians in the west of Ireland, my career and perspectives were indelibly marked by Mícheál. In 1994 an invitation was extended from Mícheál, the newly appointed chair of music at the Academy, to the Irish Chamber Orchestra (ICO). This invite resulted in a decision by Michael D. Higgins (at that time the minister for arts, culture, and the Gaeltacht, and later elected president of Ireland in 2011), on the recommendation of the Arts Council, to relocate the orchestra to the University of Limerick (UL).

The ICO, founded in 1970, had been firmly embedded in Dublin, and this brave and visionary relocation to Limerick was masterminded by Mícheál, and John Kelly, the CEO of the ICO (1993–2012). The chamber orchestra was now in a position where it could offer attractive player contracts and regular work, resulting in a strong ensemble identity. By becoming orchestra-in-residence, the ICO forged a deep and lasting partnership with the university and Limerick city that flourishes to this day. After some years based in the Foundation building, developing a loyal audience base in the University Concert Hall, in 2008 the orchestra moved to its own home on the Clare side of the campus, adjacent to the Academy.

The relationship between Mícheál and the orchestra was close and fruitful. On an organisational level he was proud that the ICO move to Limerick was so successful, but it was as a composer and performer with the orchestra that true connection and joy was found. One of my very first concerts with the ICO, aged eighteen, was a programme of Mícheál's own works in Féile an Phobail, west Belfast in 1991. The concert was memorable not only for the music, but for a dramatic incident where the fire curtain fell down halfway through, separating Mícheál and his piano from the rest of the orchestra. The show must go on, and so it did. Not even a fire curtain could repress the joy and connection we had playing together.

As well as composer and performer, Mícheál was a fervent educationalist. Central to the ethos guiding his development of the Academy was a belief in the importance of a real-life artistic surround for academic programmes, and it was not long before he realised the potential of creating a master's programme in Classical String Performance that would be linked to the ICO.

I was one of the very first cohort of four students that undertook that newly created MA programme in 1998, studying with one of the top violin professors in the world, Mauricio Fuks from Indiana in the United States. The lessons with Professor Fuks brought my playing to an even higher level of performance and enriched my musical education tenfold. The lessons were sadly not numerous, as Fuks was based in the United States and was in demand worldwide. Fortunately, I had previously studied in the UK with Wen Zhou Li, who had for many years been Mauricio's teaching assistant. The MA therefore offered me a valuable opportunity to further assimilate my learnings and consolidate the teachings of one of the world's greatest masters in violin pedagogy.

Another highlight of the MA programme, which was one year in duration at that time, was my Irish fiddle lessons. Mícheál was very amused when I asked him if an option of traditional music lessons could be added to my choice of electives. It seemed to tickle him that a member of the ICO might want to learn traditional music. Mícheál not only created the elective, but in typical fashion organised that the teacher would be one of the best fiddle players in the world, the legendary Tommie Peoples. The lessons awarded a great insight into different violin-playing styles and techniques. I recall sensing greater fluidity in my bow arm as I embraced the freedom that the traditional bowing style offered to me as a classically trained musician.

One very enjoyable outcome of this elective was that when the ICO went touring abroad, a few of us became the Irish 'trad' group in the orchestra. We never needed to be asked twice to play a few tunes at post-concert receptions and publicity events. I remember Mícheál laughing over at me during one such impromptu event, no doubt recognising the same tunes I had learnt during my MA.

The first course director appointed to establish and run the MA programme was Ferenc Szűcs, a highly accomplished cellist from Hungary whom Mícheál held in great regard. He frequently described Ferenc's audition where his rendition of a movement from Bach's unaccompanied cello suites stole his heart.

Ferenc Szűcs
Part Two: Remembering Mícheál

Mícheál Ó Súilleabháin was certainly the kind of person one does not forget in a hurry. Even if you met him once you would remember this totally unique, very colourful and rather complex man, a great musician, successful composer, dedicated scholar and educator with an engaging, warmly personal style and with highly unusual and visionary ideas.

I met him in 1998 when I was entrusted to set up and direct the new MA Classical String Performance at the Academy. Coming from a classical music background, I already had considerable experience about how music schools would operate in my area of discipline but listening to Mícheál's ideas actually turned my world upside-down. To implement these ideas was a considerable challenge for me at first but soon I was caught up with his vision and had an irresistible attraction and desire to make it work. I had the feeling in those days that whatever we were going to create in Limerick would be different from anything I had known before.

It became clear to me quite early on that our MA Classical String Performance would not try to imitate or recreate the system of a classical music conservatoire but instead would have different strengths. We were very fortunate to be able to bring to Limerick the best teachers the classical music world could offer – Mauricio Fuks from Indiana, Bruno Giuranna and Mariana Sirbu from Italy, Michael Wolf from Berlin, Hugh Maguire from London and many others. This was a brilliant experience for the students and I am very grateful to these teachers for their work and support over many years.

From the beginning the MA was closely associated with the ICO. The orchestra became resident on the UL campus a few years before the MA started and in fact the presence of the ICO was the very reason the MA existed in the first place. Over the years we used the orchestra as a resource and planned many joint projects and performances. More recently this interaction came to its fullness as following my retirement the ICO took the programme fully under its wings and its members are now actively involved in the teaching and running of the MA.

While aspiring for the highest standards in our own discipline, we would also aim to interact with all available creative performance energies and scholarly disciplines of the Irish World Academy and on occasions with the wider university. The students had and still have the opportunity to interact with other performance and academic programmes as part of their study. The co-existence of these programmes and disciplines in one place carries a very special energy and provides countless opportunities to meet, listen, learn, discuss and to understand things beyond our own horizon. As Mícheál would put it, we learn 'to think outside of the box'. I believe that the students value these creative opportunities, and over the years I also found myself performing with many colleagues, including Irish traditional musicians and contemporary dancers, comparing notes and discussing ideas. Our students arrived from all parts of the world – countries of Europe, North and South America, Australia, New Zealand, the Far East and, of course, many from Ireland. Most of them became successful in their chosen fields as teachers and performers. I am delighted to hear about their success and am very proud of them.

It all originated out of Mícheál's vision and I believe that without him none of this would exist in Limerick. He took a keen interest in the Academy programmes and we regularly discussed the finer details of the curriculum, projects, performances and further developments. He was a mentor to many, including myself. I had the privilege of working with Mícheál for nearly two decades. Apart from our interests at the Academy, he also invited me to perform with him on several occasions and perhaps the most memorable for me was our tour of China. Mícheál was a wonderful musician, it was most natural and easy to play with him and we understood each other without the need for words. I admired him for his boundless energy, his creativity and his generosity, and I think of him with gratitude.

Diane Daly

Part Three: Developing the MA Classical String Performance and realising Mícheál's vision

In 2015 Ferenc retired and it was recommended that a newly designed course incorporating a fuller partnership with the ICO would be initiated. The orchestra was by now firmly established as one of the world's leading chamber orchestras. With Limerick as the home of the ICO, it had also become the home for many members of the orchestra who decided to settle down in this beautiful part of the world. I am one of these musicians, living in the nearby picturesque village of Killaloe in County Clare, on the western bank of Lough Derg.

I was invited to coordinate the transition of the MA programme into this new immersive partnership with the ICO over a period of six months. This was a very exciting time in the history of the programme as the ICO players were all extremely motivated to spread their own love of chamber music-making and to teach the skills that had brought them such successful careers. The ICO players now do all the teaching and coaching on the course, also playing in and directing internationally acclaimed ensemble projects, such as the Irish Chamber Orchestra Academy Project 2018.

During this time I embarked on a visionary adventure led by Helen Phelan and Mícheál – the PhD Arts Practice. In 2014 I had experienced a momentous transformation in my violin performance following a day spent training in Dalcroze, a somatic music education method based on experiencing and learning music through movement and by movement. After a day of intensive training, I stayed on late in the evening to practise as I was performing the Bruch violin concerto the following week. I was struck by a perception that I was playing at a far higher level than normal. My sense was that the training exercises undertaken that day unlocked an ability for me to play from inside the body, in a holistic sense, rather than focusing on technique and specifics. It seemed that spending a day focusing on developing my active listening skills, developing my inner hearing and working on expressing the elements of music physically was a powerful way to warm up before even picking up my violin.

I jumped at the opportunity to investigate this further, with a view to establishing whether these positive benefits were real, and if so, whether they could be evaluated and subsequently harnessed more regularly and widely. The PhD programme in Arts Practice was established in 2009 as the first structured PhD programme in Ireland to support research by professional artists using their own practice. Designed and led by Professor Phelan, it attracted professional dancers, musicians, theatre directors and aerial artists. I was the first doctoral student on the programme to come from the world of professional classical music performance and the first in Ireland to receive the prestigious and highly competitive Irish Research Council funding for research in this area. Along with Dalcroze expert Jane Southcott, I asked Helen and Mícheál to be my supervisors, and thus began an exciting four-year artistic adventure, culminating in my final doctoral research being awarded the inaugural Aloys Fleischmann Prize, 2022, established by the Society for Musicology in Ireland and University College Cork to recognise outstanding practice-based research.

The Swiss educator Émile Jaques-Dalcroze 'initiated an important pedagogy that, when practised well, can cause the human organism to reach beyond understanding and appreciating music, to the maximum – living music'.[1] Classical musicians are trained to be exceptional instrumentalists and technicians, often at the expense of developing creative artists who have the freedom, autonomy and confidence to express what they feel. Musicians move, just like dancers and athletes, and the quality of our movement is integral to the quality of our sound. The findings of my research affirmed for me the importance of instilling freedom, autonomy, creativity and somatic awareness into the training of classical musicians.

In 2018 I became the new course director for the MA Classical String Performance, and have subsequently sought to integrate the learnings from my research into the design and delivery of the curriculum. Students now take weekly classes in Feldenkrais and Dalcroze as well as one-on-one classes in technique and interpretation, chamber music, baroque, Irish traditional music, improvisation and large ensemble. One of the many benefits of being based in the Academy is having access to the excellent dance studios. The classical music students have a weekly class in what I have termed creative embodied string performance, where each student can investigate the concept of inscribing the written music *into* their performing bodies[2] through exploring how the music moves. We have devised internationally acclaimed performances where we hone in on the listeners' ability to not only 'hear a performer's body in the music'[3] but also to experience it visually and kinaesthetically.

The integration of ICO players into the MA programme resulted in the possibility and creation of a number of ICO Academy projects. These annual projects bring my research directly into the MA programme as students rehearse core chamber orchestral masterpieces away from their instruments, exploring how the music moves in the space and in their bodies. They use Dalcroze techniques, using their bodies, and objects such as balls, scarves and elastics to explore and discover how the embodiment of harmony, melody, rhythm, phrasing and character as a group can enhance the ensemble sound and interpretation. The students also explore the multi-sensory performance aspects of moving in the space while playing, showing how the music moves in their performing bodies, offering both performers and audience a visual, aural and kinaesthetic experience. The impact of these projects has been powerful, to the extent that the ICO asked me in 2019 to direct a professional version of this creative way of performing, incorporating a moving (in every sense of the word) rendition of Albinoni's *Adagio in G Minor* for an ICO concert in St Mary's Cathedral, Limerick.

The MA programme curriculum responds to and develops current research in the area of somatic-based classical music performance and believes that in order to help students progress from being good instrumentalists to creative artists, we must liberate their bodies to be able to play freely, joyfully and expressively, without pain-connecting mind, body and musical intention. In the words of Mead, '[t]he study of music has its own rewards, but it is good to remind oneself occasionally that music's path to the mind is inevitably through the body'.[4]

Mícheál was incredibly supportive of my playing, teaching and research, firstly as a young violinist in the ICO, then an MA student on his new programme, twenty years later his PhD student and since 2018 the course director of his cherished MA. I know that every fibre of his body would be bursting with pride to see how the MA Classical String Performance has evolved into a journey to create musicians not only adept at playing their instruments at the highest level, but also musicians who can fully express themselves and connect with others through their art. As a result, the course has developed an international reputation not only for artistic excellence, but for adopting a 'whole musician' approach that goes beyond technical excellence to also focus on body awareness and emotional intention. The strength of this reputation can be seen from the international profile of the course cohort that commenced in September 2020. The twelve musicians who passed the stringent audition process travelled to Limerick from Mexico, Hungary, the United States, Estonia, Italy, Paraguay, the UK, Italy, Ukraine, Croatia, Denmark and Austria.

This international recognition was Mícheál's dream for the course, and it demonstrates the MA, in partnership with the ICO, as truly a leader in establishing UL as an international centre of excellence in the field of innovative, creative classical music performance. Mícheál loved to hear about the individual journey of each and every one of the students in the Academy. Below are some reflections from the cohort of students on the MA Classical String Performance, written in the autumn semester of 2020.

From the first day, despite our physical distancing, the energy was tangible. The positivity quietly circulating continued over the following weeks to encapsulate our programme, as we slowly took in and gave more, piecing together fragments of an idea; the reasons we are all here, the places we all came from and where we are up to with our journeys, how each of us expresses ourselves so very differently, soaking in our teachers' guidance on how to communicate the music that seems to be the foundation of this newly formed family.

The MA Classical String Performance is unique in comparison to other master's around the world, having a very deep artistic and mental focus. After the first few weeks of classes, I can say that I have learned far more about myself in this short time than I had learned in the last six years of higher education in classical music. Course director Dr Daly and the other Irish Chamber Orchestra musicians search for the artist that each one of us carries within us, using all the artistic elements to fully edify the student. This course will take me far beyond the goals and expectations that I had in mind for this programme.

I am reminded daily what Einstein said about vibrations – 'Everything is energy' – and therefore we cannot fail to consider our body, our mind and our heart while making music, just as we cannot forget the world. Making music requires a lot of work of connection, of integration, of discovering the truth. This MA reminds me of Pablo Casals' dictum: 'The main thing in life is not to be afraid of being human.'

In the same way that the MA in Classical String Performance is now transforming the lives of so many gifted young string players, Mícheál also changed my life and helped me believe that anything is possible. He brought me to Limerick as a young violinist with the Irish Chamber Orchestra, supported my academic development to PhD level and created the course I now direct. He once said to me he believed in enabling students to follow wherever their potential leads, and to turn dreams into reality. In this way he touched numerous lives, lit several fires and helped enhance countless futures.

33

The MA Programme in Ritual Chant and Song: A mirror of a grand spirit

Edward Foley and Sr Sidonia Freedman

Duns Scotus Professor Emeritus Edward Foley has thirty-one books, fifty-eight book chapters, forty-eight peer-reviewed articles and over 300 other published works to his credit. He has received numerous national and international awards and grants, including a major grant from the John Templeton Foundation on preaching with the sciences.

Nun Sidonia Freedman resides at the Sacred Monastery of St Nina (Georgian Patriarchate), United States. She sings contemporary eastern chant repertories, and early and folk traditions. Following a BA in music and medieval studies (St Olaf College), work at the Irish World Academy culminated in a doctoral, multi-disciplinary exploration of theology of Eastern Orthodox chant. Current work includes postdoctoral research, and various liturgical and pedagogical activities in her community.

Introduction

While we were at different stages of our careers and different places in our vocational discernment at the time, both of us were drawn to the Irish World Academy of Music and Dance (hereafter, the Academy) and its programme in Ritual Chant and Song for similar reasons. What neither of us understood at the time, however, was how the looming figure and vision of Mícheál Ó Súilleabháin was at the heart and soul of both the Academy and this unique programme.

Sr Sidonia was then Sydney Freedman, a recent graduate of St Olaf College in Northfield, Minnesota, where she had completed an interdisciplinary double major in music history and medieval studies. She had been searching for a path to continued studies in the history, musicology and primary literature of early chant. Beyond the theoretical aspects, she was also interested in stressing its ritual and religious aspects while performing it, particularly in worship. This course admirably met these criteria and fostered related work in eastern traditions which were important to her. This prompted Sydney to continue with doctoral studies focused on Orthodox chant through the Academy's Arts Practice programme. Mícheál proved to be very supportive and greatly interested in the theological and spiritual emphases in this research. Along the way, she was privileged to teach in the MA course and to work with him as a co-examiner. Her Academy affiliation branched out into broader musical activities in the community, including performances with multiple ensembles in concert and liturgical settings and participation in various seminars. Her work with Mícheál in multiple arenas brought her to a deep appreciation of his gifts as an insightful and generous scholar, educator and composer.

While Sydney arrived as a student, Ed was already a professor of liturgy and music at Catholic Theological Union in Chicago when he was invited to be an external examiner in the Ritual Chant and Song programme in 2005. Having grown up as a choir boy singing Gregorian chant, that aspect of the programme had great appeal for him. More compelling than that, however, was his research and writing over the previous decades on the nature of ritual music and the usefulness of this umbrella category for reimagining liturgical music and its various functions. As a Roman Catholic priest, akin to the interests of Sr Sidonia, he too was interested not only in the theoretical aspects of ritual chant and song but also its performance, particularly in worship. What he did not expect was Mícheál's deep involvement in and commitment to this very modest programme from its inception. Mícheál not only had a ritual sense of chant and traditional Celtic song, but a ritual sense of music more broadly and the Academy in general. Ed's tenure as an external examiner stretched over a decade, returning not only to examine students but to interview potential faculty and programme directors. Over that period he developed a deep admiration and affection for Mícheál's musical and personal hospitality.

History and description of the programme

The one-year MA Ritual Chant and Song has been offered at the Academy since 1998.[1] The multiple reflections and resources that birthed this venture are symbolic of the multifaceted vision of its progenitor and his concern to wed both theory and practice throughout his newly founded academy. Keenly interested in western plainchant, one theoretical cornerstone of this programme was Ó Súilleabháin's ethnomusicological interest in the relationship between orality and literacy. Key here was the work of Leo Treitler,[2] which Ó Súilleabháin explored beyond issues of transmission to include the actual composition and performance of music. The practice point was his long personal connection with the Benedictine community at Glenstal Abbey. His 1980 production *Caoineadh na Maighdine* featuring Nóirín Ní Riain and the monks of Glenstal Abbey is an early testament to this connection.

Already in 1994, when the newly christened Irish World Music Centre was first founded, Ó Súilleabháin proposed a postgraduate programme in chant performance. Significant groundwork for this programme developed from the series of sixteen international seminars (1996–7) funded in large part by The Atlantic Philanthropies. The seminar on chant performance brought celebrated chant scholars David Hiley and Nicholas Sandon to Limerick who together helped design an MA Chant Performance. The first director was Dr Katarina Livljani (1998–9), followed by Dr Lila Collamore (1999–2000), Dr Helen Phelan (2000–9, 2010–11, 2020-1), acting director Dr Eri Hiribayashi (2009–10), Dr Wolodymyr Smishkewych (2009–14), course coordinator Dr Hannah Fahey (2014–16) and Dr Eleanor Giraud (2016–19). It was during Phelan's tenure that the programme was expanded to include other ritual song repertoires including Irish traditional song and modules on ritual studies alongside those in historical musicology. This evolution led to a change in the programme's title, to the current MA Ritual Chant and Song. Epitomising this wedding of chant and Irish traditional song was Ó Súilleabháin's 1995 composition *Lumen*, featured at the 1995 Eurovision Song Contest in Dublin and subsequently released on CD. It is a stellar, sonic testimony to his chant-song commitment in ritual mode.

In the current design, students explore theoretical and practical aspects of chant and ritual, each in a dedicated yet overlapping module: these are distinct but not separate elements keeping to Ó Súilleabháin's integrated vision. Early western chant provides the core repertoire and is studied in its liturgical context. It is sung with a focus on the interpretation of the earliest manuscript sources while yet being put in dialogue with other musics in the course. Irish *sean-nós*, a traditional form of ornamented Irish singing, is the second major vocal practice with which students engage. These two pillars of western chant and *sean-nós* are supplemented by various other forms of singing dependent upon the interests of students, the involvement of guest performers and the expertise of course tutors and department members. In addition to the repertoire-based group lessons there is also private vocal coaching for students. These elements comprise the first module of the programme.

Developing expertise in vocal performance is enhanced by concurrent musicological and liturgical studies of the repertoire and through an immersion in ritual studies addressed in the second module of the course. This module includes surveys of liturgical history with distinctive attention to parallel Irish spiritualities and exploration of the history and methodologies of fieldwork. A pivotal practical component is the ritual laboratory in which students design and complete fieldwork in a community of their choosing as well as contribute to a joint field project within the class itself. Another example of the interplay between theory and practice is the requirement that students reconstruct, analyse and perform a historic liturgical service, employing methods from both modules. As an example, Sr Sidonia's class chose a Sarum Rite mass from the high Middle Ages. Students also participate in a variety of in-house ensembles and have opportunities to present repertoire at informal concerts. These are important parts of the preparation for final exams and juried performances. The course ends with a dissertation, recital, or combination of both, presented after a third 'summer' semester dedicated to this work.

Spiritual porosity

While it is not unusual for a secular university to offer programmes that are thoroughly interdisciplinary or that take seriously both the theory and practice of some science or art, the Academy at UL through this programme also embraced the significance of various spiritualities as they impact both the understanding and performance of the musical arts.

Traditional Roman Catholic theology considered the spiritual life as an integral element in theological discourse but for centuries did not treat it as a separate area of speculation. By the post-Reformation era, however, the distinctive discipline of mystical theology had developed, which took as its focus the soul's journey to union with God. At the same time, popular practices like the *Spiritual Exercises* of Ignatius of Loyola (d. 1556) and the largely abandoned field of ascetical theology took a more practical turn as they focused on the practices of virtues that would lead to such union with the Holy One. This shifted emphasis from abstract theories about the soul to pastoral concerns about individuals and their call to holiness. This was less an issue in eastern Christianity that maintained a closer link between theologies of 'divinisation', ascetic practice and pastoral care.

In the twentieth century spirituality increasingly came to be understood as a multidimensional reality. One celebrated tri-partite framework considered spirituality: 1) the lived experience of faith, 2) teachings about that lived experience (e.g. formulated in schools of spirituality), and finally as 3) the academic study of the first two.[3] Because of the emphasis on experience in emerging definitions of spirituality, the field migrated beyond traditional religious boundaries. What was once considered a realm primarily dominated and even controlled by Roman Catholic thought and practice has burst that boundary and is now happily appropriated by groups as diverse as Muslims, Buddhists, humanists and so many in between. For the growing number of religiously unaffiliated in the world – a religious reality to be reckoned with especially in what was considered the 'Christian West'[4] – Lionel Abadia notes that spiritual has emerged as an alternative or even substitute for institutionalised religion and has come to represent 'a modern form of sacredness, centred on the individual and oriented toward emotions and experiences rather than based on rites and aligned on norms'.[5]

Because of its distinctive history of Christianisation as well as the pluriform nature of Christianity in the West in the fifth century AD when missionaries such as Patrick and Fionnán were establishing churches and monasteries, there is a general recognition that spiritualities indigenous to Ireland have some distinctive characteristics. While sometimes labelled 'Celtic' Christianity, some scholars prefer the moniker 'insular' Christianity. Some of the characteristics of this Celtic/insular Christianity were manifest in singular ecclesial structures that emerged especially across Irish monasticism. Other distinctive features – parallel to places in Europe that experienced various waves of 'tribal' Christianity, or what James Russell considers the 'Germanization' of Christianity[6] – were the result of Celtic/insular Christians exhibiting a particular closeness to nature.[7]

The Celtic revival movements of the late nineteenth and twentieth centuries that sought to recover elements of Irish heritage from ancient sports to preserving the Irish language, also included renewed interest in so-called 'Celtic' spiritualities.[8] The confluence of this revival with growing interest in 'new age' beliefs and practices has broken open the study of such spiritualities akin to Abadia's general assessment of the nature of spirituality and its study in the early twenty-first century. For the Irish context, this hybridity and pluriformity is well summarised in the recent publication *Ireland's New Religious Movements: Alternative spiritualities, migrant religions, the new age and new religious movements*.[9]

The MA Ritual Chant and Song is a programme in which this blending of spiritualities – whether Christian and humanistic, or Buddhist and Benedictine – thrives. This respect for and even cultivation of explorations in spirituality becomes particularly obvious in the Ritual Studies module, in which social scientific approaches complement those from religious studies and even theology. This cross-fertilisation varies according to each student and tutor. In Sr Sidonia's class, for instance, Japanese Buddhism and Shinto, Eastern Orthodox Christianity and Pentecostal were some of the contexts that she and her colleagues explored. A ritual studies approach allows for an exploration of these cross-fertilising spiritualities as each student pursues their individual fieldwork, which requires contextualising their empirical observations within the various cultural and spiritual factors that shape and are shaped by the musical practices under consideration.

The previously noted core module in which students examine early western chant along with traditional forms of Irish singing already begins this process, as it provides a necessary contextualisation of such musics within both Benedictine and Celtic/insular spiritualities and practices in all of their hybridity. Glenstal Abbey provides a contemporary field setting for this work and members of its community provide lectures on topics that range from Celtic enculturation at early Christian sites to contemporary organ-accompanied chant. In the broad and variegated research and writing generated in this process – by students and faculty alike – this respect for and even nourishing of the consideration of various aspects of spirituality provides a hospitable context for exposure to and even immersion in this oft-ignored facet of musical study. In Sr Sidonia's case, this porous approach to spirituality facilitated and invited robust engagement with Orthodox theologies side by side with ritual and anthropological considerations. This respectful blending allowed the hospitable engagement of Orthodox spirituality – à la Walter Principe's tri-partite definition – as a lived faith experience, reflections about that experience as well as the academic study of the two.

While a true cosmopolite who energetically embraced his role as a citizen of the world, Mícheál Ó Súilleabháin was also a fierce advocate for all things Irish. Listening to his elegant Irish at the recital in honour of the taoiseach (prime minister) Brian Cowen at the inauguration of the new building that was to serve as the new home of the Academy (24 September 2010)[10] is symbolic of that passion. Maybe even more notable, if one samples the performances from that concert, was its musical and artistic blending of spiritualities. Sitting under the magnificent *Sionna* mosaic designed by Desmond Kinney depicting the various phases in the wisdom journey of the goddess *Sionna*, the taoiseach was greeted with musics as diverse as Claudio Monteverdi's *Psalm 150*, Hiberno-Indian instrumental music, and secular songs from Mexico and Ireland. Not to be overlooked was Mícheál's own solo piano interpretation of the traditional Irish folk song 'The Wexford Carol', a beloved Christmas carol in the Christian tradition. On the one hand, this blend of secular and sacred music and dance overseen by a mythological river goddess could be considered by some as a jarring bricolage of mismatched elements. Read more graciously, this concert, the building and the modest programme in Ritual Song and Chant might, instead, be inspired lenses allowing a privileged glimpse of Ó Súilleabháin's own porous spiritual profile.

A ritual lens

The aforementioned concert is one example of several rituals – albeit the most elaborate one – that occurred at the Academy surrounding the opening of its new building. Others included a procession across the bridge over the river Shannon, with students chanting the Marian hymn 'Ave Maris Stella', as well as a Nepalese shaman performing a chanted rite of blessing in the main hall. The students and staff who were present watched or participated to varying degrees and in different ways. Some simultaneously chose to summon their own ritual traditions around the periphery of the primary action, for example offering prayer in some Christian tradition while Nepalese chants filled the air. While this ritual counterpoint could seem even more jarring than the opening concert, it yet symbolises Mícheál Ó Súilleabháin's intrepid exploration of the power of ritual, its musics and even its architectural setting.

While the content and performance of rituals has been the focus of studies for centuries – largely by Christians under the rubric of worship or liturgy – the field of ritual studies is relatively new. Its development required an understanding of ritual not confined to Christianity or other religions. Such is already signalled in the entry 'ritual' in the 1910 edition of the *Encyclopaedia Britannica*, which demonstrates an understanding of ritual that is not so confined but newly appreciated as a symbolic activity that is an integral part of human life and a common practice that is essential to our social structure.[11] The coalescing of this new field was signalled at the 1977 American Academy of Religion (AAR) meeting in San Francisco, when scholars from various disciplines established a 'Ritual Studies Consultation'. Central here was the work of Ronald Grimes, one of the acknowledged progenitors of the field. The work of Grimes and other pioneers contributed to the development of a multidisciplinary study of ritual that was concerned with what it is, what it means, what it affords and what it does.[12] Particularly important for the programme in Ritual Chant and Song were the performative aspects of ritual,[13] especially its musics. Grimes' work not only supported the development of ritual studies in this programme, but also the creation of the MA Festive Arts programme.

Catherine Bell offers a useful framework that allows us to chart, in broad strokes, contemporary directions in ritual theories along what could be considered two axes, although she does not explicitly employ that language.[14] A first general rubric useful in creating a taxonomy of ritual theories is the distinction between 'those theories that emphasize ritual as a form of communication from those that emphasize it as a form of action'.[15]

To a large extent this communication–action axis implicitly recognises the historical development of ritual theories which, generally speaking, originated on the communication side of the axis and have increasingly moved towards the action, practice or performance side of the axis. A second axis is between 'theories that remain heavily rooted in cultural explanation and those that are recreating naturalistic (or scientific) models of explanation'.[16]

Both of these axes or strands of ritual understanding flow throughout the Academy. As Mícheál once demonstrated to us, music intersects both, providing tools and data for study. The strength in traditional Irish forms of music and dance certainly resonates with theories rooted in cultural sources and explanations. On the other hand, there is also a strong action–performance orientation throughout the Academy, especially evident in the MA Ritual Chant and Song and PhD Arts Practice programmes. The former allows students to investigate ritual musics as forms of social and spiritual technology by putting them into practice and exploring the result. Practice is not merely the enacting of some pre-existing ritual, like the previously mentioned Sarum Rite, in order to reproduce some ancient meaning. Rather, practice itself is a source of fresh data and new meanings that can produce wide-ranging and unpredictable effects. Variables that influence those effects are things such as the level of participants' engagement, the quality of the performance and even the space in which it is enacted. For some, a particular ritual may have been simply an academic exercise; for others it could and did mean more. Apart from the perceived significance of any singular ritual, it is clear that the Academy in general and the programme in Ritual Chant and Song in particular are marked by persistent yet highly diverse forms of ritualising, ranging from the tightly choreographed to the improvisatory and spontaneous.

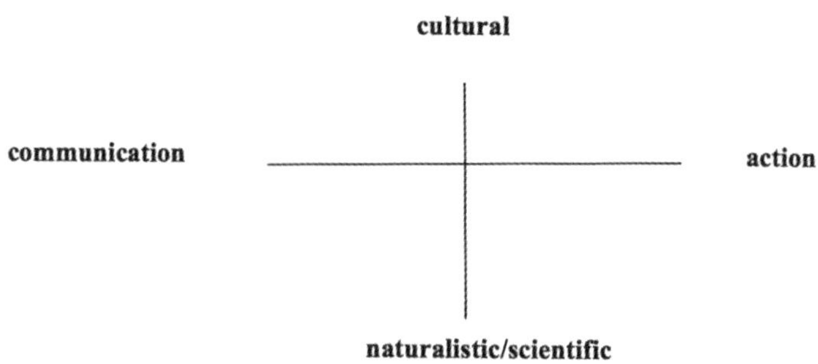

Figure 33.1: Contemporary directions in ritual theories in two axes: A communication–action axis and a cultural–naturalistic/scientific axis.

In many ways, this diversity reflects the broad ritual instincts and genius of the person and the teacher, the composer and the performer we remember and honour as Mícheál Ó Súilleabháin. He not only conceived of and fostered an environment in which students and their instructors could explore ritual musics in their untold variety, but thoroughly embodied that exploratory spirit, remarkable improvisatory skill and an amazing gift for ritual and musical choreography. This endures as a distinctive part of his rich legacy resonating throughout the Academy and in this one modest programme. *Ar dheis Dé go raibh a anam.*

34

Music Therapy at the Irish World Academy: A 'lobal' reflection

Tríona McCaffrey and Jane Edwards

Tríona McCaffrey is lecturer in music therapy at the Irish World Academy of Music and Dance. Her research primarily focuses on adult mental health with several related publications. She is founder of the Alliance for Recovery Research in Music Therapy, an international group committed to the development of recovery-oriented research in music therapy.

Jane Edwards is professor and associate dean for research in the Faculty of Humanities, Arts, Social Sciences and Education at the University of New England, Australia. She was course director for the MA Music Therapy at the University of Limerick from 1999 to 2013. She has over eighty publications with three edited books about music therapy.

Introduction

Central to the development of the Irish World Academy of Music and Dance has been the concept of 'lobality', a term Mícheál Ó Súilleabháin used to describe the local–global dynamic. The Academy's recognition of this dynamic has signified a commitment to resonate with its location in a way that also strikes resonance with a global community. An example of such 'lobal' resonance is exemplified in the Academy's development of the first degree programme in music therapy on the island of Ireland. Impassioned with the belief in music's capacity to promote health and well-being, while inspired by music therapy pioneers internationally, Micheál's leadership led to the founding of the MA Music Therapy programme in 1998. This marked a brave departure for music and arts education in Ireland whereby artistic and healthcare practices combined to create the first and only professional music therapy training in the country. These fundamental steps have led to the training of over one hundred graduates who through their practice of music therapy have touched the lives of many individuals and communities in Ireland and beyond. Written from educator, graduate and practitioner perspectives, the chapter reflects on this flagship programme and its legacy.

Programme development and foundations

The seeds for the first MA in Music Therapy training in Ireland were planted as far back as 1994 when Mícheál founded the Irish World Music Centre at the University of Limerick (UL). Together with Helen Phelan (UL) and a group of local visionaries including Mary Morgan (Lisnagry), Michael Fagan and Cathy McGahon (University Club, Plassey House, UL), and Judith Brereton (Cork), Mícheál set about creating a new third-level programme that would educate students in the use and application of music for the promotion of well-being. To say that this was uncharted territory in Ireland at that time is something of an understatement, yet the international landscape told something of a different story with a number of successful music therapy training programmes already in operation, many led by professors with strong histories of research and publications. In order to learn further about music therapy trainings, Mícheál visited courses at Ithaca College (New York) and the Southern Methodist University (Dallas). It was in Dallas that an Irish woman, Netta Blanchard, introduced Mícheál to Dr Kaja Jensen, an experienced educator and music therapist, leading the music therapy programme at Southern Methodist University, Dallas.

Kaja came to Ireland in 1998 to design the programme and then teach the firstsemester cohort of MA in Music Therapy students. Professor Wendy Magee, at that time working in the UK but now at Temple University in the United States, became the subsequent course director. She taught the second semester of the first intake and then the summer placement programme. However, she decided to move back to London and Professor Jane Edwards who was the music therapy course director at the University of Queensland agreed to support the programme for nine months to assist the students to complete the second year of the course. During the period of her visit she applied for the advertised senior lecturer in music therapy role and was appointed.

Tríona's story

Like many other graduates who have completed the MA in Music Therapy, the decision to undertake a programme of this nature was one not taken lightly. Aware of how this new field of practice was emerging internationally, I was excited for the possibilities that music therapy could offer. Following my attendance at a colloquium given by Jane at Trinity College Dublin where I completed a degree in music and Irish, I decided to apply to the MA in Music Therapy at UL. In 2004 I auditioned for the programme and was offered a place, having spent six months doing voluntary work at a care home for children and adults with intellectual and/or physical disabilities in north-eastern Argentina. This time in Argentina had been a deal-breaker in deciding to study music therapy. Having regularly played and sung with these residents I witnessed first-hand the capacity of music to engage, stimulate and create connections that overcame communicational and language barriers. I came to UL as a musician with a deep belief in music's capacity to promote well-being but with limited knowledge of this field of practice. For me, this was a step into very unfamiliar clinical and scientific territory, yet coupled with a quiet confidence that this was the right path to follow.

A striking reflection on my early days of training was the amount of public awareness of Mícheál's development of a music and dance department at UL. There was curiosity and interest around this which perhaps had not previously occurred with other music departments in the country. This may have been due to people's familiarity with Mícheál's music in the Irish traditional genre that immediately made a cultural connection between academic pursuits in UL and everyday life outside it. There was a public sense that something special was underway at UL and many people were drawn to this and the character and charisma of Mícheál who drove it. Yet despite UL developments being generally well-received by the public, there was still a long uphill journey in terms of developing the profession of music therapy in Ireland. There were very few qualified practitioners in the country which meant that clinical placements were very limited. While on clinical placement at a care facility for older adults in Limerick, I recall casually explaining to a staff member that I was a music therapy student. To my dismay he rolled his eyes and replied, 'Gosh, it gets more exotic around here every day!' In my view, this was a fair indicator of the appetite for music therapy among many health professionals in the country at that time who understandably knew little about the role or application of this practice in healthcare. It is heartening to note that now there is undoubtedly much more awareness and knowledge of music therapy at a national level. This shows that the 'exotic' seeds sown by Mícheál and other visionaries in 1994 have certainly grown!

Upon my appointment as lecturer in music therapy at the Academy in 2010, I had an opportunity to work directly with Mícheál and witness first-hand his dynamism and energy. Leaving a full-time music therapy position at Mayo Mental Health Services to embark on a career in academia marked a steep learning curve for me. During my early days at UL I distinctly recall discussing these challenges with Mícheál, who reminded me to believe in my abilities as I navigated such unfamiliar territory, and who encouraged me to bring my own unique contribution to the music therapy training. This showed his investment was not only in the music therapy training he had founded but also in those who delivered it. Since this discussion with Mícheál I have particularly drawn on my experience of closely working with various stakeholders in healthcare practice to inform service delivery. This has helped me enormously in listening to student perspectives and ensuring that they are equal stakeholders in informing programme development. This serves as a frequent reminder of the unique skills and talents that each stakeholder brings to the UL training.

Jane's story

With Mícheál's persuasion I very reluctantly came to Ireland in 1999. I was in the final year of my doctoral studies in the Faculty of Medicine at the University of Queensland (UQ) and I was a busy clinician and academic teacher in a full-time lecturer role in the Faculty of Music at UQ. I have never regretted my decision. I remember in my first year or two Mícheál would always introduce me as being from Sydney, and I would always reply, 'Mícheál wishes I was from Sydney.' Mícheál gave me such a warm welcome. He wanted music therapy, the course, and me to succeed.

Mícheál was so immensely persuasive that I should relocate to Ireland. 'You like us and we like you,' he said in one of our first meetings about possibly staying on at UL. I decided I would return if they advertised a senior lecturer role, and I was successful in attaining it. I also recall Mícheál was positively gleeful when I told him that the vice president of Finance wanted to negotiate with me as to the financial support I needed to undertake the start-up of the postgraduate allied health courses. Mícheál was no help at all; he formed the idea I should ask for a Connemara pony! He laughed a lot at this idea.

I struggled sometimes being the only academic music therapist in the country and I am grateful to many people including, among others, Tommy Hayes, Andrea Intveen, Alison Ledger, Úna McInerney, Oonagh McMahon and Jason Noone who regularly stepped up and helped with supporting the course for the nine years I worked in the sole position. It was such a relief to be able to advertise a second music therapy lecturer position in 2008, and to welcome Simon Gilbertson in the full-time lecturer role. The chapter we wrote together sets out our shared approach and style to the Limerick programme.[1]

Mícheál and I did not always see eye to eye. We are both strong and determined people and it is possibly an Australian trait to not give much care to annoying people. I remember when I was working on the development of UL's inaugural psychology courses, Professor Ciarán Benson, one of the advisors from UCD, and I were at dinner. Mícheál was also dining there. As he knew Ciarán he came over to greet him during the evening. I said to Ciarán, 'Mícheál is my boss.' Mícheál threw his head back, laughed and exclaimed, 'There is no way someone can boss her!' I still smile when I think of that.

I am always grateful to Mícheál that he allowed me time off for health reasons at a difficult juncture, and he was supportive in my frequent trips back to Australia to support my parents through various unexpected health crises. Mícheál was always in the middle of multiple projects, events and ideas but he would always slow and be calm when I needed to sit with him to tell him something. That is a much appreciated quality in a leader.

Mícheál: bringing the people with him

Mícheál had a way with words. He often would mark down a few points in a pre-speech conversation and then deliver a powerful and impactful speech, amazing the room. He liked to be loved by the audience, to win them over and bring them along with him. In this section of the essay we reflect on four speeches he made about music therapy. The first was at a small gathering of health practitioners in Limerick in 1999 who assisted placements through 1999. The second was the music therapy Christmas event that same year which included a larger number of practitioners and health leaders, many of whom now have music therapists working in their services. Then two further speeches will be recalled: one at a workshop on music and health in 2005, and the other at the inaugural meeting of the International Association for Music and Medicine in 2009.

Through the inaugural years of the music therapy course the relationship with the health services was essential to developing placements. Educating practitioners and managers about the role and potential value of music therapy was a key task. Mícheál was always willing to speak with the healthcare community. During 1999, the second year of the music therapy course, he hosted two events, one a pre-drinks social event prior to a concert of the Irish Chamber Orchestra in the UL Concert Hall, and the other a Christmas festive event in the Conservatory of the Castletroy Park Hotel. In both speeches he emphasised the humanity of music and its capacity to change hearts and minds. In the Christmas speech he talked about love, and many of the audience were so overcome by his words they were moved to tears. In the audience were practitioners and service directors from many facilities local to Limerick, and some from Dublin. At the time of writing these services have now employed music therapy practitioners for two decades. Sparked and inspired by Mícheál's words, they opened their services to music therapy.

The conviction and belief with which Mícheál spoke, coupled with the eloquent lyrical and musical delivery of his words, left an overwhelming sense of inspiration and determination among his audience, eager to find a way to support and develop music therapy. In 2005 a workshop on music and health was funded by the European Science Foundation (ESF) which partnered with UL as the lead institution in cooperation with the University of Bristol (UK) and Aarhus University (Denmark). The workshop supported music therapy researchers along with other leaders in the music and health field to come to Limerick and engage in seminars and round-table meetings to consider how we could develop a music and health network internationally. It also sought to ensure that our research was as widely available as possible, to assist health services to make good decisions about the service they wanted, and service users and their families to have advice and support as to the use of music in their care. One of the outputs from the event was an edited book with a foreword by Mícheál.[2] He was fond of the story about the little boy who after his first school music class raced home to tell his parents that he had learned to play a golden flute with a green top – an Irish whistle. Mícheál included this story in the book but when he had told it in the opening of the public seminar day which followed the workshop people roared with laughter in recognition of the joy of musical discovery. In that speech and later text he referred to the people who held the course director role at various times as 'Australian angels' who had 'flapped their wings' – an acknowledgement that at a time when the course was in its early stages, involvement from multiple people with Australian heritage was crucial to provide teaching and leadership.

During 2009 Jane was approached with an invitation to host the inaugural meeting of a new organisation, the International Association for Music and Medicine. Mícheál immediately offered support and was keen, but there were no funds available to run the event. He contacted the inaugural director of the Graduate Education Medical School at UL, Professor Paul Finucane, and asked him for funding support. Paul agreed and the meeting was initiated, the result being a busy and exciting event with participants from fourteen countries. Similarly to the ESF workshop, the closed meetings were followed by a conference. At the conference Mícheál gave the opening address, focusing on the felicitations of health and music. He inspired and thrilled the audience with his intellect and charm.

The programme

The MA in Music Therapy has grown from strength to strength since it started with its first cohort of eight students in 1998. With a cautious approach to programme numbers that aligned with limited availability of clinical placements in the early years, student intake was on a two-yearly basis. However, as the number of clinical placement sites and demand for places on the programme increased, student intake was adjusted in 2007 to a yearly intake. While the majority of students in the early years were Irish, the graduate profile of the programme has grown significantly. There are now over 150 graduates from countries including Australia, Bahrain, Canada, China, Czech Republic, Cyprus, Ecuador, Germany, Greece, Hong Kong, India, Ireland, Israel, Lithuania, Norway, Singapore, Thailand, UK and United States. Each of these graduates brought their unique worldview and life experiences to the programme, creating an international community of practice that in turn is a community of influence within music therapy worldwide. This very much reflects Mícheál's idea of 'lobality' whereby the careful establishment of meaningful local connections has resonated with a global community. In doing so, the MA in Music Therapy at UL is a well-known and much respected programme among international peers.

Of equal importance in building the international profile of the programme has been the many inspiring music therapy educators who have left their unique imprints on this training as it stands today. These include Kaja Jensen (US), Wendy Magee (Australia), Bent Jensen and Anne Steen Moeller (Denmark), Jeanette Kennelly (Australia), Kat McFerran (Australia), Vicky Abad-O'Shea (Australia), Simon Gilbertson (Germany), Alpha Woodward (Canada) and Jane Edwards (Australia) who was the programme director for over fourteen years.

The development of the MA Music Therapy was especially enhanced by Mícheál's commitment to bringing in international visitors to teach and advise, along with the careful appointment of external examiners. These external examiners to date have included Professor Tony Wigram (UK/Denmark), Professor Barbara Wheeler (US), Professor Susanne Metzner (Germany), Professor Heide Ahonen-Eerikainen (Finland/Canada) and Dr Joanne Loewy (US).

Under the current directorship of Hilary Moss (associate professor), with Tríona McCaffrey (lecturer), the MA Music Therapy remains committed to providing students with a training that is built upon the three pillars of practice, theory and research. A key marker of success has been in terms of the number of clinical placements that have been created over the past two decades, in stark comparison to the few placements there were in existence in Ireland when the programme commenced in 1998. With almost thirty clinical placement sites across Ireland and the UK, there are opportunities for students to complete supervised placements with various client groups in fields such as intellectual disability, neuro-rehabilitation, acquired brain injury, paediatrics, palliative and hospice care for both children and adults, adult mental health, older adult care, acute medical care and maternity care. Central to this development has been the investment of time and care into developing these relationships with supervisors without whom it would not be possible to expose students to music therapy practice in the 'real world'. Another contributor to the success of the programme has been through final-semester independent placements whereby students introduce music therapy to a facility that has no previous experience of providing this practice. This has led to the creation of a number of music therapy posts and subsequent employment in paediatric care, adolescent and adult mental health, neuro-rehabilitation, older adult care and maternity care.

Music therapy and arts and health research

A dynamic research culture in the Academy has been another contributing factor to the success of the MA Music Therapy. The vibrant Arts and Health Network chaired by Hilary Moss (2015 to present), with its pre-cursor, the Music and Health Research Group (Leigheas an Cheoil[3]) directed by Jane Edwards (2004–13), have collectively led numerous studies in a range of quantitative, qualitative, mixed-method and arts-based contributions to knowledge creation. Current faculty expertise has resulted in several research outputs in subject areas such as medical humanities, singing and well-being, chronic pain, dementia care, adolescent and adult mental health, music therapy service development, service user involvement, perinatal mental health care and creative arts therapy in intellectual disability services.

Over the past twelve years twelve doctoral candidates have completed research studies in areas such as music therapy service development, music therapy and anti-oppressive practice, service user experience of music therapy in mental health, anthroposophical music therapy, telehealth music therapy, self-regulatory music listening, accessible music technology, music therapy for stammering and adolescents, music therapy for chronic pain, music in dementia care, in addition to neurologic music therapy and gait. The number of doctoral students has grown significantly in recent years on a research programme that continues to develop and adapt thanks to Mícheál's vision. A key component of this programme's development has been promoting the value of interdisciplinary work across multiple professions to advance the research agenda, and to improve awareness of the role of the arts in health and social care.

Commitment to community

Still firmly rooted in the 'lobal foundations' on which the programme was founded, faculty on the MA Music Therapy programme continue to build active relationships with various local, national and international communities to promote music therapy engagement and education. Such recent initiatives include a global online skill-sharing and music therapy education programme in Ghana[4] and the establishment of the Global Music Therapy Educators Network in response to the Covid-19 pandemic.[5] These are just two examples of how local and global needs are at the heart of the development of music therapy initiatives at UL and how such actions remain true to the original guiding vision of the Academy.

Conclusion

The MA Music Therapy at the Academy continues to exponentially strengthen since its first signs of life in 1998. Mícheál remarkably dared to dream of, and bring into being, the first and still the only professional music therapy training in Ireland. His energy, dynamism and ability to bring people along with him created an unstoppable force that has made a marked contribution to third-level education and healthcare services in Ireland. His ability to nurture a shared conviction in the concept of music as a health-promoting resource, while believing in the talents and expertise of those who have been entrusted as caretakers of the MA Music Therapy ever since, ensures that his legacy continues.

35

Mícheál Ó Súilleabháin: 'Ah, sweet dancer'[1]

Mary Nunan

Mary Nunan is a dance artist. Throughout her career she has created choreographies that have been presented at national and international venues. Her career began when she joined Dublin Contemporary Dance Theatre (1981–6). She was founder/artistic director of Daghdha Dance Company (1988–99) and course director of the MA Contemporary Dance Performance, UL (1999–2016). Since 2016 she has worked as an independent artist: choreographer, performer, mentor and writer.

> 'In a reincarnation I would be a dancer, because when I'm performing I feel a huge connection between gesture and sound. I'm very interested in the connection in the musician's body movement – in other words, how gesture engenders sound. I often feel that instead of dance being a response to music, music is a response to the initial gesture which creates the sound. You can't create a sound unless you make a gesture first. I know this from sitting at the piano. A sound comes from a gesture. Then a gesture may respond to the sound. So I'm interested in something that goes deeper than music or dance.'[2]

Mícheál Ó Súilleabháin's contribution to music and music education in Ireland is well known and widely acknowledged. However, less is known about his very significant contribution to both Irish traditional dance and contemporary dance education. In this essay I discuss his role in the development of the latter, focusing specifically on his time as founding director of the Irish World Academy of Music and Dance. It was during this time that Mícheál oversaw the establishment of an MA Dance Performance.[3] This was the first full-time dance programme to be set up in a university in Ireland. It was one of a suite of nine MA programmes that marked the first phase of the development of the Academy. 1999 saw the intake of the first cohort of students. This essay is written from my perspective as a contemporary dance artist and the first course director of the MA Contemporary Dance Performance programme. There are lots of 'firsts' mentioned in this paragraph, but they were pioneering times!

The establishment of this programme was significant on a number of levels, not least because of the marginalised status of dance in Ireland at that time. The historical lack of recognition of dance, as an art form, has been highlighted in recent years by dance artists, educators and also by researchers in the relatively new field of dance scholarship in this country. Their research provides interesting perspectives on the cultural, social, artistic and epistemic politics that contributed to dance being marginalised in this way.[4]

According to McGrath and Meehan, it has always been the experience of dance practitioners and scholars in Ireland to find themselves positioned in a 'space peripheral to the hegemonic structures of cultural governance and education'.[5] Theodores goes further and locates dance beyond the peripheral, arguing that our choreographic history is largely 'an invisible history' which receives for the most part 'short-term media hype and attention rather than real recognition'.[6] This is echoed by Mulrooney who points to the absence of documentation and lack of archival records of some very significant developments in dance performance in the early twentieth century in Ireland.[7]

The fact that it was not listed in the Irish government's first arts act, which was signed into law in 1951, might go some way towards explaining the historical lack of policy and provision for dance in this country. This act, which led to the establishment of the Arts Council, defined the arts to mean painting, sculpture, architecture, music, drama, literature, design in industry and the fine arts and applied arts generally. In 1973 the list was updated to include cinema. However, it was only with the passing of the 2003 Arts Act that dance was named.[8]

Likewise Aosdána, the affiliation of creative artists established by the Arts Council in 1981, did not initially recognise choreographers as artists, arguing that choreography was not a creative but interpretative practice. They finally changed their stance on this with the election of two choreographers in 2006. However, despite the above-mentioned systemic omissions, the professional dance community in Ireland was, during these fallow years, slowly and steadily developing from the ground up and making itself visible. An aerial view of these developments would reveal many bright lights – hubs of activities – dotted around the country. Their growth pattern was necessarily rhizomatic. This term, borrowed here from Deleuze and Guattari, describes patterns that can spread, like water, across surfaces and through fissures and gaps, finding new pathways and creating new spaces in response to emergent conditions and evolving circumstances.[9] Thomond College of Education (now University of Limerick) was one such hub.

In the 1980s the Arts Council recognised the need to put in place a policy that would allow it to better respond to and support this burgeoning dance community. To this end it commissioned a report entitled *The Dancer and the Dance: Developing dance theatre in Ireland.*[10] The council's new policy was strongly informed by the recommendations of this report. New priorities and funding streams were identified including bursaries, commission schemes and choreography awards. In addition, there was a focus on dance education and dance-in-education initiatives, including funding the first ever dancer-in-residence (Mary Nunan) post jointly hosted by Thomond College of Education and Mary Immaculate College of Education, which led to the establishment of Daghdha Dance Company[11] (artistic director Mary Nunan) in 1988.[12]

This was the dance environment (nurtured in no small part by Teresa Leahy, dance lecturer in Thomond College[13]) into which Mícheál stepped when he took up his position as chair of music in 1994. He saw that contemporary dance could have a place within his overall vision for the Academy. Unencumbered by the constraints that had inhibited its development in Ireland, he did not hesitate in including it as one of the Academy's original suite of six MA programmes. And it is worth repeating that he did this despite its marginal status and the fact that there were no full-time programmes in dance at any university in Ireland at that time.[14] When viewed within this wider context it is clear that this was unquestionably a bold and indeed visionary move on Mícheál's part.

The MA in Dance Performance launched in 1999 attracted many national and international dance artists, choreographers and performers who welcomed the opportunity the programme gave them to undertake intensive periods of studio-based research (under the guidance of faculty and highly renowned guest tutors), and to integrate it into their own artistic practice. The atmosphere of experimentation and innovation that was central to the programme gave each student an opportunity to 'find their own voice'. This notion of finding one's voice was central to the ethos of the Academy and one that Mícheál spoke about with great passion at every opportunity.

Amongst the guest tutors at that time were some of the most iconic dance artists from the ground-breaking New York Judson post-modern dance movement.[15] As this was the first time these artists had come to Ireland, many members of the wider professional dance community came to the Academy to attend their workshops and lectures. The 'White Space'[16] initiative was set up to encourage and facilitate their participation. It was an exciting time and one that Mícheál actively engaged with and supported.

In a personal note sent to me at that time he wrote, 'Such a joy to be in the presence of such originality.'[17]

In 2001, in a completely unexpected turn of events, Irish traditional dancer Colin Dunne expressed an interest in undertaking the MA Contemporary Dance Performance. As course director of the programme, I wasn't entirely sure how this might 'work' given his already established and internationally recognised status as a virtuosic Irish traditional dance performer.[18] So Colin and I had many conversations about whether the MA programme could provide the right kind of environment for the research he wanted to undertake. It was hard to tell or foretell. But it was a risk he was willing to take: a leap into a somewhat familiar but simultaneously unknown landscape.

Mícheál had no such reservations. He was very excited about Colin walking 'across the line' between Irish traditional dance and contemporary dance. And he honoured Colin's already established status as an artist by offering him the position of dancer-in-residence while he was undertaking the MA. Mícheál had a great interest in all the 'turns' that were happening within Irish traditional dance at that time: the revival of interest in *sean-nós*; Siamsa Tíre, the National Folk Theatre of Ireland; and of course *Riverdance*, to name a few. Therefore, he had a strong sense of what Colin was interested in exploring within this context. However, he also saw Colin's undertaking as being unique and distinctive. According to Mícheál it was coming from an impulse for which 'words like "fusion" or "crossover" are far too small. I'm talking about the under-ground cultural well that the diviner tips into'.[19]

In an interview for this essay I asked Colin what drew his attention to the Academy in the first instance. And, not surprisingly, he spoke about Mícheál.

> Before I met Mícheál, or was aware of the Irish World Academy, he had become a massive figure to me and probably to a lot of people of my generation within traditional music and dance. He first entered my orbit as a musician with his album *The Dolphin's Way* – which blew my mind because I hadn't heard traditional music played this way before on the piano. And then as a composer with pieces like *Oileán* and through the TV series *River of Sound*. And even the fact that he was Dr Mícheál Ó Súilleabháin – that was a totally new thing in traditional music or traditional arts circles at that time. The way he talked, the vocabulary he used, all made him a fascinating figure who was both in and from the tradition yet also able to stand out of it and see it all in a wider frame.

> Then when I met him in 1999, all these things were confirmed. He was so dynamic and poetic and kind of spiritual but also really practical and maverick-like. I wanted to go where he was going and roll with it all.[20]

I then asked Colin what kind of exchanges he might have had with Mícheál – artist to artist, dancer to musician.

> Just before I came to do the MA in 2001 I had some e-mail correspondence with Mícheál in which he said he would find it fascinating for me to take on the music of Tommie Potts and to dance it. He seemed to recognise that some of my agitations and views around traditional dance aligned with Potts' own musical journey. At that time though I just didn't get it! Mícheál was sixteen years ahead of me as it turned out as I finally came to Potts in 2017.[21]

The focus of the interview then turned to the MA Contemporary Dance Performance and how Colin's experience of undertaking that programme had impacted on him as a dancer and choreographer.

> The Potts' project is probably a really good example of this. In 2001 (before doing the MA), I wouldn't have had the physical capacity, the vocabulary, the sensitivity to dance to Potts' music, or the ability to research and dig down into finding a relationship with such a unique and complex musician. On the one hand, contemporary dance is just a very humanistic way of looking at movement, and I began to discover how the body can move or speak in its most efficient way and how my previous training was physically and literally tripping me up. But more than that, the MA was really about discovering your own mode of enquiry, the permission and necessity to ask questions, and the ability to listen to and act on your own creative impulses. And so maybe paradoxically, rather than contemporary dance potentially drawing me away from the tradition, it actually landed me right back in the middle of it armed with the ability to at least know where to start digging.[22]

In this regard it was clear that he was, to use Mícheál's term, like a 'diviner' trying to tap into some well that lay under the ground of both traditions. And it has been widely recognised, nationally and internationally, that he did indeed tap into something unique, as a performer and a choreographer, the critical acclaim he received for *Out of Time* (2008)[23] and *Concert* (2017)[24] being one manifestation of this.

The MA Dance Performance was the only programme within the Academy that was comprised of two streams: Irish traditional dance and contemporary dance. In constructing the programme in this way it was clear that Mícheál was interested in providing an opportunity for interaction and exchanges between the two streams. I would go as far as to say that, as an artist and educator, he was really excited and curious about what might emerge from this. But he was also deeply respectful of both traditions and understood that the relationship between them should not be forced. In his wisdom he could see that each stream would first need time to 'bed down' and establish its own foundations. This provided the perfect environment for each stream to flourish and for the interactions and exchanges between them to emerge from the ground up rather than being imposed from the top down.

Although Colin was the first Irish traditional dancer to undertake the MA Contemporary Dance Performance, he was not the last. In the years that followed, other distinguished Irish traditional dancers undertook the programme and the dialogue across the traditions became increasingly enriched as a result. This was just one of the many exciting developments that happened, as Colin put it, 'in the magic of those early days – in terms of Mícheál being wizard-like, waving wands and buildings coming up and new courses. It just felt like anything was possible.'[25]

Since these early days, graduates of the MA Dance Performance have contributed greatly to the growth of the professional dance community in Ireland through their work as independent dance artists/choreographers, performers, academics, festival directors, writers and scholars. Some are also involved in policy-making and advocacy (in the Arts Council and Dance Ireland) and as a result contributing to the development of increased systemic support for dance. Many of the international graduates are doing likewise in their communities.

Were Mícheál to now speak to an assembly of the national and international graduates and all the faculty and guest artists who had been involved in the MA Dance Performance programmes, I have no doubt he would generously acknowledge and celebrate all our achievements to date. And I am sure he would also take the opportunity to remind us, in his inimitably poetic way, to always keep our senses open and responsive to that 'something that goes deeper than music and dance' in whatever we do.

And so we must, and so we do, and so we dance with him.

36

Conferring the Céilí: Irish traditional music programmes at the Irish World Academy

Niall Keegan

Niall Keegan is a flute player and academic at the University of Limerick where he contributes primarily to programmes in the areas of traditional music and ethnomusicology. Much of his research is concerned with cognitive structures used by traditional musicians to organise their oral music in a literate world.

The Irish World Academy of Music and Dance is an environment where an extremely diverse group of performance practices and their communities are critically and performatively engaged and honoured. However, the practices most commonly associated with the Academy are from the native traditional arts and, in particular, that contemporary behemoth of the western folk world, Irish traditional music. This is due to a number of factors: the genre focus of the founding director of the Academy, Professor Mícheál Ó Súilleabháin; the Academy's initial research focus; and the sheer strength and vitality of tradition, crying out for institutional and mainstream[1] engagement and recognition. The relationship of the institution to this community of practice and the role of Ó Súilleabháin is the focus of this short essay.

In my experience of the engagement of formal education,[2] and in particular at third level, with 'other' music practices (whether they be so-called folk musics, popular musics or basically any other music apart from western classical music), it is an endeavour fraught with distrust and difficulty. In my more limited experience of the life of classical music at third level there seems to be a longstanding happy compromise, a sort of memorandum of understanding between musicologists and musicians, resulting in the controlled interface between the conservatoire and music department at that level.

However, for popular or folk musics the relationship between community and institution is not quite as established. Communities of practice,[3] while often longing for the mainstream recognition they receive when their music appears in curricula, are often suspicious of the motivations of the academy.[4]

The communities that support these practices are usually urban and/or rural working classes, communities that only recently have started to make inroads into the institution. Society still effectively creates many barriers to this process, particularly financial ones. The spin that the academy will put onto the study of such music, like theoretical approaches from academic disciplines or developing valuative ideas around performance practice (for example, what is needed to get an A1, a C or an F in a traditional song exam), can at most reflect aspects of traditional hierarchies of value and aesthetic. Very often the academy generates avenues of research that can seem pointless to many members of the community that live the music; anecdotally I have often been in situations where an academic, explaining their research to a musician, is met by responses which amount to 'what's the point?' This is complicated by the fact that communities endeavouring to seek third-level validation develop their own hierarchies of knowledge, their own experts whose orders of knowledge and discourse can be radically different to those honoured in disciplinary academic contexts. Lectures are often a feature of the plethora of traditional music summer schools that are such a prominent feature of the Irish traditional music calendar, but experts who work outside the university or conservatoire deliver the majority of these. (In the 2015 Willie Clancy Summer School only one of seven lectures or seminars was presented or led by academics currently employed as such.) Very often the communities of practice are concerned that the academy will historicise the music – becoming a resource, an archive, a centre for archaeological endeavour, rather than a generative site for arts practice. The academy is usually quite happy to fill this role, becoming at most a resource for classical and folk musicians alike. This is not to condemn this role, as such engagement is useful and helps in the imagination of a tradition and its status; but it limits the engagement of the university with music and its communities, and it diminishes its univers(ity)ness.

Ethnomusicological inquiry into this phenomenon often throws up terms such as 'westernisation'[5], 'classicalisation'[6] or 'artification'[7] of folk music in the university or conservatoire. In these contexts it has been seen as generating changes to some obvious and fundamental aspects of a music practice – particularly, codifying and delineating folk music; the decontextualising of music; the decline of oral processes; or the promotion of 'concert' performance. I find it interesting that those ethnomusicologists writing about such processes are very often not part of the process. Of course I am not saying that their perspective is limited, rather that the perspective of the ethnomusicologist within and often instigating the process (i.e. creating these programmes) is notable by its absence. This leaves a potentially really interesting branch of applied ethnomusicology curiously silent (although the recent series of FolkMusEd conferences in Scotland and Finland have moved in some way to address this).

Traditional music at third-level institutions in Ireland

The integration of traditional music practices into third-level programmes of Irish institutions has, for nearly fifty years, been led by ethnomusicologists. Much has been said about the pivotal role of Seán Ó Riada, a lecturer at the Department of Music at University College Cork (UCC) in the 1960s, in the revival (if that is the right word) of Irish traditional music.[8] However, it is the work of one of his students, Mícheál Ó Súilleabháin, that brought Irish traditional music truly into the academy. Mícheál developed the study of traditional music in the general undergraduate music degrees of UCC and, more pivotally, accepted students on the partial basis of their traditional music performance (partial as they still needed to have a high level of western music education also). Early examples of these musicians included young traditional performers such as piper Mary Mitchell, concertina and whistle player Catherine Foley and pianist and whistle player Geraldine Cotter. In the late 1980s Ó Súilleabháin developed a research community around traditional music populated almost entirely by traditional musicians. This research was traditional (i.e. with a thesis as the sole research outcome) and a long way yet from the type of arts practice outputs we see at the Academy today. But again, it was notable that the important criterion for access to research degrees was not necessarily a schooling in classical music but in a far wider range of academic disciplines – and, most importantly, a performance and communally engaged background in traditional music. This allowed students such as myself, with a degree in history and theology and a lifetime playing traditional flute, to complete research degrees in UCC under Mícheál's guidance.[9]

In 1994 Ó Súilleabháin relocated to the University of Limerick (UL) where he took up the institution's first and only chair of music. By this time he had developed a national reputation as a performer – playing traditional and original material on the piano, often in an orchestral context – and as a writer and commentator. As Juniper Hill has discussed,[10] his educational work not only involved the development of pedagogy around traditional music but was much broader in the context of the Academy.[11] As well as being facilitated by his creative and utopian vision for the mission of the Academy and his profile as a performer, these developments were also made possible by his gregarious national profile and, very importantly, his international profile in a philanthropic context. However, within the traditional music community his reputation has been that of an innovator – he plays an instrument not commonly associated with traditional music, in a significantly different style to those players who played the instrument in that tradition, and in a fusion context engaging forms and instrumentation from classical, jazz, popular and other, more exotic traditions. In particular his solo piano album *The Dolphin's* Way (1987) and *Oileán/Island* (1999) paradoxically illustrate his virtuosity as a traditional musician and as a leading innovator, presenting traditional and newly composed Irish material in frameworks from classical and jazz.

His status as innovator was, and still is, politically situated within the tradition – he was often seen as someone who was interested in changing tradition. This association reached its height with the release of a seven-part television series he produced with Hummingbird Productions called *A River of Sound* (1995). Mícheál scripted and presented the programme. Through the extremely high level of media attention it received, it has been the high point (or low point, depending on the perspective) of the two-dimensional and oversimplified, but very real, tradition/innovation debate in Irish traditional music. It has inspired headlines in national media such as the famous *Irish Times* header 'Rivers of Dissent' where the journalist attending the McGill Summer School themed around a discussion of tradition and innovation in Irish music stated that '"River of Blood" might have been a better title for the debate'.[12] Perhaps the most significant expression of this debate was the *Crossroads Conference* held in Dublin in 1995, where traditional musicians and academics presented and debated on the nature of the Irish music tradition, the apparent crisis of the polarisation of innovation versus tradition and the television programme itself. The proceedings of this conference were published in 1996 and give a good flavour of the intensity of the debate at the time, from restrained contributions from a number of disciplinary approaches to some outraged individuals venting against the 'bastardisation' and 'mongrelisation' of tradition.[13]

For many within the tradition, this sort of controversy illustrated how the university was taking its music and changing it (and for some, destroying it in the process). It highlighted how some people identified a desire by the university to somehow own or possess the music. In 1996 at the Willie Clancy Summer School a carefully staged and much promoted debate was set up featuring alleged protagonists Ó Súilleabháin and the great fiddle player Paddy Glackin (I say alleged as the two were, in my experience, great friends and frequently performed together!). Despite what turned out to be a particularly – and perhaps to some, disappointingly – conciliatory debate, one member of the audience asked whether he would need a degree from the University of Limerick to get into one of the well-known session sites of the festival. For Mícheál and many of us working in the university sector, and in particular UL, this comment highlighted how we have had to work with the double-edged sword of engagement and advocacy. In working to bring Irish traditional music and its immense, diverse and international community to the table of institutional, mainstream pedagogy, we had, partially, alienated this community.

If the university is not trying to change the tradition into a more artful (i.e. more classical) expression or trying to possess and order the tradition into something curriculum-sized and university-complex, then why do we bring it into the university at all? Why aren't we content to fulfil the role of academic observer, where even participant observation serves the process of observation rather than the traditional role of participation? Or why don't we provide the tradition with a relatively static resource for archival information, validating tradition but not playing a real operational role in the life of the tradition? To answer this we must look to the nature of music in formal education in Ireland. Like many other places, formal (i.e. state-sponsored and institutionally based) music education has privileged classical music, the musical activities of some aspects of the middle classes of the country. Until the 1990s, to study music at secondary school you had to study instrumental classical performance privately outside of school. This changed with the new Leaving Certificate syllabus adopted in 1996 which was built on the potential of work in the school classroom rather than that purchased outside of it. However, despite this heavily critiqued move,[14] school music still tends to be a middle-class, urban and privileged activity. In the context of secondary education, music has been perceived as a particularly female concern so the predominantly male, rural performers of Irish traditional music were doubly excluded.

University music departments tended to be musicology units concerned with the study of classical music while the country's three conservatoires[15] taught classical music performance in a manner that reflected practices of European conservatoires. This had the effect of creating citadels of music education with particularly high ramparts that largely excluded musicians from by far the strongest participant tradition on the island, traditional music. At UL, and continuing his previous work in UCC, Ó Súilleabháin and the team he gathered around him decided that this situation was not satisfactory. There was a deliberately built barrier between the world of formal music education and qualification and the majority of musicians in the country from their very first engagements with formal education.

This situation not only disserved those communities of musicians but also the institutions of formal education, as they were making themselves irrelevant to the majority of music practitioners on the island. Undoubtedly the engagement of the university was reflective of and facilitated by the growing middle-class make-up and aspirations of the participants within the tradition. Whether the incentive comes from a need to democratise the world of third-level music education or the paradoxical gentrification of traditional music, the intention has been to admit to the canon of academic and performance study a music practice on its own terms – as much as possible – in the context of the intellectual and performative rigour expected within a third-level context.

Traditional music programmes at the Academy

Staff at the Academy have built programmes where the standards of entry come from aesthetics and value systems found within communities of practice. This process was first embodied in curriculum with the foundation and development of the one- or two-year-long MA Irish Traditional Music Performance with its first intake of students in September 1999. Its most recent articulation is in the new four-year BA in Irish Music (starting in September 2023) which has emerged from the Academy's first undergraduate programme, the BA in Irish Music and Dance (established in 2002). We accept students who are good performers and who can demonstrate an intelligent engagement with, and knowledge of, the community of practice that we call traditional Irish music. At no stage in our entrance procedures do we look for an understanding of western music theory. Indeed, we often take students who may have little knowledge of standard western notation. However, they almost always have experience of notational practices that have developed in the tradition.[16] This of course throws up challenges for curriculum design. Part of our mission is to train students to engage a wider musical world that is dominated by the standards and practices of western art and popular musics, so teaching traditional elements of curriculum like music theory, music history and keyboard is essential. However, we must do this in a critical manner that comes from, and remains relevant to, the practices of the community that we try to engage.

Much of the pedagogy is built around the development of the student's traditional music performance practice. Central to this development is a strongly individualistic ethos mentioned by Juniper Hill from her observances of the Folk Music programme of the Sibelius Academy in Helsinki, Finland.[17] This is central to all the approaches followed by similar initiatives in western European institutions, but perhaps not so extreme as in the Finnish case. We are aware that this is an approach perhaps idiomatically associated with western arts practice, emphasising artistry and individuality as central goals. Hill characterises this as the 'artification' of tradition,[18] and closer to home it has been described as 'classicalisation'.[19] There has certainly been an aesthetic of individuality in the Irish tradition for as long as we have records of it. For example, Nic Suibhne illustrates this in the Donegal fiddle tradition where there were different classes of fiddle player, divided according to their perceived virtuosity.[20] However, there are other aesthetics that reject virtuosity and individuality, placing higher value on community involvement and conformity (such comments are frequently to be found on social media).

However, in the traditional music programmes of the Academy we emphasise the development of these principles of artistry or individuality in context, and we look for these elements in ways reflecting wider artistic aesthetics in the tradition, which are diverse. It would be overly simple to present a spectrum of aesthetics with a single axis imagined between creativity and community. Neither can it ever be entirely oppositional and must rely on one another to be meaningful. Central to the ethos of the Academy is the slogan 'finding your own voice'. We are anxious that this happens for our students and, for example, it is a matter of great pride to me that some students have come to us from Donegal – 200 kilometres north of us – to become better Donegal fiddlers. The implication of this trope is that, yes, we aspire for an individual voice, but a voice is something that is communally meaningful. Students play a central role in the development of their own performance repertoire for examination; they influence who their tutors, and particularly visiting tutors, are; they also contribute to how their exams are structured and assessed. This kind of engagement occurs in a discursive framework whereby faculty, students, tutors and external examiners provide input to the creation of standards and the content of assessment. We are always acutely aware that there are other ways of performing traditional music in a socially meaningful way and we attempt to negotiate these ways wherever possible while remaining cognisant of the limitations of curriculum in engaging a tradition.

One of the main means of encouraging such processes is to bring members of the traditional music community into the Academy to play, teach and comment. Our teachers teach in ways that are appropriate to them, invariably in a predominantly oral manner, accentuated by various forms of notation and other more contemporary technologies (mobile phones, mp3 and video recorders, YouTube and Soundcloud are just some examples). We develop new ways of teaching traditional music. We draw on old and current pedagogical practices from within the tradition, imposing structures of assessment, semesterisation and other institutional foibles in as sensitive and appropriate a way as possible. But our strength is the community of practice we engage, not the institution. Hill speaks of a power relationship between institution and practice.[21] Certainly there are hierarchies of power but such hierarchies are multi-dimensional and are a lot more complicated than is often presented, accounting for communities without power and institutions with power. There is certainly power in the university in the areas of publishing, validating and qualifying; the university publishes the word and there is an undoubted power in the published word. But if the university makes itself irrelevant, it can be made inconsequential by the communities that it tries to engage. There is power in the word but only if we choose to read it.

Hill writes that 'it is crucial that scholars, educators and administrators, self reflexively and critically examine how their ideologies, assumptions, politics, curricula and teaching methods may impact and transform the traditions they teach',[22] and in a footnote in the same article paraphrases me saying that if the traditional music programmes of the Academy disappeared in the morning the tradition would be unaffected. This is not a boast about the institution's irrelevance or unimportance, but the opposite. All of the contemporary changes around the practice of traditional music do not emerge from the engagement of the university with the tradition; they come out of the tradition's continued relevance and engagement with modernity (of which the university is just a small part). The professionalisation of traditional music, the growth of virtuosic standards, the development of concert and more idiosyncratic performance contexts, the development of ensemble performance which has so often taken forms and practices from other traditions, the technologisation of the tradition, the development of 'musicologies' and histories to posit the tradition – these are but a few of the themes of change that have marked and transformed the tradition in the past century or so. They are not coming from the university but from the day-to-day life of this community of practice, making it relevant to the increasingly complex and diverse worlds this community lives in. An institution has to reflexively and critically engage these processes and encourage our students to do likewise. If the Academy slipped into the Shannon and out to the Atlantic, disappearing overnight, these processes would not stop. However, I would like to think that its loss would be felt, that the processes themselves may not be understood as well, and that a lot of young musicians would be less able to make their way in this world. Our intent is not to transform tradition but to understand it and give our students tools to do likewise – in order to fruitfully engage a life in this tradition.

The power of an institution like the Academy in the world of traditional music practice is inherited from tradition and this is a power that Ó Súilleabháin instinctively recognised. This power is passed from the students and the practitioners that facilitate much of our pedagogy, rather than the institution itself. UL is politically situated within tradition but I see that as a positive force – to be politically neutral in any fundamental, heart-rending context like music is to be unconnected. Mícheál Ó Súilleabháin embodied many political positions within tradition; he was never aloof or disconnected. Through our reflexive approach to the engagement with tradition as well as our reliance on a broad church of individuals from communities of practice, we believe that this institution becomes part of tradition, providing a fertile ground for some of the performers, researchers, teachers and arts organisers of the future.

37
Community Music in the Irish World Academy: Opening, inspiration, rupture

Kari K. Veblen and Kathleen Turner

Kari K. Veblen is professor emeritus of music education at Western University in Canada. Scholarship, professional service and teaching have taken her around the world. A widely cited researcher, Kari's interests include community music networks, lifespan music learning, traditional transmission, vernacular genres, interdisciplinary curriculum, musical play and social media.

Kathleen Turner is a singer, songwriter and community musician, course director of MA Community Music at the Irish World Academy of Music and Dance and commissioner for CMA, the Community Music Activity component of the International Society for Music Education. Kathleen's research interests are community music, social 'change', autoethnography, and their intersections with song.

Community music entered the Irish World Academy of Music and Dance in the 1990s as an inspiration, an opening, and a rupture of previous music education curriculum. Founding director Mícheál Ó Súilleabháin had laid the groundwork for its inclusion from the outset with his expansive vision:

> As musicians, and music researchers, and educationalists, many of us sense music not so much as something we do, but as something we are. It is this existentialistic sense of music that clearly demonstrates for us the deep connection between artistic expressions – in this case, music and dance – and human identity. By adjusting the social and cultural conditions within which people exist, we create conditions where embodied music also adjusts. Likewise, by adjusting the social and cultural conditions within which music exists, we create conditions where humans adjust socially, psychologically, and culturally.[1]

Former course director Jean Downey recalls how Ó Súilleabháin came to include community music in his vision. An impromptu conversation with Phil Mullen introduced him to this field of practice that resonated with these foundational roots of the Academy. Further conversations with Bruce

Cole and Patricia Shehan Campbell compelled him to consider a new programme that was exploratory in nature. While it was strongly established in the UK, Ó Súilleabháin wasn't sure what community music as a field of study was or could be in Ireland. However, he felt sure that the Academy could offer the place for this process of discovery.

Historical context

During 1996 and 1997 when the Academy was forming, David Elliott (University of Toronto) and Kari Veblen (then chair elect to the ISME Community Music Activity Commission) came to Limerick as curriculum advisors. Veblen had recently met Phil Mullen (the Goldsmiths' College, University of London) who proposed a series of public meetings to take the pulse of community music in Ireland. Mullen initiated and organised four seminars[2] – held at the Academy in Limerick, the Design Centre in Temple Bar, Dublin, the Clotworthy Arts Centre in County Antrim and the Cork School of Music – and then reported on these findings during a seminar held at the Academy. Each seminar attracted a cross-section of musicians working in the community who expressed appreciation in discovering that they were not alone. The Irish community music seminar series began an important dialogue in this emerging field at a time when networks were emerging in Ireland to facilitate access to music-making for Irish people. While there is no agreed-upon definition for the term 'community music' because it encompasses a wide range of activities and settings, people at the seminars agreed on certain perimeters.

The seminars encouraged members of the Academy to investigate the feasibility of offering an advanced degree in the new field of 'community music'. Kari Veblen wrote the MA programme document in consultation with David Elliott, David Price (Liverpool Institute of Performing Arts), Phil Mullen, Bruce Cole (York University), Mícheál Ó Súilleabháin and Helen Phelan.[3] As proposed, the graduate programme offered significant career options providing access to the arts and to arts organisations seeking to broaden their audience base. At the time of its generation, no course of study of this type existed in Ireland, and there were only three other programmes in the world. The proposal was accepted, and the first graduate students began the MA programme in 1999.

Ideals and principles

At the time of writing, community music has become an umbrella term to embrace practitioner-catalysed musical engagement in many contexts as well as participatory music-making in informal settings. Community musicians facilitate the expressive work of others. They may be proficient in a variety of genres and reach a broad spectrum of people across geographical communities, ages, abilities and socio-economic circumstances. The practice and the study of community music are grounded in the values of diversity, inclusion and access. These values are reflected in the student body who have studied community music at the Academy. This is not to say that these values are fully realised, but rather, as the programme grows, so too does a sense of its social responsibility and responsiveness. Matters such as climate change, forced migration and discrimination are taken up in doctoral research and the work of practitioners in the programmes at the Academy.

Programme growth: constant strands and emerging themes

Constant strands have persisted throughout the programme's growth including an initial reception of the field, engagement with practice and developing research. As well, themes have emerged such as commitment to international engagement and awareness of a collective self that is complex, grounded and distinctly Irish.

Phil Mullen facilitated the first years which were further developed by Lee Higgins, directed by Jean Downey and now by Kathleen Turner. Likewise external examiners Patricia Shehan Campbell (University of Washington), Kari Veblen (Western University, Canada), David Elliott (University of Toronto, New York University), Mary Cohen (University of Iowa) and Brydie-Leigh Bartleet (Griffith University, Australia) have guided the course.

Staying true to the 'parity of esteem' sought by Ó Súilleabháin, the programme welcomes applicants with diverse qualifications such as practising musicians already working in community settings. This is reflected in the application process, which has always welcomed students with relevant 'recognised prior learning' in a community setting, in lieu of an undergraduate degree. Consequently, students span a broad range of musical traditions; all types of musicianship are valued, multiple ways of knowing are recognised, and all musicians have space to learn and develop. Graduates of the programme Hala Jaber and Stephen Ryan are demonstrative of this approach and retain strong connections with the ongoing development of the MA Community Music as facilitators. Hala, who is currently pursuing post-doctoral research at the Academy, says she found that her personal practice of classical flute was a valid way into community facilitation:

> The programme exposed me to different ways of facilitating and reflexively helped me find my personal way of doing it. A very important highlight for me was that I can use my flute as an instrument to lead a workshop. It doesn't have to be a piano or guitar.[4]

Equally, current doctoral student and singer songwriter Stephen Ryan grounded his sense of professional identity within the programme:

> The course was a place to find words for what I do – a musician working in community and with community. When I did the course I discovered a framework for this, and found other people working in similar areas. I'd had a feeling of floating, but this gave me a definition for my work and a renewed sense of confidence going forward.[5]

As former course director Jean Downey explains, this sense of grounding and belonging was due in large part to the original vision that Ó Súilleabháin established:

> Mícheál Ó Súilleabháin recognised the discipline of community music when it was not widely identified in Ireland. He had a very broad vision and recognised the parity of esteem regarding studies of disciplines with a particular vocational ethic such as community music, music education and music therapy. There is such a variety among the student cohort that it is impossible to mention them all, but they include music teachers at first, second and third level, arts officers, Music Generation tutors, singers, instrumentalists, conductors, composers and singer-songwriters, health professionals, media presenters and outreach officers.[6]

Community musicians tend to have a sense of vocation as demonstrated in the multitude of routes that graduates have chosen. Many of the programme's graduates work as freelance community facilitators, partnering with organisations, schools and community centres. Some incorporate their practice into work as teachers, while others use their expertise in healthcare settings. Some are inspired to take this work further through additional training in music therapy.

What is true about community music in Ireland is that it is like a river that takes its own course. Those who have studied at the Academy imprint their own understandings, choices and ideals in their work. This is reflected in the growing number of doctoral and post-doctoral researchers at the Academy exploring intersections of societal issues with community music practice.[7] At the time of writing, areas of community music practice being explored at the Academy include socio-economic inequity, environmental activism and ecology, trauma-informed practice, self-care and creativity of the facilitator, experiences of migrant communities and people seeking sanctuary. These have shaped and will continue to shape the nature and value of the field in Ireland and abroad.

Facilitation, musicality, project management and emerging research remain central to the programme's delivery. Phil Mullen initiated these strands from 1999 to 2000, then continued as a visiting lecturer with the programme over the next decade. He notes:

> This was a challenging time – very diverse experiences with some students very musical but from limited backgrounds and others with advanced degrees. I thought these students were exceptional. They chose topics and projects that were ground-breaking and spoke to the Irish experience. We were well supported. There was a lot of flow and dialogue between the different master's platforms ... [We] all stepped up to the plate to expand our collective vision of what community music might be.[8]

One theme that has remained constant during the course's development is commitment to international engagement. Mullen organised an international seminar in 2000. A Palestinian group, Sabreen, was brought over along with Einar Solbu, former president of the International Society for Music Education (ISME) and director of the Norwegian Concert/Rikskonsertene. As a result of this encounter, Sabreen and Rikskonsertene formed an ongoing partnership to provide educational support in the West Bank. Mullen also organised a second Community Music Activity (CMA) conference in Limerick in 2004 with colleagues from the Goldsmiths' College, University of London and representation from ISME, the Netherlands and Scandinavia. A third conference was organised in 2018 by Hala Jaber, Frances Garry and Kathleen Turner. The event welcomed practitioners from across Ireland to engage in a day of workshops, reflection and discussion. Keynote speaker Brydie-Leigh Bartleet from Australia addressed the rather prophetic topic of 'Community Music in a Changing World'.

Issues of Irishness and identity in the modern world have also surfaced as important themes. Lee Higgins who served as course director from 2000 to 2002 found himself wondering if traditional Irish musicians could be seen as community music workers themselves:

> Explaining what constitutes Community Music practice was not an unusual experience; the challenge for me in Ireland was articulating it in the light of a strong indigenous music tradition. I would often be informed that Ireland had a strong tradition of Community Music, this was with clear reference to their traditional music … 'Communal music' and 'music of the community' were terms that I had found useful in attempts to qualify characteristic features of Community Music, could they be applied in this context?[9]

Lee Higgins' recognition of Irish-rooted communities of musical practice finds correspondence with Mícheál Ó Súilleabháin's vision of a collective identity that is rich, nuanced and complex:

> Because of their subversive and transgressive powers, their ability to break out from within while at the same time cutting through all boundaries, the performing arts of music and dance can claim a special place in the creation of a cohesive multifaceted identity – an identity which encourages new unities out of old oppositions, which honours the many voices within us, and which continues to engage us in the ongoing liberation of Irishness in an increasingly challenging global cultural environment.[10]

When this graduate programme began it came heavily stamped with global perceptions filtered through the Community Music Activity Commission of ISME. In the decades since, this field has grown as a scholarly area as well as a practice. Graduates and Academy staff have played a key role in connecting the University of Limerick to local projects and national organisations. Ireland's national performance music education programme, Music Generation, has strong local connections with the Academy.[11] The Irish Chamber Orchestra's Sing Out with Strings programme, which provides instrumental and vocal workshops for children across Limerick city, was developed with Kathleen Turner. Both Music Generation Limerick City and the Irish Chamber Orchestra have collaborated with the Academy through World Carnival. This project is based at Maria King Presentation Primary School and explores the cultures and languages of the pupils through song.

While a broader awareness continues, the programme housed at UL has generated a body of research projects from graduates, forged Irish connections, and has become a player in the international scene.

Looking forward

As of this writing, a global pandemic has brought an abrupt halt to community gatherings, necessitating swift response to ensure the university's ongoing survival and to support community practitioners. The class of 2021 will be the first cohort to study fully online, translating elements such as ensemble work and community placements into shared digital projects with community partners. While prompting students to find innovative ways to engage their collaborators, face-to-face contact is sorely missed.

The pivot online has been best demonstrated by Community Music Learning, an online project[12] which brings together staff and students from Germany, Ireland, Canada and the UK to meet, support each other's research, and listen to international experts.[13] An archive of research presentations is being generated on YouTube. This project has been an example for how rich and rewarding interactions are still possible through online forums.

As community music progresses in Ireland, there are two pressing issues identified by graduates and staff. Self-care and professional well-being are of key concern as freelance practitioners who work independently find themselves increasingly isolated; a problem which was exacerbated by the Covid-19 pandemic. Practitioners express an urgent need for access to technology, funding, networking, and strategies for professional resilience. A second concern is the establishment of a community music organisation (similar to Sound Sense (UK)) to offer professional support. An earlier website and Facebook page called Community Music was initiated but requires dedicated staffing.[14]

In closing

Some twenty-five years after its inclusion in the Academy templum, the graduate platform in community music at the Academy continues to be inspired by Mícheál Ó Súilleabháin's vision of 'the potential of music and dance to act as powerful forces of cultural mediation, redressing social – and musical – inequalities'.[15] The graduate programme provides a space for creation, exploration, access and inclusivity. Community music in Ireland is by no means limited to those who study at the university, but has been enhanced and furthered through this programme. Here practitioners meet, find new inspiration, galvanise their professional network, and critically engage with their work.

38

Moving Song: Reflections on the BA Voice and Dance

Jennifer de Brún, Hannah Fahey and Óscar Mascareñas

Jennifer de Brún is an Irish aerialist and ethnochoreologist, specialising in aerial spiral. Originally trained in Cecchetti classical ballet and contemporary dance, she is performing arts coordinator at the Irish World Academy of Music and Dance, University of Limerick, where she was awarded a PhD in Arts Practice.

Hannah Fahey is a singer, voice educator and academic who has performed internationally medieval, contemporary and Irish music as soloist and ensemble singer. She is course director of the BA Voice at the University of Limerick and her research interests are in vocal pedagogy and voice studies.

Óscar Mascareñas is a poet working in the fields of sound, light, movement and letters. He has published work in Europe, Africa and the Americas for the past twenty-six years; lectures and researches in sound and contemporary practice at the Irish World Academy of Music and Dance; and works as an independent artist internationally.

The BA Voice and Dance was established at the Irish World Academy of Music and Dance in 2008. This reflection is offered by two graduates of the programme who subsequently joined the Academy faculty, dancer Jennifer de Brún and singer Hannah Fahey. The first course director of the programme, Óscar Mascareñas, draws on his poetic voice to conclude the reflection.

Jennifer de Brún

On movement

As a dancer, born in the Republic of Ireland, the significance of being able to study dance at undergraduate level at an Irish university cannot be overstated. The BA Voice and Dance provided this opportunity for many young dancers and paved the way for specialised dance education at third level in Ireland.

I commenced my dance training in Cecchetti classical ballet in Limerick School of Classical Ballet. This training was disciplined and rigorous, with an emphasis on technical and performative excellence, in keeping with the philosophy of the Cecchetti Method. The method itself is based on theoretical principles, movement qualities and dynamics developed by Maestro Enrico Cecchetti[1] throughout his lifetime. Directly linked to Maestro Cecchetti through my ballet teacher Alice Marshall and her teacher Molly Lake, I was keenly aware of my dance lineage and developed a deep love for dance and movement from a young age. With the support of my family, I endeavoured to continue to study dance and, in time, become a professional dancer.

Until the initiation of the BA Voice and Dance in 2008, the prevailing narrative was that if one wanted to seriously pursue dance as a profession, one had to audition for a conservatoire or university overseas. This, of course, had a profound effect not only on how young dancers perceived dance in Ireland, but in turn the wider dance education environment in Ireland. When the Academy at the University of Limerick (UL) introduced the BA Voice and Dance, I knew that it was the first time an undergraduate degree with an emphasis in western theatrical dance was being offered in the Republic of Ireland. In keeping with the founding principles of the Academy, instilled by Professor Mícheál Ó Súilleabháin, the perspective that all dance is inherently valuable was deeply embedded in every facet of the programme. Hierarchical sparring between humans is nothing new and occurs within all disciplines, but the implication that some forms of dance are more 'aesthetic' or associated with 'high art' is particularly prevalent within the western theatrical dance canon. This perspective was the antithesis of the values of the Academy, and the non-hierarchical training we received reflected this. Western theatrical dance techniques were studied in tandem with a broad range of dance genres from all over the world. As a dancer with the perception of a strong singular movement identity prior to the commencement of the course, the process of broadening my dance training to include a wide variety of dance styles and body awareness approaches was exhilarating but also challenging and at times disorientating.

Another facet of the course was the interconnection of both the theoretical and practical aspects of embodying dance. This negotiation was adeptly guided by Jenny Roche, who provided a solid foundation in contemporary dance technique and choreography, and also in dance scholarship and research. In my third year of the programme I was introduced to the field of ethnochoreology and was immediately enthralled. Upon graduating from the BA programme, I enrolled in the MA Ethnochoreology

Figure 38.1: Jennifer de Brún performing on an aerial spiral in her work entitled *Spéirbhean*, 15 December 2018.
PHOTOGRAPH © TRUE MEDIA

with Catherine Foley at the same institution. Following graduation, I began working with Mícheál Ó Súilleabháin in the Academy in the role of performing arts coordinator and admired his enduring commitment to the equity of all music and dance forms. This was typified in his invitation to Fidget Feet Aerial Dance Theatre to become artist-in-residence at the Academy in 2014. Through the tenacious work of its executive creative director Chantal McCormack, Fidget Feet is Ireland's foremost aerial dance company.[2] Fidget Feet founded the Irish Aerial Creation Centre[3] in 2015 and has since provided aerial dance modules for students from UL.[4] Upon Chantal's invitation, I joined Fidget Feet as an aerialist and began engaging in a daily practice in aerial dance and aerial circus, performing in a variety of contexts including theatres, outdoor events and cranes. Through the process of learning new skills, engaging with a new discipline and creating work, questions emerged around my previously embodied training, and the negotiation of the multiplicity of my movement identities through aerial dance and aerial circus. I began to reflect on my early dance training, my experience in the BA Voice and Dance, and the conceptualisation of myself as a performer. I decided to engage in doctoral research as part of the PhD Arts Practice programme at the Academy to examine and interrogate emerging research inquiries.

My research[5] is structured around my individual phenomenological experiences as a twenty-first-century aerialist in Ireland, navigating the transition from the perception of a fixed movement identity to that of a moving identity.[6] The title of the thesis includes the Irish word *ilchruthach*, used to describe a shapeshifter, meaning 'many-shaped, multiform, polymorphic'.[7] The term aptly expresses my experience of engaging with and adapting to multiple forms of movement, both on the ground and in the air. I posit that my experience of training, in ballet and contemporary dance, to training in aerial dance and aerial circus, is not a massive leap across the chasm of style, genre and technique but rather is an adaption to another movement system that requires the utilisation of previously embodied knowledge and the acquirement of further knowledge. The theoretical and physical realisation that I am not exclusively bound to previously embodied training provides me with a sense of agency when moving and creating new work.

My collective educational experiences have refined my skills as performer, pedagogue and researcher. They have also revealed the need to critically examine this process in order to contribute to the evolving landscape of dance education in Ireland.

Hannah Fahey
On voice

I began my UL journey in 2006 as a law student and was placed in student accommodation with musicians of the BA Irish Music and Dance. Watching them perform one evening in the University Concert Hall with Mícheál Ó Súilleabháin and The Chieftains, I found myself in awe of their university experience. The Academy was then housed primarily in the Foundation building, but it projected something very special indeed. I attended law tutorials in the room adjacent to the Performing Arts Centre (PAC), which was the main performing space that the Academy had at that time. Constitutional law seemed rather dull in comparison to what was happening next door. Two years later I auditioned for the new BA Voice and Dance programme. I wasn't sure what to expect. Would it be a classical voice programme or maybe musical theatre? I prepared a folder of my classical singing certificates and awards and decided to audition with a classical song

Figure 38.2: Hannah Fahey, Locating the Gothic festival, 2014.
PHOTOGRAPH © DEIRDRE POWER

and a musical theatre song. Soon, my offer was in the post.

In the early years the BA Voice and Dance was experimental, maverick and certainly not what we expected. The course expanded our horizons and marooned us at sea, providing us with unique educational experiences and deliberately disorienting ones. Known throughout the Academy as 'The BAVaDs', we began our studies in Room C of the Foundation building, where we learned an eclectic mix of medieval chant, contemporary dance, gospel singing, Latin American song, improvisation and much more. Vocalists were challenged to think of voice beyond the parameters of any signature pedagogy or style, and we worked closely with dancers to incorporate movement and somatic knowledge into collaborative performance pieces. This earned the programme a unique identity within the broader context of voice and dance education in Ireland, but this approach also deviated from standard institutional training for these disciplines at that time. Systematic training of the singing voice has been historically conceptualised within the framework of institutionally legitimised western classical voice pedagogy.[8] It is only in the first two decades of the twenty-first century that musical theatre and popular styles of singing became part of examining boards and third-level training programmes in Ireland,[9] and this BA was among the first to depart from the status quo.

There was an awareness that the BA was different, and as the first cohort approached graduation, an anxiety permeated as we struggled to consolidate our educational experiences with the professional world beyond the institution. The pluralistic nature of the BA Voice and Dance was interesting, with many unique learning opportunities, but there were also moments of frustration. I felt the absence of a fixed specialism or performance identity. I needed to know more, to progress more, to sing more. However, I still feel this way years later, knowing now that I can never know enough. Diverse experiences and skills needed to be pieced together by each of us to forge our own paths after graduation. The biggest leaps in my education accompanied my first steps into professional performance and teaching. With no precedent to follow, I sourced work in a number of different vocal contexts: solo and ensemble singing work, choral conducting jobs and teaching for various institutions.

I developed *Sionna*, an ensemble of BA Voice and Dance graduates, and began booking concerts and workshops. The ensemble served as a vehicle for processing the wide variety of repertoire that we had learned together. Our concert programmes included chant, medieval song, Georgian polyphony and traditional song. Keen to learn more, I progressed to more specialised postgraduate study, and with a scholarship in hand, I began the MA Ritual Chant and Song. Later that year I was invited to join Cantoral under the direction of Parisienne early music singer Catherine Sergent. During my time with the ensemble, Mícheál produced our album *Let the Joyous Irish Sing Aloud!* Further along the path from BA Voice and Dance, I was moving and adapting to each performance or teaching setting, shifting between old and new worlds of singing, continuously crossing over and embracing different experiences.

I had many unresolved questions about my stylistically plural undergraduate experience on the BA Voice and Dance programme. These questions propelled me towards the doctoral research path. I had been teaching in a variety of contexts, from primary school age to third-level students, and I was now a tutor on the BA Voice and Dance. I developed a passion for voice teaching work, and I loved working with individual students. I began to read widely in vocal pedagogy and voice science, realising that this was key in working across genres effectively. My doctoral research questions centred on voice teaching culture and pedagogy in Ireland, and as I focused the lens outward, away from the Academy and my own experience, I began to understand more about music education in Ireland and the debates that had emerged in the late twentieth century around institutional change and innovation.[10] I developed a deeper understanding of the context and conceptual thinking behind a programme like the BA Voice and Dance, and more broadly, an institution like the Academy itself.

At the cusp of institutional change in Irish vocal education, the BA Voice and Dance set out to break the mould. Reflecting on this with Mícheál in my first year as a doctoral student, we spoke about navigating stylistic pluralism and digesting the 'post-BAVaD condition'. His words stay with me today: 'You have got to find your own authority.' That search has taken me to many places of interest. Explorations in voice studies, voice science and vocal pedagogy have contextualised the journey, and introducing these to the curriculum of the new BA Voice degree has been an important step towards innovation with clear purpose, context and practical application. To date, the route has been scenic, and I endeavour to keep searching.

Óscar Mascareñas

a*BaVaD*song in sixteen parts[11] – *for Mícheál*

I

What does the smell of a flower sound like? Can we touch it? Must it match the colour of the flower? And does it taste of something? Something what?

It is its sound that interests me and the way it leaves the flower

Suspended
elevated movement
Momentary

II

10 singers and 10 dancers[12]

III

eighteen

IV

Hand grabs feet grabs floor grabs breath grabs sound
Lets go
Sound displaces breath displaces floor displaces feet displaces hand
Empty space

V

A poem's words stolen briefly by a voice
swallowed whole
lung-ward

Some reaction inside the body spits them out
but now there aren't any sounds
nor any voices
Just pulsations
Body displacing air
Air re-placed
And then a sort of stillness occurs
and a mute word is stolen briefly by the voice
ciúnas ama

What silence!

VI

'*Un sarao de la Chacona*
se hizo el mes de las rosas
hubo millares de cosas
y la fama lo pregona'[13]

¡Ay qué vida! ¡Qué suerte!
Oh what life! What luck!
¡Ay! on they sang!
'A *la vida*' they relished!
'*vidita bona*' the memory!
Life
'*vámonos a Chacona*'!
Vida lets go now!

(It is gone now)

VII

New places
New names
kNew how to
New songs
New words
New steps
kNew what
New paths
New symbols
New sensations
kNew why
Learned to forget
Forgot to go back
New directions
kNew
UnKnown yet

VIII

¡Ay de mí, Llorona![14]

(One-two-three
Five-six-seven)

Te vas Alfonsina
O!
con tu soledad

Iustus ut palma florebit
Allelú

IX

The poetics of the body fermented
A long transformation ensued leaving no-body
just traces of sounds
of paths walked
of words uttered
by a breathless shadow

X

And it'll all start again
The year before
et sicut cedrus multiplicabitur[15]
Allelú

XI

UnKnown yet
kNew
New directions
Forgot to go back
Learned to forget
kNew why
New sensations
New symbols
New paths
kNew what
New steps
New words
New songs
kNew how to
New names
New places

XII

No
No third space
No combination of ways of doing
of ways of thinking
It's just body

XIII

The force of improvisation
at its core
displaces
vanishes
generates
and displaces again

One moment she is Singer
one moment Dancer
The moment after
Neither

Always a figure
bound by space
and silence
(*ciúnas ama*)

Nothing ever empty
nothing ever emptied

Always a figure pulled by
another figure
another force
a shadow following
Vibrating

What an image!

XIV

De qué callada manera[16]
it all happened
Y de qué modo sutil
it all ended
Only to start again
the day before

XV

Bodies
experiencing
experimentation
excruciating pain
after hours of
endless movement
exhaling
exhilarating
exhausted
after days
of timeless song
Exegesis
Voices
excelling
eccentric
excepted
New bodies
kNew
new Voices
Exertion
New paths
Exodus

XVI

'Te doy una canción'[17]

what is left of our times
silence and stillness
a dream lying bare

'I give you a song'

a dance in agony
a torrent of poetry
over fields of Clare

'Te doy una canción'

vestiges of memory
a voice full of hope
the ringlets of *Sionna*

'I give you a song'

33 minutes 4 seconds
twelve years now gone
an outbreath of melancholy

'yo te doy una canción'

39
Mícheál Ó Súilleabháin: My personal psychopomp

Carl Corcoran

Recently appointed University of Limerick emeritus lecturer, having managed, curated and directed the inaugural five years of the MA Songwriting, Carl is a forty-five-year veteran of the music industry. He has been involved in a wide variety of music-related activities from performing, broadcasting and academia.

It was a gorgeous autumn evening. Making my way into the radio studio for my nightly broadcast of *The Blue of the Night*[1] – a glorious and eclectic three hours of late-night music on our national broadcaster, RTÉ Lyric FM – I felt the mobile phone in my pocket vibrating. Glancing at the screen, I saw the ascribed contact information: MOS. I would later learn how appropriate it was that I labelled Mícheál's contact in my address book in the form of initials. He loved acronyms!

I have, more recently, learned that the weekly faculty meeting in the Irish World Academy of Music and Dance is known as COG, standing for Co-Ordination Group. Soon enough, after that mobile call I too was referring to the steering committee for his annual summer school 'Blas'[2] at the Academy as BAB – Blas Advisory Board. But on this autumnal evening in September 2006, MOS meant only one thing – Mícheál Ó Súilleabháin.

'Carl Corcoran!' the ever energetic and warm voice at the other end of the line exclaimed. '*Conas tá tú?*'

'*Táim go maith, a Mhíchíl, agus tú féin?*' I answered.

Once we had exchanged these customary salutations and enquiries as to our mutual well-being in our beloved 'tongue' (at which I was far from fluent, but keen to use; he on the other hand had a musical and magical mastery), it was down to business.

'I have a proposal for your consideration – I want you as the director of my Blas Summer School,' he said.

I knew even before he spoke, whatever the proposal, I was likely to accept it. Such was the power and influence Mícheál wielded – not in any forceful way but simply by his soft yet convincing ability to passionately communicate an idea; to imbue one with a desire to be on board; to be willing to gladly sign up for the project at hand, whatever it might be; but most importantly to be on a journey in the company of MOS.

'Blas' was and is exactly what its translation indicates – a 'taste' of what the Academy's suite of courses has to offer: studies in and performance of Irish music and dance, as well as incorporating an academic rigour in the writings and readings relevant to such pursuits. It was Mícheál's 'baby', a passion, a means of giving students from forty countries around the world the opportunity to visit the Academy on the banks of the river Shannon and enjoy a two-week immersion in all that the building had to offer. Managing it was simply the implementation of a 'bite-size' version of the Academy's curriculum – the creation was Mícheál's vision, assisted by a dedicated faculty; the logistics were overseen by the director, assisted by BAB. Knowing the man and his MO (another acronym), it was impossible to say no.

Mícheál Ó Súilleabháin, the artist, had appeared on my radar some ten years earlier. In America, where I spent some two decades in various guises and iterations of a career in music, the last and perhaps most influential 'hat' I wore in an exciting American sojourn was one of broadcaster. In a small rural town, some sixty miles north of New York City, I produced and presented a weekly programme aimed at the Irish American community of Orange County, New York. *A Drop of the Irish*[3] was a popular mix of Irish music of all sorts, news from Ireland, interviews with personalities, and always included 'new' material to expand the musical palette of my discerning audience. Always in search of new material, one such album arrived in my mailbox – a compilation album featuring various artists. The other contributions on the album were more jazz-influenced than the Celtic contemporary strains that emanated from this eclectic mosaic of Irish traditional jazz-tinged three minutes. Bouncing piano motifs, unique to the artist I would later come to know both personally and professionally, beautifully enhanced by the contributions of Mel Mercier and Colm Murphy on traditional Irish percussion. 'Oíche Nollag'[4] was the track and it made regular appearances on my playlist – to the delight of the listeners. I went further. My appetite was whetted. I was convinced that here was an artist who deserved a wider audience, an artist who fitted the burgeoning musical genre called 'world music crossover'. Wearing another of my multitudinous 'hats', that of promoter/artist manager, I recognised the potential of this talented musician. A series of exploratory and investigative 'searches' made it clear that this Mícheál Ó Súilleabháin was more than a 'once-off' artist.

On the next trip home to Ireland, I managed to arrange a face-to-face with 'the man', by virtue of a mutual connection and friend – the late John

Kelly. John was an old friend and the CEO of the Irish Chamber Orchestra.[5] Mícheál had convinced the ensemble to establish a 'home base' in the University of Limerick (UL) where the ever-inventive Ó Súilleabháin had founded the Academy. That August afternoon in 1996, we met, we plotted, we laughed – but most of all we became friends. In the months that followed, back in America there were sorties into the labyrinthine tunnels of music promotion, meetings with record labels, music lawyers, music publishers and agents. And while all these manoeuvres never amounted to creating the 'crossover artist', I soon realised that there was far more to this man than the one I had imagined. Here was a true communicator, a music lover, an explorer, an academic, a musical anthropologist – a man for all seasons who had bigger, better and more laudable aspirations than just being a commercial entity. Mícheál's vision and destiny were certainly global but on a different and higher plane.

Despite not scoring the goal that I had set out to achieve (for various reasons) of being his 'Brian Epstein in America', we became friends. He became an inspiration, a confidante, a source of stimulation, both intellectually and musically. In fact, that August afternoon in his office, perhaps unbeknownst to him and certainly to me, the seeds were sown, and the thought was planted that now was the time to bring the family home to Ireland. Somehow, that day he passively and maybe inadvertently (or not) convinced me to implement a career change – and it wasn't to be the last time that such intervention of his changed my life.

Three years later, my treasured family was back in Ireland. I was fortunate to secure a broadcasting position with the newly established national radio station RTÉ Lyric FM – an appointment that was surely helped by the inclusion of MOS as a referee on my application. Now I was based in Limerick! We'd meet – not that often, but always in a warm and convivial circumstance. His ability to make one feel that you were important, unique and special was empowering. I recall one afternoon visiting him in his office. I walked into the office for a chat about music, life, loves and walked out committed to doing an MA Community Music. Such was his influence. Another important and life-changing milestone in my life, under the influence and curation of this gentle giant.

A year later, postgraduate degree accomplished (during which time I was mentored in piano accompaniment by my hero), I got the call that September evening, 2006. *Would I what?* I silently thought. My audible reply was, 'Of course, Mícheál, I'd be honoured to join you.' I was. I did. And for three years I directed Blas Summer School at the Academy, managing the passage of hundreds of students, Irish and international, through the immersive and inspiring journey created, nurtured and proudly overseen by 'the Prof'. I considered it to be a role of honour, of privilege and a proud achievement that I could never match. That was until 2017 when, at Mícheál's suggestion, I was invited to become course director of the MA Songwriting programme at the Academy.[6] The course is a further example of the man's vision for his beloved Academy – an extension of his belief that the tree of music education has many branches, many tentacles that should and do reach far and wide. It has been an honour, a joy, a shining glory that was dimmed sadly by his untimely passing.

It was a sad day, the day we heard the news. And I joined the gathering to say '*slán tamall*' or 'goodbye for a while'. There was a list of roles and titles on the memoriam card that was distributed to the packed church in Kilrush, County Clare on that cold November morning. Mícheál had claimed these various listed roles throughout his life. I nodded affirmatively as I read through the list. Musician, composer, performer, educator, parent, partner, lover, friend, and more. I recognised and related to all. I saw first-hand the relationships he had nurtured with each of the connections he had made over the previous sixty-five years.

But at the end of the list was the term 'psychopomp'. I wasn't familiar with the word – mythological entities, spirits, angels or deities in many religions whose responsibility is to escort newly deceased souls from earth to the afterlife. Was this another role that Mícheál performed? My curiosity was piqued and I quickly glanced at a Google definition of this mysterious descriptor. Yes, spiritual indeed. But there is also a more temporal definition of this nomenclature – an individual who guides and assists in helping others in their transition to other experiences or periods in their life.

Whether he intended it or not, Mícheál was either present, or a presence, or indeed responsible for several changes in my life. We shared many experiences over the years. As a promoter in America at the end of the 1990s I came close to representing Mícheál the recording artist. As a broadcaster back in Ireland in the new millennium I championed his music on air. As a curious middle-aged man, at a crossroads in my life, I benefited from his advice and guidance, leading to an MA Community Music. As a contracted employee I managed his beloved Blas Summer School for three years. And finally, upon my retirement from RTÉ Radio in 2017 he invited me to be course director for his latest addition to the suite of programmes available at the Academy. This man who became my friend is, to this day, the spiritual psychopomp, guiding and influencing my daily life. He instilled me with a confidence, with a love of learning, with a love of creative expression. As I glanced at the death notice I couldn't help but remark on the final acronym attached to Mícheál Ó Súilleabháin – three letters that I never wanted to see, RIP.

Míle buíochas, a Mhíchíl – thank you Mícheál. I once thought I could 'make you a star'. It wasn't to be, nor was it necessary, for you were and still are a shining beacon, guiding, inspiring and eternal.

40

Between Worlds: Being, becoming and belonging

Mary Louise O'Donnell and Matthew James Noone

Mary Louise O'Donnell is a harpist and musicologist who has performed extensively as a soloist and with various ensembles. She has published widely on topics relating to Irish cultural history, semiotics and performance studies, and has received many awards and grants, including a Fulbright Scholar Award and Centre Culturel Irlandais Fellowship. She currently works as a creative associate with the Arts Council.

Matthew James Noone is a performer and arts practice researcher. He works in a diverse range of disciplines ranging from Irish traditional and Indian classical music to free improvisation and electroacoustic composition. He currently teaches in the Irish World Academy of Music and Dance at the University of Limerick.

For almost three decades, the Irish World Academy of Music and Dance has been a space where teachers, artists-in-residence and others have generously shared theirknowledge and wisdom with thousands of musicians and dancers; they have also drawn from that space to inform their performance and research. A space like the Academy needs to constantly replenish and regenerate so that it never stagnates but remains a dynamic space in which bodies and minds can temporarily lodge on the road to becoming. It is a unique space for creatives who 'desire for a better way of being' – it is a utopia.[1] In *Demand the Impossible*, Tom Moylan described utopias as 'images of desire' and 'figures of hope'.[2] The pioneering figure of Mícheál Ó Súilleabháin desired and envisioned a cultural and academic utopia – a space where he championed Irish music and dance studies, as well as thesis-based and arts practice research.

Through his work, and even his mere presence at the Academy, he inspired many to explore the basic human impulse to find a 'better way of being'. We were both fortunate to have shared so richly in the generous mentorship and guidance of a teacher and artist who gently, yet successfully, enabled us to embrace the challenges of graduate education and life thereafter. Doctoral and postdoctoral studies exist in a liminal space in academic development – the student/mentee/proto-academic exists between two worlds – but Mícheál was a constant figure of hope in that space. What follows is an autoethnographic account of the role Mícheál Ó Súilleabháin played as mentor and guru in our academic formation and research.

Mary Louise O'Donnell
'Call me Mícheál'

On a crisp February morning in 2004 I met Mícheál Ó Súilleabháin in person for the first time. In a strange way, I felt I already knew the man. From the first moment I heard him play Turlough Carolan's 'Sí Bheag, Sí Mhór' with Cormac Breathnach and John O'Kane on the soundtrack for *A River of Sound* in 1995, I was entranced. For three minutes the trio created a musical space in which genres collided and baroque textures and sounds were combined with moments of jazz extemporisation to create a piece of music that had a thrilling sense of immediacy. Ó Súilleabháin was at the heart of the ensemble on harpsichord playing in a style that deftly negotiated a path between baroque music of the seventeenth and eighteenth centuries and baroque pop of the 1960s. I think I listened to that track a hundred times and each time I heard a different nuance. What style of music was this? Could it even be categorised? Or, to paraphrase Ó Súilleabháin, was it the result of the 'confrontation' of 'what were once separate music systems'?[3]

I began playing the Irish harp in my teenage years and, although I learned some slow airs and dance tunes, my repertoire was dominated by the music of Carolan, Thomas Moore, transcriptions of art music, and contemporary works by Irish composers such as Gerard Victory and Brian Boydell. Nowadays, the modern Irish harp is the medium *par excellence* for the transmission of Irish traditional music (specifically dance music), but in the early 1990s there were only a handful of harpers who could truly be described as virtuosic traditional musicians.[4] My repertoire or training did not fit the category of 'harper', so I happily identified as an Irish 'harpist'. During my music studies at Trinity College Dublin I read Joan Rimmer's *The Irish Harp*, which was the most widely referenced source for the history of the instrument at that time.[5] The history of the wire-strung harp was the primary focus of the book, but a short chapter on the origin of the modern Irish harp, or 'neo-Irish harp', in the early nineteenth century was also included. It was disappointing that an academic of Rimmer's calibre could belittle the harps of John Egan, the harp maker who created the prototype for the modern Irish harp, and cavalierly dismiss over 150 years of a tradition to which I belonged. The harpist Janet Harbison best described the predicament of the (modern) Irish harp in Ireland in the mid-1990s as 'lying awkwardly between traditions, expectations and prejudices', and Rimmer's work exemplified this.[6] But this was not solely the predicament of the modern Irish harp, there were also many harpists whose musical practice lay 'awkwardly between traditions'.

For a musician, a liminal space can facilitate experimentation and creativity, but on a fundamental human level this space can be isolating and disorientating and there is often a feeling of not 'belonging'.[7] Abraham Maslow, in his discussion of a hierarchy of human needs, pointed out that belonging is an essential and prerequisite human need that must be met before one can achieve a sense of self-worth.[8] My doctoral research on the Irish harp was motivated by a strong desire to figure out where I 'belonged' in the rich musical tapestry of music in Ireland, but also to challenge the commonly held myths about the modern Irish harp tradition. It was Mícheál who helped and encouraged me to articulate the myriad protean ideas on the subject that were floating around my head. I knew that the concept of two separate Irish harp traditions, in which the Irish harp tradition in the nineteenth century was viewed as the 'other' tradition in a paradigm that defined both traditions in oppositional terms, i.e. wire-strung/strung with gut, male dominated/female dominated, oral/literate, rural/urban, was too simplistic. They were not unconnected traditions – the modern Irish harp tradition would not have come into being without the influence of the wire-strung tradition, its repertoire and even some of its practitioners. My earliest attempt to tease out some of these ideas was in a master's thesis in which I referenced all Ó Súilleabháin's research on Carolan, the wire-strung harp tradition and Edward Bunting.[9] In 2004 I emailed Mícheál a copy of this thesis. Evidently, it piqued his intellectual curiosity and a meeting was soon scheduled.

'Thanks for taking the time to meet me, Professor Ó Súilleabháin.'

'Hang on a minute there, Mary Louise, there's no formality here, you must call me Mícheál'.

And so it began.

A few months later I met with Mícheál and two of his colleagues, Ruán O'Donnell from the Department of History and Tom Moylan who was director of the Ralahine Centre for Utopian Studies. At the end of the meeting we agreed that my doctoral research would focus on a period from 1790 to 1845 and that it would highlight the role the Irish harp(s) played in political and social discourse and in the creation of Irish identities in this period. Finally, and crucially, we conceded that the concept of 'tradition' was too limiting, that it would be more beneficial to think of the Irish harp as a space, or *topos*, consisting of visual and sonic dimensions; the visual dimension would include the use of the instrument in contemporary iconography and the innovative Irish harps made by John Egan; the sonic dimension would focus on the use of the harp as a metaphor for Ireland and the Irish people in contemporary poetry and songs. Our meetings were never lengthy in the years that followed but they were always productive, and that first meeting was the genesis of an interdisciplinary project like no other.

Over the years, I applied for scholarships, fellowships and bursaries with the support of Mícheál, who always acted as a referee and cast an eye over various proposals.[10] In 2011 I was awarded an IRCHSS[11] Government of Ireland Postdoctoral Fellowship to prepare my doctoral dissertation for publication at the Academy under the mentorship of Mícheál. When I informed him of the successful outcome of my application he was exuberant and enormously proud that the pioneering research he had so carefully guided had finally been recognised at the highest levels, nationally and internationally. During 2011/12 I worked diligently on the manuscript that would eventually become *Ireland's Harp: The shaping of Irish identity c. 1780 to 1880* (2014), but Mícheál sagely advised to use the period to build a portfolio of new research, to develop skills in presentation, and to access further research opportunities. My work on the iconography of the Irish harp in the Celtic Tiger years, the harpist Owen Lloyd/Eoghan Laoide (2013), and the Bengal Subscription/the Irish Harp Society of Belfast (2015) all originated during those twelve months.

Although I did not take up a full-time position in academia, I was particularly honoured when Mícheál appointed me as the first chair of Ionad na Cruite/the Irish Harp Research Cluster at the Academy in 2013. I know he promoted my research at every opportunity, he always supported the publication of my work, and he launched my first book, *Ireland's Harp*, at the Royal Irish Academy in Dublin in 2015. I contacted him in the summer of 2018 to see if he might help me once again and, true to form, he did. I wanted to apply for a Fulbright Scholar Award at Villanova University to research the diverse ways in which the Irish harp was used in the construction of an identity among Irish emigrants and their descendants in the United States from 1780 to 1930. I did not realise how seriously ill he was at that time, but he filled out the necessary documents online and wished me well. With Mícheál's support and encouragement, my application was successful, and I officially joined the elite group of Fulbright scholars in May 2019. Seamus

Heaney wrote: 'All of us would like to have been born / Infallible, but since we knew we weren't / It's better to attend to those who speak / In honesty and good faith, and learn from them'.[12] I learned, progressed and became self-reliant under the mentorship of a gentleman I will always be proud and privileged to have called Mícheál.

Matthew James Noone
The magpie and the mongrel: an apprenticeship in-between worlds

While the point of origin is always a sacred one, the process of becoming must supersede this, in that it is a process that creates new dynamic sacred spaces within which our voices can grow and speak as they are called to do.[13] Mícheál Ó Súilleabháin had a subtle and profound influence on my 'process of becoming' an artist-scholar; finding my authentic voice both as a musician and as an academic. My point of origin is mixed, or as I like to describe it, a bit mongrel. I began my musical life as a guitar player in post-rock bands in Brisbane, Australia but also experimented with electronic music, free jazz, trip-hop, west African percussion and even Zen chant. By the time I entered the Academy as a mature student to begin an MA Ethnomusicology in 2010, my main performance practice was with the north Indian lute known as the *sarode*. A significant subtext in my early time in the Academy was trying to navigate the cultural dilemmas of being a non-native performer of an Indian classical instrument.[14] To Mícheál, however, impure musical heritage, my mongrelity, was not an obstacle but rather something to be treasured. He himself was a self-confessed 'musical magpie', an artist who openly embraced musical hybridity and moved gracefully between local practices and translocal realities.[15] In fact, Ó Súilleabháin argued that hybridity was a fundamental part of Irish traditional music, starting that 'the history of Irish music is one of fusion'.[16]

It was through my master's research that I first became aware of the discourse of connections between Irish traditional music and the classical music of India. With Mícheál's encouragement, I decided to pursue a PhD within the Academy to test the hypothesis of links between Irish and Indian music through arts practice research. Arts practice research utilises the making of artistic work as a case study to test explicit research questions. Mícheál was instrumental in establishing an environment in the Academy where arts practice research was highly valued, in which the poetic and the practical could intermingle. In my own research I utilised the somewhat poetic and tongue-in-cheek metaphor of 'mongrelity' to situate and also problematise my musical practice.[17] My intention was to find a metaphor that spoke to the embodied nature of musical hybridity rather than the more theoretical arguments that are predominant in ethnomusicology and cultural theory. Yet I was also sceptical about the validity of artistic practice as 'real' scholarship and uncertain whether the personal focus of my research was a little too 'touchy-feely'.[18] However, I was again encouraged by the work of Ó Súilleabháin, who argued that it is 'fundamentally within the individual' that hybridisation emerges, and furthermore that 'growth within the individual translates into the culture'.[19] Mícheál's own mentor, John Blacking, also reminds us that 'many, if not all, of music's essential processes may be found in the constitution of the human body'.[20] Taking heed of this advice, I doggedly pursued my mongrel trajectory.

In addition to excellent supervision from Colin Quigley, Mícheál became a sort of unofficial mentor during my research, an elder who embodied many of my interests. While I did not meet regularly with him, our interactions felt like a kind of apprenticeship, an Irish equivalent of the Indian classical music tradition of *guru-shishya parampara*. In Indian classical music a student learns by spending a long time with a guru or teacher, imitating their playing, absorbing subtle socio-cultural knowledge and eventually finding their own voice or style. This oral (and aural) model of learning has many parallels with Irish traditional music as many musicians learn their style and repertoire by ear in the company of more experienced performers. In Indian classical music, the *guru* (which translates as 'one who brings the light') is an intermediary between the ordinary world and the profound 'other world' of musical performance. Mícheál conceptualised Irish traditional music in a parallel manner to that of my teachers in Indian classical music. As Ó Súilleabháin explains, 'the musical essence is within the form rather than being the form itself'.[21] It exists in 'tension between the inaudible and the audible within music'.[22] Mícheál argued that we should view Irish music and dance as more than entertainment, as 'another form of reality itself'.[23]

Mícheál was in no doubt strongly influenced in his thinking about Indian and Irish music through his mentorship with Seán Ó Riada in University College Cork.[24] In particular, Ó Súilleabháin focused on Irish harp music as the living remnant of an ancient past and saw commonalities between medieval Gaelic courts and the classical court traditions of India. He also compared some of the fragmentary non-cyclical tunes in Bunting's *Ancient Music of Ireland* collection with the modal improvisational model of north Indian classical music.[25] Ó Súilleabháin was significantly inspired by this interpretation to compose new material which explicitly drew upon

Indian classical music theory.[26] This, he argued, was 'a practical way of putting primary creativity back in the hands of the Irish harper' through channelling 'a living musical system' and therefore 'heal[ing] a break in the oral tradition which occurred a century and a half ago'.[27]

Mícheál's ability to construct connections in the space in-between musical worlds was one of his greatest gifts. As a musical magpie, he situated himself between multiple cultural intersections – western classical, Irish traditional, jazz, and ecclesiastical music. This liminal, in-between space of cultures is what Ó Súilleabháin described as 'the crossroads of becoming where the dynamic of cultural change is being generated'.[28] He used his vision as a 'musical magpie' to find new knowledge through connections with older ways. To paraphrase Seamus Heaney,

Ó Súilleabháin's crossroads of becoming is a place where you may find 'a music that you never would have known to listen for'.[29] In 2020 I am at my own crossroads. I have just completed a two-year IRC-funded postdoctoral research fellowship (also in the Academy) which explored hybridity with a particular focus on composition and improvisation.[30] While this research was not explicitly indebted to my work with Ó Súilleabháin, it was a realisation of a musical process of becoming, a desire to find my own artistic and academic voice that was inspired by Mícheál a decade earlier. This mongrel is glad to have abided for a time at the crossroads with such a graceful guide as the musical magpie and I believe that our apprenticeship shall continue in that ephemeral space in-between worlds.

Conclusion

Music has a powerful way of shaping our sense of belonging, of heightening singular moments of being and inferring the possibility of our future becoming. These three modes of musical experience (belonging, being and becoming) form a temporal intersection between the past, the present and the future. As both musicians and scholars, we are often required to make a journey through this liminal space to try and gain greater knowledge of the musical past, develop insight into the performative present and our potential future practices: a metaphoric dancing at the crossroads of the many paths of musical inquiry. Mícheál was a master at this dance and a generous and encouraging guide. He pioneered a trail in academic research where Irish traditional music, dance and song were of equal cultural value to western art music and musicology. In establishing the Irish World Academy, Mícheál created a new academic paradigm where artistic practice and academic rigour were on the same footing; where the piper could be considered a philosopher, the singer a scholar and the dancer a text in motion. The wealth of his achievements stretches beyond his own music and the Academy itself and is also reflected in the musical and scholarly pursuits of his many, many apprentices. Through his example, let us hope that the past may be more illuminated, the present brought more alive and the future be full of hope and promise.

41

The Grace of His Teaching: Lessons from Mícheál Ó Súilleabháin

Patricia Shehan Campbell

Patricia Shehan Campbell is emeritus professor of music at the University of Washington, and author and editor of books on the pedagogy of world music cultures. She is a recipient of the 2017 Koizumi Prize for work on the preservation of traditional music through educational practice, and Fulbright fellowships in Canada, China and India.

As a revolutionary thinker in music, Mícheál Ó Súilleabháin's reach was far and wide. He interacted regularly with musical artists and aspirant musicians from across the world, and he envisioned a place in which they could gather to perform, to exchange in music and about music, to teach and to learn. Mícheál drew together a brilliant faculty of musicians, who likewise drew students from communities near and far – from the UK, Canada and the United States, Australia and New Zealand, and from parts of Africa, Asia and Latin America. He took to organising for them, composing for them and performing alongside them as an 'musical insider'. His exhaustive collection of offerings to the musical world encompassed also his teaching. As tributes to Mícheál have somewhat under-acknowledged the excellence of his contributions as tutor, trainer, mentor and model, this recognition here seems warranted.[1]

Mícheál was a force in the musical education of generations of players, singers and listening audiences. A consummate musician, Mícheál was exemplary in his capacity to enlighten and excite musicians to emulate his command of colourful and dynamic means of facilitating musical understanding among the earnest, the occasional and the unschooled musicians whom he encountered regularly in his work. He was an educator 'writ large', one who could work his magic in classrooms and concert halls, in person and on the air, in boardrooms and on professional panels, in what he conceived and carried out, and in what he designed and delivered. His brand of teaching mastery benefited from his genuine interest in all music, whether from Ireland or India, whether historic or contemporary, in its many particularities. He was as deeply knowledgeable as he was charismatic, capable of captivating the attention of learners through a particular style of communication that was exceptionally colourful and rightfully confident of the topic. He could 'read a room', and as he made it his responsibility to know his students and his audiences, his capacity to communicate in music and about music was boundless.

While he grew in the music that came at him at an early age from the family gramophone and radio, Mícheál must have tuned in to the broader web of Irish traditional and western art music that was out there, too – or perhaps it was 'in his blood', because he achieved mastery in record time. Schooled by the Irish Christian Brothers, Mícheál developed a lifelong love of poetry, and literature at large, even while he took up piano on the side and as a technical challenge to be achieved through rigorous practice. He was a 'first gen', the first in his family to attend university. There, Mícheál further honed a pianist's techniques, and as he continued to be drawn to Irish traditional music, he wondered whether he'd been 'stuck with the wrong instrument for the music I love'.[2] It seems, though, that it was also the right instrument from which he would teach, mix Irish tunes with pianistic technique, bridge gaps between the repertoires, and connect musical worlds.

Some of the qualities of Mícheál's revolutionary self extended as well to his distinctive musicological analysis of the virtuosic Irish fiddler Tommie Potts, who had managed to stitch the nuances of western art music so thoroughly into the fabric of Irish traditional music as to render it unrecognisable (yet astonishing). While he viewed Potts as a case study of a performer's transcultural musical expression, Mícheál was himself blending techniques, ideas and ideals into an innovative sound and style of his own. Certainly, his own teachers at University College Cork (UCC) were major musical influences for him too, including Aloys Fleischmann and Seán Ó Riada, both of whom instilled in him a love of Irish traditional music. He was intrigued with the musical enculturation of traditional Irish musicians whom he knew outside the academy, as he deeply valued the informal learning pathways of family, peers and local mentors who nurtured their musical, social and cultural behaviours. His later studies with John Blacking, ethnomusicologist at Queen's University Belfast, led him to deepening his own questions of musical identity.[3] The last of Blacking's students, Mícheál fostered a belief in human musicality (or musical humanity), which came shining through in his embrace of students for what musical knowledge they brought to him that he might fashion further through education and training.

Such a backdrop would explain Mícheál's enthusiastic embrace of a tertiary-level music programme that would give weight to studies in Irish traditional music, western art music and music of a wider world of sonic qualities. As a member of the UCC faculty, it was Mícheál who was instrumental in elevating the status of Irish traditional music at the piano, and who verified that any instrument that came through the door could conceivably sound the songs of the Irish. Working as a dynamic and inspirational music lecturer in UCC from 1975 to 1993, he opened up university education to traditional musicians without classical music training by devising new entry requirements and courses, and he created an ethnomusicological model that has been widely imitated in third-level education. Of course, it was Mícheál too who envisioned the Irish World Academy of Music and Dance to offer programmes of excellence in performance studies, scholarship, composition and education. He dreamed large and in living colour and galvanised a world-renowned faculty of musicians to join him in fashioning twenty innovative undergraduate and graduate programmes in music and dance, and in imagining the beautifully designed superstructure on the banks of the river Shannon from which flowed all manner of artistic beauty.

Teaching came naturally to Mícheál. His commitment to the transmission of music to others was endless and immeasurable, and he was keen to have his students learn to perform the music, musically, and to have his audiences listen to it with intelligence, sensibility and perhaps even reactivity. Mícheál's students recall his generosity of time for them, his capacity to model musically what he would have them do, and his penchant to play along with them as a means of furthering their understanding of the music's phrasing and flow, its expressive qualities, its 'spirit'. In that one of the key characteristics of music-making during ritual experience in human culture at large is the synchronic imitation of voices, instruments and gestures,[4] Mícheál's approach to teaching was akin to the sociocultural phenomenon in which he steered a course of alternating social interactions with his students that were marked by affiliative processes, emotional resonance and human respect. He would integrate stories (and histories) into a lesson or lecture, adding flavour through the telling of a context in which the music was composed or performed. As only a humanist could do, Mícheál mixed perspectives of music's sonic structures with its sociocultural meaning, doing so with eloquence, clarity and verve so as to bring engagement in music as both art and cultural heritage.

The grace of his teaching is captured in regular broadcasts on radio and TV, in which he appeared as guide to the programmed selections. A highlight of Mícheál's work as a public educator was his hosting of the 1995 RTÉ and BBC television series *A River of Sound: The changing course of Irish traditional music*. Audiences were swept along by the thoughtfully produced programme that featured Mícheál in conversation with notable musicians, and sometimes in performance with them too. Many living artists were featured in brief exchanges, among them Paul Brady, Ronan Browne, Martin Hayes, Mary MacNamara, Matt Molloy, Mel Mercier, Christy Moore, Pat Phádraic Tom Ó Conghaile, Iarla Ó Lionáird and Van Morrison. Mícheál joined with these musical insiders, clarifying the meaning of music, the sources of songs and instrumental techniques, the relationship that develops between a musician and the instrument, and the aim of musicians to allow their instruments to operate as extensions of the body that channel the music from players to their listening audience. He was uniquely interested too in the contexts in which the music was learned, who taught whom at home or in the village, and just how the tunes were fully preserved or individually personalised.

The popular series was an important journey into understanding musical tradition and change, and an acknowledgement of traditions that are alive and well in informal as well as formal learning settings. In enthusiastic support of traditional music in schools (and tertiary-level learning), Mícheál cornered a question with clarity and conviction that concerned the fear of losing the genius of individual artistry through large-group teaching and learning: 'People worry about learning traditional music in a classroom. I mean, is it possible to develop an individual style in that environment? The important thing, I feel, is that technique is being laid down, and out of that technique, a personal, individual style will come.'[5] Such a rumination is traceable to Mícheál's long-held sense of the need for a musician's musical anchoring, his/her developing of a foundational musical skill set on an instrument and within a repertoire, from which innovation of a transcultural nature may well develop. It is on this belief that rests Mícheál's philosophical framework for his vision of music in education, a value system that is the bedrock of the Academy.

In the end, Mícheál's gift to the world was a manifold capacity to make music, and to 'make' musicians as well as thoughtful listening audiences. He channelled his energy to a thoroughgoing commitment to music and its reception, to the occasional musical encounters by audiences and the extended study by those students whom he mentored. As he moved in the musical world, he revolutionised it, caring enough for the music to want to ensure its respectful passage to others. May his life in music be a part of his legacy and the lessons that he left for us: to love the music, to communicate music's essence through an irrepressible and unceasing energy, to foster tradition while facilitating creative invention, and to further the humanistic spirit of music in building long-lasting human relationships.

42

'there for the crossing': Reflections on the practical and the poetic

Anya Peterson Royce

Anya Peterson Royce is chancellor's professor emerita, Indiana University, and adjunct professor, University of Limerick. She received degrees from Stanford University (BA) and University of California, Berkeley (MA, PhD), and an honorary doctorate from the University of Limerick. Her research focuses on arts, performance, and long-term ethnography with the Zapotec of Mexico.

Mícheál Ó Súilleabháin, composer, musician, scholar, mentor and creator of the Irish World Academy of Music and Dance, lived into being that magical crossing between the poetic and the practical. And he took generations of students, colleagues, audiences and academies along with him. Poet Seamus Heaney is perhaps the most spare and eloquent in describing these two orders that make up our lives: 'Within our individual selves we can reconcile two orders of knowledge which we might call the practical and the poetic; each form of knowledge redresses the other and the frontier between them is there for the crossing.'[1]

It is rare in the academic world to find programmes that do just that. It is even more rare to find entire schools of performing arts with a global reach and mandate. The Academy is a model for us, recognising and fostering the synergy between practice and reflection that is at the heart of creative growth. This essay addresses the creation of the Academy and the philosophies and practices of learning in, with and about the performing arts that are the foundation of all its programmes. Among those, we will examine collaborations and the conversations that sustain them, mentoring, listening as a kind of conversation, the transformation that springs from practice and reflection. Each new programme added to the Academy, indeed the new building itself, reflects this core philosophy of practice and reflection, honouring the contributions of each, and of crossing the frontier between them. Mícheál was always thinking about ways to facilitate transitions between practice and reflection, the practical and the poetic. He asks whether these are parallel universes. Are they inside-out/outside-in? Or are they – as Heaney suggests – potentially fluid and open to healing transitions? Finally, he asks how can we empower a softening of these boundaries?[2] He would find the answer in his own work that thrived on hearing possibilities across genres. As early as *Lumen*, the interval act for the 1995 Eurovision Song Contest, he softened the boundaries between classical music, chant from the monks at Glenstal Abbey, song featuring Brian Kennedy, and traditional Irish music, with himself at piano. An extraordinary work! In his obituary in *The Blackpool Sentinel*, the writer describes this signature creation: 'he manages to do what he always did: turn theory on its head while minting a work of great beauty'.[3]

Living in the crossing requires journeys of transformation begun with a passion, burnished and refined by discipline and craft, pushed by curiosity and a search for that realm beyond craft where artistry and transformation lie. It takes great courage to step beyond those arenas of competency that we construct by learning our craft because we must let go of the comfort of familiarity and move into unknown territory. Turning again to Seamus Heaney, this time in his marvellous poem 'Postscript' he urges us to take the time to visit the flaggy shores of County Clare: 'You are neither here nor there, a hurry through which known and strange things pass'.[4]

Imagining the Academy

When he came to the University of Limerick (UL) in 1994 as founding chair and professor of music, Mícheál wove conversation into the very beginnings of the Academy. He began with his colleagues and quickly included others: musicians, dancers, scholars working at other institutions and in other countries. His international and respected status as a musician, composer and scholar of musical traditions gave him a worldwide network of specialists across the performing arts, performers as well as historians and scholars of performance. In the years of his leadership, the Academy created some twenty undergraduate, master's and PhD programmes that embraced traditional Irish music and dance, ritual chant, contemporary dance performance, traditional music performance, ethnomusicology, ethnochoreology, festive arts, music therapy, community music, classical string performance and both text-based and arts practice research. A fine musician spanning classical and traditional, Mícheál convinced the Dublin-based Irish Chamber Orchestra to relocate to Limerick, creating opportunities for students to interact with seasoned musicians and the wider community to hear splendid concerts. In other programmes of study, students work with visiting artists and are part of Academy-sponsored workshops and panels. Other programmes – Festive Arts, Music Therapy, Community Music – engage students with the broader Limerick community.

One of the most innovative programmes in terms of what higher education traditionally offers has been the PhD Arts Practice created in 2009 by Professor Helen Phelan working with a course team. This is the realisation of the merging of high-level performance practice with theoretical perspectives on the arts. It is a four-year programme and limited to four students a year, each of whom is already an established performing artist. In its first year, for example, students included an internationally known *sean-nós* singer, a former dancer with *Riverdance* and a highly recognised contemporary dance choreographer, an Irish harpist who worked with the harp tradition of the Karen people of Myanmar, and finally an Irish classical singer working in contemporary liturgical music. In its description of the PhD programme, the Academy addresses the mind/body disjuncture that is common across higher education: 'It examines the privileged status of writing in theory production within the academy and the importance of "the somatic turn" in contemporary research which seeks to redress the "mind/body" duality at the heart of Western philosophical traditions and re-evaluate the role of "doing" in our understanding of "knowledge".'[5]

Conversations and collaborations

Sited on the banks of the river Shannon and sprung from a landscape of curves and meanders, the Academy is a place of conversation/*comhrá*. Conversations arise from questions and passions brought by artists and scholars who come seeking a community that understands their vocations, challenges them, and burnishes their gifts. These students represent some forty countries. Conversations are created out of the rich humus of world traditions embodied in both the performing arts and those who practise and seek to understand them. These are conversations that require listening with the ear of one's heart, believing in the power of such unfettered exchange to unleash the creative spirit and refine the craft.

An excellent example of the kind of collaborative thinking that characterises the Academy was the Stepping Stones initiative begun in 2008, a marvellous multi-year set of conversations and my introduction to the creative exchange possible at the Academy. Charged with envisioning the next way stations the Academy might choose in order to expand its compass more broadly across the performing arts and community engagement, a small group of us from several countries and sets of expertise sat down together to listen and to talk. All ideas were welcome, and our wise guides gave us time to imagine, to listen to each other and, out of that mutual engagement, find new ways of seeing. Then began the process of finding a common thread, of placing ideas next to each other to see how they prospered by the proximity. Slowly, and after inviting others into the conversation, possibilities were winnowed down to a vision, an MA in Festive Arts, that had coherence and beauty and that embodied the values of community, invitation and creativity that have characterised all the Academy offerings. This was the kind of creative process followed by the American dance company Pilobolus, unique in the dance world for its embrace of collaboration and conversation. In the early stages of creating new works, their philosophy is 'say yes to everything. Saying no ends the conversation'. Listening, to oneself and to others, opens possibilities that would otherwise not be imagined.

It was in this sense of listening that Mícheál and Iarla Ó Lionáird rehearsed quietly in Mícheál's home studio in preparation for his concert on 29 June 2018 with the RTÉ National Symphony Orchestra at the National Concert Hall. Ó Lionáird is one of Ireland's finest singers of *sean-nós*, the old unaccompanied, highly ornamented singing from the west and south of Ireland. What made this collaboration so unusual then is that Ó Lionaird would sing and Mícheál would play the piano. A conversation, they both agreed. Each voice would have its own melody, but together going where the conversation took them. Similar conversations brought other musicians from traditional forms such as Mel Mercier on traditional percussion, Pádraic Keane on the uilleann pipes, Liz Doherty, Katie Boyle, Zoë Conway and Aidan O'Donnell on fiddles together with Mícheál in unlikely conversations bringing together traditional and contemporary musics. The concert was billed appropriately as *Between Worlds: The music of Mícheál Ó Súilleabháin*.

Performing artists are always in conversation; some of these are intimate and others communal but all are essential in vocations based on an interpretive role. The most intimate, the first and the last, is with their instruments. Acknowledging the daily obligation to make one's instrument as perfect as possible defines performers to themselves and to others. Mentors and teachers become partners in the process of discovery and refinement. The creators of the works performers bring alive are insistent voices, requiring their interpreters to listen into the stillnesses and the silences, to reveal the arc of the work. This is the through line that floats above the bodies, notes and technique and that leads to a resolution that is inevitable while never predictable. Performers join their colleagues in ensembles that bring together individual voices, creating something more than any single performer could have imagined or realised. Performances, the sum of all the conversations, are offered to audiences in theatres, community halls or ritual grounds, where another conversation takes place. In them, the practicalities of craft disappear into the transparency of artistry, and both performer and audience are transformed.

The Academy and its home

The Academy is one of those rare places that lives out this philosophy of conversation that crosses the known and the not yet known with a vibrancy and a generosity that continues to astonish. It is filled with creative spirits who, by their fearless exploration, give us the courage to embrace the unexpected. That fluid architecture of exploration is embodied in the splendid building – the heart-building, a jewel sprung out of the Shannon and the sea and the stone and all the stories that wrap around them. Mícheál was thrilled by the building, saying as it neared completion: 'The new building is like a poem. I am trying like mad to keep it at arm's length, but it simply overwhelms me. It is a house of light and of welcome.'[6] The building's designer, French architect Daniel Cordier, was chosen after a fierce competition, and it is clear that he and Mícheál had many conversations about what the building needed to symbolise and accomplish in order to be the physical embodiment of that philosophy of practice and reflection, of two kinds of knowledge, of being anchored yet free to fly. Mícheál describes it in his essay 'Elver Gleams', rooting it, especially its seven individual roofs, in the shape and movement of Irish set dance but also echoing medieval Irish monastic traditions. In his essay he quotes part of Cordier's description: 'to bring the performing spaces at the heart of the building and to wrap studios … around it like monastic buildings around a cloister. The full-height foyer connects cloister, performance spaces and piazza … This structure is expressed externally as a series of seven individual roofs to convey the visual concept of settlement … a dynamic *céile* [partner] for cultural and spiritual reference.'[7]

The spaces for learning craft flow into the spaces of performing, and the contiguity of performance and inquiry lets one move fluidly between these two ways of knowing and doing. Those who live, learn and work here are reminded daily of the conversations and connections there for the taking, by the architecture that reveals old traditions in modern forms. The building includes two state-of-the-art performance spaces. Theatre 1 accommodates up to 230 people and can be converted depending on the performance. Theatre 2, known as the Tower, holds ninety and is especially fine for acoustic performances. This stunning theatre rises three storeys to the open roof. Inside, the second and third storeys are cloud forests made of metal blue and silver shapes reaching all the way to the sky. It is rooted in a buried cache of treasures that represent the heritage of the Academy.

Above, Figure 42.1: Irish World Academy of Music and Dance from across the Living Bridge, 2019.
PHOTOGRAPH BY ANYA PETERSON ROYCE

Left, Figure 42.2: Tower Theatre clouds, 2010.
PHOTOGRAPH BY ANYA PETERSON ROYCE

Figure 42.3: Sionna mural, lobby of IWAMD, 2010. PHOTOGRAPH BY ANYA PETERSON ROYCE

High up on the Tower's front is a mosaic. What better image than that of the goddess Sionna so intent on seeking the hazelnuts of knowledge, wisdom and healing that she falls into the pool in which they lay. She is taken immediately away from the familiar on a long and often terrifying journey into unknown territory, encountering obstacles, being transformed and transforming all around her, creating the great river Shannon, and coming home again to the familiar as the river meets the sea.[8]

The Academy building sits on the Clare side of the Living Bridge, connecting the two parts of the university, linking counties Clare and Limerick. It is the join between the counties, between academic schools, between two kinds of knowledge. A stunningly modern building, it rises up out of the river, three storeys, rooted in ancient traditions and home to path-breaking performance and creative reflection.

Mentoring in the performing arts

Mentoring students in the arts is a privilege, a challenge, time-consuming, and it requires an investment of both knowledge and heart. It is always best done by people who themselves are dancers and musicians. In a book about artists as professors, the authors write: 'In a university, students are given their best chance if they learn philosophy from philosophers, biology from biologists not from historians and appreciators of philosophy and biology. So students have the most real introduction in the arts from artists, not from historians or appreciators of the arts.'[9] In the history of higher education, we have often been most comfortable with and appreciative of those disciplines that think about rather than those that practise. If we are to grow and learn, we need both. This is one of the great contributions of the Academy – that it sees the potential for creative growth in the synergy between practice and reflection. The Academy faculty, consummate practitioners of their art, understand this. A dear friend and colleague, cellist Janos Starker, once summed it up: 'After the standing ovation, eventually people sit down. But teaching moves through generations.'[10] Learning in the arts is a model for collaborative creativity – how to be fearless in creating new ideas, new ways of thinking and working together to distinguish which of these stands out from all the other possibilities.

The relationship between student and teacher in performance practice and reflection, at its best, is one of mutual trust and respect. That context emboldens exploration and allows students to accept and process feedback in ways that foster both mastery and creativity. My experience with the students of the Academy and with my faculty colleagues there tells me that this sort of trust and respect is nurtured and modelled. When you see students working collaboratively across quite different practices, they are modelling the same common cause and respect. The results are astonishing. Everyone benefits – the faculty mentors, the individual students and the community. Learning with is always more than the sum of the individual parts. To allow oneself to be transformed and to share that knowledge with others: this is at the heart of arts practice and reflection and its teaching and learning.

Listening: a kind of conversation

The faculty, staff and students of the Academy often discuss how this model of the arts as practice and reflection works as part of a university. In one of those gatherings, an international panel and members of the Academy took up the topic of 'Performing Arts in Higher Education: International perspectives on teaching, learning and research', at the Academy on 14 March 2013. The day-long set of panels addressed this broad topic from the point of view of students, faculty, performers who had often come to teach and perform at the Academy, visitors who held positions around the globe in schools of the arts. Some of the important themes included the nature of one-to-one or small-group teaching, the kinds of practice-based research and modes of evaluation typical of such institutions, and the need for a certain autonomy of governance. We heard extraordinary personal stories offered from many perspectives and it enlarged the ways in which we thought about what the Academy is about and why it matters as an example to the world.

In 2014, in celebration of its twentieth anniversary, the Academy held two and a half days of lectures, performances and workshops around the theme, echoing Seamus Heaney, 'Between the Poetic and the Practical'. The participants, as is the practice in the Academy, included students, faculty, invited scholars and performers who spoke and performed. Emphasising its belief in the necessity of both practice and reflection, the final panel undertook the theme 'The Role of the Artist as Citizen', highlighting both performance and scholarly approaches. These two events from 2013 and 2014, out of many, are excellent examples of why the Irish World Academy of Music and Dance is one of the world's leading academic institutions in terms of thoughtful and effective practice-based education in the performing arts.

Last words: healing, welcoming, transforming

The Academy was conceived as a place for conversations about creating arts informed by reflection. It is a site of transformation as students and faculty and staff embark together on journeys into many unknowns, given courage and inspiration by the support of each other. It is, finally, grown out of the fundamental value of radical inclusion, of creating fluid boundaries, of being citizens of the between. This is one of the great contributions of the Academy – that it sees the potential for creative growth in the synergy between practice and reflection. It can be an unsettling place, requiring courage and conviction and a strong community to withstand occasional buffetings. This Academy, both place and people, has followed the meanders, faithful in its bedrock philosophy, welcoming transformation and transforming, a sanctuary, a magical terrain – endpoint and beginning.

The Academy is a hospitable place, welcoming known and strange, in the ancient tradition of the abbeys and monasteries that line the Shannon. The Academy is a fount of creativity; those who guide it and those who pass through it bring together the poetic and the practical, performance both in the doing of it and in the thinking about it, guided always with the artist's sense of curiosity and humility. The architecture of invention spun from medieval traditions and the latest in genres and technologies honours and sustains both. The Academy is a healing place if we understand healing as a making whole. Body, mind and heart are joined here; we have only to enter the conversation.

Figure 42.4: Zen Garden, from below to the sky, 2019. PHOTOGRAPH BY ANYA PETERSON ROYCE

43

Three Meetings with Mícheál Ó Súilleabháin from 1985 to 2017

Tran Quang Hai

Tran Quang Hai is a Vietnamese musician, ethnomusicologist, educator, composer and performer. He is recipient of many honours, including the chevalier of the Legion of Honour in France. He has performed in more than 3,000 concerts in seventy countries, and recorded twenty-three LPs and CDs, five DVDs, and published four books.

Thanks to Mícheál, I discovered Ireland and the beautiful city of Limerick in 2005. I met Mícheál three times in my life, and my memory of these meetings has built my admiration for what he has done in life as a researcher, a musician, a music creator and a genius. The meetings with Mícheál started in 1985 at the late John Blacking's home in Belfast, the next in 2005 at the University of Limerick (UL), and the third in 2017 during the ICTM World Conference organised by UL.

First meeting with Mícheál in Belfast in 1985

I was invited by Queen's University Belfast (QUB) to perform at a concert of Vietnamese traditional music. I was there with my wife Bach Yen. John Blacking was my friend. I knew him when he was in South Africa and met him a few times in Paris. During my visit, John organised a party at his house and invited many friends. It was there I met Mícheál who was then a PhD student at QUB preparing his PhD with John Blacking and John Baily. Mícheál talked about the bodhrán, the Irish tambourine and the wooden beater. I was then interested in rhythms (jigs and reels) used to accompany Irish folk dances. I did not know the contents of his dissertation at that time. He attended my concert of Vietnamese traditional music at the university. He was fascinated by my spoons playing and my overtone singing. He met me again before I returned to France. Referring to the concert, he said that in Ireland the spoons were practised widely but he was surprised that in Vietnam the spoons were used in the performance of traditional music. I replied that I learnt the basic techniques of spoons in Vietnam and developed some new techniques to enrich the way of playing them. I did not meet Mícheál again during that visit to Belfast. Later I learned that he completed his PhD in 1987 on the Dublin traditional fiddle player Tommie Potts.

Second meeting with Mícheál in Limerick in 2005

Twenty years later, I received an invitation from Helen Phelan to go to Limerick to give a concert of Vietnamese music and a talk on Asian music. I was agreeably surprised about this unexpected invitation. Of course, I accepted it with pleasure. I arrived in Limerick for the first time. The university was well-equipped and the staff were very kind and helpful. I was surprised to see Mícheál as the director of the Irish World Academy of Music and Dance. My wife Bach Yen and I gave a concert of Vietnamese traditional music. Mícheál asked me to participate in an arts promotion project that included many artists from South-East Asia. In 2005 we worked together to present an artistic programme aligned with the aims of Culture Ireland.

One evening Mícheál invited me to a concert where I saw him play the piano in the style of improvised jazz music. I discovered his pianistic talent and his fantastic improvisation skills. During the concert, he invited me to join him for some duet improvisations. I was inspired by his music and joined him with jew's harp, spoons and overtone singing. This duet was acclaimed by the audience. I was happy to perform with Mícheál and it was the first time I saw Mícheál the talented pianist, and someone with a rich sense of musical creation and an amazing presence on stage to captivate the audience.

Before meeting him this time, I thought that I was the only person who was both a performing musician and researcher in the field of ethnomusicology. Most ethnomusicologists of the first generation were (only) theoreticians of music, working with the brain only and not with the heart like musicians who practised and lived with the soul of music. I studied ethnomusicology to know the methodology and techniques of research. I was also a musician of traditional music, practised many musical instruments, and gave many concerts around the world. Furthermore, with my passion and capacity for musical creation I introduced elements of traditional music into new music to enrich the music in my own way. Now, in front of me, Mícheál was researcher, educator, lecturer, music creator and music performer. He was celebrated for his fusion of Irish traditional and classical music, in particular for his unique style of piano playing. Like me, he shared his passion for music with everyone he met. He published many records and books and received many honorific awards.

Since that visit in 2005, I discovered more about his career and read articles about him. The more I read, the more I respected and loved him as an exceptional person. I considered him as a living national cultural treasure of Ireland. This title does not exist in Ireland but it does exist in Japan, Korea and Vietnam. Thanks to Mícheál, I gave a concert at University College Cork because of his connection with the university where he was previously professor.

Third meeting with Mícheál in Limerick in 2017

Twelve years later, UL organised and hosted the 44th ICTM World Conference. As I was an executive board member of this society I attended this international meeting. And there, I met Mícheál again. Although many years had passed, our friendship remained unchanged. For the inaugural speech, Mícheál gave the important paper 'The Redress of Music: Music, mediation and parity of esteem'. During the conference, I did not have an opportunity to talk to him because of my participation in many sessions. This was the last time I met Mícheál.

Figure 43.1: Tran Quang Hai and Mícheál, 2017. PERSONAL LIBRARY

The last word

One year and four months after the ICTM conference in Limerick, the emeritus professor of music at UL, the founder and director of the Academy and, above all, my dearest friend from Ireland whom I admired greatly passed away on 7 November 2018. These three meetings with Mícheál Ó Súilleabháin from 1985 to 2017 remain profoundly in my heart.

44

Mícheál Ó Súilleabháin: The candle and the light

Christopher Frayling

Christopher Frayling is former rector of London's Royal College of Art and chair of Arts Council England. An award-winning broadcaster and cultural historian, he has published twenty-five books. He is a fellow of Churchill College Cambridge. In 2000 he was knighted for 'services to art and design education'.

The first time I met Mícheál, in the early days of the Irish World Academy of Music and Dance, he presented me with a quotation from the book *Real Presences* by one of my tutors when I was at university, George Steiner. This quotation, said Mícheál, meant a great deal to him. It went like this: 'A city for painters, poets, composers, choreographers, rather than one of art, literary, music or ballet critics and reviewers, either in the market-place or in academe.'[1] Not a secondary or a tertiary city, he added with a characteristic twinkle in his eye, but a primary one, which put creation before criticism, art before the artificial, one where painters, authors, composers and dancers could form a concentrated creative community of mentors and students in a radical form of academy. It was this kind of atmosphere which he wanted the Academy to represent. Not a city for mimics, but for creatives; for teaching and learning to art and teaching and learning through art.

This was a distinction – to art and through art – coined by the poet and critic Herbert Read in his mid-1940s book *Education Through Art*,[2] a sadly neglected work these days. Teaching to art, he said, meant the professional education of the young artist – teaching the techniques and skills, attitudes, aptitudes and knowledge of how to make art, and eventually to find one's own voice; the grammar, then the usage. That aspect of art education, he added, was widely understood. Teaching through art meant the learning of a series of wider, related skills through the practice of the arts – skills that the arts seemed particularly good at bringing out. Which, he reminded his readers, was the original root meaning of the word education: *e-ducare*, signifying in Latin to lead out, to lead forth. Paraphrasing in today's less elegant language, these life skills include: problem-solving; resourcefulness; independence of mind; setting one's own agenda; flexible thinking; communication skills;

personal development, tailored to the individual, rather than to rote learning; confidence and self-esteem building; commitment and motivation; and preparation for an unpredictable world. Mícheál and I agreed that if Herbert Read was right about that in 1943 – an unpredictable world for sure – he would certainly have been right about his perceptions today. The very best form of education – concluded Read – combined the two.

As the recently appointed rector of London's Royal College of Art, I immediately spotted a kindred spirit, and over the ensuing twenty years or so there developed between us – in correspondence and meetings – a mutual understanding of this very special form of higher education. Surrounded by structuralists, reductionists, de-constructionists and all manner of other 'ists' in the late 1990s – not to mention passing celebrities and naysayers of the moment – I had sometimes felt like the protector of an endangered species. But I wasn't alone. Mícheál came to represent for me a different kind of celebrity – the right kind – firmly rooted in his own talents and contributions as a composer, a performer, a deeply committed educator – and a visionary. And his was among the strongest voices of all. George Steiner had concluded, in his Harvard lecture series *Lessons of the Masters*, about the best teachers of the arts: 'There is no craft more privileged. To awaken in another human being powers, dreams beyond one's own; to induce in others a love for that which one loves; to make one's inward present their future: that is a threefold adventure like no other.'[3] It was this sense of adventure that Mícheál evidently loved and which helped to sustain him during the formation and development of his Academy between 1994 and 2018, and beyond – years of outstanding achievement by anyone's measure. The tradition of ateliers, workshops, studios and masterclasses – which went back a long way and which, we both felt, had a rich future ahead of it. 'Radical' in the sense of back to the roots. We enjoyed the thought that, in the earliest universities of the Middle Ages, the practice of music preceded its analysis – so a 'masterpiece' would be a sort of performance.

He was a visionary, but by no means unworldly. I always sensed that – like Charles Dickens' Mrs Todgers in *Martin Chuzzlewit* – Mícheál had 'affection beaming in one eye, and calculation shining out of the other'. And I mean that as a compliment. Quite simply, he was brilliantly effective at getting things done, whether it was raising funds for the Academy – notably through The Atlantic Philanthropies – or persuading more traditional colleagues in the university of the importance of research through the arts or for the arts side by side with the better-understood research into the arts. For me, this was neatly symbolised by the Living Bridge linking the north and south campuses, overseeing the specially designed new building for the Academy in 2008, or expanding the portfolio of courses in exciting new directions until there were some twenty of them – whether it was any or all of these, his successes over the years brought to mind Jean Cocteau's famous motto: 'no one ever told me it was impossible'. And all this while composing and performing and recording his own piano music, his signature fusion of Irish traditional and classical styles. Mícheál had a prodigious supply of energy as well as of talent. He also had a special sense of humour.

He used to remind me – frequently – that English theatre was saved in the late nineteenth century by Irish writers (which was true, by the way, though I wasn't about to admit it!). That the best legends of the American Wild West (one of my enthusiasms) – Billy the Kid, Jesse James, Kit Carson – were about Irishmen. And the same went for the best music-hall songs: 'It wasn't all about the British Empire, you know, Christopher,' he'd say with a chuckle. To which I once replied, 'You were the man who nearly upstaged Queen Elizabeth II – in your tail-coat – on the stage of the National Convention Centre on 19 May 2011 – how did *that* feel ...?' I can recall in particular an animated conversation we once had about the music-hall song 'It's a Long Way to Tipperary', first performed in London in 1912 by its part-author Jack Judge. This song was at first only a modest success. Then in autumn 1914, at the start of the First World War, it was revived by the much-loved star Florrie Forde and became a phenomenon. When the volunteers of 1914 marched towards the fields of Flanders, it was to this song – about an Irishman's visit to the lights of London, and nostalgia for home – that they marched. Did the volunteers think about the words they were singing, or were they more concerned with missing the excitements of the West End of London: 'Goodbye, Piccadilly/Farewell, Leicester Square'? Whichever it was, it proved the truth of J.B. Priestley's celebrated comment, 'As soon as the English go to music-halls, they love the Irish.' Mícheál loved that line too. I'll miss his joshing. Just as I'll miss his commitment, his enthusiasm and his special kind of energy. I'll miss listening to the CDs of *Lumen* and *Templum* which he gave me, in our cottage on the Burren, knowing that the composer was on the other end of a phone-line. And I'll miss him showing me around Glenstal Abbey. Mícheál was a larger-than-life figure – and so there's now a larger-than-life Mícheál-sized hole in the universe.

Thinking last night about Mícheál's style of teaching and his style of living, as well as about his enduring legacy at the Academy, I was reminded of a short poem written by Christopher Logue in the late 1960s, as a homage to the French writer Guillaume Apollinaire.[4]

It's called 'Come to the Edge':

Come to the edge.
We might fall.
Come to the edge.
It's too high!
COME TO THE EDGE!
And they came,
and he pushed,
and they flew.

That, for me, speaks volumes about Mícheál Ó Súilleabháin as well. I'm proud to have called him my friend. With best wishes, Christopher Frayling.

45

Transmodal Curriculum Maker, Symbolic Leader

Regina Murphy

Regina Murphy is associate professor and former head of the School of Arts Education and Movement, DCU Institute of Education. Teaching and research themes span music education, creativity, critical reflection and identity. Her most recent publication is a co-edited volume, Music Education as Craft *(2021). Regina led the evaluation of Creative Schools, 2018–22.*

In this chapter, I trace the ways in which Mícheál influenced curriculum in music education in schools as well as in higher education through approaches that bridged musical modalities and ways of being a leader and a teacher. In so doing, Mícheál embodied symbolic leadership of the collective institutions that strive to guide music education in the Irish context.[1] Here, Mícheál artfully transcended structures, boundaries and standard curricula. He challenged the prevailing cultures through inspired action and through expression of his unique vision in the most creative ways possible. Like many leaders, Mícheál engaged followers, both immediate and more distal, and so many have benefited from his influence. In this personal essay, I reflect on school days and stories recounted of the young lecturer in University College Cork (UCC) who was beginning to challenge the norms of how learning ought to take place in the university. Focusing on seminal moments in Ireland's music education identity, this essay provides a vantage point to consider Mícheál's subliminal influence on curriculum in music education on many levels.

Context

As a teacher educator, theories of what one might teach and how one becomes a teacher, in any domain, invariably feature prominently in my day-to-day work. There are tried and tested approaches and received orthodoxies as to how effective teaching might occur. A standard approach might reasonably employ some well-proven techniques such as the designing of curriculum objectives, the engagement of students in curriculum subject matter, and finally the assessment of what has been learned.[2] But the science of teaching has yet to formulate ways of becoming transformational and visionary teachers who will impact positively on many others throughout the course of their career. The curriculum scholar William Pinar[3] posited a theory of curriculum as *currere*, from the Latin 'to run', as a current in a stream. *Currere* conjures up the idea of running the course of life and then, as a way of reflecting on a life's work, capturing the essence of how we carve out meaning through the rivers of our experiences, drawing from the sediment, the minerals, the flora and fauna towards what we teach. In many ways, then, a curriculum is less about course objectives and more a complicated conversation with oneself, as an ongoing project of self-understanding. The outcome of this process is in becoming mobilised for engaged pedagogical action with others – as a private and public intellectual – in the social reconstruction of the public sphere.[4]

Reflecting on the life of Mícheál Ó Súilleabháin calls to mind a multiplicity of modalities and ways of being a visionary teacher on many levels. If we were to enter into conversation with Mícheál now about his experience of *currere* and teaching, no doubt we would uncover a myriad of modalities employed at different stages in his life. Imagining his presence in such a conversation, I share personal reflections of various direct and indirect encounters with Mícheál from my childhood growing up in Cork, to later years as a teacher educator, intermingled with various direct sources from Mícheál himself, such as interviews that were broadcast nationally and various concerts, lectures, workshops and talks I attended over the years.

Institutional leadership

To so many of us, Mícheál has been something of a household name in Ireland as the 'face' of Irish music – a legacy that has its roots in the early phase of his academic career at UCC where he studied in the 'forcefield' between Aloys Fleischmann and Seán Ó Riada.[5] Here, he forged the capacity to bridge formal classical traditions and his love of the piano with the desires to engage with living, Irish traditional music. For any student, these two strands of expertise might have appeared to be quite distinctive and perhaps irreconcilable areas of curriculum, serving separate functions within a course of study. But Mícheál's capacity to transcend modalities had its genesis in this environment where both lecturers were highly influential in his emerging career as an academic and future leader.

On succeeding Ó Riada as the young lecturer in UCC in 1975, Mícheál's creativity began to blossom through an express focus on ethnomusicology – that is, studying music from the perspective of the social and cultural aspects of music makers themselves. His undertaking of doctoral studies at Queen's

University Belfast as a student of the ethnomusicologists John Blacking and John Baily marked another symbolic step. Blacking's classic study of the Venda people in South Africa, and his book *How Musical is Man?* – a mainstay of music education and ethnomusicology students worldwide – were no doubt highly inspirational for Mícheál.[6] But identifying a focus for his own study of music and culture, while already immersed in that culture, marked another ground-breaking step. Here, it was the music of a Dublin city fiddler, Tommie Potts, who served as the ethnomusicologist's area of focus. It is important to recognise that when a local figure is the subject of intense scholarship by a higher education institution, the work is assuredly propelled to a global stage. Thus, in doing this study, Mícheál not only met the doctoral requirements, but also demonstrated that a focus on music-making locally could be as worthy of in-depth scholarship as any music internationally.[7] The creativity of Tommie Potts' fiddle playing was undoubtedly unique, and the study in itself impelled other musicians to experiment creatively with style and form in ways previously unimagined. The study also prompted a host of other ethnomusicological studies of Irish traditional music that were in some way 'transmodal' – through space, time, corporeality, modality or tradition – that were to follow and, indeed, become the norm.[8]

Most significant during Mícheál's time in Cork was his founding of the highly regarded traditional Irish music programme at UCC that required academic and performance modules in both the undergraduate arts and education programmes. Undoubtedly, this was a source of joy and pride to the students who studied in the 'rebel county', as Cork was traditionally known, and envy to those in other institutions, particularly in the capital city, where Irish music was confined to a more marginal status within higher education. In conversations with my older sister, a former music graduate at UCC, she remembers lectures with Mícheál that were always expansive in their vision and captivating of students' attention. From the perspective of a young student, she recalls how he infused each lecture with progressive thinking such that each lecture was unique, fresh and original, and he often emphasised how music, as well as other areas of study, would develop in the future. In this regard, she felt he differed from others in his style and vision. To her, he brought originality to every lecture, and students were spellbound each time. But conversely, he also sought to enculturate the undergraduate students into the traditions and scholarship of ethnomusicology through authentic assignments. In this regard, as student-researchers, she and her fellow students were each tasked with gathering authentic field recordings of a traditional musician in the spirit of a true ethnomusicologist.[9]

Looking on as the younger sister, I was somewhat mesmerised by a number of dimensions of this project. Foremost was the status of the subject matter and its scholarship in UCC, as well as the signature pedagogy of the lecturer within the realms of the university who commandeered such engagement. Next, there was the issue of procuring sophisticated recording equipment as an essential tool that reflected the gravity of this musico-scientific assignment, as well as a level of dedication required to undertake it. In the days before Amazon and internet shopping, knowledge of *where* to purchase was as significant as knowing *what* to purchase. Finally, there was the execution of the research itself in the field – in this case, the challenge of travelling from east Cork to a remote hinterland in west Cork in the absence of direct public transport routes. To facilitate exceptional travel arrangements during daylight hours, my aunt, as the owner of a modest vehicle, was enlisted as the support team. Though delighted to be of help, she was also somewhat flattered that the musical tradition of her native county could be both the subject and object of attention in the university. Admittedly, for my father too there was something of a sense of disbelief turning to pride on realising that the music makers in the rural farmhouses of his childhood could hold their place in university subject matter and its assessment.

Scholarship in music also recognises the important role that music education can play beyond the local towards more global perspectives in enabling students to see how music can support their own individual lives effectively and in focusing attention on creativity and embracing diversity.[10] Mícheál had an innate sense of the power of music – its role in fostering creativity and identity, and the importance of projecting its essence onto the world stage. If, as Kertz-Welzel suggests, music education is about considering 'who we are right now and as a music education profession' and then 'figur[ing] out who we want to be', then we can see how Mícheál's work thrust issues of identity into the Irish music education picture and made those associations.[11] It was, you could say, the beginnings of a new sense of Irish identity outside of academia, inspired by the symbolic leadership of Mícheál.

Symbolic leadership

While leadership can be expressed in many forms, leadership from the top can have the greatest impact[12] and by extension, be the most empowering. Symbolic leadership, emanating from the pinnacle of the institution, can exert a powerful force.[13] Here, the symbolic dimension is expressed in its clearest form through practices that are exemplified, embodied and conveyed to those who lie within the sphere of influence. The notion of 'symbolic' is not concerned with imagery per se, but through the personification of what an organisation represents in the eyes of all participants or stakeholders. Within any organisation, members may be expected to subscribe to the philosophy, strategy and practices of the institution – typically expressed in mission statements, strategy documents and reports of implementation plans. On an individual level, an enacted dimension of leadership will see influence exerted through various cognitive and behavioural processes. But leaders can also serve a symbolic function to those who are not members of the immediate organisation but come to fall within its sphere of influence from further afield.[14] Therefore, what the organisation enacts and represents can, in turn, influence public consciousness and extend the bounds of possibility on many levels.

To undertake research in what some might consider 'ordinary places', such as rural west Cork, is to honour local musicians who might otherwise blend anonymously into a less publicly recognised musical lifeworld. Such valuing enables students to honour not just the person but the process, and is reflective of Mícheál's *symbolic leadership*. It also reflects a very contemporary notion of the diversity of knowledge existing outside of the university,[15] and the importance of representing local 'voice', through attunement, scholarship and sensitivity to place.

But even now, for those of us in music education seeking to develop new modules or pathways in our curricula at first, second or third level, Mícheál's personal and professional commitment to research, cultural context, local expertise and new modalities is among the supreme examples of the pursuit of a vision and its realisation at the highest level.

In the late 1990s I was engaged as a curriculum writer for the National Council for Curriculum and Assessment in revising the primary school music curriculum, the first revisions in almost thirty years. Capturing all that was emerging in Irish musical identity in the 1990s in particular posed a special challenge. By this time, Mícheál's presence at the Irish World Academy of Music and Dance continued to underline the status and importance of Irish music in Irish education. Thus, the inclusion of Irish music in the (new) *Primary School Curriculum*,[16] published at the turn of the century, was more assured. In that regard, the new document differed from its predecessor from almost three decades earlier, *Curaclam na Bunscoile*,[17] in that the status and centrality of music-making in the programme was so strongly articulated in the rationale and introductory statements. Moreover, Irish music could be seen to stand up to any concepts-based framework for developing musical understanding and pedagogical theories of participatory music-making, while maintaining an inclusive underpinning – not just for those born into the tradition. Music belonged to all, and Irish music – as well as music of other cultures – should therefore be valued by all. This was an evolving ideal that would ultimately survive the test of (curriculum) time.

As the curriculum-drafting process was drawing to a close, I was keen for the work to be scrutinised by an international expert, yet the opportunities for direct dialogue with an external scholar were limited for a number of reasons. In the 1996–7 academic year, Mícheál invited Professor David Elliott as visiting professor to the Academy. Elliott's recent ground-breaking book *Music Matters: A new philosophy of music education*[18] had begun to take the music education community by storm as he pointed to new ways of conceptualising music education from post-colonial and constructivist perspectives. The opportunity to engage in consultation with Elliott in Limerick through Mícheál's facilitation was timely. Elliott proved to be most affirming and influential in emphasising a praxial approach to music education, moving beyond music as aesthetic appreciation, towards one where making music itself was central and where listening to music could be a multicultural, multimodal and multi-stylistic experience. A key shift in Elliott's philosophical aims was to see musical worlds from outside the academy reflected in music curricula,[19] and his philosophical statement allowed scope for many emerging and marginalised music makers to be represented as relevant curriculum material. Moreover, Elliott's expansive ideas on music underlined the scope and focus of curriculum at a time when ideas such as exploring sound, listening and responding to diverse musics of the world, and enabling children to channel their own creative impulses through improvising and composing music appeared very alien to the teaching fraternity. Again, it was Mícheál's vision of a global music education community and his leadership in this symbolic form that enabled this work to happen.

Music Education National Debate

As debate on developments in music and music education in the mid-1990s reached new levels of intensity, reflected most of all in Frank Heneghan's Music Education National Debate (MEND)[20] initiative as another *fin-de-siècle* project, Mícheál's contribution was clearly evident in the discussion on multicultural education. Heneghan writes that the topic was dealt with 'generously and comprehensively' during MEND to extract the parameters or context of the Irish case. He emphasised that the main protagonist in effecting balanced progress on the many problems identified was Mícheál

Ó Súilleabháin, professor at the University of Limerick (UL). In this regard, it is clear to see that Mícheál did not demur from articulating the issues facing music education and demonstrated his usual perspicacity in putting forward a range of challenging questions such as:

- Is the general music education system the appropriate and natural ambience in which to promote traditional music?
- In an educational system hitherto dominated by the norms of method and repertoire derived mainly from western art music, how could already overloaded curricula be flexed to accommodate an enhanced presence of traditional music?
- How do current methods of transmission in traditional music dovetail with understandings of achievement targets such as composition/ performance?
- What is the so-called first culture musical experience of Irish children?[21]

Mícheál argued that in educational terms, and especially in pre-third-level contexts, the meaning and significance of such classifications as traditional/ folk, ethnic, 'musics of the world's cultures', multicultural, multi-ethnic, non-tonal, exotic, etc must be clearly understood in curriculum development and syllabus construction. He also set out a plan for introducing Irish traditional music to children that should include 'a balanced mix of musical repertoire', with due attention to 'the nature of performance and listening within the scheme, music and movement, literate/non-literate methods, uses of technology'.[22]

Looking back on this report some twenty years later, the key pedagogical issues are as relevant now as they were then. But most importantly, Mícheál also had the foresight and strategic vision to signal many of the related pragmatic issues, such as 'the role of culture-bearing musicians in the scheme; the method of creating authentic musical settings for the whole scheme to flourish "naturally"; the potential within the scheme to bridge the gaps between formal education and community, and between so-called high and mass culture'.[23] At the time, social media such as YouTube, Instagram or TikTok as vehicles for curation and communication of mass culture were still some years away. Even now, the ubiquity of online platforms to augment musical events has not obviated the necessity for live traditional music performances, nor for ethnomusicological research in context. The importance of pedagogical presentation and appropriate mediation and interaction with children and young people as active listeners and music makers remains as vital as ever to children's engagement with music of the world.

Symbolic leadership: keynote address at ISME's 25th world conference

It was not surprising that Mícheál's innovative work soon came to the attention of the International Society for Music Education (ISME) and he was invited to give the keynote at the biennial world conference in Bergen, Norway in 2002. As a conference delegate I was eager to hear that Mícheál would address the international audience on Thursday, 15 August 2002 in the main theatre, the Peer Gynt Hall of the resplendent Grieghallen. The conference theme was *Samspel* – a uniquely Nordic concept meaning interaction or interplay. Yet, I wondered what other delegates would make of an outsider's elucidation on this concept, and whether an Irish interpretation would sound too colloquial, or banal to others. However, Mícheál took to the stage with confidence, immediately generating rapport and capturing the imagination of the audience, characteristic of an effective communicator. He drew attention to the idea of 'global listening', and the need to develop the 'art of listening', in particular the 'art of global listening'. Here he underlined the theme of the conference of *Samspel* in emphasising the interplay between different ways of music-making: 'Whenever we respectively cross boundaries that border our musical experience from that of another, we move towards furthering something. Every movement of respectful knowing we make creates another stepping stone where another may follow – or indeed someone may come across from the other side.'[24]

My memory of this event was his confident but humble message, simple but ingenious. His words were imbued with contemporary poetry, ancient philosophy and sharp insights. In the days before TED talks, his had all the elements that would appeal to a very broad audience. He shared his dream for music: 'Imagine a new university faculty ... design a new purpose-built facility ... attract the best teachers, scholars and musicians internationally, begin with postgraduate students ... call it the Irish World Academy of Music and Dance.'[25] Mícheál's keynote was a talking point for the rest of the week and permeated conversations about music education months, years later. Those who were there commented on how mesmerised they were by such daring ambition and advocacy! Professor Magne Espeland, chair of the Bergen conference, recalls that 'Mícheál inspired the global education community profoundly through his visionary speech and showed that he is a true global pioneer for music education traditions'.[26] On a personal level,

I will forever be grateful to Mícheál for the sense of pride in being Irish that he generated on that day within the context of an international audience, and his ability to traverse time, space and place, to inspire powerful leadership for the music education community.

Society for Music Education in Ireland

Mícheál's presence and keynote contribution to ISME in 2002 encouraged my own involvement in the ISME board of directors from 2008 to 2012. In turn, this membership prompted me to find ways of establishing a national organisation in Ireland. Among the music education community, the sense of collegiality was strong, and I again have no doubt that this was inspired by Mícheál's open-minded and inclusive gestures, emanating from the Irish World Academy. Thus, the Society for Music Education in Ireland (SMEI) came into being. As a fledgling organisation, achieving international national affiliate (INA) status with the international organisation (ISME) became an important goal. To do so, support was required from key institutional leaders in music education nationally, as evidence of bona fide intentions and to ensure due diligence in the democratic process. Here, we were immensely grateful for Mícheál's support for our efforts, and following our application, SMEI succeeded in its mission in securing and maintaining an affiliation with ISME through to the time of writing. With the same generosity of spirit, Mícheál presented a spirited provocation at our SMEI 2013 conference – *The Gathering* – which was one of our most ambitious projects as a national committee in engaging debate on the nature and purpose of music education in Ireland in the post-Celtic Tiger years. Building on its original foundation, SMEI has held an annual conference each year since inception.

Yet, for each of us in SMEI, Mícheál has extended a generous spirit as a professional colleague in innumerable ways. As committee member Simeon Smith reflected: 'When I first thought about returning to education after a long spell away, Mícheál contacted me personally to encourage me, and made me feel like my story was of value, and should be shared.'[27]

It is this ability to see what might be, what we might become, individually and collectively, that has been Mícheál's gift – a love of music and all the ways of envisioning and embodying it. While the ensuing successes of the Academy in UL are legion, and are well documented in various sources, such as the university's website itself, in Fintan Vallely's *Companion to Irish Traditional Music*[28] and in resources at the Contemporary Music Centre of Ireland,[29] to name but a few, there have been numerous occasions over the past half century when those of us on this island have grown in confidence, born of the reimagining of our identity and the valuing of our musics, in all forms, such that it has enabled us to grow as musicians, as teachers and as citizens in a young republic. Returning to Pinar's[30] concept of *currere*, it is easy to see the work of the public intellectual, and the legacy of Mícheál's 'curriculum' on the education system and cultural institutions alike as sonic rivers of inspiration. His influence has been gigantic but subtle, never demanding but ever present. And in this, he endures.

In concluding these reflections, I am drawn to lines from the poem by Moya Cannon, 'Between the Jigs and the Reels', that Mícheál himself chose as part of his submitted keynote paper to the ISME conference in 2002, to illustrate the joy of bringing ideas and people together, on one artistic journey, and turning them into one. Finally, I express my gratitude to Mícheál, for an expansive vision of leadership and enduring legacy to music education in Ireland.

> Because what matters to us most
> can seldom be told in words
> the heart's moods are better charted
> In its own language –[31]

46

Mícheál Ó Súilleabháin: Encounters with a musical visionary

Svanibor Pettan

Svanibor Pettan is professor and chair in ethnomusicology at the University of Ljubljana, Slovenia, and a visiting professor in Colombo, Vienna and Zürich. His studies on music on a war–peace continuum, minorities, and applied ethnomusicology were published in various formats, countries and languages. He is the current president of ICTM.

A visionary! This was my first impression at the initial meeting with Mícheál Ó Súilleabháin at the University of Limerick (UL) in 2004. The Irish World Academy of Music and Dance, which he established a decade earlier, was clearly on its rise to excellence, and I very much enjoyed learning from him about what had been done so far and his enthusiastically delivered explanations on what was still ahead.

The story that led to our first encounter started in September 2003 when I received an invitation from the Academic Council of UL to accept a four-year appointment in the capacity of an external examiner in ethnomusicology at the Academy. Two of my respected colleagues whom I already knew from the worldwide scholarly events under the umbrella of the International Council for Traditional Music (ICTM) were in charge of ethnomusicology (John Morgan O'Connell) and ethnochoreology (Catherine E. Foley) at the Academy. Dr O'Connell and I shared the experiences of studying ethnomusicology in Europe and in the United States and of developing the study of ethnomusicology in Limerick and Ljubljana, respectively. I immediately recognised complementarity of our efforts and enthusiastically accepted the invitation.

Mícheál's vision of an integrated interplay of academic and performance excellence, strengthened through community outreach and artists in residence in the beautiful American-style campus of UL on the banks of the river Shannon was becoming reality in front of my eyes and it was a true privilege for me to be a part of this process. Every year when I returned to do the evaluation work there were noticeable novelties and improvements. After John Morgan O'Connell moved to Cardiff University, I continued evaluating the achievements of his successor Alexandra Balandina and her students. Inspiring conversations with Mícheál at both our formal and informal gatherings repeatedly revealed his great love for and internalised understanding of music. A composer, performer, thinker and educator creatively coexisted in him, complementing each other and encouraging new musical encounters across cultural specifics, always rooted in a sense of an underlying humanity.

My next visit to Limerick in 2009 was related to the search for a new ethnomusicologist. Mícheál invited me to serve as an external member in the selection committee since I was already reasonably familiar with the Academy and the needs of the programme and was delighted to continue working with Dr Colin Quigley following his appointment.

In the period 2011–17 I served as secretary general of the ICTM and my further visits to UL were related to this role. It was a pleasure to experience the new representative building of the Academy and to use the Living Bridge to get there. It was a pleasure to meet a growing number of colleagues and an increasingly international student population in and around the building. It was a pleasure to add a few more flowers to Mícheál's blossoming bouquet.

In 2015 the Academy hosted a historic event: the first ever forum of the two leading societies in the field, the ICTM and the Society for Ethnomusicology, joined by the European Seminar in Ethnomusicology (see Figure 46.1). In 2016 the ICTM Executive Board held its annual meetings at the Academy, at which the old constitutional document was reworked, and approved at the general assembly the following year. Finally, in 2017 ICTM celebrated its seventieth anniversary with the 44th World Conference hosted by the University of Limerick. Working with Catherine E. Foley (member of the ICTM Executive Board) and Colin Quigley, along with other faculty and staff of the Irish World Academy chaired by Sandra

Figure 46.1: Mícheál Ó Súilleabháin with colleagues at the SEM/ICTM Joint Forum held at the University of Limerick, 13–16 September 2015. PHOTOGRAPH PROVIDED BY ELLIE BYRNE

Joyce, was a truly amazing experience and so was the resulting event. Mícheál had lost some weight and I learned with much sadness that his health had deteriorated, but he bravely accepted the invitation to give a plenary presentation.

In his convincing, personalised presentation, well received by the audience, Mícheál investigated the power of music in redressing cultural and social imbalances. With this act, I felt, he left the stage through a big door. This turned out to be the last time we saw each other. The last sentence I received from him via email was: 'Thank you as always for your support and enthusiasm for our shared vision.' Mícheál the visionary closed his eyes for the last time the following year.

Thank you for everything, dear Mícheál!

47

'My Love is in America': Mícheál brings Irish music to Boston College

Elizabeth Sweeney and Christian Dupont

Elizabeth Sweeney has served as Irish music librarian at Boston College's Burns Library since 1999. Her previous library positions included cataloguing, reference and collection development. In curating Burns Library's Irish Music Archives, she has collaborated on several initiatives with fiddle player and former BC Sullivan artist-in-residence Séamus Connolly.

Christian Dupont is associate university librarian for collections and Burns librarian at Boston College, where he has led the development of John J. Burns Library's renowned Irish special collections since 2014. He previously held administrative and curatorial roles at the University of Virginia, Syracuse University and University of Notre Dame.

In June 2018, while travelling through Ireland in the days before the American Conference for Irish Studies annual meeting at University College Cork (UCC), we had a rare opportunity to make a number of site visits to colleagues, friends and institutions on behalf of the John J. Burns Library at Boston College (BC). A memorable highlight was visiting with Mícheál at Dromore House, the country estate he shared with Helen and Luke and their instruments in County Tipperary. Over coffee, we reminisced about how Irish music had taken root and flourished over the years at Boston College – in no small part due to his presence and influence.

Mícheál's first visit to BC was in March 1979 during the week-long Irish Fortnight series co-sponsored by BC and the Irish American Cultural Institute. For the closing event Nóirín Ní Riain and Mícheál presented 'The Irish Woman in Song', a two-hour programme echoing the series theme of 'The Irish Woman'.[1] At BC Nóirín and Mícheál met professors Adele Dalsimer and Kevin O'Neill, who just a few months earlier had founded BC's Irish studies programme around their respective disciplines of literature and history.[2] They had already collaborated with BC's Fine Arts Department, and Kevin recalls how the Irish Fortnight event brought music into the conversation as well: 'We had no budget so Mick and Nóirín stayed at my place and we had a chance to get to know each other, and to know that there was a real need and opportunity to bring more Irish music to BC.'[3]

A few years later, Kevin and Adele went to Cork to expand BC's Irish studies offerings by setting up a Junior Year Abroad programme at UCC. As it happened, Mícheál was launching an Irish music programme at UCC, and so they had occasion to renew their acquaintance and earlier conversation. 'Mick wanted to make sure that the traditional Irish music programme he was launching there would be available to our students,' recalls Kevin. 'No one could fail to be struck by the enthusiasm and love that he had for the music. We agreed that we should work on ways to connect BC and UCC via music.'[4] An opportunity to expand BC's music offerings came in 1989 when the university's music programme became a department.[5] The Music Department's inaugural chair was Anne Dhu McLucas (previously Anne Dhu Shapiro), whose research interests included the traditional music of Ireland and Scotland. Synergy between Anne, Adele, Kevin and others led to BC extending to Mícheál a joint visiting appointment in music and Irish studies for the spring semester of 1990.

Mícheál's six months at BC were highly productive and formative. As a visiting professor of ethnomusicology he taught courses in Irish music, brought guest artists to the classroom, and organised the landmark fiddle festival My Love is in America, which took place in the university's historic main building in a large hall that had been given by Boston's Irish community. Among other stellar musicians, Mícheál recruited Clare-born fiddle champion Séamus Connolly, who was living and working in the Boston area, to perform in the festival and to assist with engaging other players.

The Boston College Irish Fiddle Festival weekend in March 1990 featured sixteen of the finest traditional Irish fiddle players then living in the United States, accompanied by Mel Mercier on bodhrán. 'The musicians gathered the day before the concert to work with Mick on setting the programme for the following night,' Kevin remembers. 'I was a bit apprehensive as I wondered how sixteen musicians, some of whom had never met, could organise themselves into a coherent concert in a few hours. Obviously, I was unduly worried. As Mick worked his magic, the many different personalities became a community,' adding reflectively, 'I was aware that I was witnessing a historic moment ... the reconnection of strands of traditional culture that had been severed by the diaspora.'[6]

Mícheál arranged to have the festival recorded, alongside oral history interviews he conducted at Burns Library with a few of the performers. From the audio tapes of the final concert he produced a critically acclaimed CD, *My Love is in America*. He transferred the master tapes to Burns Library and advocated for BC to create an archive focusing on Irish music in America, which was officially established in Burns Library later that year.[7]

Following Mícheál's professorship, the 1990s were a period of growth for Irish music classes and programming at BC. Séamus Connolly received an appointment in the Music Department in autumn 1990 to teach weekly Irish fiddle classes to the BC community and to help coordinate public events. Soon afterwards, the Music Department began recruiting instructors to teach weekly classes in tin whistle and Irish dance. BC students also had opportunities to enrol in academic courses such as Celtic Folk Music and Introduction to Irish Folk Music. With the support of the Boston community, BC hosted a *sean-nós* singing festival in 1991 and a Celtic harp festival in 1992 that commemorated the 1792 Belfast Harp Festival. Séamus recalls how these festivals 'brought the attention of the community at large, who asked that we bring musicians playing different instruments, such as fiddle, accordion, flute, pipes and tin whistle – instruments in the idiom of Irish music, as well as singers and Irish dancers. I did so in the fall of 1993 under the heading of Gaelic Roots. That broadened the programme, and it was a very successful weekend of classes, concerts, and lectures'.[8]

Séamus' decision to name BC's festival Gaelic Roots and to incorporate various musical traditions was influenced by UCC's traditional music offerings, which during Mícheál's tenure had included a festival of music from Cape Breton Island.[9] After BC's second Gaelic Roots weekend festival in 1995, Séamus joined the Irish studies faculty full time and began organising an annual Gaelic Roots summer school and festival that would last a full week. From 1997 to 2003, students of all ages came to campus each June to learn music, song and dance from faculty hailing from Ireland, Scotland, England, Canada and the United States.

In March 2003 Séamus invited Mícheál back to BC to mentor BC student musicians and perform a concert with members of the BC community. The *Between Worlds* concert featured traditional music alongside some of Mícheál's classical compositions and arrangements. Later that year, after the Gaelic Roots festivals ended due to changes in United States visa programmes, Séamus began hosting events in an academic year series that continued the Gaelic Roots name.

In 2004, BC appointed Séamus as the inaugural holder of the Sullivan artist-in-residence chair sponsored by BC graduate and benefactor G. Craig Sullivan and his wife Maureen Sullivan. The following year, Séamus invited Mícheál back to BC to perform in the Gaelic Roots Music, Song, Dance, Workshop and Lecture Series. In the Irish Room of Gasson Hall, site of the 1990 fiddle festival, Mícheál accepted an honorary alumnus award for contributions to the university. He then performed his piano variations on a twelfth-century Irish plainchant tune, followed by a few of his arrangements of Irish traditional melodies. He would return to Gasson Hall once more, in autumn 2012, to give a Gaelic Roots concert featuring some of his piano compositions and arrangements on solo piano, in a duet with Séamus on fiddle, and in a collaboration with string quartet.

In keeping with the precedent that Mícheál set in 1990, recordings from BC's Gaelic Roots festivals and the ongoing Gaelic Roots series are routinely added to Burns Library's Irish Music Archives. The collecting ideas he articulated for the archives included other types of material as well.[10] In recent years the library has been fortunate to expand its Irish music holdings with manuscript collections, such as the personal papers of Séamus Connolly, Mary O'Hara and others; collections of rare audio, published and unpublished; and rare printed materials.

During our summer 2018 conversation at Dromore House, Mícheál enthusiastically gave permission to the library to add his four oral history video interviews from the 1990 fiddle festival to the YouTube channel of Burns Library's Irish Music Archives. Sadly, it would be our last meeting with him. We were preparing these videos for release in the autumn of that year when Irish folk singer Karan Casey, during a special Gaelic Roots memorial concert honouring Craig Sullivan, broke the news of Mícheál's passing. She offered a spontaneous and moving tribute, followed by a plaintive vocal/piano performance of 'Siúil a Rúin'.

In a more recent conversation, Robert Savage, a historian of modern Ireland who since the 1990s has held various administrative roles in the Irish studies programme, offered us his summary perspective on Mícheál's influence at BC and beyond:

> Mícheál's reputation as an innovative composer and musician is well established. But an important aspect of his legacy is the work he did to bring performance, especially music and dance, into the discipline of Irish studies. He was a passionate and highly successful advocate for Irish performance both at home and abroad where his charisma and energy proved tremendously effective. At Boston College he enhanced Irish studies by successfully arguing that Irish culture was more than Yeats, Joyce, Beckett and the great dramatists and figures from Irish history. The co-founders of the program, Adele Dalsimer and Kevin O'Neill, agreed with him that the study of Ireland had to recognise and embrace a rich and complicated tradition of music and dance as an essential aspect of a complex culture. Mícheál brought us a brilliant artist, Séamus Connolly,

and with Séamus came a critical appreciation of traditional music that forms an important part of the Irish studies programme at Boston College. Gaelic Roots, the continued concert series and especially the Irish Music Archive would never have been possible without Mícheál's foresight, charm and persistence. He was a formidable artist, academic and intellectual who left a critical imprint on the field of Irish studies.[11]

48

Mícheál Ó Súilleabháin, Music Educator: Local accent, global vision

Marie McCarthy

Marie McCarthy is professor of music education at the University of Michigan. She has been a regular contributor to music education in Ireland for over three decades. Her awards include honorary life member of the Society for Music Education in Ireland and the International Society for Music Education.

Mícheál Ó Súilleabháin embodied the attributes of visionary artist-teachers. His charisma inspired action, his powers of communication drew people into the circle of his teaching and mentoring, and his presence was animated by curiosity and creative energy. His educational vision emerged from and was integral to his practice as a creative and performing musician. In this essay, I address the implementation of his vision and illustrate how his philosophy of music education was global in vision and local in context and accent.

My first correspondence with Mícheál was in early 1990 when I was completing a dissertation on Irish music education at the University of Michigan. Inspired by his writings and innovative thinking, I sent him a draft of the dissertation to review at a time when he was visiting professor at Boston College. Later I met him at the Music Education National Debate (MEND) international symposia held in Dublin in 1995 and 1996. I spent a sabbatical leave at the Academy in autumn of 1997 during a semester when the first programmes were implemented at the Academy and others were in development. Even in those early days it was clear that his vision for music in higher education was progressive, expansive, interdisciplinary and cross-cultural.

While Mícheál was expanding the horizons of music curriculum in university settings in Cork and Limerick in the 1980s and 1990s, modelling pathways for traditional music and dance to enter the academy and find a home there, scholars around the world were engaged in similar quests.[1] They began to challenge the status quo of formal education and to search for authentic ways to include folk, traditional and popular musics in the curriculum. Mícheál was a luminary in that movement, facing into the cross-currents that accompanied such reform efforts, introducing new curriculum models and building bridges between music in the academy and the community. His contributions to reform in music education were not limited to locating traditional music in formal education. He contributed also to scholarship and practice on the creative process; holistic approaches to music learning that unified practice, theory and reflection; and dialogue on the relationship between music education in local and global contexts. At one level, his pedagogical intuitions and educational vision were aligned with contemporary innovations in music education but at another level the curriculum models he created and guided towards implementation were ahead of their time.

Leading the change: lessons for international music education

Efforts to transform philosophy, curriculum content and approaches to pedagogy were widespread in music education. In light of those changes, I discuss four aspects of Mícheál's contribution: music in higher education; inclusive approaches to music in education; community engagement; and local accent in a global context.

Re-envisioning music in higher education

The relationship of practice to theory is reflected in how music schools organise academic divisions and enact curriculum.[2] Instruction in music performance and in music studies (e.g. history, theory) frequently occurred in separate institutions in the past, with performance granted lowly status in universities.[3] Reflecting on his belief about the pedagogical relationship between practice and theory, Mícheál said:

> I believe that performance should continue to be put to the fore in music. At some point, the theorisation of music nearly took over and the playing of the damn thing became almost secondary. I think kids want to perform, to get inside the music first, before they can get hooked into it.[4]

Cultures of music instruction had become mired in sets of binaries – practice and theory, formal and informal, sound and symbol, or notation-based learning and oral learning. He approached music holistically as a practice rooted in place and culture, a medium of creative expression, and an activity integrated with other art forms. Music education contexts, then, needed to reflect the diverse nature of music-making as an artistic practice. Breaking away from the literate- and theory-based curriculum typical of university music curricula in Ireland, he embraced a new curricular model. Academic coordinator at the time of the founding of the Academy and creator of

The PIPA Report, Helen Phelan, later described Mícheál's efforts to create 'a centre of learning that sought to redress these biases and to develop an approach to music education that would bring performance back into the heart of the educational process'.[5]

He found support for his beliefs in current ideas at the forefront of international scholarship, particularly David Elliott's praxial philosophy of music teaching and learning. This people-centred, practice-based approach to music education, with a strong focus on the education of reflective practitioners and teachers, influenced the shaping of curriculum at the Academy and clarified relationships between the worlds of doing and thinking, performing and reflecting.[6] The creative process was at the heart of Mícheál's life in music, evident in his creative output, in-depth analysis of the creative process in the music-making of Tommie Potts, and interest in 'the dynamic between tradition received and tradition reinvented'.[7] In addition to the creative process, the musical creativity of the individual student was in the foreground of his pedagogy. He found an image in Seamus Heaney's poem 'At the Wellhead' to capture the process in poetic form: 'Sing yourself to where the singing comes from'.[8] It was not enough for the student to find their 'unique and precious' voice or 'fingerprint'; 'it must meet other fingerprints if it is to make a way in the world, to acquire external meaning'.[9] Mícheál's approach to and analysis of the creative process in music deserves further study and application to music teaching and learning.

As degree programmes developed their niche in the Academy, the bridging of practice, teaching and research was embedded across the curriculum, culminating in the introduction of a PhD in Arts Practice in 2009. It takes a special academic environment in higher education to achieve a confluence of teaching, practice and research. In the Academy, that outcome was achieved in part by a focus on interdisciplinary ways of studying music, innovative research methodologies that placed practice at the heart of inquiry, and recognition and respect for all musical traditions and their transmission processes.

Inclusive approaches to music in education

One of the most persistent themes of music education in the last fifty years has been the inclusion of diverse musical traditions in the curriculum. Mícheál was at the forefront, calling for the 'redress of music', for 'parity of esteem', and for the equal recognition of all musical traditions in education. As far back as the mid-1980s he recognised that the challenge facing Ireland in the field of music education 'is such that if we succeed in reconciling the opposing forces in our musical life [classical and traditional], we will have hit upon a formula which may well prove to have an international significance'.[10] There is abundant evidence that this reconciliation was lived out in the curriculum he envisioned and the educational spaces he facilitated.

Speaking in Beijing in 2003 on the preservation of traditional music, he concluded that it is possible 'to honour tradition while at the same time encouraging reinvention' and 'to integrate traditional music with an academic environment such as a university – without compromising the essence of the music'.[11] In the published summary of the address, he provided a valuable guide for educators considering the appropriation of a musical practice in the space of a traditional western curriculum. Among the points he highlighted, he encouraged 'a shared educational space for musicians from all available traditions; avoidance of the imposition of the aesthetic norms of one music tradition upon another; encouragement of a deep respect for all music traditions; and recognition that any knowledge increase in cross-cultural awareness of global music traditions is by definition a movement towards combating racism'.[12] These insights evolved over twenty-five years, evident in the ways he influenced the development of curriculum in higher education and in the school he co-founded in Ennis, County Clare – Maoin Cheoil an Chláir.

Redressing the imbalance of musical traditions taught in higher education and creating new and equitable contexts for transmission was a goal he sought to advance throughout his career. It was expressed with clarity in his article 'The Redress of Music: Music, mediation and parity of esteem' (2018). He described entry into university teaching at UCC as 'the beginning of a career spent redressing imbalances in access to higher level music education for traditional and classical musicians in Ireland',[13] and the Academy as 'a working laboratory of cultural redress' with music and dance holding potential to act as 'powerful forces of cultural mediation, redressing social and musical inequalities'.[14] An inclusive approach to musical traditions was at the heart of his disposition, which he compared metaphorically to 'many rivers of sound'.[15] The scope of inclusion extended beyond traditional music and dance to embrace all musical traditions and their related arts.

Community engagement

The first community of music-making Mícheál Ó Súilleabháin encountered was in his hometown of Clonmel. He recalled in great detail events and people associated with music in that community – from playing in the pipe band for the Corpus Christi procession, the music from the local dancehall he heard at night, playing pop music on guitar with school pals in the Sea Cliffs group they formed, to the gigs that he was invited to play as a young musician.

With knowledge of the musical resources available in the community, confirmed during his time teaching in Clonmel and Ring, the scope of his musical cosmos extended outwards from the educational institution into the community. In both Cork and Limerick he strategised to create and sustain pathways between school and community. In Cork he hired traditional performers to teach students at UCC. This continued in Limerick with expansion of the community-based model. Collaborating with local artists (Daghdha Dance Company, Glenstal Abbey, Irish Chamber Orchestra) was influential in the development of several degree programmes. Such collaborations anchored learning in living communities of practice beyond the Academy. The unique resources of the local community served an important role in inspiring, energising and validating the direction of the curriculum. In the same time period, community music was coming into its own as a practice with a pedagogy, literature, professional identity, research base and degree programmes. Early in the development of the Academy, the MA in Community Music was established, attracting students with a diverse portfolio of musical backgrounds, experiences and career goals.

Local accent in a global context

As music from a variety of traditions and cultures began to be integrated into music education, the question of whose music ought to receive priority was central to the discourse. Mícheál adopted a broad view of music and identity formation, concluding that musically, 'we must go further to embrace the globe if we are to spark the necessary fire of self-knowledge'.[16] It was reflected in the juxtaposition of 'Irish' and 'World' in the naming of the Irish World Music Centre.

> [T]he performing arts of music and dance can claim a special place in the creation of a cohesive multifaceted identity – an identity which encourages new unities out of old oppositions, which honours the many voices within us, and which continues to engage us in an ongoing liberation of Irishness in an increasingly challenging global cultural environment.[17]

Over the years he refined his thinking about the local–global relationship in music education, continuing to focus on identity formation as well as musical self-knowledge. He continued to advocate for 'a shared community of sound between Irish classical and traditional musicians' which would serve as 'an ideal local laboratory for a cultural bridge-building that might be applied globally'.[18] Understanding the dynamic between the local and the global, he wrote, was 'part of the necessary wisdom of the times we live in'.[19] In that space, the musician is listening respectfully, searching for 'the common ground of human heritage' and also 'the boundaries of difference, which unite us as a truly global community'.[20] And similar to Mícheál's approach to the creative process, 'the art of global listening' was also an individual journey facilitated by mediators who 'hold the light steady' for the listener. For the music teacher, then, the musical challenge we face in our own time is

> to address the global multiplicity of voices as never before. To continue to work like a good cartographer drawing the educational map of the location of the stepping-stones. Everyone must find them in the end for themselves for the experience to be wholesome as it should be, and everyone *will* find them in their own way and at their own rate – something that must also be respected.[21]

To gain understanding of the synergy between the local and the global in musical experience, Mícheál provided perspective for the teacher, the 'good cartographer'[22] whose role as cultural mediator enables access to the world of music.

Reflection

The present essay set out to capture some of the fundamental aspects of Mícheál Ó Súilleabháin's philosophy of music education. His wisdom about music education and its role in culture was centrally located in the human dimensions of music and dance. Conversations around music and identity formation, the dominance of place in music-making, his sensitivity to musical personality and his interest in how the individual searches for their voice through creative music-making all attest to an artist-educator who was grounded in the human significances of music.

Although his life in music was predominantly played out in the context of an island culture, the essence of his understanding and insight about music and other arts as sources of meaning have universal soundings. It behoves music educators in each nation or cultural group to dig deep into its musical practices to find the stories that make music education vital to its further development. Mícheál illustrated this by showing that the artistic tensions played out in music education in Ireland offer inspiration for music educators elsewhere.

The narrative of his life in music also shows that early childhood music is vitally important in stimulating latent musicality and encouraging the young to find their musical voice. Mícheál found music, music found him. Related to this point is the importance of access to music education. There are many moments of 'what if' in the story of this iconic figure. What if he didn't discover music as an academic subject to pursue for Leaving Certificate? What if there was no teacher qualified to prepare him for the examination? As a profession, one of the goals must be to recognise and encourage individual musicality. The role of informal music education in his community was highly influential in Mícheál's development as a musician during childhood and youth. This aligns with research findings pointing to the need for music education in the early years of life.

As a reformer and change agent for music in education, his story demonstrates clearly the slow pace of change, as well as the gift of 'right fit' in the context of institutional climate and receptivity to individuals with innovative and entrepreneurial ideas. The development of an academy for music and dance grounded his educational vision in concrete and artistic form. It was a place where many 'rivers of sound' met and flowed together, some with deep resonances in the past living alongside state-of-the-art contemporary practices – the diachronic and the synchronic in tension, the practical and the poetic.

PART III
CULTURAL MEDIATOR

Foreword

Helen Phelan

While the core of Mícheál Ó Súilleabháin's contributions resides in the areas of music-making (performing, composing, recording) and education (first at University College Cork and then through the development of the Irish World Academy of Music and Dance at the University of Limerick), it is impossible to offer a comprehensive picture of his legacy without also exploring the wider context of his role as a cultural mediator. This is the most difficult aspect of his work to categorise, embracing his wide-ranging engagement with Irish politics, history, language and the media as well as other art forms including poetry, painting, film, literature, theatre and academic writing.

A key area of mediation involved his engagement with the Irish language, particularly through his interest in Irish-language song and poetry. In the first section of Part III, Casadh/Turning, Lillis Ó Laoire, Áine Uí Cheallaigh and Tríona Ní Shíocháin explore this mediation. Lillis Ó Laoire and Áine Uí Cheallaigh share memories of their own engagement with Mícheál through his lifelong interest in *sean-nós* singing, and its impact on his compositional work. Tríona Ní Shíocháin traces the evidence of his interest in the Irish-language poetic heritage from his earliest research, as part of his MA thesis, on the songs of three eighteenth-century Munster poets, arguing that poetry and music formed interlocking aspects of his wider philosophy, embracing multivocality and embodiment.

This mediation between music and poetry is the focus of the second section of Part III, Gaiseadh/Flowing. From Heaney to Rilke, Larkin and Ó Ríordáin, Mícheál repeatedly drew on the poetic voice in his essays, lectures, performances and media interviews to enhance communication between the head and the heart. He was also interested in the poet's understanding of music, believing that one entered the poetic and musical realm through the same door. He was fascinated by the poets who wrote about Ó Riada – Montague, Kinsella, Lucy and Heaney, among others – and often incorporated their work into his performances, suggesting that they may have grasped the essence of what Ó Riada was struggling to achieve better than many of his musical contemporaries. Fióna Bolger, John McAuliffe and Vincent Woods helped us to connect with the poetry community in Ireland and abroad and the response was extraordinary, with twenty-two poets – Paula Meehan, Thomas McCarthy, Joseph O'Connor,

Tom French, Paddy Bushe, Vincent Woods, Eva Bourke, Enda Wyley, Eiléan Ní Chuilleanáin, Moya Cannon, Michael Coady, Paul Muldoon, Peter Sirr, Mícheál 'Moley' Ó Súilleabháin, Áine Uí Fhoghlú, Fióna Bolger, David Whyte, Gerard Smyth, John McAuliffe, Bernard O'Donoghue, Theo Dorgan and Martin Dyar – offering poems for the book, most of which are newly composed.

The final section of Part III, Oileán/Island, explores Mícheál's mediation of other areas of cultural life, from his work with Culture Ireland to his regular presence in the national media, as well as his academic and compositional interactions with film, theatre, visual arts and scholarly publications. Nuala O'Connor and Philip King offer poignant and often humorous memories of their work with Mícheál on the ground-breaking production *A River of Sound*. Aodán Ó Dubhghaill recalls a lifelong engagement with RTÉ Radio and Television and particularly with Lyric FM in the context of its move to Limerick. Mícheál's work with film, visual arts, storytelling and theatre are examined by Rod Stoneman, Timothy Emyln Jones and Page Allen, while sustainable economist Finbarr Bradley explores the Irish World Academy as an example of regenerative innovation. John O'Flynn's essay provides an in-depth review of Mícheál's engagement with academic publication. Méabh Ní Fhuartháin's and Cathal Goan's essays highlight the important contribution Mícheál's work made to the growth of Irish studies in America, while using this as a springboard into their own research on representations of Irishness in American film, and 'planxty' as a newly coined word for a new kind of composition. Owen Ó Súilleabháin and Fintan Vallely offer perspectives on Ó Súilleabháin as both a figure of mediation and controversy, while Johanne Devlin Trew and Harry White explore the parallels between Heaney and Ó Súilleabháin as cultural mediators. While Part III concludes with White's essay, the epilogue which follows draws the book to a close with the text of the homily delivered by Mark Patrick Hederman OSB at Mícheál Ó Súilleabháin's funeral.

49

Memories of Mícheál: Cuimhní cinn ar Mhícheál

Lillis Ó Laoire

Lillis Ó Laoire is emeritus professor of Irish, formerly at Roinn na Gaeilge, University of Galway. He is a Donegal native and acclaimed sean-nós *singer. A prolific writer, he is co-author, with Sean Williams, of the award-winning book* Bright Star of the West, *on the great Connemara singer Joe Heaney.*

It is a pleasure, inflected by sorrow, to write about Mícheál Ó Súilleabháin and to remember the ways in which our work and lives intersected and interacted in the twenty-six years that I personally knew him. *Bóithrín na smaointe*, the little lane of thought or memory, brings a reflection on my good fortune to have met and worked with Mícheál through song and music. To have a chance to express these memories in writing is a great opportunity, also providing a chance to contemplate my own life and work. Mícheál's energy had the character of a force of nature, and in his exuberant presence, things were always in motion and flux. The first time I met him properly was on the Cork train from Dublin in 1987. Both of us had attended the launch of the Irish Traditional Music Archive in the Guinness Storehouse on 19 November and we happened to catch the same late train south from Heuston Station, both of us having to be back at work the next day, a Friday.

I nGaeilge a labhair muid agus phléigh muid cúrsaí amhránaíochta agus ceoil go dtí gur fhág mise an traein ag Gabhal Luimnigh. Níor smaoinigh mé an oíche sin go mbeadh baint an-mhór aige le mo shaol lá ní b'fhaide anonn. Ina dhiaidh sin, i 1994, ceapadh Mícheál ina ollamh le Ceol in Ollscoil Luimnigh, cathaoir nua Cheoil a chuir cor úr i gcinniúint léann an cheoil in Éirinn. Níor luaithe istigh an doras i Luimneach é ná a bhí grúpa ceoltóirí ón Eoraip bailithe le chéile aige – Carlos Núñez, Mercedes Péon ón Ghailís, Solen Piriou agus Charles Quimbert ón Bhriotáin, agus Brendan Ring, an píobaire, chomh maith liom féin, Niall Keegan, Sandra

Joyce, agus Desi Wilkinson, triúr a bhí díreach tagtha go Luimneach mar mhic léinn iarchéime. Rinne muid dhá cheolchoirm agus rinneadh ceirnín den cheolchoirm dar teideal *Fonn*. Tá mo chóip agam go fóill agus is mór an áilleacht an dearadh clúdaigh deas a rinne David Lilburn, chomh maith leis an cheol bhreá atá air. Seod é nach bhfuil an oiread sin cóipeanna de ar fáil.

In 1991, I first won Corn Uí Riada, the top prize for *sean-nós* singing, a trophy named in honour of Seán Ó Riada, after his death in 1971. It was a satisfying victory, not least because it was unexpected. I remember the singers that night were outstanding and still recall the one whom I favoured for first prize. It was the culmination of over ten years of study, learning, practice and performance. I had been seriously infected by a deep attraction to Irish-language song and to the unaccompanied singing style known as *sean-nós* from early in my university days because of the influence of Breandán Ó Madagáin, my teacher and mentor at University College Galway, himself a leader in research on song and an advocate for an appreciation of the centrality of music in the study of traditional poetry in Irish. Breandán ceaselessly argued that music had to be considered as a central part of this body of literature. In university Irish departments, on the Leaving Certificate curriculum, even in primary schools, texts such as 'Droimeann Donn Dílis', 'An Droighneán Donn' and 'Bean Dubh an Ghleanna', to name only three, were studied only as texts with seldom any reference to music. To Breandán this was a travesty. Separating the texts from their music did the poetry – a unity of music and words – a grave disservice. This argument resonated strongly with me. I remembered studying texts such as the great love song 'Dónall Óg' and one of Eoghan Rua Ó Súilleabháin's aislingí, 'Im Aonar Seal ag Siúl Bhíos' at secondary school. Vaguely, there was some understanding that these were informed by music but no emphasis was placed on it. It remained out of sight, hidden away, an insignificant detail. Breandán's advocacy had a strong effect upon me, making me reassess my interest in such texts. In understanding that they were not only to be read, but to be said, to be voiced, to be sung, this rich and diverse body of poetry took on new meaning for me. I became excited by the idea of a melding of music and text. I certainly had liked the poetry before, but had been drawn more to modern post-revival literature, Seán Ó Ríordáin's poetry being a good example. My new understanding of poetry as song changed everything, and set me firmly on the path of attempting to enact these texts myself. Breandán was an accomplished musician as well as a scholar of language and text and, influenced by his reading in ethnomusicology, he believed firmly that learning to do, acquiring performance skills could lead to a deeper understanding of the poetry. I readily accepted this and started to learn songs as fast as I could. My efforts were faltering at first but as time went by I began slowly to improve and gather confidence. This brought me almost inevitably into the ambit of competitive singing, which culminated in my twice winning of Corn Uí Riada.

Ionad na nAmhrán – Lá na nAmhrán

After returning to work following the weekend of the Oireachtas in Dungarvan, County Waterford in 1994, a few days passed before I received a note from Ed Walsh, president of the University of Limerick (UL), in his characteristic handwriting with trademark purple ink, congratulating me on my achievement. That year also inaugurated Mícheál's professorship of music at Limerick and a beginning that marked another important departure in my journey into the world of Irish song. Mícheál contacted me soon after that and we met. His enthusiasm and energy drew me in at once. He was truly delighted that someone with passion about song was on the UL staff and immediately set to planning for how this could be activated and made productive. The idea of a song centre came to the fore quite quickly and before I knew it I was organising what became the first of several annual days of song, called Lá na nAmhrán, a vehicle to generate archive footage for Ionad na nAmhrán, a centre for the study of song. These were one-day festival seminars, celebrating the contemporary song traditions of Ireland and, in the case of one of the days, Scotland. In 1995, the first group included singers from different parts of Ireland, representing both Irish language and English singing traditions. The singers included Treasa Ní Mhiolláin, Maighread Ní Dhomhnaill, Róisín White, Paddy Berry and John Tunney. We discussed the need for more research and performance opportunities for traditional song.

In 1995, we invited a number of singers from Tory Island, Donegal, where I was then conducting doctoral research. As a direct result of Mícheál's agency, Hummingbird Productions, a television company run by Philip King and Nuala O'Connor, became involved to make a film of the proceedings and thereby to create archive footage. A bus came from Donegal with the singers. The great patriarch of the Donegal fiddle, Proinsias Ó Maonaigh, and his wife Kitty came as well. We were also joined by Gearóidín Breathnach, Caitlín Ní Dhomhnaill and Máire Ní Choilm. My research focused on one family from Baile Thoir, the east end of Tory, eight Duggan sisters whose parents and other relatives were renowned singers in their time. We managed to get five of them, Bríd, Kitty, Hannah with her husband Antoin, Teresa and Gráinne and Gráinne's husband Jimmy to come to Limerick, hosting them in the Glentworth Hotel. The event drew a capacity crowd. On the day prior to the concert there was a welcome reception in the Bourn Vincent Gallery. Francis (Proinsias) played the fiddle and the islanders began to dance. At one point as they were dancing an elegant stately walking dance to the tune of 'O'Donnell Abú', Sandra Joyce leaned in and remarked in delight, 'That looks like an eighteenth-century court dance.' Excerpts from the concert made it into the final cut of a film called *Bláth Gach Géag dá dTig*, a fifty-minute documentary on the Gaelic song tradition of Donegal, including a focus on Tory Island. The film first aired on TG4 during the first year of its life in 1996 and has been broadcast to acclaim on several occasions since then. It was the first hour-long film to treat the subject of song in the Donegal Gaeltacht in a sympathetic and serious way and brought many faces and voices to the screen that had not previously been seen or known. It was both aesthetically and archivally important. This event would not have happened but for Mícheál's presence in Limerick and his unflagging support for such initiatives.

A special highlight of those annual days was the one dedicated to Traveller traditions in 2001. I remember well the night of the concert in the City Art Gallery in Pery Square, Limerick. Mary Frances Keenan, the youngest of the singers, began to interact with the art work in the front gallery. This was a huge ball, by the artist Andrew Kearney, that moved across from one side of the softly lit space to the other making a gentle rustling sound as it progressed. Totally unfazed by this extraordinary sight, Mary Frances sat down and began to play her guitar and sing. The others joined her and accompanied her in the chorus of her songs. The space became instantly reanimated, turning from a rather formal gallery configuration into an intimate campfire setting that emanated a sense of easy camaraderie, the ball functioning as a kind of representation of the moon. It made a very good beginning, setting the scene for the concert that followed, the main event, that went off very well.

Another of the Lá na nAmhrán days happened in tandem with the annual day of dance, Tráth na gCos, organised with Catherine Foley, course director of the MA Ethnochoreology. We had a wonderful group of Scottish singers and dancers with both singers and dancers performing very happily together, the variety enhancing each aspect. This was the first visit of Mats Melin to Limerick where he later became a staff member. A standout memory for me that night was Kathleen MacInnes' singing of 'Òran Tàlaidh na Mnà-sìdhe' ('Lullaby of the Fairy Woman'), a song from the Tolmie Collection, afterwards included on her album. It presents a dialogue in which the fairy woman utters magic formulae in order to entice the baby away from its mother. The mother counters with equally strong formulaic language to protect a baby from fairy interference. With Allan MacDonald as tutor, Kathleen's reanimation of the old song carried immense appeal. According to tradition, it had been one of the tests for women applying for a position as a nurse in MacLeod of Dunvegan's noble household on the Isle of Skye. Kathleen's striking singing brought out the full potential of the item.[1] (Figure 49.1)

Figure 49.1 '"Òran Tàlaidh na Mnà-sìdhe" from Songs of Rest and Recreation', *Journal of the Folk Song Society*, vol. 4, no. 16, 1911, pp. 174–5.

With film-maker, broadcaster and musician, Philip King (l), *River of Sound*, 1995.
PHOTOGRAPHER: COLM HENRY

With Eileen Ivers and the Irish Chamber Orchestra. PHOTOGRAPHER: COLM HENRY

With singer Brian Kennedy, *Lumen*, 1995.

With Seamus Heaney, honorary conferring, University of Limerick, 1996.
PHOTOGRAPHER: EOIN STEPHENSON

With (l-r) Nicholas Carolan, Nóirín Ní Riain, President Mary McAleese, Michael Mortell, Martin McAleese and Paul McGettrick, launch of Fleischmann's *Sources*, University College Cork, 1999.

With businessman and philanthropist Tim Mahony, Toyota Arts Initiative.
PHOTOGRAPHER: EOIN STEPHENSON

With Helen Phelan and first graduating music education class, University of Limerick, 1998.
PHOTOGRAPHER: EOIN STEPHENSON

With the Irish Chamber Orchestra CEO John Kelly (centre) and writer Brian Keenan.
PHOTOGRAPHER: EOIN STEPHENSON

With dancer and choreographer Colin Dunne. PHOTOGRAPHER: MAURICE GUNNING

With The Chieftains, University of Limerick President Edward Walsh, and Irish World Academy students. PHOTOGRAPHER: MAURICE GUNNING

With Indian Ambassador and guests, University of Limerick. PHOTOGRAPHER: EOIN STEPHENSON

With singers Maighread Ní Dhomhnaill and Lillis Ó Laoire (co-founder of Ionad na nAmhrán) and colleagues. PHOTOGRAPHER: EOIN STEPHENSON

With banjo player Barney McKenna, Sionna Festival, 2006. PHOTOGRAPHER: MAURICE GUNNING

With Mícheál 'Moley' and Eoin, 'Squeal Amach', Sionna Festival, 2004.
PHOTOGRAPHER: MAURICE GUNNING

With composer Bill Whelan and singer-musician Andy Irvine. PHOTOGRAPHER: EOIN STEPHENSON

With singer Joan Armatrading, 2006. PHOTOGRAPHER: MAURICE GUNNING

With musician Pecker Dunne. PHOTOGRAPHER: MAURICE GUNNING

With Catherine Foley, Irish World Academy. PHOTOGRAPHER: MAURICE GUNNING

With President of Ireland, Michael D. Higgins. PHOTOGRAPHER: MAURICE GUNNING

At the piano. PHOTOGRAPHER: COLM HENRY

Dara Bán Mac Donnchadha: Amhránaí cónaitheach

Thar aon ghné eile de thionchar dhearfach Mhíchíl ar an cheol agus ar an cheol Ghaelach go háirithe bhí an sciar de mhaoiniú Toyota Ireland a chuir sé ar leataobh don amhránaí cónaitheach sean-nóis. Bhí ceapachán Dhara Bháin Mhic Dhonnchadha (1939–2009) ar cheann de na buaicphointí dom féin le mo linn i Luimneach. Is iomaí éileamh a bhí ar mhaoiniú Toyota

* *Mingiliseach* is from a side form of the root in *meann*, kid, whence the diminutive *minnein*, a small kid; the ending seems founded on *leis* or *slios*. Hence *minnleiseach*, save that the sound is influenced by the following *maingiliseach*, from *mang-leis-ach*. The *i* before the *l* is a parasitic vowel.—G. H.

TRANSLATION.

[*Fairy sings*] "1. Behold my child, limbed like the kid and fawn, smiting the horses, seizing the accoutrements of the shod horses, the spirited steeds. My little child! 2. Oh, that I could see thy cattle-fold, high up on the mountain-side; a green, shaggy jacket about thy two white shoulders, with a linen shirt. My little child! 3. Oh, that I could behold thy team of horses: men following them; serving-women returning home, and the Catanaich † sowing the corn." [*His mother sings*] "4. O tender hero [*sing thrice*] whom my womb did bring forth, who didst swallow from my breast, who on my knee wast reared. 5. My child it is, my armful of yew [bows and arrows], merry and plump, my bulrush, my flesh and eggs, that will soon be speaking. Last year thou wast beneath my girdle, plant of fertility! and this year, fair and playful on my shoulder, thou wilt be going round the homestead. 6. (Obh, i-rinn obh-o!) Oh! let me not hear of thy being wounded. (Obh, etc.) Grey do thou become duly. (Obh, etc.) May

† *i.e.* men of the Clan Chattan, or here possibly Cattanachs.

175 C

ach rinne Mícheál cinnte go dtiomnófaí cuid de d'amhránaí ar an sean-nós. Nuair a phléigh muid cé a bheadh i gceist, i ndiaidh mo mhachnamh a dhéanamh ar an cheist, dar liom gurbh é an té ba mhó arbh airí air an gradam, Dara Bán, as an Aird Thoir i gCarna, Contae na Gaillimhe. Ba chomharsana béil dorais iad teaghlach Sheosaimh Uí Éanaí agus teaghlach Dhara Bháin, muintir Sheáin Choilm Mhic Dhonnchadha. B'as an dúchas céanna a fáisceadh an péire, cé go raibh Seosamh fiche bliain ní ba shine ná Dara. Bhí tuiscint faighte agam ar an saibhreas amhrán a bhí ag Dara Bán ag an Oireachtas. Chomh maith leis sin ag féilte éagsúla, bhí eolas agam ar an chumas a bhí ann mar amhránaí ar a theacht i láthair, ar bhinneas a ghutha agus ar chruinneas a stíle. Is iomaí ainm eile a rith trí m'intinn, ach dar liom go fírinneach gur deis ar leith a bhí ann aitheantas a thabhairt don chaighdeán iontach amhránaíochta a bhí ag Dara agus aitheantas a thabhairt chomh maith don cheantar de bharr shaibhreas an traidisiúin ann. Bhí Margaret O'Sullivan lárnach sa togra chomh maith agus gan a cuidiú leis an eagrúchán agus gach gné den tionscnamh ní éireodh leath chomh maith leis. Tháinig Dara Bán agus a dheartháir cleamhnais, Seán Ó Madaoin, go Luimneach agus chaith muid trí lá iontacha ina theannta agus sinn ag éisteacht lena chuid amhrán, lena chuid seanchais agus ag cur aithne air de réir a chéile. Bhí an t-amhránaí Celia Ní Fhatharta, as Cois Fharraige, Conamara, inár measc chomh maith, rud a thug sásamh ar leith do Dhara Bán. Fear ciúin a bhí ann ach ba léir gur duine diongbháilte a bhí ann chomh maith. Thuig sé ina chroí go raibh rud luachmhar, rud annamh, aige agus bhí bród speisialta air as sin. Ba é an té a d'fhan sa bhaile nuair a scaip formhór a chuid siblíní ar imirce go Sasana agus go Boston, agus níor chaith sé mórán ama ar an scoil. Michael Mháire Ghabha Ó Ceannabháin an comrádaí mór a bhí aige i rith a shaoil, agus bhí an bheirt an-mhór lena chéile. Léiríonn an caradas sin neart an dúchais ar an Aird Thiar agus ar an Aird Thoir. Tá clann Mhichael ar fad geall leis sáite i gcúrsaí ceoil agus amhránaíochta ar bhealach amháin nó ar bhealach eile. B'iontach an t-oideachas dúinn i Luimneach cuairt Dhara Bháin.

Bhí gné eile ag baint leis an tréimhse chónaitheach, chomh maith leis na hamhráin a thaifeadadh. Bhí scannán le déanamh. Leis an chomhlacht JDM Productions thosaigh muid orainn agus chuir muid scannán leathuaire le chéile faoi Dhara Bán. Bhí fúinn ceann ní b'fhaide a dhéanamh ach sa phlé a bhí againn le TG4, socraíodh gur fiche sé nóiméad a bheadh ann. Chuaigh an clár amach ar dtús i 1998 agus bíonn sé á chraoladh ó am go ham ó shin. Nuair a bhuaigh Dara Bán gradam amhránaí na bliana ó TG4 sa bhliain 2007, cuireadh sleachta as an scannán sin amach mar thaca leis an taispeántas ag an bhronnadh.

Dara Bán's legacy of song was recorded on film and sound for posterity and remains in the Glucksman Library Special Collections at UL. It is a very satisfying thought that his songs and his artistic commitment to them, stemming from a strong continuous family tradition, received recognition from a university with a new forward-looking music faculty. The residency acknowledged Dara Bán as an individual and valued his artistry and excellence in the present. While recording the material for future use and paying homage to its importance as belonging to a distinct time and place, it could also be celebrated as belonging to and inhering in the present. This highlighting of the contemporary relates directly to Mícheál's vision for traditional music and indeed all music. His time in An Rinn, when he came to know Nioclás Tóibín personally, was undoubtedly influential, as was his own identity as a performer and his respect for others who shared a similar identity. Is mór an chomaoin a chuir Mícheál orm féin agus ar an amhránaíocht ar an *sean-nós* dá bharr sin.

Mícheál had a deep and abiding interest in the Irish language and *sean-nós* song since his youth. Undoubtedly stimulated by Seán Ó Riada's championing of the style and the songs, he broadened and deepened his knowledge because of his own interest in it. He encouraged his students to do the same, making them listen closely to songs on their personal stereos as part of his course on traditional music in Cork. In 1995, when composing *Missa Gadelica*, he gathered a group of traditional singers together, including myself, to form a core part of the ensemble. Using religious poetry by Seán E. Ó Cearbhaill (1922–2011), he set some to traditional airs and composed new melodies for parts of the liturgy. The rehearsals in Dromore were highly enjoyable gatherings where everyone had a lot of fun while also working hard. During a tea break, I happened to sing him a short sacred text. Seán Ó hEochaidh had ensured that Séamus Ennis wrote down the music of seven sacred songs during a collecting trip to Donegal in 1944 for Coimisiún Béaloideasa Éireann. I first became aware of them through Angela Bourke's (Partridge) work on the oral poetry of Jesus' passion. I sought them out and learned some of them with help from Teresa Doohan, a neighbour in Gort A' Choirce, Donegal, who could read music. I had begun performing one in particular, a 'Gloria' that I called 'Glóir Nóra Ní Ghallchobhair', after the woman from whom it had been recorded. I sang the 'Gloria' for Mícheál and he was very taken with it. It became part of *Missa Gadelica* almost immediately (see Figure 49.2).

That song remained a connection between us over the years after I left Limerick finally to take up a position in Galway in 2006. When, in 2017 he was planning a major concert at the NCH with the RTÉ

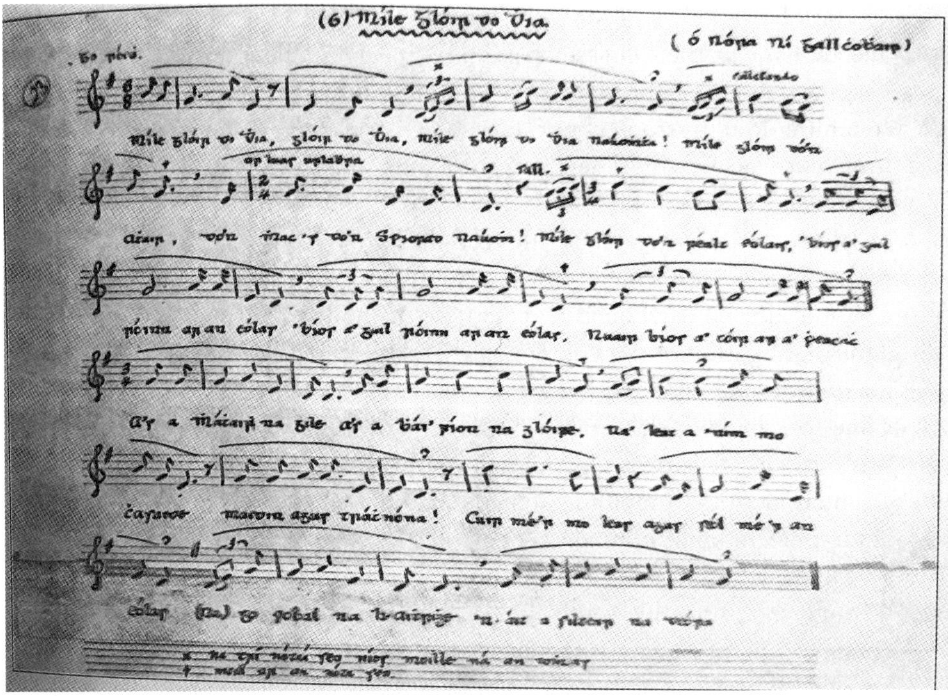

Figure 49.2: '"Míle Glóir do Dhia" ó Nóra Ní Ghallchobhair'. A fair copy of a transcription by Séamus Ennis based on his own recording of the piece from Nóra. (National Folklore Collection) CC 020.023. Used by permission.

Symphony Orchestra, he asked me to sing it again in a new full orchestral arrangement he had written for the piece. In his introductory essay for the programme, characteristically, he remembered Nóra, Séamus Ennis and Seán Ó hEochaidh. It was an incredible bringing together and merging of disparate traditions in a distinctive and beautiful arrangement. For this unforgettable concert he also wrote new orchestral arrangements for three poems by Seán Ó Ríordáin that he had set to music many years previously, 'Seachtain', 'Colm' and 'Fill Arís'. He also gathered Iarla Ó Lionáird and Síle Denvir to him and we all engaged with the complex settings Mícheál had composed for these song-poems. Mícheál presided over our meetings, remaining unfailingly patient and buoyant. The night in Dublin was a great occasion full of joy and celebration. Although Mícheál was clearly not well, his exuberant spirit never flagged during rehearsals, and he remained cheerful and present throughout. I learned later that he was working on arrangements for all seven of Nóra's sacred songs. Sadly, his time ran out before he finished this work. I was humbled to sing the 'Gloria' again at his funeral in Kilrush in November 2018. A few nights before that, I had been participating in an event to honour the late Siobhán McKenna, Galway's own actor, director and passionate advocate for Irish language and culture. The beginning of November made me especially mindful that it was Mí na Marbh, the month of the dead. After opening remarks by University of Galway president Ciarán Ó hÓgartaigh, I introduced Lelia Doolin, who gave a splendid lecture on Siobhán's legacy. There were also wonderful musical performances from Johnny Óg Connolly and from Rita Connolly and the Shaun Davey Ensemble. Just as we finished after a very cheering night, the news came that Mícheál had died. It seemed uncanny, given where we were. An Taibhdhearc, the National Irish Language Theatre, venue for countless performances of drama, music, song, dance, poetry and literature over the ninety years seemed, in the dimness before we started, to recollect the passage from Joyce's famous story 'The Dead' in which those gone ahead hovered near, in some kind of intimate but fleetingly unfathomable rapport.

The day of his funeral saw the hosts descend on the beautiful church of St Senan's in Kilrush to bid farewell to someone who had been a major force for good on Irish music for forty years and whose influence will continue for much longer. The ritual clown, a representation of the Archangel Michael, reminded us that a new journey had begun and that the playfulness of life continued regardless. It was by turns humbling and thrilling to be a part of the day. Writing now about Mícheál's life and my experiences with him on his journey makes me understand with greater clarity what a great and positive influence he had on my life and career, a gift for which I remain deeply grateful and one that increases in value with the passing of time.

50
Cófra na mBeart Caillte
Áine Uí Cheallaigh

Áine Uí Cheallaigh is from Belfast but has lived most of her life in Gaeltacht na nDéise where she was principal of Meánscoil San Nioclás for twenty-two years. She has won Corn Uí Riada twice and performed in Riverdance *and in the musical* The Pirate Queen *on Broadway. She holds an MA Chant and Ritual Song from the University of Limerick.*

'In ainm Dé, a Áine, cad is brí leis sin?'

Sin an beannú a thug Mícheál dom agus é ag seoladh isteach doras Mheánscoil San Nioclás sa Rinn, mí Eanáir, 2006. Bhí sé de dhánaíocht agamsa a iarraidh air teacht i gcomhpháirt liom agus saothar ilghnéitheach á léiriú agam, eisean i bhfeighil an cheoil agus mar chrann seasta na hoibre. Níl mórán daoine dá leithéid, ollamh, cumadóir agus ceoltóir i mbarr a réime, a thoilfeadh a bheith páirteach i dtogra i scoil bheag tuaithe, ach bhí a chroí istigh sa scoil áirithe seo agus ghlac sé go fonnmhar leis an gcoimisiún beag, rud ná díolfadh riamh é as a chuid ama ná a chuid cruthaitheachta; ach ba bheag leis é sin.

Tháinig Mícheál go dtí Gaeltacht na nDéise chun cónaí ann ar feadh seal i 1973 agus, mar sin, bhí a cháil amuigh air i bhfad sular tháinig mise chun cur fúm ann. Chloisinn na scéalta faoi agus é ina fhear óg ag múineadh sa scoil agus an cór sa tséipéal faoina stiúir; an tslí ina mbíodh sé ag cuimsiú an tsean-nóis leis an méarchlár, an tsuim a léirigh sé sa chanúint agus go háirithe an meas a bhí aige ar Nioclás Tóibín. Bhí an-chuimhneamh ag an bpobal áitiúil air ó thaobh an cheoil de, ach bhíodar tógtha chomh maith leis an ngreann agus an deisbhéalacht a bhain leis, agus lena phearsantacht gheal spreagúil. D'fhág sé a rian ar na daoine agus níor chaill seisean riamh a ghean dóibhsan. Ní raibh uair gur bhuail mé leis nach raibh cuimhne cinn le riaradh aige nó nár fhiaraigh sé faoi chlann éigin den dúiche.

Scríobh Áine Uí Fhoghlú, file ón Rinn, an dán 'Duan Déiseach' mar bhunábhar an tsaothair nua. Thaitin an dán go mór le Mícheál. Is cuimhin liom go maith é ag léamh na bhfocal seo thíos agus sinn go léir timpeall an bhoird san oifig an chéad lá, Fearghus Ó Conchúir, an rinceoir a bhí i mbun cóiréagrafaíochta, farainn chomh maith:

Fuinfead duit fáinne fí
fífead duit fleasc focal
is maiseod le féithleog
feileastram is an conrós cumhra.

Léigh Mícheál go mall cúramach, ag baint suilt as fuaimeanna na bhfocal. Ba léir nár thuig sé gach rud, dála gach éinne a bhí i láthair ach an file í féin. Ar deireadh, d'ardaigh sé a cheann. Bhí miongháire ar a aghaidh agus lasair ina shúile le teann fiosrachta, é cíocrach chun brí iomlán na bhfocal a bhaint amach agus a mhaisiú lena ealaín féinig. Spreag na focail chun ceoil é.

Bhí daltaí na scoile chun a bheith lárnach sa saothar agus bhídis ag pléascadh do chuairteanna Mhíchíl, mar a bheadh seanchara ag teacht chucu. D'aithin sé cuid acu as a muintir agus cheistíodh sé iad mar gheall orthu. Thuig sé a nginealach agus a n-oidhreacht; bhí sé féin ag baint sásaimh as glúin eile ag síolrú ón bhfód céanna agus bhí meas aige orthu dá réir. Bhí dáimh aige leo. Ní bhfaighfeá luach a chur ar an maitheas a dhein sé ins na míonna sin. Thuirlingíodh sé mar spéirling ag líonadh an halla. Léirigh sé féin an uaisleacht agus an t-údarás lena raibh sé ag súil uathusan. Mheall sé chun misnigh iad sa tslí is gur chuaigh siad i bhfad thar aon acmhainní a cheapadar a bheith iontu féin roimhe sin. Ardoideachasóir ba ea é.

Samhlaigh an chíor thuathail lá nó dhó roimh ré agus nócha dalta ina mbuíonta éagsúla: an cór, cór labhartha agus ceoltóirí traidisiúnta na scoile; Mícheál ag an mórphianó mar thionlacóir agus é ag stiúradh téadcheathairéid; mé féin fós ag foghlaim na n-amhrán; an bhuíon rince mar scata ghéanna ar strae; an chóir stáitse fós á réiteach........ Shíl mé go rabhamar in umar na haimléise, ach má cheap Mícheál go raibh cúrsaí in

Figure 50.1: Postaer don seó Duan Déiseach.

Figure 50.2: Fearghus Ó Conchúir, Áine Uí Cheallaigh, Mícheál Ó Súilleabháin agus Áine Uí Fhoghlú.

amhréidh, níor lig sé air. Thug sé ugach don bhfoireann uilig agus d'ardaigh sé ár meanma.

Bhí an aimsir niamhrach ar fad gach aon oíche den taispeántas, dul faoi na gréine taobh thiar dínn agus an spéir ina lasair ag na tinte ealaíne a chuir críoch spleodrach leis an seó; gach duine cruinnithe timpeall an easa nua amuigh a bhí ina chaise den chéad uair. Bhí Mícheál ina sheasamh i measc an tslua. D'aithin sé go leor a bhí ann; d'éist sé leis na léirmheasanna ar a chuid oibre. Bhí sé níos fearr ná na Tonys! Gan dabht, bhí a chuid cumadóireachta aoibhinn álainn, ach ar shlí, ba chuma san; ba é an t-aitheantas a thug sé do dhúchas na háite ba mhó a shásaigh agus a mheall na daoine chuige. Ba léir air go raibh sé 'sa mbaile'.

Maidr leis an bprios úd, Cófra na mBeart Caillte, a bhíodh ag cur thar maoil le truflais agus farasbarr na ndaltaí: shádh Mícheál a cheann isteach ann go minic amhail is gur phúicín draíochta a bhí ann agus é ag lorg seoidín éigin laistigh.

Bhí cúpla nóta siar is aniar eadrainn tar éis 'Duan Déiseach' agus seo mar a scríobh sé i gceann acu:

> Obair sa bhreis le déanamh againn go léir fós. Idir an dá linn, deireann an foghlaí mara eile, (Ó Foghlú) go bhfuil Rap na mBeart Caillte tosnaithe aici. Athbheochaint na nDéise le teacht fós. 'Sé Rap (=Reacaireacht) ná, Cantaireacht na cistine comhaimseartha.

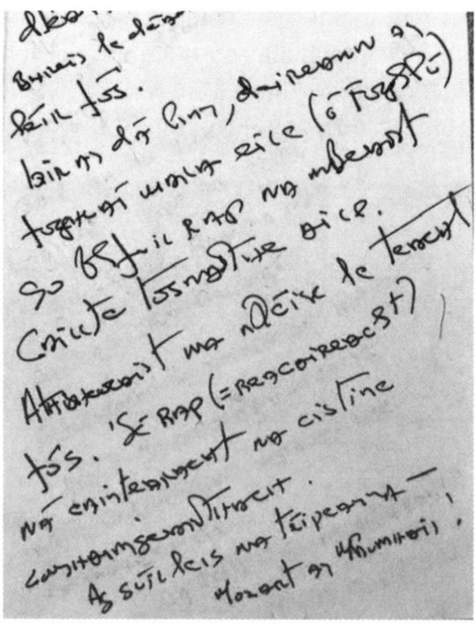

Figure 50.3: Nóta ó Mhícheál.

Shínigh sé é féin: 'Mozart na Mumhan!' Bhí sé cliste leis an teanga agus féith an ghrinn de shíor ann.

Luadh sé an Ríordánach go minic. Scríobh sé na líntí seo ó 'Fill Arís' i gceann eile de na nótaí: 'Buail is osclófar/ D'intinn féin is do chló ceart'. D'aithin Mícheál a fhíorchló agus d'fhíoraigh sé go mórtasach é.

... dein
Síocháin led ghiniúin féinig
Is led thigh-se féin is ná tréig iad
Ní dual do neach a thigh ná a threabh a thréigean.

Is mó gradam agus ardmholadh a fuair sé i rith a shaoil ach níor dhearúd Mícheál riamh an dream ar díobh é. Gael dílis ba ea é, agus ní beag san.

This piece recalls several of Mícheál's visits to the secondary school Meánscoil San Nioclás in An Rinn during 2006. He worked there, in collaboration with a poet, musicians and dancers, to compose a memorable and inspiring work which was performed to great excitement to packed houses. It describes his love for the Irish language and the Gaeltacht, his sense of fun, his ability to connect with people of all ages, and his great curiosity about everything, including the school's lost property cupboard.

51
Téada Machnaimh agus Téada Gutha: Ceist na teangan sa cheol Gaelach

Tríona Ní Shíocháin

Tríona Ní Shíocháin is a sean-nós *singer, whistle player and interdisciplinary scholar of music and Irish. She is currently professor of modern irish and performing arts at Maynooth University, and previously was head of the Department of Music at University College Cork where she was also a lecturer in Irish traditional music.*

Léirigh Mícheál Ó Súilleabháin suim dhoimhin in oidhreacht na filíochta Gaelainne go luath agus é ar bhóthar an cheoil, mar is léir ón dtráchtas máistreachta a chuir sé i gcrích i gColáiste na hOllscoile, Corcaigh, i 1973, dar teideal 'The Songs of Three Eighteenth-Century Munster Poets'. D'fhéadfaí a rá dá réir go raibh an fhilíocht agus an ceol ag tionnscailt a chéile ina shaothar agus ina mhachnamh ó thús. Ba léir go raibh nasc ann i gcónaí in intinn Mhichíl idir an teanga féin agus an ceol, idir an chruthaitheacht agus an traidisiún béil, idir an fás agus an fhréamh. Spreagann na téada machnaimh sin a d'fhorbair Mícheál ina shaol acadúil agus ina shaothar cruthaitheach a thuilleadh ceisteanna fén ngaol idir an bhéalaireacht agus an chumadóireacht, agus idir an teanga agus an ceol. Ag tógaint ar theoiricíocht úd an tSúilleabhánaigh, déanfar plé insa chaibidil seo ar cheist na teangan i ndomhan inmheánach na cumadóireachta, agus ar an ngaol idir an teanga fhileata agus struchtúr na séise ceoil sa traidisiún Gaelach. Seachas féachaint ar an ngaol idir an teanga agus an ceol mar rud dénártha, is féidir an gaol casta céanna san a thuiscint mar ghné bhunaidh de mhodh machnaimh comhtháite comhthrasnach lena mbaineann idir ilghuthacht agus ionchollú. Creidim go bhfreagraíonn an teoiricíocht so d'aestéitic na béalaireachta atá le sonrú ar shaothar cruthaitheach an tSúilleabhánaigh, go mba ghné speisialta í den taighde ealaíonta a chuir sé chun cinn trí mheán an chleachtais chruthaithigh i gcaitheamh a shaoil. Mar chlabhsúr ar an aiste seo, fillfead ar choincheapa fileata de chuid Sheáin Uí Ríordáin a chuimsíonn gnéithe lárnacha de mhachnamh cruthaitheach an tSúilleabhánaigh.

It was very early in his career that Mícheál Ó Súilleabháin demonstrated a deep interest in Irish-language poetic heritage as part of his studies in music, as demonstrated by his 1973 MA thesis entitled 'The Songs of Three Eighteenth-Century Munster Poets' (University College Cork). One could go so far as to say that Irish-language poetry and music accompanied one another in his work and thought even from his earliest years as a composer and academic, and it was clear that the language and the music were interlocking components of Mícheál's broader philosophy. Similarly, the value he placed on oral vernacular practices within Irish traditional music was key to the innovations he pioneered as a university teacher while also underpinning his own creative practices. Inspired by those téada machnaimh *or 'strings of thought' as developed by Mícheál in his life and work, this essay will briefly explore the relationship of the Irish language to music. Drawing on Ó Súilleabháin's analysis of the life and work of Seán Ó Riada, I will firstly discuss the place of the Irish language within the liminal post-colonial conceptual world of the composer and in the work of Ó Súilleabháin himself. I will then focus specifically on the relationship of poetic language to musical structure in the oral tradition. I argue that this consideration of language and music ultimately moves us away from binary or polarising distinctions, and more towards an enmeshed and interlocking mode of creative thought that encompasses multivocality and embodiment. This, I believe, corresponds to the oral aesthetics of Ó Súilleabháin's compositional practice, which was integral to the distinctive artistic research conceptualisation he communicated through his creative work. To conclude, I will consider some poetic concepts of Seán Ó Ríordáin, inspired by the Corca Dhuibhne Gaeltacht, which resonate strongly with Ó Súilleabháin's artistic and scholarly practice.*

Téada machnaimh

D'athchruthaigh an tOllamh Mícheál Ó Súilleabháin paraidímí oideolaíochta an cheoil ó bhonn le linn do a bheith ina léachtóir i Roinn an Cheoil i gColáiste na hOllscoile Corcaigh, agus ina dhiaidh sin arís nuair a ceapadh é ina ollamh le ceol in Ollscoil Luimnigh, áit inar bhunaigh sé Dámh Chruinne Éireann.[1] Dlúthchuid dá fhealsúnacht ba ea an tábhacht ollmhór a bhaineann leis an dtuiscint ar leith a eascraíonn as an gcleachtas féin, agus na slite machnaimh is dual don traidisiún beo béil go speisialta.[2] Cheangail téada machnaimh a shaothair an t-eolas ealaíonta leis an eolas stairiúil, an traidisiún béil leis an gcumadóireacht chomhaimseartha, agus tuiscintí sainiúla na teangan le tuiscintí sainiúla an cheoil. Díol suime ba ea an tslí inar nasc sé sanasaíocht na Gaelainne go minic leis na coincheapa ceoleolaíochtúla a bhí á bhforbairt aige: na nathanna cainte 'ag casadh ceoil' agus 'cas amhrán' a bhí mar bhunús leis an gcoincheapú íogair a dhein sé ar phróiseas cruthaitheach an cheoil thraidisiúnta, mar shampla.[3] Ar an gcuma chéanna is ea a thagair sé don dul cainte 'ag déanamh ceoil' agus síothlú á dhéanamh aige ar choincheap na cumadóireachta laistigh de chultúr an cheoil dhúchais, cumadóireacht nárbh ionann í agus cleachtais chumadóireachta cheol ealaíne Iarthar na hEorpa.[4] Roimis sin arís i 1973, agus é ag tosnú amach ar bhóthar an léinn an chéad uair is ea a dhírigh a thráchtas máistreachta i Roinn an Cheoil, Coláiste na hOllscoile, Corcaigh, ar fhilí Gaelacha ón ochtú haois déag.[5] Mar sin tá tionchar na Gaelainne le brath ar chroílár a chuid teoiricíochta ar struchtúir agus ar nósanna an cheoil Ghaelaigh féin ó thús. Díol suime leis is ea an saothar ceoleolaíochta a d'fhoilsigh sé as Gaelainn in *Comhar* i 1977, alt dar teideal 'Gnéithe Áirithe de Cheardaíocht Phádraig Uí Cheallaigh (Patrick Kelly): Fidléir ó Chontae an Chláir', saothar luath uaidh ina bhfaighimid léargas ar a chuid machnaimh ar phróiseas cruthaitheach an cheoil thraidisiúnta, machnamh a d'fhorbrófaí go mór mar chuid dá shaothar dochtúireachta ina dhiaidh sin.[6] Mionanailís cheoleolaíoch ar an bpróiseas cruthaitheach a chleacht sé, ónar fhás meititheoiric ar an gceol traidisiúnta, agus ina mbíodh coincheap na teangan féin go minic mar ghléas anailíse aige: 'The player manifests firstly his musical idiolect, secondly his musical dialect, and finally the musical language itself which we identify as Irish traditional music.'[7] Ba chuige seo an cheoleolaíocht i gcás Mhichíl Uí Shúilleabháin: chun iniúchadh a dhéanamh ón dtaobh laistigh ar theangain an cheoil thraidisiúnta, cé nach 'teanga uilíoch' d'aon tsaghas a bhí i gceist leis an gcoincheapú áirithe sin ar an gceol.[8]

Insan aiste ghairid seo, ba mhaith liom tógaint ar theoiricíocht an tSúilleabhánaigh ar phróiseas cruthaitheach na béalaireachta sa cheol agus í a nascadh le coincheap na teangan féin. Díreofar ar dtúis ar thábhacht na Gaelainne i ndomhan iarchoilíneach tairseachúil an chumadóra; agus ina dhiaidh sin déanfar iniúchadh ar ionad na teangan fileata i struchtúr na séise saor-rithimiúla ceoil, ina n-áitím gur féidir an teanga fhileata féin a thuiscint mar 'fho-intinn' cheoil de shórt. Ní hann do thraidisiún teibí teoirice sa cheol traidisiúnta ó dhúchas: is amhlaidh a mhair córais shofaisticiúla an cheoil, idir rithim agus séis agus stíl, sa traidisiún béil agus sa chleachtas cruthaitheach féin.[9] Córas smaointeoireachta ann féin ba ea an ceol dúchais riamh anall nár lean tráchtaireacht ar bith é ar uairibh ar an abhar gur mhinic a mhair an t-eolas cuí sa chleachtas féin amháin.[10] Eolas ionchollaithe a rith tríd an gcorp, tríd an gcluais, agus tríd an mbéalaireacht ba ea é. Bhain téada gutha go dlúth le téada machnaimh ionchollaithe seo an cheoil le hoidhreacht, téada atá le sonrú chomh maith céanna ar shaothar cruthaitheach an tSúilleabhánaigh féin.

An teanga, an tairseachúlacht, agus domhan coincheapúil na cumadóireachta

Is minic a shamhlaítear ceol ealaíne na hEorpa a bheith bun os cionn le cleachtais dhúchais an cheoil Ghaelaigh agus d'fhéadfaí a áiteamh gur domhan coincheapúil ceoil ann féin a bhí le fáil sa traidisiún Gaelach.[11] Ba léir, áfach, gur tuigeadh tábhacht ana-mhór a bheith le hoidhreacht na Gaelainne i ré na hathbheochana nuair a tugadh fé cheol ealaíne de chuid na hÉireann a athchruthú agus a athGhaelú,[12] cé nach i gcónaí a d'éirigh leis na hiarrachtaí sin, áfach, mar a d'áitigh Ó Súilleabháin: 'Fruitless efforts were made to force a wedding between the Irish language and the European art-music tradition in the interest of de-anglicisation.'[13] Ba léir, mar sin féin, gur tuigeadh don Súilleabhánach ó thus go mba dhlúthchuid den cheol féin í ceist na teangan, agus go raibh tochailt le déanamh i ndomhan na Gaelainne chun go bhféadfaí stair chasta an cheoil Ghaelaigh a thuiscint agus iniúchadh a dhéanamh ar chleachtais agus ar bhrí an cheoil féin. Ba léir an méid sin óna thráchtas MA, 'The songs of three eighteenth-century Munster poets', a bhí dírithe ar Aindrias Mac Craith, ar Sheán Ó Tuama an Ghrinn, agus ar Sheán Clárach Mac Domhnaill, agus inar chnuasaigh sé oiread fianaise agus arbh fhéidir ar chleachtais cheoil na bhfilí sin ó fhoinsí sna lámhscríbhinní agus ó shaothar na mbailitheoirí ceoil araon. Ba léir arís é i bhfad ina dhiaidh sin fós in 2004 ina pháipéar cáiliúil dar teideal 'Ceol na nUasal: Seán Ó Riada and the search for a native irish art music' a thug sé ar ócáid Léacht Chomórtha an Riadaigh i gColáiste na hOllscoile, Corcaigh, inar thagair sé don dán 'Fill Arís' agus an gaol idir an cultúr dúchais agus cleachtais chumadóireachta an Riadaigh fé chaibidil aige. Féineolas, féintuiscint, agus iniúchadh ar dhomhan eile a bhí á lorg ag an gcumadóir, mar a áitíonn an Súilleabhánach, agus macalla ba ea turas ceoil an Riadaigh de mheanmain an dáin cháiliúil sin de chuid an Ríordánaigh:

> Sin é do dhoras:
> Dún Chaoin fé sholas an tráthnóna
> Buail is osclófar
> D'intinn féin is do chló ceart.[14]

Murab ionann agus cumadóirí na hEorpa sa tréimhse chéanna san, turas isteach seachas turas amach a bhí á thabhairt ag an Riadach, dar leis an Súilleabhánach: 'While Ó Riada was travelling inwards – to borrow the words of Seán Ó Ríordáin "[ag dul] faobhar na faille siar tráthnóna gréine go Corca Dhuibhne" – composers like Stockhausen and John Cage were travelling outwards to Japan, Indonesia and India in search of another voice.'[15] In ionad tabhairt fé oirthearachas na nEorpach agus na Meiriceánach, is amhlaidh a bhí turas go dtína fhochomhfhios ceoil déanta ag an Riadach: 'He had made the journey inwards to his native tradition – like a visit to his own musical subconscious.'[16] Dlúthchuid den aistear suibiachtúil ceoil seo don Riadach ba ea an Ghaeltacht féin. Bhain an Ghaelainn dá réir sin le díchoilíniú nó le frithchoilíneachas, le frithbheartaíocht i gcoinnibh an chultúir oifigiúil. Eochair ba ea an Ghaelainn do 'chló ceart' an cheoil, cló ceoil ná beadh á smachtú ag gnásanna cheol ealaíne na hEorpa. Fealsúnacht chomh maith le teangain ba ea an Ghaelainn dá réir; ba ghréasán tuiscintí í an teanga féin a d'fhéadfadh machnamh nua ceoil a sholáthar a bheadh nasctha leis an dtraidisiún beo béil agus ag freagairt do staid chomhaimseartha na Nua-aoise ag an am gcéanna. Bhí brí feasta le baint as an dteannas nach beag idir an dá thraidisiún ceoil seo – an ceol ealaíne agus an ceol dúchais – agus tábhacht ar leith ag baint leis an staid idir eatarthu inar mhair lucht cumadóireachta, dála an Riadaigh, mar a áitíonn an Súilleabhánach: 'For Ó Riada to be positioned in mid-stream between both traditions in such a manner as to be increasingly aware of their separateness even as his need to find a link between them also increased was a kind of cultural crucifixion.'[17]

Ceist ana-chrosta a bhí le réiteach ag an gcumadóir dá réir: conas a thabharfaí an dá thraidisiún so le chéile chun síochána, agus an bhféadfaí go brách talamh slán a dhéanamh de ná plúchfaí aeistéitic an cheoil Ghaelaigh fé ualach agus fé stádas cheol ealaíne na hEorpa? Cuid d'fhealsúnacht chasta na cumadóireachta sa tsaol comhaimseartha ba ea domhan na Gaelainne don Riadach dá réir sin, agus do bb'amhlaidh dá dhalta, Mícheál Ó Súilleabháin, ina dhiaidh, cé nárbh ionann ar fad an dearcadh a bhí acu. Tá ionad tábhachtach ag amhráin na Gaelainne agus na Gaeltachta i gcleachtais chumadóireachta Mhichíl Uí Shúilleabháin sa tslí is go mba chuid lárnach de dhomhan coincheapúil a shaothair an Ghaelainn féin. Cuímhním, mar shampla, ar 'Casadh na Gráige' ón albam *Templum* in 2001, saothar a thógann ar leagan Sheáin de hÓra ó Chloichear den amhrán 'Iníon an Fhaoit' ón nGleann'. Do bhí 'faobhar na faille siar tráthnóna gréine go Corca Dhuibhne' á leanúint aige féin trí mheán an cheoil: ag filleadh ar dhomhan Gaelach na béalaireachta a bhí an cumadóir sa chás so, agus struchtúir chasta áille na saor-rithime agus na séise ó thraidisiún beo na hamhránaíochta ina lóchrann ina chuid cumadóireachta aige. Mar sin a bhí leis i gcás na bpíosaí dar teideal 'Bean Dubh an Ghleanna' agus 'Aisling Gheal' (a tiomnaíodh don Riadach) ar an albam céanna. Ach dála an Riadaigh a tháinig roimis, do bhí an áit idir eatarthu le sonrú go láidir chomh maith ar phróiseas cruthaitheach an tSúilleabhánaigh: is amhlaidh a bhíodh an tairseachúlacht chomhaimseartha iarchoilíneach agus tairseachúlacht oidhreachtúil na filíochta agus an cheoil féin ag cothú a chéile ina chuid cumadóireachta. Más fíor gur bhain ciapadh nó 'psychic distress' nó 'psychomusical struggle' áirithe leis an spás idir eatartha san idir saol an Bhéarla agus saol na Gaelainne don Riadach,[18] níorbh ionann é agus an Súilleabhánach ón dtaobh san de. Is amhlaidh a dheineadh an Súilleabhánach an spás idir eatarthu san a iniúchadh agus a cheiliúradh, mar a bhí le clos ina shaothar *Between Two Worlds* a eisíodh i 1995, mar shampla, agus cuid lárnach dá chleachtas cruthaitheach ba ea an comhnascadh nó an t-agallamh idir traidisiúin dhifriúla cheoil. Chímid téama na tairseachúlachta go láidir chun cinn ina cheolchoirm cháiliúil *Between Worlds: The music of Mícheál Ó Súilleabháin. Exploring the space between traditions* sa Cheoláras Náisiúnta i samhradh na bliana 2018, mar shampla, achar gearr sarar imigh sé féin ar shlí na fírinne. Mar a dúirt sé féin i bhfíseán poiblíochta don cheolchoirm sin, is é a bheadh le clos inti ná 'the sound of different cultures meeting', agus go bhfaighfí éachtaint ann ar 'the various worlds of music and how they talked to each other in a kind of liminal threshold space and the magic that happens in the space between night and day, in the space between different polarities and opposites'.[19] Míníonn Ó Súilleabháin an caidreamh idir na córais dhifriúla smaointeoireachta ceoil seo le linn an taibhithe féin mar chomhrá: 'I always feel myself it is like a conversation going on.'[20] Cumarsáid ba ea í seo a dhéanfaí trí mheán an chleachtais chruthaithigh féin, nó mar a dúirt sé féin agus é i mbun comhráidh le hIarla Ó Lionáird fé cheol an phianó a nascadh leis an amhránaíocht ar an sean-nós díreach sarar thugadar fén amhrán 'An Buachaill Caol Dubh' le chéile: 'Well, will we have a little conversation on this song purely through the music and the words?'[21] D'fhág a ghrá d'amhráin agus d'fhoinn na Gaeltachta go mbíodh cuisle na teangan féin i gcónaí lárnach sa domhan cruthaitheach cumarsáide a d'fháisc sé as spás tairseachúil na cumadóireachta comhaimseartha.

Téada gutha: an teanga fhileata agus struchtúr na séise ceoil

Léiríonn saothar Mhichíl Uí Shúilleabháin tábhacht agus luach aeistéitiúil na béalaireachta ina phróiseas cruthaitheach agus ina fhorbairtí nuálacha curraclaim araon. D'fhág an cur chuige oideolaíochta aige, inar leagadh béim ar leith ar an gcleachtas, go bhféadfadh an traidisiún béil labhairt uaidh féin gan traidisiún nodaireachta Iarthar na hEorpa a bheith á smachtú ná á chur as a riocht;[22] d'fhág ionad lárnach na bhfonn traidisiúnta ina shaothar mar aon leis an neamhspleáchas a thugadh a chuid cumadóireachta do phróiseas cruthaitheach an cheoltóra nó an amhránaí thraidisiúnta féin go bhféadfadh cleachtais bheo an traidisiúin bhéil a bheith ag labhairt uathu féin i gcomhthéacs na nua-chumadóireachta, gan umhlú do nósanna clasaiceacha ach a bheith i gcomhpháirt nó i gcomhimeartas leo.[23] Spás cruthaitheach ab é seo ina raibh domhan samhailteach na Gaelainne agus na Gaeltachta lárnach, é ar aon chéim agus ar aon stáitse le ceol ealaíne ardréimneach na hEorpa. Spás chun cumarsáide agus spás chun imeartha a chruthaigh sé, spás a bhí ag tarrac ar choincheapa traidisiúnta na tairseachúlachta i gcosmeolaíocht dúchais na hÉireann ar thaobh amháin agus ar thualangacht chruthaitheach na tairseachúlachta comhaimseartha ar an dtaobh eile. Sa tslí seo, is féidir linn saothar cumadóireachta an tSúilleabhánaigh a thuiscint mar shaothar taighde ealaíonta a chuir mórán i dtuiscint dúinn trí mheán an cheoil agus na hamhránaíochta amháin, beag beann ar an dtráchtaireacht féin.

Teastaíonn uaim filleadh anois ar ghné amháin des na téada éagsúla machnaimh a d'fhorbair sé ina shaothar cruthaitheach agus ceoleolaíochta, ag díriú go speisialta ar bhuncheist taighde a chuir sé roimis ina thráchtas MA i 1973, is é sin le rá, cad é an gaol idir an fhilíocht agus an ceol sa traidisiún Gaelach? Baineann téada gutha go mór le saineolas ceoil ó dhúchas sa domhan Gaelach. Bíonn gluaiseacht ar leith fén saor-rithim ar dlúthchuid d'aeistéitic an cheoil í, agus is iad na focail féin a rialaíonn eispéireas san na rithime agus an ama.[24] Mar sin cé nach ann do theoiric theibí le hoidhreacht sa cheol traidisiúnta, do mhair córais agus rialacha coimpléascacha an cheoil sna cleachtais chruthaitheacha féin.[25] Idir phortaireacht agus amhránaíocht, traidisiún ceoil is ea é seo ina bhfuil an guth féin lárnach, ina dtreoraíonn cleachtais ghutha dul na hornáidíochta agus na rithime agus struchtúir shéiseacha an cheoil. Do thagair Seán Ó Ríordáin tráth do choincheap na fo-intinne ina dhán dar teideal 'Na Blascaodaí': 'An chuimhne fho-intinneach lean / Ag fo-chogarnach ionainn go ciúin … / Chuaigh ár gcúrintinn éadrom go tóin / Nocht ár bhfo-intinn folaigh mar chúr …'[26] Bun-eisint is ea an fho-intinn seo a bhíonn i bhfolach ar uairibh ach gurb ann di agus dá tionchar mar sin féin; b'fhéidir gurb ionann an fhilíocht agus fo-intinn an cheoil sa traidisiún Gaelach. Áitím gurb ann do bhun-nasc idir an ceol agus an teanga go doimhin ar leibhéal na haeistéitice: tá struchtúr casta na saor-rithime ceangailte go dlúth le friotal agus le meadarachtaí na Gaelainne, agus anuas air sin, tá próiseas cruthaitheach an amhránaí ag brath ar mháistreacht a bheith aige/aici ar an ngaol casta san idir an fonn agus rithimiúlacht na bhfocal. Nó mar a dúirt an scoláire iomráiteach, Donncha Ó Cróinín, ó Ghaeltacht Mhúscraí tráth, ní mór 'fonn is focail a tháthadh go ceart'.[27] Tá ollstruchtúr an cheoil pósta leis an dteangain fhileata sa tslí is nach fuirist iad a dheighilt. Mar a dúirt an tOllamh Breandán Ó Madagáin tráth i dtaobh choibhneas na filíochta leis an gceol sa traidisiún Gaelach, '[níorbh] fhéidir neamhshuim a dhéanamh de thaobh amháin den aonad gan an ealaín a chur as a riocht a bheag nó a mhór'.[28] Is fada an fhilíocht agus an ceol ag tionnscailt a chéile sa traidisiun Gaelach,[29] agus leagann Ó Súilleabháin ana-bhéim ar 'the everpresent connection between poetry and music in the Irish tradition' i réamhrá a thráchtais MA.[30] Díol suime, mar shampla, is ea an méid a bhí le rá ag an bhfile Gaelach, Pádraig Ó Crualaoi (Gael na nGael) ar thábhacht an cheoil i bpróiseas cumadóireachta na filíochta:

> Is minic a bheadh filíocht ag duine agus ná beadh aon cheol aige. D'fhéadfá 'breacfhile' a thúirt ar a lithéid sin. Ní bheadh an buala ró-chruínn aige. Bheadh sé achrannach anso is ansúd aige, agus loitfeadh san an t-amhrán. An file a bhíonn go maith dineann sé an ceol leis na focail agus leis a' gcaint: bíonn said a' freagairt a chéile i gcónaí.[31]

Is dlúthchuid í an teanga féin de dhomhan inmheánach coincheapúil an cheoil dá réir sin, idir bhealaí sainiúla na séise agus phoncaíocht shainiúil na rithime, ar an abhar nach féidir an tsaor-rithim a scarúint ón tslí ina bhfitear focail le fonn. Ina theannta san, ní hann go beacht do struchtúr an fhoinn cheoil go dtí go dtugann an t-amhránaí uaidh/uaithi é – is athchumadóir le ceart é an t-amhránaí, seachas 'seachadóir' amháin, ealaíontóir a mhúnlaíonn an tséis agus an rithim de réir a stíle féin agus de réir a t(h) uisceana aeistéitiúla féin.[32] Ní gá ach éisteacht le leaganacha difriúla na n-amhránaithe féin chun an flosc cruthaitheach so is bunús le struchtúir na séise féin i dtraidisiún an tsean-nóis a thuiscint: mar shampla, leagan Sheosaimh Uí Éanaí den amhrán 'Dónal Óg' a chur i gcomparáid le leagan Bhríd Ní Mhaoilchiaráin den amhrán céanna,[33] ina dtéann stíl shainiúil álainn na beirte i bhfeidhm ar an bhfonn ar bhealaí difriúla; nó leagan Sheáin de hÓra den amhrán 'Maidin Álainn Ghréine' le Máire Bhuí Ní Laeire, ina gcloisimid beart dhochreidte chruthaitheachta sa gheábh aoibhinn ard uaidh i dtosach an tríú véarsa.[34] Fágann an cleachtas dúchais cruthaitheach san bun-nasc idir an taibhiú féin agus struchtúr an cheoil nach féidir a scarúint ó chéile choíche. Sin é an taobh go luann an Súilleabhánach nach ann do choincheap an chumadóra sa traidisiún Gaelach fé mar a thuigtear an focal san sa cheol clasaiceach, agus gur tábhachtaí coincheap an fhile sa traidisiún.[35] Cumadóir fé cheilt is ea an t-amhránaí féin taobh leis an bhfile áfach, nó mar a déarfadh an Súilleabhánach: 'The non-literate oral-tradition music of this country regenerates itself through creative performance, not through composition …'[36] Braitheann láimhseáil éifeachtach na séise saor-rithimiúla ar thuiscint inchollaithe an amhránaí (nó an fhile) ar shoshínteacht na bhfocal agus na meadarachta. Eolas meadarachta is ea é seo atá nasctha leis an gceol agus a mhaireann ní ar phár ach i gcorp agus i dtéada gutha an amhránaí. D'fhéadfaí a rá gurb í an teanga fhileata féin cuisle an cheoil, nuair is ceol saor-rithimeach é. Fiú amháin i gcás fonn ná fuil focail ag gabháil leo, bíonn nósanna na hamhránaíochta chomh mór san in uachtar go gcloistear a dtionchar ar chúrsaí frásaíochta, fiú amháin nuair nach ann dos na focail in aon chor. Mar seo atá aon uair a chloistear fonn amhráin á fhí ar an gcóiriú clasaiceach i saothar an tSúilleabhánaigh. Is amhlaidh a thaibhsíonn an fhilíocht sa cheol, más fé cheilt féin í: nó go nochtann fo-intinn fhileata an cheoil mar chúr.[37]

Conclúid

Maireann ilghuthacht i saothar an tSúilleabhánaigh a fhágann gur mó ná an cumadóir aonair a bhíonn laistiar de: bíonn athchumadóireacht bheo an amhránaí nó an cheoltóra le sonrú ann, chomh maith le macallaí d'athchumadóireacht an phobail féin mar is dual do shéiseanna traidisiúnta na Gaeltachta agus na hÉireann trí chéile. Ní saothair chalcaithe ba ghnáthach leis, ach saothair a chothaigh cur is cúiteamh an cheoil, saothair lenar bhain daonnacht bheo, saothair a chruthaíodh domhan tairseachúil idir eatarthu a chumasaíodh an ceoltóir. Ba léir go mba chuid thábhachtach den chultúr cumadóireachta a chleacht an Súilleabhánach, agus an Riadach roimis, cultúr beo na Gaeltachta. Fealsúnacht chumadóireachta a chleachtadar a bhain macalla as saothar ceannródaíoch ceisteach comhaimseartha an Ríordánaigh féin, agus do bhí 'mianach macalla sa bhfuaim'.[38] Sa tslí seo, ba dheocair gluaiseachtaí cumadóireachta an cheoil Ghaelaigh a scarúint ó ghluaiseachtaí intleachtúla frithchoilíneacha na Gaelainne sa tréimhse chéanna.

Ní hamháin go bhfuil téagar machnaimh le sonrú ar shaothar ceoleolaíochta an tSúilleabhánaigh, ach díol suime ar leith is ea an machnamh a cuireadh in iúl dúinn trí mheán an chleachtais chruthaithigh féin i gcaitheamh a shaoil. Sa tslí sin, creidim go bhféadfaí a shaothar cumadóireachta a thuiscint mar thaighde ealaíonta a dhein coincheapú íogair ar an mbéalaireacht, ar an dteangain, ar an bhféiniúlacht, agus ar an staid idir eatarthu iarchoilíneach. Coincheapú ba ea é seo a bhí agus atá fós réabhlóideach. Samhlaím spiorad na gcoincheap so a leanas de chuid an Ríordánaigh go láidir ar shaol agus ar shaothar an tSúilleabhánaigh dá réir: 'imigéiniúlacht 'nár n-aice / Is aisiompú eagair san aer'.[39] Maireann teanga fhileata na Gaelainne mar fho-intinn cheoil ina shaothar sa tslí is gurb ann i gcónaí í, fiú más fé cheilt féin. Cothóidh na téada machnaimh agus na téada gutha a d'fhorbair sé ina shaothar léannta agus cruthaitheach scoláirí agus ealaíontóirí araon go ceann i bhfad.

Gaiseadh/Flowing

52

Listening to Mícheál Ó Súilleabháin Play 'Carolan's Farewell to Music' on the Piano

Paula Meehan

Paula Meehan is Irish poet whose work has garnered critical and popular acclaim locally and internationally. Recent publications include As If By Magic: Selected Poems, *and* The Solace of Artemis. *Her poems have been scored for and sung by many choirs; they've been danced, filmed, put to music by divers artists ranging from the folk traditions to the avant garde.*

In the stillness after
the last note resonates to nothing,
the light fades, November's moon waxes
over the rooftops
and night has all my care.

*

Amongst the shelved poetry books
I fancy birdlife prisoned in the leaves,
the woodpulp's dim memory of trees:
my workroom suddenly an aviary,
the poets ghost warblers,
the chittering, chirruping, chirring, cawing, honking, clucking,
hooting, tooting, murmuring, whistling, piping, trilling, shrilling,
twittering, tweeting,

the swan song.

*

I remember that 'truth' to the ancient Greeks
is literally 'not forgetting': and the word *swan*,
does not forget it once meant *sound*,
mouth to ear, mouth to ear across the millennia
from the grandmother tongue.
Hence: assonance, consonant, dissonant,
unison, sonata, sonic, sonnet –

my own humble trade.

To write a farewell to music,
to be overcome with endings:
thanatography.

*

Once by a mountain tarn in snowlight
I watched nine swans lift from the water
their wakes lapping the grasses at my feet
long after they were no longer
even shadows over the snowfield.

*

When synchronicity is flowing:
writing this poem and the postman delivers rhizomes
of the salt tolerant anemone, *Wild Swan*.

I dream it next year Japanese in the garden
its white petals true windflowers,
feathery, yes, and angelic.

*

Digging out the compost in frosty weather,
mulching the beds,
Mars as close to us as it ever will be
in my mortal span.
In the voided time of Covid, I sweep the garden,

over my head five swans bronzed by sunset,
I vow to be peaceful, daughter of earth.

*

In from the orchard at dusk,
thawing my icy fingers at the hearth,
drying my mittens, my scarf,
I track the moonrise, her full face serene,
her maria and craters visible to the naked eye.

My hand too cold to write
I dream images in the flames,
the music of the settling logs,
murmurings from my bookshelves,
the poets restless
in their bindings.

*

Think in triplicities, in triads, in trinities:
to triangulate where you are in the infinity of time
take the last note of 'Carolan's Farewell to Music',
the solitary swan on Baldoyle estuary,
the last line of the last poem you will write.

Are you any the wiser?

*

Whatever wings that beat & beat & lifted
 from this our broken earth
 with the last mortal beating
 of your heart
were bound for summer skies,
 between the stars Albireo & Deneb
 the full galactic nourishment
 of the Milky Way.

*

I desire a music that is fractal –
as sure as the snowflake melting on my boot,
as sure as the pattern the ripple makes on water,
as sure as that swan's song,
the creature who carries our yearning across the generations,
heart and soul given in the art we are in bondage to,

before spirit lifts and leaves
your name in my mouth as prayer,
and the tarn's still water is mirror
to the fated constellations of our stars.

53

Elegy Between Worlds (*In Memoriam* Mícheál Ó Súilleabháin)

Thomas McCarthy

Thomas McCarthy was born in County Waterford. He has published ten collections of poetry including Merchant Prince, The Last Geraldine Officer, Pandemonium and Prophecy. *He has won the Patrick Kavanagh Award, the Alice Hunt Bartlett Prize, the O'Shaughnessy Prize for Poetry and the Ireland Funds Annual Literary Award. He is a member of Aosdána.*

i. Idir Eatarthu

At the turning of the road, a piano, a goldcrest,
A golden bird that finds the bass notes to begin
At the heart of a life that had depths. Three shafts
Of death disturb us, as death cannot be governed
By our prepositions; nor can its wings signify

Possession in the way Mícheál was possessive.
The wine-glass of one life is emptied now, but still
Songs come up out of the wind like the ghost
Of a hedge-school near Clonmel. There is no end
To the knowledge he left on these ivories; even

Tipperary hedge-rows whistle his name
And music he possessed possesses us still.
The vibrations left behind in the frame,
The tremble and variations, they assert again
The movement of his eye, his hands' assertion.

ii. Heartwork

At the racing heart of *Heartwork* is a musical fox
Fabulously escaping: no piper shall have him
At the end of his piping, none but the scales
That protect living things. The metrical forms
Have a wildness within. Or such passions as
You knew, Mícheál, when the hunt was in you
Between isle and marsh, piano and bodhrán.

iii. Templum

The high curling notes and the notes in restraint
Rise and fall between such veils of sound
As part in that space where a piano is found,
As part in the space where you played. Such saints
Of the Gael where you were a prince are a comfort
In this terrible era. Mícheál, you were the scribe
With a keyboard for pen, and a soul transcribed
Into celestial notations. And there too, without effort,

A great procession of gifted women, Fanny Power,
Lady Maisterton, attend to you in the fading hours,

Telling you yet again of collectors of music, of
The soul of all Ireland that folded into you.
Scholar-soloist, maestro from Clonmel, it's true
Skylarks rose when you played. The skies moved.

54
A Planxty for Mícheál Ó Súilleabháin
Joseph O'Connor

Joseph O'Connor holds the Frank McCourt chair of creative writing at the University of Limerick. His novels include Ghost Light, Shadowplay *and* Star of the Sea. *His work has been published in forty languages and has received many awards, including the American Ireland Fund Literary Award 2022.*

In the summer of 1978, when I was aged fifteen, I got a job washing dishes in an upmarket restaurant in Killiney, south Dublin. The work was hot and tedious and the hours were long, but I loved being up late and getting paid even the pittance I was paid, and the roaring furnace and banter of kitchen life. One of the great pleasures of the job was listening to the radio. I stood at the sink, arms in suds, washing glasses and plates all night, and the tiny transistor on the shelf in front of my face brought sounds from the wide world beyond.

1978 was a fantastic time to be young and into music. Late punk, early new wave, some of Dylan's greatest work, The Boomtown Rats, British ska and two-tone. For some time, I had loved Irish traditional music also. I was doing a project in school about Carolan, whose work I had fallen in love with. I never missed Marian Richardson's Thursday-night folk and blues show on RTÉ Radio.

One evening, at that sink, I heard the extraordinary beauty and elegant power of Mícheál Ó Súilleabháin playing 'Bonaparte ag Trasnú na Réine' from his Gael Linn album *Jockey to the Fair*, the right hand so bright and impish and extraordinarily vivid, the left hand bamming out a simple bassline that set your heart on fire.

There was no Carolan on that album, but there would be, in his future recordings, when he would reveal wonders and majesties about Ireland's greatest ever composer, in his utterly unique and beautiful style. No one has ever played quite like Mícheál.

On that night among the suds, for a fifteen-year-old kid, worlds opened. Clouds parted. I've loved his playing all my life since that electrifying moment. This poem is my attempt at a thanks.

Spangling arpeggios. Nimble glints of harmony
Eddying his melodies. Fiery right hand.
Quavering, crotchety, felt-hammered plinkettings.

Bold, building basslines. One-man band.

Carolan's Ellington.

Sharps of sonic starburst
Avid for elegance. Jazzy, zinging buzz.
Impossible to make a keyboard laugh.
He does.

Reacher. Teacher. Syncopating preacher.
Juicy spumes of blues-chords; a harper's weeping fingertips
Coaxing out grace notes, eight to the bar.
Maestro. Scholar.

Counterpointed waterfalls.

Bonaparte ag Trasnú na Réine.

Maith an fear.

55

Irish Destiny (1926)

Tom French

Tom French's The Last Straw *was shortlisted for the Irish Times/Poetry Now award in 2019. His work has received the O'Shaughnessy Award for poetry 2016, the Dermot Healy Award 2015, and the Forward Prize for Best First Collection 2002. His book* Company *(Gallery Press, 2022) received 'The Pigott Prize at Listowel Writers' Week 2023.*

> Other scenes from the film may well have appeared elsewhere purporting to be genuine images of the War of Independence but matters are complicated by the fact that *Irish Destiny* is intercut with contemporary newsreel footage of the conflict.
>
> *History Ireland*, May/June 2010

You wouldn't put it past them to have slipped
a re-cut under another moniker
under the eye of the Board of Film Censors
but how Eppel's epic ever could've given

Gilbert and Garbo in *Flesh and the Devil*,
Jean Renoir's *Nana*, Karloff in *The Bells*,
von Sternberg's *A Woman of the Sea*,
a run for their money is beyond me.

*

That single nitrate print of rushes
sat in the vault of the Library of Congress
a blessèd age without turning it,
as it threatened to at every instant,
into a veritable museum of ashes.

*

It wasn't his stagecraft that landed
Paddy Dunne-Cullinan the lead.
It was rather, they say, because he knew,
from time served as ostler and groom,
fetlock from forelock, wither from poll,
gaskin from stiffle, hock from croup.

*

So *Irish Destiny* was hacked to ribbons
to earn, as *An Irish Mother*, its censor's *U*,
despite jump cuts every couple of minutes
as iron is unholstered and hell breaks loose.

56
The Rags of Time
Paddy Bushe

Paddy Bushe lives in Kerry. Peripheral Vision, *a collection in English, and* Second Sight, *a selection of his poems in Irish with his own translations, appeared from Dedalus in 2020.* The Amergin Step, *an exploration of the landscape and literature of Iveragh, is forthcoming. He is a member of Aosdána.*

> Love, all alike, no season knows, nor clime,
> Nor hours, days, months, which are the rags of time.

At first I couldn't understand why, after the concert, those lines of John Donne, unbidden and for no apparent reason, insistently and continually resonated with me. I was exultantly aware that the music had been great, I was pleased and flattered that Mícheál Ó Súilleabháin had asked me to read a poem as part of a concert he and Mel Mercier had given in Waterville, County Kerry, and I felt reinforced in my belief that music and literature – indeed art in all its forms – is of fundamental and necessary importance to our well-being, both individual and societal. I felt personally validated for having made a small contribution to the night. But I still couldn't figure out why Donne's lines kept on insinuating themselves into my celebratory mindset.

Let me rewind, and give a context to these memories. The concert took place on 21 September 2001, part of an ESB Music Network tour that had already been described by Siobhán Long in *The Irish Times* as 'an unforgettable evening, a mixture of madness, mania and sheer musical ebullience'.[1] And indeed it had been like that in Waterville. Fíona and myself were as high as kites long after we came home. The terms 'world music' and 'fusion' had been concepts I had resisted. But that night, mesmerised by the percussive rhythms of Mercier's bones and bodhrán and by the lyrical flights of Ó Súilleabháin's keyboards, and by the catholicity (small *c*) of material in their repertoire, I felt my conservative (very small *c*) resistance dissolve in one great universal dance, like the pure and graceful exhilaration painted by Henri Matisse. Jazz danced with traditional, the meditative opened its ears to clapping hands and stamping feet, and Ireland opened itself to the world at large. Seán Ó Riada and Scott Joplin shared space on a brightly painted upright piano, and 'The Foxhunt' ran in wild and wonderful circles around the rippling 'Woodbrook', all sent cheerfully and rhythmically packing with 'Bye Bye Blackbird'.

The date of the concert, 21 September, meant, of course, that it coincided with the autumn equinox. The word suggests balance: the balance of time, of the year, above all the balance between light and dark. I think of equidistance, of equipoise, of equality and, especially, of equanimity. Equanimity: a balance of the soul. A sense of balance facing into the winter, a confidence that the year will turn again towards the light – all of this mirrors the equanimity we need in the face of time. I usually manage to persuade myself towards this equanimity around these seasonal turnings of solstice and equinox. But that particular equinox I was, like so many others, deeply and overwhelmingly fearful. Because 21 September 2001 was just ten days after the 9/11 attacks on the twin towers in New York. The world was in horrified shock, and there was a palpable apprehension and unease in the air. Nobody knew what was going to happen. I remember how Fíona and myself had gloomily seen the Florida re-count hand the United States presidency to George W. Bush and his shadowy neoconservative backers in December 2000 and concluded that the world had become a far more dangerous place than it had been. The following months and years were to bear witness to the accuracy of this conclusion. This is not the place to go into all of that; I just want to establish the wider universal context in which I and others were privileged to hear Mícheál and Mel play, as Siobhán Long put it, 'with surprising tinctures of grace and danger'.[2] The grace showed itself in Waterville Community Centre that night; the danger was in the ominous air enveloping the whole world. For that night, at least, the grace dominated over the danger.

When we got home, my head was, as they say, in a *rírá* with all these conflicting feelings. I needed to shape them, to express them and, for all the fear, to celebrate what I had heard. I wrote and rewrote for a few hours. The next morning, somewhat bleary-eyed, I drove up to the Bayview Hotel where Mícheál and Mel were staying and interrupted their breakfast to give them copies of the poem I had written, unusually quickly for me. It is not perhaps the poem I would write today, over twenty years later, in a world in the grip of not only seemingly intractable conflicts, but of climate change and threatened biodiversity with a consequent pandemic. But it does, I hope, express the wonder, appreciation and gratitude I felt that night, as well as the need to continually reach towards the spiritual and moral insights that art can give us.

Equinox Concert

for Mícheál Ó Súilleabháin and Mel Mercier

Light and darkness are in balance
All over the globe tonight, the world
Shrinking into itself like a nut
Hardening into its winter shell.

Years turn, and millennia, and ten
Days after the towers burned,
The spheres are grinding out of tune
And time, and cannot find a measure.

But tonight I heard the world's music
Shake hands with itself, old marches
Jazzed into new rhythms, bodhrán
And bones clatter out their resurrection.

So may the world's axis still hold true,
The pole star be constant, our slow
Turning from west to east lead us
Daily from darkness towards the light.

That night was the first time I met Mícheál Ó Súilleabháin. A few years later, in 2006, at a festival in Waterville, he presented a setting of my poem 'Freagra Scéine ar Aimhirghín', a setting that was beautifully and soaringly sung by Róisín Elsafty. It was the same poem I had read at the equinox concert. I last met him, briefly, with Fíona, after a concert of Carolan music in Valentia Island, when he held a capacity audience spellbound in the parish church. Although I didn't know him well, he enriched my life, as he did the lives of so many.

And the rags of time? Much later, I figured it out. During the concert, Mícheál had more than once played and talked about ragtime music. I had, as I have indicated, been contemplating seasonality and time, and how love, individual and universal, is our bulwark against the inescapable consequences of the passing of time, our perhaps illusory way of experiencing the eternal in the face of time. And I had been thinking how war and its terrors are the deliberate refusal of, and subversion of, individual and universal love. I had been contemplating too how art, like religious belief, can enhance, intensify and universalise spiritual experience, however irrational it may be in purely materialistic terms. And somehow the word 'ragtime' must have chimed with Donne's 'rags of time', a serendipity that played and replayed itself in the back of my mind until it eventually made its way to the front. Donne's great lines have since become part of how I experienced that night, its darkness and its light (the lines come from a poem called 'The Sun Rising') and, above all, its celebration of the universality of art. And those rags of time have transformed themselves into somethings like prayer flags waving in the wind, allowing their reaching towards the spiritual to be lifted and spread by winds that encircle the wide earth. For this experience, and my continued reliving of it, I will always be grateful to Mel Mercier and Mícheál Ó Súilleabháin, for whose soul, I hope, a rag of time continues to flutter.

57
Across the Plains of Boyle
(*In Memoriam* Mícheál Ó Súilleabháin)
Vincent Woods

Vincent Woods is a writer and broadcaster whose publications include The Turning Wave: Poems and songs of Irish Australia, *co-edited with Colleen Burke, and* Fermata: Writings inspired by music, *co-edited with Eva Bourke. The connections between poetry and music are explored in Vincent's poetry, prose writing and film work. He is a member of Aosdána.*

Edwina Guckian and I are filming for *Bealach an Fhéir Ghortaigh/ Hunger's Way*, our film of poetry connected to Ireland's Great Hunger. We're in search of the great singer Mai Malone (Mai Reynolds) who has been living in Woodbrook House for years. It turns out she has moved, temporarily, to nearby Cootehall. As we stand at the gate of the house made famous by David Thomson's memoir *Woodbrook* which inspired Mícheál Ó Súilleabháin's tune of the same name, a flurry of sleet changes the landscape and drives this poem into my mind.

Woodbrook is dark, the gate to the driveway padlocked
and raw to the touch.
The singer who lives here now is wintering out.
We drive away, sleet blowing heavy across the plains of Boyle;
A breath away – Alderford and Kilronan, the separation of body and soul.
And Lasair, the flaming saint who lit many a good fight –
Not to mention the bare head of Ben Bulben and the bones that lie beneath.

Your music swoops to mind, catches the white rhythm of the windscreen wipers,
So car and evening and the blurring world become one with Easter Snow.
The tune you're playing moves quick as a magpie, lingers on a grace
note, and away. Deep in all the loughs nearby eel are turning –
elver-light invisible between worlds.

I stop near the Shannon and listen to the river flow – piano and water;
Like Ó Riada, you made things happen – west to east, the greatest
music.

58

Where Music Begins (*In Memoriam* Mícheál Ó Súilleabháin)

Eva Bourke

Eva Bourke is a poet and translator. Her eight collections of poetry include the recently published Tattoos. *She co-edited* Landing Places: Immigrant poets in Ireland *with Borbála Faragó and* Fermata: Writings inspired by music *with Vincent Woods. She is a winner of the Michael Hartnett Poetry Prize and a member of Aosdána.*

> Consider this: you are at the edge of a cliff and your task is to leap across the void onto a safe landing place opposite you. You must land firmly on your feet … and pick up the same speed you had … Too short a leap will have you dashed on the rocks below. Too long a leap will have you flat on your face … This is a fermata in music, a magic moment when there is an enormous build-up of tension …
>
> Mícheál Ó Súilleabháin

Berlin in lockdown, the concert halls deserted,
pianos on stages standing in half light, lids closed,
fallboards down. There's a quarantine silence
in the city's long streets and wide, open squares
and to defeat it a young man has invited the world
into his room where he will play the Sonata for Hammerklavier,
written by Beethoven in anticipation of a generous gift,
a new-fangled piano from London with a six octave claviature,
two pedals and ebony and ivory keys, sent to him
by master piano builder and devotee John Broadwood.
The young man has set up his camera and microphone and now
he launches into the fanfare, seven spirited chords
throwing open the splendid doors on the first movement.
We don't know what music is, but we understand
that its desire for freedom is unrestrainable,
it roams far and wide, sometimes stopping

for just a few moments at the edge of a cliff
to gaze into the void before taking a wild leap across, landing
with precision and ease on the other side and
gathering speed from there to its natural destination
in the ears of his listeners where music begins.

II

Twice being labelled an 'enemy' cost my father two pianos.
Back from the Great War, years of saving as much as he could
from his meagre pay had bought him the first one,
a third-hand concert grand; it had a sweet, light touch, he said.
When the brownshirts came for him, the 'enemy of state'
who loved Schubert and Chopin, he left it behind and fled.
Years later, deported from Jerusalem, he lost the second,
a baby grand he'd bought from a colleague,
an 'enemy alien' like himself. Fingers press the keys,
hammers touch the strings, the mechanism sets
the notes in motion. The music is transparent, flowing
like the amber-coloured bog stream beside which I stand
watching it progress downhill from one little waterfall
to the next below the bridge where the meadow pipit
takes a dip. The river is so clear each pebble is visible
on the bottom and now and then the silver flash of a trout.
The night my father died, Schubert was on the stereo,
the Sonata D-960 in B Flat Major. *Molto moderato*. He'd played it
the day before on his Steinweg, his third and final piano.
The last sense to go is the ear, I am told.
How much did my father hear in the end, I wonder,
did he hear the music streaming over granite boulders
to the turn in the river where the moorhen nests?
Did he hear the skylark rise up fast and straight
from the marshy ground into the sky singing loudly
unable to contain the notes of joy in his small heart?

59
Eurydice Speaks
Enda Wyley

Enda Wyley has published six collections of poetry from her debut Eating Baby Jesus, *through to* New and Selected Poems *and recently,* The Painter on His Bike. *A seventh collection,* Through the Window, *is due 2025. She teaches poetry and co-hosts the podcast* Books for Breakfast, *about writing. Enda lives in Dublin and is a member of Aosdána.*

Knowing how much Mícheál loved Rilke's *Sonnets for Orpheus*, I offer this poem of mine, 'Eurydice Speaks', in memory of Mícheál Ó Súilleabháin who was an Irish Orpheus.

At the edge of my new life, in the early hours,
a message comes to me: *Follow the passage*
of light up to your old world and stop halfway.

I don't understand why, but I do it –
walk and walk, then wait in that strange
space that's divorced me from you.

And waiting alone, I feel nervous like when
I'd been human and you'd run your hand
for the first time gently down my throat,

down from the tip of my chin through the valley
of my breasts to that dark place below my navel,
which I remember allowing only you to find.

The tunnel's midway point charges with your energy
and I realise I've been given a second chance –
sent here to catch one more sighting of you, up ahead.

I'd know your back anywhere, the fallen coat hem
that I'd promised to stitch – too late, the snake

took me from you – your face resolutely forward,

your shoulders hunched in the uphill climb.
I trace your footprints marked in damp clay,
softly follow them. I can wait for you.

The light ahead will make me woman again.
But you haven't changed. The warning's ignored;
your impatience takes over. You turn around your face

and I can't help it, cry out, immediately become shadow,
a ghost of a song you'll sing forever. You can't return twice
to where you found me. One look from you and I know this.

60

Air: The map of the world

Eiléan Ní Chuilleanáin

Eiléan Ní Chuilleanáin was born in 1942 in Cork. She taught at Trinity College Dublin from 1966 to 2011 and was Ireland chair of poetry from 2016 to 2019. She has published eleven collections, as well as translations from Irish, Italian and Romanian. She edits the literary journal Cyphers *and was recently elected saoi of Aosdána.*

The map had told us already what would happen to the peoples of the west –
long promontories hurrying them out into the salty ocean fields,
roads that twisted around inlets constantly promising a place to rest –
and yet invention does not falter,
just feel the tailor's clutch of the variously woven tweeds
ready for the scissors, the tacking, the silky lining, listen.
as the echoes are twisting into a macaronic language,
listen to the places we came from, their stories elbowing each other out of the way
(can you recall the dripping walls of the library, the lads
who were thought to be studying grammar to prepare for Maynooth,
but they were planning their forays across the plains of Argentina?)
Up comes the prophecy I heard in the train making the slow journey
from Fishguard as far as the junction, when the big woman with red hair
in the green and white dress with a gold belt, and red shoes,
told us over and over, *they don't come back from America,*
they comes back from England, not America, they never comes back –
and along the carriage a man was playing an accordion,
the cards were slapped down on suitcases, do we not know
about those journeys now? or how the accordion's long note
spoke up in agreement? so that I could not have recalled her voice
except for that music, its delays and provisos,
dividing up the time.

61
Between the Jigs and the Reels
Moya Cannon

Moya Cannon was born in County Donegal and lives in Dublin. Her Collected Poems *brings together poems from six previous books. A winner of the Brendan Behan Award and the O'Shaughnessy Award, she is a member of Aosdána.*

Mícheál Ó Súilleabháin's debut album, issued by Gael Linn in 1976 with a wonderful Jack Yeats print of racing horses on the sleeve, was one of the iconic LPs of the Irish traditional music revival. Its opening salvo, *Bonaparte Crossing the Rhine*, played on the harpsichord, still makes my blood run a little faster and freer when I play it. This was an album, as Jack Yeats himself might have put it, 'full of the living ginger of life'. Through it, the airs and tunes of the seventeenth- and eighteenth-century Irish harpers and composers – Cornelius Lyons, William Connellan and others unknown – in addition to the great airs of the Déise, were revivified. They resonated through student bedsits in Rathmines, Ranelagh and elsewhere, as well as through concert halls at home and abroad.

It was an extraordinary debut to a career in performance, composition and teaching which culminated in his foundation, with the support of philanthropist Chuck Feeney, of the visionary Irish World Academy of Music and Dance. I met Mícheál Ó Súilleabháin only once at a concert/reading in that Academy but have much to thank him for. He has left us greatly enriched. Wherever his spirit has flown, I hope that it is in the company of many great harpers and, of course, other musicians, singers and dancers!

Between a jig and a reel
what is there?
Only one beat
escaped from a ribcage.
Tunes are migratory
and fly from heart to heart
intimating
that there's a pattern

to life's pulls and draws.
Because what matters to us most
can seldom be told in words
the heart's moods are better charted
in its own language –
the rhythm of Cooley's accordion
which could open the heart of a stone,
John Doherty's dark reels
and the tune that the sea taught him,
the high parts of the road and the underworlds
which only music and love can brave
to bring us back to our senses
and on beyond.

62

Between the Beats at The Moorings Bar

Michael Coady

Michael Coady lives in Carrick-on-Suir. Writer, photographer and musician, he is a member of Aosdána and a recipient of both the Patrick Kavanagh and the O'Shaughnessy Poetry Awards. Coady has collaborated with contemporary composers including Bill Whelan and Wolfgang Sauseng. His most recent book from Gallery Press is Given Light.

'Will you chance the waltz?'

It isn't a waltz.
But he'll dance a waltz to it anyway,
knowing no better, and she'll chance it

along with him, neither aware of how hard
it would be to do what they're doing
if they knew what it is they are doing

which is dancing together
in irregular three-four time
to a steady four in the bar

while at the same time
facing opposite ways
but towards each other

not yet glimpsing anything of all
they begin to dance into being
between the beats

including those still unconceived
who in time will stand and weep
over each in turn.

63
Anonymous: A blackbird
Paul Muldoon

Paul Muldoon is an Irish poet, editor, critic, playwright, lyricist and translator. He has published over thirty poetry collections and is a recipient of the T.S. Eliot Prize and the Pulitzer Prize for Poetry. He has been professor of poetry at Oxford University, poetry editor at The New Yorker, *and currently teaches at Princeton University.*

That this one smallish bird might fill
an amphitheatre with the trill
of notes from its yellow bill
is truly awesome –

a shock
wave over Belfast Lough
from a branch already chockablock
with whin blossom.

64

Interludes
(*In Memoriam* Mícheál Ó Súilleabháin)

Peter Sirr

Peter Sirr's most recent books are The Swerve *and* Intimate City: Dublin essays, *both published by The Gallery Press. He is a member of Aosdána, and lives in Dublin.*

I got to know Mícheál when I served under his chairmanship on the first board of Culture Ireland. I was greatly impressed by his enthusiasm, energy and good humour and offer this series of music-inspired pieces as a small tribute to his positive and generous spirit.

1. *Cello Life*

Today I choose you cello life
your shadows and lightenings your plunges
and somehow ascents I'll walk
your woody depths, come

darkened lit darkened lit
black white browns and blues
stretched and drawn leaping and standing
almost completely still. Here I am

gravely sarabanding, making room
for the Bach breath of Pablo Casals
wounded joyful morning evening
the light closing the light opening again

2. *Mahleresque*

I am lost to the world
unhanded

I am loosed
let slip
I am unsteady in it
I have so long been writing to it
but now
now it hears nothing from me
and must think me
strayed unsighted fallen
over the edge
let it
let it think what
it will I am truly gone
from dark to dark
faltered
I am sleeping
in the throat
of the song
stretched
from note to note
stranded
to the last breath
abandoned
Ich bin
Ich bin der Welt
abhanden gekommen

3. *No Journey's End*
(*Michael O'Shea*)

A music you hardly bothered to record
swamps my ears

the hammered strings and dinking riffs
of percussion pouring, trancing

yet still keeping itself to itself
like something less listened to than overheard

but reached for urgently and wondered at
a flaunted secret

or careless privacy
We knew, didn't we, the instrument was made

from a door found in a Munich skip
Mo Chara – in every note

the doorway stages, the street corners
the black concealing hat, head bent low

in a West End Tube station
Krishna in a tweed suit

or bangles and heels if the day decided
The point was to go or stay, to sit still or not

You fill the room now despite yourself
the vision caught

just the music again and again
flying out from the chopsticks to make

its own city, to twist and climb, fade and press
a noise we had always imagined, rippling through us

as a hurry gathers, pauses, moves on

65
Early Music
Mícheál 'Moley' Ó Súilleabháin

Mícheál 'Moley' Ó Súilleabháin is a poet and singer. He holds an MA Ethnomusicology with a specialisation in Irish rap. He inherited a store of songs from his parents, Rev. Nóirín Ní Riain and Mícheál Ó Súilleabháin, and performs regularly with his brother, Owen. His first book of poetry, Early Music, *was published in 2021.*

I learned to make music when I was alone,
revering the moment before I began
to sing, then break the solitary silence.

I learned to love my own voice,
making a friend of it,
fashioning a fountain pen to master
the phantom language,
each Brandenburg concerto
furrowing ground, turned up
loud, while my father drilled
his impossibly strong fingers
on the steering wheel,
careening the back roads
of Birdhill.

My mother would sing alone for hours,
Hildegard and sean nós, seamlessly sung.
Light would stream in the sash window
while she scribbled illegibly,
preparing for a performance.

I would drum my hands on my thighs
till they were hot and red, repeating
the same beat thousands of times,
honing the same phrase.

And in the evening we would gather
around two candles and
Early Music on cassette.
Before the dissonance and serialism,
an early music to keep us company.

An instrumental combination
to unlock conversation and
make the silences dance
like shadows in candlelight.

No vocal music to deflect and distract
from a small family huddled
around only food and flame,
and the warm faint sound
of wood and gut string.
Deepening every narrative,
sharing harmony and conversation.

A family that feels safe is sacred.
Embryonic echo soundings
still bounce back,
reflected in the sound
of Early Music.

66

Tigín i gCnocán a' Phaoraigh (i gcuimhne ar Mhícheál Ó Súilleabháin)

Áine Uí Fhoghlú

Poet and writer Áine Uí Fhoghlú comes from An Rinn in County Waterford. Among her many published works are four collections of poetry. She has won various awards including Oireachtas na Gaeilge, Listowel Writers' Week and the Michael Hartnett Poetry Award, as well as literature bursaries from An Chomhairle Ealaíon/The Arts Council and Ealaíon na Gaeltachta.

Tuairim na bliana 1974 tháinig Mícheál Ó Súilleabháin agus Nóirín Ní Riain chun cónaithe sa Rinn agus chuireadar fúthu i dtigh Uí Aonghusa ar Bhóthar na Sop. Ba chuí gur ann a lonnaíodar, mar bhí stair ceoil ag góilt leis an dtigh úd. Sa mbliain 1936, is ann a bhí cónaí ar Shéamus Ó hAonghusa, fear an phoist agus a chéile Máire, bean chabhrach an cheantair. An bhliain chéanna fuair beirt de shár-amhránaithe na Rinne, Máiréad de Nógla agus Pádraig Tóibín, cuireadh dul go dtí Corcaigh agus amhráin a chanadh ar chlár a bhí ag Peadar Ó Cearnaigh ar Raidió Éireann. Ó ba rud é gur sa tigh seo a bhí an t-aon raidió sa pharóiste ag an am, is ann a bhailigh na comharsain go léir chun go gcloisfidís an craoladh beo. Bhí an slua chomh mór sin gur líonadar an clós agus bhí ar chuid acu suí ar an gclaí lasmuigh ag éisteacht leis an gcraoladh trí fhuinneog oscailte an tí.

Bhí cáil na hamhránaíochta ar An Rinn le fada. Bhí Nioclás Tóibín in ard a réime agus bhí a ghlúin siúd a d'fhoghlaim a gcuid amhrán cois tine nó amuigh sna goirt, fé mheas mór ag Mícheál. Níorbh fhada gur bhailigh sé féin agus Nóirín fearaibh is mná an pharóiste le chéile agus gur chuireadar cór ar bun. Thugadar beirt ana-spreagadh dúinne a bhí i mbun ceoil agus ba mhinic iad ar cuairt go dtí mo thuismitheoirí sa Linn Bhuí mar a mbíodh plé ar cheol domhanda agus ar bhailitheoirí amhrán. Bhláthaigh an ceol sa Rinn. Bhíodh Halla de Hindeberg lán go doras dos na coirmeacha ceoil a chuireadar ar stáitse. Bhunaigh siad an grúpa ceoil Tiompán le ceoltóirí ón gceantar máguaird agus eisíodh an céirnín fadseinnte *Óró Damhnaigh*. Im dhéagóir dom, ba dhraíochtúil an t-am é. Bhíodh fáilte i gcónaí romham féin is mo chairde sa tigín úd ar Bhóthar na Sop. Nuair a d'fhreastail mé ar Choláiste na hOllscoile i gCorcaigh roinnt blianta ina dhiaidh san, bhí áthas orm Mícheál a bheith mar léachtóir agam agus sa mbliain 2006 bhí sé d'onóir agam comhoibriú leis féin agus le healaíontóirí aitheanta eile i léiriú stáitse mar ar chuir Mícheál ceol le dán fada liom ('Duan Déiseach'), coimisiún a bhronnadh orm don ócáid.

Tugann an dán nua-scríofa seo chun cuimhne teacht Mhíchíl go dtí An Rinn agus an rabharta ceoil a bhíodh ar bun sa tigín úd i gCnocán an Phaoraigh.

Sometime around 1974 Mícheál Ó Súilleabháin and Nóirín Ní Riain arrived in An Rinn and found that the cottage known locally as 'Hennessy's' on Bóthar na Sop was available to rent. It was a fitting house for them to find, as it had a significance in the musical history of the parish. In 1936 it was owned by postman James Hennessy and his wife Mary, the local midwife. That year, two of the best singers from the area, Máiréad de Nógla and Pádraig Tóibín, were invited to participate in a radio programme in Cork, hosted by Peadar Kearney on the newly established Radio Éireann. The prospect of hearing your neighbours singing on the radio was a real fascination back then, and as the Hennessys owned the only radio in the parish, it was to their kitchen that people flocked from every corner of the parish to hear the broadcast. The crowd spilled out into the yard and onto the road where many sat on the ditch listening to the programme through the open kitchen window.

The young couple's enthusiasm and talent sparked a flame in an area already known for its singing and musical tradition. Mícheál had a huge regard for sean-nós singer Nioclás Tóibín and those of his generation who had learned their singing at the firesides and in the fields. It wasn't long before Mícheál and Nóirín gathered together the men and women of the parish and formed a choir. They encouraged and taught music to those of us eager to learn and were frequent visitors to my parents' home in An Linn Bhuí where long discussions were held about world music and song collectors. Music blossomed in the area. The local hall, Halla de Hindeberg, was packed to capacity for the concerts they organised. The music group Tiompán was formed, composed of musicians from neighbouring areas, and the LP Óró Damhnaigh was issued. As a teenager, eager and enthusiastic about music, this was a magical time for me. My friends and I were always welcome in the cottage on Bóthar na Sop and when I attended University College Cork a few years later I was thrilled to have Mícheál as a lecturer. In 2006 I was honoured to participate in a collaboration with Mícheál and a number of other well-known artists and performers when a poem of mine ('Duan Déiseach'), commissioned for the occasion, was set to music by him for a stage performance.

This poem, a newly written tribute to Mícheál, recalls his arrival in An Rinn and the cascade of music which flowed from the cottage in Cnocán an Phaoraigh while he lived there.

Nuair a ghíosc an doras thuig na fallaí go raibh an t-am tagtha
le greim a scaoileadh ar a gcuimhní. Dhúisigh na frathacha
as a dtromshuan, léim doirse dá mbacáin, chrioth cathaoireacha
iad féin is thosnaigh ag luascadh na gcos.

Bhíomarna ann, déagóirí, is bhlaiseamar de. Fínnéithe na súl
lánleathan fé bhriocht ag gliogarnach an *shekere*, binneas
an ucailéile, cársán na harmóine.

D'fholcamar sinn féin sa rabharta siansach, chomh saonta
san gur chreideamar ná tráfadh an tuile úd go deo.

Inniu is mé ag siúl thar bráid, airím a chuid ceoil ina thonnta
cúracha ag briseadh ar charraigreacha mo chuimhne

ina thráithníní buí ag séideadh soir siar
ar Bhóthar na Sop.

67

For Mícheál

Fióna Bolger

Fióna Bolger is a poet, writer and facilitator who has lived mainly in Ireland and India. She was wearing almost all green when she first met Mícheál and Helen. They laughed.
www.fionabolgerpoetry.com

The farmer's pitchfork becomes a tuning fork
in the master's hands. These fingers gripping
a pen are not yours dancing across piano keys.
Let these symbols scratched on paper translate
to a music of the mind and between these lines
may a perfectly timed pause, build tension until –

You spoke of choice in every moment
of the making, life as an abundance
of creation, until you shimmy
out of earshot, somewhere becoming –

68
The Music of the Morning Sun (Elegy for Mícheál Ó Súilleabháin)
David Whyte

David Whyte grew up with a strong, imaginative influence from his Irish mother among the hills and valleys of his father's Yorkshire. The author of eleven books of poetry and four books of prose, including Consolations, *he holds a degree in marine zoology, and honorary degrees from Neumann University and Royal Roads University.*

You have been woken and placed
in a street walking toward the morning
sun, with both those hands lifted, hearing
the music everywhere, you are walking
toward the sea, though you do not know
exactly where you are, though you do not
know what an extraordinary city this might
be, but you can see above you the ruffling
tessellation of leaves against the sky; you
can hear the birdsong and the exuberant
note of a ship's horn and that particular pale
reflection a sea can make above its calm
sunlit self, telling you it is there and also
that it is just beyond you, over the high
buildings of the waking town.

You can see and hear so clearly now,
you can see and hear music everywhere
and you understand at last how you have
always heard music everywhere, but now
you hear the essential incantatory
invitation in all things, you understand
the wordless music of all words;
and that through all the years of practice

and playing and secret praying, that
you never minded not knowing
as you played, knowing as you did
that whenever you played music
you played as a wanting-to-know
miracle amongst other miracles,
all wanting to know you,
and all wanting to hear you
and like your music, you have
achieved the unachievable, you have
become unclassifiable, un-nameable
and free; people walking toward you
see every line in your upturned face,
people walking behind you find
a happy silhouette, sometimes a man,
sometimes a young woman,
walking out on a first spring day,
someone, no matter their outward form
with a rhythm in their step,
haloed by the sun, called by every
distant strain of notes.

You are on your way somewhere,
drawn by an air you are just beginning
to sing your self, though you do
not know fully where you are going,
though you do not know anything
anymore, though you only know
you can walk, you can talk, you can
wave a cheery hello to complete
and utter strangers, overwhelmed
as they are by your untrammelled joy,
so that you look down as if concentrating
on the inner keys of your body
in just the same way as you played
head bent as if in prayer
so as not to burden the world
with your happiness, though
you never say a word
about the source of your joy,

though you cannot say a word
on any subject at all,
though you understand only as you did
as a child, when you first sat down
before the ivory whiteness
and touched the first black keys
that you were on your way home
to the very place you find yourself now
and are just on the edge of reaching.

Walking toward the river and the sea
today, you see your hands at last
as a marvel, doing what they
have always done, you stop
in the street and open them
as silhouettes to the noon-day sun,
the light coming to find you
through outstretched fingers,
and in their outline, you understand
from the very first, every last thing
they created, how they leapt like a child
from stepping stone to stepping stone
as easy and as nimble as dancers.

Your hands, outlined by the light
of music have always been beacons:
they led every building theme,
and every theme of building,
they led the sincerity of every student,
they led your own sons through
the music of the morning light,
filling the waking house
with the unanswerable, tidal run
of sky and sea and the swelling,
rising sun, and now, walking toward
this western light, this sun-lit city
by the river, you are playing
as closely and as faithfully
as you ever will to the world's
tidal reach, and as you catch

the last, faint call of the waiting sea,
you guide the river of notes
to the last dolphin gleam
touching the sun-line of the west.

You lean forward, silhouetted
by the dying Atlantic sun,
true and faithful and outlined
as ever, in our memory,
your firm, outstretched hands
working on our behalf,
still sure of everything,
holding the chords to the last.

69
Ceol
Gerard Smyth

Gerard Smyth's poetry has appeared in journals in Ireland, Britain and the United States as well as in translation. He has published ten collections, including The Sundays of Eternity *and* The Fullness of Time: New and selected poems *both published by Dedalus Press. He is a member of Aosdána.*

The subject of these two interlinked poems is music and its makers. The first is set in the Dublin locality where I was born and grew up, the second begins in an area of County Meath close to my grandmother's farm in Knightstown where my mother was born and on which I spent the summers of my childhood and adolescence.

The area of Dublin known as the Liberties, where my Meath mother settled with my Dublin father, was home to a great music tradition that included the famous pipers' club Na Píobairí Uilleann, in Thomas Street. The most legendary figures among local musicians came from the Potts family on the Coombe, around the corner from where I lived in Pimlico. Seán Potts was a founding member of The Chieftains, and according to the plaque on the wall of St Catherine's church on Thomas Street the group played their debut gig there under the clock made famous in the poem by Thomas Kinsella and mentioned here in 'The House on the Coombe'.

But before Seán there was his uncle Tommie Potts, another son of the Coombe whose influence on traditional fiddle playing has been far-reaching and continues in the present time among contemporary players. All in all, Biddy Mulligan's Coombe has had a significant role in Irish traditional music, and central to that was Number 6.

Mícheál Ó Súilleabháin clearly revered the innovative musician and senior member of the Potts dynasty as was obvious in the documentary he made about the musician with Philip King and in his writings about Potts.

Growing up in that part of old Dublin in the 1950s and '60s it was impossible to be unaware of Number 6 the Coombe and its significance at the heart of traditional music, a house honoured in the title of the final album recorded by Seán Potts, *Number 6*. Music did indeed come out of the walls of that house, and occasionally some of us passers-by were lucky to catch a tune in the Coombe air.

The second poem here begins in 'his father's forge' in Nobber, County Meath, where Carolan was born. During my summer sojourns with my grandmother – again in the '50s and '60s – Nobber entered my imagination mainly because directly outside a window of the farm cottage stood a road sign telling the passing traveller that Nobber was six miles further on up the road. Back then I had no sense of the connection between this part of the Royal County and the harper whose tunes have been constantly renewed in the hands of succeeding generations of musicians, including Mícheál Ó Súilleabháin and Seán Potts and his fellow Chieftains, all of whom became exponents and revivalists of Carolan's music.

The house at Number 6 the Coombe, known locally as Watkins Buildings (there had been a Watkins brewery nearby) stood on land that had once been granted to the Brabazon family (earls of Meath). The local place names are still reminders of that connection: Brabazon Square, Meath Street, Ardee Street. In his time in Mayo and Roscommon one of Carolan's chief patrons was George Brabazon for whom he wrote some of his most frequently performed planxties. A chain of coincidences perhaps, but one linking music makers as well as city and country locations.

CEOL

1 *The House on the Coombe*

Passing that house we wanted to dance.
Music came out of the walls at night –
tunes that were buried and dug up again.
A lullaby for the newborn, dozing and swaddled
in the lying-in hospital a few doors away.

The first notes were barely audible,
reticent as morning sun behind morning cloud.
Then the sound of a full house,
the clear run of a long finish that kept circling
and circling but never landing on ground.

There was story-telling when the music stopped
for a sip, a swig, a cigarette outside under the moon.
One sad neighbour always dropped in
when she heard the tin whistle beginning its dirge.

The last fling went on and on
until the morning chill when the milkman came
with his bottles of milk and stars were gone
from the sky above St Catherine's Clock.

2 *The Road from Nobber*

The first rhythms he heard rang clear in his father's forge:
hammer on anvil, stress of the chisel, clatter of tongs.

With hands that were blind he knew only by touch
what others could see: his smallpox scars,
the dripping rain, sun glinting on glass,
frost in the air on the first cold morning
when the strings of his harp became bad-tempered.

When he started his travels his walking stick was cut
from a tree that grew between salt sea air and mountain drizzle.
Some women were trouble –
Fanny Power and *Eleanor Plunkett*.

And when he grew tired of hearing them say *Play us that tune*,
he took up his instrument and moved on
to wherever a lord of the manor might pay for a planxty
to rouse his guests, make them drum the bare boards
with their quicksteps, warm the cold air of his house.

70
Church Music
John McAuliffe

John McAuliffe's books include Selected Poems *and* The Kabul Olympics. *John grew up in County Kerry and has lived in Manchester since 2004. He is professor of poetry at the University of Manchester's Centre for New Writing and associate publisher at Carcanet.*

'But all is cleansed when the marble weeps' – George Herbert

1. *St Patrick's Chapel, Paris*
   17.7.2013

At a round table, the talk
starts to sound responsible, a *performance*,
as if the old piece being read
is a bath the sainted blackbird
lands on and dips into.
Its airs. Scattering water everywhere.

Or, the choir in the old seminarians' library
stand up to the notes; and suddenly
something unearthly:
the library *in* the choir.

2. *All Saints', Braunston, Devon*
   (after William Trevor Cox)

Copied across from the Book of Kells,
his images hardly register
the history they preside over
but know the wooden grain they're imposed on,
and made from. Each lined, knotted evangelist's face
is opaque and broad, so the lectern

shines flatly, its brown sloping panels
a pulpit where their author
reserves *judgment* for later,
taking on board the possibility of forgiveness
and what the text's long resonance
distorts.

3. *Manchester Cathedral*
    11.3.2012

It was not exactly
                    church music,
but 'Oileán' – on flute McGoldrick,
Sinead Hayes conducting – reeled in
some crowd – a congregation.

At the interval
I was remembering the cassette version,
how the piece could shuffle
tune and orchestration
when the MC pointed to this place's oldest part,
the 'angel stone', a Saxon fragment.

Going back to it,
I see the angel reads from a scroll, a sort of vertical banner,
which the text (roughly from the Latin –
'Into your hands I commend my spirit')
spills over,
            spilling over

            like how a tune will originate
in a certain place, a set form, or the soul alone,
and be re-shaped, as it was that night,
by whatever course its players could unravel,
bending frail dotted lines into the cathedral's marble.

71

Back on the Island
(*In Memoriam* Mícheál Ó Súilleabháin)
Bernard O'Donoghue

Bernard O'Donoghue was born in Cullen, County Cork, and he still lives there for part of the year. Since 1965 he has lived in Oxford where he taught medieval English and modern Irish poetry. His most recent book of poems was The Seasons of Cullen Church.

Behind the mysterious ground of the cellos,
tunes were secreted, waiting to break out
and dance on the keys: 'The Three Sea-Captains',
'Cooley's', or 'Killarney Boys of Pleasure'.
So how did he know where they were?
He must have put them there himself:
it's the only explanation. When things are lost,
we keep on looking in places where we know
they are not because we've looked there already.
But they remain the most likely places
so we'll look there again, back on the island.

72
Marbhna on a Grand Piano (for Mícheál Ó Súilleabháin)
Theo Dorgan

Theo Dorgan is a poet, and also a translator, librettist, novelist, non-fiction author, essayist, editor and documentary screenwriter. He is a member of Aosdána.

The left hand falls, drawing dark chords from the air,
heavy and slow, heavy and slow; the right hand hovers …

the pianist leans back, arms braced, face a pale mask,
then something changes in his breath, the right hand falls,

his eyes flick open, he leans forward, all intent,
and cold clarity fills out the room, light and dark

drawing one into the other, hand conjuring with hand
what was there in the silence, what's here now

in the blood – melody, a pulse of grief, climbing urgent
over the dark chords, stubborn percussive insistence,

a run of notes crisp as frost – lament
and resolution, not grief but the called-in memory of grief.

Thunder and lightning from the black grand,
and all of us there, holding our breath, while the human,

the all too human, maestro draws dark chords from the air,
ancestral pain from memory – then soothes it away

into the silence after, the dying hum of the hammered strings,
the ripples lapping the walls, as we repossess our hearts.

73

Like a Soul (*In Memoriam* Mícheál Ó Súilleabháin)

Martin Dyar

Martin Dyar's first book of poems Maiden Names *was shortlisted for the Pigott Poetry Prize. He is the editor of the anthology* Vital Signs: Poems of Illness and Healing. *He teaches in the School of Medicine at Trinity College Dublin.*

We'll speak now, for a brief moment, although,
you understand, I would prefer not to
have to press you again on the question
of your self-confidence. You're supposed to be
past all of that. Remember what I said
on the first day. I have a role. *Professor*
fits by sleight of hand only, but we must
for practical purposes use that word. We'll
also use *mentor*, another wiry title,
which you must think of as equivalent
to your solid demon of encouragement.
I am here for you. And yet, the nameless
pilot in your heart is the primary
authority in all of this. Make no
mistake, that little man knows our business.
After today, I won't repeat myself.
Today we cross the Rubicon of music.
But I'll spell it out for you now, one more time:
you were born for magic, and born for this.
Pack all of your faith into that queer notion.
You were born for and born of magic. Of course,
we'll be keeping this to ourselves. There are some
who at the faintest scent of our ideals
will begin to orchestrate our downfall.
The sweet juice of hatred is plentiful
hereabouts. But that is for down the line.

This morning, let your writing be a war
for the territory of concentration.
Go back to the irrational daydream
that the songs you are trying to attain
are a means to part the veil of the West.
Stay with the coastal hills. Marry their slopes
and marry their streams. What was your Pied Piper
image? Something about imagination
being a cave in Limerick? Don't dare let go
of that romantic fragment. In fact, repeat
it to me for the remainder of the year.
Give it to me a hundred different ways.
Relentlessness deserves to be in the room.
Sit at the piano now, and begin
with a pair of chords. Play them, mind you, gently.
Let's aim to reach the most original
gentleness by midday. Pied Piper stuff.
Subtle, careful, merry, plain, and true.
A tune that makes the heart look like a soul.

74

Mícheál Ó Súilleabháin and Seamus Heaney: Boundaries, mediation and redress

Johanne Devlin Trew

Johanne Devlin Trew is a musician, and lecturer at Ulster University, Belfast. Her doctoral research at the University of Limerick was supervised by Mícheál Ó Súilleabháin. Her publications include Leaving the North: Migration and memory, Northern Ireland, 1921–2011 *(2016); and (co-edited with M. Pierse)* Rethinking the Irish Diaspora (2018).

In an essay published in 2018, the composer and educator Mícheál Ó Súilleabháin acknowledged the influence of his mentor John Blacking's 'utopian charge' – the belief in the potential of art forms to become 'forces of cultural mediation' that may act to redress inequalities in the social and political spheres.[1] Ó Súilleabháin enthusiastically thus took up the role of cultural mediator and, inspired by Seamus Heaney's notions of *crossing* or *bridging* knowledges and of passing through a boundary (*terminus*), encouraged us to *redress* imbalances and to listen to voices previously unheard.[2] As the island of Ireland arrives at a new crossroads of rapidly changing politics and demographics, this essay is a personal reflection on the example of Ó Súilleabháin's own crossing of boundaries within Ireland North and South, in the Irish diaspora, and further afield. Might Ó Súilleabháin's vision of 'art as prophetic', a notion he shared with Heaney, shine a light to show us the way forward?[3] The essay begins with a personal reflection on Mícheál Ó Súilleabháin as an educator, especially as an *enabler* of his students. Secondly, consideration is given to Ó Súilleabháin as a cultural mediator and his own crossing of boundaries to redress imbalances. Comparison is made with the work of Seamus Heaney, who was a seminal influence in Mícheál Ó Súilleabháin's work and life.

Following the light

On a dark evening in early December 1993, with some trepidation I entered the Department of Music at University College Cork (UCC), then located in a large and rather dilapidated three-storey house just across the street from the Western Road gate to the main campus. The entry hall was dimly lit and there was no one about, although I could make out the muffled sounds of musical instruments playing from somewhere deep inside the building. I carefully made my way up the creaking staircase which turned and narrowed considerably as I continued upwards after the first floor. As I headed up the final flight of narrow stairs, the only dim light available to me appeared to come from the attic floor above and when I arrived at the top I could see that it emanated from a small desk lamp in an otherwise unlit room across the landing. I followed the light and knocked timorously on the open door. In my somewhat hazy vision of that memory, my mind replays the scene of Mícheál Ó Súilleabháin getting up from the chair behind the desk, necessarily stooping slightly due to the steeply pitched gabled attic ceiling, and then coming towards me smiling widely, extending his hand of greeting.

My appointment that evening was my first meeting with Mícheál Ó Súilleabháin which had been arranged by telephone the week before with the purpose of discussing the possibility of pursuing doctoral studies. Having relocated from Canada to Cork via Belfast a few months earlier and enrolled myself in an intensive programme of Irish-language study at UCC, it had taken several weeks to build up the courage to make the initial phone call to Ó Súilleabháin 'out of the blue' fearing that my entire future depended upon the reception. I need not have worried. As I recall, Ó Súilleabháin picked up the phone after a few rings – I had caught him late in the day in his office – and his welcome could hardly have been more magnanimous, expressing keen interest with the offer to meet up the following week. From the outset of our first meeting, there appeared to be no question in his mind of whether I – the daughter of mixed marriage parents from Belfast[4] – would take on doctoral studies and I left Ó Súilleabháin's office that evening having made the firm commitment to submit a PhD proposal the following month to the University of Limerick (UL), where he was to take up the post of professor in January 1994 to establish what would become the Irish World Academy of Music and Dance.

Thus, my first experience of Mícheál Ó Súilleabháin as an enabler of others reveals an important aspect of his legacy. That he shone a light for others to follow was linked strongly with his intellectual curiosity, and indeed personal courage, to cross boundaries to seek inspiration and new knowledge, which often came from voices unfamiliar to him, as evidenced in the research topics he supported his students to undertake beyond the shores of Ireland.[5] He shared this openness with the poet Seamus Heaney (1939–2013), who like Ó Súilleabháin was an artist, an educator, a cultural mediator and by many accounts an enabler of others. It is the connection between these two artists that warrants further investigation and which I address in the rest of this essay, in particular the influence on Ó Súilleabháin of Heaney's ideas on cultural mediation, boundaries and redress.

'Holding the light steady': Mícheál Ó Súilleabháin and Seamus Heaney as cultural mediators

In his 2018 essay referenced at the beginning of this essay, Mícheál Ó Súilleabháin outlines the core proposal:

> that music and dance hold potential to act as powerful forces of cultural mediation, redressing social – and musical – inequalities. The influence of Seamus Heaney and his *The Redress of Poetry* on my thinking should be clear at this point … the idea of the role of music in cultural and social mediation with a view to achieving a parity of esteem for world cultures.[6]

Ó Súilleabháin's admiration of Heaney's work actually dates back well before *The Redress* of 1995; indeed, his connection to Heaney is demonstrated in the several instances that he employed (with permission) Heaney's poetry in his music production, for example the albums *The Dolphin's Way* (1987) and *Elver Gleams* (2010).[7] He also frequently drew on Heaney's ideas in his academic writing. I am not suggesting that Ó Súilleabháin simply appropriated ideas and metaphors from Heaney, but rather that coming across Heaney's work in the mid-1980s resonated strongly with his own thinking developing at that time in his work, particularly in the study of the music of Tommie Potts for his PhD at Queen's University Belfast.[8] Indeed, as Ó Súilleabháin later recounted, 'my direct research engagement with Potts in the early to mid 1980s coincided exactly with the development of the traditional piano material that was to appear on my album entitled *The Dolphin's Way*'.[9] Perhaps it was his crossing of the border to the 'troubled' North to study at Queen's in 1984 and encountering Heaney's work of that period that provoked new thinking on nation, identity, borders and boundaries, and the potential of the arts to influence societal change. Indeed, it is the northern poet Heaney as he emerges from the darkness of his earlier poetry collections – *Death of a Naturalist* (1966), *Door into the Dark* (1969), *Wintering Out* (1972) and *North* (1975) – and 'writing in subdued light' during the 1980s, who holds up a lamp or lantern to shine a light on the bitter political climate of that 'troubled' decade (e.g. in his collection *The Haw Lantern*, 1987).[10]

The work of Mícheál Ó Súilleabháin and Seamus Heaney shares many features. Firstly, Heaney peppered his writing with the terminology and sound imagery of music and rhythm, while Ó Súilleabháin made frequent use of the poems and prose of poets.[11] Moreover, Ó Súilleabháin took a deep interest in the poets that Heaney cited, especially T.S. Eliot, W.B. Yeats and Václav Havel, and the psychoanalyst Carl Jung, notably the latter's ideas on reconciling opposites.[12] Secondly, there is considerable use of nature metaphors in the work of both artists. For Heaney it is primarily landscape, particularly the metaphors of digging or unearthing hidden layers, buried histories or meanings, of the bog as 'landscape that remembered everything that happened in it and to it'.[13] For Ó Súilleabháin, nature provides powerful evidence of an afterlife, of 'some sort of continuity after death',[14] and he cites as influential Estyn Evans' notion of the 'intelligence of the landscape'.[15] However, in his work it is water metaphors (river, ocean, wave, flow, well, island) that predominate – *The Dolphin's Way* (1987), *Oileán/Island* (1989), *Gaiseadh/Flowing* (1992); *The River of Sound* (1995), *Elver Gleams* (2010).[16] Thirdly, concepts of duality (or 'doubleness' or 'betweenness' or 'two-mindedness') are likewise shared by both artists. In Heaney's work, it is exemplified in his uncovering/recovering of the Gaelic Irish placenames in Ulster that were supplanted by English names, while at the same time wrestling with his 'dual' identity as a northern nationalist, what he called 'the minority citizen in oneself'.[17] With Ó Súilleabháin, the duality is expressed in his work *Between Worlds* (1995) and *Becoming* (1998), in his 'dual' identity as a musician and composer involved in both art music and traditional music, as a performer and an academic, and as a fluent speaker of Irish and English. Fourth, the understanding that the locus of creativity resides in performance (or process) was shared by both artists. In his early poems, for example, Heaney described the value of process over product with reference to the traditional practices of the thatcher, the diviner and the poet.[18] For Ó Súilleabháin, performance is 'an intelligence and a knowledge in its own right' and he emphasises that in Irish traditional music it is in the moment of performance when creativity takes place.[19] While Heaney sought to nourish his own creativity free of the push and pull demands of society, to create an 'elsewhere' from which to write,[20] Ó Súilleabháin recounted, 'Whenever I perform, I experience a sensation of "going *somewhere else*" … what might be termed either "out of body", or "into body" experiences of performers in action'.[21] Fifth, while both Ó Súilleabháin and Heaney returned for inspiration again and again to the well of tradition, they were nevertheless keenly aware of, and felt somewhat constrained by, the conservative nature of their environment and both pushed against the boundaries or expectations of the local canon. In several publications, for example, Ó Súilleabháin traced the experience of a number of important figures – Turlough Carolan, Thomas Moore, Seán Ó Riada and fiddler Tommie Potts – and their attempts to mediate change, successfully or unsuccessfully, within the Irish music tradition.[22] In the context of the emotionally charged tradition/innovation debate of the 1990s, Ó Súilleabháin described Potts as 'operating of necessity, if not by choice, within the general cultural confines of his inherited tradition'.[23] Seamus Heaney likewise noted in his 1995 Nobel lecture how he had internalised conservative attitudes that were prevalent in Northern Ireland 'to censure any flourish of rhetoric or extravagance of aspiration' to the point that for many years he avoided 'the opulence and extensiveness' of much poetry literature.[24]

Perhaps the most important connection between the two artists, however, concerns their own significance as cultural mediators. Accordingly, cultural mediation occurs where cultural practices serve a particular cause with the aim of political or social transformation. A mediator, then, is the actor in the scenario who intervenes to resolve some form of conflict, argument or tension between opposing sides or forces.[25] While mediation bears some relation to the duality expressed in the individual identities of Ó Súilleabháin and Heaney, as discussed above, the direction of cultural mediation is outward, aimed towards the community. Ó Súilleabháin describes the cultural mediator as:

> that middle voice which opens up a channel of communication between separate energies .... The musical mediator can be viewed as a bridge which allows listeners access to parts of their society and their experience of which they were unaware or perhaps just suspicious. And like any bridge, people walk across it – often with little regard for that which conveys them to another place, another world.[26]

During such boundary crossings, the task of the mediator, as Ó Súilleabháin points out, borrowing from Heaney, 'is to hold the light steady'.[27] But as music education specialist Marie McCarthy has articulated, the cultural mediator must possess particular characteristics and attitudes, including: curiosity and openness towards the viewpoints of others, respect for diverse values, desire to expand their own knowledge, and willingness to reflect on their own potential biases and suspend judgement where appropriate. This requires the mediator to be critically aware of political agendas that may operate through society, education and the arts to foster nationalisms, sustain colonialisms, or reproduce class divides. The cultural mediator thus necessarily becomes an agent of change in the mediation process, empowering others forward into 'a future that is a creative and dynamic fusion of past and present'.[28]

Key to successful cultural mediation, the goal of which is to arrive at better equilibrium between sides, is the concept of redress, a form of 'counter-weighting' to mitigate existing imbalances.[29] In his 1995 essay *The Redress of Poetry*, Heaney defines redress in three ways: firstly as a form of reparation or compensation for a wrong or loss sustained; secondly, to restore or to re-establish; and lastly, to bring [a tradition, an artform, etc] back to its proper course from where its full potential can be achieved. For Ó Súilleabháin, redress is required, firstly, for a problem to be resolved, and secondly, to rectify a missed opportunity.[30] He reflected on how redress might have operated in the Irish music tradition historically:

> If Heaney speaks of a 'redress of poetry' within English language tradition, can we view Potts and Ó Riada as being involved in some way in 'a redress of music'? What came up and out of music in Ireland during that period [1950s and 1960s] that made traditional music so central to a resurrection of an Irish psyche? Has some imbalance been addressed?[31]

Clearly, Ó Súilleabháin was engaged in cultural mediation from early on in his career with the obvious example being his role in the development of undergraduate and postgraduate degrees in music and Irish studies at UCC, and subsequently at UL, that redressed the omission of traditional musicians in third-level music education and brought them together with students studying jazz and classical music.[32] Indeed, he later commented that, 'this lifelong obsession with bringing the literate and the oral together in a performative situation is demonstrative of my role as a cultural mediator'.[33] But the mediation of differing traditions also occurred early on in his musical composition. Although his teachers and mentors Aloys Fleischmann and Seán Ó Riada also attempted mediation within the Irish music tradition – the former in the lifelong pursuit of 'Gaelic art music', the latter on a search for 'native Irish art music' and Ó Súilleabháin 'walked into the forcefield between them'[34] – it is clear that from early on he already held a somewhat different vision, as exemplified by his *Concerto for Traditional*

Musician and String Orchestra (1979), later reworked as *Oileán/Island* (1989). For, unlike his mentors, who aimed to achieve some form of musical synthesis, Ó Súilleabháin sought rather to bring the Irish art and traditional music systems 'into dialogue' in a manner that 'respected the boundaries of each'.[35] Thus in the *Concerto* he kept the traditional flute unscripted and distinct from the playing of the classical strings. Similarly, Seamus Heaney was concerned with how to mediate opposing forces without bringing them together in synthesis, noting that compromise was not necessarily the best way forward. This, he observed, was relevant to the political sphere and was where art and poetry could perhaps exert some positive influence.[36]

However, both Heaney and Ó Súilleabháin distanced themselves from any explicit involvement in politics, especially the thorny constitutional question of the North. Heaney noted in the context of the ongoing political violence in Northern Ireland 'feeling challenged yet steadfast in my noncombatant status' and that he was 'neither internee nor informer; / An inner émigré' who firmly resisted being placed into 'the political positions variously approved by mutually disapproving groups'.[37] But Roy Foster has pointed out that 'the restraint which he [Heaney] generally practised when addressing politics ... raised sensitive questions' and he endured criticism from within the Northern nationalist community and some of his contemporaries in the arts and academia.[38] Reflecting on the role of poetry in society in his 1995 essay 'Frontiers of Writing', Heaney envisioned the 'idea of poetry as an answer ... as a responsible poetry'. Poetry, he maintained in his Nobel lecture, may be credited 'for its truth to life', and the contribution of poets and writers in society was such that 'the Ireland I now inhabit is one that these Irish contemporaries have helped to imagine'.[39] But Heaney also emphasised that poetry must maintain its independence, and not be compromised or overly influenced by societal forces, as 'being given in its own language rather than in the language of the world that provokes it'.[40]

Similarly, Ó Súilleabháin expressed reluctance to engage directly in the political arena, preferring to keep his cultural distance though noting that it is the artist in each of us that 'senses *an ideal truth* somewhere out there like a distant yet bright light'.[41] He recounted the example of W.B. Yeats and his distrust of politics, concluding that Yeats' vision of Ireland as an independent nation with a loyal diaspora around the world was more about community than politics. Nevertheless, both Ó Súilleabháin and Heaney were similarly convinced of the power of the arts to achieve social change, often ahead of what might eventually become possible in the political sphere. Heaney's expression on this point is direct, writing that 'poetic fictions, the dream of alternative worlds, enable governments and revolutionaries ... [and] compel society to take on the shape of their imagining'. For his part, Ó Súilleabháin explains, 'I understand art as prophetic – as having a capacity to intuit happenings before the reality catches up … a political or social movement might be enacted first through art … The suggestion here is that by setting a cultural imbalance right, any social or political imbalance might also be at least partially addressed.'[42] However, Ó Súilleabháin recognised that the contribution of the non-verbal arts of music and dance in creating an emerging new vision of Ireland and Irish identity around the world had not been fully acknowledged especially in academia, that 'as usual we are faced with the problem of translating an idea, an intuition, into the world of action which is the world of politics'.[43] Significantly, it is such participatory non-verbal art forms that are often more easily accessible to newcomers and new citizens of Ireland, on the island and out in the greater diaspora.[44] As far back as the early 1980s, Ó Súilleabháin wrote that 'such great sections of the material on which traditional music in Ireland is built have come from outside the culture'.[45] Thus, the importance of openness towards, and inclusion of, many voices within and without Ireland is crucial to Mícheál Ó Súilleabháin's cultural vision of the way forward and he employs the metaphor of 'light' to describe it: 'Within our light there is a world of different lights. Within that world of different lights there is a shared brightness, a luminosity.'[46]

Clearly, Mícheál Ó Súilleabháin and Seamus Heaney were deeply committed to the emerging new cultural vision of Ireland in the 1990s – a vision both artists helped to create – that took firm hold with the majority approval of dual North/South referenda on the Good Friday Agreement (1998). It further encouraged them to come into what Ó Súilleabháin described as 'the sacred space of boundaries and thresholds' (*terminus*), whether encountered on the ground, in institutions or in people.[47] It is significant that both Ó Súilleabháin and Heaney participated in official events during the visit of Queen Elizabeth II to Ireland in May 2011. As an honoured guest, Seamus Heaney was seated at the queen's table at the state banquet in Dublin Castle (May 18), and as a featured performer at the concert in the National Convention Centre (May 19), Mícheál Ó Súilleabháin was presented to the queen on stage at the end of the event.[48]

Conclusion: lighting the way forward

The imagery and metaphors of vision and light, including, for example, the pursuit of knowledge as illumination, are associated with healing, forgiveness, hope and justice, and pervade the work of Seamus Heaney and Mícheál Ó Súilleabháin. Gradually from the 1990s, Heaney's work becomes suffused with light as optimism about the peace process in the North takes hold, with images of electric light and sunlight replacing the lantern light of old, most notable in the poetry collections *Seeing Things* (1991), *The Spirit Level* (1996) and *Electric Light* (2001).[49] Similarly, the image of Heaney's lamp light borrowed by Ó Súilleabháin increasingly becomes a 'bright, distant light', in the aisling/vision of *Oileán/Island* (1989) to works such as *Lumen* from *Between Worlds* (1995).[50] Heaney's preoccupation with the image of unroofed dwellings, notable in his poem 'The Skylight' (1991), recalling the open-roofed Roman temple where the stars could be read and the future foretold – the inspiration for Ó Súilleabháin's *Templum* (2001) – represents the vision of an unroofed, limitless world, an Ireland without boundaries.[51] The ongoing work of culture, 'by breaking the repressive forms and liberating new potential' as Heaney signifies, is 'helping the future to be born'.[52] But recognising that the future Ó Súilleabháin envisioned might not get here on its own, he was aware that others – notably his students – could be enabled to find the way forward. Hence, returning to the metaphor of the lantern held aloft, projecting light that is muted, not blinding, indicates the respect for each individual's unique path, the recognition that they must have the freedom to find their own way in life: as Heaney wrote of his own experience, 'a journey where each point of arrival – whether in one's poetry or one's life – turned out to be a *stepping stone* rather than a destination'.[53] Encompassing several of the concepts outlined in this essay – mediation, redress, the crossing of boundaries – Mícheál Ó Súilleabháin borrows Seamus Heaney's metaphor of the 'stepping stone' to reveal an enduring aspect of his legacy – that of enabling others:

> Whenever we cross the boundaries that border our musical experience from that of another, we move something on. Every movement of respectful knowing we make creates another *stepping stone* where someone may follow – or indeed someone may come across from the other side.[54]

75
Turas go Tír na nÓg: A personal reflection

Nuala O'Connor

Nuala O'Connor is an Emmy award-winning documentary film maker working in the area of music and arts documentaries. In 1994 she was the producer and writer for television with Mícheál Ó Súilleabháin and Philip King of A River of Sound.

I first met Mícheál during the making of our documentary series *Bringing It All Back Home* in 1990. The occasion was the filming and recording of the second and third movements of his composition *Oileán/Island* in the long-gone Windmill Lane studio in Kildare Street, Dublin. My sense of him then, which never changed over the following years, was of a hugely energetic force of positivity, an artist of deep creative resources and unfailing good cheer. Also, as became apparent very quickly, he was a very playful, humorous person and in his company we laughed a lot.

However, there was never any doubt that he was a serious, thoughtful man, deeply committed to two things: his work as a creative artist and teaching. Composing, arranging and performing were central to his creative process and, within the field of education, he worked ceaselessly to bring traditional music into the academy, not as a dry, theoretical, objectified field of study, but as the living thing experienced by real musicians and listeners. On that afternoon in Kildare Street I was simply thrilled to be there when, with Mícheál conducting, Johnny McCarthy played on flute the plaintive opening phrase of *Oileán* and the orchestra, like a swelling ocean, came in behind him and held him until the last phrase resolved, leaving that silence in which the heart and soul absorbs the profound beauty of what it has encountered.

This piece had emerged from a commissioned work, *Concerto for Traditional Musician and String Orchestra*, written by Mícheál in 1979. The original flute player was Matt Molloy and, as Mícheál explained, the orchestral part was composed to create a fabric around the playing of the flute. In this movement, consisting entirely of original music, the flute line is slow and the atmosphere dark. The swelling strings elaborate the sombre theme. The traditional musician is given space to exploit the full vocabulary of ornamentation within the piece. The final jaunty *Idir Eatarthu/Between Worlds* reiterates the dualities of *Oileán/Island* in the dialogue between two musical forms or two cultures and is based on a traditional song tune 'Jockey to the Fair' now restated as a single jig. In its liveliness and exuberance it very much bore the characteristics of its creator.

I have never forgotten that day and luckily I was to have the same experience again several times in the following years when we collaborated on *A River of Sound*, a six-part series for television. This involved many opportunities to watch and hear Mícheál play in many different contexts: in rehearsal, in full performance mode, solo, in ensemble, with orchestra and many times just for fun.

Between 1990 and 1994 I got to know him very well and spent a significant amount of time with him. This was when he was in transition to the University of Limerick from University College Cork to head up the newly established Irish World Academy of Music and Dance.

This was also when Philip King and I, then directors in Hummingbird Productions, embarked on our second documentary series, this time with Mícheál presenting a version of his foundation course in Irish traditional music, adapted for television. This was jointly commissioned by RTÉ and the BBC and was broadcast in 1995. As researcher and scriptwriter with Mícheál, I visited him frequently in the years running up to the filming of the series in his house in Murroe, County Limerick and then in Newport, County Tipperary. The challenge for us was somehow to distil an academic programme of lectures into an accessible, informative series with which the audience could identify. Although it was to became the subject of some controversy, sparking a sometimes heated debate about innovation and tradition, our intentions were to present and re-present/represent the world of traditional music as it appeared at that time: a snapshot of the culture, in other words, and not a tablet of stone delivered from on high.

Having worked in radio and television, it often fell to me to test our ideas from the perspective of the viewer. Mícheál would critique the developing film scripts against rigorous standards of ethnomusicological scholarship. Our relationship was, I think, fruitful for both of us and we were temperamentally well suited to working together. We argued, but most arguments ended in a laugh, and by that magical syncretic process which happens when collaboration works at its best, we produced a script that satisfied both of us.

He told me quite early on in the course of our work that he realised he would have to cede some control and that he was prepared to do this. That he trusted us to deliver what essentially was his vision of a traditional music series for television was humbling and daunting.

Once we had finished the script, set up the production, engaged with all the musicians and made final decisions on performances, interviews and locations, the shoot began and rolled out over a few memorable months in 1994. We became a travelling company of artists and film crew with Mícheál as the presiding ringmaster. This bit of the production involved travelling all over the country filming and recording musicians, sometimes with Mícheál playing, Mícheál interviewing people, Mícheál demonstrating and illustrating aspects of traditional music practice at the piano, and Mícheál doing what are known as PTCs or 'pieces to camera': addressing the viewer directly. Because of his style of communicating and years of teaching he was a natural communicator. Nonetheless there were times when multiple takes had to be filmed to get a fluff-free piece to camera, and uncontrollable laughter frequently brought work to a halt. In my memory those days are light-filled and happy and brimming with wonderful music; sometimes even too wonderful. Many a time I ended the day emotionally wrung out from over-exposure.

Two experiences stand out from that time. One was in Ballinlough House, County Westmeath with the Irish Chamber Orchestra, Eileen Ivers and Mícheál at the piano. The Nugent family who were our hosts had allowed us to recondition the beautiful old grand piano for Mícheál. As no member of the family played, the piano had been silent for decades and had been used for holding family photographs and vases of flowers. When the first notes of 'Ah Sweet Dancer' sounded on the piano followed by Eileen on fiddle with the orchestra, it was as if we entered a dreamtime when the seventeenth-century Nugent ancestors, maybe even Carolan himself, were present in the candlelit room. The contemporary Nugents who were actually present were overcome by emotion not having heard music in the room in their lifetime.

Lastly, there was the occasion when we filmed Mícheál himself playing 'Turas go Tír na nÓg' on his own grand piano in his home at Dromore House, a place he absolutely loved. Although there was a full crew working around him, he was completely unaware of anything other than the music he was making. He was 'gone'; fully submerged, a precious thing to see and hear. And then, as Prospero says at the end of *The Tempest*, 'Our revels now are ended'. This was the stuff that dreams are made of, now only revisited in memory and dreams.

76
A River of Sound
Philip King

Philip King is a film director, writer, musician, broadcaster and commentator. He is producer of the music series Other Voices, *co-founder of the radio programme* South Wind Blows, *and producer of* A River of Sound, *written and presented by Mícheál Ó Súilleabháin. He holds an honorary doctorate in music from University College Cork.*

I heard him before I saw him. It was 1970 in University College Cork (UCC). I was drawn by the sound of a piano playing an air in the most beautiful way. I sat at the back of the Aula Maxima and watched this thin, elegant figure lean into the piano and produce a sound I have never forgotten. Twenty years later, back in the same room, at the same piano, Mícheál played the air for me again, this time for a series of films we were making called *Bringing It All Back Home*. It was 'Bean Dubh an Ghleanna':

> Tá bó agam ar a' sliabh
> Is táim le seal 'na diaidh
> Ó chailleas-sa mo chiall le nuachar.

Mícheál spoke the words to me, taking delight in the sound and the cadence of each phrase. His sensitivity of touch and his natural empathy for the air were remarkable. Here now was a musician fully formed, an inspirational teacher and a man beginning a musical expedition that would take him right to the source of the 'river of sound' that is Irish music. He was to take me and so many more with him on that magical journey. On the journey to record the documentary *A River of Sound*, Mícheál said to me:

> 'Music in this our own time is like an ocean of sound. Travelling back upstream will help us to find parts of ourselves which may lie hidden. Traditional music is at the quick of our being. For those who grow to know to love it, the music becomes the heartbeat of our lives. As we make this journey, we will be searching out the deepest parts of a unique musical language.'[1]

This was 1994 and so off we went on what was to be the most inspirational, insightful and enriching journey of my life. We went everywhere across the island of Ireland and Mícheál talked and played with dozens of musicians, dancers, young and old, historians and people from every walk of life. For me it was a revelatory and life-changing experience and, as it turned out, an occasion of great argument and debate about the state and role of our music: a music that is the inspired music of generations and not the music of any one individual.

Passions, theories, beliefs and ambitions were captured in the words of those we met and recorded. Individual voices stay in my mind, like Donnchadh Ó Corráin, saying, 'I have an instinctive feeling that *sean-nós* is the lineal descendent of Irish church music and it is far too much a music of art to be the simple music of untrained people.' A very young and brilliant Laoise Kelly voiced her passion: 'I want to go out there on my own and do as well as anybody else on a solo instrument and I think the harp has its place not just traditionally but in all sorts of music.' The figure of Tommie Potts loomed large. Mícheál stood outside Tommie's house in Dublin and said to me:

> 'Here in this house in Dublin lived one of the most extraordinary Irish traditional musicians: Tommie Potts. In my mind, he ranks with Carolan and Seán Ó Riada as one of our greatest musical innovators. Yet so few people seem to know who he was and even less seemed to understand the nature and depth of his musical genius. You see, Potts did something that no outsider can do … he exploded the music from within. History may show him to be a brilliant cul de sac or it may show him to be a musical prophet.'

We visited the east Clare family home of P.J. Hayes and his son Martin who had recently returned from Chicago. They sat and played beautifully together and Mícheál asked Martin if he had any sense of where the music came from. Martin replied:

> 'Well, the music must come out of the souls of the people. I mean in this locality they lost a language and with it much of the poetry. But the music is something that was retained very strongly here and it's the only means left to express soulfully what's important to the community here.'

All of this material and my memory of it is but one part of Mícheál's legacy and a gift to us all. Mícheál's gift as a musician, composer and performer could have brought him great universal acclaim but he chose a different river to navigate and to go deep within himself to search for the heart and the soul of the music that informed every aspect of his life.

I hear his voice again now – energetic, playful and wise – as I sit here in west Kerry not far from Casadh na Gráige and within earshot of Port na bPúcaí, and he is telling me:

> 'Traditional music is as delicately balanced as the earth's ecological system. It is essential that we recognise this because in recognising it we will know what to do when traditional music meets education, meets all kinds of commercial demands, digital transmission and so much more. Our music is a music to live and die for. Like all true music, it carries the spirit of truth and freedom.'

Bhí an ceart aige.

77

A Constant Companion in Music

Aodán Ó Dubhghaill

Aodán Ó Dubhghaill worked with Ireland's national public service broadcaster Raidió Teilifís Éireann (RTÉ) for forty-three years. He was appointed head of RTÉ Lyric FM in 2002 and managing director of RTÉ's orchestras, quartet and choirs in 2016. Following retirement, he completed the MA Irish Traditional Music Performance at the University of Limerick.

I was reared in a household steeped in the Irish language and culture and filled with music, traditional and classical. I participated in competitions as a boy soprano (An t-Oireachtas and Feis Ceoil), fiddler (feiseanna in Galway, Cork and Dublin) and violin player (a member of the Irish Youth Orchestra). It was no accident that my teenage working career started in the 1970s working for the record company run by Gael Linn Teo. I managed their retail record division, a shop called Fónodisc, which was based in the Creation Arcade off Grafton Street in Dublin. It had three main specialisms: classical music, Irish music (including the full range of Irish traditional music) and folk music (which would later branch out to incorporate the descriptor 'world music').

These were minority sectors of the booming record industry at the time. In western Europe, classical music held an approximate 9 per cent share of the record market. In Ireland, the market share held by classical records did not exceed 5–6 per cent and the market share for Irish traditional music records was in the region of 5 per cent.

My first introduction to Mícheál Ó Súilleabháin was when his self-titled album of keyboard music was launched on the Gael Linn label in 1976 and became a favourite on the turntable in Fónodisc. I was intrigued by how the harmonium could sound like the uilleann pipes (including drones), or the harpsichord could develop from the traditional style of playing that Ó Riada had brought to the keyboard in his 1972 LP Ó Riada's *Farewell to Music*. Since that time Mícheál has been a part of musical life in Ireland and has had an immense influence on the sonic landscape of our small island, with tentacles spreading far across the globe.

The development of Irish music, in all its forms, from those folk-frenzied days of the 1970s to today, is mirrored in everything Mícheál undertook in his varied, eclectic compositions, traditional arrangements, and performances. Traditional music merged into folk music, which in turn melded into world music, and he somehow fused these idioms with jazz and western art music influences.

Many of the tunes featured on his first album appear in compositions and arrangements later in his career, always with a new twist. The second album (*Óró Damhnaigh*), which was released a year after the first, featured arrangements that are quite traditional in places but venture also into jazz idioms, which Mícheál would later develop.

In 1996, twenty years after the release of his first album, I was a producer/sound engineer for a radio broadcast (on RTÉ FM3, a forerunner of RTÉ Lyric FM) from the RTÉ/Bank of Ireland Proms in the RDS, Dublin. Mícheál introduced his group Hiberno Jazz (featuring Eileen Ivers and Therese Timoney on violins, Niall Keegan on flute, Kenneth Edge on saxophone, Mel Mercier on spoons and bodhrán and Andy Baker on bass). As well as featuring guest artists in his own concerts, Mícheál would also appear as a guest himself on many recordings by other artists as well as on concert platforms with orchestras, choirs, chamber ensembles and a variety of musical groups. He was also a talented media performer and being bilingual (in Irish and English) was in demand as a presenter and contributor on RTÉ television and radio channels including Lyric FM and Raidió na Gaeltachta (RnG), as well as TG4.

I was privileged to play music with Mícheál on two occasions and both stay etched in my memory. As a shy (non-professional) musician he made me feel totally at ease. The first time was in 2002 during a live broadcast from Limerick of the Vincent Browne radio programme where we played 'Eleanor Plunkett' together (piano/fiddle) and then later I recall a mega-session in his home and we played a few songs with Andy Irvine and Dónal Lunny. During that evening we talked about playing and I related to him my reticence about playing in public. It was interesting for me to hear his own thoughts on the piano and its place in Irish traditional music. Many commentators credited him with changing the mindset on how the piano was regarded in the context of 'traditional' instruments in Irish folk music. He didn't regard himself as a 'traditional Irish musician', rather an interpreter of Irish traditional music. He felt as nervous playing with a group of traditional musicians as he did playing with a group of classical musicians in an orchestra/ensemble setting. He spoke about the grounding he got as a musician and composer in the early years with Ó Riada and Fleischmann in Cork and how this background prepared him well for his future lifelong journey exploring the trans-musical impact of traditional and classical musicians sharing the same acoustic. During an interview in 1991 with Paddy Glackin for *The Pure Drop* programme on RTÉ television he said, 'I came to traditional music, and found myself with the wrong instrument … so what I'm playing is a working out of that dilemma.' Ten years later he was still discussing that 'dilemma', a theme we often returned to when we met.

Alongside his prolific musical output as a performer, Mícheál was an active composer. Speaking with him in later years as we worked on several concerts with the RTÉ National Symphony Orchestra and the RTÉ Concert Orchestra, I got the impression that it was composition that gave him the most satisfaction, with each commission presenting its own challenges. Throughout his career he was commissioned to write several large-scale works, usually featuring piano with string orchestra or concert orchestra, but also more intimate works such as *Fidelio Unsung*, commissioned by RTÉ Lyric FM and receiving its premiere at King's Palace, London in 2010. His interpretation of songs 'Míle Buíochas Leatsa', 'An Buachaill Caol Dubh' and 'Port na bPúcaí' for *sean-nós* singer and orchestra was commissioned by the RTÉ Concert Orchestra and first performed at the National Concert Hall, Dublin in September 2013. Some years later in 2017 we opened our RTÉ National Symphony Orchestra season of concerts on Friday, 8 September with *Elver Gleams: A celebration of the music of Mícheál Ó Súilleabháin*. This concert presented his newly composed and newly scored works, together with a *sean-nós* arrangement that fused traditional and orchestral styles.

During our conversations about what might be included in the concert, Mícheál relished the prospect of working with the larger forces of a symphony orchestra and was keen to rewrite some of the earlier pieces for piano as well as new compositions. He had written pieces for symphony orchestra previously (for example, *Gellan*) but these pieces did not include traditional musician soloists and he was keen to continue making work wherein traditional and classical musicians shared the same stage. He described the pieces featuring *sean-nós* singer Iarla Ó Lionáird as miniature tone poems and used the new Irish term *ceoldán* to describe this new genre, which he also called 'orchestral *sean-nós*'.

For this concert Mícheál also revisited *Oileán/Island* (composed originally in 1979 for traditional flute and string orchestra, re-emerging in 1989 under this title). In programme notes for the concert he described the piece as being 'about the redress of balance between oppositional forces – in this case formal and informal, literate and oral, classical and traditional, playing by eye/ear and playing entirely by ear. The piece has now been lifted once again onto the wider palette of full orchestra', and harmonica player Brendan Power took the solo line.

Piper Pádraic Keane finished the concert with a commemorative piece for pipes and orchestra on the tenth anniversary of 9/11. This concert was conducted by Sinead Hayes from Galway and I've no doubt the success of the evening was helped by the fact that she is also a traditional fiddle player!

The influence Mícheál has had on the musical landscape of our island may not be fully appreciated for many years to come but I have no doubt that his music will touch many generations. He communicated through music, but I also liked the way he could speak about the 'space' where art is created – he was very aware of the sounds, frequencies and echoes in wood, stone and nature. Listening to his music, incorporating other idioms into the Irish tradition (rather than the other way around), is still a joyful and enlightening experience and I hope that through the many written scores and recordings of his music, many generations of musicians and interpreters will discover new and enlightening aspects of his output that have yet to be discovered, as I am doing myself as I re-listen to his early recordings as I write.

78
History Lessons
Rod Stoneman

Rod Stoneman is an emeritus professor at the University of Galway. A documentarian and author, he served as director of the Huston School of Film & Digital Media, chief executive of Bord Scannán na hÉireann/The Irish Film Board, and as a deputy commissioning editor at Channel 4 Television.

A *Vertical Man*, Christopher Swann's documentary on Seán Ó Riada, included sections of a long interview with Mícheál Ó Súilleabháin talking about his mentor.[1] I had been working at Bord Scannán na hÉireann/The Irish Film Board since 1993 and, as we contributed to the film's production costs, I saw several early versions and learned a little about Ó Riada's complex artistic trajectory reinventing himself as artist through different generic explorations of jazz, the avant garde, Irish traditional music and classical liturgical music.

Getting to know Mícheál Ó Súilleabháin a few years later and collaborating by organising symposia on practice-based research in the west of Ireland, it was clear that the ebullient personality suggested in his filmed interview was combined with energy and focus that encouraged joint enterprise across disciplines and between institutions.[2] Practice-based research in the arts, combining creative work with written reflection and analysis, is a relatively recent academic space and offers a range of opportunities for innovation and transformative knowledge. The diversity of material engaged in a project of enquiry stimulates movement between disciplines and encourages encounters between the diverse art forms.[3] A clear example of such creative practice is the conjunction of musical composition with the images of a silent film, a process that enacts a subtle transformation in the viewer's experience of pre-existent images. Ó Súilleabháin was conscious of Ó Riada's previous work in this field and was interested in the possibilities of the combination of art forms involved in writing music for film; remarking on the significant differences involved when 'something has been made by someone else and then you are brought into the process afterwards'.[4] He approached this process of composition for a finished film in a specific and historically conscious way.

Film music is a powerful element in the ensemble of signs and the construction of meaning in cinema.[5] Used to support on-screen action, it is generally subordinated to both picture and narrative, sustaining and heightening psycho-dramatic effects. In mainstream cinema this aural transmission of meaning and emotion works on the spectator's unconscious mind and achieves its effects through largely standard musical means: calculated, evocative use of instrumental colour, harmonic tension and release (dissonance-consonance, sudden modulations, tension-building clichés like the diminished seventh chord), recurring melodic leitmotifs and patterns. In commercial cinema the effect of musical sound on the image with which it is juxtaposed is usually to restrict ambiguity and close off the range of possible meanings which could be produced. Looking at many old films, one is struck by the trivialising and sedative effects that narrative music has on potent imagery, and how abstract sounds have become culturally codified and irretrievably loaded with connotation. These subtle effects are generally naturalised and imperceptible to the viewer. As the philosopher Theodor Adorno and the composer Hanns Eisler wrote: 'One of the most widespread prejudices in the motion picture industry is the premise that the spectator should not be conscious of the music … the thesis that film music should be unobtrusive is questionable.'[6]

Seán Ó Riada wrote the score for *Mise Éire*, George Morrison's 1959 documentary which assembled archival footage to tell the story of the moment of Irish revolutionary nationalism in 1916 and its historical context. Some thirty years later, Mícheál Ó Súilleabháin composed a new score for a restored version of silent feature film *Irish Destiny*, with a starting point after Sinn Féin's electoral victory in 1918, combining a fictional narrative with actuality footage of the War of Independence. This combination of disparate material shifts registers between a love story, with oedipal drama attached, and the large-scale historical events depicting the violence in the moment of national formation. The film's use of newsreel footage of actual historical events is interposed in the fictionalised, restaged military action and domestic drama, questioning the categorical division of fiction and documentary (Figure 78.1).

Figure 78.1: The loving couple and the British burning of Cork city, reduced to 'A City of Ashes' on 11–12 December 1920.

Written and produced by Isaac J. Eppel and directed by George Dewhurst in 1926, an extant copy of this film had been disinterred from the vaults of the Library of Congress in Washington in 1991 by the Irish Film Archive.[7] Tinted and toned, the print retained its original textures: the orange/gold colour of the countryside gives way to a deep blue for night scenes and unexpected flare of scarlet flames and smoke bursting from the screen in several sequences – a strange effect disrupting the surface of the image. Although the film was shot only a few years from the events portrayed – viewed nearly 100 years after it was made – the representations appear anachronistic, the melodramatic gestures of heroic motion and emotion appear overstated as the chronological distance brings the means of representation into focus.

Ó Súilleabháin was commissioned to compose a soundtrack for the restored film, performing it live at the National Concert Hall in Dublin on 11 December 1993.[8] His musical versatility works across the diverse registers of the film as he developed inventive orchestration and compositional structure. After an overture with elements directly borrowed from Bach's *Brandenburg Concerto No. 5*, the music builds into the love theme, which Ó Súilleabháin described as 'a deconstructed version of the National Anthem'.[9] The orchestration articulates delicate movements between a plaintive piano and a full orchestra. The single piano notes played over original newsreel footage of military and Black and Tan reinforcements in Dublin is framed by a succession of ominous orchestral chords. A variation of these leitmotifs is heard for the first time when we see the IRA officer Tom Kelly, with an intertitle to explain that he is a 'Captain in the Irish Republic [*sic*] Army'.[10] Ó Súilleabháin noted that 'the feelings of pride are always subverted in the music by deeper feelings of love and hope in a gesture of yearning'.

Anticipation of the raid at Vaughan's Hotel in Dublin is built with strings and mournful woodwind notes, playing under the gunfight where Denis O'Hara is shot, and over the large crowds in framing scenes made possible by utilising actuality footage. Rhythmic patterns playing alongside the battle sequences are punctuated by an ominous warning signal, a horn motif leading to a return to the piano. These were forms of orchestration connected with the diversity of musics and instruments Ó Súilleabháin had encountered early in his career, encouraged by Ó Riada's mixing traditional Irish music with wider and non-traditional instrumentation.

Ó Súilleabháin was acutely aware of the historical frames of reference that preceded his work and the contemporary context for composition of a new soundtrack for the film in 1991. He wrote a prefatory note invoking the precedents: 'I wrote the music for *Irish Destiny* some thirty years after Seán Ó Riada wrote the score for *Mise Éire* (1959) – a time when self-pride was a necessary stage on the path to self-esteem; and Ó Riada's score is unequivocal in its emotions. He, in turn, wrote that score thirty years after *Irish Destiny* was made – so in a sense this work salutes both those moments, drawing wisdom from them both.'[11]

Ó Súilleabháin was precise in his description of the way in which '[t]he feelings of national pride, which the film seeks to exploit, are allowed partial expression in a series of variations on *Amhrán Dóchais/Song of Hope*, the official state music which is played in the presence of An Taoiseach in our own times'.

As his note indicates, Ó Súilleabháin wanted to enunciate the relation with Ó Riada's music for *Mise Éire* as an important frame of reference at a different stage of Irish cultural and political development and aimed to achieve something that would be appropriate for *Irish Destiny* at a later point in history. Perhaps one should be reminded that in 1991, ninety-six people died in the Troubles. Making the changed conceptions and emotions precise, he conceived the score with a wider and more international reference: 'My hopes for the music are that it is questioning without being apologetic; that it is proud without being arrogant; that above all else, it praises the human spirit of freedom in whatever tradition it is found.' Interestingly, one of the film's intertitles also touches on a broader perspective: 'They're thinking of nothing but war – will fighting in this world never cease?' When the Haunted Mill is burnt and traitors destroyed at the end of the film, red flames, powerfully contrasting with the purple filtered interior, spring from the illegal poteen still. The blaze can be understood to stand for the IRA attack on Dublin's Custom House before the ceasefire in July 1921 and is followed by the intertitle: 'The dawn of a new era – peace and happiness to all mankind'.

A further thirty years after Ó Súilleabháin's score was originally composed, and nearly 100 years after the film was shot, we can view the images of *Irish Destiny* in conjunction with it as an exact index of the complex shifting layers in Irish self-image. There are moments where Ó Súilleabháin's music seems almost to challenge or doubt the very images he is scoring. Music is generally understood as an abstract art form but it is deployed as part of the ensemble of representations in film and in this case it explicitly calibrates the changing political emotions of a specific nation state. The conjuncture of the present inflects our selective understandings of the past, and the film and its score allows us insight into how people understand themselves in history.

Irish Destiny is part of a set of divided and contested representations of that pivotal revolutionary moment in modern Irish history. Mícheál Ó Súilleabháin's music articulates intricate undercurrents in the depiction of the War of Independence that the image track supresses through the disposition of stereotypes: the villainous traitor and the heroic IRA volunteer (who is also a devoted son and lover). As Walter Benjamin proposed: 'To articulate what is past does not mean to recognise "how it really was". It means to take control of a memory as it flashes in a moment of danger.'[12] Ó Súilleabháin's nuanced score for *Irish Destiny* uses unique musical means to enunciate a complex version of the contradictions of a politically violent moment of history.

79

'Too-Ra-Loo-Ra-Loo-Ral': Musical priests on screen and Irish-American identity

Méabh Ní Fhuartháin

Méabh Ní Fhuartháin is head of Irish studies at the University of Galway. Specialising in Irish music and dance studies, she has co-edited special issues of Ethnomusicology Ireland *and* Éire-Ireland: An interdisciplinary journal of Irish studies *and published widely on Irish popular and traditional musics.*

Prologue

Based on his commitment to parity of esteem for traditional music in an Irish music world, Mícheál Ó Súilleabháin challenged his students to think about traditional music in new and critical ways. My longstanding interest in music in a diasporic setting stems directly from a conversation I had with Mícheál in 1989, as the end of my primary degree was looming. A notice for a graduate fellowship at Boston College was posted in the foyer of the Old Rectory, then the Department of Music, in University College Cork. I tentatively asked him if I should apply; he responded with confidence, 'Sure, why wouldn't you?', illustrating his capacity to recognise potential in people who perhaps did not yet recognise it themselves. My move to the United States for graduate study, on foot of an application encouraged by Mícheál, opened my ears (and intellect) to a broader church of Irish music where the intersectional sounds of popular culture, immigrant and dominant worlds meet. In Mícheál's memory, this essay explores such a sound space, exploring the complexities of music, meaning and identities in the mediated world of American musical film and in particular the figure of the musical priest as personified by Bing Crosby.

Introduction

Discourses of Irish music in America from 1920 to 1950 have two particular themes: the evolution of an ethnic recording industry during that period (with instrumental music dominating those discussions), and popular Irish song.[1] Building on these areas, this essay explores film, music and Irish-America.

I argue that during the twentieth century the figure of the singing, Irish(-American), Catholic priest on screen became an essentialised and essentialising representation of Irish-America in the American popular culture imagination. Simultaneously, this sounded image of masculine Irish-America also represented the ordinary American, thereby appealing to both the particular and the universal experience. Set in the wider context of changing American society, the popularity of singing priests in the golden era of Hollywood musicals and musical movies, from the late 1930s to the 1950s, was made possible due to a generational remove from Irish origins and upward mobility of the Irish in America during the period. Important too is the historical context of Irish contributions to the development of popular song in America from the nineteenth and early twentieth century and the animation of Ireland as a musical nation. Irish, musical, singing, Catholic and priest: all intersect to produce a super-ethnic constellation which functions as a foil for the ordinary American experience. Examined here in particular is the soundscape of Irish-America within American popular culture as performed by Bing Crosby as melodious cleric. Arguably, this is the final ethnic flourish of late-stage post-Famine Irish-America as it became part of mainstream American identity.

(Irish-)America 1920–50

The period from 1920 to 1950 in America was one of Prohibition, Depression and yet another world war. It was also when 'the American Irish left behind much of the discrimination and impoverishment' of the previous century.[2] Emigration from Ireland to America dropped significantly with coeval upward mobility of second and subsequent generations. Despite ongoing anti-Catholic sentiments and pockets of prevailing nativism, Irish-America achieved 'rough occupational and educational equality with the American population as a whole' with an 'increasingly elective nature of Irish ethnicity in mainstream American thought'.[3]

In 1908, Pope Pius X decreed that the Catholic Church in the United States was no longer a missionary church, recognising the parity of the American church with that of Europe.[4] Notwithstanding the presence of other Catholic emigrant groups (Italian-Americans, for example), the Catholic Church in the United States during this period was an Irish one: institutionalised through a private Catholic school and college system, and to a lesser extent a Catholic-orders medical system. The construction of Irish-American identity as a Catholic one stems from Famine and post-Famine migrations, belying the statistical reality of an Irish-American majority self-identifying within a broad category of Protestant.[5] Nonetheless, a Catholic priest was de facto an Irish priest in the American cultural imagination. This is demonstrated in the multiple Irish priest figures featured in movies from the 1930s onwards including Pat O'Brien playing priests in *Fighting Father Dunne* (1940), *Angels with Dirty Faces* (1938) and *The Fighting 69th* (1940), and Spencer Tracy as Fr Flanagan in *Boys Town* (1938) and its sequel, *Men of Boys Town* (1941).

The emergence of sound in film by the end of the 1920s was transformative not just for the evolving film industry but for society. In 1927, the first film with sound, *The Jazz Singer*, had music and ethnic identity politics as essential narrative building blocks. Advancing sound technology led to the emergence of film genres specifically built around music, among them musical films and film musicals. Within this developing canon, Fergal Lenehan notes the disproportionately large number of Irish-themed films in the golden age of this genre, from the 1930s to the 1950s.[6] Some are located partially or fully in rural Ireland, but the majority are situated in urban emigrant settings in the United States.[7] In contrast to the fiddle recordings of Michael Coleman and others, the music in these films and the characters' singing is not (primarily) directed inward to Irish-America, though they may appeal to that assimilating constituency. Rather, as Christopher Shannon recognises, the success of these films lay in their seeming counterintuitive capacity to 'present the Irish as representative of a broader vision of the city as an urban village – fully ethnic, yet fully American'.[8]

What remains unacknowledged in scholarship is the meaning generated through, and in, the ethnically bonded music repertoire of these movies and the foil of the Irish-American priest character who essentialised and sounded those meanings. Within these films, the character of priest is ever-present and frequently a singing one. The most effective and successful Irish singing priest of them all was Bing Crosby whose 'portrayal of a wise, warm, Irish Catholic patriarch' was his 'longest-running, most convincing role'.[9]

Bing Crosby: American and Irish

Born and raised in Spokane, Washington, Harry Lillis (Bing) Crosby (1903–77) was the son of second- and fourth-generation Irish emigrants. Crosby was educated at a Jesuit high school and even considered becoming a priest; he became one of the highest-profile lay Catholics of the twentieth century in the United States.[10] His professional success can be traced in several different phases as his career intersects with, and drives, the rapidly expanding entertainment industry. Crucially, Crosby was one of the key architects of a new kind of crooner voice which developed in the 1930s. This crooner was a response to the vocal and presentational style of men crooner performers that developed in the previous decade primarily through radio that had offered 'new possibilities for intimacy between singers and their audiences, especially a female audience'.[11] The 1930s crooner regained a more overt masculinity in presentation while retaining the gentle, sonorous quality of the vocal sound developed in the 1920s.[12] When Crosby signed with Decca Records in 1934 his distinctive sound was crafted carefully, capitalising on his natural ability and previous vocal experience. Songs were selected to use his lower voice, foregoing the upper register which he had used heretofore. Crosby avoided stretching his voice, a key to the 'crooner' sound aesthetic, and emphasised a repertoire of 'confident love songs ("It's Been a Long, Long Time"), seasonal anthems ("White Christmas"), nostalgic tributes to home and family ("Dear Hearts and Gentle People") and upbeat inspirational tunes ("Accentuate the Positive")'.[13] This new, refined Crosby 'was forthrightly masculine yet intimate in scale' and delivered a 'comfortable repose' to put the 'listener wholly at ease'.[14]

Crosby was an unrivalled marquee draw for any movie in which he appeared. During the 1930s, as movie musicals (at MGM and Fox) and musical movies (at Paramount) developed, he excelled in the latter, often playing different versions of his own affable stock character.[15] Both music-film sub-genres provided 'primal popular music moment[s] when a song everyone knows was sung into the culture by a singer everyone knows'.[16] Additionally, 'relatively slight films' were vehicles 'that showcased a new [original] batch of potential hit songs'.[17] By the early 1940s, 'Crosby held a dominant position in radio, records, and film simultaneously' with a 'command over all three entertainment media'.[18] Crosby was therefore well established in his career when he first drew explicit attention in performance to his ethnic Irishness.

Rejecting the advice of record company executives at Decca, he recorded 'Did Your Mother Come from Ireland/Where the River Shannon Flows' in 1941, which was the first of several Irish-themed hits over the next decade and a half. During the same period, Crosby played several screen roles as an Irish-American priest, in what Eric Mazur terms the 'Fr Crosby' movies, singing his way through admittedly thin plot lines in *Going My Way* (1944), *The Bells of St Mary's* (1946) and *Say One for Me* (1959).[19] The characterisation and sound of Fr Chuck O'Malley in the first of these, *Going My Way* (a role reprised in *The Bells of St Mary's*), resonated profoundly with the wartime audience, as Fr Chuck became a 'test case for America's emerging conception of itself as a pluralist democracy'.[20]

Going My Way: (Irish-)America on screen

On its release in 1944, *Going My Way* was seen by over a million people (just in New York) and won a record-breaking seven of ten Oscar nominations received.[21] Crosby won Best Actor and the Irish actor Barry Fitzgerald won for Best Supporting Actor (he was also nominated for Best Actor). Linda Dowling Almeida writes that the success of the movie 'suggested that the American public was ready to accept the Irish, their priests and communities as part of the larger culture and consider them lovable rather than dangerous'.[22] But it was not just a matter of being allowed in the door upon which Irish-Americans had been knocking, there were changes afoot from within Catholic Irish-America too. *Going My Way* is directed at a broad public, declaring that Catholic Irish-Americans are just like everyone else.[23] Fr Chuck, most often in ath-leisure wear rather than priestly garb, is selling and singing a non-threatening Catholicism. No religious sacraments are performed on screen, and scenes within the church building display soft-focus Catholicism as a universal experience relatable to all Americans. Todd Decker, writing of another Crosby movie, comments on the 'conjunction of song, singer, and historical moment', an intersection which is also exploited in *Going My Way*.[24] Written, made and released after Pearl Harbor and the subsequent declaration of war by the American government, Crosby was a significant figure in selling 'the war to the average, middle-class American', and further 'he sold pleasurable respite from the total war'.[25]

In addition to the universal Catholicism on screen, this is a movie which foregoes or reimagines many tropes of Irish ethnicity: it is without violence; the use of alcohol is benign (though significant in one scene); and for the most part has Irish-American rather than first-generation emigrant characters. The plot, such as it is, centres around the younger Fr Chuck who arrives at the New York parish of St Dominic's (located ten blocks from the Metropolitan Opera) to rescue the parish finances and assume responsibilities from the older parish priest Fr Fitzgibbon. A set of oppositions are immediately constructed: Fr Chuck represents a younger generation of Irish-America, modern and forward-looking, in comparison to Fr Fitzgibbon as old, Irish-born and unwilling to avert his gaze away from the past and to the future. Other supporting characters include an Irish-American cop (Pat McCarthy), another younger Irish-American priest (Fr Doyle), a historical love interest for the pre-priest Fr Chuck, and a number of secondary Irish female characters (including the housekeeper, Mrs Carmody). Obvious, but important to note, is that ethnicity is marked by patrilineal naming assuming absolute intra-ethnic marriage practices. There are two female songstresses (neither Irish), their religion undeclared, but as Fr Chuck is an ecumenical pastor to one and all, this reasserts the suitability of (Irish) Catholicism to the grand urban American project.

As its default soundscape, *Going My Way* has Irish and Irish-American voices both spoken and sung. Irish and Irish-American sounds, particularly spoken accents, are the bedrock of the film's identity-making. Irish accents of Irish-born actor-characters (Fr Fitzgibbon), accents of Irish characters (Mrs Carmody) and Irish-American accents of the Bowery are interspersed and overlap with stage Irish accents and phrasing of secondary characters. Similar to the use of the iconic phrase 'Now you has jazz' in *High Society* as Morris B. Holbrook notes, sound patterns of language in *Going My Way* act as signifiers, unlocking and reinforcing ideas about place, belonging and identity.[26] 'Sure and Father O'Malley has a strong pair of shoulders', and 'Do you have a wee drop of the craythur about?' locate the film and its cast of characters in urban Irish-America, a microcosm of wider American society. In 1944, Irish-American representations on screen fulfilled the dual functions of demarcating Irish-American as its own distinct identity, but also one which was increasingly part of the universal American experience to which all could relate, as presented in the voices and sounds of St Dominic's parish.

Categorised as a musical movie, *Going My Way* disrupts the 'girl meets boy, girl/boy does silly things, girl and boy finally unite' dramatic structure typical of this genre. A family movie without a family, according to Shannon, the primary relationship explored is that between two (celibate) generationally distinct characters, Fr Chuck and Fr Fitzgibbon.[27] Songs function as narrative scaffolding, amplifying dramatic moments and feelings, offering carefully paced musical explanations, pauses and/or transitions. Fr Chuck (Crosby) performs five songs, including the Oscar-winning 'Would You Like to Swing on a Star?' However, in the context of the movie and this essay, 'Too-Ra-Loo-Ra-Loo-Ral' is the song which carries the weight of meaning and affect.

'Too-Ra-Loo-Ra-Loo-Ral' as super-ethnic expression

'Too-Ra-Roo-Ra-Loo-Ral (That's an Irish Lullaby)' is not the theme song of *Going My Way*, nor is it the Oscar-winning song of the film. However, it is the climax of super-ethnic expression in the movie and operates as a sonic site in which key emotional questions of the story are explored and, to some degree, resolved. Used as a structuring and ambidiagetic device, it 'advances the dramatic development' in this film and signals 'other important cinematic elements'.[28] The song's first iteration takes place at a pivotal moment of reconciliation between the two priests. Up to this point, tension between them has been building in the film as the older Fitzgibbon resists ceding any control of the parish to the younger priest. In a fit of pique, Fitzgibbon is caught outdoors in a rainstorm and returns home to take to his bed. Fr Chuck checks on the older priest and in a gesture of ethnic stereotypical peace-making asks if Fitzgibbon has 'a drop of the wee craythur about' that they might share. Directed to a music-box, when opened the music box plays the melody of the song 'Too-Ra-Loo-Ra-Loo-Ral' (1:01:15) for the first time in the movie. Fr Chuck describes the melody as a 'little bit of old Ireland'. Also revealed is a bottle of whiskey secreted within.

Originally written in 1913 by James Royce Shannon for the Tin Pan Alley musical *Shameen Dhu* (and recorded by Chauncey Olcott in the same year), 'Too-Ra-Loo-Ra-Loo-Ral' is a quintessential Irish-American popular song, with sentimental, nostalgic lyrics and a strong melodic line. The whiskey music-box is a recurring gift which Fitzgibbon's mother sends him each Christmas and symbolises that mother–child bond. The mother figure is implicit in the lullaby genre and explicit in the original song ('My mother sang a song to me in tones so sweet and low … And I'd give the world if I could hear that song of hers today'). In this scene, Fitzgibbon reveals he has not seen his mother for four and a half decades. The nostalgic yet poignant loss which Fitzgibbon experiences by this prolonged separation from his mother is encapsulated in the lullaby, the chorus of which Fr Chuck then sings.

The mother image, dramatically introduced through the music box and through the Irish(-American) lullaby played, is simultaneously an avatar of Ireland herself, a powerful image used in Irish-American stage and popular song of the nineteenth and twentieth centuries. Fr Chuck, assuming the maternal role and inverting the generational reality of the characters, sings the older Fr Fitzgibbon, now reverted to child, to sleep. The image of the younger priest consoling and comforting the older figure, together with their juxtaposition of origins (Irish-America and Ireland), subverts expectations, but they are united in grief and longing for their respective mothers (one dead, one far away).

Following this initial sounding, the song assumes a highly charged symbolic role in the film. When Fr Chuck is given instructions to move to another parish towards the end of the movie, the music box is pulled out, opened and 'Too-Ra-Loo-Ra-Loo-Ral' is again heard while the two priests drink to another leaving, another loss (2:01:50). There is one more, meaning-filled performance of 'Too-Ra-Loo-Ra-Loo-Ral' (2:05:20) in the very final scene. This time the scrappy boys' choir, which Fr Chuck has under his wing throughout the film, sing the chorus of 'Too-Ra-Loo-Ra-Loo-Ral' as Fr Fitzgibbon's aged mother enters the church, a miracle of sorts. In an act of restorative nostalgia, her surprise arrival from Ireland is Fr Chuck's parting gift to Fitzgibbon, filling an emotional void with both song and mother. Rather than boy gets girl, as is the norm for the end of movie musicals and musical movies, it is priest sees mother as a climactic emotional end. Its sounding evokes the Irish mother figure certainly, but also the generic American mother figure and the experience of loss in the war period.

Conclusion

The nature of the relationship between music and identity revealed here contributes to critical mediations of cultural meaning, a theme which Mícheál Ó Súilleabháin explored through his own music-making, teaching and writing.[29] 'Too-Ra-Loo-Ra-Loo-Ral' suggests the distance not just between immigrants and their origins, but also the distance felt by all during this period as a universal American experience, evoking a continuous cycle of loss and leaving. Carefully deployed in *Going My Way*, the song asserts the strength of generational bonds while recognising that inevitably age must yield to youth. This song is central to what Lenehan identifies as the semantics of migration, so often found in Irish-themed musicals of the period.[30] The motif of longing for home (in this case, home being Ireland and, simultaneously, America) is contained and registered in, through and by the song. Ultimately, however, the success of the singing Irish priest as super-ethnic in 1940s Hollywood film indicates that the Irish-American experience was no longer outside, but within, mainstream construction of a universal American identity.

80

The Gleam of the Elver and the Work of the Heart: Reflections on Mícheál Ó Súilleabháin

Timothy Emlyn Jones

Timothy Emlyn Jones is an artist of dual Welsh–Irish citizenship. His work is represented in several public collections, including the Irish State Art Collection, and the UK's Government Art Collection and Royal Collection. An early pioneer of practice-based research, his extensive teaching career includes his appointment as dean of the Burren College of Art, Ireland.

The perspective taken in this essay on Mícheál Ó Súilleabháin's contributions to Irish and world culture is that of an artist and educationalist with a shared interest in introducing doctoral programmes to the study of art. For me, this was primarily the visual, plastic and media arts, and for Mícheál, mainly music and dance, and I was fortunate to work with him and others as a professional colleague in that project over several years. What he and I shared, beyond our passions for our own art, was what the arts have in common, and how they can learn from each other, and I appreciated his generosity of spirit in sharing his thinking with me, just as his music seems to me to convey his warmth of personality.

Doctoral education provides new and unique ways into understanding how art works, in that a doctoral student in any discipline is required to give an account of methods used, and in the practice-oriented arts these are most often creative methods on which there has not been much published, and on which there is a great deal of misunderstanding. This may seem a minor concern to some, but in this essay I use Mícheál's achievements to show how that insight goes straight to the heart of how art is made, whether the art be music, dance, poetry, film, drawing, painting, sculpture, performance art or theatre, or any other.

All doctorates, across all university disciplines, have in common the generation of new knowledge or contribution to understanding, together with an account of how that contribution was generated. The latter is new to the arts and much of what emerges goes across and counters the stereotypical accounts of creative process, notably that of the expressive

Romantic genius who is beyond understanding.[1] This is the conflict of enquiry as an alternative to expressionism, the latter being resistant and sometimes hostile to explication. There is a long and respectable tradition of artists leaving interpretation and explanation to others, yet all high-level artists are capable of explaining their art if and when they choose, many choosing silence. The difference between choosing to be silent and simply being inarticulate is crucial to the intelligence of art, yet it is often not understood, notably amongst students who lack confidence and seek shelter behind a mask of *hauteur*. The potential ambiguity in this, combined with the difficulties of explaining intuition and ideation, has famously been exploited by some artists to their personal advantage in claiming the status of genius. Picasso was possibly the most thorough of liars when it comes to accounts of his own artistic production, as I have shown,[2] and the normalising of intelligence in artistic discourse as required in PhD culture is progressively making the obsolescence of such claims visible.

Mícheál's investments in doctoral programmes placed him firmly on the side of openness and attempted transparency, while also recognising the difficulties of understanding what appear to be mysteries. Evidence of his interest in how creative process may be understood can be seen in his fascination with what may be learnt of creative process from other arts. This was evident in our conversations at his college or mine, but most notably in his love of poetry, and in particular the two poems discussed below, Seamus Heaney's 'Station Island', and Rainer Maria Rilke's 'Turning-Point', both of which inspired compositions that can be found in Mícheál's final collection *Elver Gleams*, which he kindly gave me as a gift.

Elver Gleams[3] demonstrates Mícheál's passion for poetry and particularly for the poetry of Seamus Heaney and Rainer Maria Rilke, whose concern for the character of creative process that can be found throughout their work reflects Mícheál's own. Heaney's concern is evident in 'Postscript' in which he captures the central moment of sacrifice of ego in which artistic transformation takes place, and his collection of essays in which that point of interest is made most explicit in his oeuvre *The Government of the Tongue*.[4] Mícheál was delighted and generous in accepting an invitation to open an art exhibition, 'Postscript', of which I was the curator, that celebrated the Heaney poem of that name, at an exhibition at the Russell Gallery, located at the Flaggy Shore in New Quay, County Clare, which is the setting of 'Postscript'.[5] In his opening speech Mícheál alluded to how in that poem Heaney enigmatically captures that experience of the heart which the poem suggests cannot be captured, demonstrating Mícheál's own self-awareness of process that he then displayed in an extended improvisation on the low whistle, which he referred to that evening as his 'flute' in response to the paintings of the exhibition.

In the recording *Elver Gleams* the final track bears the same title as the collection, providing insight on his thinking. The phrase is taken from the twelfth part of Seamus Heaney's long poem 'Station Island',[6] which Heaney describes as 'more like an examination of conscience than a confession'.[7] In this poem, the poet returns from a pilgrimage to St Patrick's Purgatory on Lough Derg, County Donegal, to be met by the ghost of another poet, who provides him with the secret of what he has been seeking (creative process) but failed to find on the pilgrimage. Heaney's notes confirm that the ghost in the poem is that of James Joyce, and the five lines that Mícheál quotes in the sleeve note (reproduced below) represent the core of the ghost's advice and represent that key stage of creative process at which the mature artist abandons the deliberations of what should or should not be the case so as to express his or her evolved creative autonomy. This can be seen as Mícheál's testimony to his own achievement, *Elver Gleams* being not only a summative self-assessment, or a best-of collection, but also – since it was his last publication – a valediction:

> ... it's time to swim
> out on your own and fill the element
> with signatures on your own frequency,
> echo-soundings, searches, probes, allurements,
> elver-gleams in the dark of the whole sea ...

Elver Gleams contains other signals of the character of creative process, notably in the composition 'Heartwork', which too is accompanied with a sleeve note. Here too Mícheál looks to poetry for an explanation of creative process in Rainer Maria Rilke's poem 'Turning-Point'. This provides not just the title of one of Mícheál's compositions, 'Heartwork', but also insight into Mícheál's own view of creative process as he follows Rilke's example. The original poem[8] is prefaced by a quotation from Rilke's contemporary, the Austrian writer Rudolf Kassner (1873–1959), 'The road from intensity to greatness / Passes through sacrifice', observing how artistic standing progresses from an internal stimulus to external recognition through an intensely personal inner transformation and it is that which Rilke calls the 'turning point'. Here too, as in Heaney's 'Station Island', artistic standing is achieved through an inner journey that involves transformation, not only of the artist's materials but also the artist personally. This transformative stage in creative process is documented elsewhere too, as in Joseph Campbell's account[9] of what Otto Scharmer later called the 'U process',[10] and as one of three stages of design method in John Chris Jones' account of creative process – divergent-transformative-convergent.[11] In his sleeve notes for *Elver Gleams*, Mícheál quotes the final stanza of Rilke's poem, translated by Michael Hamburger:[12]

> Work of seeing is done,
> now practice heart-work
> upon those images captive within you

Here we can see the artist's progress from taking in what is seen to its transformation into art through the artist's subjective immersion in emotional intelligence. In the fuller context of the eight-stanza poem this emotional experience is characterised as part of a process that transforms the artist through new perceptions of self and gender at the same time as transforming the artist's images into something of their own standing, independent of the artist yet still connected to the artist in the manner of what Donald Winnicott called a 'transitional phenomenon':

> Learn inner man, to look on your inner woman,
> The one attained from a thousand
> Natures, the merely attained but
> not yet beloved form.

Mícheál's fascination for the connections between the arts is what brought him into a collaborative project with Burren College of Art, where I was then the college dean, and the Huston School of Film and Digital Media at NUI Galway, where Rod Stoneman was the head. Knowing of my earlier involvement in the pioneering of so-called 'practice-based' doctorates in art at several art schools and a music academy in the UK, since the late 1980s, Mícheál and Helen Phelan invited me to address their own developing PhD community at the Irish World Academy of Music and Dance on two occasions. Since my own interests at that time centred on developing an epistemology of artistic enquiry and production – an aesthetics of method – a strong connection immediately transpired. On the second occasion, I took with me Rod Stoneman, with the shared intention to invite Mícheál and Helen to participate in a collaborative project Rod and I called *Same But Different*, which brought together academic practitioners of as many of the arts as possible within the orbit of the doctoral programmes at NUI Galway and Burren College of Art. Rod and I saw the inclusion of the University of Limerick's burgeoning arts doctoral programme as a natural extension of that, and the collaborative but more prosaically named Practice-Based Research Forum was born.

The union of Mícheál and Helen, Rod Stoneman, myself and later Conor McGrady, who took over from me as dean, led to three annual conferences, one each at the World Academy, the Huston School and Burren College of Art, the name subsequently changing once again at Mícheál's instigation to *Bresal*. Each conference explored (and, as Mícheál insisted, also celebrated) a theme of common interest to the three PhD centres, thus establishing a west coast community of interest which also brought in University College Cork and Belfast College of Art (University of Ulster) with further attendees from all over Ireland. The new name that Mícheál introduced proved apposite as well as revealing his fondness for enigma. In mythology, Bresal, also known as Hy Brasil, is an island off the west coast of Ireland that periodically appears and disappears. Its existence was extended beyond mythology in the early twentieth century with the objective account of antiquarian, folklorist and archaeologist T.J. Westropp (1860–1922) observing and testifying to its actuality, together with drawings made from observation. The most likely explanation for this phenomenon is that it is one example of the optical illusion or mirage that results from different densities of warm and cold air resting one above the other at sea, bending the rays of light. The effect of the illusion is a mirage of a real phenomenon such as a ship or a land mass otherwise invisible across the water due to the curvature of the planet Earth made visible by such bending of light rays. In this instance what periodically appears as an island off the Clare coast may be the coast of Nova Scotia, although, as the name suggests, it has been thought to be Brazil. Perhaps the best-known example is on Lake Michigan when the skyline of Chicago is occasionally clearly visible from the eastern shore of the lake despite it normally being out of sight. It is apposite that the common name for this mirage, the Fata Morgana, is derived from Celtic mythology. The fairy Morgan Le Fay appears and disappears at will, like the conferences that appeared without a regular schedule, and as does the transformative core of creative process, as any artist who has dried up will know.[13] Mícheál brought a singular sensibility to its proceedings – as well as musical performances – which contributed to its success.

Just as Mícheál's music brought a new dimension to Irish culture, leading to new perceptions of the traditional Irish repertoire and its connections to the other musical modes such as jazz, so he also contributed to how creative processes may be understood, through the example of his own work as well as the Academy's doctoral programmes. The constantly growing understanding of creative process in the new culture of doctoral arts education, of which he was an important part in Ireland, does not make art any less mysterious. Instead, it helps us to understand and thus savour more fully the character of intuition, the ways in which its mystery may be articulated, understood, savoured and worked on, as the examples taken from Mícheál's own oeuvre show. Every person's potential to immerse in and benefit from Mícheál's music means his influence will continue long after his death, but his legacy is larger than his music. He set an example of the importance of embracing the diversity and the unity of the arts. This is evidenced by not just how he was drawn to poetry and the visual arts, but also by how visual artists have been drawn to him as an example of warmth, inclusion and inspiration.

81

A Journey of the Soul

Page Allen

Page Allen is a painter and writer, living in the American south-west. She has shown her work in New York, Chicago, Montana and Santa Fe. Allen's first illustrated book, Madison's Descent, *was adapted for stage with music by Mícheál Ó Súilleabháin. Page is represented by The Owings Gallery, Santa Fe.*

My great adventure with Mícheál began with the creation of my book *Madison's Descent.*

I am a painter and an author-illustrator of books. I work and have lived these many years in Santa Fe, New Mexico. In 1996 I made my first visit to Ireland. As many have before me, I was moved and inspired by the land and the sense of ancient spirit within the earth, and thus also within our own bodies. I began to imagine the first of my *Passageway Books*, to be *Madison's Descent*, telling of a child's journey down the 'River of Stars', on her way to be born.

In 1998 I shared the not quite complete book with my friend, Jedediah Wheeler, a New York-based creative producer. He imagined its adaptation as a piece for stage, with music and other theatre arts. Since the story had found its birth for me in the myth-fertile land of Ireland, Jed reasoned that he should invite an Irish composer to consider it. With great good fortune, he was led to Mícheál Ó Súilleabháin.

Mícheál seemed to embrace the story in immediate familiarity. He greeted the river and the journey of a soul as true to himself and the myth of the Shannon. There was indeed a quick recognition of creative truth in him, and thus a creative trust, which was a more important quality between us, or better described, than that of our being kindred artists.

Though we were, when I think back, kindred. What was this kinship? We were two very different personalities, with different work processes, it seemed. Next to his stature, I felt shy. And yet, both of us held deep beliefs in the ancient truths and the individual power to make new versions out of the old knowledge, old stories, each in our own way. We both had a passion for spirit and beauty and meaning in our work. This came naturally to culturally rooted, Irish Mícheál, but not to an American of a contemporary culture of doubt. I was grateful for his birthright. And he must have recognised this intuitive truth-telling in me, this trust in the language of the soul, whether in music or in painting. We each took to ourselves the right and privilege as artists. Not shy.

As our working unfolded over the years, I was lifted by his tacit kinship and respect. Mícheál worked hard with those he respected. From our first meeting with Jed at Dromore, when Mícheál proclaimed with relish the line from Seamus Heaney's 'The Cure at Troy', 'Greeks with a job to do!' he never wavered. As *Madison's Descent* for concert and stage took shape, it refused to take shape easily. We asked question after question, as we gathered more multidisciplinary artists to its creation. Mícheál continued in his strong voice and bright intuition, finding our path. In our first auspicious days getting to know each other, 1 and 2 February 2001, I came to Limerick to hear the solo songs that Mícheál had composed for the singer Brian Kennedy. We all met in a recording studio at the University of Limerick and listened.

It is rare that an artist in one medium is invited to interpret the art of one in another, and very rare to feel that one's own creation has been completely met by the other, without any distortion or diminishment. I felt with Mícheál, in the meeting of my painting and his music, there was extraordinary mutual illumination.

A bridge between paintings and music was the written story, answered by his lyrics. I have found in my work as a visual artist that adding words can amplify the paintings. This is different from much illustration, in which text and image serve a narrative. It is more like illuminations within a manuscript, in which both forms serve to amplify a greater spirit, side by side. Mícheál's lyrics also accomplish the highest art of choral music, in which music and verse raise each other.

In the National Concert Hall (NCH), during a concert of Mícheál's music, the section devoted to the songs from *Madison's Descent* brought absolute silence to the full audience. The lyrics sung, joined with the instrumental music, were so moving, so expressive.

Madison's Descent: A masque in ten movements was first performed on the great stage at the Kasser Theater of the University of Montclair, New Jersey in 2006. The choreography and stage direction was done by David Bolger of Cois Céim Dance, Dublin. The puppetry was by Michael Curry of Michael Curry Design. Animation design was by Misha Films and the music, of course, composed and conducted by Mícheál Ó Súilleabháin. In 2014 the adaptation *Madison Songs* was made by Mícheál for orchestra, chorale and soloist, performed at the NCH.

As the river runs deep and runs wide
The flow of the stars will decide
When the moment to move has begun
And the moon must give rise to the sun.

It's your time, it's your time to let go,
Your time to sing yes and not no.
On the river so dark yet so right,
It's your time to be born this night.

('Song of the Moon' from *Madison's Descent*, lyrics by Mícheál Ó Súilleabháin and Page Allen)

Still now, his spirit, of belief in good work, in sharing art, is with me.

82

Learning from Mícheál: Placing culture at the heart of regenerative innovation

Finbarr Bradley

Finbarr Bradley is a visiting professor at Aalto University, Finland, and a former professor at Dublin City University, where he was also founding director of the Irish-medium centre, Fiontar. He authored or co-authored several books including Capitalising on Culture, Competing on Difference *(2008). He has a PhD in international finance from New York University.*

Introduction

I first met Mícheál in October 2009 at the Douglas Hyde Conference (Comhdháil an Chraoibhín) in Ballaghadereen, County Roscommon. My talk was on the topic of culture and innovation in a post-boom Ireland. As Mícheál seemed taken by my contribution, he later commissioned me to write a report for the Irish World Academy of Music and Dance. My brief was to investigate the contribution that arts practice education, with special emphasis on the Academy itself, might play in the reversal of Ireland's economic fortunes.

My key finding was that the work of the Academy had positive implications for stimulating innovation in other sectors of Irish society. The following piece draws on what I discovered during my visits to the Academy and in several discussions I had with Mícheál himself. I argue below that Ireland's prospects of becoming a 'knowledge' economy would be greatly enhanced if conventional approaches to innovation drew on the arts programmes and practices initiated by Mícheál in the Academy.

Irish university leaders are adept at promoting the idea that innovation starts with scientific research. The arts, especially the traditional arts, are relegated to a minor peripheral role even when considered at all. These leaders also assert that innovation and economic competitiveness depend on the amount of money spent on research and development (R&D) within their institutions. Such thinking is seriously flawed, outdated and largely discredited internationally. In fact, there is little evidence of any relationship between the money spent on R&D in universities and the economic prosperity of a country, city or region. Prosperity depends more on learning and the acquisition of tacit skills and know-how than on research per se.[1]

Creativity and innovation have the greatest potential to flourish if a learning environment is embedded within a community that emphasises tradition while also being receptive to outside influences. For example, valuable traditional knowledge can be transformed through design to develop sustainable innovative products that improve people's lives.[2] As Mícheál held about the Irish music tradition, creative reworking of global ingredients has a major revitalising effect.[3] The research and arts practices nurtured at the Academy clearly demonstrate this.

Tradition works, not just in the arts but also in business. This is especially true in the food, drink, tourism, design and craft sectors. For instance, a Bord Bia/Irish Food Board study found that celebrating and harnessing the best of tradition to meet modern tastes now constitutes a key consumer food trend.[4] In tourism, the *albergo diffuso* hotel model in Italy consists of lodging and dining physically dispersed in remote villages or towns.[5] International tourists are drawn to the historic cultural traditions they experience during their stay.

It is a flawed dichotomy to suggest that Ireland must choose between being internationally 'progressive' or remaining faithful to 'backward' native values. No country can be truly innovative if its people do not appreciate who they are, where they come from and where they are trying to go. Grounded in their own culture, they appreciate diversity and the cultural values of those with whom they must cooperate and compete. They learn to identify difference and appreciate distinctiveness, absorbing different ideas, yet are not dominated by globalised cultural influences.

Paradigm shift

In today's economy, making 'sense' matters more than making 'stuff'. A search for meaning is becoming a core economic driver as societies undergo a paradigm shift from a techno-economic age founded on physical goods to a regenerative age of intangible experiences. The word regenerative is used here to emphasise that it lies beyond conventional terms like green or sustainable. It refers to the flourishing of life, both human and non-human. Regenerative innovation in turn describes the process of creating real value, that is value that lies beyond mere monetary value. Real value is a far deeper and broader concept than today's financially dominated definition of value suggests.[6]

In their quest for self-realisation, individuals wish to spend time and money on compelling transformative experiences. In the experience economy, the predominant economic offering is an 'experience'. The demand for personalised and unique experiences has grown out of informed, connected, empowered and active consumers weary of globalised, mass-produced goods. Empathy and emotion support the delivery of sensation-filled experiences that engage people in memorable ways. Experiences are inherently personal and exist only in the mind of an individual engaged on an emotional, physical, intellectual and spiritual level. As with a stage production, for example, no two people have the same experience; this derives from the relationship between the act and the audience member's response to it.

There is an urgent need for a paradigm shift in the mission, purpose and values of Irish businesses to counter social and environmental problems such as wealth inequality, biodiversity loss and global warming. As the significance of the material diminishes and capacities of the mind become a crucial competitive factor, meaning, experience and identity are becoming key to regenerative innovation. Imagination, perhaps the most valuable resource of all, is driven by emotions and feelings, the heart rather than the rational mind, and is mostly nurtured through the arts. It is a resource founded on inspiration, empathy, tradition and trust, rooted in the social and economic fabric of relationships.

Aptitudes such as empathy, performance and interpretation are increasingly needed to excel in business. Ireland possesses such resources in abundance, ideal for the regenerative age. Corporate value is increasingly tied up not in tangibles like buildings but in intangibles such as culture, relationships and brands.[7] For many companies, intangibles are their great untapped source of competitive advantage. A different mindset is needed to create real value, and heightened sensitivity to cultural uniqueness is especially critical. Progressive businesses realise that the best way to differentiate their goods and services is to infuse them with emotion and artistry. It is no surprise that IT companies often spend more on the symbolic aspects of products than on technical development. Apple is a good example, when during its Steve Jobs-led years its mission statement didn't describe what the company did, instead it talked about what the company believed in.[8]

Creative learning

Breakthrough ideas require intelligence of the heart and hand, not just intelligence of the head. Emotions, tastes, sensations and feelings which come from the heart rather than the rational mind are primary drivers of creativity and innovation. The most valuable resources in sectors like food or tourism, for instance, are founded on empathy and tradition, rooted in the social and economic fabric of relationships. So, a sense of place, belonging and shared meaning are at least as important as skills in science or mathematics in developing an innovative ethic. Yet many students graduate today from academic environments shaped largely by the old industrial model, out of step with the learning required for the regenerative age. The influential United States business magazine *Fortune* argues that in future the most valuable skills in highest demand will be those that people can do better than computers. These include forming emotional bonds, making human judgements and being sensitive to cultural difference. *Fortune* says tomorrow's most valuable engineers will not be geniuses in cubicles. Instead, they'll be those who can build relationships, brainstorm and lead.[9]

The industrial age heralded the loss of intimate knowledge that mattered so much to traditional craftsmen. Poignant accounts of their lost skills are recorded in books such as Seamus Murphy's *Stone Mad* and George Sturt's *The Wheelwright's Shop*.[10] Their tacit knowledge of materials has been lost through mass production. Moreover, true understanding was traditionally associated not with the de-contextualised setting of the classroom or the university lecture hall, but in a more integrated process, involving the scholar working with the master, or the craftsman working with the apprentice. In today's networked world, the essence of an innovative learning community is not, as many politicians and policy makers assert, the science lab, but the small-scale craft workshop, ideal for co-creating value through continuous interaction and feedback between say the customer and supplier.

Excellence in education is a practice where three elements feature: craft (or experience), art (or imagination) and science (or analysis). This approach to learning is encapsulated in the concept of apprenticeship. The benefits of apprenticeship include pride in work and enhanced motivation as individuals work in practical situations. In such situated learning, students discover the appropriate circumstances to apply what they are taught. They learn where, when and why some concept fits or does not fit a particular situation.

Mícheál was in the vanguard with his adventuresome approach to learning and innovation. He understood how to develop a powerful milieu where creative acts were imbued with strong feeling and emotion, so conversation, reflection, discussion, shared meaning and performance were central. At the Academy, the performing arts and research sit side by side in an empowering relationship, or as Mícheál put it in an email to me in October 2011, 'global listening out of a local stance'. He rejoiced in his invention of a word he called 'lobal'. He said the word lobal was softer than glocal and more redolent of the lobe of the ear and therefore it was what he termed a 'listening' word. He saw that the poetic (global listening) and practical (feet on the ground) have fused, linking heavens (counting) and earth (dancing). He put it, 'lobality is the new locality'. Elsewhere, he liked to quote poet Seamus Heaney speaking on his seventieth birthday to illuminate this same spirit: 'We should keep our feet on the ground to signify that nothing is beneath us but we should also lift up our eyes to say nothing is beyond us.'[11]

In the potent learning environment Mícheál created, and that lives on in the Academy, students engage in discussions, practice, make decisions, and both compete and cooperate within a mutually supportive environment, while drawing on and learning from each other. Such environments tend to be founded on self-discovery, that is *learning to be* rather than *learning about*. Because of this kind of learning, students have more practice exploring their inner emotional world. Hence, they more confidently and creatively deal with change and are open to new possibilities. Exposure to self-discovery helps them explore for themselves, perform their own research, solve real-life problems and make decisions. In other words, they learn to 'create themselves'.

Judgements about 'qualitative reasoning', or ordering relationships of qualities, were central to the performing arts programmes that Mícheál developed. By inquiring qualitatively, students learn to think but do so in a form which engages the senses and improves technique. Students thrive in such an atmosphere since qualitative reasoning nurtures imagination, personal development and mutual respect.

Students largely learn for themselves rather than receive information and knowledge from lecturers, which is often just instructive and imposed. Instead, the student is engaged in transformative learning and active listening, usually in small groups. Improvisation in music sessions, for instance, shares many of the same characteristics as managing complexity and uncertainty through collaborative innovation in business, where few rules and regulations apply. What students know cannot easily be separated from how they act. A sense of community is cultivated, not accumulation of facts, within this type of experiential-learning supportive community.

Students experience the world through their bodies; with hearts as well as minds engaged, and interpretation balanced with analysis. While working with music and dance, they are inspired to receive meaning through their actions, which helps them understand more about themselves. Reflection and highly developed hand and body skills help foster a sense of identity, thereby spurring the creative spirit. In many conventional programmes students fail to see connections and patterns.

This suggests that Mícheál's insights could similarly light the way for how Irish educational institutions might better develop creative learning environments. In the emerging regenerative age, the emphasis is on relationships. Meaning and purpose, which emerge from a student's sense of connectedness to who they are and where they have come from, can help create and share real value by building a flourishing authentic life to counter the worst elements of today's market-driven world such as consumerism, materialism and individualism.

Regenerative innovation

In essence, two fundamental processes lie at the heart of innovation.[12] One, analysis or rational decision-making. The other, what might be called irrational, inspirational or intuitive thinking, is what MIT researchers Richard Lester and Michael Piore call 'interpretation'. This is more about orchestrated conversations that emerge from community.[13] What is required is a balance between analytical, interpretive and improvisational processes but Irish policymakers, loath to embrace this perspective, see science-based research alone as key to achieving the vaunted innovation society.[14]

Innovation has more to do with qualitative factors, founded on memory and belonging, such as meaning, purpose, level of trust and sense of community than on expenditures on university research per se. Doing and valuing are critical in innovation, distinguishing it from research which centres on thinking and reflection. The heart of innovation is not discovery of new knowledge but identifying connections between all sources of knowledge to create real value. Therefore, feelings of belonging that lead to cooperative relationships are more crucial than scientific research on its own in stimulating innovation.

Scientific research has no monopoly on the ways in which humans inquire; arts-based research in music and dance equally helps people understand and 'know' the world in which they live. Rather than research being a species of science, as Elliot Eisner wrote, 'science is one, and only one, species of research'.[15] The innovative idea and its development has many inputs, not just scientific research; breakthrough ideas require intelligence of the heart and hand, not just intelligence of the head. Innovation is shaped by deep characteristics founded on values, norms and habits. Emotions, taste, sensations and feelings are its primary drivers. The new usually begins with an unspecified emotion or feeling which then morphs into an insight or idea that is then related to a problem or context; only then does it get framed by a rational structure or form.[16]

Mícheál's thinking and practice, illustrated by his work on innovating tradition, contain significant lessons on how regenerative innovation can be fostered in Irish society. A critical economic and social lesson is that Ireland's traditional arts must play a more central role if we hope to develop a regenerative innovation society. Through immersion in music, song and dance experiences, Mícheál created a dynamic environment through the interaction of people with different backgrounds, skills and countries, coming together to share ideas. Driven by the goal of creating real value, they learned from and related to one another.

If Ireland is ever to make its innovation economy more than mere rhetoric, it must draw on its own rare, unique and inimitable resources, no matter how 'soft' these are perceived to be. Yet Irish research and innovation policy suffers many of the same pathologies which the 2011 Nyberg Report said delivered gross errors in property and banking during the Celtic Tiger boom: hubris, pervasive pressure for consensus, an echo-chamber closed to debate, and hostility to contrarian views. It's a policy castigated as 'full of far-flung aspirations, wholly argument and arbitrary targets that ultimately fail to mask the self-seeking behaviour of politicians, business interests and lobbies'.[17]

Innovation is really about stories and the Irish are great storytellers. Ireland's heritage provides an ideal base for creativity with different traditions leading to diversity in meaning. Integrating science and technology with a tradition of metaphors and narrative offers Ireland a huge competitive advantage. Take Irish mythology: it is not linear but has a meandering interconnectedness, ideal for a sustainable age where conversation, empathy and relationships are critical innovative resources.

Internationally, a shift is taking place from supremacy of the theoretical to a growing appreciation of the practical, with acceptance that innovation is as likely to emanate from dynamic learning communities as from lab-based research. However, the Irish higher education model of innovation is still largely conceptualised as a linear one comprising scientific research leading to commercialisation through technology transfer. This is choking off support for vital interpretative places and the discovery of new forms of meaning-making, two elements that Mícheál promoted so well.

Conclusion

Tradition is not some dead artefact but a living national resource that drives the creation of economic value by fostering meaning. By presenting a compelling view of the past, it provides a guide to the future. It offers people an opportunity to reflect on their place in the world, helping them better manage uncertainty, which harnesses a spirit of self-discovery and an innovative mindframe.

Cultural identity contributes to integrity, civic responsibility, aesthetic sensibility, ecological stewardship, ethical behaviour and resourcefulness. A country's wisdom and cultural self-knowledge offer breadth, purpose and confidence. Individuals with meaning in their lives, with a sense of continuity between past and present, create more trusting and caring communities. Standards become internal, deriving impetus from personal values, integrity, community, and intergenerational solidarity.

In today's world of globalised markets and climate crisis, economic advantage is driven by local distinctiveness. But at a time when Irish public policy remains focused upon foreign direct investment as the primary engine, if not the saviour, of the Irish economy, home-grown enterprises that are intimately rooted in both the soil and culture of Ireland are often overlooked. Yet it is precisely these characteristics and values which underlie significant, inimitable and very real competitive advantages for Irish enterprises based on culture, authenticity and a sense of place.

It is difference, not sameness, which matters in global markets, a fact scarcely appreciated in contemporary Ireland. Regenerative, innovative and indigenous ventures are essential to build a successful, vigorous and diverse economy that is no less globally competitive for being distinctively Irish. Mícheál would be proud that his path-breaking ideas can help us imagine how such Irish enterprises can be nurtured in the years to come.

83

Planxty: A newly coined word for a new kind of composition?

Cathal Goan

Cathal Goan worked in broadcasting as an archivist and a radio and television producer. He was the founding director of TG4 and the director-general of RTÉ. He has had a lifelong interest in Irish music, contributing occasional pieces to Breandán Breathnach's journal CEOL, *and teaching annually at Scoil Samhraidh Willie Clancy.*

The last time I heard Mícheál Ó Súilleabháin in recital was in the DeBartolo Performing Arts Center at the University of Notre Dame in Indiana in 2013.[1] The programme for the recital consisted of works by Turlough Carolan, played with gusto on grand piano and with Mícheál's customary wit and playfulness. I have a memory that Mícheál suggested this recital offered a short preview of his intended comprehensive revisiting of Carolan's compositions.[2] Looking back to Carolan's time of ferment and change in Irish music and its patronage no doubt appealed to Mícheál with his own innovations in form and presentation of various strands of music in a changing Ireland. Unfortunately the proposed exploration was not to be. In celebration of Mícheál's musical talents, his interest and enthusiasm for finding links across boundaries, his collegial generosity and leadership skills, I offer this short speculative paper on the word *planxty*, a word intimately connected with Carolan's compositions.[3]

The designation of a particular kind of merry tune as a *planxty* is originally and most commonly associated with Carolan. The word's first known appearance in print is in 1724 in an English-language context in the Neals' *A Collection of the Most Celebrated Irish Tunes*[4] where 'Planksty Plunket' (no. 8) and 'PLANKSTY' (no. 32), both associated with Carolan, occur. The word order of the first title indicates an Irish-language usage or origin. It appears regularly in print in journals such as *Saunders's News Letter* in the final quarter of the eighteenth century in a manner that suggests its ready recognition and acceptance, as in this example for instance from that newspaper of 8 April 1779:

> For the benefit of Mr. OWENSON
> On Friday the 30th of April, 1779, will be performed
> A PRELUDE
> Mr. Wallis, Servant Mr. Burke, and Darby Hoolaghan (an Irish Actor) Mr. Owenson, in which will be introduced some original Planxties written by Carolan, the celebrated Irish Bard, particularly Planxty Kelly, &c. &c. and a new song called Darby Hoolaghan's Description of Donnybrook Fair; with an occasional Prologue (in Character) by Mr. Owenson …

In his introduction to the facsimile re-publication of the Neals' *Collection* referred to above, Nicholas Carolan details the evolving musical landscape in which Carolan the harper worked and travelled. Changed and changing patterns of patronage, land-ownership, religion and language are the backdrop to a dwindling harp tradition that could nonetheless still produce virtuosi, versed in the old and receptive to the new in musical taste.[5]

Mícheál Ó Súilleabháin gave a paper to the University College Cork (UCC) Irish Traditional Music Society in 2004 that linked the work of Seán Ó Riada with the traditional ensemble Ceoltóirí Chualann to an ambition on the composer's part to develop a native 'art' music.[6] The composer had an association with the music of Carolan largely through arrangements of some pieces he had made for Ceoltóirí Chualann. Ó Riada, who had been Mícheál's teacher in UCC, is credited with one explanation of a possible origin for the word *planxty*. The word was used in the title of a number of Carolan compositions and Ó Riada argued it was derived from a misreading of the Irish-language word *sláinte* (health). The drift of the argument was that the Gaelic font for 's' (s) was mistaken for 'p' and accordingly *sláinte* became *pláinte* and then became *planxty*.

The tune called simply *Hewlett* by Donal O'Sullivan,[7] in his two-volume study of Carolan and his music, has words which begin:

> *Sláinte bhreagh Hiúlit, sgaoil chugain é gan mhaill,*
> *'S ná césaigidh dúbailte lionn, punch is meadhar*
>
> (Hewlett's good health, send him to us without delay,
> And don't complain about porter, punch or mirth)

In Cork in June 1970, at a concert with Ceoltóirí Chualann to celebrate the compositions of Carolan, this derivation for the word *planxty* served as the starting-off point for Ó Riada when he introduced the tune as *Sláinte Bhreá Hewlett*.[8]

In favour of the argument is the apparent synonymous import of both words in this context as celebrating a patron. Patronage formed a central theme in Carolan's music-making. Against the argument is its exceptional nature; this would be a singular example of such a misreading of Gaelic fonts. Added to this is the otherwise unknown sound shift from / 't'ji/ to / ksti:/. Other theories and opinions as to its origin and meaning have surfaced over the almost three hundred years now since the word first appeared in print.

In 1855, George Petrie opined that the *planxty* tune-type was a 'harp-tune of a sportive and animated character'.[9] He wrote that it was a tune in 6/8 time and, along with the term 'Pleraca', owed its existence to Carolan and together [they] 'are to be regarded as a class of festive harp-tunes composed in honour of his patrons or hospitable entertainers'. Petrie mentions English language 'prance' or 'prank' or Eugene O'Curry's suggestion of 'flaxsaraidh' as possible origins for the word. Donal O'Sullivan, just over one hundred years later, suggested the word 'may come from the Latin *plangere* (supine, *planxtum*) on the model of the existing Irish word *planncaim* which means to strike (the harp)'. He was dismissive of Petrie's attempt to categorise the tunes as all being in jig time; likewise he rejected Petrie's identification of *planxty* and *pléaráca* as synonyms and he was much more conservative in using the word *planxty* in the titles of numerous tunes where it had previously been deployed.[10]

In the period between the two, and indeed since, others like Ó Riada, as mentioned above, have not been slow to offer suggestions. In 1871, in the journal *Notes and Queries*, for instance, 'The Knight of Inishowen' asserted ancient origins for the word, meaning 'a harp air of grand and elevating character', adding that it celebrated 'a victory and the virtues of the victor chief'. But it also meant 'the nuptial song of a royal hero's bridal, or the revengeful and defiant strain upon his fall in battle'. The author mentions potential derivations from Latin *planctus*, 'the noise of the tempestuous waves dashing on a rock-bound coast', or the more popular Latin meaning of *planctus*, 'as we all know is a plaint or complaint', or indeed from ancient Greek πλαγκτός (plaxktos), meaning vagrant. The writer dismisses both Latin and Greek sources 'as the Celtic is of older stock than either'.[11] This display of fanciful and bogus erudition finds more playful and mischievous expression in a twenty-first-century digital descendant of *Notes and Queries* – thesession.org. In that forum, we are informed that, 'contrary to all other speculation, the word derives from the German physicist Max Planck who, while taking tea, would often listen to these tunes, thus begetting *Planck's*

Tea tunes'.[12] Hopefully this current attempt at an explanation may provide some diversion – if not quite the same enjoyment.

Donal O'Sullivan's observation, cited above, that the word may derive from the Irish verb 'planncaim' (modern spelling 'plancaim') is an interesting starting point. Dinneen's fabled dictionary offers: 'Planncaim … I beat, strike violently, pommel, plank down on the table; p. téad I play up music on a stringed instrument … *al.* pleanncaim'.[13] There is, however, no evidence for the verb in older Irish-language sources and it is absent from the *Dictionary of the Irish Language* which examines sources up to 1600.[14]

The first use of the verb recorded in the *Historical Irish Corpus 1600–1926*,[15] an online database of Irish-language texts, is in a poem by Séafradh Ó Donnchadha, *Sgiathlúireach Shíle Róisde*, said to have been composed in 1656:

Ná raibh fa chnapaibh a chúntair
ag ceannaighe géar mhaith dá thrúncaibh;
ná raibh fear círéibe ar campa
ag pleanncadh a príléide ar plúncaibh.[16]

In a series of verses, the poet looks at potential scenarios in which the young woman's virginity might be robbed. In this verse we hear 'May no clever sharp merchant [draw] from under bundles on his counter out of his trunks (?), and may no ruffian in camp assault her honour on the boards'. Here both *pleannc* and *plúnc*, according to Dinneen's dictionary,[17] appear to share a common origin.[18] In any event, the verb appears to come into Irish language usage only in the seventeenth century.

It is to be found in more Irish-language sources from the eighteenth century, but there is no attestation with a musical context before the period in which the tune titles associated with Carolan are first recorded. In a macaronic poem by Aindrias MacCraith composed c. 1735 we find:

Is feas gurb umhal dom rún do shléachtas,
do ghlacas dúil im shiúir do bhréagadh,
do phreab chun siúil, do liúigh le héigean
's is pras a dúirt an plancadh:

(It's known I affected to posture in desire / I took a fancy to seduce my kinswoman [sister?] / She jumped away and howled with force / And quickly uttered a pommelling:)

Keep off, I say, you raking rogue,
have a care, don't tear my cloak,
or I'll vow and swear I'll break your nose
if you abuse my gown, sir![19]

The first Irish-language reference with a musical connotation is attributed to Carolan himself:

A Chupid bhéasach, mharuigh na céadta
A phlancadh an téad go ceolmhar[20]

(Oh mannerly Cupid who has slain hundreds by dint of striking the string musically.)

Likewise

Le Gaedhilg, le damhsa,
le Béarla gach aimsir,
ól choidhche 'na dteanta
agus ceolta dhá bplancadh.[21]

(With Irish and dance and with English at any time, drinking for ever in their company, tunes are struck.)

'Planc' and associated words, therefore, seem to have been relatively recent arrivals in Irish and not to have been much in evidence before Carolan's time (1670–1738).

On the face of it, 'planc' seems to offer the best explanation for the initial syllable of the word *planxty*. Whether it, in turn, is a borrowing from Latin *plangere* (to strike) as suggested by O'Sullivan or from English-language alternatives such as 'plonk' or 'plank' or even 'pluck' will remain a moot point.[22] I have always, perhaps unthinkingly, accepted the Latin source as its basis.

As to the second part of the word *planxty/plancstaí*, the particle *sty* or *staí/stí* also occurs in other Irish-language contexts. Admittedly there are not abundant examples but there are, I think, sufficient to discern a pattern. Briefly they are: *bacstaí*[23](boxty), *cucstí*[24] (a mess), *creaicstí*[25] (a devil-may-care person), *plucstaí*[26] (a child with puffy cheeks), *hacstaí*[27] (a filler-word of no apparent meaning in a song chorus), *ruicstí*[28] (a commotion, a fight), *brocstaí*[29] (bad, rotten food). What is noticeable in all these cases is that the root-word is monosyllabic and ends in a final /k/ or hard 'c'. The second element, variously /sti:/, /ʃt'i:/ and /ʃti:/, seems to act as an intensifier, emphasising the inherent meaning of the first element of the new word and, perhaps, additionally giving a degree of humour or mild mockery. Boxty and, to a lesser extent, craxty or cracksty are known and used in the English of Ireland today.[30]

So, we may speculate along with others that *planxty* indicates a tune which is played with gusto on the harp. It might also hint that it is a tune of no great import, a light-hearted but spirited tune for a generous patron. The designation and the type of tune it connotes first appears in print at the end of the first quarter of the eighteenth century where it is almost exclusively connected with Carolan. It may not be such a stretch to suppose that not alone did he come up with these kinds of composition in the evolving milieu of patronage but that Carolan or his circle also coined the name for them. It may be a stretch to suggest he was influenced in making up the new word by the triad model for categorising Irish music already well known from early sources. Here the monosyllabic roots *suan*, *gean* and *gol* were appended with the *traighe*, or later *traí*, to mean music of sleep, music of laughter and music of lament. In the case of *planxty*, this argument would run, the root word 'planc' is suffixed with 'staí' in the same manner to mean jolly music of the harp.

As Professor Aloys Fleischmann suggested to O'Sullivan, the *toccata* is to the keyboard as the *planxty* is to the harp.[31] *Planxty* might also be compared to Italian *divertimento*, a term from the same period, meaning a light and entertaining composition. We might translate that into the English of Ireland as a *divarsion*. We do not know fully how Mícheál Ó Súilleabháin envisaged his revisiting of Carolan's compositions but we may assume he would have embraced the dynamic nature of eighteenth-century Ireland's differing cultures (*Between Worlds*), both native and new, with integrity, wit and invention. Looking at his early treatment of traditional tunes such as 'Merrily Kiss the Quaker', his orchestral arrangement of 'Carolan's Concerto', his own later contemporary compositions such as '(must be more) Crispy', his evident appreciation of word-play in a title like 'flowansionnamare', we may be sure an intuitive sympathy for his sources, and a melodic sense of mischief, would have guaranteed *divarsion* in any new undertaking of this kind.

84

'The local is the path to true globalisation': Mícheál as musical mediator and the redress of the Irish psyche

Owen Ó Súilleabháin

Owen Ó Súilleabháin is a singer, composer, teacher and leadership coach. He is founder of 'Dámh Imeall' – the (h)Edge School, offering creative and spiritual courses with his mother Nóirín Ní Riain, and brother Mícheál. He has worked with world-renowned artists including Steven Spielberg, Russell Crowe, Nigel Kennedy, David Whyte and his father, Mícheál Ó Súilleabháin.

Introduction

Mícheál was my father, and he was just as brilliant a father as he was at so many other things in his life. He brought such playfulness, curiosity, educational encouragement and love to his fatherly role. The arts were central to our home life. The parity of esteem for arts of all cultures was the common theme. The house was stuffed full of instruments and books, and from the earliest age I was soaking it all up. While I was always singing and engaging with the arts on a deep creative level, I was also driven to read philosophy, history and social theory. I studied philosophy and Greek and Roman civilisation at University College Dublin and peace and development studies at the University of Limerick.

At home Mícheál would often launch into the elucidation of a certain theory or the historical context of a certain subject and instantly my brother and I would roll our eyes and teasingly drone, 'I feel a *léacht* coming on.' In truth our feigned cynicism was nothing less than a rousing admonition for him to launch on, and on it would come, and a powerful discussion was sure to follow.

The great underlying theme to our conversations always assumed that the arts are at the vanguard of any society. Artists are scouts that are compelled to venture forth and return with reconnaissance from over the horizon. The artist is also the conscience of the society, the voice of a society's soul, the voice that redresses imbalance and tips the scales of justice towards equilibrium. We were always deciphering the sounds and signs of art from our own place and time, but also artists from other places and other times.

But our most profound discussions were around our own creative impulse and artistry. That was always approached with a kind of reverence that acknowledged a holy kind of ineffability, and there were very few items for debate that were ever left to pass over in silence.

In this essay I want to begin to put words to my reflections on what Mícheál's position as a 'mediational' artist can teach us, and what is has to say about the conversation in Ireland in particular, as well as the lessons this case study may have to impart to other parts of the world. This article will not articulate these lessons explicitly, but it is a beginning, and an invitation to you, the reader, to also voice your own ideas about what Mícheál's work meant to Ireland finding its place in the world, both in the past and today.

'All our central fire'

In 1994, Mícheál published the article '"All our central fire": Music, mediation and the Irish psyche' in *The Irish Journal of Psychology*.[1] In it, he introduces certain artists who, during pivotal moments in the history of Ireland, created what he describes as 'mediational art' that transformed the Irish psyche into a 'new and necessary consciousness'.[2] Mícheál explores the work of four 'musical mediators' who could speak 'to opposite sides'[3] (oral/literate; Hiberno/Anglo-Irish) in Irish society: blind itinerant harper Turlough Carolan (1670–1738), writer and lyricist Thomas Moore (1779–1852), traditional fiddler Tommie Potts (1912–88) and composer Seán Ó Riada (1931–71).

Using this essay as a touchstone, I would like to explore the proposal that Mícheál was himself a 'musical mediator' in this lineage. His artistic, educational and cultural work mediated between opposing aspects of the 'Irish psyche' in his own time. In his exploration of Carolan, Moore, Potts and Ó Riada, Mícheál wrote:

> By mediation, I mean that middle voice which opens up a channel of communication between separate energies ... The musical mediator can be viewed as a bridge which allows listeners access to parts of their society and their experience of which they were unaware or perhaps just suspicious. And like any bridge, people walk across it – often with little regard for that which conveys them to another place, another world.[4]

Mícheál proposed that music could not only reflect the culture and time it is in, but also reveal new and emerging collective identities. It is important, as he put it, 'to consider what it is that music in Ireland can tell us about ourselves'. He wrote, '[T]he secret power of music as a healing force may lie in its ability to bring together opposites in the form of a sonic encodement which in turn invites a psychic response from the composer, performing musician, or sympathetic listener.'[5]

During Mícheál's life, Ireland was struggling in a space between local identity and the forces of globalisation.[6] He was intensely interested in the Irish psyche and how it was changing. Of the thousands of books in our house, the majority concerned some aspect of Irish culture. Of the hundreds of titles of poetry books, the overwhelming majority were by Irish poets, many of them in the Irish language. Drawing on these sources, Mícheál actively sought to mediate a new Irish identity, bridging the local and the global, in his composition, performance and music education.

Between worlds: bridging local and global, oral and literate

During Mícheál's life, Ireland was struggling between local identity and the more global forces of American influence and power, European integration, and a new world economy. Mícheál's work mediated between the worlds of local and global, helping to forge an inclusive Irish nationalism that valued tradition while simultaneously embracing new cultures. This divide between the local and global can also be described as the gap between the oral and literate in music and it is striking how mediating between these dynamics remained a key motif throughout his life's work. In his keynote address to the International Council for Traditional Music (ICTM) delivered in 2017, he reflected on his decades of uniting the two spheres of culture:

> ... many of my performances, compositions, and recordings present a shared platform for both literate classical musicians and oral-tradition musicians ... [T]his lifelong obsession with bringing the literate and the oral together in a performative situation is demonstrative of my role as a cultural mediator.[7]

In the following section I will reflect briefly on examples of Mícheál's compositions ('Oíche Nollag'), musical collaborations (Hiberno Jazz) and educational work (Irish World Academy) to examine this lifelong record of cultural mediation more closely.

Composition: 'Oíche Nollag'

Mícheál's seminal album *The Dolphin's Way* (1987) captures some of the mediational mix of sonic ingredients that he was working with at that time. In the opening bars of 'Oíche Nollag' (Christmas Eve), Mícheál plays what sounds like electric guitar power chords with his left hand, while holding a syncopated sequence of octaves on the right hand, then breaking into a torrential jazz ragtime before finally landing at a gallop into an Irish traditional dance tune. This is part rock and roll, part jazz, part ragtime mixed up with a dash of the theatricality of The Beatles' *Sgt Pepper's* project.

Here is Irish traditional music played with the brilliance and virtuosity of the greatest Irish traditional musicians of the past, played for the first time with that kind of fluency on the piano – an instrument representing the height of European classical art music. But Mícheál is bringing it further than that. He is opening and closing the piece with strong, bold chords from the rock-and-roll tradition and adding in a further layer of complexity with jazz idioms. With 'Oíche Nollag', Mícheál created a signature blend of Irish traditional music mixed not only with European art music but also with the sounds and energies of rock and roll and jazz.

The addition of percussion on the bones and bodhrán, played by Mel Mercier and Colm Murphy respectively, with such a rare and expert precision, added another layer of mediation in itself. Martin Hayes described how surprising he found this the first time he listened to *The Dolphin's Way*:

> … the use of the bones and the bodhrán with the piano would have seemed like a new dish with ingredients that you'd think, they should never be together, ever; they should be on separate plates at all times. You would have thought the same about the bodhrán and the bones and the piano – that they absolutely had no relationship sonically, and that they were from different worlds. But somehow because of the way [Mícheál] had devised his playing on the piano, and the more staccato way he had of articulating, suddenly it created that possibility for the bones and the bodhrán to work in it. So it was a new sound, it was a new way of doing things, especially for the piano.[8]

Collaboration: Hiberno Jazz

As well as his own compositional and performative practices, Mícheál's musical collaborations also evidence his interest in musical mediation. In 1993 he formed an ensemble called Hiberno Jazz. This was a group of extraordinarily virtuosic musicians who were able to keep up with

Mícheál's dizzyingly fast playing of Irish traditional melodies, relentless jazzy harmonies, rock and roll power chords, chordal stabs, and frenetic, breathtaking flourishes of syncopation. With Mícheál's classical piano and scoring at the helm, the ensemble brought together an array of classical, traditional and jazz musicians including Ken Edge on saxophone, Niall Keegan on wooden flute, Mel Mercier on bones and bodhrán, and Andy Baker on double bass.

The use of the word 'Jazz' in the title of the ensemble is telling. Hibernia was the ancient Roman name for Ireland, while jazz is a uniquely American art form, an improvisational one, and oral at its core. For Mícheál, jazz also meant energy, exuberance, drive, and there was an unstoppable liveness to the music.

But for Mícheál, it wasn't about the music alone. It was the special energy created by bringing together musicians from different traditions. According to Mícheál, this was a mediational act – and one with implications beyond the music or the performance itself. In the ICTM keynote, he wrote:

> In my case, searching out strategies of cultural mediation that enabled classical and traditional musicians to perform together across the orality/literacy divide was an attempt to redress imbalances that might exist between different voices, different traditions, different points of view. The suggestion here is that by setting a cultural imbalance right, any social or political imbalance might also be at least partially addressed.[9]

Education: a 'community of sound' at the Irish World Academy

In Mícheál's words, his higher-education career was dedicated to 'redressing imbalances in access to higher-level music education for traditional and classical musicians in Ireland'.[10] First at University College Cork and later at the University of Limerick, Mícheál created programmes in Irish traditional music and dance performance alongside degrees in western classical music, world music, world dance and contemporary dance. This not only elevated traditional arts to what Mícheál often called a 'parity of esteem' with other cultural practices, it also created new higher-education opportunities for traditional musicians and dancers. Mícheál amended the entrance criteria for music degrees; with the traditional music focus in place, oral musicians could play traditional music in their auditions to enter the university. As Mícheál later noted, 'the rural social context'[11] of traditional music drew in a higher percentage of students who were the first in their family to attend university:

> In our experience at the Irish World Academy, a focus on achieving parity of esteem for traditional music and dance served dramatically as an invitation to a population group whose performance traditions have historically been marginalised from higher education. By facilitating the inclusion of a music and dance genre hitherto excluded, the inclusion of performers who embody these traditions has naturally followed.[12]

Mícheál was a first-generation university student himself, the beneficiary of a national scholarship access programme in the late 1960s. He went on to do his PhD in ethnomusicology at Queen's University Belfast, where he had many conversations with Professor John Blacking around what Blacking called a 'sound community'. Mícheál reflected, 'For me, the creation of a shared "community of sound" between classical musicians and traditional musicians in Ireland served as an ideal local laboratory for a cultural bridge-building that might be applied globally.'[13]

Musical mediation and social change

In considering Mícheál as a cultural and musical mediator, we must explore his commitment to justice and inclusion. In his ICTM keynote, Mícheál defined mediation as 'a middle way, an acoustic that exists in the liminal space between perceived realities. It is literally the medium through which issues of injustice are addressed and put right'.[14] In the arena of cultural injustice, he said, certain voices are bypassed and a musical imbalance results. Mícheál, as he once stated about Blacking, was 'surely fuelled by his deep belief that social change could be achieved through the human creation of culture'.[15]

As noted throughout the examples above, Mícheál's mediation was not only about the music that resulted; at its core, it was about the creators and carriers of music and tradition. To be a true mediator, one must not only transfer local or oral culture to the global or classical stage. One must recognise that music and culture are embodied, carried by individual people, and they must be included as equals. Ultimately, Mícheál's mediational work was made up of acts of inclusion. He expanded our social and political understanding of who was qualified to enter university, who was qualified to perform and teach there, and who was qualified to play or sing with national and international orchestras. He described this work with traditional music as redressing an imbalance:

> … to bring things back into a just line, to provide leadership, articulation, and order in any perceived cultural aggression, to set something

> right, to stand up for somebody and something, to repair a broken tradition, to rectify a cultural injustice, to mediate a cultural resolution that facilitates the free growth of apparently opposing traditions – all of these and more sustain us in our calling.[16]

For Mícheál, the exchange resulting from this mediation was mutually beneficial to both established cultural forces and 'newly arrived voices',[17] creating a cultural parity of esteem that would in turn influence the social and political domains.

Conclusion

Mícheál was a musical mediator of the Irish psyche for all of the complex realities that the nation was experiencing during his lifetime. He did this not only through composition and performance, but also through his work as founder and director of the Irish World Academy of Music and Dance and his work in the broader Irish cultural space. Through his composition, his performance collaborations and his educational work, Mícheál mediated a new Irish identity that valued local and traditional culture, welcomed multiculturalism and world cultures in a changing Ireland, and stood as equal to European classical high art.

Mícheál was always fascinated by the image of the estuary, the place where the inland river enters into a transitionary, tidal state as it flows out into the ocean. Estuaries are places of extraordinary biodiversity and abundant natural activity. Mícheál wanted his funeral to be held in a church by the great Shannon estuary and I think we can take this thought as his final great teaching to us: *Remember where you have come from and honour it. You will need all that precious memory and identity when the time comes to flow out and enter the ocean. The destination is the ever-flowing journey, ever renewed, living and in awe.* Our art, like our lives, must be lived in this dynamic paradox, each side redressing the other, each foot following the other, each breath in and out: a parity of esteem across every cell of our body leaving the 'new and necessary consciousness' emerging in our wake.

Mícheál stated that his work with traditional music empowered him to 'find parts of my cultural self that lay hidden, to find the words to articulate my emerging cultural beliefs …' He said, 'The intimate connection between all of that and my music making – both as a performer and a composer – are too deep for me to articulate.'[18]

Mícheál was my father, but he was also very much my avid, boisterous and constructively argumentative conversational companion. We spoke all the time about culture – its symbols and its meanings. In retrospect,

I believe that what he said about his cultural beliefs – that they were too deep for him to articulate – is what I observed and heard over our years of conversation. Ultimately, he had the wisdom to let his art and actions do the talking. This was all part of his great teacherly personality, urging us on to do the work ourselves – to uncover our own interpretation, in our own voice; a voice that has been patiently waiting within us to emerge.

85
Irish Music (Re-)Defined: The writings of Mícheál Ó Súilleabháin

John O'Flynn

John O'Flynn is professor of music at Dublin City University. His publications include three monographs and five co-edited volumes and numerous articles/chapters on film music, popular music, music in higher education, and music in Ireland. He was founding chair of the Society for Music Education in Ireland (2010–13), and served as president of the Society for Musicology in Ireland (2021–4).

Introduction

Among his considerable achievements and outputs as a leading performer, composer, educator and advocate for music in Ireland, it would be fair to say that Mícheál Ó Súilleabháin was primarily concerned with artistic and creative practice. He referred to this at many scholarly occasions as 'the thing itself'. One such event was his welcome address to those who attended the 6th International Symposium on the Sociology of Music Education at Mary Immaculate College in Limerick in 2009 (having presented the keynote address at the previous biennial symposium at St John's, Newfoundland in 2007). Yet, while musicking in one shape or another was at the heart of his endeavours, the University of Limerick's first chair of music greatly understood the importance of words, not just to inform various musical, cultural and educational debates but also, critically, to change hearts and minds, and ultimately to realise his transformative vision for music in Ireland. So, while Ó Súilleabháin may have left research studies based on Pierre Bourdieu's theories of cultural capital to those versed in the sociology of music education, from early on in his career he adumbrated a similar critique of received socio-cultural hierarchies and mechanisms that perpetuated such distinctions, and never tired in his quest for a parity of esteem for different genres of music, and for their associated cultural histories and creative practices.

As other chapters in this book attest, Ó Súilleabháin had a deep well of knowledge in music, Irish cultural history, ethnomusicology and anthropology that he drew on throughout his career. At the same time he regularly dialogued with a wide range of scholarly and creative disciplines, from philosophy, psychology and postcolonial studies to engagement with practices and perspectives from dance, poetry and visual arts. Many of his essays were inspired by Irish poetry; for example, in his Ó Riada memorial lecture 'Ceol na nUasal' delivered in 2003, he referred to texts by five poets: Michael Hartnett, Seamus Heaney, Thomas Kinsella, John Montague and Seán Ó Ríordáin. Much earlier, in a short *Irish Times* article published in 1977, Ó Súilleabháin astutely observed how Ó Riada, his former lecturer at University College Cork (UCC), 'had a much greater influence on his poet contemporaries than on other composers'.[1]

Ó Súilleabháin also clearly enjoyed words and narrative forms in and for themselves, as suggested by his opening statement to a note to accompany *Phoenix Rising*, the score he produced for the documentary feature *Pioneers and Aviators: A century of Irish aviation*, released in 2013 and directed by Alan Gilsenan:

> I was on the train to Dublin when my phone sprang into life. My ringtone choice is always 'French Horns' with their cool mellow outdoor pastoral timbre. A tally-ho kind of sound, a sound commanding a journey.[2]

This is one of myriad examples of Ó Súilleabháin's humanistic approach to a subject, drawing the reader into a lived journey with its own soundtrack, before going on to describe a conversation about the scoring brief and his eventual compositional approach to the film production.[3]

The remainder of this chapter presents an overview of writings by Ó Súilleabháin from his earliest publications in the mid-1970s to the mid-2010s. Drawing on a range of sources from journals, book publications and magazine and newspaper archives, it addresses the corpus of Ó Súilleabháin's published writings. These are organised thematically, while also following a broad chronological order, through the following subheadings: defining Irish music; the bodhrán; collections and editions; reviews; music education; traditional players and individual style; innovation, tradition and mediation; and twenty-first century reflections on Irish music and culture, including writings centred on the Irish World Academy of Music and Dance (henceforth, the Academy). As may already be evident, several of these themes overlap. A select bibliography of Ó Súilleabháin's published and unpublished writings is provided at the end of the book.

Defining Irish music

Among Ó Súilleabháin's earlier articles were two position pieces published in *The Crane Bag*, a critical Irish studies journal published from 1977 to

1985 under the editorship of Richard Kearney. Ó Súilleabháin's 1981 article 'Irish Music Defined' was provocative and aspirational for its time, and signalled the author's capacity to break new ground in ways that music in Ireland could be imagined and ultimately, *re-defined*, as the title to the present chapter suggests. In it, he discusses the problems associated with delineating Irish music and suggests that the principal difficulties arise from the separate traditions, discourses and performance practices that are associated with the three main style categories of traditional, classical and popular. Taking an inclusive and pragmatic approach, he proposes that Irish music be defined as '... encompassing all creative music-making in Ireland',[4] qualifying this by pointing out that all genres of domestic music have continuities and connections with music systems outside of Ireland.

His second short *Crane Bag* article, 'The Art of Listening', was a response to composer Frank Corcoran's argument, published earlier in the same journal, that Irish classical music was historically undervalued by the Irish state and was marginalised in contemporary articulations of Irish cultural identity. Ó Súilleabháin's alternative view listed specific socio-historical factors for this state of affairs, provocatively suggesting that rejection of or indifference to the traditions of European classical music was not necessarily problematic.[5] While lauding the new music produced by Corcoran and other contemporary Irish composers, he critiqued earlier aspirations towards an Irish school of classical music in the emerging nation-state, noting failed attempts of both *translation* ('impossible from one system of music to another') and *transference*, especially when the rhythms and tones of traditional music were extrapolated from 'more "meaningful" non-literate elements such as timbre'.[6] Furthermore, and as noted by Thomas Johnston,[7] in the same article, Ó Súilleabháin also contemplates the relevance or otherwise of the terms 'composer' and 'composition'[8] – a comparative perspective that informs some of his later writings on Irish traditional music in education, discussed below.

The bodhrán

Prior to entering debates over Irish musical identities, Ó Súilleabháin's first publications were focused on the history and performance style of bodhrán playing. His two short articles in 1974 for *Treoir*, the Irish-language newsletter of Comhaltas Ceoltóirí Éireann (CCÉ), provide insights into his capacity for considering local traditions and practices in light of comparative music studies. The first article situates the instrument in a historical and cross-cultural discussion of frame-drums, before going on to describe bodhrán making and playing and associated cultural traditions in areas of Munster, notably, north Kerry, south Tipperary and west Limerick.

In the second *Treoir* article, largely based on his observations of individual players, Ó Súilleabháin next describes and notates featured rhythm patterns for the bodhrán and associated beating patterns, according to region. For this, he adapts symbols from classical string bowing to indicate single down-, double down- or up-strokes, pointing to regional variations in how the instrument is beaten by upper or lower knob sticks. He employs standard rhythm notation to illustrate his description, all the while stressing that this does not accurately reflect 'the element of "swing" that is in Irish dance music',[9] and providing more nuanced notations to suggest uneven realisations of standard durations.

A decade later, he authored a book-length guide to the bodhrán, published by Waltons in 1984. Its opening chapters expand on the ideas explored in the earlier *Treoir* articles, albeit now aimed at a much wider global readership and learnership, and incrementally introducing more advanced techniques, some of which reflected contemporary developments in the wake of traditional music's widespread popularity by the mid-1980s. The publication also includes a selection of dance tunes with accompanying bodhrán patterns notated. As Niall Keegan records, the book was translated into several languages and was pitched to adult beginners who were likely already performers in another musical style.[10]

Collections and editions

In 1976 a pair of songs that Ó Súilleabháin collected and notated from the singing of Pilib Ó Laoghaire was published in a newsletter of the local history society Cuimhneachán Chois tSiúire. This was a fitting tribute to the Cork-born traditional singer, song collector, choral conductor, teacher and part-time lecturer who died in the same year and who undoubtedly influenced Ó Súilleabháin while a student at UCC. Following his appointment as music lecturer to that institution in 1975, Ó Súilleabháin undertook the challenging task of completing the editorial work that renowned folk music scholar Donal O'Sullivan (1893–1973) had begun decades earlier, based on the original manuscripts by Edward Bunting.[11] It culminated in the publication of *Bunting's Ancient Music of Ireland* by Cork University Press in 1983. About the same time, Ó Súilleabháin provided an informative introduction to the 1982 reprint of the *Frank Roche Collection* of dance tunes, airs and marches, originally published by Roche in 1912 and revised in 1927. For the 1982 publication, Ó Súilleabháin interprets the tune types that were more popular according to historical period and/or regional practice, the addition of piano accompaniments, and Roche's Irish-language and educational activism within the Gaelic League movement.

Ó Súilleabháin later oversaw the editorial completion of the two-volume *Sources of Irish Traditional Music c. 1600–1855*. It was eventually published in 1998 as part of Garland's Reference Library of the Humanities, six years after the death of its principal editor, the UCC Professor of Music, Aloys Fleischmann (1910–92), with Paul McGettrick as associate editor. This was another extensive project cataloguing and annotating centuries of Irish oral-tradition sources. It included an index of melodic incipits for each tune or air, transposed to a G-centred tonality for comparative purposes.[12] Ó Súilleabháin also wrote a preface to the book, which detailed the many people involved in a venture that began through a project initiated by one of Fleischmann's students, Annette de Foubert, and continued for almost half a century:

> From de Foubert's initial project in the 1950s, the springing into life of Fleischmann's project in the 1960s with [Seán] Ó Riada and [Pilib] Ó Laoghaire, and the work of the many dedicated research assistants who rallied round the project throughout the 1970s and 1980s, a great oak tree has grown in this the final decade of the 20th century.[13]

Also acknowledged in the same preface is the extensive involvement of Nicholas Carolan and the Irish Traditional Music Archive.[14]

Later collaborations with traditional music scholars included selected proceedings from *Blas: The local accent in Irish traditional music*, published in 1997, and which Ó Súilleabháin co-edited with Thérèse Smith (and assistant editors Sandra Joyce and Niall Keegan). This followed a conference at the University of Limerick in November 1995 that was co-sponsored by the Irish Folk Music Society and the Academy. It was the first of several international academic conferences in the 1990s that focused exclusively on Irish traditional music, whether in Ireland, among the Irish diapsora or further afield. Ó Súilleabháin also presented a keynote paper at the *Crosbhealach an Cheoil, The Crossroads Conference* that took place in Dublin in 1996, leading to his 1999 'Crossroads or Twintrack?' article that is considered below.

Reviews

The select bibliography of Ó Súilleabháin's writings at the end of the book includes references to two reviews that do not appear to have been published. The first, titled 'Guides for Young Traditional Players', was based on three out of the four volumes of *Music from Ireland* compiled and edited by Dave Bulmer and Neil Sharpley, and published in 1974. In contrast to the historical collections cited in this chapter's previous section, Bulmer and Sharpley's books contained notations of tunes from live sessions. While many of these were the same as or variants of those published in the canonical volumes of dance tunes by Chief Francis O'Neill and later by Breandán Breathnach, they reflected more contemporary styles of playing. Similarly, in 1977 Ó Súilleabháin drafted a review of *Irish Tunes by the 100*, vol.1 (1975) compiled by the renowned fiddlers Seán McGuire and Josephine Keegan; and an undated manuscript on Robin Williamson's annotated collection *English, Welsh, Scottish & Irish Fiddle Tunes* (1976), aimed at existing as well as newly converted folk music enthusiasts.

That Ó Súilleabháin studied and reviewed these materials during the mid-1970s was significant on several counts: first, it demonstrated a capacity to interpret historical sources alongside contemporary performances based on those sources; second, it reflected his awareness of new tunes emerging across a now vibrant traditional music network; and third, his reviews recognised the increasingly transnational and inter-generational appeal of contemporary traditional and folk scenes.

Ó Súilleabháin later reviewed three books concerning Irish music subjects. The first review was of James Cowdery's *The Melodic Tradition of Ireland*, published in 1993 in *Ethnomusicology*, the journal of the Society for Ethnomusicology. Although Ó Súilleabháin is somewhat critical of Cowdery's reductive book title, conservative analytic approach, reliance on outdated historical sources and buy-in to orientalist ideas of Irish traditional music, he is also sympathetic to the author's 'poetic insight' and 'his own obviously deep emotional response to Irish musical tradition'.[15]

His second book review, on Séamas de Barra's monograph *Aloys Fleischmann, 1910–92*, was published in the *Journal of Music* in 2007. Ó Súilleabháin is highly complimentary of de Barra's analysis and discussion of the composer, conductor, teacher and musicologist, and identifies the book project as 'a labour of love' for its author who also studied under Fleischmann at UCC. The same could be said of Ó Súilleabháin's article which mostly historicises his former professor's academic and aesthetic positions – including those pertaining to folk music – while also revealing the reviewer's fond memories of 'a seminal figure in Irish musical life'.[16]

In November 2013, Ó Súilleabháin articulated a resounding endorsement for the landmark publication *The Encyclopaedia of Music in Ireland* in a review published by *The Irish Times*. His appraisal of the substantial two-volume publication considered contemporary debates regarding the representation of different musics in Ireland, and the complex issues facing general editors Harry White and Barra Boydell and the wider editorial board in negotiating such a terrain. Ó Súilleabháin concluded that the *Encyclopaedia* successfully transformed 'a labyrinth into a readable map'.[17]

Later, his review of Martin Dowling's *Traditional Music and Irish Society* was published by *The Irish Times* in January 2015. This was significant, not only because it appeared in the main reviews section of a leading newspaper, but also because Dowling, like Ó Súilleabháin, was a musician-academic, in his case a socioeconomic historian 'with fiddle in hand'. Although the review is relatively short, Ó Súilleabháin considers each chapter of Dowling's substantial history in turn. Reflecting on the author's concluding aspiration that musicians be free from the constrictions of previous political movements and ideologies, the reviewer comments: 'As a primary perspective on history, that is spoken like a true creative artist.'[18]

While Ó Súilleabháin's occasional reviews of musicians and recordings in traditional and folk genres might be expected (for example, his joint *Irish Times* article on Dónal Lunny in 2007), his review of the Oasis album *Be Here Now* for *The Irish Times* in 1997 may have surprised some readers. Adopting an auto-ethnographic approach that opens with the statement, 'I was a Beatles fan', the article first offers a brief account of Ó Súilleabháin's rock and pop youth experiences. He then interprets the album as a type of rock oratorio, with a 'basic musical language still rooted in the blues' and with some of Noel Gallagher's ideas 'redolent of the Irish song tradition'.[19]

Music education

As noted in the introduction, although Ó Súilleabháin was primarily concerned with the advancement of music (and dance) per se, he recognised the centrality of music education in realising his long-term artistic and cultural vision. While not an educationalist in the disciplinary sense, he engaged widely with music education philosophy and literature throughout his career, and displayed a deep understanding of the importance of teaching and learning systems and processes for various groups and individuals within society. Some of this was gained from first-hand experience as a music teacher in a vocational school in Cork, immediately after graduating with a BMus from UCC in 1973.

His first published writings on the subject of music education in Ireland were short letters to *The Irish Times*, respectively, in 1977 and 1981. In the first, titled 'Folk Music Studies', he prophetically advocated for a three-to-four-year course specialising in Irish traditional music performance that also included modules in ethnomusicology, European art music and contemporary music.[20] Arguing that UCC would be the ideal location for such a programme, given its existing modules in folk and traditional music, he also envisioned full-time teaching positions for traditional music graduates in post-primary schools. The 1981 letter, 'Irish Music',[21] was a response to the opening address given by An tAthair Pádraig Ó Fiannachta to the Willie Clancy Summer School that year. While sharing Ó Fiannachta's critical stance in regard to the marginalisation of traditional music in music degree programmes, Ó Súilleabháin rejected the vehemence of the former's tone, again pointing to developments at UCC.

Some of those curricular changes were outlined in the leaflet 'University Music Courses and the Irish Traditional Musician', published by CCÉ in 1984. It advertised scholarships to entice traditional musicians to undertake formal music studies at UCC, and detailed the technical requirements for entrance examination to the BMus and BA (music) programmes. Ó Súilleabháin ended the CCÉ piece by considering the relevance of university-level education for musicians from all backgrounds. His statement reflected the influence of his ethnomusicology studies at Queen's University Belfast (QUB) and his consistent philosophical consideration of listening as inherent to musicality and to humanity:

> … an individual must not only possess a degree of excellence in his own music, but more importantly must be able to cultivate an ability to listen beyond his own experience, and beyond the experience of his social group. Such an ambitious and exciting educational endeavour should result not only in a greater degree of self-knowledge but also of a greater awareness of the musical needs of the community within which we live.[22]

A seminal paper in the context of Irish music education was Ó Súilleabháin's article 'Out of Tune with Reality: Music and the school in Ireland', published in *Irish Educational Studies* in 1985.[23] Drawing on his own experiences as learner and teacher, his engagement with contemporary music education literature, and a paper he had presented at the International Folk Music Council (UK) conference at the University of Durham in 1982, the article explored the alienation of second-level students from the music syllabuses of state examinations, in large part due to what the author interpreted as residual colonial constructions of a classical music canon in most third-level institutions. Ó Súilleabháin's advocacy for the inclusion of aurally based music materials and encounters in school music was a multifaceted one that, while championing Irish traditional music, also rejected narrow curricula based on essentialist tenets of cultural nationalism.

Convened by Frank Heneghan at Dublin Institute of Technology over three phases from 1994 to '96, and at the time of the establishment of the Irish World Music Centre (later Irish World Academy) at the University of Limerick, the Music Education National Debate (MEND) involved the largest gathering to date of national and international music educators in Ireland. Its published proceedings were for the most past interpreted through Heneghan's well-intentioned but ultimately conservatoire-oriented vision of a national music education system. Ó Súilleabháin's individual contributions to the proceedings of MEND are documented in two appendices to Heneghan's main report.[24] However, for the main report, his ideas concerning traditional music in education are paraphrased by Heneghan,[25] and as such are subsumed within the latter's agenda to accommodate some 'multicultural' elements in a notation-centred classical model. This goes against Ó Súilleabháin's reservations, expressed during his first contribution to MEND, concerning the assimilation of aural-tradition music styles into existing music education frameworks without addressing more fundamental curricular, cultural and pedagogical issues.[26]

From the mid-1990s onwards and as later discussed, Ó Súilleabháin's writings on music education were mostly concerned with higher education. However, he maintained links with schools and community initiatives, including his support of the independent music school Maoin Cheoil an Chláir in Ennis, County Clare. As he observed in a brief letter to *The Irish Times* in 2001, that school provided a unique bi-musical instrumental music programme (incorporating both classical and traditional courses). He went on to suggest that: 'A network of such schools across Ireland would make significant inroads into broadening access to music education, combating issues related to elitism in the music education system.'[27] It is perhaps worth noting that this was almost a decade before the establishment of Music Generation in 2010 and its subsequent rollout of multi-genre, county-level music education partnerships throughout the country.

Traditional players and individual style

A consistent theme throughout Ó Súilleabháin's academic writing was that of the individual style of traditional musicians, including several auto-ethnographic reflections on his own piano playing. The major opus in this regard was his PhD on innovation and tradition in the music of renowned fiddler Tommie Potts, carried out under the supervision of John Blacking and John Baily at Queen's University Belfast (QUB). This led to the subsequent publication of chapters and other articles based on sections and/or concepts from that ethnomusicological research. Yet Ó Súilleabháin had a demonstrated interest in individual style prior to embarking on doctoral studies; one of his earliest publications comprised a short piece in 1977 for *Comhar* on the fiddle playing of Patrick Kelly from west Clare.[28] Acknowledging earlier research on Kelly's tunes by Séamus Mac Mathúna in the mid-1960s, Ó Súilleabháin adopted a mix of folk and classical music terminology to interpret some of the renowned fiddler's preferred techniques. These included: homophones, *scordatura*, octaves, double stops, inversions, slow introductions and endings to dance tunes; melodic variations; and use of variable (chromatic) tones.

Well before writing up his thesis and the award of PhD from QUB in 1987, in 1982 Ó Súilleabháin had a short article based on Potts' music published in *An Fhidil Ghaelach*.[29] It focused on the fiddler's 'melodic deviation' and 'programmatic' playing of the reel 'My Love is in America' on his celebrated LP *The Liffey Banks*, released in 1972. The article included a standard notated version of the tune alongside Ó Súilleabháin's transcription of Potts' highly individual rendition of it, and an analysis of the latter based on 'formal' and 'tonal' aspects. As the author later recalled,[30] it was after reading this short article that Potts agreed to meet Ó Súilleabháin for an extensive series of meetings and interviews.

He next contributed an article on improvisation for the French-language collection *L'improvisation dans les musiques de tradition orale*. Its publication in 1987 followed two sessions on the subject of improvisation at the European Seminar on Ethnomusicology, respectively, in Cologne (1983) and Tours (1984). Ó Súilleabháin's article begins by introducing his international readers to the model structures or received settings of Irish traditional dance tunes; he then continues with some notes on the use of bodhrán before interpreting Potts' playing through a theoretical frame of improvisation.[31]

Post-award publications based on his PhD began with an extended chapter in 1990 for the inaugural volume of the peer-reviewed book series *Irish Musical Studies* (1990). Titled 'The Creative Process in Irish Traditional Dance', this was a highly significant inclusion given that the book represented the first-ever collection of essays 'designed to offer a conspectus of musicology in Ireland'.[32] Here it can be noted that Ó Súilleabháin was a member of the steering committee that led to the establishment of the Society for Musicology in Ireland (SMI) from 2002 to 2003 and was subsequently elected to the first SMI Council (2003–6). His chapter in *Irish Musical Studies 1* is a seminal essay that comprehensively explores the social and aesthetic relationships between, on one hand, the framework for traditional dance tunes and rounds, and on the other hand, performer creativity. Illustrated by many notated examples and tables, it proposes and utilises the idea of set accented tones, and deviations from these, in appraising individual performances by Potts and fellow fiddlers Paddy Glackin and Patrick Kelly, and by the flute player J.P. Downes.

Much later, Ó Súilleabháin contributed to *Dear Far-Voiced Veteran*, a *festschrift* published in 2007 in honour of folk song collector Tom Munnelly. His chapter, '"Traditional Ears": Perception and analysis in Irish traditional music', constitutes another original contribution from his PhD, once again focusing on the case of Tommie Pots but now comparing how his music might be heard differently by those from a classical background (as discussed below, Potts absorbed many classical influences) and those with insider knowledge of Irish traditional music. This article provides an in-depth consideration and glossary of the terms developed throughout Ó Súilleabháin's writings on traditional music (comparing these with equivalent 'folk terms') and furthers draws on his engagement with literature from ethnomusicology, notably Bruno Nettl's concepts of model audibility and model density.[33]

In his 2007 essay, Ó Súilleabháin replaces his use of the term 'deviation' (from models of set accented tones) to the more fluid and creative idea of 'alteration' – a concept for interpreting traditional music performance that ascribes more individual agency than that of tune variation.[34] This concept had been explored earlier in his 'Crossroads or Twintrack?' paper,[35] in which Ó Súilleabháin employed John Blacking's idea of objective/subjective perspectives on change in musical style.[36] It led to a research focus on 'the five central pieces' by Potts,[37] that is, on recordings that exemplified the fiddler's unique individual style. Similar to the 1990 chapter in *Irish Musical Studies*, the 'Crossroads or Twintrack?' paper contains an extended discussion on processes of the round in traditional dance music, this time further illuminated through comparisons of different recordings by Potts and illustrated with analytic figures.[38]

A further substantial article based on his PhD thesis, 'The Litany of the Saints', appeared in a 2010 issue of *Inbhear*, the Academy's journal of music and dance. Its title not only refers to the deep impression that Catholic liturgical music made on Potts, but also to the litany of composers that were quoted or adapted in, or that more generally inspired, the music-making of the featured fiddler.[39] Covering some of the material considered in his chapter for Tom Munnelly's *festschrift*, the *Inbhear* article is comprehensive in its analytic comparison of, on one hand, original classical pieces (notably, those of Chopin and Liszt), Romani-inspired music and popular jazz, and on the other hand Potts' integration of diverse idioms, techniques and 'moods' from those pieces into his own playing. The article ends with a consideration of the very different musical identities and pathways pursued by Potts and his contemporary, Seán Ó Riada.

Tradition, innovation and mediation

Though centred on a single case study, Ó Súilleabháin's doctoral research, like his own music-making, was consistently engaged with a dialectics of innovation and tradition. Although this was a perspective that informed many articles already cited in this chapter, this section now explores his writings that engaged with broader musical and cultural debates, including those addressing issues of tradition/innovation, mediation and musical-national identities.

In 'All our central fire', published in *The Irish Journal of Psychology* in 1994, Ó Súilleabháin draws on Jungian theory – specifically, the concept of tension between 'structure' and 'dynamic' – to present the idea of an Irish psyche and its relation to music. Once again referring to the figures of Potts and Ó Riada, as well as Turlough Carolan and Thomas Moore, he interprets musical mediation in Irish cultural history (in each case between Irish traditional/aural and European classical/literate) as:

> that middle voice which opens up a channel of communication between separate energies ... musicians who, through a mix of artistic talent, temperamental disposition and what some would call historical accident, find themselves in a position where their natural accent speaks to opposite sides ... The musical mediator can be viewed as a bridge which allows listeners access to parts of their society and their experience of which they were unaware or perhaps just suspicious.[40]

In a later chapter for the book *Music in Ireland: 1848–1998*, Ó Súilleabháin contemplates how different traditions and innovations (classical, popular, traditional) can be accommodated in contemporary society, suggesting a psychoanalytical sense of healing through integrations of diverse identities and 'the sounds which can represent them'.[41] Along with his 'Crossroad or Twintrack?' article, these published writings by Ó Súilleabháin in the 1990s interpret innovative practices and cultural entrepreneurship within the 'art world' of traditional music, to adapt Howard Becker's concept.[42] Within this world he interprets 'media-friendly' progressions in traditional music that can be distinguished from more introspective innovative developments based on the solo performer.[43]

Appraising Seán Ó Riada

Similar to Ó Riada, Ó Súilleabháin's artistic work and advocacy was of the 'media-friendly' sort. However, in contrast to the angst and perceived failure of Ó Riada in accommodating different musical-historical traditions, Ó Súilleabháin advanced an alternative compositional principle founded on the anthropological idea of syncretism, a process that 'seems to seek out shared elements in the cultural organisms which on the surface may appear to be in total conflict'.[44] His idea of musical syncretism not only linked sounds, but also involved the broader idea of cultural mediation.

Some of these ideas informed Ó Súilleabháin's appraisal of Ó Riada's oeuvre and his wider cultural contribution through broadcasts and writings. In his lecture 'Ceol na nUasal', delivered at the annual Ó Riada Memorial Lecture at UCC in 2003, Ó Súilleabháin historicised Ó Riada's musical and ideological influences and convictions, interpreting the very opposite to syncretism in the latter's various creative projects and cultural enterprises. This culminated in Ó Riada's eventual declaration of an incompatibility between an aurally based, Irish art music of a past Gaelic aristocracy (termed by Ó Súilleabháin as a 'broken harp tradition'[45]) and modern literate music with historical continuities to Britain and continental Europe. Ó Súilleabháin regards Ó Riada's rejection of that heritage as in some respects comparable with radical ideas proposed by other post-Second World War composers who challenged the hegemony of western music theory and history, notably Stockhausen. However, the published lecture also deconstructs the speculative orientalism and 'cultural fundamentalism' that imbued many of Ó Riada's statements and actions.[46]

Arguably, Ó Súilleabháin's critique of Ó Riada acts to strengthen his admiration of a figure who for much of his short adult life negotiated two parallel musical worlds – as twentieth-century European composer and as leader of a newly imagined traditional-art music ensemble (Ceoltóirí Chualann) – while also developing a 'third voice' as documentary score composer, notably for *Mise Éire*.[47] Critically, Ó Súilleabháin interprets that Ó Riada's quest for a utopian, indigenous art music, 'ceol na n-uasal', was impeded by his primary perspective, namely that of an educated composer.[48] Consistent with his 1990s publications that address key mediators in Irish music history, he goes on to compare the composer's frustrations with the more low-key artistic revolutions that were concurrently emerging through the performer creativity of Tommie Potts and others. Ó Súilleabháin's appraisal of Ó Riada is a sophisticated one that does not shy away from 'the darkness' of the composer's personal journey. At the same time, he notes his enormous contribution to the practice and reception of Irish traditional music, contributing 'something essential to the release of that music to a renaissance of international dimensions'.[49]

The interlacing themes of tradition, innovation and mediation were constant threads in oral presentations and writings by Ó Súilleabháin. One of his last pieces in this regard was his contribution to a co-authored chapter for the edited volume *Harp Studies: Perspectives on the Irish harp*.[50] Published in 2016, it contemplated mutual influences of Irish cultural heritage, globalisation and contemporary artistic practice.

Twenty-first-century reflections on Irish music and culture

Another consistent thread running through Ó Súilleabháin's writings over several decades was his anti-essentialist position vis-à-vis music and national identity. This came to the fore from the mid-1990s, whether through his keynote addresses, audiovisual productions or published writings. Significantly, he was invited to contribute an article on the theme of creativity, tradition and innovation for *The Irish Times* on 30 December 1999, just before the dawn of the new millennium. Employing the then current terms of 'local' and 'global', he introduced the idea of 'lobal' as a preferred portmanteau for interpreting transnational cultural intersections. He also drew on Edward Said's musings in *Culture and Imperialism* when proposing:

> While the point of origin is always a sacred one, the process of becoming must supersede this, in that it is a process which creates new and dynamic sacred spaces within which our voices can grow and speak as they are called to do.[51]

Several of Ó Súilleabháin's ideas in his *Irish Times* piece were later expanded on in his essay 'An Island Sound: Reflections on music, politics and identity in contemporary Ireland' for the edited volume *Ireland in the New Century: Politics, culture and identity*, published in 2003.[52] In common with several of his other publications, this essay also involved a dialogue with modern poets, in this instance with Nuala Ní Dhomhnaill, Seamus Heaney, W.B. Yeats and T.S. Eliot. In the same article, Ó Súilleabháin further reflected on his composition for traditional flute and classical orchestra that he originally wrote in 1979 but later reworked into the piece *Oileán/Island* that was released by Virgin Records in 1989.

He developed a more spiritual approach to writing about music in his chapter 'The Singing Body' for the collection *Anáil Dé/The Breath of God*, published in 2001. Among many philosophical reflections, perhaps the most pertinent to the subject of this chapter is the following analogy:

> The singing body is the body in prayer. We are here in the domain of action. What the reflection of theology brings to prayer, that of musicology brings to music. Reflection may lead us towards a better and more successful singing and praying, but it still is not that which it reflects upon.[53]

This statement poetically articulates the distinction made in the introduction between phenomenological engagement with, and academic approaches to, 'the thing itself'.

Ó Súilleabháin's chapter 'Listening to Difference: Ireland in a world of music', published in the 2004 collection *Global Aspirations and the Reality of Change*, followed his address at the annual Céifin Summer School in County Clare.[54] In it, he combines earlier expounded ideas of different cultural traditions in 'lobal' contexts with inspirations from poetic texts; additionally, he draws on Irish mythological sources, referring to tales of the goddesses Céifin and Sionna (the latter giving her name to the river Shannon). The entire piece is imbued with a humanist, spiritual perspective that is enriched by allusions to local experience and ontology.

The Irish World Academy

As a leading figure in the development of Irish traditional music and other musics in third- and fourth-level education, Ó Súilleabháin was actively involved in representing the Academy. This included occasional letters to the press, such as in 1997 when he responded to concerns raised about the Academy's new summer school, *Blas*, arguing that its international attendance would complement rather than compete with the Willie Clancy Summer School or with similar community-based enterprises.[55] By the 2010s, the Academy was well established in the Irish cultural and educational life, an achievement that along with Ó Súilleabháin's own maturity afforded substantial reflections from an auto-ethnographic perspective. His chapter 'Elver-Gleams: Sub-marine soundings from the Irish World Academy', which was published in 2013 in the edited volume *Music and the Irish Imagination*,[56] followed an Irish studies conference that took place at the University of Caen, Normandy in 2008. Here, Ó Súilleabháin argues for the integration of performing arts into Irish studies, giving examples of undergraduate and postgraduate programmes offered at the Academy. He also refers to its e-journal *Inbhear*, with links to audio recordings of fieldwork integrated with academic texts; and to *Comhaimseartha/Of Our Times*, the Academy's biannual publication bringing together abstracts and resumés of its various concerts, seminars and workshops across a range of music and dance genres. The final section of his chapter outlines the architecture and concept of the new Academy building on the County Clare side of the University of Limerick campus.

In 2013, Ó Súilleabháin presented a keynote paper at The Music Education Gathering (3rd Annual Conference of the Society for Music Education in Ireland) hosted by St Patrick's College, Drumcondra. Among several themes, The Music Education Gathering reflected on changes in Irish music education since the MEND debate of 1994–6, and in his paper 'MENDing Music Education? Some progress at the Irish World Academy', Ó Súilleabháin documented the development of undergraduate and postgraduate programmes at the Academy. It was later re-written as a co-authored chapter with Helen Phelan for the inaugural volume of the book series *Studies in Irish Music Education*.[57]

Ó Súilleabháin presented the opening address at the 44th World Conference of the International Council for Traditional Music (ICTM) which was hosted by the Academy in July 2017. His keynote paper 'The Redress of Music: Music, mediation, and parity of esteem' was subsequently published in the ICTM's *Yearbook for Traditional Music* in 2018. Adapting the idea of redress from Seamus Heaney's writings,[58] Ó Súilleabháin's paper offered a subjective view on 'practical' and 'poetic' aspects of his agency as performer, composer and music educator and referred to various developments that he led, first at UCC and, from 1994, at the Academy. Returning to his oft-cited theme of cultural mediation, he now reflected on his life's work in that role – between aural and literate musical traditions; between music, dance and other arts; between arts practice and research; and across various cultural and educational institutions. He closed his address to the international ICTM gathering by contemplating the societal benefits of interpreting music – and in particular, oral tradition music – through a range of humanities, social sciences and creative practice perspectives:

> … we may be heartened in the belief that the redress of music leads through a process of mediation towards a cultural parity of esteem, and that resonances in social and political domains will follow.[59]

Ó Súilleabháin's essay 'Cultural Redress and the Growth of Love' was published posthumously in 2021 in the edited volume *The Artist and Academia*. It followed a convocation in 2014 to celebrate the first twenty years of the Academy. Also adapting Heaney's idea of cultural redress, Ó Súilleabháin's chapter is presented as 'a guided autoethnography' that focuses on his later years as a UCC lecturer (1987–93), prior to moving to Limerick. His story interprets how 'the integration of Irish traditional music studies and performance within the University music curriculum … released a new energy previously unrecognised', and represented a significant postcolonial moment in Irish cultural history.[60] While the chapter focuses on Ó Súilleabháin's agency, several 'spirit guides' accompany him on this narrative journey. These are Aloys Fleischmann and Seán Ó Riada at UCC, and his PhD supervisors at QUB, John Blacking and John Baily. Here, Ó Súilleabháin not only describes the particular milieu and set of circumstances that inspired the curricular innovations he led at Cork, and that subsequently blossomed at the Academy, but also poignantly suggests that his role as cultural mediator is contingent on crossing paths with many others.

Concluding note

Common to the various themes emerging from Mícheál Ó Súilleabháin's writings are his aspiration to transform the landscape of music in Ireland, and a belief in the importance of words to realise that vision. Although not the first scholar to focus on process as opposed to product in Irish traditional music, he was the first to do so comprehensively. Before, during and after his PhD studies, his writings on various topics illustrated an understanding of the dynamic relationships between discourses *of* and *about* music, and how praxial theories of music could also invoke discourses of advocacy, aesthetics, spirituality and, when necessary, politics. While always giving prominence to 'the thing itself' and to the various cultural manifestations and value systems associated with performing arts, he was astutely aware of the potency of both spoken and written word in his lifelong quest to re-define music in Ireland.

86

The Daring Young Man on the Flying Trapeze: A personal recollection and evaluation by a musician and educator

Fintan Vallely

Fintan Vallely is a musician and writer on Irish traditional music. He was the Irish Times *correspondent for music in the 1990s, and lectured in NUI Maynooth, Ulster University and Dundalk Institute of Technology. His major work is the encyclopaedia* Companion to Irish Traditional Music *(1999, 2011, 2024).*

I began playing Irish traditional music in 1963, and inside the following decade took part in fleadhs, concerts and sessions in every part of the island, a scene which was so compact that we all knew, or knew of, each other. It was driven by passion and dedication, yet was full of exciting newness to me as a gauche teenager. I dropped out for a few years, and when I came back to it in 1977 I found it a different experience – quite commercialised, with celebrities, rationally organised, and involving large numbers of younger players. But it was still a thrilling place to be, now with new opportunities too, outside the country in Europe and America. Working at printing when not playing and teaching music led me to produce a tutor for the flute,[1] one result of which was being asked to start teaching at Scoil Samhraidh Willie Clancy in 1986, and, subsequently, led me to academic research into attitudes to the music in northern counties. This admitted me to the new sphere of third-level teaching, and to reviewing concerts and albums for *The Irish Times*, through which I met Mícheál Ó Súilleabháin, then a charismatic dynamo in University College Cork (UCC).

I had heard his music on radio and had learnt much about him on the hoof – through conversations, opinions, brief interviews and conversations with his students – but meeting him was different. We did not see eye-to-eye on everything, but this new, real dimension of the man opened me to appreciation of the value of – and need for – his kind of nerve and fresh ideas in what had hitherto been a quite defensive realm of culture. It was clear that he had swung into the once-so-staid traditional music scene as a left-field interloper, entering our sight-line with a flourish, his energised playing of 'Bonaparte Crossing the Rhine'[2] on harpsichord demonstrating a new potential in old material. That iconic Gael Linn performance served to seduce some of us self-perceived guardians of 'the pure drop' out from behind the palisades of our reclamation zones to consider a new vista of potential. Broadcast often by Radio Éireann in the late 1970s, this buzzing expression of popular music from the past, on a four-centuries-old instrument type, mediated traditional, classical and popular tastes. Ó Súilleabháin took off from the shoulders of Seán Ó Riada,[3] so to speak, but he had a unique amalgam of personal, intellectual and aesthetic instincts and abilities that made his flight remarkable. As with Ó Riada, but deliberately without the concept of 'folk orchestra', his music ignored the established safety net that was the unison, céilí band format, its function, instrumentation and repertoire style. Yet his transformative re-envisaging did not devalue or sideline the extraordinary achievements of Leo Rowsome, Comhaltas Ceoltóirí Éireann and Breandán Breathnach or those of Ó Riada himself. Organically embedded in education, this was not combative. He simply opened up another 'way', unobtrusively softening and dissolving the competing, defensive cultural borders which were the fallout from Ireland's pre-1921 colonial status.

Formerly, the traditional musician's boast was of having had no formal music education, that their music was superior to all else. Post-Ó Súilleabháin's initiatives, many of us found ourselves somewhat eating the words of our certainties, for it is now study, if not a degree, that is almost the norm in traditional music. And, though the soundly established sophistication and integrity of the 'core' remains a deeply appreciated and still necessary anchor and lodestone, the now much more diverse, expanded clientele routinely chooses to relish or question music exploration. This is in addition to understanding and appreciating old repertoire and styles as a constructive buffer of enduring potential in what Alan Lomax had worried might become a blended 'grey-out' in today's music cosmopolitanism.[4] In this way, Mícheál Ó Súilleabháin's following of his muse psychologically endorsed and boosted the interplay of positives that mark the evolution of new-age, Irish cultural confidence since the 1970s.

I had heard Mícheál on radio in that decade, long before I ever had occasion to come across him in the flesh near the turn of the 1990s. This was after my cousin Niall Vallely had gone to study with him in UCC in 1988, something of a courageous destination for a young traditional musician at that time. Also in UCC then was Paul McGettrick, whose interviewing me for a UCC dissertation on the flute further shook up my assumed absolutes: we had few college-educated precedents among traditional players up to then. I don't recall Mícheál proselytising for his courses, rather he just 'went at it', and students came to him, as filtered-out awareness or parental confidence directed them. His reputation was established unaggressively, not least through the energetic spark of his recordings, in particular the drama of the escalating-pitched, plucked-string keyboards on 'Bonaparte', which on Mike Murphy's pre-news, RTÉ morning programme woke us up often in the 1970s. Mícheál's subsequent music gave visibility to a new form of legacy – a university teacher basing his image and composition in indigenous music. In this, he was following the direction and awareness mapped by both Ó Riada and Aloys Fleischmann before him in UCC. Precedents in orchestral arrangement of the traditional had already been established there by Annie Patterson from 1927 to '34, and we were familiar too with the work of Éamonn Ó Gallchobhair with the Radio Éireann Light Orchestra in the 1950s,[5] and of David Curry with the BBC Northern Ireland Orchestra.[6] The difference was that Ó Súilleabháin started from within the traditional idiom, thus giving due respect to vernacular music sophistry.

The 'writing on the wall', subtle though it was, of which Mícheál was part author had already imperceptibly nudged me (to my great surprise for one who saw himself primarily as 'musician') into postgraduate study via the same John Blacking legacy which had inspired Mícheál himself. That opened me to a vast, until-then-unknown literature and way of intellectualising traditional musics in both the Irish music-establishment and the modern world. My view, like that of others, shifted from the stoic, endangered-species pride of the 'there's only a few of us left' variety to 'this can become open to widespread, popular appreciation and uptake'. As a result of my shift I was asked by Paddy Woodworth to write on the music for *The Irish Times* and, later, by Diarmuid Doyle for the *Sunday Tribune*. This further expanded my critical and aesthetic headspace by permitting me to experience the variety and great number of both passion-driven and commercial music events around the country. Prime among these was UCC's Éigse na Laoi series which ran from the early 1980s until 1996. The festivals addressed the spread of Irish and Irish-related music, drawing in the diaspora regions: Fiddlesticks: Fiddle music from Donegal and Shetland (1991); Dear Old Erin's Isle: Irish music from America (1992); Traditional Music and Dance of Cape Breton Island (1993); Across the Waters: Irish music from England (1994); The Gathering (1995); and the Seán Ó Riada commemoration (1996). Memorable among these tremendous, participatory events were those held in the years when fiddler Liz Doherty was, first, a student, then, from 1994, lecturer, the first woman appointed to such a position in traditional music. Working on these events too, with other staff and students, was Niall Vallely until 1993. My memory of visits to the UCC Music Department in its original building at that time is one of an ebullient Mícheál Ó Súilleabháin with an armful of documents and tremendous energy, endlessly on the move all over campus, conducting meetings on the hoof, spiritedly shouting cogent advice, discussing, confirming and approving, seemingly always trailed by a wake of questioning or fascinated students; such charisma was amazing to behold, of itself stimulating, enervating and enabling, exceptional for a college environment.

Mícheál was of course headstrong, a hallmark of his self-confidence, certainties and powers of persuasion. His contribution to debates indicated that he was perpetually thinking ahead and outside of the box, typically with a broader or deeper view. In this way he was able to spark and stimulate as well as contribute much to debate, dealing with controversy succinctly by his pragmatic clarity, something I saw and could appreciate on panels and at seminars. Not unsurprisingly for one in power, and with such fresh, eager ideas, in addition to considerable praise and renown, he also had to face diverse criticism, challenges and decision-making crises – ideological, pedagogic and, internally, employment-related. These he dealt with logically, but not always impressively, and occasionally with an impatience, or with doubt. One such example was the 1996 *Crosbhealach an Cheoil* conference, the first event of its kind to be held in traditional music, organised by a group who felt the need for new developments to be debated in public by a broad spectrum of opinions, rather than griped about privately; in this, we organisers were somewhat disappointed that he could not engage with its opportunity fully.

Mícheál took a deep interest in his staff appointments, seeing harmony and compatibility as vital to student confidence. Inevitably, some discord could colour this, difficult to avoid for a creative director who was also an administrator, for his decision-making had to juggle personal compatibilities along with funding, achievement-targets and student-number constraints. His visibility as a shaper of young traditional-music minds also made him a target for a tough, but good-natured, slagging as much as other ideologues in the music. But his success and fulfilment enabled him to shrug this off, dealing with both it and a greater academic-world reticence by simply *doing*. Of significance in this has been his presentation of analytical ideas with enduring value for academic teaching. These were published in different volumes – for example his fresh bodhrán rationale in *Treoir* magazine[7] and his research on creative process in his 1987 PhD thesis[8] and in an article that year in *An Fhidil Ghaelach*;[9] this was covered also in *Irish Musical Studies 1*.[10] In 1999, in *Crosbhealach an Cheoil*, he also addressed innovation, structure and creative process based on the study of Dublin fiddler Tommie Potts' music.[11] *Dear Far-voiced Veteran: Essays in honour of Tom Munnelly*[12] carried this further in '"Traditional Ears": Perception and analysis in Irish traditional music' wherein he laid out analytical process and terms valuable to description of analysis and variation in traditional music. His editing most notably includes the bringing to print of the mammoth, 1,419-page Aloys Fleischmann *Sources of Irish Traditional Music*, a task achieved with Paul McGettrick in 1998.[13]

Thus Mícheál prevailed, and went on to further astonish the field by having a fabulous music department constructed from scratch at the University of Limerick, a veritable monument to the music he espoused as well as to his confidence and achievements in it. At conferences he subtly promoted the importance and existential, mythological and cultural significance of this tiered hall of learning and practice in a technologically disruptive, material world. We met at an International Society for Music Education Colloquium in Bergen, 2002, where I personally was merely addressing the *classicisation* of traditional music, but Mícheál was a veritable pied piper to hundreds of international music educators who were fascinated by the bricks and mortar realisation of his concept of music education. Yet he also found time to compose, arrange and perform, and participate in the world of music education in Ireland. In later years he was able to calm the waters between himself and RTÉ's pioneering television broadcaster Tony MacMahon. This was around the time of his warm, deeply appreciative participation in *The Friendly Visit* house-concert series in which I had the privilege of playing with him at Liz McManus' home in Bray; there he also played some of his long-gestating Carolan arrangements, undeterred that it had to be done on an upright piano. His penultimate performance, with leading players including many former students, at the National Concert Hall in 2018, also featured this music. It brought together a large assembly of varied voices in the educational, professional, historical and aesthetic dimensions of the music, an event which deeply moved everyone present, as – for many of us – we knew it was nearing his finale.

These practical, personal and emotional markers shape my projection of the map of Mícheál Ó Súilleabháin's journey – a mixture of the 'street' and the 'satellite' views, so to speak. But the Irish World Academy of Music and Dance is his monument, a spiritual as well as analytical and developmental hub to Irish traditional music, an artform which, pre-Covid, was an island-and-diaspora-wide, world-reaching, year-round practice. Outside of that building's student achievements, and even beyond the prestige accorded traditional music itself in education today, to which Mícheál contributed so much, there are of course his recordings which are every bit as enduring as the concrete, steel and glass on the banks of the Shannon.

87

Tradition and the Individual Talent: Ó Súilleabháin in the light of Heaney

Harry White

Harry White is professor of music at University College Dublin and a fellow of the Royal Irish Academy of Music. He was inaugural president of the Society for Musicology in Ireland (2003–6) and general editor (with Barra Boydell) of The Encyclopaedia of Music in Ireland *(2013). His publications include five monographs and two collections of poetry.*

Throughout their working lives, both Seamus Heaney and Mícheál Ó Súilleabháin were preoccupied by the claims of Irish cultural sovereignty. In Heaney's case, these claims were contextualised by a critical reception which tended to suppress the poet's classical and central European inherences (notably Virgil, Dante, Zbigniew Herbert and Czesław Miłosz) in favour of his Irish and English forbears (including Yeats, Kavanagh and the English Romantics). By contrast, Ó Súilleabháin contended with the sounding form of Irish traditional music as an immutable and collective presence which, almost by definition, either resisted or problematised the individual claims of the composer. Ó Súilleabháin interrogated this resistance, partly through the agency of his own compositions (in which the tradition was boldly reconceived and imaginatively enlarged), and partly by means of his scholarly deliberations, which at least on occasion memorably challenged the cultural authority of the tradition itself.[1] By reading Ó Súilleabháin's creative estate in the light of Heaney's self-aware emancipation from an 'Anglo-centric Protestant tradition' (*The Redress of Poetry*), we can more narrowly than otherwise explain the conflict between 'composer' and 'tradition' through which Ó Súilleabháin stringently tested his own response to the cultural sovereignty of Irish music as an artist, educator and writer. In this enterprise, we can also briefly enlist Ó Súilleabháin's formative (and decisive) relationship with Seán Ó Riada.

In a passage from the last of Heaney's lectures in *The Redress of Poetry* (1995), entitled 'Frontiers of Writing', the poet summons 'five towers' which locate different phases of Irish literary culture, the fourth of which belongs to James Joyce. This is the Martello tower, on Dublin Bay. Heaney identifies this tower as:

> … the setting of the opening chapter of *Ulysses* and symbol of Joyce's attempt to 'Hellenise the island', his attempt to marginalise the imperium which had marginalised him by replacing the Anglocentric Protestant tradition with a newly forged apparatus of Homeric correspondences, Dantesque scholasticism and a more or less Mediterranean, European, classically-endorsed world-view.[2]

It is not difficult to sense the tone of approbation which underlies this reading, at least insofar as Heaney's work, like Joyce's, drew its authority in significant measure from these classical and European antecedents. This does not mean that Heaney disdained inherences which lay closer to home (as in Kavanagh, Yeats and Wordsworth), but his poetry acknowledges and engages with a conspicuously European tradition nevertheless, both as to technique and subject matter. The translator of Virgil, *Beowulf* and Dante, to cite three prominent instances, deeply imbued his original verse with an inflection of tone and voice that is unmistakably classical. As Colin Burrow recently observed (in a review of Heaney's posthumously published translation of Book VI of the *Aeneid*), 'Joyce, who offers the final word to Heaney in "Station Island" ("You've listened long enough. Now strike your note"), enabled Heaney to use Virgil in two ways: as a bridge to a wider tradition of Western verse, and as a means of rejoicing in the particularity of his Irishness'.[3] We might even suggest that Virgil (and the classical literary tradition which he inaugurates) allowed Heaney to be Irish and European at one and the same time.

This affordance has proved much more elusive within the domain of Irish music. If ever a composer rejoiced in the 'particularity of his Irishness', it was Mícheál Ó Súilleabháin. But we can also enlist evidence to suggest that *as* a composer, Ó Súilleabháin sought for much of his life to locate that particularity not only in relation to Irish traditional music, but also to other musical practices which gained his attention. Indeed, 'You've listened long enough. Now strike your note' might legitimately be tendered as the watchword which governed Ó Súilleabháin's lifelong quest for voice as a composer, not least by his own admission. At the outset of his first concert with the National Symphony Orchestra of Ireland, held on 7 September 2017 (very sadly, his second and last appearance with the NSO would take place in June 2018, a few months before his death), Ó Súilleabháin graciously invoked 'Station Island' as a poem about finding one's voice, and added that he was still embarked on that process himself. This concert amply demonstrated, moreover, the collaborative condition of Ó Súilleabháin's compositional enterprises, which for the purposes of this brief essay we might resolve as the condition of creative *listening*. More narrowly still, I would propose that this fundamental impulse, this auditory prowess and responsiveness to other musicians, to other traditions and to pre-existing music (through the agency of improvisation and variation) effectively defined the nature of Ó Súilleabháin's artistic imagination. Through the agency of such listening, Ó Súilleabháin intervened in anterior musical processes with such consistency that these interventions became the essence of his own musical utterance.

It is for this reason that his compositions resist the self-standing agency of the musical work in favour of a more pliant and (once again) more collaborative engagement with other musics. To borrow a phrase, one is constantly aware of the wider 'river of sound' from which these compositions originate, and to which they return. This resistance to the finished work, constantly attested to by Ó Súilleabháin's habitual re-casting of his music (as in the freshly conceived versions of work from his 2010 CD *Elver Gleams* in the 2017 NSO concert) also prompts me to consider Ó Súilleabháin as a composer-performer, first and last. But even this category (which summons a long and distinguished list of precedents from within the folds of European art music no less than it does the more immediate example of jazz) scarcely does justice to the meditative and expressly contingent condition of Ó Súilleabháin's compositional estate. For all the lustre, fame and sheer popularity which Ó Súilleabháin enjoyed as a professional musician, the greater reverence on his part lay not with the finished work but with the existential process of listening to and thereby improvising upon a pre-existent music.

The implications of this process and its ascendancy as a consideration in Ó Súilleabháin's musical career bear further scrutiny. Both in relation to Irish traditional music (in which the sovereignty of the air remained undisturbed) and to other traditions (notably jazz and north Indian classical music), Ó Súilleabháin's deference to the idea of tradition entailed a corresponding dissent from the absolute sovereignty of the original musical work. It is in this sense that Ó Súilleabháin himself problematised the role of the composer. It is in this sense, too, that we must perforce distinguish between Heaney's constant assent to the jurisdiction and legitimacy of fixed forms and literary genres, and Ó Súilleabháin's more provisional and more contingent interpretation of the artist's role. In Heaney's case, the singular evolution of his art was mediated through the governance and prescriptive authority of the collection as a generic ingathering. From *Death of a Naturalist* (1966) to *Human Chain* (2010) it is not only possible but necessary to read his twelve collections as 'stepping stones' (to borrow another germane phrase) on account of their graduated deepening of engagement with the idea of poetry itself.[4] Taken together, these collections comprise a kind of *Biographia Literaria* which affords evidence of the 'growth of a poet's mind' with such a degree of purposefulness that both thematically and technically we cannot resist their attestation of early, middle and late styles and preoccupations. Each of these twelve collections, to say little else of them, breaks new ground. Each promotes original invention as the legitimating claim to our attention.

The twelve albums (or collections) recorded by Ó Súilleabháin, from the eponymous *Mícheál Ó Súilleabháin* (1976) to *Elver Gleams* (2010), argue a different posterity. This is not to dispute either their stylistic integrity or their circulatory power and success. But these albums do not function in the same way as Heaney's collections, precisely because original invention is *not* their legitimating claim. Instead, one finds throughout these recordings two prevailing constants: one is a pervasively consistent and immediately recognisable style of pianism in which Ó Súilleabháin (despite his own assertions to the contrary) found his abiding signature, if not his voice. The other is a variation technique which characteristically defers to other people's music. For my part, the tension between these two governing agencies (a stylistic signature of uncanny staying power and a deliberated reliance on Irish traditional melody in particular)[5] is what lends Ó Súilleabháin's musicianship its enduring interest. This tension promotes an unusual degree of intimacy between Ó Súilleabháin as concert artist and as composer. Both categories are virtually indistinguishable from each other in Ó Súilleabháin's case (whether in live performance or in recording), so that the music that arises from these categories is itself a composite. This is especially (and perhaps self-evidently) clear when Ó Súilleabháin is at the keyboard, but it is a feature that pervades his music generally.

Two examples (among many such) will allow me to press this home. The first is from the NSO concert in 2017, and is an arrangement of 'Bean Dubh an Ghleanna' ('The Dark Maiden of the Valley') for saxophone, strings and horns.[6] The arrangement is itself a modification of an earlier version by Ó Súilleabháin written for the uilleann piper Liam Óg O'Flynn and included in *Elver Gleams*. Indeed the provenance of this version of the air appears to originate with the great piper Séamus Ennis, although variants of the tune have been traced to Edward Bunting's *Ancient Music of Ireland* (1840).[7] It is not in the smallest degree a disservice to Ó Súilleabháin's 2017 arrangement of this air to observe that 'original composition' is at most a peripheral consideration in this hauntingly beautiful enterprise.

Ó Súilleabháin's consummate musicianship lies elsewhere: in the tact and discretion of his orchestral textures (which to my ear summon an unmistakable allusion to the opening of Sibelius' second symphony at the outset); in the artistry of his executants (notably the saxophonist Kenneth Edge), and in the unobtrusive transition of the air itself from pipes to saxophone, specifically for this occasion. This is composition as supremely skilful representation, as an exceptionally attentive contemplation of the original air. The delicacy of this retrieval, which also affords a subtle salute to Ó Riada's arrangement of 'Róisín Dubh', exemplifies an auditory prowess on Ó Súilleabháin's part which quietly departs from what Mark Evan Bonds has described as 'the imperative of originality' in European art music.[8] This departure is decisive to the success of Ó Súilleabháin's arrangement. Another imperative is in its stead. This is the abiding imperative to listen, in which listening itself becomes the creative enterprise.

My second example is an arrangement of 'Fáinne Geal an Lae' ('The Dawning of the Day') which Ó Súilleabháin recorded for the Patrick Weston Joyce microsite project in 2014.[9] Ó Súilleabháin at the piano was often extrovert, his bravura performances in later years (especially with the RTÉ Concert Orchestra) acclaimed as media events in themselves. But these ebullient entertainments did not perhaps comprehend the interiority of his musical deliberations elsewhere. Once again, the conventional rhetoric and understanding of 'composition' defers in this performance of 'Fáinne Geal an Lae' to a notably intense synthesis of deep listening and representation. Meditation, repetition, doubling, turning: throughout this performance, Ó Súilleabháin's representation of the integrity of the original air is everywhere apparent, but so also is the integrity of Ó Súilleabháin's own technique, which mirrors the structural intelligence of the air in its systematic ornamentation, variation, symmetry and harmonic undertow. It is a technique which is also attentive to the traditional air as a *somatic* experience whose morphology induces meaning through the agency of repetition. In this key respect, it seems to me entirely valid to privilege Ó Súilleabháin's arrangement as one which reflects his abiding interest in north Indian classical music, not as a scholarly consideration but as an expression of kinship, aesthetics, artistic identity and sheer experience. To compose in the context of this experience is evidently to immerse the performer (and the listener) in a mesmeric iteration of the pre-existing air.

This is a delicate matter. Ó Súilleabháin was such a public figure, so emblematic of Irish music as a cultural phenomenon of the highest lustre and prestige, as well as a public entertainer whose unabashed engagement with popular culture was as (apparently) effortless as it was novel, that he often seemed pressed for time.[10] But in solo piano works such as this arrangement of 'Fáinne Geal an Lae', the gravity and composure of Ó Súilleabháin's performance promote an atemporal and deliberately indefinite engagement with the air which draws sharply inwards. The soft imperative which underlies this performance is not 'You've listened long enough', but 'Listen now, again'.[11]

The introspection and intimacy of these engagements also afford new meaning to Irish traditional music, precisely through the agency of Ó Súilleabháin's individual talent: 'What happens next / Is undiminished for having happened once, / Twice, ten, a thousand times before'. The virtue vested in repetition which is sacralised in these lines from Heaney's poem 'The Rain Stick' creates a literary analogue for the virtue of repetition in Ó Súilleabháin's music. And repetition itself privileges listening, both as a means of meditation and as a mode of (re-)composition.[12]

The persistence of this engagement with traditional music, and in particular with the prior authority of the air as an agent of meditative repetition, was complicated by Ó Súilleabháin's scholarly heft as a musicologist and theorist, as well as by his brilliant media presentations, above all the television series *A River of Sound* (1995). In these domains, Ó Súilleabháin did not especially problematise the status and function of the composer, but rather the creative processes by which the tradition could be more boldly (and less rigidly) imagined. Although it is not part of my brief here to assess Ó Súilleabháin's scholarship or his broadcasts, both of which richly merit sustained appraisal as independent entities, they do have considerable bearing on his legacy as an artist.[13]

So also does Ó Súilleabháin's sensitive and self-aware recognition of Ó Riada and Turlough Carolan as his true forbears, especially towards the end of his life. This, too, is a matter of some delicacy. Whereas the lineage itself is obvious – Ó Riada was Ó Súilleabháin's teacher, and long after his death in 1971 he retained the status of mentor to his former student, and Carolan was a venerated presence throughout Ó Súilleabháin's career – the implications of this lineage are less easy to understand. This is partly because Ó Súilleabháin was undecided as to his own status as a contemporary Irish composer, specifically in relation to a growing repertory of Irish art music in which the tradition was of remote concern.[14] But he was not in the least undecided about the imperative of creating a reception history adequate to this tradition as a creative presence of equal stature to this repertory: 'Until the idea of "contemporary music" in Ireland is widened to include Irish traditional music – as it should be – any attempted understanding of music and contemporary identity in Ireland can only fly on one wing.'[15] The obvious rejoinder to this imperative is work for another day. Ó Súilleabháin's own understanding of this tradition, however, was anything but defensive or chauvinist. It lay open, to his mind, not as a fossilised resource, but as a creative, living estate through which his own impulses as a composer were not only renewed, but refined. In this process he reimagined the conceptual authority of composition (as I have tried to suggest here) by listening to this music afresh through the agency of his own arrangements and meditations. But he did so not as a rebuke to the legitimacy of composition itself, but as a means of apprehending other musical practices which might enrich his auditory imagination. This enrichment emancipated Ó Súilleabháin from the acute crisis fomented by Ó Riada's abandonment of composition. It also allowed him to bypass to a significant extent the throes of a musical modernism which, for the most part, has remained invisible (or inaudible) to Irish cultural history.

Epilogue

Homily at the Funeral Mass for Mícheál Ó Súilleabháin, St Senan's Church, Kilrush, County Clare, 12 November 2018

Mark Patrick Hederman OSB

Mark Patrick Hederman is a Benedictine monk of Glenstal Abbey, Limerick. His doctorate is in the philosophy of education. Former abbot of the monastery and headmaster of the school, he was a friend of Mícheál Ó Súilleabháin's for forty years. They worked together on several projects both musical and educational.

Aisling ghéar do dhearcas féin
im leaba 's mé go lagbhríoch:
ainnir shéimh darbh ainm Éire
ag teacht im ghaor ar marcaíocht.[1]

For many of us Mícheál Ó Súilleabháin was a hero, a contemporary Orpheus, who brightened our paths with heart-rending music. For others he was a teacher, a guru, a guide.

For very few of us he was a brother, a husband, a father, a step-father; to all of these we extend our sympathy in a very special way. Their sorrow at his departure is deeper than anything we can pretend to understand.

But our focus today is celebration of the great gift of love, of friendship, of music, and of creativity that was Mícheál Ó Súilleabháin as a blessing for the whole world.

Mícheál planned this funeral ceremony with as much detailed precision as he would have when organising one of his own concerts. Everything has a meaning and a personal message directed at each one of the wonderful people who surround this altar today. I have no doubt that you will find your own special gift from him in some of the people you meet, the readings you hear, the prayers you say, or the music which he has chosen.

Why are we here in the Church of St Senan at Kilrush? Surely it is another symbol of everything that Mícheál stood for and gave his life to: this is the estuary where the Shannon river meets the vastness of the Atlantic Ocean. Estuaries form a transition zone between the riverine and the maritime. Mixing sea water with fresh water provides a high level of nutrients which make estuaries among the most productive natural habitats in the world. In 1831, Captain Mudge (as he is named in the Commissioners' report of the time)[2] was not impressed by Kilrush. It was a backwater, he said, and could never be turned into a viable transition between the Shannon and the ocean; we shouldn't be bothered throwing good money after bad in so benighted a cause.

In the meantime, however, genius has been born and ingenuity has provided what is called 'a lock-gate', an ingenious engineering feat which allows access to the Shannon from myriad watercraft on the ocean and vice versa. Nor would it have escaped Mícheál's notice that there is here a resident group of bottlenose dolphins in the estuary which needed to be accommodated when creating this 'dolphin's way'.

Mícheál created a similar estuary further up the Shannon where Limerick and Clare are joined on a living bridge, and where traditional Irish music and dance gain access to, and at the same time hugely enrich, the vast body of classical and worldwide music from which they had previously been excluded. The Irish World Academy of Music and Dance, created under his guidance from a zero base only twenty-five years ago, is an estuary where the culture of Ireland can meet and mingle with the culture of the universe. From the early 1960s Mícheál 'relished the adrenalin rush in the energy field between … the classical and the traditional'.[3] He spent much of his life forging a 'lock-gate' between them. And yet, for this magnanimous musician, culture was never something to be hoarded or stockpiled with jealous proprietorial exclusivity; it was to be cherished, preserved, nurtured, ripened and then opened to be shared.

But the end has not come. We believe, as he indeed believed, because no one with such creativity and generosity can be unaware of the creator of everything that is. There is a God, and Mícheál Ó Súilleabháin is with that God today. Both are present here as we celebrate God's real presence in the Eucharist; and I am perfectly sure that Mícheál Ó Súilleabháin is at this moment creating an estuary in heaven where the pure and robust music of our humanity can mingle with the heavenly music of the angels, without losing a leaf or spilling a drop. We look forward to hearing Saint Cecilia singing some *sean-nós* and King David playing the bodhrán. Perhaps, indeed, under Mícheál's inspiration we are hearing some of this heavenly music in this church today?

Conducting the Carolan String Orchestra with singer Grace Toland (seated) and members of the Armagh Pipers Club at the William Kennedy International Piping Festival, 2009.
PHOTOGRAPHER: PAUL ELIASBERG

With piper and broadcaster Peter Browne. PHOTOGRAPHER: MAURICE GUNNING

With singers Bobby McFerrin and Iarla Ó Lionáird. PHOTOGRAPHER: MAURICE GUNNING

With saxophonist Kenneth Edge and the Carolan String Quartet, Glenstal Abbey.
PHOTOGRAPHER: MAURICE GUNNING

With the Irish Chamber Orchestra. PHOTOGRAPHER: MAURICE GUNNING

With the Mayor of Clonmel, Pat English, Helen and Luke Phelan, Freedom of Clonmel, 2016.
PHOTOGRAPHER: JOHN KELLY

With colleagues and students, Irish World Academy. PHOTOGRAPHER: MAURICE GUNNING

With singer Karan Casey. PHOTOGRAPHER: MAURICE GUNNING

With colleague and musical collaborator Mel Mercier. PHOTOGRAPHER: MAURICE GUNNING

With violinist and conductor Gábor Takács-Nagy, 2014. PHOTOGRAPHER: MAURICE GUNNING

Mícheál conducting. PHOTOGRAPHER: MAURICE GUNNING

With the Mayor of Limerick, Kieran O'Hanlon, Helen and Luke Phelan, Mayoral Reception, 2017. PHOTOGRAPHER: LIAM BURKE

Above: Kate Ellis, Mel Mercier, Iarla Ó Lionáird, Mícheál, Miriam O'Callaghan and Martin Hayes, RTÉ Radio Centre, 2016.
PHOTOGRAPHER: MAURICE GUNNING

Left: With artist Desmond Kinney, 2011.
PHOTOGRAPHER: MAURICE GUNNING

With UCC and UL graduates, David Brophy (conductor) with National Concert Orchestra, *Elver Gleams* concert, University Concert Hall, Limerick, 2016.
PHOTOGRAPHER: MAURICE GUNNING

Mícheál with Luke, Mícheál 'Moley', Eoin, and the National Concert Orchestra, University Concert Hall, Limerick, 2016. PHOTOGRAPHER: MAURICE GUNNING

With singers Síle Denvir, Iarla Ó Lionáird, and Lillis Ó Laoire, Dromore House.
PHOTOGRAPHER: MAURICE GUNNING

With broadcaster Áine Hensey. PHOTOGRAPHER: MAURICE GUNNING

Honorary doctorate, Royal Conservatoire of Scotland, with Helen and Luke Phelan, 2017.

With the National Symphony Orchestra, *Between Worlds* concert, National Concert Hall, 2018.
PHOTOGRAPHER: MAURICE GUNNING

Mícheál, *Between Worlds* concert, National Concert Hall, 2018. PHOTOGRAPHER: MAURICE GUNNING

WORKS BY MÍCHEÁL Ó SÚILLEABHÁIN: DISCOGRAPHY, WRITINGS AND SELECT SCORES

Mícheál Ó Súilleabháin: Discography

Nicholas Carolan

Over the course of forty years Mícheál Ó Súilleabháin made commercial long-playing recordings on which he featured as performer, composer, arranger, conductor and producer. Commercial recording, separate from but linked at times with his parallel academic, performing and composing careers, was important to him. At first it provided his calling card to the world outside academia. It proclaimed to a listening public that there was a startling new voice in Irish traditional music, one which had been mainly heard before then in intriguing arrangements of traditional tunes made for Irish radio. From there it tracked his musical developments and his ever-widening musical involvements, from postgraduate traditional music experiments with friends in County Waterford to fronting large-scale orchestral and choral forces in performances of his own compositions before international audiences. His commercial recordings, listed below, form to an extent an archive of his various musical lives.

Mícheál began in 1976 in a world of recording in which a few gatekeeper commercial companies decided who would record, or not record, and in which a buying public eagerly awaited the results. Records, especially the long-playing 12-inch LP discs with their impressive graphics and their capacity for presenting extensive sleevenote information, were important. Mícheál had had by then, in University College Cork where he was now a lecturer in music, the good fortune of two academic mentors and role models: the professor Aloys Fleischmann and the lecturer Seán Ó Riada. Both would influence his recording career, Fleischmann by his imparting of the arcana of orchestration and his research interests in historic collections of Irish music, Ó Riada by the example of his public performing life and his interests in traditional and classical music. Mícheál, with his arresting skills on a variety of keyboard instruments and his fresh musical arrangements as heard on radio and in live performance, was taken up by Ó Riada's record company Gael Linn and the manager of its record division Riobard Mac Góráin. Gael Linn, essentially a cultural organisation for the promotion of the Irish language, was a perfect starter home. *Mícheál Ó Súilleabháin*, his first experimental LP with the company, opening with an explosive harpsichord solo, was a sonic manifesto. Every piece on it came from the Irish oral tradition of the previous three centuries, as he made clear in his historical source-notes, but his renewing of this old material was highly original, even transgressive in the opinion of some. Harp, fiddle, flute and uilleann pipe timbres were remade on harpsichord, clavichord, piano, pedal organ and synthesiser. The making of a new Irish keyboards style was under way. Mícheál remained with Gael Linn as his record publisher until 1981, by which time he was already branching out into film music, but he stayed with it as an arranger, accompanist and producer on the recordings of others, chiefly those of the singer Nóirín Ní Riain, until 1989. The company continues to reissue the early recordings in new formats as they arise and to license tracks to other record companies.

In 1987, with his doctorate achieved, Mícheál moved forward in his recording career. At the invitation of Declan Colgan of London's Virgin Records, a company which had by then an international reach, he signed with its new subsidiary Virgin Venture, a label intended to feature ethnic-progressive music. The LP was still the leading publishing format but it would soon be overtaken and eventually replaced by the CD or digital compact disc. Mícheál's first recording for Virgin, *The Dolphin's Way*, unveiled a new fast, highly rhythmical, virtuoso Irish piano style which combined traditional music with elements of jazz and classical music. The piano would henceforth be his main recording instrument; it would bring him new and enthusiastic audiences inside and outside Ireland. Mel Mercier, a frequent co-performer on percussion instruments, provided accompaniment on bones, Colm Murphy on bodhrán. The remaining six Virgin recordings (not counting a compilation album) document the increasing appearance of new compositions by Mícheál and increasing orchestral collaboration with his own piano playing, and his restless remaking of earlier pieces. The compositions, often inspired by a traditional music underlay, were mainly the fruit of commissions. The orchestral collaboration was mainly with the Irish Chamber Orchestra, based in the University of Limerick since 1995, after Mícheál left Cork to become professor of music in Limerick in 1993. Particularly notable among the commissions was one to provide the ambitious vocal and instrumental interval piece *Lumen* for the Eurovision Song Contest, hosted by Ireland in 1995 and viewed by tens of millions. Since 2012 Virgin Records has been part of the Universal Music Group, a global American music corporation with French and Chinese involvement, and Mícheál's recordings are still published by it in a variety of formats.

From the late 1990s, with the rise of social media and streaming services, the traditional recording industry began a slow collapse. Cheap digital technology enabled musicians to record and define themselves musically in their own bedrooms. This was not a route that Mícheál took. The ambition and scale of his recordings and their increasingly orchestral nature demanded commercial sound studios to accommodate the large forces involved. In that sense he finished his main recording career in the studio recording world in which he had begun for Gael Linn in 1976. But the record industry, trying to survive and reinvent itself in the 2000s, would no longer commit to such expense and those years saw only three of his orchestral recordings appear, one for Virgin, one for EMI Ireland (which closed in 2013) and the last, *Phoenix Rising*, in 2015 from a sponsored film score. At the time of his death he was actively working on a solo recording for future issue of the music of the eighteenth-century harper-composer Turlough Carolan.

Mícheál also had a secondary recording career which lasted almost to the end of his life, one in which he took part variously on the recordings of others, as a performer, arranger, conductor, music director and producer. Beginning in 1977 as an accompanist and arranger on Gael Linn for the fiddle player Paddy Glackin, a colleague of his early radio days, and as producer on Gael Linn and other labels for the singer Nóirín Ní Riain, he went on for more than three decades to feature by invitation on the recordings of friends and colleagues. Some arose from his academic work: the Nimbus recordings which were made at an early 1990s series of Éigse na Laoi festivals in which his students were blooded in the realities of festival and record production; these would not have been made without his initiative and guiding hand. Also particularly notable are recordings which arose from two television series produced by Philip King and Nuala O'Connor: the BBC's *Bringing It All Back Home* (1991) and RTÉ–BBC Northern Ireland's *A River of Sound* (1995–6) in which Mícheál was central as presenter, writer, composer and musician.

This discography is a chronological listing of 'real' recordings issued as physical objects as opposed to one of 'virtual' computer files. No pointless attempt has been made to list the constantly shifting number of recordings legally available as computer downloads from the commercial websites of their original publishers or from licensed affiliates, or the impossible tsunami of legally and illegally copied files which are daily shared on a huge variety of social media platforms. The listing is divided into two sections – the first of the recordings on which Mícheál is the main performer (original issues and reissues), the second of recordings to which he contributed as a performer or producer or otherwise (original issues). Tracks in the relevant sections are indicated by a semicolon.

SECTION A. AS SOLO OR LEAD PERFORMER, ARRANGER, CONDUCTOR, COMPOSER

A1: Mícheál Ó Súilleabháin

Gael Linn, Dublin, LP CEF 046, 1976; CD reissue CEFCD 046, 1990

Mícheál Ó Súilleabháin, harpsichord, pedal organ, piano, clavichord, mini-moog synthesiser, arranger

Engineer John Penrose; Producer Tony MacMahon. Historical notes on material by Mícheál Ó Súilleabháin

Side A. 1 Bonaparte ag trasnú na Réine/Bonaparte crossing the Rhine, hornpipe; 2 Salamanca, reel; 3 Carúl Loch Garman/The Wexford carol, song air; 4 Miss Hamilton, harp piece; 5 An marcach chun an aonaigh/Jockey to the fair, set dance; 6 Suí síos fá mo dhídean/Sit down under my protection, harp piece; 7 Le hAis na Siúire and Cois Abha Móire na nDéise, song airs; 8 An nóta fada/The long note, single jig

Side B. 1 Cailleach an túirne/The maid of the spinning wheel, double jig; 2 Treascairt Phárais/The downfall of Paris, set dance; 3 Bruacha gleoite glasa na Siúire/The lovely sweet banks of the Suir, song air; 4 Bantiarna Uíbh Eachach/Lady Iveagh, harp piece; 5 An seanphláta copair/The old copper plate, reel; 6 Oíche Nollag/Christmas Eve, single jig; 7 Na Géanna Fiáine/The Wild Geese, harp piece

A2: Óró Damhnaigh

Gael Linn, Dublin, LP CEF 056, 1977; CD reissue CEFCD 056

Mícheál Ó Súilleabháin, harpsichord, arranger, conductor; Nóirín Ní Riain, singing in Irish; Tomás Ó Catháin/Tommy Keane, whistle; Tommy Kearney, uilleann pipes; John Dwyer, fiddle; Matt Fahy, flute (formerly the members of the group Tiompán) with Paul Mercier, bodhrán; Mel Mercier, bodhrán, bones

Engineer John Penrose; Producer Mícheál Ó Súilleabháin. Historical notes on material by Mícheál Ó Súilleabháin. Song texts on inner sleeve

Side A. 1 Larry O'Gaff, double jig; 2 An buachaillín bán/The white-haired boy, air, and The flogging reel; 3 Ím bím babaró, Ailiú éanaí, Óró Damhnaigh, songs; 4 The pigeon on the gate, The Galway rambler, reels; 5 Cornphíopa Phortláirge/The Waterford hornpipe; 6 Eibhlín a rúin, air; 7 Madame Bonaparte, set dance

Side B. 1 The Waterford waltz; 2 Paddy Ryan's dream, Fair-haired Mary, reels; 3 Seoithín seó, Seoithín agus seó, songs; 4 Ceolsraith/Suite (Ril Mhic Dhiarmada/McDermott's reel, the reel as a double jig, Ril Mhic Dhiarmada, Gilbert Clancy's reel played simultaneously with Bímis ag ól, double jig); 5 Seacht ndólás na Maighdine Muire/The seven sorrows of the Virgin Mary, song; 6 Téama breachnaithe/Theme and variations (Dives and Lazarus/Star of the County Down as air, double jig, air, polka, slip jig, song Gleanntán Airiglín aoibhinn, air), instrumental and vocal piece

A3: Cry of the Mountain

Gael Linn, Dublin, LP CEF 079, 1981; CD reissue CEFCD 079, 2012, as *Cry of the Mountain: Ceol Scannáin agus Raidió/Music for Film and Radio 1974–1978*

Engineers John Penrose, Harry Bradshaw, Gerry Fitzgerald; Producer [Riobard Mac Góráin], radio producer Tony MacMahon, film producers Tommy McArdle, Éamon de Buitléar; Notes on music of Mícheál Ó Súilleabháin by Gerard Victory

Mícheál Ó Súilleabháin, harpsichord, mbira, bow, sitar, whistles, arranger, composer; Mary Bergin, whistle; Michael Crehan, whistle; Michael Gavin, flute; Paddy Glackin, fiddle; Dave Hennessy, melodeon; Paddy Keenan, uilleann pipes; Mel Mercier, bodhrán, bones; Paul Mercier, bodhrán; Matt Molloy, flute; Nóirín Ní Riain, vocals; Seamus Tansey, flute, bodhrán; Ursula Willis, bass viola

Side A. 1 The Green Linnet, radio programme (An mháirseáil mhór/The grand march; set dance Treascairt Phárais/The downfall of Paris, hornpipe Napoleon ag trasnú na Réine/Napoleon crossing the Rhine, set dance Madame Bonaparte); 2 The Kinkisha (Collage no. 1), film score

Side B. 1 Seán Ó Duibhir an ghleanna ('concertino for fiddle'), radio programme; 2 Cry of the mountain (Collage no. 2), film score

A4: The Dolphin's Way

Virgin Venture, London, LP VE 1 and CD CDVE 1, 1987

Mícheál Ó Súilleabháin, piano, arranger; Colm Murphy, bodhrán; Mel Mercier, bones

Engineer Bill Somerville-Large, Windmill Lane Studios, April 1987; Producer Declan Colgan

Side A. 1 Oíche Nollag/Christmas Eve, reel; 2 Magh Luirg/The plains of Boyle, air/hornpipe; 3 Eibhlí gheal chiúin/Gentle fair Elly, song air; 4 An tseanghé liath/The old grey goose, double jig; 5 An cailín deas crúite na mbó/The pretty milkmaid, song air; 6 Péarla an bhrollaigh bháin/The snowy-breasted pearl, song air; 7 Carolan's Concerto, harp piece

Side B. 1 Merrily kiss the Quaker, single jig; 2 An páistín fionn/The little fair-haired child, song air; 3 Fiach an mhadra rua/The fox chase (set-off, chase, kill, lament for the fox, triumphant jig, return home), descriptive piece; 4 Mollaí Ní Ailpín/Molly Halpin, song air; 5 Planxty Irwin, harp piece; 6 An mhaighdean cheansa/The gentle maiden, song air [CD has two additional tracks: solo piano versions of Oíche Nollag/ Christmas Eve; Péarla an bhrollaigh bháin/The snowy-breasted pearl]

A5: Oileán/Island

Virgin Venture, London, LP VE 40 and CD CDVE 40, 1989

Mícheál Ó Súilleabháin, piano, conductor, arranger, composer; Irish Chamber Orchestra; Matt Molloy, flute; Mel Mercier, bones; Colm Murphy, bodhrán; Tony MacMahon, button accordion

Engineer Bill Somerville-Large, Windmill Lane 2 Studio, Dublin, 17–19 January 1989; Producer Declan Colgan

Side A. 1 Heartwork, instrumental piece; 2 Ah sweet dancer, instrumental piece; 3 Idir eatarthu/Between worlds, instrumental piece; 4 Carolan's farewell to music, instrumental piece

Side B. 1–3 Oileán/Island a; b; c, instrumental piece in three movements; 4 Ah sweet dancer, instrumental piece

A6: Casadh/Turning

Virgin Venture, London, LP VE 904 and CD CDVE 904, 1990

Mícheál Ó Súilleabháin, piano, harpsichord, arranger, conductor; Andrew Baker, bass; John Kelly, viola; Johnny McCarthy, flute; Tony MacMahon, button accordion; Mel Mercier, bodhrán, bones; Matt Molloy, flute; Colm Murphy, bodhrán; Adele O'Dwyer, cello; Therese Timoney, violin

Engineers Brian Masterson, Windmill Lane Studios, Dublin; Tadhg Kelleher, Sulán Studios, Ballyvourney, County Cork; Producers Declan Colgan, Mícheál Ó Súilleabháin. Source notes on material by Mícheál Ó Súilleabháin

Side A. 1 By golly!, air/double jig; 2 The Wexford carol, song air; 3 Brian Boru, march; 4 An londubh agus an chéirseach/The blackbird and the thrush, air; 5 The rolling wave, air; 6 Casadh na Gráige/The turning of the road, instrumental piece

Side B. 1 King of the blind; 2 The fairy queen; 3 Planxty Irwin; 4 Fanny Power; 5 Cearc agus coileach/The hen and cock; 6 Lady Maisterton (all harp pieces)

A7: Gaiseadh/Flowing

Virgin Venture, London, CD CDVE 915, 1992

Mícheál Ó Súilleabháin, piano, midi-piano, tapes, tanpura, surpeti, arranger, composer; Irish Chamber Orchestra; Neil Martin, uilleann pipes; Mel Mercier, bodhrán, bones, tabla

Engineer Tadhg Kelleher, Sulán Studios, Ballyvourney, County Cork; Producer Mícheál Ó Súilleabháin; Notes by Mícheál Ó Súilleabháin

1 Woodbrook, instrumental piece; 2 flowansionnamare (i Flowan, ii Sionna, iii Mare), instrumental piece; 3 Eleanor Plunkett, song air; 4 (must be more) Crispy, instrumental piece; 5 Through an eye of stone, instrumental piece; 6 At the still point of the turning world, instrumental piece

A8: Lumen

Virgin Venture, London, CDs CDVEND 5 and CDVENDX 5, 1995

Mícheál Ó Súilleabháin, piano, harpsichord, arranger, composer; Andy Baker, bass; John Bargamo, frame drum; Kenneth Edge, saxophone; Evelyn Glennie, percussion; Gary Hastings, flute; Eileen Ivers, fiddle; Niall Keegan, flute; Laoise Kelly, harp; Cyprian Love, organ; Mel Mercier, bodhrán; Brendan Ring, uilleann pipes; RTÉ Concert Orchestra; Singers: Glenstal Abbey Senior Boys Choir, Brian Kennedy, Monks of Glenstal Abbey, Máire, Brídín, Olive and Deirdre Ní Bhraonáin, Nóirín Ní Riain, Peadar Ó Ceannabháin, Pádraig Ó Cearbhaill, Antaine Ó Faracháin, Lillis Ó Laoire

Engineers Brian Masterson and Bill Somerville-Large, Glenstal Abbey, County Limerick, and Windmill Lane Studios, Dublin; Tadhg Kelleher, Sulán Studios, Ballyvourney, County Cork; Producers Mícheál Ó Súilleabháin, Philip King, Declan Colgan

Lumen, vocal and instrumental piece; Woodbrook, instrumental piece; Eibhlí gheal chiúin/Gentle fair Elly, song air; The Wexford carol, song air

A9: Between Worlds: The Music of Mícheál Ó Súilleabháin

Virgin Venture, London, CD CDVE 926, 1995 [compilation from A4–8 and B27]

Mícheál Ó Súilleabháin, piano, harpsichord, arranger, composer; Andy Baker, bass; John Bergamo, frame drum; Nollaig Casey, fiddle; Kenneth Edge, saxophone; Evelyn Glennie, percussion; Gary Hastings, flute; Irish Chamber Orchestra; Eileen Ivers, fiddle; Niall Keegan, flute; Laoise Kelly, harp; Cyprian Love, organ; Dónal Lunny, bouzouki, bodhrán; Mel Mercier, bones; Colm Murphy, bodhrán; Brendan Power, harmonica; Brendan Ring, uilleann pipes; RTÉ Concert Orchestra; Strings: K. Rice, A. Veckes, J. O'Kane, J. Kelly, M. Robinson; Singers: Glenstal Abbey Senior Boys Choir, Brian Kennedy, Monks of Glenstal Abbey, Máire, Brídín, Olive and Deirdre Ní Bhraonáin, Nóirín Ní Riain, Peadar Ó Ceannabháin, Pádraig Ó Cearbhaill, Antaine Ó Faracháin, Lillis Ó Laoire; Frank Torpey, bodhrán

1 Oíche Nollag/Christmas Eve, reel; 2 An tseanghé liath/The old grey goose, double jig; 3 Cailín deas crúite na mbó/The pretty milkmaid, song air; 4 Casadh na Gráige/The turning of the road, instrumental piece; 5 An mhaighdean cheansa/The gentle maiden, song air; 6 Fiach an mhadra rua/The foxchase, descriptive piece; 7 Brian Boru, march; 8 Idir eatarthu/Between worlds, instrumental piece; 9 Woodbrook, instrumental piece; 10 Ah, sweet dancer, instrumental piece; Eleanor Plunkett, harp piece; 11 Heartwork, instrumental piece; (must be more) Crispy, instrumental piece; 12 A river of sound, instrumental piece; 13 Lumen, vocal and instrumental piece

A10: Becoming

Virgin Venture, London, CD CDVE 937, 1998

Mícheál Ó Súilleabháin, piano, arranger, composer; Irish Chamber Orchestra; members of the National Symphony Orchestra of Ireland

Engineer Brian Masterson, Windmill Lane Studios, Dublin; Producers Declan Colgan, Mícheál Ó Súilleabháin

1 So merrily dance; 2 Letting go; 3 *Irish Destiny* film score (i Destiny, ii Anthem, iii Story, iv Rising, v Hope, vi Goodbye, vii Flowan);

4 Becoming; 5 Around the house, set dance; 6 Salve (all instrumental pieces)

A11: Templum

Virgin Venture, London, CD CDVE 955, 2001

Mícheál Ó Súilleabháin, piano; Irish Chamber Orchestra; National Chamber Choir; Kenneth Edge, saxophone; Mel Mercier, bones, bodhrán; Sandra Joyce, bodhrán

Engineers Brian Masterson, Windmill Lane Studios, Dublin; Bill Somerville-Large, Cuan Studios, County Cork; Producer Mícheál Ó Súilleabháin

1 In search of ancient Ireland (score for television series of same title; includes song air Barbara Allen, march Marcshlua Uí Néill/O'Neill's cavalcade, song air Dóchas linn Naomh Pádraig/St Patrick our hope, Brian Boru's march, descriptive piece The fox chase); 2 Session, instrumental piece; 3 Templum/Temple, instrumental piece; 4 Seachtain/Sabbath, instrumental piece; 5 Casadh na Gráige/Turning, instrumental piece; 6 Maranatha/Come, Lord, choral piece; 7 Bean dubh an ghleanna/Dark woman of the glen, instrumental piece; 8 Aisling gheal/Bright vision, instrumental piece; 9 Turas go Tír na nÓg/Journey to the Land of Youth, song air; 10 Streetwalk, instrumental piece; 11 Ave, Maris Stella/Hail, Ocean Star, chant air

A12: Elver Gleams: New and Selected Recordings

EMI Music Ireland, Dublin, CD CDMOS 1, CDEG 1, 2010

Mícheál Ó Súilleabháin, piano; Irish Chamber Orchestra

1 Christmas Eve/Oíche Nollag, reel; 2 The fox chase/Fiach an mhadra rua, descriptive piece; 3 The Wexford carol, song air; 4 Woodbrook, instrumental piece; 5 Heartwork, instrumental piece; 6 Eibhlí gheal chiúin/Gentle fair Ellie, song air; 7 Dark woman of the glen/Bean dubh an ghleanna, instrumental piece; 8 Hope, instrumental piece; 9 Flowan, instrumental piece; 10 Casadh na Gráige/Turning, instrumental piece; 11 Limerick's lamentation, harp piece; 12 (must be more) Crispy, instrumental piece; 13 So merrily dance, instrumental piece; 14 Turas go Tír na nÓg/Journey to the Land of Youth, song air; 15 Ah! sweet dancer, instrumental piece; 16 Elver gleams, instrumental piece

A13: Phoenix Rising: Music for the film *Pioneers and Aviators: A century of Irish aviation*

Avolon, Ennistymon, CD [unnumbered], 2015

Mícheál Ó Súilleabháin, piano; RTÉ Concert Orchestra

Film score: 1 Phoenix rising; 2 Uplifting; 3 What's the story?; 4 Inflight; 5 Flying boat; 6 Engine room; 7 Flight transfer; 8 Phoenix rising 2 (all instrumental pieces)

SECTION B. AS PERFORMER, ARRANGER, CONDUCTOR, MUSIC DIRECTOR, PRODUCER ON RECORDINGS OF OTHERS

B1: Glackin: Ceol ar an bhFidil. Gael Linn, Dublin, LP CEF 060, 1977. Paddy Glackin, fiddle, and others. Mícheál Ó Súilleabháin, harpsichord accompaniment, arrangements

B2: Seinn Aililiú. Gael Linn, Dublin, LP CEF 067, 1978. Nóirín Ní Riain, vocals, and others. Mícheál Ó Súilleabháin, harpsichord, piano, pedal organ accompaniment

B3: 10 Gorey Years. LÁR, Gorey, County Wexford, LP LLP001, 1979. Various performers. Mícheál Ó Súilleabháin, harpsichord accompaniment to Nóirín Ní Riain, vocals

B4: Caoineadh na Maighdine. Gael Linn, Dublin, LP CEF 084, 1980. Nóirín Ní Riain and Monks of Glenstal Abbey, vocals. Mícheál Ó Súilleabháin, musical director, producer

B5: Good People All, Glenstal Records, Glenstal, County Limerick, LP GR 01, 1982. Nóirín Ní Riain and Monks of Glenstal Abbey, vocals. Mícheál Ó Súilleabháin, producer

B6: **Seoda from the Irish Tradition**, vols 2–3. Gael Linn, Dublin, LP CDT 002–003, 1985. Various performers. Mícheál Ó Súilleabháin, harpsichord: Napoleon crossing the Rhine, hornpipe (vol. 2); piano: The Waterford waltz (vol. 3)

B7: Stór Amhrán: A wealth of songs from the Irish tradition. Ossian, Cork, audio cassette OSS 7, 1988 (with book of same title). Nóirín Ní Riain and Monks of Glenstal Abbey, vocals. Mícheál Ó Súilleabháin, organ accompaniment

B8: Liam O'Flynn. Liam O'Flynn, Kildare, LP LOF 1, 1988. Liam O'Flynn, uilleann pipes, and others. Mícheál Ó Súilleabháin, harpsichord accompaniment, arrangements

B9: Vox de Nube. Gael Linn, Dublin, LP CEF 144, 1989. Nóirín Ní Riain and Monks of Glenstal Abbey, vocals. Mícheál Ó Súilleabháin, musical director, producer

B10: Voyage. WEA Ireland, Dublin, LP WX 286 LP, 1989. Christy Moore, vocals, and others. Mícheál Ó Súilleabháin, piano accompaniment

B11: Enlightenment. Caledonia/Polydor, London, LP 847 100–1, 1990. Van Morrison, vocals, and others, Mícheál Ó Súilleabháin, piano

B12: Bringing It All Back Home. BBC, London, LP REF 844 (2nd disc), 1991 (from television series of same title). Various performers. Mícheál Ó Súilleabháin, piano, with Irish Chamber Orchestra: Oileán/Island, instrumental piece; Idir eatarthu/Between worlds, instrumental piece

B13: An Rás. Mulligan Records, Dublin, CD LUNCD 055, 1991. Tommy Hayes, percussion, and others. Mícheál Ó Súilleabháin, piano lead and accompaniment

B14: The My Love is in America Boston College Irish Fiddle Festival. Green Linnet, United States CD GLCD 1110, 1991. Various performers. Mícheál Ó Súilleabháin, producer

B15: Fiddle Sticks: Irish traditional music from Donegal. Nimbus Records, Herefordshire, CD NI 5320, 1991. Various performers. Mícheál Ó Súilleabháin, piano accompaniment, producer with Robin Broadbank

B16: Dear Old Erin's Isle: Irish traditional music from America. Nimbus Records, Herefordshire, CD NI 5350, 1992. Various performers. Mícheál Ó Súilleabháin, producer with Robin Broadbank

B17: Lament. Real World Records, Wiltshire, CD CDRW 27, 1992. Various performers. Mícheál Ó Súilleabháin, piano: Plunkett, song air

B18: East Wind. Tara Records, Dublin, CD TARACD 3027, 1992. Davy Spillane, uilleann pipes; Andy Irvine, bouzouki, and others. Mícheál Ó Súilleabháin, piano accompaniment

B19: Idir Dhá Chomhairle/In Two Minds. Gael Linn, Dublin, CD CEFCD 158, 1992. Áine Uí Cheallaigh, vocals, and others. Mícheál Ó Súilleabháin, arrangement

B20: Soundings. Ossian, Cork, CD OSS CD 88, 1993, Nóirín Ní Riain, vocals; Irish Chamber Orchestra. Mícheál Ó Súilleabháin, producer

B21: Traditional Music from Cape Breton Island. Nimbus Records, Herefordshire, CD NI 5383, 1993. Various performers. Mícheál Ó Súilleabháin, producer with Robin Broadbank

B22: Chatterbox. Dara Records, Dublin, CD DARACD 052, 1993. Máirtín O'Connor, button accordion, and others. Mícheál Ó Súilleabháin, piano accompaniment

B23: Clarity. Streamline Productions, Minneapolis, CD SL 103CD, 1993. Karen Mueller, dulcimer, harp, and others. Mícheál Ó Súilleabháin, piano accompaniment

B24: A Treasury of Irish Traditional Music, vol. 1. His Master's Voice Ireland, Dublin, CD HMVCD 001, 1993. Various performers. Mícheál Ó Súilleabháin, harpsichord: Bonaparte crossing the Rhine

B25: Across the Waters: Irish traditional music from England. Nimbus Records, Herefordshire, CD NI 5415, 1994. Various performers. Mícheál Ó Súilleabháin, producer

B26: I Won't Be Afraid Any More. Solid Records, Dublin, CD ROCD 16, 1994. Nomos (group). Mícheál Ó Súilleabháin, piano accompaniment

B27: A River of Sound: The changing course of Irish traditional music. Hummingbird Records, Dublin, and Virgin Records, London, CD

CDV2776, 1995 (from television series of same title). Various performers. Mícheál Ó Súilleabháin, harpsichord, piano, conductor, arranger, composer: Ah! sweet dancer, instrumental piece; piano accompaniment to Christy Moore, vocals; River of sound, instrumental piece; Turas go Tír na nÓg, song air

B28: L'Imaginaire Irlandais. Keltia Musique, France, CD KMCD 63, 1996. Various performers. Mícheál Ó Súilleabháin, piano, Irish Chamber Orchestra: Idir eatarthu/Between worlds, instrumental piece

B29: A Treasury of Irish Traditional Music, vol. 2. His Master's Voice Ireland, Dublin, CD HMVCD 004, 1997. Various performers. Mícheál Ó Súilleabháin, piano, with Tommy Hayes, percussion: The molka, dance tune

B30: Sticking Out a Mile: Celtic music. Castleview Records, Chicago, CD CVCD 1001, 1997. Seán O'Driscoll, accordion, vocals, and others. Mícheál Ó Súilleabháin, piano accompaniment

B31: Celtic Moods. Virgin Records America, United States, CD 7243 8 44951 2 1, 1997. Various performers. Mícheál Ó Súilleabháin, piano with orchestra: Woodbrook

B32: A Taste of Ireland. Nimbus Records, Herefordshire, CD NI 7035, 1997. Various performers, reissued from Nimbus. Mícheál Ó Súilleabháin, producer with Robin Broadbank

B33: The Gathering. Real World Records, Wiltshire, CD CDRW 62, 1997. Various performers. Mícheál Ó Súilleabháin, producer with Mel Mercier and Niall Vallely

B34: The Piper's Call. Tara Records, Dublin, CD TARACD 3037, 1998. Liam O'Flynn, uilleann pipes, and others. Mícheál Ó Súilleabháin, orchestral arrangements

B35: Don't Touch the Elk. Elk Records, Limerick, CD ELK 009, 1999. Niall Keegan, flute, and others. Mícheál Ó Súilleabháin, piano accompaniment

B36: From a Distant Shore: Irish and Cape Breton traditional music live from the Cork University traditional music festivals 1–4. Nimbus Records, Herefordshire, CD set NI 1752 (reissued from Nimbus), 1999. Mícheál Ó Súilleabháin, accompaniment on piano, producer

B37: Ceol Reoite. RTÉ, Dublin, CD RTÉ 240 CD, 2000. Various performers. Mícheál Ó Súilleabháin, piano: Limerick's lamentation, air

B38: Amhráin Uilliam English agus a Chairde. CD accompanying book *Canfar an Dán: Uilliam English agus a chairde* by Úna Nic Éinrí (An Sagart, An Daingean/Dingle, 2003). Pádraig Ó Cearbhaill, vocals. Mícheál Ó Súilleabháin, music advisor

B39: Music in Ireland: Experiencing music, expressing culture. CD accompanying book of same title by Dorothea E. Hast and Stanley Scott (Oxford and New York: Oxford University Press, 2004). Various performers. Mícheál Ó Súilleabháin, piano: The old grey goose, double jig

B40: The Chieftains Live in Dublin: A tribute to Derek Bell. Sony/BMG RCA Victor CD 82876 67137 2, 2005. The Chieftains and various performers. Mícheál Ó Súilleabháin, piano: Oíche Nollag/Christmas Eve, reel

B41: The Fiddler's Choice: In aid of Nenagh Hospital. Eileen O'Brien, Nenagh, County Tipperary, CD EOBCD001, 2006. Various performers. Mícheál Ó Súilleabháin, piano: Eibhlí gheal chiúin Ní Chearbhaill, song air

B42: Éistigí: The essential traditional music collection. Dara Records, Dublin, CDs 1–2 TORTV2CD1187, 2008. Various performers. Mícheál Ó Súilleabháin, piano: Brian Boru, march (CD 1)

B43: Nollaig: Essential Irish Christmas. All Media Entertainment, Dublin, double CD CACD 9903, 2009. Various performers. Mícheál Ó Súilleabháin, piano: Oíche Nollag/Christmas Eve, reel

B44: Go Mairir i bhFad: Long life to you. New traditional Irish music for fiddle and guitar. Tara Music, CD TARACD 4025, 2012. Zoë Conway, fiddle, and John McIntyre, guitar. Mícheál Ó Súilleabháin, composer: Bóthar na sop

B45: *Anything But Love*, a play by Mary Coll, directed by Joan Sheehy, produced for radio by Kevin Brew. Featuring a live soundtrack by Mícheál Ó Súilleabháin. RTÉ Radio 1 *Drama on One* series 2012. Available at: https://www.rte.ie/radio/dramaonone/647041-genres-life-anythingbutlove https://librivox.bookdesign.biz/de/book/166760

B46: Ark of Tides. Inishowen Traditional Music Project, Inishowen, County Donegal, CD ITMP 002, 2013. Dinny McLaughlin, fiddle, vocals, etc., and others. Mícheál Ó Súilleabháin, piano accompaniment

B47: Filleadh: Sacred songs. Echoes from ancient Ireland and around the world. Owen and Moley Ó Súilleabháin, County Limerick, CD unnumbered, [2013]. Mícheál Ó Súilleabháin, whistle: Irish whistle improvisation

B48: Let the Joyous Irish Sing Aloud/Laetabundus Decantet Hybernicorum Cetus. Irish World Academy, University of Limerick, CD CDVE 915, 2014. Cantoral. Mícheál Ó Súilleabháin, producer

B49: Pondelorum. Eoin Dillon, Dublin, CD EDCD 01, 2016. Eoin Dillon, uilleann pipes, whistle, and others. Mícheál Ó Súilleabháin, harpsichord accompaniment

With thanks to the Irish Traditional Music Archive, Dublin, where these recordings can be heard by the general public. Mícheál Ó Súilleabháin was chairman of the board of the Archive for two terms, 1993–99.

Mícheál Ó Súilleabháin: Writings

John O'Flynn, Helen Phelan, Marie McCarthy, Nicholas Carolan

'The Bodhrán: Its history and construction', *Treoir: Journal of Comhaltas Ceoltóirí Éireann*, vol. 6, no. 2, 1974, pp. 4–7

'The Bodhrán: Traditional performance techniques', *Treoir: Journal of Comhaltas Ceoltóírí* Éireann, vol. 6, no. 5, 1974, pp. 6–10

'Guides for Young Traditional Players' [review], *Music from Ireland*, vols 1, 2, 3, compiled and published by Dave Bulmer and Neil Sharpley (Leeds: Celtic Music, 1974)

'The Bodhrán', *Ais-Éirí*, vol. 1, no. 3, summer 1975, pp. 38–42 [reprint of 1974 *Treoir* articles without rhythm notations]

Irish Tunes by the 100, vol. 1 [review], compiled by Sean McGuire and Josephine Keegan (Leeds: Celtic Music, 1975) (typed manuscript dated 1977)

'High-class Superficiality' [review], in Robin Williamson (ed.), *English, Welch, Scottish and Irish Fiddle Tunes* (New York: Oak Publications, 1976)

'Two Songs Collected and Notated by Mícheál Ó Súilleabháin from the Singing of Pilib Ó Laoghaire', in Rev. W.J. Hayes (ed.), *Tipperary Remembers: Cuimhneachán chois tSiúire* (Tipperary: Tipperary Remembers Society, 1976), pp. 84–5

'A Man and His Music', *The Irish Times*, 27 August 1977, p. iv

'Folk Music Studies', Letters to the Editor, *The Irish Times*, 24 February 1977, p. 9

'Gnéithe Áirithe de Cheardaíocht Phádraig Uí Cheallaigh: Fidléir ó Chontae an Chláir', *Comhar*, vol. 36, no. 10, October 1977, pp. 26–7

'Oasis Look Fertile in a Modern Desert', *The Irish Times*, 23 August 1977, p. 9

'University College Cork Music Department', *International Folk Music Council UK Committee Newsletter*, no. 18, April 1979, pp. 2–3

'Theses at University College Cork', *Ceol Tíre*, no. 16, April 1980, pp. 16–17

'Contemporary Developments in Bodhrán Performance Technique', *International Folk Music Council UK Committee Newsletter*, no. 27, July 1981, pp. 12–14

'Irish Music Defined', *The Crane Bag*, vol. 5, no. 2, 1981, pp. 83–7

'Irish Music', Letters to the Editor, *The Irish Times*, 26 July 1981, p. 9

'The Art of Listening', *The Crane Bag*, vol. 6, no.1, 1982, pp. 59–61

'My Love is in America: Melodic deviation and the programmatic in the fiddle playing of Tommie Potts', *An Fhidil Ghaelach*, vol.1, no.1, 1982, pp. 17–22

'Music in Ireland since 1600: A typological model', paper read at the annual conference of the International Folk Music Council (UK chapter), University of Durham, 1–4 April 1982

'Ó Riada, Right or Wrong' [letter], *Soundpost*, no. 9, August 1982, pp. 2, 28

'The Roche Collection: An introduction', in Francis Roche (ed.), *The Roche Collection of Traditional Irish Music*, vols 1–3 (new edn) (Cork: Ossian Publications; New York: Oak Publications, 1982), [unnumbered page after title]

Bunting's Ancient Music of Ireland, edited with Donal O'Sullivan (Cork: Cork University Press, 1983)

The Bodhrán: A practical introduction (Dublin: Waltons, 1984)

'The Irish Traditional Musician and University Music Courses' (Dublin: Comhaltas Ceoltóirí Éireann, 1984)

'Out of Tune with Reality: Music and the school in Ireland', *Irish Educational Studies*, vol. 5 no. 1, 1985, pp. 44–57

'Innovation and Tradition in the Music of Tommie Potts', unpublished PhD thesis, Queen's University Belfast, 1987

'"Tourner" un Air: L'improvisation dans la musique traditionelle Irlandais', in Bernard Lortat-Jacob (ed.), *L'improvisation dans les Musiques de Tradition Orale*, Ethnomusicologie 4 (Paris: SELAF, 1987), pp. 211–20

'The Creative Process in Irish Traditional Dance Music', in Gerard Gillen and Harry White (eds), *Irish Music Studies 1: Musicology in Ireland* (Dublin: Irish Academic Press, 1990), pp. 117–30

'An Orient of Time', in Tomás Ó Canainn (ed.), *The Cork Review: Music in Cork* (Cork: Triskel Arts Centre, 1992), pp. 45–6

'Review: The melodic tradition of Ireland by James R. Cowdery', *Ethnomusicology*, vol. 37, no. 1, 1993, pp. 109–12

'"All our central fire": Music, mediation and the Irish psyche', *The Irish Journal of Psychology*, vol. 15 nos 2 & 3, 1994, pp. 331–53

'Willie Clancy Summer School', Letters to the Editor, *The Irish Times*, 22 July 1997, p. 17

The Local Accent: Selected proceedings from Blas: The Local Accent Conference, edited with Thérèse Smith (Dublin and Limerick: The Folk Music Society of Ireland and the Irish World Music Centre, University of Limerick, 1997)

'"Around the house and mind the cosmos": Music, dance and identity in contemporary Ireland', in Richard Pine (ed.), *Music in Ireland: 1848–1998* (Cork: Mercier Press, 1998), pp. 76–86

Mícheál Ó Súilleabháin (asst. ed.) with Aloys Fleischmann (ed.) and Paul McGettrick (assoc. ed.), *Sources of Irish Traditional Music c. 1600–1855*, vols I & II (New York and London: Garland Press, 1998)

'Preface', in Aloys Fleischmann (ed.), Mícheál Ó Súilleabháin (asst ed.), and Paul McGettrick (assoc. ed.), *Sources of Irish Traditional Music* (New York: Garland Publishing, 1998), pp. xi–xiv

'Bobby Gardiner's "Clare Shout"', *Treoir*, vol. 30, no. 2, 1999, p. 15

'The Becoming Thing: Composer Mícheál Ó Súilleabháin salutes an Ireland in which the tension between tradition and novelty in the arts is increasingly a creative one', *The Irish Times*, 30 December 1999, p. 12

'Crossroads or Twin Track? Innovation and tradition in Irish traditional music', in Fintan Vallely, Hammy Hamilton, Eithne Vallely and Liz Doherty (eds), *Crosbhealach an Cheoil, The Crossroads Conference 1996: Tradition and change in Irish traditional music* (Dublin: Whinstone Music, 1999), pp. 175–98

'Conair an Cheoil: Smaointe faoi fhorás an cheoil Ghaelaigh', in Ruairí Ó hUiginn and Liam Mac Cóil (eds), *Bliainiris 2000* (Meath: Carbad, 2000), pp. 80–90

'The Singing Body: Music, spirit and creativity', in Helen Phelan (ed.), *Anáil Dé /The Breath of God: Music, ritual and spirituality* (Dublin: Veritas Press, 2001), pp. 140–7

'State of Music Education', Letters to the Editor, *The Irish Times*, 31 January 2001, p. 17

'Many Rivers: Towards a global listening', in *Samspel ISME 2002: Abstracts and sessions guide*, 25th Biennial World Conference of the International Society for Music Education (Bergen, Norway: International Society for Music Education, 2002), https://www.isme.org/other-publications/25th-isme-world-conference-2002-proceedings

'The New, the Old, and the Learned: Issues of innovation, tradition and education in traditional music in our times', in *Preservation of Traditional Music: Report of the Asia-Europe training programme Beijing, China, 30 March–6 April 2003* (Beijing: China Academy of Arts, 2003), pp. 199–201

'An Island Sound: Reflections on music, politics and identity in contemporary Ireland', in Robert Savage Jr (ed.), *Ireland in the New Century: Politics, culture and identity* (Dublin: Four Courts Press, 2003), pp. 189–97

'A Strategy for the Promotion of Traditional Music in Formal Music Education Contexts', in Frank Heneghan (ed.), *Music Education National Debate*, Document 306, III P/vi (Dublin: Dublin Institute of Technology, 2004)

'Ceol na nUasal: Seán Ó Riada and the search for a native Irish art music', *Ó Riada Memorial Lecture 15* (Cork: Traditional Music Archive and Irish Traditional Music Society, University College Cork, 2004)

'Irish Traditional Music in Education', in Frank Heneghan (ed.), *Music Education National Debate*, Document 120, Ref. I P/DN (Dublin: Dublin Institute of Technology, 2004)

'Listening to Difference: Ireland in a world of music', in Harry Bohan and Gerard Kennedy (eds), *Global Aspirations and the Reality of Change: How can we do things differently?* (Dublin: Veritas, 2004), pp. 20–35

'The Truth of Beauty: Towards a global listening', Sabhal Mòr Ostaigh Lecture (Isle of Skye, Scotland: Sabhal Mòr Ostaigh, 2004)

'Fírinne na hÁilleachta i dtreo Éisteacht Domhanda', in Séamus de hÍde (ed.), *Daonscoil na Mumhan: Imeachtaí 2005* (Dublin: Coiscéim, 2006), pp. 79–83

'Mícheál Ó Súilleabháin, Director, Irish World Academy of Music and Dance, University of Limerick', in Deirdre Mulrooney, *Irish Moves: An illustrated history of dance and physical theatre in Ireland* (Dublin: The Liffey Press, 2006), pp. 228–32

'A Wealth of Songs', in Nóirín Ní Riain (ed.), *Stór Amhrán: A wealth of songs from the Irish tradition* (new edn) (London: Ossian Publications, 2007), p. 3

'Ní ón ngaoth a fuair sé é: Aloys Fleischmann, 1910–92', review of Séamas de Barra, *Aloys Fleischmann*, *Journal of Music*, 1 May 2007, https://journalofmusic.com/focus/ni-ngaoth-fuair-se-e-aloys-fleischmann-1910-92

'"Traditional Ears": Perception and analysis in Irish traditional music', in Anne Clune (ed.), *Dear Far-Voiced Veteran: Essays in honour of Tom Munnelly* (Miltown Malbay, County Clare: Old Kilfarboy Society, 2007), pp. 249–76

With Nuala O'Connor, Noel Eccles and Nicholas Carolan, 'Pulling the Strings: How Lunny took the music from black-and-white to colour', *The Irish Times*, 10 March 2007, p. C7

'A Thread Across the Ocean', in Brian A. Roberts (ed), *Sociological Explorations: Proceedings of the 5th International Symposium on the Sociology of Music Education, Memorial University of Newfoundland, July 2–5, 2007* (St John's, Newfoundland: The Binder's Press, 2008), pp. 9–12

'Parallel Universes: The state of play', keynote address, *Arts Research: The state of play*, GRADCAM conference, Dublin, 8–9 May 2008

'The Litany of the Saints: Quotations and borrowings in the music of Tommie Potts', *Inbhear: Journal of Irish music and dance*, vol. 1, no. 1, Irish World Academy of Music and Dance, University of Limerick, 2010, pp. 1–46

'Elver-Gleams: Sub-marine soundings from the Irish World Academy', in Thierry Dubost and Alexandra Slaby (eds), *Music and the Irish Imagination: Like a language that we could all understand* (Caen: University of Caen Press, 2013), pp. 15–27

'Hallelujah: A book to celebrate', review of Harry White and Barra Boydell (eds), *The Encyclopaedia of Music in Ireland*, *The Irish Times*, 23 November 2013, p. 11

'Between the Jigs and the Reels: From the Famine to the peace process', review of Martin Dowling, *Traditional Music and Irish Society: Historical perspectives*, *The Irish Times*, 10 January 2015, p. B10

'Blacking, Baily and Belfast: An autoethnographic journey', The John Blacking Annual Memorial Lecture, 31st European Seminar in Ethnomusicology, Irish World Academy of Music and Dance, 16–20 September 2015

'A Note on the Score', in Irish Film Institute, *Irish Destiny* (DVD booklet), 2011, n.p.

'Phoenix Rising', in Mark Quinn (ed.), *Pioneers and Aviators: A century of Irish aviation* (Dublin: Avolon, 2015), p. 7

In conversation with Hilary Fennell, 'This Much I Know: Musician, composer and academic Mícheál Ó Súilleabháin', *Irish Examiner*, 19 November 2016, https://www.irishexaminer.com/lifestyle/arid-20431249.html

With Aaron Lawless, Niamh NicGhabhann and Helen Phelan, 'The Harp of Aaron: The Irish harp as shopping trolley', in Sandra Joyce and Helen Lawlor (eds), *Harp Studies: Perspectives on the Irish harp* (Dublin: Four Courts Press, 2016), pp. 270–93

'The Redress of Music: Music, mediation and parity of esteem', *Yearbook for Traditional Music*, vol. 50, 2018, pp. 1–14

'Between the Poetic and the Practical: An address by Professor Mícheál Ó Súilleabháin on the acceptance of the 2018 SMEI Award', 8th Annual Conference of the Society for Music Education in Ireland, Royal Irish Academy of Music, Dublin, 2 November 2018, https://www.smei.ie/smei-events/8th-annual-conference

'Cultural Redress and the Growth of Love: A guided autoethnography', in Helen Phelan and Graham F. Welch (eds), *The Artist and Academia* (London and New York: Routledge, 2021), pp. 205–18

'MENDing Music Education? Some progress at the Irish World Academy' (with HelenPhelan), in John O'Flynn and Patricia Flynn (eds), *Music Education for the 21st Century: Legacies, conversations, aspirations* (*Studies in Irish Music Education*, vol. 1) (Cork: Cork University Press, 2023), pp. 31–50

Micheal Ó Súilleabháin: Select Scores

Contemporary Music Centre

The Contemporary Music Centre (CMC) is the all-Ireland body that represents almost two hundred composers born or based on the island of Ireland. The centre is a relevant, resourceful and recognisable force in the documentation, development and promotion of new music from Ireland, at home and abroad. CMC meets the needs of a wide variety of interest groups – composers, performers, musicologists, teachers, students – and reaches a wide range of audiences – music enthusiasts, other art forms, children and young people, general public – in its support to contemporary music. CMC acknowledges the support of the Arts Council Ireland/An Chomhairle Ealaíon through annual strategic funding and the Arts Council of Northern Ireland (ACNI), through the lottery project funding.

Preface

One of the most challenging aspects of compiling this book was the creation of a list of compositions. There are several reasons for this. Chief among these was Mícheál's own understanding of composition, which was not limited to the standard western conceptualisation of 'the work' as a fixed, discrete, sole-authored output. It is not that he didn't have pieces which fit this description, but he also relished older and more culturally diverse understandings of composition which included borrowings, live improvisation, multi-authorship, and the constant recycling of key ideas across pieces. Throughout his life, he resisted scoring his own piano playing, preferring the freedom of the performer-composer to improvise, in situ, at any given performance. He only scored those aspects of his output which were created for notation-based western art musicians. A second challenge is the number of variations he produced around most of his compositions. 'Oíche Nollag' exists, for example, for solo piano, string quartet, string orchestra, jazz ensemble, concert orchestra and symphonic orchestra. Several versions of pieces are still emerging from his vast personal archive and it will be many years before a complete list can be created. For this publication, we decided to limit the list of works to those pieces which exist as scores, and which Mícheál shared with the library of the Contemporary Music Centre, Dublin. (Helen Phelan)

Introduction

Whilst delivering the keynote address at the International Association of Music Information Centres (IAMIC) annual conference in 2010, hosted by the Contemporary Music Centre (CMC) in Dublin, Mícheál Ó Súilleabháin reflected: 'Let me explore that liminal point between the poetic and the practical where I'm suggesting here music information centres live. I want to imagine these centres as embassies of sound.'

Mícheál Ó Súilleabháin was a represented composer of the CMC and also served on the CMC board of directors between 2009 and 2013. Mícheál deposited a number of scores in the library of CMC which are detailed in this select annotated bibliography of his work, compiled by CMC library coordinator Susan Brodigan. These works represent a selection of Mícheál's overall compositional output.

Evonne Ferguson, director of CMC, reflects on his contribution to the Centre, both as a composer and as a board member:

> Throughout many years Mícheál remained an unwavering source of support to the team and board. Like so many other organisations, CMC was the beneficiary of Mícheál's expert guidance, thoughtful advice and kind-hearted encouragement. In CMC, when we remember Mícheál, we think of a warm, passionate, generous musician who engaged and nurtured so many areas of musical life on this island and internationally, as a composer, pianist, educator, advocate and mentor of so much musical talent. Mícheál Ó Súilleabháin was a cultural leader and leaves an enduring legacy. Those of us who have been touched by his music and his generosity of spirit have been honoured in a special way.

Speaking at the 2010 IAMIC annual conference, Mícheál Ó Súilleabháin said of music information centres: 'You increase our circle of friends, and allow us to hopefully extend yours in a community of common cause and call.' As one of these 'embassies of sound', CMC hopes that this select annotated bibliography will further extend Mícheál's music to new performers, new audiences and new perspectives.

Micheal Ó Súilleabháin scores in CMC Library

Carolan's Farewell to Music (1988)
Instrumentation: Solo piano and string orchestra
Duration: 6 minutes

Premiere: June 1989. National Concert Hall, Dublin. Irish Chamber Orchestra, conductor Mícheál Ó Súilleabháin.
Score details:
Pages: 6
Note on score: Arrangement of a composition by O'Carolan; Críoch 15/9/1988 MÓS.

Oileán/Island (1988)
Instrumentation: Solo flute (traditional) and string orchestra
Duration: 19 minutes
Movements: 3
Premiere: June 1989. National Concert Hall, Dublin. Irish Chamber Orchestra, conductor Mícheál Ó Súilleabháin.
1988 version
Note on score: The flute line may be taken by Irish traditional flute, fiddle, pipes, concertina or button accordion. Under no circumstances should the flute line ever be played as written. It is intended only as a general guide for the conductor, and will vary according to the style of the soloist.
Score details:
Pages: 59
Programme note: The work is based on an earlier work entitled Concerto for Traditional Musician and String Orchestra written in 1979. Commissioned by the Gorey Arts Festival and first performed there conducted by Proinsias Ó Dúinn with Matt Molloy as soloist. The concert was recorded by RTÉ Radio for broadcast in a series entitled An Droichead Beo.

Oileán/Island (1988, rev. 2007 and 2016)
Instrumentation: Solo flute (traditional) and symphony orchestra with optional harp (2222 4331 time 2 per hrp [opt] str)
Duration: 19 minutes
Movements: 3
Commissioned by: RTÉ Lyric FM (2007)
Score details:
Pages: 41
Typeset
Dated 2007 and 2016 (when harp part was added for National Youth Orchestra of Ireland)
Programme note: The work is based on an earlier work entitled Concerto for Traditional Musician and String Orchestra written in 1979.

Commissioned by the Gorey Arts Festival and first performed there conducted by Proinsias Ó Dúinn with Matt Molloy as soloist.
The concert was recorded by RTÉ Radio for broadcast in a series entitled An Droichead Beo.

Oíche Nollag (Christmas Eve) (February 1989)
Instrumentation: Solo piano and string orchestra
Duration: 3 minutes
Premiere: June 1989. National Concert Hall, Dublin. Irish Chamber Orchestra, conductor Mícheál Ó Súilleabháin.
Score details:
Pages: 26
Handwritten
Note on final page of score: Críoch Mícheál Ó Súil. Corcaigh, Feabhra 1989.

Oíche Nollag (Christmas Eve) (September 1989)
Instrumentation: Solo piano and string orchestra
Duration: 3 minutes
Premiere: December 1989. St. Nicholas' Church, Galway. London Chamber Orchestra, conductor Mícheál Ó Súilleabháín.
Score details:
Pages: 26
Handwritten
Dated September 1989
Note on final page of score: Críoch Mícheál Ó Súil, Corcaigh, Fomhar 1989. This is a second orchestration of the original piano piece for the LCO. MÓS.

Session #1 (1991)
Instrumentation: Solo percussion, solo piano and string orchestra
Duration: 18 minutes
Movements: 3 – Homo Ludens; Streetwalk; Session
Premiere: 7 March 1992. National Concert Hall, Dublin. Dublin Orchestral Players, Mícheál Ó Súilleabháin.
Commissioned by: Dublin Orchestral Players, 1991, with funds provided by the Arts Council/An Chomhairle Ealaíon
Score details:
Pages: 40
Handwritten

Note on score: Percussion is optional and may consist of one, two or three bodhráns with one player doubling on bones if desired. The notated rhythm is only intended as a general guide.
Note at end of score: Críoch 20/12/91 MÓS.

Woodbrook / The Plains of Boyle (1992)
Instrumentation: Piano and string orchestra
Duration: 3 minutes
Score details:
Pages: 14
Typeset
Per composer: '… first appeared under that title in a piano and string orchestra version on my album entitled *Gaiseadh/Flowing* (Virgin Records) with Irish Chamber Orchestra'.

Woodbrook (1992)
Instrumentation: Solo piano
Duration: 3 minutes
Premiere: RTÉ studios, Union Quay, Cork. Mícheál Ó Súilleabháin (pf).
Commissioned by: RTÉ Radio producer Julian Vignoles
Score details:
Pages: 5
Typeset
Note: Used in a 1986 RTÉ Radio programme called *Woodbrook*. Solo piano version originally entitled *Magh Luirg/The Plains of Boyle*.

Woodbrook (1992 rev. 2016)
Instrumentation: Solo piano and chamber orchestra (4 hn, hrp, str)
Duration: 3 minutes
Score details:
Pages: 25
Typeset

FLOWAN (1993 rev. 2016)
Instrumentation: Solo piano and orchestra (2222 4231 timp perc str)
Duration: 3 minutes
Premiere: December 1993. National Concert Hall, Dublin. Mícheál Ó Súilleabháin (pf), RTÉ Concert Orchestra, conductor Proinnsias Ó Duinn.
Score details:

Pages: 15
Typeset
Note from composer: From the film music *Irish Destiny*.

Story (1993 rev. 2016)
Instrumentation: Solo piano and orchestra (2222 2000 timp hrp str)
Duration: 6 minutes
Premiere: December 1993. National Concert Hall, Dublin. Mícheál Ó Súilleabháin (pf), RTÉ Concert Orchestra, conductor Proinnsias Ó Duinn.
Score details:
Pages: 31
Typeset
Note from composer: From the film music *Irish Destiny*. The piece *Story* is entitled *Clonmore* in the *Irish Destiny* score and is the third movement of *Irish Destiny*.

So Merrily Dance (1997)
Instrumentation: Solo piano and string orchestra
Duration: 3 minutes
Premiere: January 1998. Celtic Connections Festival, Royal Festival Hall. Mícheál Ó Súilleabháin (pf), Irish Chamber Orchestra.
Score details:
Pages: 10
Handwritten
Note on final page of score: Fine 21/7/97. Dromore.

So Merrily Dance (1997 rev. 2016)
Instrumentation: Solo piano and orchestra (2222 4321 timp perc hrp [opt] str)
Duration: 3 minutes
Premiere: January 1998. Celtic Connections Festival, Royal Festival Hall. Mícheál Ó Súilleabháin (pf), Irish Chamber Orchestra.
Score details:
Pages: 13
Typeset

Salve (1997)
Instrumentation: Solo piano and string orchestra
Duration: 7 minutes

Premiere: March 1998. Barbican Hall, London. Mícheál Ó Súilleabháin (pf), Irish Chamber Orchestra.
Score details:
Pages: 9
Handwritten
Note on final page of score: Críoch MÓS 1/4/97. (c. 6'30") Dromore.

Becoming (1997)
Instrumentation: Solo piano and string orchestra
Score details:
Pages: 6
Handwritten
Note on final page of score: MÓS 7/97 Dromore.

Maranatha (1999)
Instrumentation: Mixed choir (SATB)
Duration: 12 minutes
Premiere: 27 April 2000. Cork International Choral Festival, Cork. National Chamber Choir, conductor Colin Mawby.
Commissioned by: Cork International Choral Festival for the 27th Seminar on Contemporary Choral Music, with funds provided by the Arts Council/An Chomhairle Ealaíon
Language: Latin, sacred text (anon.)
Score details:
Pages: 28
Typeset
Programme note (on CMC catalogue): Commissioned by the Cork International Choral Festival for its contemporary music seminar, and given its first performance there by the National Chamber Choir in 2000, *Maranatha* strikes a note of de profundis juxtaposed with the expectant hope of the O antiphons of Advent. The word 'maranatha' (which may have been used as a form of greeting by early Christians) is Aramaic and means 'Come, Lord'. The O antiphons all commence with the word 'veni' meaning 'come', and this plea resonates throughout the piece. The cry 'jubilate Deo' (praise God) breaks through the darkness and ultimately leads to a catharsis towards the end with the exclamation 'O!' The tonal ending seems to herald a coming, perhaps in the form of acceptance.

Madison's Descent (a masque in ten movements for voice, choir and orchestra) (2006)

Instrumentation: Voice, mixed choir and chamber orchestra
(Ct-solo, vn-solo, satb ssax 2 hn pf str)
Duration: 50 minutes
Movements: 10 – Asculta; The Song of the Moon; Heart of Stillness; River of Stars; The Wish; Unfolding; That Kind of Person; River of Stars Reprise; So Love Returns; Becoming
Premiere: 2006. Alexander Kasser Theater, Montclair University, New Jersey. Angelo Smimmo (counter-tenor solo), Fionnuala Hunt (violin solo), Montclair Chorus, conductor Mícheál Ó Súilleabháin.
Commissioned by: Peak Performances at Montclair State, New Jersey, United States
Score details:
Pages: 248
Typeset
Composer note: Based on the book and paintings by Page Allen. The premiere had choreography by David Bolger. Two dancers from CoisCéim dance company, a semi-theatrical production by Jed Wheeler.

Fidelio Unsung (2010)
Instrumentation: Piano trio
Duration: 7 minutes
Premiere: 23 April 2010. King's Place, London, England. Fidelio Trio.
Commissioned by: RTÉ Lyric FM
Score details:
Pages: 25
Typeset

Port na bPúcaí (The Island's Cry) (2012)
Instrumentation: Piano solo
Duration: 10 minutes
Premiere: 5 July 2013. Clonmel Junction Festival, Clonmel, County Tipperary. Mícheál Ó Súilleabháin (pf).
Score details:
Pages: 4
Typeset
Note on cover page: Traidisiúnta ó na mBlascaodaí. Dedicated to John O'Sullivan.

An Buachaill Caol Dubh (2013)
Instrumentation: Voice (*sean-nós*) and symphony orchestra (2222 3330

timp 2 perc hrp str)
Duration: 10 minutes
Premiere: 12 September 2013. National Concert Hall, Dublin. Iarla Ó Lionáird (voice) RTÉ Concert Orchestra, conductor David Brophy.
Language: Irish (Fonn traidisiúnta. Focail le Seán Ó Seanacháin (18ú aois))
Score details:
Pages: 16
Typeset

Míle Buíochas Leatsa (2013)
Instrumentation: Voice (*sean-nós*) and symphony orchestra (2222 3330 timp 2 perc harp str)
Duration: 10 minutes
Premiere: 12 September 2013. National Concert Hall, Dublin. Iarla Ó Lionáird (voice), RTÉ Concert Orchestra, conductor David Brophy.
Commissioned by: RTÉ Concert Orchestra
Language: Irish (Focail: Traidisiúnta. Fonn: '*Sliabh na mBan*')
Score details:
Pages: 11
Typeset

Port na bPúcaí (symphony orchestra) (2013)
Instrumentation: *Sean-nós* singer and orchestra
Duration: 10 minutes
Premiere: 12 September 2013. National Concert Hall, Dublin. Iarla Ó Lionáird (voice), RTÉ Concert Orchestra, conductor David Brophy.
Commissioned by: RTÉ Concert Orchestra
Language: Irish (Féach: Fearghal Mac Amhlaoibh, *An Caomhnóir*, Meán Fómhair, 1989, lch. 14/15)
Score details:
Pages: 12
Typeset

Phoenix Rising (2013)
Instrumentation: Symphony orchestra (2222 3330 timp 2 perc pf str)
Movements: 8 – Phoenix Rising 1; Phoenix Rising 2; What's the Story?; Inflight; Flight Transfer; Engine Room; Uplifting; Flying Boat
Premiere: Recorded by the composer on piano with RTÉ Concert Orchestra, conductor Robert Houlihan, in September 2013

Commissioned by: AVOLON for the film documentary by Alan Gilsenan
Score details:
Pages: 261
Typeset
Per composer November 2013: 'I am in the process of producing a concert version of the film music which will be performed by the RTECO at the NCH in January 2014 as part of an occasion when the film will also be shown.'

Letting Go (no date)
Instrumentation: Solo piano and string orchestra
Duration: 3 minutes
Premiere: March 1988. Barbican Hall, London.
Score details:
Pages: 6
Handwritten

Notes

Introduction *Helen Phelan*

1. See 'Irish World Academy Recital in Honour of President' (2011), https://www.youtube.com/watch?v=QP0MaSCj5Ws&list=UUUW1fIRLyvCeZ4e6TefB1xQ&index=18 (accessed 20 May 2020).

2. Seamus Heaney, 'Postscript', in *The Spirit Level* (London: Faber & Faber, 1996), p. 70.

3. Mícheál Ó Súilleabháin, '"Around the house and mind the cosmos": Music, dance and identity in contemporary Ireland', in Richard Pine (ed.), *Music in Ireland: 1848–1998* (Cork: Mercier Press, 1998), pp. 76–86.

4. Bill Meek, 'On the Keyboard', *The Irish Times*, 31 August 1976, p. 8. The 'problems of the KB [keyboard] family' referred to by Meek include issues of harmonic accompaniment on an instrument positioned at the periphery of Irish traditional music practice. Meek's reference to 'Mick Sullivan' alludes to Mícheál's birth name, Michael O'Sullivan, shortened to 'Mick Sullivan' during his student years in Cork before he changed to the use of the Irish-language form of his name, Mícheál Ó Súilleabháin.

5. See, for example, Edward Said, *Music at the Limits* (New York: Columbia University Press, 2007).

6. Ó Súilleabháin, 'Around the House', p. 80. The 'bomb' described by Ó Súilleabháin in this quote refers to the explosive impact of creating a point of entry for traditional musicians into the music programmes in UCC, leading to a root and branch change in every aspect of the music curriculum from this point onwards.

7. Rob Adams, 'Celtic Connections', *The Herald* (Glasgow), 24 January 2005.

8. Interview with Noeleen Dowling, *Evening Press*, 21 July 1989.

9. Mícheál Ó Súilleabháin, 'The Becoming Thing', *The Irish Times*, 30 December 1999, p. 12.

10. Mícheál Ó Súilleabháin, 'The Redress of Music: Music, mediation and parity of esteem', *Yearbook for Traditional Music*, vol. 50, 2018, pp. 1–14 (p. 4).

11. Seamus Heaney, 'The Rain Stick', in *The Spirit Level* (London: Faber & Faber, 1996), p. 1.

12. Seamus Heaney, *The Redress of Poetry: Oxford lectures* (London: Faber & Faber, 1995), p. xiii.

13. Seamus Heaney, '70th Birthday Speech', Irish Museum of Modern Art, Dublin, 2009, https://www.rte.ie/archives/exhibitions/681-history-of-rte/708-rte-2000s/289812-heaney-at-70 (accessed 20 May 2020).

14. Heaney, *The Redress of Poetry*, p. 203.

Mícheál Ó Súilleabháin: A biography *Helen Phelan*

1. Baptised Michael O'Sullivan, he would not publicly change his name to Mícheál Ó Súilleabháin until 1976.

2. Excerpt from two personal narrative interviews with Mícheál Ó Súilleabháin by Nicholas Carolan, recorded in the studio of the Irish Traditional Music Archive, 63 Merrion Square, Dublin 2, on 6 June 1996 and 24 June 1997 (324-ITMA-DAT & 325-ITMA-DAT). Transcribed by Orla Henihan.

3. Ibid.

4. Ibid.

5. See https://www.rte.ie/archives/profiles/healy-shay/ (accessed 20 May 2020).

6. Carolan interview, 1996.

7. Ibid.

8. Ibid.

9. Ibid.

10. Mícheál Ó Súilleabháin, 'Out of Tune with Reality: Music and the school in Ireland', *Irish Educational Studies*, vol. 5 no. 1, 1985, pp. 44–5 (p. 45).

11. Charles Acton, 'Two Traditions', *The Irish Times*, 9 August 1976, p. 8.

12. See, for example, Séamus Ennis performing on 'An Fear agus a Chuid Ceoil', https://www.rte.ie/archives/2015/0916/728180-master-musician-seamus-ennis (accessed 20 May 2020).

13. Excerpt from Carolan interview, 1996. The article referred to by Ó Súilleabháin is 'The Creative Process in Irish Traditional Dance Music', in Gerard Gillen and Harry White (eds), *Irish Music Studies 1: Musicology in Ireland* (Dublin: Irish Academic Press, 1990), pp. 117–30.

14. Mícheál Ó Súilleabháin, *The Bodhrán: A practical introduction* (Dublin: Waltons, 1984).

15. Mícheál Ó Súilleabháin, *Bunting's Ancient Music of Ireland*, edited with Donal O'Sullivan (Cork: Cork University Press, 1983).

16. Brian Trench, 'Interview with Mícheál Ó Súilleabháin', *Magill*, October 1987. 'Ven001' was the first recording of the new Venture label.

17. Mícheál Ó Súilleabháin, personal communication, 7 February 1992.

18. Helen Phelan, *The PIPA Report* (Limerick: Irish World Academy, University of Limerick and the Irish Chamber Orchestra, 1995).

19. David J. Elliott, 'Artful Knowing', Irish World Academy, University of Limerick, unpublished report, 1997.

20. David J. Elliott, *Music Matters: A new philosophy of music education* (Oxford and New York: Oxford University Press, 1995).

21. For the development of the Irish World Academy vision, see Helen Phelan, 'Voicing *Imbas*: Performing a philosophy of music education', in Wayne Bowman and Ana Lucía Frega (eds), *Oxford Handbook of Music Education Philosophy* (Oxford: Oxford University Press, 2012), pp. 63–85.

22. Ciara Ferguson, interview with Mícheál Ó Súilleabháin, *Sunday Independent*, 13 June 1999.

23. Dearbhla Acheson, 'Mícheál Tipps His Hat Towards Clare Music', *Clare Champion*, August 2005.

24. *Sources of Irish Traditional Music c. 1600–1855*, vols I and II, Aloys Fleischmann (ed.), Mícheál Ó Súilleabháin (asst. ed.) and Paul McGettrick (assoc. ed.) (New York and London: Garland Press, 1998).

25. 'In Search of Ancient Ireland', https://www.imdb.com/title/tt0836660 (accessed 20 May 2020).

26. Eamonn Lacey, 'Supreme Bard of Fleadh Honour for Composer', *The Nationalist*, 5 July 2003.

27. Jill Sheehy, 'Irish Arts Minister John O'Donoghue Announces New Initiative to Promote Irish Culture Abroad', *Irish Echo*, 2–8 March 2005, p. 5.

28. Earle Hitchner, '*Irish Echo*'s Traditionalist of the Year', *The Irish Echo*, 30 January–5 February 2008.

29. Gordon Deegan, 'Music Academy Plan Gets Green Light', *Irish Examiner*, 27 November 2007, p. 11.

30. http://archiseek.com/2011/2010-irish-world-academy-music-dance-limerick (accessed 20 May 2020).

31. Colette Sheridan, 'Mel Mercier's Musical Journey from UCC to UL', *Irish Examiner*, 28 April 2016.

32. Cian O'Broin, 'Limerick-based Professor is New Director for the Irish World Academy', *Limerick Leader*, 3 August 2022.

33. https://irishstudies.nd.edu/news/tributes-for-micheal-o-suilleabhain-emeritus-professor-of-music-at-the-university-of-limerick-and-founder-director-at-the-irish-world-academy-of-music-and-dance (accessed 20 May 2020).

34. https://www.thejournal.ie/musician-and-composer-micheal-o-suilleabhain-has-died-4328706-Nov2018 (accessed 20 May 2020).

5. 'Let's start with an improvisation': Playing the saxophone for Mícheál Ó Súilleabháin *Kenneth Edge*

1. From the programme notes for the world premiere performance of Mícheál's work *Madison's Descent*, which took place at the Alexander Kasser Theater of Montclair State University, New Jersey, on 12 May 2006.

2. Mícheál Ó Súilleabháin, 'The Art of Listening', *The Crane Bag*, vol. 6, no. 1, 1982, pp. 59–61 (p. 59).

3. Ibid.

4. Christopher Small, *Musicking: The meanings of performing and listening* (Connecticut: Wesleyan University Press, 1998).

5. Ibid., p. 9.

6. Mícheál Ó Súilleabháin's works featuring the saxophone as a solo instrument include *Templum* (1994), *Missa Gadelica* (1994), *Lumen* (1995), *A River of Sound* (1995), *Bean Dubh an Ghleanna* (1998), *Madison's Descent* (2006) and *The Brook of Donode* (2014).

7. *Missa Gadelica* was commissioned by the Irish Christian Brothers and first performed in Westland Row Church, Dublin, in 1994.

8. Mícheál Ó Súilleabháin, *Templum*: Kenneth Edge (soprano saxophone), Mícheál Ó Súilleabháin (conductor), Irish Chamber Orchestra, National Chamber Choir of Ireland, CD, Virgin Records Ltd, CDVE955, 2001.

9. Seamus Heaney, 'In Memoriam Seán Ó Riada', in *Field Work* (London: Faber & Faber, 1979).

10. Performers involved in *Lumen* included Mícheál on piano and harpsichord, me on soprano sax, Mel Mercier and Evelyn Glennie on percussion, the RTÉ Concert Orchestra conducted by Proinnsías Ó Duinn, Niall Keegan on flute, the monks of Glenstal Abbey and the vocal soloists Nóirín Ní Riain, Brian Kennedy, Máire Ní Bhraonáin and Lillis Ó Laoire.

11. Mícheál Ó Súilleabháin, personal communication, 6 January 2014.

16. The Mediator and the 'Disappointment': Understanding Mícheál Ó Súilleabháin's contribution to Irish composition *Toner Quinn*

1. Mícheál Ó Súilleabháin, 'Hallelujah: A book to celebrate', review of Harry White and Barra Boydell (eds), *The Encyclopedia of Music in Ireland*, *The Irish Times*, 23 November 2013, https://www.irishtimes.com/culture/books/book-reviews/hallelujah-a-book-to-celebrate-1.1600077 (accessed 10 March 2021).

2. Helen Phelan, *Anáil Dé, the Breath of God: Music, ritual and spirituality* (Dublin: Veritas, 2001).

3. Mícheál Ó Súilleabháin, 'Fleischmann', *JMI – The Journal of Music in Ireland*, vol. 7, no. 3, May–June 2007, pp. 6–9.

4. Toner Quinn, 'Mícheál Ó Súilléabháin's Example will Continue to Inspire', *The Journal of Music*, 8 November 2018, https://journalofmusic.com/focus/micheal-o-Súilleabhain-s-example-will-continue-inspire (accessed 10 March 2021).

5. Mícheál Ó Súilleabháin, 'Crossroads or Twin Track? Innovation and tradition in Irish traditional music', in Fintan Vallely, Hammy Hamilton, Eithne Vallely and Liz Doherty (eds), *Crosbhealach an Cheoil, The Crossroads Conference 1996: Tradition and change in Irish traditional music* (Dublin: Whinstone Music, 1999), pp. 175–98 (p. 196).

6. Harry White, *The Keeper's Recital: Music and cultural history in Ireland, 1770–1970* (Cork: Cork University Press, 1998), p. 149.

7. Axel Klein, 'Roots and Directions in Twentieth-Century Irish Art Music', in Gareth Cox and Axel Klein (eds), *Irish Music in the Twentieth Century*, Irish Musical Studies Series 7 (Dublin: Four Courts Press, 2003), pp. 168–82.

8. Interview by the author with Mícheál Ó Súilleabháin, Newport, County Tipperary, 3 November 2016.

9. Ibid.

10. Liam Cagney, 'Metamorphoses in a New Millennium', in Michael Dervan (ed.), *The Invisible Art: A century of music in Ireland 1916–2016* (Dublin: New Island, 2016), pp. 217–38 (p. 229).

11. Sean Williams, 'Ó Súilleabháin, Mícheál', in Harry White and Barra Boydell (eds), *The Encyclopaedia of Music in Ireland*, vol. 2 (Dublin: UCD Press, 2013), pp. 811–12.

12. 'Mícheál Ó Súilleabháin Obituary: Exceptional musician who straddled classical and Irish traditional music', *The Irish Times*, 10 November 2018, https://www.irishtimes.com/life-and-style/people/micheal-o-suilleabhain-obituary-exceptional-musician-who-straddled-classical-and-irish-traditional-music-1.3692385 (accessed 10 March 2021).

13. Benjamin Dwyer, 'Irish Music in the 20th Century', *The Journal of Music in Ireland*, vol. 3, no. 6, September–October 2003, pp. 18–25 (p. 19).

14. Benjamin Dwyer, *Different Voices: Irish music and music in Ireland* (Hofheim: Wolke Verlag, 2014), p. 61.

15. Ó Súilleabháin, 'Crossroads or Twin Track?', p. 177.

16. Interview by the author with Mícheál Ó Súilleabháin.

17. Ó Súilleabháin, 'Crossroads or Twin Track?'

18. Ibid, p. 177.

19. Ibid.

20. Ibid.

21. Toner Quinn, 'A New Irish Musical Language is Developing', *The Journal of Music*, 10 October 2019, https://journalofmusic.com/focus/new-irish-musical-language-developing (accessed 10 March 2021).

17. Reflections from the Well *Mel Mercier*

1. Mícheál Ó Súilleabháin, interview with Mel Mercier (Dromore, Newport, County Tipperary), 6 October 2015.

2. *Peadar Mercier*, RTÉ *Doc on One*, produced by Mel Mercier with Liam Ó Brien, RTÉ Radio 1, 10 September 2016.

3. Ó Súilleabháin, interview.

4. Ibid.

5. Ibid.

6. A range of musical instruments, including bodhráns from the old and new worlds of the instrument, and drums of many shapes and sizes, including circular, square and diamond-shaped frame drums from many far-flung places, adorned the walls and shelves of Mícheál's office in University College Cork (UCC) and the music room in his home in Tipperary. I marvelled at how he could knock a sound out of them all, especially the bodhrán, from which, employing basic technique, he could elicit elemental rhythms.

7. A student of ethnomusicologist John Blacking, Nzewi was awarded his PhD in 1977 from Queen's University Belfast, where, ten years later, in 1987, Mícheál completed his own PhD dissertation on the music of Tommie Potts under the supervision of Blacking and John Baily.

8. Clement Chukuemeka Ezegbe, 'Igbo Ubo-aka: Its role and music among the Nri people of Nigeria', unpublished MA thesis, University of British Columbia, 1977.

9. Meki Nzewi, 'Melo-Rhythmic Essence and Hot Rhythm in Nigerian Folk Music', *The Black Perspective in Music*, vol. 2, no. 1, spring 1974, pp. 23–8.

10. Nóirín learned the song from Pilib Ó Laoghaire between 1967 and 1970 and she published the version in *Stór Amhrán: A wealth of songs from the Irish tradition* (Cork: Mercier Press, 1988), p. 28.

11. The trip was supported by the Indian embassy in Ireland.

12. Nóirín Ní Riain, personal communication, 2 January 2021.

13. Charles Acton, *The Irish Times*, 17 September 1979. Beginning with the line, 'Standards were the big problem about the Padraig [*sic*] Pearse Centenary Concert presented by Coiste Comóradh an Phiarsaigh at the Gaiety Theatre', Acton's review is fascinating and entertaining in equal measure. One of its most extraordinary passages is his critique of how the musicians presented themselves on stage: '… in the formal presence of our President … it seems inadequate to me that, while the keyboard player was in suit and colourful tie, shirt and footwear, the fiddler had an open-neck shirt, with (mostly) rolled up sleeves and not very well polished boots; the flute player had a tie but unbuttoned cuffs; the percussionist wore rolled up jeans and a shirt open to reveal his underwear'. On 17 September 2002, twenty-three years to the day after the review was published, I received a yellowed, signed and framed original copy of it from Mícheál, with the handwritten inscription, 'Mel – in future when you perform with me I would be most obliged if you would check your underwear …'.

14. Ó Súilleabháin, interview. Mícheál suggested that the performance may have been presented by the Listowel Players.

15. Ibid.

16. Ibid.

17. Ibid.

18. These are Mícheál's first published articles and, to my knowledge, the first papers about the bodhrán ever published.

19. Mícheál Ó Súilleabháin, 'The Bodhrán: Its history and construction', *Treoir: Journal of Comhaltas Ceoltóirí Éireann*, vol. 6, no. 2, 1974, pp. 4–7.

20. Mícheál Ó Súilleabháin, 'The Bodhrán: Traditional performance techniques', *Treoir: Journal of Comhaltas Ceoltóirí Éireann*, vol. 6, no. 5, 1974, pp. 6–10.

21. Ó Súilleabháin, interview.

22. Ibid.

23. In 1971, at the time of his death, Seán Ó Riada held the position of statutory (senior) lecturer in music at UCC.

24. Mícheál Ó Súilleabháin, 'Contemporary Developments in Bodhrán Performance Technique', *International Folk Music Council UK Committee Newsletter*, no. 27, 1981, pp. 12–14.

25. Mícheál Ó Súilleabháin, *The Bodhrán: A practical introduction* (Dublin: Waltons, 1984).

26. I am grateful to Olga Barry, the current director of Kilkenny Arts Festival (KAF), for retrieving the programme information from the KAF archives.

27. The programme note goes on to say: 'Mícheál Ó Súilleabháin is a senior lecturer in music at University College Cork. As a musician equally talented in the classical and traditional modes, he is unique in using the cosmopolitan piano to reproduce the traditional rhythms, percussive tone, accentuations and ornamentations of Irish music.'

28. Ó Súilleabháin, interview.

29. Ibid.

30. When I finished secondary school in 1979 I trained and worked in the field of digital telephony with the French company CIT Alcatel. In 1984 I left the company and went to work for the next two years as a volunteer with Dublin Simon Community and the Ana Liffey Drug Project.

31. My father and I performed four short, improvised bodhrán duets as part of the performance, playing for a total of twenty minutes over the course of the sixty-minute piece.

32. I was twenty-six years of age. As a mature student I was eligible for entry to the programme without having taken the Leaving Certificate music examination.

33. During my time at UCC (1986–2016), many students who identified themselves as traditional musicians also played classical, popular and non-western musics (and the same was true in reverse), and this is still the case today. When Mícheál introduced Mantle Hood's concept of 'bi-musicality' in his ethnomusicology lectures, he knew that he was holding up a mirror to many of his Cork students; see Mantle Hood, 'The Challenge of "Bi-Musicality"', *Ethnomusicology*, vol. 4, no. 2, May 1960, pp. 55–9.

34. I am grateful to Mary Mitchell-Ingoldsby for this information. Mícheál Ó Riabhaigh taught for just one year at UCC.

35. In 2015, when I was writing a short introduction to the online publication of a new collection of Connie's original tunes, *Bóithrín na Smaointe*, I asked Mícheál to recount the history of Connie's role as a fiddle tutor at UCC. My account here is based on what I wrote in that introduction. Connie O'Connell's *Bóithrín na Smaointe* (Cork: UCC, 2015) is available at http://epu.ucc.ie/connieoconnell.

36. Mel Mercier, 'About the Project', in Connie O'Connell, *Bóithrín na Smaointe* (Cork: UCC, 2015).

37. Ibid.

38. Ibid.

39. Paul Everett, one of Mícheál's colleagues at UCC, recalls that there were two similarly sized lecture rooms in the building: the 'Ó Riada Room' (named after Seán Ó Riada) on the ground floor and the 'Bax Room' (named after the composer Arnold Bax, who had served as external examiner in the 1970s) on the first floor.

40. In addition to the lectures that took place there, the 'Ó Riada Room' was often used as a practice, rehearsal and performance space.

41. Ó Riada's death mask was made by Cork sculptor Seamus Murphy.

42. Mary Mitchell-Ingoldsby was the uilleann pipes and tin whistle tutor at the Department of Music at this time, a position she took up in 1982. In 1999 she was appointed as lecturer in music, with primary teaching and research interests in Irish traditional music.

43. In 1990, while I was at CalArts, I travelled to Boston College where Mícheál was a visiting professor, to take part in the Boston College Irish Fiddle Festival. In that same

period, Mícheál came to Los Angeles where we performed a concert in Hollywood as part of a CalArts music festival.

44. 'Bagedi', a companion piece to 'Crispy', was composed in a similar fashion in the late 1990s, but we rarely performed it.

18. The Scholar's Harvest Home: Mícheál Ó Súilleabháin and the student experience of traditional music at third level
Sandra Joyce

1. Jack Talty, 'The Ivory Tower and the Commons: Exploring the institutionalisation of Irish traditional music in Irish higher education (discourse, pedagogy and practice)', unpublished PhD thesis, University of Limerick, 2019, https://researchrepository.ul.ie/articles/thesis/The_Ivory_tower_and_the_commons_exploring_the_institutionalisation_of_Irish_traditional_music_in_Irish_higher_education_discourse_pedagogy_and_practice_/19834171/1.

2. Ethical approval was sought and attained from the University of Limerick (UL), information letters were given to participants and consent forms were signed. I contacted five males and eight females, a gender balance reflective of my own experience as a student in the 1980s – my memory is that there were more females than males studying music in UCC at that time. Most are friends on social media platforms or who I am in contact with outside of my daily work at UL. In the case of some informants, I have not been in contact with them for many years, while others I have seen more regularly in formal (conferences, performances, for example) and informal, social contexts.

3. Heewon Chang, *Autoethnography as Method* (Walnut Creek, CA: Left Coast Press, 2008), p. 40.

4. Ibid., p. 52.

5. At the time, the Department of Music was based at the building called the Rectory, on Western Road, Cork.

6. A discussion of the history of music at UCC, as well as developments at this time in relation to the history and context of Irish traditional music at third level in Ireland, is beyond the scope of this paper, but see Talty, 'The Ivory Tower', pp. 24–7 and pp. 81–134 for a recent review of this area.

7. Ibid., pp. 89–90.

8. Harry White, *The Keeper's Recital: Music and cultural history in Ireland, 1770–1970* (Cork: Cork University Press, in association with Field Day, 1998), p. 149.

9. *Oxford English Dictionary* defines cult of personality as 'a collective obsession with, or intense, excessive, or uncritical admiration for, a particular public figure, esp. a political leader; the instigation of such an obsession', https://www.oed.com/search/dictionary/?scope=Entries&q=cult%20of%20personality.

10. Natalie S. Royston and Ryan A. Fisher, 'A Comparison of Collegiate Ensemble Members' Preferences of Teacher Interpersonal Behaviors', *Contributions to Music Education*, vol. 43, pp. 77–94 (p. 78), https://www.jstor.org/stable/26478000

11. Marie McCarthy, *Passing It On: The transmission of music in Irish culture* (Cork: Cork University Press, 1999), p. 139.

21. 'The Dolphin's Way': Mícheál Ó Súilleabháin's pioneering work at the Department of Music, University College Cork (1975–93)
Mary Mitchell-Ingoldsby

1. Documents held in the Irish Traditional Music Archive, Department of Music, UCC.

2. The Seán Ó Riada Collection/Bailiúchán Sheáin Uí Riada, Boole Library, UCC.

3. John Fitzpatrick, personal communication, March 2022.

4. Mícheál Ó Súilleabháin, speech 'Launch UCC Website: The fiddle compositions of Connie O'Connell', 26 March 2015, UCC, unpublished document.

5. Matt Cranitch, personal communication, March 2022.

6. Paul Everett, personal communication, February 2022.

7. Ibid.

8. Nóirín Ní Riain, personal communication, February 2022.

9. Taken from Mícheál Ó Súilleabháin's papers held at the Traditional Music Archive, Department of Music, UCC.

10. Mícheál Ó Súilleabháin, letter to Mrs Kathleen White, secretary, Cultural Relations Committee, Department of Foreign Affairs, Dublin, 2 and dated 3 March 1984, housed in the Traditional Music Archive, Department of Music, UCC.

11. Paul O'Donnell, personal communication, December 2020.

12. Nóirín Ní Riain, personal communication, February 2022.

13. Taken from Mícheál Ó Súilleabháin's papers held at the Traditional Music Archive, Department of Music, UCC.

14. My *Love is in America*, sleeve notes (Danbury, CT: Green Linnet Records, 1990).

15. Taken from Mícheál Ó Súilleabháin's papers held at the Traditional Music Archive, Department of Music, UCC.

16. Nicholas Carolan, personal communication, June 2022.

17. Paul McGettrick, 'Introduction', Ó Riada Memorial Lecture 1 (Cork: UCC, 1986). McGettrick was the auditor of the Irish Traditional Music Society from 1985 to '86.

18. George Cronin, *The Cork Examiner*, 6 January 1984.

19. Taken from Mícheál Ó Súilleabháin's papers held at the Traditional Music Archive, Department of Music, UCC.

20. Niall Vallely, personal communication, March 2022.

21. Taken from Mícheál Ó Súilleabháin's papers held at the Traditional Music Archive, Department of Music, UCC.

22. Mícheál Ó Súilleabháin, letter to Mícheál Walsh, cultural affairs officer, Federation of Irish Societies, Manchester and dated 5 December 1992.

23. Taken from Mícheál Ó Súilleabháin's papers held at the Traditional Music Archive, Department of Music, UCC.

24. *UCC Staff Newsletter*, located in Mícheál Ó Súilleabháin's papers held at the Traditional Music Archive, Department of Music, UCC.

25. Marian Ingoldsby, personal communication, December 2020.

26. Some of these included members of the editorial board: Annette de Foubert, Seán Ó Riada, Pilib Ó Laoghaire, Nóirín Ní Riain, Marie Neville and Mary Bollard. Helpers also included Sarah Collins and Helen Walsh.

27. Mícheál Ó Súilleabháin, 'Preface', in Aloys Fleischmann (ed.), Mícheál Ó Súilleabháin (assist. ed.) and Paul McGettrick (assoc. ed.), *Sources of Irish Traditional Music* (New York: Garland Publishing, 1998).

28. Mary McAleese, 'The Scholar', in Ruth Fleischmann (ed.), *Aloys Fleischmann (1910–92): A life for music in Ireland remembered by contemporaries* (Cork and Dublin: Mercier Press, 2000), pp. 252–4.

22. Mícheál Ó Súilleabháin, Ethnomusicology and Queen's University Belfast *John Baily*

1. A succinct biography of John Blacking can be found in Reginald Byron (ed.), *Music, Culture and Experience: Selected papers of John Blacking* (Chicago: University of Chicago Press, 1995), pp. 1–28.

24. Always Unfolding Knowing: Toyota Performing Arts Initiative as curriculum of event, cultural object and lived experience *Margaret O'Sullivan*

1. From a townland outside Doolin, the Russell family is celebrated for its music. Micho's mother was a concertina player and singer who lived into her nineties, and their father was a noted *sean-nós* singer. Micho was born in 1915, the first of five children. All three brothers were professional musicians, while it is not recorded whether their two younger sisters played or sang.

2. Carolyn Ellis, 'There Are Survivors: Telling a story of sudden death', *The Sociological Quarterly*, vol. 34, no. 4, 1993, pp. 711–30; Carolyn Ellis, *The Ethnographic I: A methodological novel about autoethnography* (Walnut Creek, CA: Altamira, 2004); Howard L. Goodall, *A Need to Know: The clandestine history of a CIA family* (Walnut Creek, CA: Left Coast Press, 2006).

3. Madeleine Grumet, 'The Politics of Presence', in Mary Aswell Doll (ed.), *The Reconceptualization of Curriculum Studies: A festschrift in honor of William F. Pinar* (New York: Routledge, 2016), pp. 76–83.

4. Ibid., p. 78.

5. Ibid., p. 81.

6. Madeleine Grumet, Amy Anderson and Chris Osmond, 'Finding Form for Curriculum Research', in Kathleen Gallagher (ed.), *The Methodological Dilemma: Creative, critical and collaborative approaches to qualitative research* (Abingdon, UK: Routledge, 2008), pp. 136–56.

7. Footage from the short film forms part of a half-hour documentary, *Dara Bán* (1997), subsequently commissioned by TG4, directed by Michael Ruane and produced by JDM

Productions, which can be viewed on YouTube: https://www.youtube.com/watch?v=VqHSIaLHx9c&t=1622s (1 December 2022).

8. The University of Limerick art trail booklet can be found here with information on its impressive collection: https://isb11dotcom.files.wordpress.com/2017/01/ul-art-trail.pdf. It contains no information on the huge model of Leonardo da Vinci's flying man, but there is a description of the second of two venetian glass mosaics created by Desmond Kinney, an evocation of the goddess Sionna, commissioned for the Irish World Academy of Music and Dance building. *Buile Shuibhne* in the atrium of the Foundation building is the mosaic mentioned here.

9. Events and experiences that formed the Toyota Performing Arts Initiative (1995–2000) are documented in *Bosca*, a limited-edition artbook designed by David Lilburn, with photos by Amelia Stein, and a CD of selected recordings.

10. David Lilburn (1950–2021) was a renowned artist working in the medium of print. See https://www.davidlilburn-archive.com for a repository of David Lilburn's work.

11. Grumet, 'The Politics of Presence', pp. 76–83.

12. Dylan Robinson, *Hungry Listening: Resonant theory for indigenous sound studies* (Minnesota, MN: University of Minnesota Press, 2020). Robinson uses the term 'inclusionary' to signal how indigenous musics and musicians have been structurally accommodated to 'fit' within classical music systems and contexts, without altering the structures themselves.

26. The CÉILÍ and the HOUSE OF LIGHT *Daniel Cordier*

1. Sinann is the goddess of the river Shannon in Ireland and the granddaughter of the sea god Lir. She is associated with Connla's Well, a mythical spring that is a source of inspiration and deep wisdom. Around the well grew nine hazel trees; the trees dropped hazelnuts into the well which were then eaten by the salmon there. Anyone who drank the water or ate the salmon or hazelnuts would receive wisdom and inspiration. In the usual story, Sinann approached the well but broke some (unknown) taboo, and the water rose up against her, drowning her and forming a river which was then named after her – the Shannon. As Sinann is the granddaughter of the sea god and would therefore be expected to have an affinity with water, it seems likely this is a patriarchal retelling; I have drawn on her then as the goddess of both the river and the well, and a goddess of that deep knowledge and wisdom symbolised by the well.

27. Of Our Times *David J. Elliott*

1. This piece was published as 'Introduction', *Of Our Times/Comhaimseartha*, autumn 2015, pp. 2–3.

2. See *The PIPA Report: Towards an institute of performing arts*, compiled by Professor Helen Phelan (Limerick: Irish World Academy, University of Limerick and the Irish Chamber Orchestra, 1996), which captured the essence of our conversations at the time and upon which the Irish World Academy was built.

3. Tia DeNora, *Music in Everyday Life* (Cambridge: Cambridge University Press, 2000), pp. 152–3.

28. Towards a National Ethnomusicology *John Morgan O'Connell*

1. This is a revised version of a paper presented at the Irish World Academy of Music and Dance (28 February 2018) to mark the twentieth anniversary of the MA in Ethnomusicology. In it I adopt a number of conventions. I represent Irish (traditional) music by placing the word 'traditional' in parenthesis cognisant of the fact that other classifications are used to represent this style (such as 'folk music' and 'ethnic music'). I am also aware that the terms 'traditional' and 'tradition' have been the subject of critical scrutiny. See, for example, Anthony McCann, 'A Tale of Two Rivers: *Riverdance*, *A River of Sound* and the ambiguities of "tradition"', in Diarmuid Ó Giolláin (ed.), *Irish Ethnologies* (Notre Dame, IN: University of Notre Dame Press, 2017), pp. 203–19. I assume that the field of ethnomusicology is widely understood to be an anthropology of music. However, the discipline acknowledges (especially in Europe) other academic fields such as music folklore and music ethnology.

2. The meeting was convened at the University of Limerick (22 February 2006). For a published report of this symposium, see John M. O'Connell, 'National Symposium: Towards a national ethnomusicology', *Bulletin of the International Council for Traditional Music*, vol. 109, 2006, pp. 61–2. For a published report of an international symposium on a related topic with respect to the European perspective, see John M. O'Connell, 'International Symposium in European Ethnomusicology', *Bulletin of the International Council for Traditional Music*, vol. 111, 2007, pp. 50–2. Significantly, the theme 'national ethnomusicologies' was the subject of a plenary session at the bi-annual world conference of the International Council for Traditional Music (ICTM) which was held in Vienna (4–11 July 2007).

3. ICTM Ireland was formally recognised as a national committee at a meeting of the ICTM Executive Board in Sheffield (2–3 August 2005). In fact, the first scheduled meeting of a national committee for ethnomusicology in Ireland occurred in conjunction with the bi-annual ICTM Colloquium, an international symposium which took place at the Hunt Museum in Limerick (3–6 September 2003). For a relevant report, see John M. O'Connell, 'The 15th ICTM Colloquium: Identifying conflict in music, resolving conflict through music', *Bulletin of the International Council for Traditional Music*, vol. 106, 2005, pp. 55–7. At another meeting of the national committee (19 February 2005) the anodyne name 'ICTM Ireland' was chosen specifically to obviate the anticipated sensitivities associated with the concept of a 'national committee' on the island of Ireland. It is noteworthy that ICTM Ireland is still thriving. For further information on ICTM Ireland see www.ictm.ie (accessed 30 December 2020).

4. Mícheál often employed the phrase 'parity of esteem' in his bid to establish an equality of opportunity for the 'traditional' and the 'classical' in Ireland. See also Mícheál Ó Súilleabháin, 'The Redress of Music: Music, mediation, and parity of esteem', *Yearbook for Traditional Music*, vol. 50, 2018, pp. 1–14.

5. Originally Mícheál aimed to establish a college of performing arts (abbreviated in the relevant documentation as 'COPA'). However, this vision was superseded by the establishment of the Irish World Academy of Music and Dance.

6. In his review of *The Melodic Tradition of Ireland* by James R. Cowdery (1990), Mícheál offers an overview of the oriental debate in Irish music citing Seán O Riada and Breandán Breathnach as principal exponents of this position. Although his review of Cowdery's monograph is not always complimentary, Mícheál also critiques Cowdery's comparative analysis of Indian and Irish tune families. See Mícheál Ó Súilleabháin, 'Review of *The Melodic Tradition of Ireland* by James R. Cowdery', *Ethnomusicology*, vol. 37, no. 1, 1993, pp. 109–12.

7. See Edward Said, *Orientalism* (New York: Pantheon Books, 1978) for a critical appraisal of orientalism and colonialism. See Joseph A. Lennon, *Irish Orientalism: A literary and intellectual history* (Syracuse, NY: Syracuse University Press, 2004) for an important discussion of orientalism in Irish literature. See John M. O'Connell, *Commemorating Gallipoli through Music: Remembering and forgetting* (Lanham, MD: Lexington Books, 2017) for a distinctive consideration of orientalism in Irish music. See John M. O'Connell, 'Sir William Jones: Welsh orientalist and comparative musicologist', in William J. Morgan and Fiona Bowie (eds), *Social Anthropologies of the Welsh: Past and present* (London: Royal Anthropological Institute, 2021) for a comparable study of orientalism in Welsh literature and music.

8. See, for example, James R. Cowdery, *The Melodic Tradition of Ireland* (Kent, OH: The Kent State University Press, 1990).

9. See, for example, Bob Quinn, *Atlantean: Ireland's north African and maritime heritage* (London: Quartet Books, 1986).

10. 'Celtitude' is a term used by Desi Wilkinson to describe the notion of 'Celticness' in the musical traditions of Brittany. See Desi Wilkinson, '"Celtitude", Professionalism and the Fest Noz in Traditional Music in Brittany', in Martin Stokes and Philip V. Bohlman (eds), *Celtic Modern: Music at the global fringe* (Lanham, MD: Scarecrow Press, 2003), pp. 219–56.

11. Drawn from the Geertzian notion of 'thick description'; see Clifford Geertz, 'Thick Description: Toward an interpretive theory of culture', in *The Interpretation of Cultures: Selected essays* (New York: Basic Books, 1973), pp. 3–30.

12. Martin Heidegger, *Sein und Zeit* (Tübingham: Max Niemeyer Verlag, 1927).

13. See, for example, David Cooper, *The Musical Traditions of Northern Ireland and its Diaspora: Community and conflict* (Farnham, Surrey: Ashgate, 2009).

14. Andrée Grau, personal communication, 5 September 2003.

15. As representative examples, the anthropologist Ronald Frankenberg with respect to Wales and the folklorist Richard Dorson with regard to Japan come to mind. See Ronald Frankenberg, *Village on the Border: A social study of religion, politics and football in a north Wales community* (London: Cohen & West, 1957) and Richard Dorson, *Folk Legends of Japan* (Rutland, VT: Charles E. Tuttle, 1962).

16. Henry Glassie, *Passing the Time in Ballymenone* (Bloomington, IN: Indiana University Press, 1982) and *Turkish Traditional Art Today* (Bloomington, IN: Indiana University Press, 1993).

17. Diarmuid Ó Giolláin (ed.), *Irish Ethnologies* (Notre Dame, IN: University of Notre Dame Press, 2017), p. 14.

18. Diarmuid Ó Giolláin, *Locating Irish Folklore: Tradition, modernity, identity* (Cork: Cork University Press, 2000), p. 5.

19. Gearóid Ó Crualaoich, 'Folkloristic-Ethnological Studies in Ireland', in Diarmuid Ó Giolláin (ed.), *Irish Ethnologies* (Notre Dame, IN: University of Notre Dame Press, 2017), pp. 75–89 (p. 81).

20. Ó Giolláin, *Irish Ethnologies*, p. 12.

21. Ibid., p. 13.

22. As the relevant *ICTM Bulletin* (no. 59, October, p. 3) attests, the expanded remit of the Council included 'folk, popular, classical and urban music', a wider definition of traditional music of which Ó Giolláin (*Locating Irish Folklore*) would have approved – that is, given his explicit recognition of popular culture and subaltern studies in his ground-breaking representation of Irish folklore. That being said, the designation 'folk music' was adopted by the Folk Music Society of Ireland, an organisation that continued for more than thirty years (1971–2003), the last issue of its journal *Éigse Cheol Tíre* appearing in 2001.

23. Béla Bartók, 'Comparative Music Folklore', in Benjamin Suchoff (ed.), *Béla Bartók Essays* (New York: St Martin's Press, 1976 [1919]), pp. 159–63.

24. See Aloys Fleischmann, (ed.) *Sources of Irish Traditional Music c. 1600–1855: An annotated catalogue of prints and manuscripts* (New York: Garland, 1998).

25. McCann, 'A Tale of Two Rivers'.

26. Ibid., p. 209.

27. Cowdery, *The Melodic Tradition*.

28. McCann, 'A Tale of Two Rivers', p. 216.

29. Ibid., p. 217.

30. Ó Giolláin, *Locating Irish Folklore*, p. 8.

29. Engaging Traditional Ears in the Irish World Academy's Ethnomusicology Programme *Susan H. Motherway*

1. *Riverdance* began as the Eurovision interval act in 1994 and evolved into a full dance show in 1995.

2. I met Mel Mercier and Mícheál Ó Súilleabháin while accompanying a friend to the open day at the Department of Music at UCC. They both encouraged me to give the entrance examination a try, noting their desire to have Irish traditional musicians on the programme. I was later awarded the Comhaltas Ceoltóirí Éireann student award for my performance at the entrance examination.

3. Festivals were presented under the title Éigse na Laoi.

4. This work was being premiered in Ireland ahead of its performance at the Seville Expo '92. It was later recognised as the precursor to *Riverdance*.

5. Society for Musicology in Ireland and the Anthropological Association of Ireland.

6. Mícheál Ó Súilleabháin, 'Innovation and Tradition in the Music of Tommie Potts', unpublished PhD thesis, Queen's University Belfast, 1987.

7. Mícheál Ó Súilleabháin, 'Creative Process in Irish Traditional Dance Music', in Gerard Gillen and Harry White (eds), *Irish Musical Studies 1: Musicology in Ireland* (Dublin: Irish Academic Press, 1990), pp. 117–30.

8. Mícheál Ó Súilleabháin, '"Traditional Ears": Perception and analysis in Irish traditional music', in Anne Clune (ed.), *Dear Far-Voiced Veteran: Essays in honour of Tom Munnelly* (Miltown Malbay, County Clare: Old Kilfarboy Society, 2007), pp. 249–76 (pp. 273–4).

9. Mícheál Ó Súilleabháin, 'The Singing Body', in Helen Phelan (ed.), *Anáil Dé/The Breath of God: Music, ritual and spirituality* (Dublin: Veritas, 2001), pp. 140–7.

10. See Mícheál Ó Súilleabháin, 'Crossroads or Twin Track? Innovation and tradition in Irish traditional music', in Fintan Vallely, Hammy Hamilton, Eithne Vallely and Liz Doherty (eds), *Crosbhealach an Cheoil, The Crossroads Conference 1996: Tradition and change in Irish traditional music* (Dublin: Whinstone Music, 1999), p. 179.

11. See Susan Motherway, *The Globalisation of Irish Traditional Music* (Farnham, Surrey: Ashgate Publications, 2013).

12. See Susan Motherway and John O'Connell, *Staged Folklore: The National Folk Theatre of Ireland 1968-1998* (Cork: Cork University Press, 2022).

30. Ethnochoreology and Traditional Dance in the Irish World Academy
Catherine E. Foley, Orfhlaith Ní Bhriain and Mats Melin

1. Catherine E. Foley, 'The Notion and Process of Collecting, Recording and Representing Irish Traditional Music, Song and Dance: The Muckross House Collection', in Therese Smith (ed.), *Ancestral Imprints: Histories of Irish traditional music and dance* (Cork: Cork University Press, 2012), pp. 107–17.

2. Catherine E. Foley, *Irish Traditional Step Dancing in North Kerry: A contextual and structural analysis* (book and accompanying DVD) (Listowel: North Kerry Literary Trust, 2012 [1988]); Catherine E. Foley, *Step Dancing in Ireland: Culture and history*, Ashgate Popular and Folk Music Series (Farnham, Surrey: Ashgate, 2013).

3. When offered the appointment, Mícheál encouraged me to take it, adding that if I didn't take it, he would not go down the dance route. Also, see Catherine E. Foley, 'Ethnochoreology', in Janet Sturman and J. Geoffrey Golson (eds), *The Sage Encyclopedia of Music and Culture* (print and electronic) (Thousand Oaks, CA: Sage Publications, 2019), pp. 844–6.

4. Catherine E. Foley, 'Maintaining, Redefining and Challenging Dance Boundaries: Irish traditional dance within third level education', in Catherine E. Foley (ed.), *At the Crossroads: Dance and Irish culture*, proceedings of 1st DRFI International Conference (Limerick: Dance Research Forum Ireland, 2007), pp. 63–70; Catherine E. Foley, 'The Roots and Routes of Irish Step Dancing: Issues of identity and participation in a global world', in Ian Russell and Chris Goertzen (eds), *Roots and Routes: Fiddle and dance studies around the North Atlantic 4* (Aberdeen: The Elphinstone Institute, University of Aberdeen, 2012), pp. 145–56.

5. Catherine E. Foley, 'Percussive Relations: An exploration of percussive dance at *Tráth na gCos* 2002', in Mick Moloney, J'aime Morrison and Colin Quigley (eds), *Close to the Floor: Irish dance from the boreen to Broadway* (Madison, WI: Macater Press, 2008), pp. 47–56.

6. The 2003 DRFI board of directors were: Catherine Foley (chair), Olive Beecher, Frank Hall, Gráinne McArdle, Risteárd Mac Aodha, Victoria O'Brien, Barbara O'Connor, Patrick O'Dea, Moira Ruff and Michael Seaver.

7. See Dance Research Forum Ireland, https://www.facebook.com/DanceResearchForum Ireland.

8. See Victoria O'Brien, *Memory Dance: The case for a national dance archive at the University of Limerick library. A feasibility report for Dance Research Forum Ireland* (Limerick: Dance Research Forum Ireland, 2009).

9. See Mícheál Ó Súilleabháin, 'The Redress of Music: Music, mediation and parity of esteem', *Yearbook for Traditional Music*, vol. 50, 2018, pp. 1–14.

10. See Catherine Foley, *The Sionna Set Dance: Newly commissioned set dance for the Sionna Festival of Music and Dance 2005* (Limerick: The Irish World Academy of Music and Dance, University of Limerick, 2007).

11. See Mats Melin, *One with the Music: Cape Breton step dancing tradition and transmission* (Sydney, Canada: Cape Breton University Press, 2015).

31. Music Education at the Irish World Academy
Jean Downey and Ernestine Healy

1. https://greenvillecottagesite.wordpress.com/2017/09/08/micheal-o-suilleabhaingrounded-with-vision.

2. Maoin Cheoil an Chláir homepage, http://homepage.eircom.net/~mcac (accessed 17 January 2021).

3. https://greenvillecottagesite.wordpress.com/2017/09/08/micheal-o-suilleabhain-grounded-with-vision.

4. Maoin Cheoil an Chláir homepage, http://homepage.eircom.net/~mcac/ (accessed 17 January 2021).

5. Ibid.

6. An Roinn Oideachais, *The Leaving Certificate Syllabus* (Dublin: Stationery Office, 1996), p. 11.

7. Marie McCarthy, *Passing It On: The transmission of music in Irish culture* (Cork: Cork University Press, 1999), p. 160.

8. The William V. Shannon Fellowship at Boston University was established in 1989 in memory of William Shannon to commemorate his dedication to education and to Ireland.

9. http://www.umuksoundfoundation.com (accessed 28 July 2022).

10. https://www.irishworldacademy.ie/wp-content/themes/IWA/pdf-flipbook/ (accessed 20 February 2021).

11. *The Late Late Show* is an Irish chat show produced by public service broadcaster Raidió Teilifís Éireann (RTÉ). It is screened live on Friday nights from September to May.

12. *A River of Sound* was a television series, a joint production by RTÉ and BBC Northern Ireland. It was written and devised by Mícheál Ó Súilleabháin, and Philip King and Nuala O'Connor from Hummingbird Productions.

13. *Junior Cycle Music*, page 6, https://www.curriculumonline.ie/Junior-cycle/Junior-Cycle-Subjects/Music.

14. Regina Murphy, 'On the Bestowing of Honorary Life Membership by the Society for Music Education in Ireland to: Mícheál Ó Súilleabháin – I gCónaí ag Cruthú, ag Casadh is ag Gaiseadh Idir Eatarthu', 8th Annual Conference of the Society for Music Education in Ireland, Royal Irish Academy of Music, Dublin, 2 November 2018, https://www.smei.ie/smei-events/8th-annual-conference

15. Ruth Fleischmann, *Aloys Fleischmann (1910–1992): A life for music in Ireland* (Cork: Mercier Press, 2000), p. 99.

32. Lighting the Fire: Perspectives on the development of the Classical String Performance programme at the Irish World Academy *Diane Daly and Ferenc Szűcs*

1. Patricia S. Campbell, 'Dalcroze Reconstructed: An application of music learning theory to the principles of Jaques-Dalcroze', in Darrel L. Walters and Cynthia Crump Taggart (eds), *Readings in Music Learning Theory* (Chicago: GIA Publications, 1989), pp. 301–15 (p. 304).

2. Darla Crispin, 'Artistic Research and the Musician's Vulnerability', *Musical Opinion*,vol. 132, 2009, pp. 25–7.

3. Wayne Bowman, 'Cognition and the Body: Perspectives from music education', in Liora Bresler (ed.), *Knowing Bodies, Moving Minds: Towards embodied teaching and learning* (Dordrecht: Kluwer Academic Publishers, 2004), pp. 29–50 (p. 41).

4. Andrew Mead, 'Bodily Hearing: Physiological metaphors and musical understanding', *Journal of Music Theory*, vol. 43, no. 1, 1999, pp. 1–19 (p. 15).

33. The MA Programme in Ritual Chant and Song: A mirror of a grand spirit *Edward Foley and Sr Sidonia Freedman*

1. The authors are grateful to Professor Helen Phelan for her aid in shaping this narrative, as well as long-time administrator and colleague Paula Dundon of the Academy.

2. For example, 'The "Unwritten" and "Written Transmission" of Medieval Chant and the Start-Up of Musical Notation', *The Journal of Musicology*, vol. 10, no. 2, 1992, pp. 131–91.

3. Walter Principe, 'Toward Defining Spirituality', *Studies in Religion/Sciences Religieuses*, vol. 12, no. 2, 1983, pp. 127–41 (pp. 135–7).

4. On this situation in the US, for example, see Derek Thomson, 'Elite Failure has Brought Americans to the Edge of an Existential Crisis', *The Atlantic* (September 2019), https://www.theatlantic.com/ideas/archive/2019/09/america-without-family-god-or-patriotism/597382/. This trend was signalled decades ago for the UK by Grace Davie in her *Religion in Britain since 1945: Believing without belonging* (Oxford: Blackwell, 1994); relevant to the Irish context, see David McClendon and Conrad Hackett, 'When People Shed Religious Identity in Ireland and Austria: Evidence from censuses', *Demographic Research*, vol. 31, no. 43, 2014, pp. 1297–310, https://www.demographic-research.org/volumes/vol31/43/31-43.pdf.

5. Lionel Abadia, 'Spirituality', in Bryan S. Turner (ed.), *The Wiley-Blackwell Encyclopedia of Social Theory*, 5 volumes (2017), https://doi.org/10.1002/9781118430873.est0373.

6. James Russell, *The Germanization of Early Medieval Christianity* (New York: Oxford University Press, 1994).

7. Patrick Wormald, 'The Venerable Bede and the "Church of the English"', in Stephen Baxter (ed.), *The Times of Bede: Studies in early English Christian society and its historian* (Oxford: Blackwell Publishing, 2006), pp. 207–28 (pp. 223–4).

8. See the final three chapters of Ian Bradley, *Celtic Christianity: Making myths and chasing dreams* (New York: St Martin's Press, 1999).

9. Edited by Olivia Cosgrove, Laurence Cox, Carmen Kuhling and Peter Mulholland (Newcastle upon Tyne: Cambridge Scholars, 2013); particularly useful for this discussion is Chapter 16 of that volume, Boozena Gierek's 'Celtic Spirituality in Contemporary Ireland', pp. 300–17.

10. Available online at https://www.youtube.com/watch?v=MHWfPHwXfR4 (accessed 2 December 2022).

11. Talal Asad, *Genealogies of Religion: Discipline and reasons of power in Christianity and Islam* (Baltimore and London: Johns Hopkins University Press, 1993), p. 57.

12. Catherine Bell, *Ritual: Perspectives and dimensions* (New York and Oxford: Oxford University Press, 1997), pp. 61–164.

13. Richard Schechner, 'From Ritual to Theatre and Back: The structure/process of the efficacy-entertainment dyad', *Educational Theatre Journal*, vol. 26, no. 4, 1974, pp. 455–81.

14. See Edward Foley, 'Ritual Theory', in Bonnie Miller McLemore (ed.), *Wiley-Blackwell Companions to Religion: A companion to practical theology* (Oxford: Blackwell Publishing, 2012), pp. 143–52.

15. Catherine Bell, 'Ritual [Further Considerations]', in Lindsay Jones (ed.), *Encyclopedia of Religion*, 2nd edn, vol. 11 (Detroit: Macmillan Reference United States, 2005), p. 2849.

16. Ibid.

34. Music Therapy at the Irish World Academy: A 'lobal' reflection *Tríona McCaffrey and Jane Edwards*

1. Jane Edwards and Simon Gilbertson, 'Exploring Resistance and Change in Music Therapy Learning', in Karen Goodman (ed.), *International Perspectives in Music Therapy Education and Training: Adapting to a changing world* (Springfield, IL: Charles C. Thomas, 2015), pp. 219–41.

2. Jane Edwards (ed.) *Music: Promoting health and creating community in healthcare contexts* (Cambridge: Cambridge Scholars Publishing, 2009).

3. Irish term for 'Music Medicine'.

4. Hilary Moss, 'Global Community Engagement through Online Skill Sharing and Music Therapy Education', unpublished PhD thesis, University of Limerick, 2020.

5. Tríona McCaffrey, Katrina McFerran, Gustavo Gattino and Sumathy Sundar, 'The Global Music Therapy Educators Network', *British Journal of Music Therapy*, vol. 34, no. 2, 2020, pp. 80–1, https://doi.org/10.1177/1359457520969322.

35. Mícheál Ó Súilleabháin: 'Ah, sweet dancer' *Mary Nunan*

1. The title for this essay, 'Ah, Sweet Dancer', is a reference to a composition by Mícheál Ó Súilleabháin (*Oileán/Island*, Virgin Records, 1989).

2. 'Mícheál Ó Súilleabháin, Director, Irish World Academy of Music and Dance, University of Limerick', in Deirdre Mulrooney, *Irish Moves: An illustrated history of dance and physical theatre in Ireland* (Dublin: The Liffey Press, 2006), pp. 228–32 (p. 228).

3. The MA Dance Performance consisted of independent streams – MA Contemporary Dance Performance and MA Irish Traditional Dance Performance.

4. Aoife McGrath, *Dance Theatre in Ireland: Revolutionary moves* (Houndmills: Palgrave, 2013); Aoife McGrath and Emma Meehan (eds), *Dance Matters in Ireland: Contemporary dance performance and practice* (Cham: Palgrave Macmillan, 2018); Mulrooney, *Irish Moves*; Diane Theodores (ed.), *Dancing on the Edge of Europe: Irish choreographers in conversation* (Cork: Institute of Choreography and Dance, 2003).

5. McGrath and Meehan, *Dance Matters in Ireland*, p. 4.

6. Diane Theodores, 'Choreographers Under Cover: An introduction', in *Dancing on the Edge of Europe*, pp. 16–32 (p. 20).

7. Mulrooney, *Irish Moves*.

8. Dance Ireland, *Dance Ireland: Our story. The history of Dance Ireland from its establishment in 1989 to the present day* (Dublin: Dance Ireland, 2019), https://www.danceireland.ie/content/pubs/Dance_Ireland_History_2019.pdf (accessed November 2020).

9. Gilles Deleuze and Felix Guattari, *A Thousand Plateaus: Capitalism and schizophrenia*, translated by Brian Massumi (Minneapolis: University of Minnesota Press, 1980), cited in Mary Nunan, *The Dance of the Poetic and the Practical (Reflections on Dance-in-Education in Ireland* (2016), http://artsineducation.ie/wp-content/uploads/The-Dance-of-the-Poetic-and-the-Practical.pdf (accessed 10 November 2020).

10. Peter Brinson, *The Dancer and the Dance: Developing dance theatre in Ireland* (Dublin: Arts Council of Ireland, 1985), http://www.artscouncil.ie/uploadedFiles/Main_Site/Content/Research_and_Publications/Dance/The_Dancer_and_the_Dance.pdf (accessed 10 November 2020).

11. Daghdha Dance Company was based at the University of Limerick from 1988 to '99. Mary Nunan was its founder, artistic director and principal choreographer. During her tenure the company's distinctive artistic identity received much recognition nationally and internationally. The success of the company during this time was reflected, in part, by the steady increase in Arts Council funding from £6,000 in 1988 to a three-year funding commitment of £1 million in 1999. Yoshiko Chuma was artistic director from 1999 to 2002 and Michael Kliën from 2002 to 2011. The company ceased operating in 2011 due to the loss of public funding.

12. Dance Ireland, *Dance Ireland: Our story*.

13. Teresa Leahy was a passionate advocate for dance education. She established an MA (part-time) in Dance at Thomond College in the late 1980s. It was she who sourced the Arts Council's funding for the first dancer-in-residence position in Ireland.

14. Anne Leatherdale and Victoria Todd, *Shall We Dance: A report on vocational dance training in Ireland* was commissioned by The Arts Council/An Chomhairle Ealaíon in collaboration with the Arts Council Northern Ireland (Dublin: The Arts Council, 1998).

15. Judson Dance Theatre was a collective of avant-garde experimentalists (dancers, composers and visual artists in New York City, 1962–4). Yvonne Rainer and Steve Paxton, two of the most iconic artists associated with Judson, were guest artists on the MA.

16. White Space was an initiative set up in 2000 by Yoshiko Chuma (artistic director of Daghdha Dance Company) and Mary Nunan (course director MA Contemporary Dance Performance). It comprised a series of curated events: performances, workshops and

seminars presented by prestigious artists including Rosemary Butcher, Lisa Nelson, Steve Paxton and Yvonne Rainer.

17. Mícheál Ó Súilleabháin, personal communication, 10 October 2000.

18. Dunne was a nine-times world champion Irish dancer and principal male lead in *Riverdance: The Show* from 1995 to '98.

19. Mulrooney, *Irish Moves*, p. 231.

20. Colin Dunne, interview with Mary Nunan, 11 November 2020.

21. Ibid.

22. Ibid.

23. Dunne was nominated for the UK Critics' Circle National Dance Award and an Olivier Award for this solo choreography.

24. Dunne's solo show, based on the music of Tommie Potts, won the 2018 TG4 Gradam Ceoil for Musical Collaboration with Sinéad Rushe and Mel Mercier.

25. Colin Dunne, interview.

36. Conferring the Céilí: Irish traditional music programmes at the Irish World Academy *Niall Keegan*

1. For an interesting discussion of the engagement of a folk tradition with one of the more problematic constructs, 'the mainstream', see Simon Keegan-Phipps, 'Folk for Art's Sake: English folk music in the mainstream milieu', *Radical Musicology*, vol. 4, 2009, http://www.radical-musicology.org.uk/2009/Keegan-Phipps.pdf

2. It is beyond the scope of this essay to examine the nature of 'formal' and 'informal' modes of learning but in this context it is certainly worthy of further work, drawing on (among others) the contributions of Lucy Green. See Green, *Music, Informal Learning and the School: A new classroom pedagogy* (Farnham, Surrey: Ashgate, 2008).

3. See Etienne Wenger, *Communities of Practice* (Cambridge: Cambridge University Press, 1998).

4. For the purposes of this paper, I will use the term 'academy' to describe third-level education more generally, and 'the Academy' when referring specifically to the Irish World Academy of Music and Dance.

5. Bruno Nettl, *The Western Impact on World Music: Change, adaptation and survival* (New York: Schirmer, 1985); Jonathan Stock, 'Peripheries and interfaces: The western impact on other music', in Nicholas Cook and Anthony Pople (eds), *The Cambridge History of Twentieth-Century Music* (Cambridge: Cambridge University Press, 2004), pp. 18–39.

6. Jasmine Hornabrook, 'Cultural Engagement, Intercultural Musical Exchange and Dialogue in "Songs of the Saints: Tamil Traditions and New Creativities"', *The World of Music – Sharing Space? Sharing Culture? Applied experiments in music-making across borders*, vol. 7, nos 1/2, 2018, pp. 135–54.

7. Juniper Hill, 'The Influence of Conservatory Folk Music Programmes: The Sibelius Academy in comparative context', *Ethnomusicology Forum*, vol. 18, no. 2, 2009, pp. 207–41.

8. See Tomás Ó Canainn, *Seán Ó Riada: His life and work* (Cork: Collins Press, 2003); Mícheál Ó Súilleabháin, 'Ceol na nUasal: Seán Ó Riada and the search for a native Irish art music', *Ó Riada Memorial Lecture* 15 (University College Cork: Traditional Music Archive and Irish Traditional Music Society, 2004); Harry White, *The Keeper's Recital: Music and cultural history in Ireland, 1770–1970* (Cork: Cork University Press, 1998).

9. Other researchers included piper Brendan Ring, whose research was on the contemporary 'travelling style' piper Paddy Keenan: see Brendan Ring, 'Travelling Style: The uilleann piping of Paddy Keenan', unpublished MA thesis, University College Cork, 1992; whistle player Damhnait Nic Suibhne whose research was on the repertoire of the Donegal fiddle tradition: see Damhnait Nic Suibhne, 'Repertoire in the Donegal Fiddle Tradition', unpublished master's thesis, University College Cork, 1993; fiddle and concertina player Colette Moloney who worked on the eighteenth- and nineteenth-century Bunting manuscripts: see Colette Moloney, 'An Edition of the Bunting Manuscripts', unpublished PhD thesis, University of Limerick, 1995.

10. Hill, "The Influence of Conservatory Folk Music Programmes', p. 222.

11. In the chronology of the development of programmes at the Academy, those in traditional music and dance performance came later in the process, after programmes in ethnomusicology, ethnochoreology, classical string performance, music education and ritual chant.

12. Gerry Moriarty, 'Rivers of Dissent', *The Irish Times*, 15 August 1995, p. 6.

13. Seamus Tansey, 'Irish Traditional Music, the Melody of Ireland's Soul: Its evolution from the environment, land and people', in Fintan Vallely, Hammy Hamilton, Eithne Vallely and Liz Doherty (eds), *Crosbhealach an Cheoil, The Crossroads Conference 1996: Tradition and change in Irish traditional music* (Dublin: Whinstone Music, 1999), pp. 212–13.

14. For example, see Barra Boydell, 'Third-Level Music and the Leaving Certificate', *Journal of Music in Ireland*, July/August 2001, pp. 14–16.

15. Cork School of Music at Munster Technological University, the Conservatoire at Technological University Dublin and the Royal Irish Academy of Music.

16. See Niall Keegan, 'Literacy as a Transmission Tool in Irish Traditional Music', in Patrick F. Devine and Harry White (eds), *Irish Musical Studies 4: The Maynooth International Musicological Conference 1995. Selected proceedings, part one* (Dublin: Four Courts Press, 1996), pp. 335–42; Matt Cranitch, 'The Sliabh Luachra "Code"', in *Irish Musical Studies 4: The Maynooth International Musicological Conference 1995. Selected proceedings, part one*, pp. 343–53.

17. Hill, 'The Influence of Conservatory Folk Music Programmes', p. 216.

18. Ibid., p. 208.

19. See Fintan Vallely, 'Authenticity to Classicisation: The course of revival in Irish traditional music', *The Irish Review (Cork): Global Ireland*, no. 33, 2005, pp. 51–69.

20. Damhnait Nic Suibhne, 'The Donegal Fiddle Tradition, an Ethnographic Perspective', in William Nolan, Liam Ronayne and Mairead Dunlevy (eds), *Donegal: History and society. Interdisciplinary essays on the history of an Irish county* (Dublin: Geography Publications, 1995), pp. 713–42 (pp. 721–3).

21. Juniper Hill, 'Rebellious Pedagogy, Ideological Transformation, and Creative Freedom in Finnish Contemporary Folk Music', *Ethnomusicology*, vol. 53, no. 1, 2009, pp. 86–114.

22. Hill, 'The Influence of Conservatory Folk Music Programmes', p. 236.

37. Community Music in the Irish World Academy: Opening, inspiration, rupture *Kari K. Veblen and Kathleen Turner*

1. Mícheál Ó Súilleabháin, 'The Redress of Music: Music, mediation and parity of esteem', *Yearbook for Traditional Music*, vol. 50, 2018, pp. 1–14 (pp. 7–8), https://*doi*.org/*10.5921/yeartradmusi.50.2018.0001*.

2. Mullen was joined in organising the seminars by colleagues Caoimhe O'Shea, Georgette Mulheir (MA Ethnomusicology student at UL), and with encouragement from Veblen and Elliott. There was support and participation from both arts councils from Northern Ireland and the Republic of Ireland, representatives of many arts organisations, and local musicians. The Irish World Music Centre, as it was initially titled, donated space, staff and resources.

3. Kari K. Veblen, CMA proposal and curriculum for University of Limerick (1998).

4. Hala Jaber, personal communication, 2020.

5. Stephen Ryan, personal communication, 2020.

6. Jean Downey, personal communications in 2020 and 2022.

7. Lee Higgins was the first community music doctoral graduate from the Academy (supervised by Patricia Shehan Campbell and Helen Phelan); other graduates of the programme who have completed doctoral research include Kathleen Turner (current course director, supervised by Helen Phelan), Fran Garry and Hala Jaber (both currently postdoctoral researchers working with Phelan on community music and migrant research).

8. Phil Mullen, personal communication, 2020.

9. Lee Higgins, 'Towards Community Music Conceptualizations', in Huib Schippers and Nina Kors (eds), *Proceedings of the 2002 ISME Commission on Community Music Activity* (Rotterdam: NK, 2012), p. 7, https://blogs.bu.edu/higginsl/files/2009/11/higgins-Towards-CM-Conceptualizations1.pdf (accessed 6 June 2022).

10. Mícheál Ó Súilleabháin, '"Around the house and mind the cosmos": Music, dance and identity in contemporary Ireland', in Richard Pine (ed.), *Music in Ireland 1848–1998: Thomas Davis Lectures* (Dublin: Mercier Press, 1998), pp. 76–86.

11. Helen Phelan, Jean Downey and Mícheál Ó Súilleabháin were all involved at early stages of the programme's development for County Clare, through music school Maoin Cheoil an Chláir. Phelan was later commissioned to develop County Clare's bid for Music Generation partnership, working closely with Sean Conlan, education officer with the Clare Vocational Education Committee. Many Music Generation facilitators in Limerick and Clare are graduates of the MA Community Music, including Limerick County's Music Generation coordinator, Patrick O'Brien.

12. Led by Alicia de Banffy Hall (Katholische Universität Eichstätt-Ingolstadt, Germany) in association with Kathleen Turner (University of Limerick), Lee Willingham (Wilfrid Laurier University, Canada) and Lee Higgins (York St John's University, UK).

13. The students from the community music programme at the Katholische Universität Eichstätt-Ingolstadt in Germany collaborate online with their cohorts from the Irish World Academy of Music and Dance, the International Centre of Community Music at York St John's University in the UK, and Wilfrid Laurier University in Canada. Building organically on smaller digital projects, in November 2020 participants from all four institutions met online for three days of community music research. The seminars provided students with the opportunity to 'meet', support each other in their research, and to hear

from international voices in the field such as Te Oti Rakena (New Zealand) and Gerard Yun (Canada).

14. Community Music Ireland was established as a website and Facebook page by practitioner Paul Facey Hunter to host news and events of activities in Ireland. The provision of the website and Facebook group has been kindly passed to the Academy, but not further developed. While both the CM Ireland website and the CM in Ireland symposium galvanised interest and enthusiasm, it has become clear that the provision of both a virtual and a live space for CM professionals in Ireland requires its own specific energy and staff. This is an ambition for the Academy to support in the future.

15. Ó Súilleabháin, 'The Redress of Music', p. 1.

38. Moving Song: Reflections on the BA Voice and Dance *Jennifer de Brún, Hannah Fahey and Óscar Mascareñas*

1. Commemorated as one of the eminent dance pedagogues of the nineteenth and twentieth centuries and founder of this renowned method of ballet training, Enrico Cecchetti's illustrious dance career traversed some of the most celebrated and decisive periods of ballet history, including the bravura tradition in Italy, Petipa's Imperial Ballet and Diaghilev's Ballet Russes; see Toby Bennett, 'The Articulate Lower Leg: An exploration into the effects of changes of jumping technique in ballet', *Proceedings, Society of Dance History Scholars, Twenty-Sixth Annual Conference, University of Limerick, Limerick, Ireland, 26–29 June 2003* (Stoughton, WI: The Printing House, 2003), pp. 1–7.

2. Fidget Feet Aerial Dance Theatre, *Fidget Feet 20 Year Anniversary Booklet* (Limerick: Self-published, 2018).

3. The Irish Aerial Creation Centre is an aerial dance training and performance space located in the Old Burlington Industrial Estate, Gillogue, Corbally, County Clare, Ireland, https://irishaerialcreationcentre.com/professionals/creative-intensive (accessed 2 April 2019).

4. Currently I teach modules in aerial dance to students at the Irish Aerial Creation Centre.

5. Jennifer de Brún, 'Ilchruthach (Shapeshifter): An autoethnographic examination of self-defined movement identity in aerial dance and aerial circus in Ireland', unpublished PhD thesis, University of Limerick, 2021.

6. Jenny Roche, 'Embodying Multiplicity: The independent contemporary dancer's moving identity', *Research in Dance Education*, vol. 12, no. 2, 2011, pp. 105–18; Jenny Roche, *Multiplicity, Embodiment and the Contemporary Dancer: Moving identities* (London: Palgrave Macmillan, 2015).

7. 'Ilchruthach', in Niall Ó Dónaill (ed.), *Foclóir Gaeilge–Béarla* (1977), https://www.teanglann.ie/en/fgb/ilchruthach (accessed 29 February 2020).

8. Scott Harrison and Jessica O'Bryan, 'Positioning Singing in the Twenty-First Century', in Scott Harrison and Jessica O'Bryan (eds), *Teaching Singing in the 21st Century* (New York: Springer, 2014), pp. 1–9; Matthew Hoch, 'Historical Landmarks in Singing Voice Pedagogy', *Voice and Speech Review*, vol. 13, no. 1, 2019, pp. 61–76.

9. Hannah Fahey, 'Stylistic Pluralism and the Experiences of Classically Trained Teachers of Singing in the Republic of Ireland', *International Journal of Music Education*, vol. 39, no. 3, 2021, pp. 301–12.

10. Frank Heneghan, 'Music in Irish Education', in Gerard Gillen and Harry White (eds), *Music and Irish Cultural History* (Dublin: Irish Academic Press, 1995), pp. 153–98; Marie McCarthy, *Passing It On: The transmission of music in Irish culture* (Cork: Cork University Press, 1999).

11. BaVaD – Mícheál used to write the acronym for BA Voice and Dance in this way.

12. During the promotion of the programme, Mícheál spoke about it being a space for ten singers and ten dancers (as the projected number was twenty), who would come together to learn from each other's disciplines and create new interdisciplinary work for voice and dance. The first year there were eighteen students: fifteen singers and three dancers.

13. Opening lines of the four-part song *Chacona* by Juan Arañés (Catalunya, seventeenth century). 'A feast of the chacona / took place in the month of the roses / a thousand things happened / and fame heralds it'. The poem also features lines from the chorus, '*A la vida, vidita bona, Vida vámonos a chacona*': 'To life, the good life, Life let's go to chacona'. This and other songs featured in this poem were taught to students of the BA Voice and Dance programme as part of the western choral and Latin-American song classes.

14. '*Ay de mí, Llorona*', 'Woe to me, *Llorona*', from *La Llorona*, a traditional Mexican song from Oaxaca, Mexico. (One two three / Five six seven) refers to the counting of steps in Latin-American dance class. 'Te vas Alfonsina / con tu soledad'; 'Off you go Alfonsina, with your solitude', from *Alfonsina y el mar*, a song by Alfonsina Storni, Ariel Ramírez and Félix Luna. 'O' is the first word of the antiphon O *cruor sanguinis*, written by Hildegard von Bingen, a German abbess from the twelfth century. '*Iustus ut palma florebit*', 'The righteous like the palm tree shall flourish', from the Gregorian chant *Alleluia V. Iustus ut palma.*

15. 'And like the cedar [s/he / it] shall grow', from *Alleluia V. Iustus ut palma.*

16. From the poem *Canción*, written by Cuban poet Nicolás Guillén. The poem became the lyrics of the song '*De qué callada manera*' composed by Cuban singer-songwriter Pablo Milanés. The two lines featured in section XIV respectively translate as 'In such a quiet way' / 'and with such a delicate touch'.

17. '*Te doy una canción*' is the title of a song by Cuban singer-songwriter Silvio Rodríguez. It translates as 'I give you a song', which, in the context of the present work represents an offering, a memorial, a homage. The line 'of our times' is written in reference to the Irish World Academy of Music and Dance brochure *Comhaimseartha/Of Our Times*, which is published twice every year. To my knowledge, Mícheál was very proud and fond of such a publication, and in the context of this poem its name is used to represent all life and existence in times present and gone. *33 minutes 4 seconds* refers to the performance titled *33' 04" for John Cage* which was presented as a homage to Cage during the year that marked the centenary of his birth. It was performed by fourth-year students of the BA Voice and Dance programme at the Academy in May 2012. The title refers to Cage's seminal work *4' 33"*.

39. Mícheál Ó Súilleabháin: My personal psychopomp *Carl Corcoran*

1. *The Blue of the Night* is a late-night eclectic mix of music broadcast weeknights on Ireland's arts and culture radio station RTE Lyric FM, https://www.rte.ie/radio/lyricfm. Carl curated and presented the programme for ten years from 2007 to '17.

2. Blas is a two-week summer school of music, song and dance hosted annually by the Irish

World Academy of Music and Dance at the University of Limerick, http://www.blas.ie (accessed 2 December 2022).

3. *A Drop of the Irish* was a weekly magazine programme produced and presented by Carl Corcoran for five years, 1994–8, on WTBQ, a local radio station in Orange County, New York.

4. The 'Oíche Nollag' track was also featured on Mícheál Ó Súilleabháin's CD *The Dolphin's Way*, https://www.qobuz.com/ie-en/album/the-dolphins-way-micheal-o-suilleabhain/5099951319458.

5. https://www.irishchamberorchestra.com/about/history (accessed 2 December 2022).

6. For details of the course curriculum, see https://www.irishworldacademy.ie/programmes/postgraduate/ma-songwriting (accessed 2 December 2022).

40. Between Worlds: Being, becoming and belonging
Mary Louise O'Donnell and Matthew James Noone

1. Ruth Levitas, *The Concept of Utopia* (Syracuse, NY: Syracuse University Press, 1990), p. 8.

2. Tom Moylan, *Demand the Impossible: Science fiction and the utopian imagination* (New York: Methuen, 1986), pp. 1–2.

3. Mícheál Ó Súilleabháin, 'Irish Music Defined', *The Crane Bag*, vol. 5, no. 2, 1981, pp. 83–7.

4. These harpers included Máire Ní Chathasaigh, Janet Harbison, Noreen O'Donoghue and Laoise Kelly.

5. Joan Rimmer, *The Irish Harp* (Cork: Mercier Press, 1969). Rimmer's most impressive and influential research can be found in her contributions to journals and collected editions; see Rimmer, 'The Morphology of the Irish Harp', *The Galpin Society Journal*, vol. 17, February 1964, pp. 39–49; 'Patronage, Style and Structure in the Music Attributed to Turlough Carolan', *Early Music*, vol. 15, no. 2, 1987, pp. 164–74; and 'Harp Repertoire in Eighteenth-Century Ireland: Perceptions, misconceptions and reworkings', in Martin van Schaik (ed.), *Proceedings of the International Harp Symposium, Utrecht 1992* (Utrecht: STIMU Foundation for Historical Performance Practice, 1994), pp. 73–85.

6. Janet Harbison, 'Harpists, Harpers or Harpees?', in Fintan Vallely, Hammy Hamilton, Eithne Vallely and Liz Doherty (eds), *Crosbhealach an Cheoil, The Crossroads Conference 1996: Tradition and change in Irish traditional music* (Dublin: Whinstone Music, 1999), pp. 94–100. In this essay Harbison classified performers on Irish harp as follows: the 'singing harpee' who performs in 'stage-Irish tourist-oriented cabarets'; the 'hippy harper' who plays dance tunes and frequents festivals and fleadhs; and the 'classical harpist' who performs 'in more formal surrounds with the background training of a classical musician reading from texts'.

7. For a stimulating account of the transformative possibilities of a liminal space in making and experiencing music, see June Boyce Tillman, 'The Transformative Qualities of a Liminal Space Created by Musicking', *Philosophy of Music Education Review*, vol. 17, no. 2, 2009, pp. 184–202.

8. Abraham H. Maslow, 'A Theory of Human Motivation', *Psychological Review*, vol. 50, no. 4, 1943, pp. 370–96.

9. See Mary Louise O'Donnell, 'The Anglicisation of the Irish Harp: A history of the Irish harp from 1800 to the present day', unpublished MA thesis, University College Dublin, 1999.

10. I was the recipient of several awards and bursaries, including an Irish Research Council for the Humanities and Social Sciences postgraduate award and postdoctoral fellowship, a grant from the Society for Musicology in Ireland (2012), an Ireland Canada University Foundation Dobbin Scholarship (2014), Fulbright Scholar Award (2019) and a fellowship to research at the Old Library and Historical Archives of the Centre Culturel Irlandais (2019).

11. Irish Research Council for the Humanities and Social Sciences is now known as the Irish Research Council (IRC).

12. Seamus Heaney, *The Burial at Thebes: A version of Sophocles' Antigone* (London: Faber & Faber, 2004).

13. Mícheál Ó Súilleabháin, 'An Island Sound: Reflections on music, politics and identity in contemporary Ireland', in Robert Savage Jr (ed.), *Ireland in the New Century: Politics, culture and identity* (Dublin: Four Courts Press, 2003), pp. 189–97 (p. 192).

14. Matthew Noone, 'North Indian Classical Music and the Kolkata Experience: Alchemical schismogenesis and being-in-the world in a musical way', *Ethnomusicology Ireland*, vol. 2, no. 3,
2013, pp. 22–37.

15. Mícheál Ó Súilleabháin, interview with Matthew Noone, Irish World Academy of Music and Dance, 2013.

16. Ibid.

17. Matthew 'Mattu' Noone, 'The Mongrel Metaphor: An arts practice response to understanding musical hybridization', *Ethnomusicology Ireland*, vol. 4, 2016, pp. 1–23.

18. Mike Crang, 'Qualitative Methods: Touchy, feely, look-see?', *Progress in Human Geography*, vol. 27, no. 4, 2003, pp. 494–504.

19. Mícheál Ó Súilleabháin, 'An Island Sound', pp. 193 and 196.

20. John Blacking, *How Musical Is Man?* (Seattle: University of Washington Press, 1973), p. 6.

21. Mícheál Ó Súilleabháin, 'The Creative Process in Irish Traditional Dance Music', in Gerard Gillen and Harry White (eds), *Irish Musical Studies: Musicology in Ireland* (Dublin: Irish Academic Press, 1990), pp. 117–30 (p. 120).

22. Ibid., p. 130.

23. Mícheál Ó Súilleabháin, '"Around the house and mind the cosmos": Music, dance and identity in contemporary Ireland', in Richard Pine (ed.), *Music in Ireland: 1848–1998* (Cork: Mercier Press, 1998), pp. 76–86 (p. 74).

24. In fact, the idea that there is a connection between Ireland, Indian music and the 'Orient' has its origins long before Ó Riada. See Aileen Dillane and Matthew Noone, 'Irish Music Orientalism', *New Hibernia Review*, vol. 20, no. 1, 2016, pp. 121–37.

25. He argues that Bunting's manuscripts are evidence that the harping tradition in ancient court life 'was not harmonically based at all but … found its logic in the melodic line itself: see Mícheál Ó Súilleabháin, 'Crossroads or Twin Track? Innovation and tradition in Irish

traditional music', in Fintan Vallely, Hammy Hamilton, Eithne Vallely and Liz Doherty (eds), *Crosbhealach an Cheoil, The Crossroads Conference 1996: Tradition and change in Irish traditional music* (Dublin: Whinstone Music, 1999), pp. 175–98 (p. 179). In particular he has suggested that the melody of 'The Dark Slender Boy' lends itself to an improvised modal structure more so than a dance tune.

26. He has composed pieces with sitar and used tambura drones to accompany an alap-style introduction in *Still Point of the Turning World* and appropriated Indian rhythms with Mel Mercier in the piece '(must be more) Crispy'.

27. Mícheál Ó Súilleabháin, '"All our central fire": Music, mediation and the Irish psyche', *The Irish Journal of Psychology*, vol. 15 nos 2 & 3, 1994, pp. 331–53, (p. 346).

28. Mícheál Ó Súilleabháin, 'An Island Sound', p. 192.

29. Seamus Heaney, *The Spirit Level: Poems* (New York: Macmillan, 1997), p. 3.

30. Matthew James Noone, '(De)composing the Mongrel: Improvisation and the (un) known', *Performance Research*, vol. 26, no. 2, 2022, pp. 104–9.

41. The Grace of His Teaching: Lessons from Mícheál Ó Súilleabháin *Patricia Shehan Campbell*

1. This essay reflects my collegial interactions with Mícheál and some of his students over the course of twenty years of external examining activity at the Irish World Academy of Music and Dance. I was also informed by the podcast 'Between Worlds: The life of Mícheál Ó Súilleabháin', produced by Padraic Flaherty, Clare FM, 1 January 2021; Toner Quinn, 'Mícheál Ó Súilleabháin's Example Will Continue to Inspire', *The Journal of Music*, 8 November 2018, https://journalofmusic.com/focus/micheal-o-suilleabhain-s-example-will-continue-inspire (accessed 13 June 2022); and by ongoing conversations with Mícheál's faculty colleagues.

2. Damian Corless, 'Interview with Mícheál Ó Súilleabháin', *In Dublin*, vol. 20, no. 20, 1995, p. 11.

3. John Blacking, *How Musical Is Man?* (Seattle: University of Washington Press, 1973).

4. Ellen Dissanayake, 'Ritual and Ritualization: Musical means of conveying and shaping emotion in humans and other animals', in Steven Brown and Ulrik Voglsten (eds), *Music and Manipulation: On the social uses and social control of music* (Oxford: Berghahn Books, 2006), pp. 31–56; Bruno Nettl, 'An Ethnomusicologist Contemplates Universals in Musical Sound and Musical Culture', in Nils. L. Wallin, Björn Merker and Steven Brown (eds), *The Origins of Music* (Cambridge, MA: MIT Press, 2000), pp. 463–72.

5. Michael Dervan, 'Mícheál Ó Súilleabháin Put Traditional Music Centre Stage', *The Irish Times*, 10 November 2018.

42. 'there for the crossing': Reflections on the practical and the poetic *Anya Peterson Royce*

1. Seamus Heaney, *The Redress of Poetry* (London: Faber & Faber, 1995), p. 203.

2. Mícheál Ó Súilleabháin, 'Parallel Universes: The state of play', keynote address, *Arts Research: The state of play*, GRADCAM conference, Dublin, 2008.

3. *The Blackpool Sentinel*, 8 November 2018.

4. Seamus Heaney, 'Postscript', from *The Spirit Level* (London: Faber & Faber, 1996), p. 70.

5. 'MD8001 Arts Practice I and MD8002 Arts Practice II', https://www.irishworldacademy.ie/programmes/postgraduate/phd-arts-practice (accessed 10 July 2022).

6. Mícheál Ó Súilleabháin, personal communication, 2009.

7. Mícheál Ó Súilleabháin, 'Elver Gleams', unpublished essay.

8. Anya Peterson Royce, 'Taking the Long Way Around: Journeys of transformation', in *Of Our Times/Comhaimseartha*, Irish World Academy of Music and Dance, autumn 2013.

9. Morris Risenhoover and Robert Blackburn, *Artists as Professors: Conversations with musicians, painters, sculptors* (Urbana: University of Illinois Press, 1976), p. 9.

10. Janos Starker, *Indiana Daily Student*, 14 September 1999, p. 9.

44. Mícheál Ó Súilleabháin: The candle and the light *Christopher Frayling*

1. George Steiner, *Real Presences* (Chicago: University of Chicago Press, 1991), p. 6, where Steiner imagines the triumph of creativity over criticism.

2. Herbert Read, *Education Through Art* (London: Faber & Faber, 1943), especially pp. 1–15 and pp. 296–302.

3. George Steiner, *Lessons of the Masters* (Cambridge, MA: Harvard University Press, 2003), pp. 183–4. This theme is related to music on pp. 59–62, 119–21, 132–7 and 163–7.

4. Christopher Logue after Guillaume Apollinaire, 'Come to the Edge' (originally a poster-poem for an exhibition at the Institute of Contemporary Arts, London, in spring 1968), https://www.poemhunter.com/poem/come-to-the-edge.

45. Transmodal Curriculum Maker, Symbolic Leader *Regina Murphy*

1. T.E. Deal and K.D. Peterson, 'Eight Roles of Symbolic Leaders', in M. Fullan (ed.), *Educational Leadership*, 2nd edn (San Francisco: Jossey-Bass, 2007), pp. 197–210.

2. A. Vic Kelly, *The Curriculum: Theory and practice* (London: Sage, 2009).

3. William F. Pinar, 'The Method of "Currere"', paper presented at the Annual Meeting of the American Research Association, Washington, DC, April 1975, https://files.eric.ed.gov/fulltext/ED104766.pdf

4. William F. Pinar, *What Is Curriculum Theory?* (Mahwah, NJ: Lawrence Erlbaum Associates Publishers, 2004).

5. Mícheál Ó Súilleabháin, 'This Much I know', *Irish Examiner*, 16 November 2016.

6. John Blacking, *How Musical Is Man?* (Seattle: University of Washington Press, 1974).

7. Mícheál Ó Súilleabháin, 'Innovation and Tradition in the Music of Tommie Potts', unpublished PhD thesis, Queen's University Belfast, 1987; 'A Litany of the Saints: Musical quotations and influences in the music of Tommie Potts', *Inbhear*, vol 1, no. 1, 2010, pp. 1–46, https://www.irishworldacademy.ie/wp-content/inbhear/volume-1/Inbhear-Volume-1-Issue-1.pdf.

8. See Jessica Cawley, *Becoming an Irish Traditional Musician: Learning and embodying musical culture* (London: Routledge, 2021); Daithí Kearney, 'Towards a Regional Understanding of Irish Traditional Music', unpublished PhD thesis, University College Cork, 2009; Daithí Kearney, 'Listening for Tradition: Contributing to a regional musical identity through higher education and research', special issue, 'Geography, Music, Space', *Musicology Research*, vol. 4, no. 2, 2018, pp. 387–424; Mary Nugent, 'Instrumental Music Learning in an Irish Bimusical Context', unpublished PhD thesis, Technological University Dublin, 2019; Kari Veblen, 'Perceptions of Change and Stability in the Transmission of Irish Traditional Music: An examination of the music teacher's role',unpublished PhD thesis, University of Wisconsin, 1991; Kari Veblen, 'The Teacher's Role in the Transmission of Irish Traditional Music', *International Journal of Music Education*, vol. 24, no. 1, 1994, pp. 21–30; Francis Ward, 'Processes of Transmission in Irish Traditional Music: Approaching a virtual orality', unpublished PhD thesis, University of Limerick, 2016.

9. Carmel Murphy, personal communication, October 2020.

10. Alexandra Kertz-Welzel, *Globalising Music Education* (Bloomington, IN: Indiana University Press, 2018).

11. Ibid., p. 6.

12. Richard H. Hall, *Organizations: Structures, processes, and outcomes*, 4th edn (Englewood Cliffs, NJ: Prentice-Hall, 1987).

13. Terrence E. Deal and Kent D. Peterson, 'Eight Roles of Symbolic Leaders', in M. Fullan (ed.), *Educational Leadership*, 2nd edn (San Francisco: Jossey-Bass, 2007), pp. 197–209.

14. Ricky W. Griffin, Kristen Dahlen Skivington and Gregory Moorhead, 'Symbolic and International Perspectives on Leadership: An integrative framework', *Human Relations*, vol. 40, no. 4, 1987, pp. 199–218.

15. See James A. Banks and Cherry A. McGee Banks, *Multicultural Education: Issues and perspectives* (Hoboken, NJ: Wiley, 2019).

16. Government of Ireland/National Council for Curriculum and Assessment, *Primary School Curriculum* (Dublin: The Stationery Office, 1999).

17. Department of Education, *Curaclam na Bunscoile* (Dublin: The Stationery Office, 1971).

18. David J. Elliott, *Music Matters: A new philosophy of music* education (New York: Oxford University Press, 1995).

19. Graham McPhail and Elizabeth Rata, 'The Knowledge Democracy Connection and Music Education', *Philosophy of Music Education Review*, vol. 27, no. 2, 2019, pp. 112–32.

20. Frank Heneghan, *MEND: A review of music education in Ireland, incorporating the final report of the Music Education National Debate (MEND – Phase III)* (Dublin: Dublin Institute of Technology, 2001).

21. Ibid., pp. 20–1.

22. Ibid.

23. Ibid.

24. Mícheál Ó Súilleabháin, keynote address, 'Many Rivers: Towards a global listening', in *Samspel ISME 2002: Abstracts and sessions guide*, 25th Biennial World Conference of the International Society for Music Education (Bergen, Norway: International Society

for Music Education, 2002), https://www.isme.org/other-publications/25th-isme-world-conference-2002-proceedings.

25. Ibid.

26. Magne Espeland, personal communication, 2 November 2018.

27. Simeon Smith, personal communication, 2019.

28. Fintan Vallely, *Companion to Irish Traditional Music*, 3rd edn (Cork: Cork University Press, 2024).

29. https://www.cmc.ie/composers/micheal-o-suilleabhain.

30. Pinar, 'The Method of "Currere"'; Pinar, *What Is Curriculum Theory?*

31. Moya Cannon, 'Between the Jigs and the Reels', in *Collected Poems* (Manchester: Carcanet Press, 2021), p. 93.

47. 'My Love is in America': Mícheál brings Irish music to Boston College *Elizabeth Sweeney and Christian Dupont*

1. 'Irish Fortnight Opens March 19', *Boston College Colleague*, vol. 4, no. 7, 1 March 1979, pp. 1–2.

2. Nancy Raferty, 'Celebrating Twenty Years of Irish Studies: A symposium', *Boston College Irish Studies*, vol. 2, no. 2, spring 1999, p. 5.

3. Kevin O'Neill, personal communication to Elizabeth Sweeney, 2 October 2020.

4. Ibid.

5. Virginia Ryan, 'Music to Her Ears: Anne Dhu Shapiro raises the baton as music is elevated from program to department', *Boston College Biweekly*, vol. 9, no. 17, 11 May 1989, p. 8.

6. O'Neill, personal communication.

7. Robert K. O'Neill, letter to Mícheál Ó Súilleabháin, 24 September 1990.

8. Séamus Connolly and Elizabeth Sweeney, 'Irish Music at Boston College, 1990–2015', unpublished report.

9. Séamus Connolly, personal communication, 15 June 2022.

10. Mícheál Ó Súilleabháin, memo and enclosure to Mary Cronin, 10 April 1990. Dr Mary Cronin was university librarian at Boston College. In Mícheál's memo to Dr Cronin he mentioned that the digital audio tape recordings from the 1990 fiddle festival were 'already deposited in Burns [Library]'. The enclosure is a one-page proposal, outlining Mícheál's vision for 'My Love is in America: An archive of irish traditional music in America'. Memo and enclosure in possession of Elizabeth Sweeney.

11. Robert Savage, personal communication, 29 September 2020.

48. Mícheál Ó Súilleabháin, Music Educator: Local accent, global vision *Marie McCarthy*

1. For example, David J. Elliott, *Music Matters: A new philosophy of music education* (New York: Oxford University Press, 1995); Lucy Green, *Music, Gender, Education* (Cambridge:

Cambridge University Press, 1997); Estelle R. Jorgensen, *In Search of Music Education* (Urbana and Chicago: University of Illinois Press, 1997); Patricia Shehan Campbell, *Songs in Their Heads: Music and its meanings in children's lives* (New York: Oxford University Press, 1998).

2. Bruno Nettl, *Heartland Excursions: Ethnomusicological reflections on schools of music* (Urbana, IL: University of Illinois Press, 1995).

3. Helen Phelan, 'The PIPA Report: An Irish Chamber Orchestra/Irish World Music Centre report' (University of Limerick, May 1996), pp. 9–12.

4. 'This Much I Know: Musician, composer and academic Mícheál Ó Súilleabháin', in conversation with Hilary Fennell, *Irish Examiner*, 19 November 2016, https://www.irishexaminer.com/lifestyle/features/this-much-i-knowmusician-composer-and-academic-micheal-o-suilleabhain-431249.html

5. Helen Phelan, 'Voicing *Imbas*: Performing a philosophy of music education', in Wayne. D. Bowman and Ana Lucia Frega (eds), *The Oxford Handbook of Philosophy in Music Education* (New York: Oxford University Press, 2012), p. 78.

6. Ibid.

7. Mícheál Ó Súilleabháin, '*The New, the Old, and the Learned:* Issues of innovation, tradition and education in traditional music in our times', in Mei Xiao, Gang Zhang and Delfin Colomé (eds), *Preservation of Traditional Music: Report of the Asia-Europe training programme* (Beijing: China Academy of Arts; Asia-Europe Foundation, 2003), p. 199.

8. Mícheál Ó Súilleabháin, 'Listening to Difference: Ireland in a world of music', in Harry Bohan and Gerard Kennedy (eds), *Global Aspirations and the Reality of Change* (Dublin: Veritas, 2004), p. 32.

9. Mícheál Ó Súilleabháin, '"Around the house and mind the cosmos": Music, dance and identity in contemporary Ireland', in Richard Pine (ed.), *Music in Ireland: 1848–1998* (Cork: Mercier Press, 1998), pp. 77–8.

10. Mícheál Ó Súilleabháin, 'Out of Tune with Reality: Music and the school in Ireland', *Irish Educational Studies*, vol. 5, no. 1, 1985, p. 46.

11. Ó Súilleabháin, '*The New, the Old, and the Learned*', p. 199.

12. Ibid., p. 200.

13. Mícheál Ó Súilleabháin, 'The Redress of Music: Music, mediation and parity of esteem', *Yearbook for Traditional Music*, vol. 50, 2018, p. 5.

14. Ibid., p. 13.

15. Ó Súilleabháin, '*The New, the Old, and the Learned*', p. 200.

16. Ó Súilleabháin, '*Out of Tune* with Reality', *p*. 47.

17. Ó Súilleabháin, '"Around the House"', p. 86.

18. Ó Súilleabháin, 'The Redress of Music', p. 5.

19. Ó Súilleabháin, 'Listening to Difference', p. 24.

20. Ibid., p. 31.

21. Ibid., p. 26.

22. Ibid.

49. Memories of Mícheál: Cuimhní cinn ar Mhícheál *Lillis Ó Laoire*

1. Frances Tolmie, A.G. Gilchrist, George Henderson, Lucy E. Broadwood and J.A. Fuller-Maitland, 'Songs of Rest and Recreation', *Journal of the Folk-Song Society*, vol. 4, no.16, 1911, pp. 157–95 (pp. 174–5). See also Kathleen MacInnes, *Òg-Mhadainn Shamhraidh*, CDTRAX294 (Cockenzie: Greentrax Recordings, 2006), track 9.

51. Téada Machnaimh agus Téada Gutha: Ceist na teangan sa cheol Gaelach *Tríona Ní Shíocháin*

1. Mícheál Ó Súilleabháin, 'Cultural Redress and the Growth of Love: A guided autoethnography', in Helen Phelan (eag.), *The Artist and Academia* (Londain agus Nua-Eabhrac: Routledge, 2021), lgh 205–18.

2. Ibid., lgh 206–9.

3. Mícheál Ó Súilleabháin, 'Creative Process in Irish Traditional Dance Music', in Gerard Gillen agus Harry White (eag.), *Irish Musical Studies 1: Musicology in Ireland* (Baile Átha Cliath: Irish Academic Press, 1990), lgh 117–30 (lch119).

4. Mícheál Ó Súilleabháin, 'The Art of Listening', *The Crane Bag*, iml. 6, uimh. 1, 1982, lgh 59–61 (lch 59).

5. Gabhaim buíochas le Mary Mitchell-Ingoldsby, stiúrthóir Chartlann an Cheoil Thraidisiúnta i Roinn an Cheoil, Coláiste na hOllscoile, Corcaigh, a chuir ábhar luachmhar ar fáil dom a bhaineann le tráchtas MA Mhichíl Uí Shúilleabháin.

6. Mícheál Ó Súilleabháin, 'Innovation and Tradition in the Music of Tommie Potts', tráchtas neamhfhoilsithe PhD, Roinn na hAntraipeolaíochta Sóisialta, Ollscoil na Banríona, Béal Feirste, 1987.

7. Ó Súilleabháin, 'Creative Process in Irish Traditional Dance Music', lch 130.

8. Mícheál Ó Súilleabháin, 'Irish Music Defined', *The Crane Bag*, iml. 5, uimh. 2, 1981, lgh 83–7 (lch 83).

9. Tríona Ní Shíocháin, 'Mother Music: Socially embedded creative practice and the marketisation of Irish traditional music', *Ethnomusicology Ireland*, iml. 7, 2021, lgh 110–22 (lgh 110–12).

10. Ó Súilleabháin, 'Cultural Redress and the Growth of Love', lch 209.

11. Féach Mícheál Ó Súilleabháin, '"All our central fire": Music, mediation and the Irish psyche', *The Irish Journal of Psychology*, iml. 15, uimh. 2 & 3, 1994, lgh 331–53 (lgh 337–43).

12. Martin Dowling, *Traditional Music and Irish Society: Historical perspectives* (Farnham Surrey: Ashgate, 2014), lgh 162–3.

13. Ó Súilleabháin, 'Irish Music Defined', lch 84.

14. Mícheál Ó Súilleabháin, 'Ceol na nUasal: Seán Ó Riada and the search for a native Irish art music', *Ó Riada Memorial Lecture* 15 (University College Cork: Traditional Music Archive and Irish Traditional Music Society, 2004), lgh 4–5.

15. Ó Súilleabháin, '"All our central fire"', lch 344.

16. Ibid., lch 245.

17. Ó Súilleabháin, 'Ceol na nUasal', lch 8.

18. Ibid., lch 8; Mícheál Ó Súilleabháin, '"All our central fire"', lch 331.

19. Mícheál Ó Súilleabháin, 'Mícheál Ó Súilleabháin on "Between Worlds" with the National Symphony Orchestra', https://www.youtube.com/watch?v=oN0Gojn-f5c (faighte 15 Meitheamh 2021).

20. Mícheál Ó Súilleabháin, 'Between Worlds: Mícheál Ó Súilleabháin and Iarla Ó Lionáird', https://www.youtube.com/watch?v=rqFIMi0_QqA (faighte 15 Meitheamh 2021).

21. Ibid.

22. Ó Súilleabháin, 'Cultural Redress and the Growth of Love', lch 209.

23. Paul Clesham, 'Between Worlds: An examination of the intersection of Irish traditional music and western art musical traditions through orchestral arrangements of Irish traditional music', tráchtas neamhfhoilsithe MA, Roinn an Cheoil, Coláiste na hOllscoile, Corcaigh, 2017, lgh 31–5.

24. Tríona Ní Shíocháin, *Bláth 's Craobh na nÚdar: Amhráin Mháire Bhuí* (Baile Átha Cliath: Coiscéim, 2012), lgh 156–8; féach chomh maith Lillis Ó Laoire, *Ar Chreag i Lár na Farraige: Amhráin agus amhránaithe i dToraigh* (Indreabhán: Cló Iar-Chonnacht, 2002), lch 207.

25. Ní Shíocháin, 'Mother Music', lgh 111–18.

26. Seán Ó Ríordáin, *Seán Ó Ríordáin: Na dánta*, in eagar ag Seán Ó Coileáin (Indreabhán: Cló Iar-Chonnacht, 2011), lgh 98–9.

27. Donncha Ó Cróinín (eag.), *Seanachas Phádraig Í Chrualaoi* (Baile Átha Cliath: Comhairle Bhéaloideas Éireann, 1982), lch xxx.

28. Breandán Ó Madagáin, 'Coibhneas na Filíochta leis an gCeol, 1700–1900', in Pádraigín Riggs, Seán Ó Coileáin agus Breandán Ó Conchúir (eag.), *Saoi na hÉigse: Aistí in ómós do Sheán Ó Tuama* (An Daingean: An Sagart, 2000), lch 83.

29. Ibid.; Méadhbh Nic an Airchinnigh agus Lillis Ó Laoire, 'Caointe agus Amhráin Chrúite: 'Is le gach bó a lao agus le gach caoineadh a cheol', *Aiste*, iml. 4, uimh. 1, 2014, lgh. 155–76.

30. Mícheál Ó Súilleabháin, 'The Songs of Three Eighteenth-Century Gaelic Poets', tráchtas neamhfoilsithe MA, Roinn an Cheoil, Coláiste na hOllscoile, Corcaigh, 1973, lch 8.

31. Pádraig Ó Crualaoi in Donncha Ó Cróinín (eag.), *Seanachas Phádraig Í Chrualaoi* (Baile Átha Cliath: Comhairle Bhéaloideas Éireann, 1982), lch 67.

32. Tríona Ní Shíocháin, 'Filí agus Amhránaithe, Foinn agus Focail: *Maidean álainn ghréine* agus ionad an cheoil i dtraidisiún na n-amhrán', *Béascna*, iml. 5, lgh 37–57; Ní Shíocháin, *Bláth 's Craobh na nÚdar*, lch 141; Tríona Ní Shíocháin, *Singing Ideas: performance, politics and oral poetry* (London and New York: Berghahn, 2018), lgh 36–9.

33. Is féidir éisteacht le leagan de chuid Sheosaimh Uí Éanaí anso, https://www.joeheaney.org/ga/donal-og, agus le leagan de chuid Bhríd Ní Mhaoilchiaráin anso, https://seannos.tg4.ie/baile/amhranaithe/brid-ni-mhaoilchiarain/donal-og-fonnadoiri-na-hairde-2. (faighte 15 Meitheamh 2021).

34. Ní Shíocháin, *Bláth 's Craobh na nÚdar*, lch 165, traic 5.

35. Ó Súilleabháin, 'The Art of Listening', lch 60.

36. Ibid., lch 59.

37. Ó Ríordáin, *Seán Ó Ríordáin: Na dánta*, lch 99.

38. Ibid.

39. Ibid.

56. The Rags of Time *Paddy Bushe*

1. See https://www.irishtimes.com/newspaper/archive/2001/0913/Pg014.html#Ar01401 for the article published on Thursday, 13 September 2001.

2. Ibid.

Paddy Bushe, 'Equinox Concert', *To Ring in Silence: New and selected poems* (Dublin: Dedalus Press, 2007) by kind permission of Dedalus Press.

57. Across the Plains of Boyle *Vincent Woods*

Vincent Woods, 'Across the Plains of Boyle (i.m. Mícheál Ó Súilleabháin)', March/April 2021.

59. Enda Wyley, 'Eurydice Speaks'

from *The Painter on His Bike* (Dedalus Press, 2019)

60. Air: The map of the world *Eiléan Ní Chuilleanáin*

(from *The Map of the World*, The Gallery Press, 2023)

61. Between the Jigs and the Reels *Moya Cannon*

Moya Cannon, 'Between the Jigs and the Reels', *Carrying the Songs* (Carcanet Press, 2007), by kind permission of Carcanet Press Ltd., Manchester

62. Between the Beats at The Moorings Bar *Michael Coady*

By kind permission of the author and The Gallery Press, Loughcrew, Oldcastle, County Meath, from *Going by Water* (2009).

65. Early Music *Mícheál 'Moley' Ó Súilleabháin*

'Early Music', reprinted with permission from Many Rivers Press, Langley, WA

68. The Music of the Morning Sun *David Whyte*

David Whyte, 'The Music of the Morning Sun', from *Still Possible* © 2022 and *The Seven*

74. Mícheál Ó Súilleabháin and Seamus Heaney: Boundaries, mediation and redress *Johanne Devlin Trew*

1. Mícheál Ó Súilleabháin, 'The Redress of Music: Music, mediation, and parity of esteem', *Yearbook for Traditional Music*, vol. 50, 2018, pp. 1–14 (pp. 6, 1).

2. Mícheál Ó Súilleabháin, 'Listening to Difference: Ireland in a world of music', in Harry Bohan and Gerard Kennedy (eds), *Global Aspirations and the Reality of Change: How can we do things differently?* (Dublin: Veritas, 2004), pp. 20–35 (p. 24).

3. Ó Súilleabháin, 'Redress of Music', p. 4.

4. My father, from the Shankill Road in Belfast, had strong loyalist credentials in the family as his grandfather, Arthur Trew (1866–1943), was a notable figure in Belfast and Ulster politics from the 1890s to the 1930s (see Patrick Maume, 'Arthur Trew', *Dictionary of Irish Biography*, https://www.dib.ie/biography/trew-arthur-a9287). My mother grew up in a working-class Catholic family in Belfast, though her mother was from Newry, County Down and her father came from a rural townland near Toome, County Antrim, approximately three miles down the road from Mossbawn, Seamus Heaney's childhood home in south Derry.

5. Among Ó Súilleabháin's original cohort of IWMC students at the University of Limerick, for example, Liz Doherty researched the Cape Breton musical tradition, Desi Wilkinson researched that of Brittany and my own research was in the Quebec/Ontario border area of the Ottawa Valley. Significantly, other students of that cohort embarked on studies of musicians who had themselves crossed boundaries and were agents of change, for example work on Edward Bunting (Colette Moloney), Turlough Carolan (Sandra Joyce) and the pre-famine piper Paddy Conneely (Jimmy O'Brien Moran). Attracting students (and staff) from around the world, regardless of their ethnic or national background, was to become the norm in the Academy.

6. Ó Súilleabháin, 'Redress of Music', p. 13, my emphasis.

7. Mícheál Ó Súilleabháin, '"Traditional Ears": Perception and analysis in Irish traditional music', in Anne Clune (ed.), *Dear Far-Voiced Veteran: Essays in honour of Tom Munnelly* (Miltown Malbay: The Old Kilfarboy Society, 2007), pp. 249–76. *The Dolphin's Way* (1987) album title is taken from an extract from the poem 'Station Island, part XII' by Seamus Heaney, which is reproduced in the sleeve notes of the CD. It was originally published in the collection *Station Island* (Faber & Faber, 1984) and later also in the collection *Opened Ground* (Faber & Faber, 1998). The term 'Elver-Gleams' begins the fourth line of the poem extract and became the title of Ó Súilleabháin's later album (2010).

8. Mícheál Ó Súilleabháin, 'Innovation and Tradition in the Music of Tommie Potts', unpublished PhD thesis, Queen's University Belfast, 1987.

9. Ó Súilleabháin, '"Traditional Ears"', p. 261.

10. Stephen Regan, 'Lux Perpetua: The poetry of Seamus Heaney, from *Door into the Dark* to *Electric Light*', *Romanticism*, vol. 22, no. 3, 2016, pp. 322–30 (p. 330). In his academic writing Ó Súilleabháin cited Heaney's work of the 1980s, specifically the poetry collections

Station Island (1984), *The Haw Lantern* (1987) and the prose collection *The Government of the Tongue* (1988), all published by Faber & Faber.

11. Ruth Macklin, 'Seamus Heaney and the "Place of Writing": Technique as evidence of redress as a construct', *Irish Studies Review*, vol. 25, no. 1, 2017, pp. 56–70. Heaney's interest in traditional music is exemplified in the partnership with uilleann piper Liam O'Flynn, and the album that they recorded together entitled *The Poet and the Piper* (Dublin: Claddagh Records, 2003).

12. Ó Súilleabháin, 'Redress of Music,' p. 11. His interest in poetry, philosophy and psychology was also stimulated by his involvement with Richard Kearney and Patrick Hederman in the context of *The Crane Bag* journal (credit to Helen Phelan on this point).

13. Seamus Heaney, 'Feeling into Words', in *Preoccupations: Selected prose 1968–1978* (London:
Faber & Faber, 1980), p. 54; on this point see also Duc Dau, 'Seamus Heaney's Religious Redress', *Literature & Theology*, vol. 17, no. 1, 2003, pp. 32–43.

14. Ó Súilleabháin quoted in Hilary Fennell, 'This Much I Know: Musician, composer and academic Mícheál Ó Súilleabháin in conversation with Hilary Fennell', *Irish Examiner*, 19 November 2016.

15. Mícheál Ó Súilleabháin, '"Around the house and mind the cosmos": Music, dance and identity in contemporary Ireland', in Richard Pine (ed.), *Music in Ireland, 1848–1998: The Thomas Davis Lectures* (Cork: Mercier Press & RTÉ, 1998), pp. 76–86 (p. 83).

16. Mícheál Ó Súilleabháin, *A River of Sound: The changing course of Irish traditional music* [television series] (Dublin: Hummingbird Productions, BBC NI & RTÉ, 1995). Heaney, however, also employs water metaphors, for example in 'The Cure at Troy' (1990): tidal wave, sea-change, floodtide, watermark and miraculous healing-wells.

17. Seamus Heaney, 'Crediting Poetry: The Nobel lecture, 1995', in *Opened Ground* (London: Faber & Faber, 1998), pp. 445–67 (p. 455).

18. Ahmed Badrideen, 'The Will to Believe: Heaney's pragmatic marvels', *Literature & Theology*, vol. 31, no. 1, 2017, pp. 99–114; Roy Foster, *On Seamus Heaney* (Princeton, NJ: Princeton University Press, 2020), p. 2, notes that the 'process over product' approach was also characteristic of Heaney as a teacher.

19. Ó Súilleabháin, 'Redress of Music', p. 11.

20. Macklin, 'Seamus Heaney and the "Place of Writing"', p. 57.

21. Mícheál Ó Súilleabháin, 'The Singing Body: Music, spirit and creativity', in Helen Phelan (ed.), *Anáil Dé/The Breath of God: Music, ritual and spirituality* (Dublin: Veritas, 2001), pp. 140–7 (p. 141) (emphasis added). Heaney, 'Crediting Poetry', p. 449, notably described the act of delivering the 1995 Nobel lecture as 'walking on air'.

22. Mícheál Ó Súilleabháin, '"All our central fire": Music, mediation and the Irish psyche', *The Irish Journal of Psychology*, vol. 15 nos 2 & 3, 1994, pp. 331–53; Ó Súilleabháin, '"Around the house and mind the cosmos"'; Ó Súilleabháin, 'The Litany of the Saints: Musical quotations and influences in the music of Tommie Potts', *Inbhear: Journal of Irish Music and Dance*, vol. 1, no. 1, 2010, pp. 1–46. In the publications after 1994, Ó Súilleabháin omits Moore from the list of mediators, associating him more with the literary tradition rather than the music which 'fell out of fashion' and 'led nowhere' ('"All our central fire"', p. 340). However, according to William H. Williams, *'Twas Only an Irishman's Dream': The image of Ireland and the Irish in American popular song lyrics,*

1800-1920 (Urbana: University of Illinois Press, 1996), p. 29, *Moore's Melodies* was so enormously popular in Irish America during the nineteenth century, with over thirty separate editions published in the United States by 1900, that it mediated the artistic, the sentimental, the historical and the political in ways that were to prove very influential in maintaining support in the diaspora for the struggle for Irish independence. Indeed, Ó Súilleabháin, '"All our central fire"', p. 339, hinted at this, noting that 'it may be that an artistic integrity allowed him [Moore] to mediate sufficient energy between traditions *to encourage others to participate*' (my emphasis).

23. Mícheál Ó Súilleabháin, 'Crossroads or Twin Track? Innovation or tradition in Irish traditional music', in Fintan Vallely, Hammy Hamilton, Eithne Vallely and Liz Doherty (eds), *Crosbhealach an Cheoil, The Crossroads Conference 1996: Tradition and change in Irish traditional music* (Dublin: Whinstone Music, 1999), pp. 175–98 (p. 193).

24. Heaney, 'Crediting Poetry', p. 451.

25. Jonathan Veillette, 'Quand la Culture Fait Médiation …', *Liens Social et Politiques*, vol. 60, automne 2008, pp. 105–15.

26. Ó Súilleabháin, '"All our central fire"', p. 336; Ó Súilleabháin, '"Around the house and mind the cosmos"', p. 77.

27. Ó Súilleabháin, 'Listening to Difference', p. 26.

28. Marie McCarthy, 'The Artist-Teacher as Cultural Mediator', in Helen Phelan and Graham F. Welch (eds), *The Artist and Academia* (London and New York: Routledge, 2021), pp. 100–16 (p. 111).

29. Brenda Carr Vellino, 'Seamus Heaney's Poetic Redress for Post-conflict Societies', *Peace Review*, vol. 20, no. 1, 2008, pp. 49–57. Seamus Heaney, *The Redress of Poetry: Oxford lectures* (London: Faber & Faber, 1995), p. 3, reports having been strongly influenced by Simone Weil for these ideas of counterweighting, redress and balance, specifically her book *Gravity and Grace* (London: Routledge, 1963), where Weil declares that if justice is to be achieved, obedience to the force of gravity is the greatest sin. However, there is criticism of Heaney's interpretation of Weil's ideas in Neil Corcoran, *The Poems of Seamus Heaney: A critical study* (London: Faber & Faber, 1998), p. x.

30. Heaney, *Redress of Poetry*, p. 15; Ó Súilleabháin, 'Redress of Music', p. 7.

31. Ó Súilleabháin, 'Litany of the Saints', p. 42.

32. Mícheál Ó Súilleabháin, 'Irish Music Defined', *Crane Bag*, vol. 5, no. 2, 1981, pp. 83–7.

33. Ó Súilleabháin, 'Redress of Music', p. 3.

34. Mícheál Ó Súilleabháin, 'Ní ón ngaoth a fuair sé é: Aloys Fleischmann, 1910–92', review of Séamas de Barra, *Aloys Fleischmann*, *Journal of Music*, 1 May 2007, https://journalofmusic.com/focus/ni-ngaoth-fuair-se-e-aloys-fleischmann-1910-92 (accessed 31 December 2020); Fennell, 'This Much I Know'.

35. Mícheál Ó Súilleabháin, 'An Island Sound: Reflections on music, politics and identity in contemporary Ireland', in Robert J. Savage (ed.), *Ireland in the New Century: Politics, culture and identity* (Dublin: Four Courts Press, 2003), pp. 189–97 (p. 189).

36. Steven Rizzo, 'The Paradox of Spiritual Matter and the Spiritual Matter of Paradox in Seamus Heaney and Robert Boyle', *Literature & Theology*, vol. 22, no. 4, 2008, pp. 458–74; Heaney, 'Crediting Poetry'.

37. Lines from Heaney's poem 'Exposure', quoted in the 1995 Nobel lecture 'Crediting Poetry', p. 453 but originally published in the collection *North* (1975); 'Crediting Poetry', p. 451.

38. Foster, *On Seamus Heaney*, p. 1; Paul Breslin, 'Heaney's Redress', *Poetry*, vol. 168, no. 6, 1996, pp. 337–51, noted that some writers and academics were critical of Heaney's stance on the North. For example, with reference to Heaney's series of bog poems (in *Wintering Out* and *North*), David Lloyd, '"Pap for the Dispossessed": Seamus Heaney and the poetics of identity', *Boundary 2*, vol. 13, nos 2–3, 1985, pp. 319–42 (p. 331), argued that it was 'to reduce history to myth' to symbolically link the sacrificial practices of ancient bog people with the killing then taking place in Northern Ireland.

39. Heaney, *Redress of Poetry*, p. 191; ibid., 'Crediting Poetry', pp. 450, 463.

40. Heaney, *Redress of Poetry*, p. 191.

41. Ó Súilleabháin, 'An Island Sound', p. 195 (emphasis added).

42. Heaney, *Redress of Poetry*, p. 1; Ó Súilleabháin, 'Redress of Music', p. 3.

43. Ó Súilleabháin, 'An Island Sound', p. 195.

44. By 'greater diaspora', I mean both the diaspora that is created by kinship, together with the diaspora created by 'affinity' – that is, including people who have established a connection with Ireland, or an interest in Irish culture, but who are not necessarily of Irish descent. See discussions in Johanne Devlin Trew and Michael Pierse (eds), *Rethinking the Irish Diaspora* (Basingstoke: Palgrave Macmillan, 2018).

45. Ó Súilleabháin, 'Irish Music Defined', p. 83.

46. Ó Súilleabháin, 'Listening to Difference', p. 21.

47. Mícheál Ó Súilleabháin describing his composition *Termon* (2011) for uilleann pipes and string orchestra, composed for the 9/11 commemoration, quoted in 'The American Ireland Fund 9/11 Anniversary' (press release), RDS, Dublin, 11 September 2011, https://www.irelandfunds.org/news/the-american-ireland-fund-911-anniversary. Video of Ó Súilleabháin describing the piece at that performance is available at: https://www.youtube.com/watch?v=AM2dGMVTNIs&list=RDAM2dGMVTNIs&start_radio=1&rv=AM2dGMVTNIs&t=3 (both sites accessed 16 June 2022).

48. Video footage of Ó Súilleabháin taking the queen's hand on stage after the concert (at 1:40) is available on Youtube at: https://www.youtube.com/watch?v=anFrTmr9ilA (accessed 8 January 2021).

49. Badrideen, 'The Will to Believe'; Regan, 'Lux Perpetua'.

50. Ó Súilleabháin, 'An Island Sound', p. 195.

51. Ó Súilleabháin, 'Listening to Difference', p. 24; Regan, 'Lux Perpetua' provides as an example 'The Skylight', a poem originally published in Heaney's collection *Seeing Things* (1991).

52. Heaney, 'Crediting Poetry', p. 457.

53. Ibid., p. 449. Note the use of the metaphor as the title of the book by Dennis O'Driscoll, *Stepping Stones: Interviews with Seamus Heaney* (London: Faber & Faber, 2009) (emphasis added).

54. Ó Súilleabháin, 'Listening to Difference', p. 24 (emphasis added).

76. A River of Sound *Philip King*

1. All quotations in this piece come from personal memory recall or are excerpted from the series *A River of Sound: The changing course of Irish traditional music.*

78. History Lessons *Rod Stoneman*

1. Christopher Swann, *A Vertical Man* (Ireland, 1998).

2. There were early collaborations and then we formally set up Bresal as an annual symposium focused on practice-based doctoral research involving the Burren College of Art, the Huston School of Film & Digital Media at NUIG and the Irish World Academy of Music and Dance at UL. It ran from 2013 to 2016.

3. Rod Stoneman, '*Screen Production Research: Creative practice as a mode of enquiry*, edited by Craig Batty and Susan Kerrigan' (review), *Alphaville: Journal of film and screen media*, no. 17, 2019, pp. 215–20, http://www.alphavillejournal.com/Issue17/HTML/ReviewStoneman.html (accessed 25 May 2022).

4. Mícheál Ó Súilleabháin in an Irish-language interview with Seán Ó Mealóid on *Cúrsaí*, RTÉ, broadcast 9 December 1993, https://www.rte.ie/archives/2018/1205/1015261-micheal-o-suilleabhain-composer (accessed 24 November 2020).

5. Chris Garratt and Rod Stoneman, 'Film Music', *Arnolfini Review*, January 1982.

6. Theodor Adorno and Hanns Eisler, *Composing for the Films* (Oxford and New York: Oxford University Press, 1947; London and New York: Continuum, 2007), p. 9. This analysis clearly draws blood from supporters of mainstream modes as they feel they have to dismiss it aggressively: 'Hanns Eisler in his otherwise testy and relatively valueless book' – see Roy M. Prendergast, *Film Music: A neglected art* (New York: Norton, 1992), p. 3.

7. *Irish Destiny* plays out a romance between an IRA member and his lover against a backdrop of intrigue and violence. Leaving his beloved Moira (Frances MacNamara) behind, Denis O'Hara (Paddy Dunne Cullinan) travels to the IRA's Dublin headquarters, evading British pursuit. Eventually wounded, captured and interned, Denis escapes to rescue Moira from unscrupulous poteen brewer Gilbert Beecher (Brian Magowan).

8. The interview with Seán Ó Mealóid on *Cúrsaí* was broadcast on 9 December 1993 in anticipation of the concert, https://www.rte.iearchives/2018/1205/1015261-micheal-o-suilleabhain-composer (accessed 24 November 2020).

9. *Hymnen*, composed by Karlheinz Stockhausen in 1966–7, is an extended deconstruction of national anthems.

10. Kit O'Malley who plays the role had been an IRA captain in the War of Independence, recalling the Algerian FLN (*Front de Libération Nationale* or National Liberation Front) guerrilla fighters re-enacting their roles in Gino Pontecorvo's *Battle of Algiers* (Algeria/Italy, 1966).

11. Mícheál Ó Súilleabháin, 'A Note on the Score' (booklet included with Irish Film Institute DVD, Dublin, 2009).

12. Walter Benjamin, *On the Concept of History*, Section VI, https://www.marxists.org/reference/archive/benjamin/1940/history.htm (accessed 24 November 2020).

79. 'Too-Ra-Loo-Ra-Loo-Ral': Musical priests on screen and Irish-American identity *Méabh Ní Fhuartháin*

1. See in particular Mick Moloney, *Far from the Shamrock Shore* (Cork: Collins Press, 2022), *Across the Western Ocean: Songs of leaving and arriving* (CT: Quinnipiac University Press, 2016) and 'Harrigan, Hart and Braham: Irish America and the birth of the American musical', in John Harrington (ed.), *Irish Theatre in America: Essays on Irish theatrical diaspora* (Syracuse, NY: Syracuse University Press, 2009), pp. 1–18. For select research on recording in Irish traditional music up to 1950 see Colin Hamilton, 'Continuity and Change in Irish Traditional Music', unpublished PhD thesis, University of Limerick, 1996 and Jimmy O'Brien Moran, 'Capturing Diversity whilst Creating Canon: The advent of sound technology in Irish traditional music', in Thérèse Smith (ed.), *Ancestral Imprints: Histories of Irish traditional music and dance* (Cork: Cork University Press, 2012), pp. 83–104.

2. Kevin Kenny, *The American Irish* (New York: Routledge, 2000), p. 181.

3. Ibid.; Sean Griffin, 'The Wearing of the Green: Performing Irishness in the Fox wartime musical', in Diane Negra (ed.), *The Irish in Us: Irishness, performativity and popular culture* (Durham: Duke University Press, 2006), pp. 64–83 (p. 65).

4. Kenny, *The American Irish*, p. 204.

5. Michael P. Carroll, 'How the Irish became Protestant in America', *Religion and American Culture: A journal of interpretation*, vol. 16, no. 1, 2006, pp. 25–54 (p. 25).

6. Fergal Lenehan, 'Singing in the Rain: The Irish-themed film musical and Schlager's Hibernian moment', in Barry Monaghan (ed.), *Ireland and Cinema: Culture and contexts* (London: Palgrave Macmillan, 2015), pp. 149–57 (p. 149).

7. Ibid.

8. Christopher Shannon, *Bowery to Broadway: The American Irish in classic Hollywood cinema* (Scranton: University of Scranton Press, 2010), p. xiv.

9. Haller and Wilhelm quoted in Morris B. Holbrook, 'Ambi diegetic Music in the Movies: The Crosby duets in *High Society*', *Consumption, Markets and Culture*, vol. 8, no. 2, 2005, pp. 153–82 (p. 162).

10. Eric Mazur, 'Going My Way? Crosby and Catholicism on the road', in Ruth Prigozy and Walter Raubicheck (eds), *Going My Way: Bing Crosby and American culture* (New York: University of Rochester Press, 2007), pp. 17–34 (p. 20).

11. Allison McCracken, '"God's gift to us girls": Crooning, gender, and the re-creation of American popular song, 1928–1933', *American Music*, vol. 17, no. 4, 1999, pp. 365–95 (p. 368).

12. Ibid., p. 386.

13. Roger Gilbert, 'Beloved and Notorious: A theory of American stardom, with special reference to Bing Crosby and Frank Sinatra', *Southwest Review*, vol. 95, no. 2, 2010, pp. 167–84 (pp. 179–80).

14. Terry Teachout, 'Whatever Happened to Bing Crosby?', *Commentary*, April 2001, pp. 48–52 (pp. 50–1); Gilbert, 'Beloved and Notorious', p. 177.

15. Todd Decker, 'On the Scenic Route to Irving Berlin's Holiday Inn (1942)', *The Journal of Musicology*, vol. 28, no. 4, 2011, pp. 464–97 (p. 466); Bernard Dick, 'Crosby at

Paramount: From crooner to actor', in Ruth Prigozy and Walter Raubicheck (eds), *Going My Way: Bing Crosby and American culture* (New York: University of Rochester Press, 2007), pp. 87–98 (p. 88).

16. Decker, 'On the Scenic Route', p. 474.

17. Ruth Prigozy and Walter Raubicheck (eds), *Going My Way: Bing Crosby, and American culture* (New York: University of Rochester Press, 2007), p. xvii.

18. Decker, 'On the Scenic Route', p. 466; Gary Giddins, *Bing Crosby: A Pocketful of Dreams. The early years 1903–1940* (Boston, MA: Little, Brown & Co., 2001), p. 6.

19. Mazur, 'Going My Way?', p. 23.

20. Shannon, 'Bowery to Broadway', p. 120.

21. Mazur, 'Going My Way?', p. 22.

22. Linda Dowling Almeida, 'Irish America, 1940–2000', in J.J. Lee and M. Casey (eds), *Making the Irish American* (New York: NYU Press, 2006), pp. 548–73 (p. 550).

23. Mazur, 'Going My Way?', p. 22.

24. Decker, 'On the Scenic Route', p. 475.

25. Mary Anne Schofield, 'Marketing Iron Pigs, Patriotism, and Peace: Bing Crosby and World War II – a discourse', *Journal of Popular Culture*, vol. 40, no. 5, 2007, pp. 867–81 (pp. 869–70).

26. Holbrook, 'Ambi-diegetic Music in the Movies', p. 166.

27. Shannon, 'Bowery to Broadway', p. 143.

28. Holbrook, 'Ambi-diegetic Music in the Movies', p. 153.

29. Mícheál Ó Súilleabháin, 'The Redress of Music: Music, mediation and parity of esteem', *Yearbook for Traditional Music*, vol. 50, 2018, pp. 1–14.

30. Lenehan, 'Singing in the Rain', p. 150.

80. The Gleam of the Elver and the Work of the Heart: Reflections on Mícheál Ó Súilleabháin *Timothy Emlyn Jones*

1. See Timothy Emlyn Jones, 'The Studio Art PhD Revisited', in *Artists with PhDs: On the new doctoral degree in studio art*, 2nd edn (Washington: New Academia Publishing, 2014).

2. Ibid., pp. 100–1.

3. Mícheál Ó Súilleabháin, *Elver Gleams*, EMI, CD, 2010.

4. Seamus Heaney, *The Government of the Tongue* (London: Faber & Faber, 1988).

5. *Postscript: Visual artists respond to Seamus Heaney's poem*, 2015, an exhibition held jointly at The Russell Gallery, New Quay, Clare and Burren College of Art, Clare. Curated by Timothy Emlyn Jones. The Russell Gallery exhibition was launched by Mícheál Ó Súilleabháin, and the Burren College of Art exhibition by Fintan O'Toole.

6. Seamus Heaney, *Station Island* (London: Faber & Faber, 1984).

7. Dennis O'Driscoll, *Stepping Stones: Interviews with Seamus Heaney* (New York: Farrar, Straus & Giroux, 2008).

8. Rainer Maria Rilke, *Turning Point: Miscellaneous poems 1912–1926*, translated by Michael Hamburger (London: Anvil Press, 1981).

9. Joseph Campbell, *Hero with a Thousand Faces* (New York: Pantheon, 1949; Novato, CA: New World Library, 2012).

10. C. Otto Scharmer, *Theory U: Leading from the future as it emerges* (London: Berrett-Koehler Publishers, 2009).

11. John Chris Jones, *Design Methods*, 2nd edn (New York: John Wiley & Sons, 1992).

12. Ibid.

13. See https://epod.usra.edu/blog/2020/04/chicago-fata-morgana.html and https://www.britannica.com/topic/Fata-Morgana-mirage (accessed 20 June 2022).

82. Learning from Mícheál: Placing culture at the heart of regenerative innovation *Finbarr Bradley*

1. Gerry Sweeney, 'The Skillbeck Report and the Need for Change', *Céide: A review from the margins*, April/May 2002, p. 19.

2. Adhi Nugraha, 'Transforming Tradition for Sustainability', Joining Forces, International Conference on Design Research, Aalto University School of Arts, Design and Architecture, Helsinki, 22–24 September 2005.

3. Mícheál Ó Súilleabháin, 'Irish Music Defined', *The Crane Bag*, vol. 5, no. 2, 1981, pp. 83–7.

4. Bord Bia/Irish Food Board, *Consumer Lifestyle Trends* (Dublin: Bord Bia, 2002).

5. Dante Di Gregorio, 'Place-based Business Models for Resilient Local Economies', *Journal of Enterprising Communities: People and places in the global economy*, vol. 11, no. 1, February 2015, pp. 123–4.

6. Dietmar Sternad, James J. Kennelly and Finbarr Bradley, *Digging Deeper: How purpose-driven enterprises create real value* (Saltaire, Yorkshire: Greenleaf Publishing, 2016).

7. Manuel Castells and Pekka Himanen, *The Information Society and the Welfare State: The Finnish model* (Oxford: Oxford University Press, 2004), p. 154.

8. Scott Goodson, 'Is Brand Loyalty the Core to Apple's Success?', *Forbes*, 27 November 2011.

9. Geoff Colvin, 'In the Future, Will There Be Any Work Left for People to Do?', *Fortune*, 2 June 2014.

10. Seamus Murphy, *Stone Mad* (Belfast: Blackstaff Press, 1997); George Sturt, *The Wheelwright's Shop* (Cambridge: Cambridge University Press, 1993).

11. Pamela Duncan, 'Heaney Receives DCU's Highest Award', *The Irish Times*, 11 May 2011.

12. Finbarr Bradley and James J. Kennelly, *Capitalising on Culture, Competing on Difference: Innovation, learning and sense of place in a globalising Ireland* (Dublin: Blackhall Publishing, 2008).

13. Richard K. Lester and Michael J. Piore, *Innovation: The missing dimension* (Boston, MA: Harvard University Press, 2006).

14. Refer, for example, to the recent strategy document by the Department of Further and Higher Education, Research, Innovation and Science: *Impact 2020: Ireland's research and innovation strategy*, https://www.gov.ie/en/publication/27c78-impact-2030-irelands-new research-and-innovation-strategy/ (accessed 18 May 2022).

15. Elliot W. Eisner, *The Arts and the Creation of Mind* (New Haven, CT: Yale University Press, 2002), p. 213.

16. C. Otto Scharmer, *Theory U: Leading from the future as it emerges* (Oakland, CA: Berrett-Koehler Publishers, 2016).

17. Eoin O'Leary, 'Prosperity Hinges on Lean, Smart Government', *The Irish Times*, 24 March 2010.

83. *Planxty*: A newly coined word for a new kind of composition? *Cathal Goan*

1. Mícheál and I, both, were fortunate to be visiting fellows there at the Keough-Naughton Institute for Irish Studies, where hospitality and intellectual curiosity made for a rewarding time.

2. Nicholas Carolan has confirmed to me in private conversation his own impression that this was Mícheál's intention.

3. Variously spelt, *planckst*y, *planksty*, *planxty*, *plangstaí*, *plancstaí*.

4. Nicholas Carolan (ed.), *John and William Neal: A collection of the most celebrated Irish tunes proper for the violin, German flute or hautboy*, Dublin, 1724 (Dublin: Irish Traditional Music Archive in association with the Folk Music Society of Ireland, 2010).

5. Ibid., pp. 3–37.

6. Mícheál Ó Súilleabháin, 'Ceol na nUasal: Seán Ó Riada and the search for a native Irish art music', *Ó Riada Memorial Lecture* 15 (University College Cork: Traditional Music Archive and Irish Traditional Music Society, 2004). See also Ó Riada interview with Charles Acton in *Éire-Ireland*, vol. 6, no. 4, 1970, pp. 106–15.

7. Donal O'Sullivan, *Carolan: The life and times of an Irish harper*, vols 1–2 (London: Routledge and Kegan Paul, 1958), vol. 2, p. 35.

8. Gael Linn CEF032. The translation here is by this writer. See also Máire Nic Fhinn, *Riobard Mac Góráin: Ceannródaí ildánach* (Baile Átha Cliath: Coiscéim, 2018), pp. 78–80.

9. George Petrie (ed.), *The Petrie Collection of the Ancient Music of Ireland* (Dublin: Society for the Preservation and Publication of the Melodies of Ireland, 1855), p. 13.

10. O'Sullivan, *Carolan*, vol. 1, pp. 150–4. Tomás de Bhaldraithe offers a thorough analysis of the meaning and usage of *pléaráca* in *Éigse*, vol. 27, 1993, pp. 133–6. He notes that evidence for the word begins in the early eighteenth century and its primary usage was in relation to an occasion rather than a dance measure.

11. *Notes and Queries*, series 4, vol. VII, 14 January 1871, p. 42.

12. https://thesession.org/discussions/1970.

13. Rev. Patrick S. Dinneen, *Foclóir Gaedhilge agus Béarla; An Irish–English Dictionary* (Dublin: Irish Texts Society, 1927), p. 845.

14. *Dictionary of the Irish Language: Based mainly on old and middle Irish materials* (various editors) (Dublin: Royal Irish Academy, 1913–76).

15. corpas.ria.ie also known as Corpas na Gaeilge. The source given on the database for the poem as quoted is an unpublished thesis by Eoghan Ó Raghallaigh, 1998. The translation offered here is by this writer.

16. See corpas.ria.ie: *pleanncadh*.

17. It is more probable *plúnc* is a direct borrowing from English 'plank'.

18. This poem of Ó Donnchadha's was adjudged unsuitable for inclusion in Fr Dinneen's edition of some of his poetry. See Ó Donnchadha's entry in ainm.ie.

19. Máire Comer Bruen and Dáithí Ó hÓgáin (eds), *An Mangaire Súgach: Beatha agus saothar* (Baile Átha Cliath: Coiscéim, 1996), p. 71. My translation of the Irish quatrain.

20. Tomás Ó Máille, *Amhráin Chearbhalláin/The poems of Carolan* (London: Irish Texts Society, 1916), p. 155. My translation.

21. Ibid. p. 170. My translation.

22. See *Oxford English Dictionary*, 2nd edn, 1989, https://www.oed.com/search/dictionary/?scope=Entries&q=plonk: '*Plonk, v. dial. and colloq* (1.**a**. *trans*. To hit or strike with a plonk. Chiefly *dial*. **b.** *intr*. To emit or cause to emit an abrupt vibratory sound, *spec*. in playing a musical instrument'. All examples are from the late nineteenth and twentieth centuries. Might *plonk* itself be a borrowing from Irish? *Plank* seems to enjoy no other older association than with bits of wood. *Pluck* could conceivably offer a genesis with nasalisation before the 'k'.

23. See Niall Ó Dónaill, *Foclóir Gaeilge Béarla* (An Gúm: Baile Átha Cliath, 1977), p. 74.

24. Ibid., p. 259.

25. Heard frequently in English usage by this writer.

26. Noted in Ranafast, County Donegal by the writer. See also Corpas na Gaeilge entry at corpas.ria.ie.

27. 'Fuaireas-sa cuireadh dul ar an bpósadh': Colm Ó Lochlainn, *An Claisceadal: Díoghluim amhrán d'Oireachtas 1941* (Dublin: Three Candles Press, 1941).

28. Brian Ó Curnáin, *The Irish of Iorras Aithneach, County Galway* (Dublin: School of Celtic Studies, Dublin Institute for Advanced Studies, 2007), p. 2320.

29. I am grateful to Máire Glackin and Cití Ní Ghallchóir, Dobhar, County Donegal for confirmation of this word. See also corpas.ria.ie under *brocstaigh*: 'same as *brocach*, the face marked by small-pox'.

30. All the examples cited above are from the last one hundred years or so and differ in that respect from *plancstaí/planxty*. The *staí/sty* element may itself be a borrowing but, in any event, requires further research.

31. O'Sullivan, *Carolan*, vol. 1, p. 152. I am grateful to Nicholas Carolan, ITMA, and Charles Dillon, RIA, for helpful suggestions.

84. 'The local is the path to true globalisation': Mícheál as musical mediator and the redress of the Irish psyche *Owen Ó Súilleabháin*

1. See Mícheál Ó Súilleabháin, '"All our central fire": Music, mediation and the Irish psyche', *The Irish Journal of Psychology*, vol. 15 nos 2 & 3, 1994, pp. 331–53.

2. Ibid. p. 351.

3. Ibid. p. 336.

4. Ibid.

5. Ibid. p. 332.

6. See, for example, Finbarr D. Bradley and James J. Kennelly, *The Irish Edge: How enterprises compete on authenticity and place* (Dublin: Orpen Press, 2013) for further discussion on this.

7. Mícheál Ó Súilleabháin, 'The Redress of Music': Music, mediation, and parity of esteem', *Yearbook for Traditional Music*, vol. 50, 2018, pp. 1–14. (p. 4).

8. See Pádraic Flaherty, *Between Worlds* (2021) radio documentary, https://www.clare.fm/podcasts/worlds-life-micheal-osuilleabhain (accessed 1 November 2022).

9. Ó Súilleabháin, 'The Redress of Music', p. 4.

10. Ibid. p. 5.

11. Ibid. p. 9.

12. Ibid.

13. Ibid. p. 5.

14. Ibid. p. 7.

15. Ibid. p. 6.

16. Ibid. p. 8.

17. Ibid. p. 7.

18. Ibid. p. 4.

85. Irish Music (Re-)Defined: The writings of Mícheál Ó Súilleabháin
John O'Flynn

1. Mícheál Ó Súilleabháin, 'A Man and His Music', *The Irish Times*, 27 August 1977, p. iv.

2. Mícheál Ó Súilleabháin, 'Phoenix Rising', in Mark Quinn (ed.), *Pioneers and Aviators: A century of Irish aviation* (Dublin: Avolon, 2015), p. 7.

3. See John O'Flynn, *Music, the Moving Image and Ireland, 1897–2017* (London and New York: Routledge, 2022), pp. 193–4.

4. 'Irish Music Defined', *The Crane Bag*, vol. 5, no. 2, 1981, pp. 83–7 (p. 87).

5. Mícheál Ó Súilleabháin, 'The Art of Listening', *The Crane Bag*, vol. 6, no. 1, 1982, pp. 59–61 (p. 60).

6. Ibid., p. 61.

7. Thomas Johnston, 'The Bloom of Youth: Conceptualising a theory of educative experience for Irish traditional music in post-primary music education in Ireland', unpublished PhD thesis, University of Limerick, 2013, p. 30.

8. Ó Súilleabháin, 'The Art of Listening', p. 59.

9. Mícheál Ó Súilleabháin, 'The Bodhrán: Traditional performance techniques', *Treoir: Journal of Comhaltas Ceoltóirí* Éireann, vol. 6, no. 5, 1974, pp. 6–10 (p. 8).

10. Niall Keegan, 'The Art of Juncture: Transformations of Irish traditional music', unpublished PhD thesis, University of Limerick, 2012, p. 163.

11. See Breandán Ó Madagáin, 'Bunting's *Ancient Music of Ireland* by Bunting, Donal O'Sullivan and Mícheál Ó Súilleabháin (book review)', *Studia Hibernica*, no. 22/3, 1982/3, pp. 174–80.

12. See Anne Buckley, '*Sources of Irish Traditional Music c. 1600–1855: An annotated catalogue of prints and manuscripts 1583–1855*' (book review), *Yearbook for Traditional Music*, vol. 31, 1999, pp. 165–7.

13. Mícheál Ó Súilleabháin, 'Preface', in *Sources of Irish Traditional Music c. 1600–1855*, vols I & II, Aloys Fleischmann (ed.), Mícheál Ó Súilleabháin (asst ed.) and Paul McGettrick (assoc. ed.) (New York and London: Garland Press, 1998), p. xvii.

14. Ibid., p. xvi.

15. Mícheál Ó Súilleabháin, 'Review: *The Melodic Tradition of Ireland* by James R. Cowdery', *Ethnomusicology*, vol. 37, no. 1, 1993, pp. 109–12 (p. 109).

16. Mícheál Ó Súilleabháin, 'Ní ón ngaoth a fuair sé é: Aloys Fleischmann, 1910–92', review of Séamas de Barra, *Aloys Fleischmann*, *The Journal of Music*, 1 May 2007, https://journalofmusic.com/focus/ni-ngaoth-fuair-se-e-aloys-fleischmann-1910-92 (accessed 31 March 2021).

17. Mícheál Ó Súilleabháin, 'Hallelujah: A book to celebrate', review of Harry White and Barra Boydell (eds), *The Encyclopedia of Music in Ireland*, *The Irish Times*, 23 November 2013, p. 11.

18. Mícheál Ó Súilleabháin, 'Between the Jigs and the Reels: From the Famine to the peace process', review of Martin Dowling, *Traditional Music and Irish Society: Historical perspectives*, *The Irish Times*, 10 January 2015, p. B10.

19. Mícheál Ó Súilleabháin, 'Oasis Look Fertile in a Modern Desert', *The Irish Times*, 23 August 1977, p. 9.

20. Mícheál Ó Súilleabháin, 'Folk Music Studies', Letters to the Editor, *The Irish Times*, 24 February 1977, p. 9.

21. Mícheál Ó Súilleabháin, 'Irish Music', Letters to the Editor, *The Irish Times*, 26 July 1981, p. 9.

22. Mícheál Ó Súilleabháin, 'The Irish Traditional Musician and University Music Courses', an explanatory leaflet published by Comhaltas Ceoltóirí Éireann, Dublin, 1984, p. 4.

23. Mícheál Ó Súilleabháin, 'Out of Tune with Reality: Music and the school in Ireland', *Irish Educational Studies*, vol. 5, no. 1, 1985, pp. 44–57.

24. Frank Heneghan, MEND: *A review of music education in Ireland, incorporating the final report of the Music Education National Debate* (MEND – Phase III, 1996), rev. edn (Dublin: Dublin Institute of Technology, 2004).

25. Johnston, 'The Bloom of Youth', pp. 35–6.

26. Mícheál Ó Súilleabháin, 'Irish Traditional Music in Education', in Frank Heneghan

(ed.), *MEND Proceedings*, Document 120, Ref. I P/DN (Dublin: Dublin Institute of Technology, 2004).

27. Mícheál Ó Súilleabháin, 'State of Music Education', Letters to the Editor, *The Irish Times*, 31 January 2001, p. 17.

28. Mícheál Ó Súilleabháin, 'Gnéithe, Áirithe de Cheardaíocht Phádraig Uí Cheallaigh (Patrick Kelly): Fidléir ó Chontae an Chláir', *Comhar*, vol. 36, no. 10, 1977, pp. 26–7.

29. Mícheál Ó Súilleabháin, 'My Love is in America: Melodic deviation and the programmatic in the fiddle playing of Tommie Potts', *An Fhidil Ghaelach*, vol. 1, no. 1, 1982, pp. 17–22.

30. Mícheál Ó Súilleabháin, 'Crossroads or Twin Track? Innovation and tradition in Irish traditional music', in Fintan Vallely, Hammy Hamilton, Eithne Vallely and Liz Doherty (eds), *Crosbhealach an Cheoil, The Crossroads Conference 1996: Tradition and change in Irish traditional music* (Dublin: Whinstone Music, 1999), pp. 175–98 (p. 178).

31. Mícheál Ó Súilleabháin, '"Tourner un Air": L'improvisation dans la musique traditionnelle irlandais', in Bernard Lortat-Jacob (ed.), *L'improvisation dans les musiques de tradition orale*, Ethnomusicologie 4 (Paris: SELAF, 1987), pp. 211–20.

32. Gerard Gillen and Harry White, 'Preface', in Gerard Gillen and Harry White (eds), *Irish Musical Studies 1: Musicology in Ireland* (Dublin: Irish Academic Press, 1990), pp. 11–12 (p. 11).

33. Bruno Nettl, 'Thoughts on Improvisation: A comparative approach', *The Musical Quarterly*, vol. 60, no. 1, 1974, pp. 1–19.

34. Mícheál Ó Súilleabháin, '"Traditional Ears": Perception and analysis in Irish traditional music', in Anne Clune (ed.), *Dear Far-Voiced Veteran: Essays in honour of Tom Munnelly* (Miltown Malbay: The Old Kilfarboy Society, 2007), pp. 248–76 (p. 265).

35. Ó Súilleabháin, 'Crossroads or Twin Track?', pp. 184–5.

36. John Blacking, 'Some Problems of Theory and Method in the Study of Musical Change', *Yearbook of the International Folk Music Council*, vol. 9, 1977, pp. 1–26.

37. Ó Súilleabháin, '"Traditional Ears"', pp. 262–5.

38. Ó Súilleabháin, 'Crossroads or Twin Track?', pp. 188–93.

39. Mícheál Ó Súilleabháin, 'The Litany of the Saints: Quotations and borrowings in the music of Tommie Potts', *Inbhear: Journal of Irish music and dance*, vol. 1, no. 1, 2010, pp. 1–46 (p. 41).

40. Mícheál Ó Súilleabháin, '"All our central fire": Music, mediation and the Irish psyche', *The Irish Journal of Psychology*, vol. 15, nos 2 & 3, 1994, pp. 331–53 (p. 336).

41. Mícheál Ó Súilleabháin, '"Around the house and mind the cosmos": Music, dance and identity in contemporary Ireland', in Richard Pine (ed.), *Music in Ireland: 1848–1998* (Cork: Mercier Press, 1998), pp. 76–86 (p. 83).

42. Howard Becker, 'Art Worlds and Social Types', *American Behavioral Scientist*, vol. 19, no. 6, 1976, pp. 703–18.

43. Ó Súilleabháin, 'Crossroads or Twin Track?', p. 198.

44. Ó Súilleabháin, '"All our central fire"', p. 337.

45. Mícheál Ó Súilleabháin, 'Ceol na nUasal: Seán Ó Riada and the search for a native Irish art music', *Ó Riada Memorial Lecture* 15 (University College Cork: Traditional Music Archive and Irish Traditional Music Society, 2004), p. 2.

46. Ibid., p. 5.

47. Ibid., pp. 7–8.

48. Ibid., p. 11.

49. Ibid., p. 17.

50. Mícheál Ó Súilleabháin, 'The Harp of Aaron: The Irish harp as shopping trolley' (with Aaron Lawless, Niamh NicGhabhann and Helen Phelan), in Sandra Joyce and Helen Lawlor (eds), *Harp Studies: Perspectives on the Irish harp* (Dublin: Four Courts Press, 2016), pp. 270–93.

51. Mícheál Ó Súilleabháin, 'The Becoming Thing: Composer Mícheál Ó Súilleabháin salutes an Ireland in which the tension between tradition and novelty in the arts is increasingly a creative one', *The Irish Times*, 30 December 1999, p. 12.

52. Mícheál Ó Súilleabháin, 'An Island Sound: Reflections on music, politics and identity in contemporary Ireland', in Robert Savage (ed.), *Ireland in the New Century: Politics, culture and identity* (Dublin: Four Courts Press, 2003), pp. 189–97.

53. Mícheál Ó Súilleabháin, 'The Singing Body: Music, spirit and creativity', in Helen Phelan (ed.), *Anáil Dé/The Breath of God: Music, ritual and spirituality* (Dublin: Veritas Press, 2001), pp. 140–7 (pp. 143–4).

54. Mícheál Ó Súilleabháin, 'Listening to Difference: Ireland in a world of music', in Harry Bohan and Gerard Kennedy (eds), *Global Aspirations and the Reality of Change: How can we do things differently?* (Dublin: Veritas, 2004), pp. 20–35.

55. Mícheál Ó Súilleabháin, 'Willie Clancy Summer School', Letters to the Editor, *The Irish Times*, 22 July 1997, p. 17.

56. Mícheál Ó Súilleabháin, 'Elver-Gleams: Sub-marine soundings from the Irish World Academy', in Thierry Dubost and Alexandra Slaby (eds), *Music and the Irish Imagination: Like a language that we could all understand* (Caen: University of Caen Press, 2013), pp. 15–27.

57. John O'Flynn and Patricia Flynn (eds), *Music Education for the 21st Century: Legacies, conversations, aspirations* (*Studies in Irish Music Education*, vol. 1) (Cork: Cork University Press, 2023).

58. Seamus Heaney, *The Redress of Poetry* (London: Faber & Faber, 1995).

59. Mícheál Ó Súilleabháin, 'The Redress of Music: Music, mediation and parity of esteem', *Yearbook for Traditional Music*, vol. 50, 2018, pp. 1–14 (p. 13).

60. Mícheál Ó Súilleabháin, 'Cultural Redress and the Growth of Love: A guided autoethnography', in Helen Phelan and Graham F. Welch (eds), *The Artist and Academia* (London and New York: Routledge, 2021), pp. 205–18 (p. 207).

86. The Daring Young Man on the Flying Trapeze: A personal recollection and evaluation by a musician and educator *Fintan Vallely*

1. Fintan Vallely, *Timber: The concert flute tutor* (Dublin: Waltons, 1986).

2. 'Bonaparte ag Trasnú na Réine/Bonaparte Crossing the Rhine', *Mícheál Ó Súilleabháin* (Gael Linn, Dublin, LP CEF 046, 1976).

3. In his own writings, Ó Súilleabháin also acknowledged the seminal influence of Aloys Fleischmann, John Blacking and John Bailey. See, for example, the posthumous essay 'Cultural Redress and the Growth of Love: A guided autoethnography', in Helen Phelan and Graham F. Welch (eds), *The Artist and Academia* (London and New York: Routledge, 2021), pp. 205–18.

4. See, for example, Alan Lomax, 'Appeal for Cultural Equity', *The World of Music*, vol. 14 no. 2, 1972, pp. 3–17.

5. Clem Mac Mánuis, 'Ó Gallchobhair, Éamonn', *Companion to Irish Traditional Music* (Cork: Cork University Press, 2011), pp. 514–15.

6. John Moulden, 'Curry, David', *Companion to Irish Traditional Music* (Cork: Cork University Press, 2011), pp. 177–8.

7. 'The Bodhrán' [1], *Treoir*, vol. 6, no. 2, 1974, pp. 4–7 and 'The Bodhrán' [2], *Treoir*, vol. 6, no. 5, 1974, pp. 6–10.

8. Mícheál Ó Súilleabháin, 'Innovation and Tradition in the Music of Tommie Potts', unpublished PhD thesis, Queen's University Belfast, 1987.

9. Mícheál Ó Súilleabháin, 'My Love is in America: Melodic deviation and the programmatic in the fiddle-playing of Tommie Potts', *An Fhidil Ghaelach*, vol. 1, no. 1, 1982, pp. 17–22.

10. Mícheál Ó Súilleabháin, 'The Creative Process in Irish Traditional Dance Music', in Gerard Gillen and Harry White (eds), *Irish Musical Studies 1: Musicology in Ireland* (Dublin: Irish Academic Press, 1990), pp. 117–30.

11. Mícheál Ó Súilleabháin, 'Crossroads or Twin Track? Innovation and tradition in Irish traditional music', in Fintan Vallely, Hammy Hamilton, Eithne Vallely and Liz Doherty (eds), *Crosbhealach an Cheoil, The Crossroads Conference 1996: Tradition and change in Irish traditional music* (Dublin: Whinstone Music, 1999), pp. 175–98.

12. Mícheál Ó Súilleabháin, '"Traditional Ears": Perception and analysis in Irish traditional music', in Anne Clune (ed.), *Dear Far-voiced Veteran: Essays in honour of Tom Munnelly* (Miltown Malbay: The Old Kilfarboy Society, 2007), pp. 249–76.

13. Aloys Fleischmann (ed.), with Mícheál Ó Súilleabháin (asst ed.) and Paul McGettrick (assoc. ed.), *Sources of Irish Traditional Music* (New York: Garland, 1998).

87. Tradition and the Individual Talent: Ó Súilleabháin in the light of Heaney *Harry White*

1. See especially Mícheál Ó Súilleabháin, 'Crossroads or Twin Track? Innovation and tradition in Irish traditional music', in Fintan Vallely, Hammy Hamilton, Eithne Vallely and Liz Doherty (eds), *Crosbhealach an Cheoil, The Crossroads Conference 1996: Tradition and change in Irish traditional music* (Dublin: Whinstone Music, 1999), pp. 175–98. See also Sean Williams, 'Ó Súilleabháin, Mícheál', in Harry White and Barra Boydell (eds), *The Encyclopaedia of Music in Ireland* (Dublin: UCD Press, 2013), pp. 811–12.

2. Seamus Heaney, 'Frontiers of Writing', *The Redress of Poetry* (New York: Farrar, Straus & Giroux, 1995), p. 199. It is not too much to add that these lectures (given while Heaney was professor of poetry at Oxford) were a touchstone for Ó Súilleabháin.

3. See Colin Burrow, 'You've Listened Long Enough', *The London Review of Books*, vol. 38, no. 8, 21 April 2016, https://www.lrb.co.uk/the-paper/v38/n08/colin-burrow/you-ve-listened-long-enough (accessed 27 October 2020).

4. *Stepping Stones* is the title of Dennis O'Driscoll's extensive series of interviews with Seamus Heaney published by Faber & Faber (London) in 2008.

5. While Ó Súilleabháin also discussed the importance of harmonic and structural elements in his compositional process (see for example 'The Creative Process in Irish Traditional Dance Music', in Gerard Gillen and Harry White (eds), *Irish Musical Studies 1: Musicology in Ireland* (Dublin: Irish Academic Press, 1990), pp. 117–30), these are not germane to my reading of his work for this essay.

6. The concert was broadcast by RTÉ Lyric FM as part of *The Lyric Concert* with Paul Herriott series: https://www.rte.ie/radio/lyricfm/lyric-live/2017/1229/930167-the-lyric-concert-with-paul-herriott-friday-29-december-2017 (accessed 11 July 2024).

7. See the Traditional Tune Archive preserved by the Irish Traditional Music Archive online at https://tunearch.org/wiki/Bean_Dubh_a%27_Ghleanna_(1)_(An) (accessed 27 October 2020).

8. See Mark Evan Bonds, *After Beethoven: The imperative of originality in the symphony* (Cambridge, MA: Harvard University Press, 1997).

9. See https://www.youtube.com/watch?v=9Bd9Kbn2Fbc (accessed 27 October 2020).

10. Beyond the sphere of his public engagements and his work as a composer and performer, Ó Súilleabháin's achievements as a university professor, as founding director of the Irish World Academy of Music and Dance (University of Limerick), as a broadcaster and producer and as a constant advocate on behalf of Irish musical scholarship were exceptionally prodigious. If I may be allowed one personal comment in this essay, it is to marvel at the unremitting generosity, eloquence and constancy of Ó Súilleabháin's enterprises on behalf of music in Ireland. As a music educator, his record of innovation is well-nigh peerless.

11. A line from Heaney's poem 'The Rain Stick', published in *The Spirit Level* (London: Faber & Faber, 1996).

12. Ó Súilleabháin's setting of 'An Buachall Caol Dubh', which was originally commissioned by Iarla Ó Lionáird and the RTÉ Concert Orchestra, also featured as part of the NSO concert referenced in note 6 above (https://www.rte.ie/radio/lyricfm/lyric-live/2017/1229/930167-the-lyric-concert-with-paul-herriott-friday-29-december-2017). In his introduction to this performance, Ó Súilleabháin explicitly acknowledges his attempt in this setting to contextualise the Irish air in a 'symphonic response' that is in turn inflected by his retrieval of north Indian classical textures and techniques.

13. Ó Súilleabháin's study of the life and music of Tommie Potts (1912–88), on whose work he was the foremost authority, is especially important in this regard.

14. See Harry White, 'The Divided Imagination: Music in Ireland after Ó Riada', in Gareth Cox and Axel Klein (eds), *Irish Music in the Twentieth Century*, Irish Musical Studies Series 7 (Dublin: Four Courts Press, 2003), pp. 11–28.

15. See Mícheál Ó Súilleabháin, 'The Litany of the Saints: Musical quotations and influences in the music of Tommie Potts', *Inbhear: Journal of Irish music and dance*, vol. 1, no. 1, 2010, pp. 1–46 (p. 43). See https://www.irishworldacademy.ie/wp-content/inbhear/

volume-1/m-osuilleabhain/pdf/Inbhear-V1-I1-OSuilleabhain.pdf (accessed 27 October 2020).

Epilogue: Homily at the Funeral Mass for Mícheál Ó Súilleabháin
Mark Patrick Hederman OSB

1. Aogán Ó Rathaille, 'Mac An Cheannaí', in Patrick Dinneen and Tadhg O'Donoghue (eds), *Dánta Aodhagáin Uí Rathaille/The Poems of Egan O'Rahilly*, Irish Texts Society, vol. 3, 2nd edn (London: David Nutt for the Irish Texts Society, 1911), p. 12.

2. *Report of the Commissioners Appointed Pursuant to the Act 5 & 6 William IV. C. 67, for the Improvement of the Navigation of the River Shannon*, Whitehall, Treasury Chambers, 28 March 1836.

3. Quoted by Toner Quinn in 'Mícheál Ó Súilleabháin's Example Will Continue To Inspire', *The Journal of Music*, 8 November 2018, https://www.journalofmusic.com/focus/micheal-o-suilleabhain-s-example-will-continue-inspire.

Bibliography

Adorno, Theodor W., and Hanns Eisler, *Composing for the Films* (Oxford and New York: Oxford University Press, 1947; London and New York: Continuum, 2007)

Becker, Howard, 'Art Worlds and Social Types', *American Behavioral Scientist*, vol. 19, no. 6, 1976, pp. 703–18

Blacking, John, *How Musical Is Man?* (Seattle: University of Washington Press, 1973)

______, 'Some Problems of Theory and Method in the Study of Musical Change', *Yearbook of the International Folk Music Council*, vol. 9, 1977, pp. 1–26

Bradley, Finbarr D., and James J. Kennelly, *Capitalising on Culture, Competing on Difference: Innovation, learning and sense of place in a globalising Ireland* (Dublin: Blackhall Publishing, 2008)

_________, *The Irish Edge: How enterprises compete on authenticity and place* (Dublin: Orpen Press, 2013)

Breslin, Paul, 'Heaney's Redress' [review article], *Poetry*, vol. 168, no. 6, 1996, pp. 337–51

Brinson, Peter, *The Dancer and the Dance: Developing dance theatre in Ireland* (Dublin: Arts Council of Ireland, 1985), https://www.artscouncil.ie/uploadedFiles/Main_Site/Content/Research_and_Publications/Dance/The_Dancer_and_the_Dance.pdf

Bruen, Máire Comer, and Dáithí Ó hÓgáin (eds), *An Mangaire Súgach: Beatha agus saothar* (Baile Átha Cliath: Coiscéim, 1996)

Buckley, Anne, 'Sources of Irish Traditional Music *c.* 1600–1855: An annotated catalogue of prints and manuscripts 1583–1855' [book review], *Yearbook for Traditional Music*, vol. 31, 1999, pp. 165–7

Bulmer, Dave, and Neil Sharpley, *Music from Ireland* (4 volumes) (Leeds: Celtic Music, 1974–6)

Byron, Reginald (ed.), *Music, Culture and Experience: Selected papers of John Blacking* (Chicago: University of Chicago Press, 1995)

Carolan, Nicholas (ed.), *John and William Neal,* A Collection of the Most Celebrated Irish Tunes Proper for the Violin, German Flute or Hautboy, *Dublin 1724* (Dublin: Irish Traditional Music Archive in association with the Folk Music Society of Ireland, 2010)

Carr Vellino, Brenda, 'Seamus Heaney's Poetic Redress for Post-Conflict Societies', *Peace Review*, vol. 20, no. 1, 2008, pp. 49–57

Carroll, Michael P., 'How the Irish became Protestant in America', *Religion and American Culture: A journal of interpretation*, vol. 16, no. 1, 2006, pp. 25–54

Cawley, Jessica, *Becoming an Irish Traditional Musician: Learning and embodying musical culture* (London: Routledge, 2021)

Clesham, Paul, 'Between Worlds: An examination of the intersection of Irish traditional music and western art musical traditions through orchestral arrangements of Irish traditional music', unpublished MA thesis, University College Cork, 2017

Cooper, David, *The Musical Traditions of Northern Ireland and Its Diaspora: Community and conflict* (Farnham, Surrey: Ashgate, 2009)

Corcoran, Neil, *The Poetry of Seamus Heaney: A critical study* (London: Faber & Faber, 1998)

Cowdery, James R., *The Melodic Tradition of Ireland* (Kent, OH: Kent State University Press, 1990)

Cox, Gareth, and Axel Klein (eds), *Irish Music in the Twentieth Century*, Irish Musical Studies Series, 7 (Dublin: Four Courts Press, 2003)

Crispin, Darla, 'Artistic Research and the Musician's Vulnerability', *Musical Opinion*, vol. 132, 2009, pp. 25–7

Dau, Duc, 'Seamus Heaney's Religious Redress', *Literature & Theology*, vol. 17, no. 1, 2003, pp. 32–43

de Barra, Séamas, *Aloys Fleischmann, 1910–92* (Dublin: Field Day Publications in association with the Keough-Naughton Institute for Irish Studies at the University of Notre Dame, 2006)

de Brún, Jennifer, '*Ilchruthach* (Shapeshifter): An autoethnographic examination of self-defined movement identity in aerial dance and aerial circus in Ireland', unpublished PhD thesis, University of Limerick, 2021

Dervan, Michael, 'Mícheál Ó Súilleabháin Put Traditional Music Centre Stage', *The Irish Times*, 10 November 2018

——— (ed.), *The Invisible Art: A century of music in Ireland 1916–2016* (Dublin: New Island, 2016)

Devine, Patrick F., and Harry White (eds), *Irish Musical Studies 4: The Maynooth International Musicological Conference 1995. Selected proceedings, part one* (Dublin: Four Courts Press, 1996)

Dick, Bernard, 'Crosby at Paramount: From crooner to actor', in Ruth Prigozy and Walter Raubicheck (eds), *Going My Way: Bing Crosby and American culture* (New York: University of Rochester Press, 2007), pp. 87–98

Dillane, Aileen, and Matthew Noone, 'Irish Music Orientalism', *New Hibernia Review*, vol. 20, no. 1, 2016, pp. 121–37

Dowling Almeida, Linda, 'Irish America, 1940–2000', in J.J. Lee and Marion R. Casey (eds), *Making the Irish American* (New York: NYU Press, 2006), pp. 548–73

Dowling, Martin, *Traditional Music and Irish Society: Historical perspectives* (Farnham, Surrey: Ashgate, 2014)

Dwyer, Benjamin, *Different Voices: Irish music and music in Ireland* (Hofheim: Wolke Verlag, 2014)

———, 'Irish Music in the 20th Century', *The Journal of Music in Ireland*, vol. 3, no. 6, Sept.–Oct. 2003, pp. 18–25

Edwards, Jane (ed.), *Music: Promoting health and creating community in healthcare contexts* (Newcastle: Cambridge Scholars Publishing, 2009)

Edwards, Jane, and Simon Gilbertson, 'Exploring Resistance and Change in Music Therapy Learning', in Karen Goodman (ed.), *International Perspectives in Music Therapy Education and Training: Adapting to a changing world* (Springfield, MA: Charles C. Thomas, 2015), pp. 219–41

Eisner, Elliot W., *The Arts and the Creation of Mind* (New Haven, CT: Yale University Press, 2002)

Elliott, David J., *Music Matters: A new philosophy of music education* (New York: Oxford University Press, 1995)

Emlyn Jones, Timothy, 'The Studio Art PhD Revisited', in James Elkins (ed.), *Artists with PhDs: On the new doctoral degree in studio art*, 2nd edn (Washington, DC: New Academia Publishing, 2014)

Fahey, Hannah, 'Stylistic Pluralism and the Experiences of Classically Trained Teachers of Singing in the Republic of Ireland', *International Journal of Music Education*, vol. 39, no. 3, 2021, pp. 301–12

Fleischmann, Aloys (ed.), *Sources of Irish Traditional Music c. 1600–1855: An annotated catalogue of prints and manuscripts* (New York: Garland, 1998)

Fleischmann, Ruth (ed.), *Aloys Fleischmann (1910–92): A life for music in Ireland remembered by contemporaries* (Cork: Mercier Press, 2000)

Foley, Catherine E., *Irish Traditional Step Dancing in North Kerry: A contextual and structural analysis* (book and accompanying DVD) (Listowel: North Kerry Literary Trust, 2012 [1988])

______, *Step Dancing in Ireland: Culture and history*, Ashgate Popular and Folk Music Series (Farnham, Surrey: Ashgate, 2013)

Foley, Edward, 'Ritual Theory', in Bonnie Miller McLemore (ed.), *Wiley-Blackwell Companions to Religion: A companion to practical theology* (Oxford: Blackwell Publishing, 2012), pp. 143–52

Foster, Roy F., *On Seamus Heaney* (Princeton, NJ: Princeton University Press, 2020)

Geertz, Clifford, *The Interpretation of Cultures: Selected essays* (New York: Basic Books, 1973)

Giddins, Gary, *Bing Crosby: A pocketful of dreams. The early years 1903–1940* (Boston, New York and London: Little, Brown & Co., 2001)

Gilbert, Roger, 'Beloved and Notorious: A theory of American stardom, with special reference to Bing Crosby and Frank Sinatra', *Southwest Review*, vol. 95, nos 1 & 2, 2010, pp. 167–84

Gillen, Gerard, and Harry White (eds), *Irish Musical Studies 1: Musicology in Ireland* (Dublin: Irish Academic Press, 1990)

________ (eds), *Irish Musical Studies 3: Music and Irish Cultural History* (Dublin: Irish Academic Press, 1995)

Glassie, Henry, *Passing the Time in Ballymenone* (Bloomington, IN: Indiana University Press, 1982)

Green, Lucy, *Music, Informal Learning and the School: A new classroom pedagogy* (Farnham, Surrey: Ashgate, 2008)

Griffin, Sean, 'The Wearing of the Green: Performing Irishness in the Fox wartime musical', in Diane Negra (ed.), *The Irish in Us: Irishness, performativity and popular culture* (Durham, NC: Duke University Press, 2006), pp. 64–83

Hamilton, Colin, 'Continuity and Change in Irish Traditional Music', unpublished PhD thesis, University of Limerick, 1996

Heaney, Seamus, *Opened Ground: Poems 1966–1996* (London: Faber & Faber, 1998)

________, *Preoccupations: Selected prose 1968–1978* (London: Faber & Faber, 1980)

________, *The Government of the Tongue: The 1986 T.S. Eliot Memorial Lectures and other critical writings* (London: Faber & Faber, 1988)

________, *The Redress of Poetry: Oxford lectures* (London: Faber & Faber, 1995)

Heneghan, Frank, *MEND: A review of music education in Ireland, incorporating the final report of the Music Education National Debate, Phase III* (Dublin: Dublin Institute of Technology, 2001)

Hill, Juniper, 'The Influence of Conservatory Folk Music Programmes: The Sibelius Academy in comparative context,' *Ethnomusicology Forum*, vol. 18, no. 2, 2009, pp. 207–41

Hood, Mantle, 'The Challenge of "Bi-Musicality"', *Ethnomusicology*, vol. 4, no. 2, May 1960, pp. 55–9

Johnston, Thomas, 'The Bloom of Youth: Conceptualising a theory of educative experience for Irish traditional music in post-primary music education in Ireland', unpublished PhD thesis, University of Limerick, 2013

Kearney, Daithí, 'Towards a Regional Understanding of Irish Traditional Music', unpublished PhD thesis, University College Cork, 2009

Keegan, Niall, 'The Art of Juncture: Transformations of Irish traditional music', unpublished PhD thesis, University of Limerick, 2012

Kenny, Kevin, *The American Irish* (New York: Routledge, 2000)

Kertz-Welzel, Alexandra, *Globalising Music Education* (Bloomington, IN: Indiana University Press, 2018)

Lenehan, Fergal, 'Singing in the Rain: The Irish-themed film musical and Schager's Hibernian moment', in Barry Monaghan (ed.), *Ireland and Cinema: Culture and contexts* (London: Palgrave Macmillan, 2015), pp. 149–57

Lennon, Joseph A., *Irish Orientalism: A literary and intellectual history* (Syracuse, NY: Syracuse University Press, 2004)

Lester, Richard K., and Michael J. Piore, *Innovation: The missing dimension* (Boston, MA: Harvard University Press, 2006)

Lomax, Alan, 'Appeal for Cultural Equity', *The World of Music*, vol. 14 no. 2, 1972, pp. 3–17

Macklin, Ruth, 'Seamus Heaney and the "Place of Writing": Technique as evidence of redress as a construct', *Irish Studies Review*, vol. 25, no. 1, 2017, pp. 56–70

Mazur, Eric, 'Going My Way? Crosby and Catholicism on the road', in Ruth Prigozy and Walter Raubicheck (eds), *Going My Way: Bing Crosby and American culture* (New York: University of Rochester Press, 2007), pp. 17–34

McCarthy, Marie, *Passing It On: The transmission of music in Irish culture* (Cork: Cork University Press, 1999)

McCracken, Allison, '"God's gift to us girls": Crooning, gender, and the re-creation of American popular song, 1928–1933', *American Music*, vol. 17, no. 4, 1999, pp. 365–95

McGrath, Aoife, *Dance Theatre in Ireland: Revolutionary moves* (Houndmills, UK: Palgrave, 2013)

McGrath, Aoife, and Emma Meehan (eds), *Dance Matters in Ireland: Contemporary dance performance and practice* (Cham, Switzerland: Palgrave Macmillan, 2018)

McGuire, Seán, and Josephine Keegan (eds), *Irish Tunes by the 100*, vol. 1 (Leeds: Celtic Music, 1975)

Melin, Mats, *One with the Music: Cape Breton step dancing tradition and transmission* (Sydney, Canada: Cape Breton University Press, 2015)

Mercier, Mel, with Liam Ó Brien (producers), *Peadar Mercier*, RTÉ *Doc on One*, 10 September 2016, https://www.rte.ie/radio/doconone/812103-peadar-mercier

'Mícheál Ó Súilleabháin Obituary: Exceptional musician who straddled classical and Irish traditional music', *The Irish Times*, 10 November 2018, https://www.irishtimes.com/life-and-style/people/micheal-o-suilleabhain-obituary-exceptional-musician-who-straddled-classical-and-irish-traditional-music-1.3692385

Moloney, Colette, *The Irish Music Manuscripts of Edward Bunting (1773–1843): An introduction and catalogue* (Dublin: Irish Traditional Music Archive, 2000)

Moloney, Mick, *Across the Western Ocean: Songs of leaving and arriving* (Hamden, CT: Quinnipiac University Press, 2016)

______, *Far From the Shamrock Shore* (Cork: Collins Press, 2022)

______, 'Harrigan, Hart and Braham: Irish America and the birth of the American musical', in John Harrington (ed.), *Irish Theatre in America: Essays on Irish theatrical diaspora* (Syracuse: Syracuse University Press, 2009), pp. 1–18

______, 'Irish American Popular Music', in J.J. Lee and Marion R. Casey (eds), *Making the Irish American* (New York: NYU Press, 2006), pp. 381–405

Motherway, Susan, *The Globalisation of Irish Traditional Music* (Farnham, Surrey: Ashgate Publishing, 2013)

Motherway, Susan, and John O'Connell, *Staged Folklore: The National Folk Theatre of Ireland 1968–1998* (Cork: Cork University Press, 2022)

Mulrooney, Deirdre, *Irish Moves: An illustrated history of dance and physical theatre in Ireland* (Dublin: The Liffey Press, 2006)

Nettl, Bruno, *Heartland Excursions: Ethnomusicological reflections on schools of music* (Urbana, IL: University of Illinois Press, 1995)

______, 'Thoughts on Improvisation: A comparative approach', *The Musical Quarterly*, vol. 60, 1974, pp. 1–19

Ní Bhriain, Orfhlaith, and Michael McCabe, *Jigs to Jacobites* (Dublin: Independent Publishing Network, 2018)

Ní Riain, Nóirín, *Stór Amhrán: A wealth of songs from the Irish tradition* (Cork: Mercier Press, 1988, reprint Ossian Publications, 2007)

Ní Shíocháin, Tríona, *Bláth 's Craobh na nÚdar: Amhráin Mháire Bhuí* (Baile Átha Cliath: Coiscéim, 2012)

______, 'Filí agus Amhránaithe, Foinn agus Focail: *Maidean álainn ghréine* agus ionad an cheoil i dtraidisiún na n-amhrán', *Béascna*, iml. 5, lgh 37–57

______, 'Mother Music: Socially embedded creative practice and the marketisation of Irish traditional music', *Ethnomusicology Ireland*, vol. 7, 2021, pp. 110–22

______, *Singing Ideas: Performance, politics and oral poetry* (London and New York: Berghahn, 2018)

Nic an Airchinnigh, Méadhbh, agus Lillis Ó Laoire, 'Caointe agus Amhráin Chrúite: "Is le gach bó a lao agus le gach caoineadh a cheol"', *Aiste*, iml. 4, uimh. 1, 2014, lgh 155–76

Nic Fhinn, Máire, *Riobard Mac Góráin: Ceannródaí ildánach* (Baile Átha Cliath: Coiscéim, 2018

Nic Suibhne, Damhnait, 'Repertoire in the Donegal Fiddle Tradition', unpublished MA thesis, University College Cork, 1993

Noone, Matthew James, '(De)composing the Mongrel: Improvisation and the (un)known', *Performance Research*, vol. 26, no. 2, 2021, pp. 104–9

Nugent, Mary, 'Instrumental Music Learning in an Irish Bimusical Context', unpublished PhD thesis, Technological University Dublin, 2019

Nunan, Mary, *The Dance of the Poetic and the Practical (Reflections on Dance-in-Education in Ireland)*, 2016, http://artsineducation.ie/wp-content/uploads/The-Dance-of-the-Poetic-and-the-Practical.pdf

O'Brien Moran, Jimmy, 'Capturing Diversity whilst Creating Canon: The advent of sound technology in Irish traditional music', in Thérèse Smith (ed.), *Ancestral Imprints: Histories of Irish traditional music and dance* (Cork: Cork University Press, 2012)

Ó Canainn, Tomás, *Seán Ó Riada: His life and work* (Cork: Collins Press, 2003)

O'Connell, Connie, *Bóithrín na Smaointe* (Cork: UCC, 2015), http://epu.ucc.ie/connie oconnell/

O'Connell, John M., *Commemorating Gallipoli through Music: Remembering and forgetting* (Lanham, MD: Lexington Books, 2017)

______, 'National Symposium: Towards a national ethnomusicology', *Bulletin of the International Council for Traditional Music*, vol. 109, 2006, pp. 61–2

Ó Cróinín, Donncha (eag.), *Seanachas Phádraig Í Chrualaoi* (Baile Átha Cliath: Comhairle Bhéaloideas Éireann, 1982)

Ó Crualaoich, Gearóid, 'Folkloristic-Ethnological Studies in Ireland', in Diarmuid Ó Giolláin (ed.), *Irish Ethnologies* (Notre Dame, IN: University of Notre Dame Press, 2017), pp. 75–89

Ó Curnáin, Brian, *The Irish of Iorras Aithneach, County Galway* (Dublin: School of Celtic Studies, Dublin Institute for Advanced Studies, 2007)

O'Donnell, Mary Louise, 'Custodians of Culture: A social, political, musicological and cultural history of the Irish harp and its patronage from 1790 to 1845', unpublished PhD thesis, University of Limerick, 2009

______, *Ireland's Harp: The shaping of Irish identity c. 1780 to 1880* (Dublin: UCD Press, 2014)

O'Driscoll, Dennis, *Stepping Stones: Interviews with Seamus Heaney* (London: Faber & Faber, 2009)

O'Flynn, John, *Music, the Moving Image and Ireland, 1897–2017* (London and New York: Routledge, 2022)

Ó Giolláin, Diarmuid (ed.), *Irish Ethnologies* (Notre Dame, IN: University of Notre Dame Press, 2017)

———, *Locating Irish Folklore: Tradition, modernity, identity* (Cork: Cork University Press, 2000)

O'Keeffe, John, *The Masses of Seán and Peadar Ó Riada: Explorations in vernacular chant* (Cork: Cork University Press, 2017)

Ó Laoire, Lillis, *Ar Chreag i Lár na Farraige: Amhráin agus amhránaithe i dToraigh* (Indreabhán: Cló Iar-Chonnacht, 2002)

Ó Madagáin, Breandán, 'Bunting's *Ancient Music of Ireland* by Bunting, Donal O'Sullivan and Mícheál Ó Súilleabháin' [review], *Studia Hibernica*, nos 22–3, 1982/3, pp. 174–80

———, 'Coibhneas na Filíochta leis an gCeol, 1700–1900', in Pádraigín Riggs et al. (eag.), *Saoi na hÉigse: Aistí in ómós do Sheán Ó Tuama* (An Daingean: An Sagart, 2000), lgh 83–104

Ó Máille, Tomás, *Amhráin Chearbhalláin/The poems of Carolan* (London: Irish Texts Society, 1916)

Ó Ríordáin, Seán, *Seán Ó Ríordáin: Na dánta*, in eagar ag Seán Ó Coileáin (Indreabhán: Cló Iar-Chonnacht, 2011)

O'Sullivan, Donal, *Carolan: The life and times of an Irish harper*, vols 1–2 (London: Routledge & Keegan Paul, 1958)

Petrie, George (ed.), *The Petrie Collection of the Ancient Music of Ireland* (Dublin: Society for the Preservation and Publication of the Melodies of Ireland, 1855)

Phelan, Helen (ed.), *Anáil Dé, the Breath of God: Music, ritual and spirituality* (Dublin: Veritas, 2001)

______, *The Pipa Report: Towards an institute of performing arts* (Limerick: Irish World Music Centre, University of Limerick and the Irish Chamber Orchestra, 1996)

______, 'Voicing *Imbas*: Performing a philosophy of music education', in Wayne Bowman and Ana Lucía Frega (eds), *Oxford Handbook of Music Education Philosophy* (Oxford: Oxford University Press, 2012), pp. 63–85

———, and Graham F. Welch (eds), *The Artist and Academia* (Abingdon, Oxon: Routledge, 2021)

Prendergast, Roy M., *Film Music: A neglected art. A critical study of music in films* (New York: W.W. Norton & Company, 1992)

Quinn, Toner, 'A New Irish Musical Language is Developing', *The Journal of Music*, 10 October 2019, https://journalofmusic.com/focus/new-irish-musical-language-developing

______, 'Mícheál Ó Súilleabháin's Example Will Continue to Inspire', *The Journal of Music*, 8 November 2018, https://journalofmusic.com/focus/micheal-o-Súilleabhain-s-example-will-continue-inspire

Regan, Stephen, 'Lux Perpetua: The poetry of Seamus Heaney, from *Door into the Dark* to *Electric Light*', *Romanticism*, vol. 22, no. 3, 2016, pp. 322–30

Rilke, Rainer Maria, and Michael Hamburger, *Turning-Point: Miscellaneous poems 1912–1926* (London: Anvil Press Poetry, 1981)

Rimmer, Joan, 'Patronage, Style and Structure in the Music Attributed to Turlough Carolan', *Early Music*, vol. 15, no. 2, 1987, pp. 164–74

———, *The Irish Harp* (Cork: Mercier Press, 1969)

Ring, Brendan, 'Travelling Style: The uilleann piping of Paddy Keenan', unpublished MA thesis, University College Cork, 1992

Risenhoover, Morris, and Robert Blackburn, *Artists as Professors: Conversations with musicians, painters, sculptors* (Urbana, IL: University of Illinois Press, 1979)

Rizzo, Steven, 'The Paradox of Spiritual Matter and the Spiritual Matter of Paradox in Seamus Heaney and Robert Boyle', *Literature & Theology*, vol. 22, no. 4, 2008, pp. 458–74

Robinson, Dylan, *Hungry Listening: Resonant theory for indigenous sound studies* (Minneapolis, MN: University of Minnesota Press, 2020)

Roche, Frank (ed.), *The Roche Collection of Traditional Irish Music*, 2 vols (Dublin: Pigot, 1912; 2nd edn in 3 vols, 1927; repr. Cork: Ossian, 1982)

Roche, Jenny, *Multiplicity, Embodiment and the Contemporary Dancer: Moving identities* (UK: Palgrave Macmillan, 2015)

Royce, Anya Peterson, 'Taking the Long Way Around: Journeys of transformation', *Of Our Times/Comhaimseartha*, Irish World Academy of Music and Dance, autumn 2013, www.irishworldacademy.ie

Said, Edward, *Culture and Imperialism* (London: Chatto & Windus, 1993)

Scharmer, C. Otto, *Theory U: Learning from the future as it emerges* (London: Berrett-Koehler Publishers, 2009)

Sewell, Frank (ed.), *Selected Poems: Seán Ó Ríordáin* (New Haven, CT: Yale University Press, 2014)

Shannon, Christopher, *Bowery to Broadway: The American Irish in classic Hollywood cinema* (Scranton: University of Scranton Press, 2010)

Small, Christopher, *Musicking: The meanings of performing and listening* (New Haven, CT: Wesleyan University Press, 1998)

Steiner, George, *Real Presences* (Chicago: University of Chicago Press, 1991)

Sternad, Dietmar, James J. Kennelly and Finbarr Bradley, *Digging Deeper: How purpose-driven enterprises create real value* (Saltaire: Greenleaf Publishing, 2016)

Stokes, Martin, and Philip V. Bohlman (eds), *Celtic Modern: Music at the global fringe* (Lanham, MD: Scarecrow Press, 2003), pp. 219–56

Stoneman, Rod, 'Screen Production Research: Creative practice as a mode of enquiry', edited by Craig Batty and Susan Kerrigan, *Alphaville: Journal of film and screen media*, no. 17, 2019, pp. 215–20

Sweeney, Gerry, 'The Skillbeck Report and the Need for Change', *Céide: A review from the margins*, April/May 2002, p. 19

Talty, Jack, 'The Ivory Tower and the Commons: Exploring the institutionalisation of Irish traditional music in Irish higher education. Discourse, pedagogy and practice', unpublished PhD thesis, University of Limerick, 2019

Tolmie, Frances, A.G. Gilchrist, George Henderson, Lucy E. Broadwood and J.A. Fuller-Maitland, 'Songs of Rest and Recreation', *Journal of the Folk-Song Society*, vol. 4, no. 16, 1911, pp. 157–95

Vallely, Fintan (ed.), *Companion to Irish Traditional Music*, 2nd edn, 2011; 3rd edn, 2024. (Cork: Cork University Press)

———, *Timber: The concert flute tutor* (Dublin: Waltons, 1986)

———, Hammy Hamilton, Eithne Vallely and Liz Doherty (eds), *Crosbhealach an Cheoil, The Crossroads Conference 1996: Tradition and change in Irish traditional music* (Dublin: Whinstone Music, 1999)

Veblen, Kari, 'Perceptions of Change and Stability in the Transmission of Irish Traditional Music: An examination of the music teacher's role', unpublished PhD thesis, University of Wisconsin, 1991

Ward, Francis, 'Processes of Transmission in Irish Traditional Music: Approaching a virtual orality', unpublished PhD thesis, University of Limerick, 2016

Weil, Simone, *Gravity and Grace* (London: Routledge, 1963)

Wenger, Etienne, *Communities of Practice* (Cambridge, MA: Cambridge University Press, 1998)

White, Harry, *The Keeper's Recital: Music and cultural history in Ireland, 1770–1970* (Cork: Cork University Press, in association with Field Day, 1998)

White, Harry, and Barra Boydell (eds), *The Encyclopaedia of Music in Ireland* (Dublin: UCD Press, 2013)

Williams, William H., *'Twas Only an Irishman's Dream': The image of Ireland and the Irish in American popular song lyrics, 1800–1920* (Urbana: University of Illinois Press, 1996)

Index

Note: Page locators in bold refer to photographs and illustrations.